Fundamentals of Investments

Valuation and Management

The Irwin/McGraw-Hill Series in Finance, Insurance and Real Estate

Stephen A. Ross
Franco Modigliani Professor of Finance and Economics
Sloan School of Management
Massachusetts Institute of Technology
Consulting Editor

Financial Management

Benninga and Sarig
Corporate Finance: A Valuation Approach

Block and Hirt
Foundations of Financial Management
Ninth Edition

Brealey and Myers
Principles of Corporate Finance
Sixth Edition

Brealey, Myers and Marcus
Fundamentals of Corporate Finance
Second Edition

Brooks
FinGame Online 3.0

Bruner
Case Studies in Finance: Managing for Corporate Value Creation
Third Edition

Chew
The New Corporate Finance: Where Theory Meets Practice
Second Edition

Graduate Management Admissions Council,
Robert F. Bruner, Kenneth Eades and Robert Harris
Finance Interactive: Pre-MBA Series 2000
Second Edition

Essentials of Finance: With an Accounting Review
Fully interactive CD-ROM derived from Finance Interactive 1997 Pre-MBA Edition

Grinblatt and Titman
Financial Markets and Corporate Strategy

Helfert
Techniques of Financial Analysis: A Guide to Value Creation
Tenth Edition

Higgins
Analysis for Financial Management
Fifth Edition

Hite
A Programmed Learning Guide to Finance

Kester, Fruhan, Piper and Ruback
Case Problems in Finance
Eleventh Edition

Nunnally and Plath
Cases in Finance
Second Edition

Ross, Westerfield and Jaffe
Corporate Finance
Fifth Edition

Ross, Westerfield and Jordan
Essentials of Corporate Finance
Second Edition

Ross, Westerfield and Jordan
Fundamentals of Corporate Finance
Fifth Edition

Schall and Haley
Introduction to Financial Management
Sixth Edition

Smith
The Modern Theory of Corporate Finance
Second Edition

White
Financial Analysis with an Electronic Calculator
Fourth Edition

Investments

Bodie, Kane and Marcus
Essentials of Investments
Third Edition

Bodie, Kane and Marcus
Investments
Fourth Edition

Cohen, Zinbarg and Zeikel
Investment Analysis and Portfolio Management
Fifth Edition

Corrado and Jordan
Fundamentals of Investments: Valuation and Management

Farrell
Portfolio Management: Theory and Applications
Second Edition

Hirt and Block
Fundamentals of Investment Management
Sixth Edition

Jarrow
Modelling Fixed Income Securities and Interest Rate Options

Morningstar, Inc. and Remaley
U.S. Equities OnFloppy Educational Version
Annual Edition

Shimko
The Innovative Investor
Excel Version

Financial Institutions and Markets

Cornett and Saunders
Fundamentals of Financial Institutions Management

Johnson
Financial Institutions and Markets: A Global Perspective

Rose
Commercial Bank Management
Third Edition

Rose
Money and Capital Markets: Financial Institutions and Instruments in a Global Marketplace
Seventh Edition

Rose and Kolari
Financial Institutions: Understanding and Managing Financial Services
Fifth Edition

Santomero and Babbel
Financial Markets, Instruments, and Institutions

Saunders
Financial Institutions Management: A Modern Perspective
Third Edition

(Continued)

Fundamentals of Investments

Valuation and Management

Charles J. Corrado
University of Missouri-Columbia

Bradford D. Jordan
University of Kentucky

Boston   Burr Ridge, IL   Dubuque, IA   Madison, WI   New York   San Francisco   St. Louis
Bangkok   Bogotá   Caracas   Lisbon   London   Madrid   Mexico City   Milan   New Delhi   Seoul
Singapore   Sydney   Taipei   Toronto

McGraw-Hill Higher Education
A Division of The McGraw-Hill Companies

FUNDAMENTALS OF INVESTMENTS: VALUATION AND MANAGEMENT

Copyright © 2000 by The McGraw-Hill Companies, Inc. All rights reserved. Printed in the United States of America. Except as permitted under the United States Copyright Act of 1976, no part of this publication may be reproduced or distributed in any form or by any means, or stored in a data base or retrieval system, without the prior written permission of the publisher.

This book is printed on acid-free paper.

1 2 3 4 5 6 7 8 9 0 VNH/VNH 9 0 9 8 7 6 5 4 3 2 1 0 9

ISBN 0-256-15423-6

Vice president/Editor-in-chief: *Michael W. Junior*
Publisher: *Craig S. Beytien*
Senior sponsoring editor: *Randall Adams*
Developmental editor: *Michele Janicek*
Senior marketing manager: *Katie Rose Matthews*
Senior project manager: *Jean Lou Hess*
Production supervisor: *Michael R. McCormick*
Designer: *Jennifer McQueen Hollingsworth*
Interior designer: *Mary Sailer*
Cover illustrator: *Otto Steininger*
Supplement coordinator: *Cathy L. Tepper*
Compositor: *Black Dot*
Typeface: *10/12 Times Roman*
Printer: *Von Hoffmann Press, Inc.*

Library of Congress Cataloging-in-Publication Data

Corrado, Charles J.
    Fundamentals of investments: valuation and management/Charles
J. Corrado, Bradford D. Jordan
        p. cm.—(The Irwin/McGraw-Hill series in finance,
insurance, and real estate)
    Includes index.
    ISBN 0-256-15423-6
    1. Investments. 2. Jordan, Bradford D.   II. Title.   III. Series.
HG4521.C66   2000   99-27709
332.6—dc21

www.mhhe.com

**To my parents, Charles and Clotilda,
who sacrificed for my benefit; I miss them dearly.**

CJC

**To my late father, S. Kelly Jordan, Sr.,
a great stock picker.**

BDJ

About the Authors

Charles J. Corrado

University of Missouri-Columbia

Charles J. Corrado is Associate Professor of Finance at the University of Missouri. He has taught investments during his entire academic career at undergraduate through doctoral levels. Professor Corrado has published numerous research articles on various topics related to financial derivatives, statistical methods in financial research, and financial market efficiency.

Bradford D. Jordan

Carol Martin Gatton College of Business and Economics, University of Kentucky

Bradford D. Jordan is Professor of Finance and Gatton Research Fellow at the University of Kentucky. He has a long-standing interest in both applied and theoretical issues in investments, and he has extensive experience teaching all levels of investments. Professor Jordan has published numerous articles on issues such as valuation of fixed income securities, tax effects in investments analysis, and the behavior of security prices. He is coauthor of *Fundamentals of Corporate Finance,* Fifth Edition, and *Essentials of Corporate Finance,* Second Edition, two of the most widely-used finance textbooks in the world.

Preface

So why did we write this book?

As we toiled away, we asked ourselves this question many times and the answer was always the same: *Our students made us.*

Traditionally, investments textbooks tend to fall into one of two camps. The first type has a greater focus on portfolio management and covers a significant amount of portfolio theory. The second type is more concerned with security analysis and generally contains fairly detailed coverage of fundamental analysis as a tool for equity valuation. Today, most texts try to cover all the bases by including some chapters drawn from one camp and some from another.

The result of trying to cover everything is either a very long book or one that forces the instructor to bounce back and forth between chapters. The result is frequently a noticeable lack of consistency in treatment. Different chapters have completely different approaches, some are computational, some are theoretical, and some are descriptive. Some do macroeconomic forecasting, some do mean-variance portfolio theory and beta estimation, and some do financial statements analysis. Options and futures are often essentially tacked on the back to round out this disconnected assortment.

The goal of these books differs from the goal of our students. Our students told us they come into an investments course wanting to learn how to make investment decisions. As time went by, we found ourselves supplying more and more supplemental materials to the texts we were using and constantly varying chapter sequences while chasing this elusive goal. We finally came to realize that the financial world had changed tremendously and investments textbooks had fallen far behind in content and relevance.

What we really wanted, and what our students really needed, was a book that would do three key things:

- Focus on the students as investment managers, giving them information they can act on instead of concentrating on theories and research without the proper context

- Offer strong, consistent pedagogy, including a balanced, unified treatment of the main types of financial investments as mirrored in the investment world

- Organize topics in a way that would make them easy to apply—whether to a portfolio simulation or to real life—and support these topics with hands-on activities

We made these three goals the guiding principles in writing this book. The next several sections explain our approach to each and why we think they are so important.

Who Is This Book For?

This book is aimed at introductory investments classes with students who have relatively little familiarity with investments. A typical student may have taken a principles of finance class and had some exposure to stocks and bonds, but not much beyond the basics. The introductory investments class is often a required course for finance majors, but students from other areas often take it as an elective. One fact of which we are acutely aware is that this will be the only investments class many students will ever take.

We intentionally wrote this book in a relaxed, informal style that engages the student and treats him or her as an active participant rather than a passive information absorber. We think the world of investments is exciting and fascinating, and we hope to share our considerable enthusiasm for investing with the student. We appeal to intuition and basic principles whenever possible because we have found that this approach effectively promotes understanding. We also make extensive use of examples throughout, drawing on "real-world" material and familiar companies wherever appropriate.

By design, the text is not encyclopedic. As the table of contents indicates, we have a total of 19 chapters. Chapter length is about 30 pages, so the text is aimed at a single-term course. By design, most of the book can be covered in a typical quarter or semester.

Aiming the book at a one semester course necessarily means some picking and choosing, both with regard to topics and depth of coverage. Throughout, we strike a balance by introducing and covering the essentials while leaving some of the detail to follow-up courses in security analysis, portfolio management, and options and futures.

Relevance to the Student

Fundamental changes in the investments universe drive our attention to relevance. The first major change is that individuals are being asked to make investments decisions for their own portfolios more often than ever before. There is, thankfully, a growing recognition that traditional "savings account" approaches to investing are decidedly inferior. At the same time, the use of employer-sponsored "investment accounts" has expanded enormously. The second major change is that the investments universe has exploded with an ever-increasing number of investment vehicles available to individual investors. As a result, investors must choose from an array of products, many of which are very complex, and they must strive to choose wisely as well.

Beyond this, students are more interested in subjects that affect them directly (aren't we all!). By taking the point of view of the student as an investor, we are better able to illustrate and emphasize the relevance and importance of the material.

Our approach is evident in the table of contents. Our first chapter is motivational; we have found that this material effectively "hooks" students and even motivates a semester-long discourse on risk and return. Our second chapter answers the student's next natural question, "How do I get started investing and how do I buy and sell securities?" The third chapter surveys the different types of investments available. After only three chapters, very early in the term, students have learned something about the rewards and risks from investing, how to get started investing, and what investment choices are available.

We close the first part of the text by a detailed examination of mutual funds. Without a doubt, mutual funds have become the most popular investment vehicles for individual investors. There are now more equity mutual funds than there are stocks on the NYSE! Given the size and enormous growth in the mutual fund industry, this material is important for investors. Even so, investment texts typically cover mutual funds in a cursory way, often banishing the material to a back chapter under the obscure (and obsolete) heading of "investment companies." Our early placement lets students quickly explore a topic they have heard a lot about and are typically very interested in.

A Consistent, Unified Treatment

In most investments texts, depth of treatment and presentation vary dramatically from instrument to instrument, stranding the student without an overall framework for understanding the many types of investments. We stress early-on that there are essentially only four basic types of financial investments—stocks, bonds, options, and futures. In parts 2 through 5, our simple goal is to take a closer look at each of these instruments. We take a unified approach to each by answering these basic questions:

1. What are the essential features of the instrument?
2. What are the possible rewards?
3. What are the risks?
4. What are the basic determinants of investment value?
5. For whom is the investment appropriate and under what circumstances?
6. How is the instrument bought and sold and how does the market for the instrument operate?

By covering investment instruments in this way, we teach students what are the questions to ask when looking at any potential investment.

Unlike other introductory investments texts, we devote several chapters beyond the basics to the different types of fixed-income investments. Students are often surprised to learn that the fixed-income markets are so much bigger than the equity markets and that money management opportunities are much more common in the fixed-income arena. Possibly the best way to see this is to look at recent CFA exams and materials and note the extensive coverage of fixed-income topics. We have placed these chapters toward the back of the text because we recognize not everyone will want to cover all this material. We have also separated the subject into several shorter chapters to make it more digestible for students and to allow instructors more control over what is covered.

Applying Investments Knowledge

After studying from this text, students will have the basic knowledge needed to move forward and actually act on what they have learned. We have developed two features to encourage making decisions as an investment manager. Learning to make good investment decisions comes with experience, while experience (regrettably) comes from making bad investment decisions. As much as possible, we press our students to get those bad decisions out of their systems before they start managing real money!

Not surprisingly, most students don't know how to get started buying and selling securities. We have learned that providing some structure, especially with a portfolio simulation, greatly enhances the experience. So, we first have a series of *Get Real!* boxes. These boxes (at the end of each chapter) usually describe actual trades for students to explore. The intention is to show students how to gain real experience with the principles and instruments covered in the chapter. The second feature is a series of *Stock-Trak®* exercises that take students through specific trading situations using *Stock-Trak® Portfolio Simulations*. More detail concerning *Stock-Trak®* and these features appears in the next section dealing with pedagogy.

Because we feel that portfolio simulations are so valuable, we have taken steps to assist instructors who, like us, plan to integrate portfolio simulations in their course. Beyond the features mentioned above, we have organized the text so that the essential material needed before participating in a simulation is covered at the front of the book. Most notably, with every book, we have included a *free* subscription to *Stock-Trak®* *Portfolio Simulations. Stock-Trak®* is the leading provider of investment simulation services to the academic community; providing it free represents a significant cost savings to students. To our knowledge, ours is the first investment text to offer a full-featured online brokerage account simulation directly with the book at no incremental cost.

Pedagogical Features

From your feedback, we included many pedagogical features in this text that will be valuable learning tools for your students.

Chapter Openers (see pages 3, 275, and 431)   These one-paragraph introductions for each chapter present facts and misconceptions that may surprise you. An explanation is more fully developed in the respective chapter.

Anyone can retire as a millionaire!

Consider this: If you invest $2,500 per year while earning 12 percent annual returns, then after 35 years you will have accumulated $1,079,159. But with annual returns of only 8 percent you will have just $430,792. Are these investment returns realistic over a long period of time?

Key Terms (see pages 37, 243, and 463)   Key terms are indicated in bold and defined in the margin. The running glossary in the margin helps students quickly review the basic terminology for the chapter.

margin call A demand for more funds that occurs when the margin in an account drops below the maintenance margin.

A typical maintenance margin would be 30 percent. If your margin falls below 30 percent, then you may be subject to a **margin call**, which is a demand by your broker to add to your account, pay off part of the loan, or sell enough securities to bring your margin back up to an acceptable level. If you do not or cannot comply, your securities may be sold. The loan will be repaid out of the proceeds, and any remaining amounts will be credited to your account.

Check This! (see pages 7, 287, and 491) Each major section in each chapter ends with questions for review. This feature helps students test their understanding of the material before moving on to the next section.

CHECK THIS

1.1a What are the two parts of total return?

1.1b Why are unrealized capital gains or losses included in the calculation of returns?

1.1c What is the difference between a dollar return and a percentage return? Why are percentage returns usually more convenient?

Investment Updates (see pages 48, 223, and 461) These boxed readings, reprinted from various business press sources, provide additional real-world events and examples to illustrate the material in the chapter. Many articles are from the past two years to highlight very recent events, while others present events of more historical significance.

Investment Updates

Time for Investing's Four-Letter Word

What four-letter word should pop into mind when the stock market takes a harrowing nosedive?

No, not those. R-I-S-K.

Risk is the potential for realizing low returns or even losing money, possibly preventing you from meeting important objectives, like sending your kids to the college of their choice or having the retirement lifestyle you crave.

But many financial advisers and other experts say that these days investors aren't taking the idea of risk as seriously as they should, and they are overexposing themselves to stocks.

"The aim is always to find the fine line between greed and fear," he says.

To that end, many financial advisers, brokerage firms and mutual-fund companies have created risk quizzes to help people determine whether they are conservative, moderate or agressive investors. Some firms that offer such quizzes include **Merrill Lynch, T. Rowe Price Associates** Inc., Baltimore, **Zurich Group** Inc.'s Scudder Kemper Investments Inc., New York, and **Vanguard Group** in Malvern, Pa.

"The typical investor may not have ever experienced a negative turn in the stock market. They need to be pre-

Numbered Examples (see pages 6, 278, and 494) Separate numbered and titled examples are integrated throughout the chapters. Each example illustrates an intuitive or mathematical application in a step-by-step format. There is enough detail in the explanations so the student doesn't have to look elsewhere for additional information.

Example 1.1   **Calculating Percentage Returns**

Suppose you buy some stock for $25 per share. After one year, the price is $35 per share. During the year, you received a $2 dividend per share. What is the dividend yield? The capital gains yield? The percentage return? If your total investment was $1,000, how much do you have at the end of the year?

Your $2 dividend per share works out to a dividend yield of

$$\text{Dividend yield} = D_{t+1} \,/\, P_t$$
$$= \$2 \,/\, \$25$$
$$= 8\%$$

Numbered Equations (see pages 149, 468, and 518)   Key equations are highlighted and numbered sequentially in each chapter for easy reference.

$$V(0) = \frac{D(0)(1 + g)}{k - g} \qquad g < k \qquad\qquad \textbf{6.3}$$

Figures and Tables (see pages 19, 126, and 216)   This text makes extensive use of real data and presents them in various figures and tables. Explanations in the narrative, examples, and end-of-chapter problems will refer to many of these exhibits.

Table 1.4

Annual Returns Statistics, 1926–1997		
Asset Category	**Average**	**Standard Deviation**
Large-cap stocks	12.83%	20.38%
U.S. Treasury bonds	5.41	8.35
U.S. Treasury bills	4.10	3.25
Inflation	3.20	4.52

Figure 1.9   Risk-Return Trade-Off

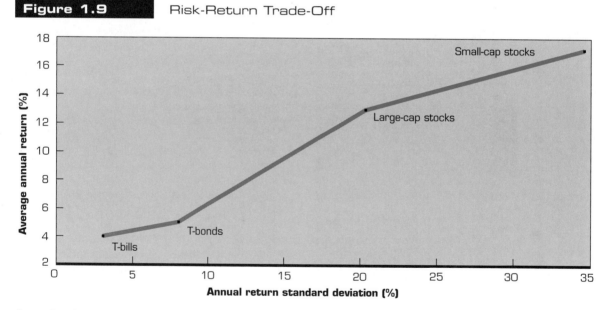

Source: Data from Global Financial Data, reprinted with permission.

Summary and Conclusions (see pages 22, 106, and 360) Each chapter ends with a summary that highlights the important points of the chapter. This provides a handy checklist for students when they review the chapter.

 # Summary and Conclusions

This chapter explores financial market history. Such a history lesson is useful because it tells us what to expect in the way of returns from risky assets. We summarized our study of market history with two key lessons:

1. Risky assets, on average, earn a risk premium. There is a reward for bearing risk.

2. The greater the potential reward from a risky investment, the greater is the risk.

When we put these two lessons together, we concluded that there is a risk-return trade-off: The only way to earn a higher return is to take on greater risk.

Get Real! (see pages 22, 231, and 297) For instructors looking to give their students a taste of what it means to be an investment manager, this section (at the end of each chapter) acts as that first step by explaining to students how they can actually apply the material they just learned. They encourage students—whether for practice, in a trading simulation, or with real money—to choose investments and make investment decisions and also give some helpful tips to keep in mind.

This chapter took you through some basic, but important, investment-related calculations. We then walked through the modern history of risk and return, both in the United States and elsewhere. How should you, as an investor or investment manager, put this information to work?

The answer is that you now have a rational, objective basis for thinking about what you stand to make from investing in some important broad asset classes. For the stock market as a whole, as measured by the performance of large-company stocks, you know that you can realistically expect to make 13 percent or so per year on average.

Review Problems and Self-Test (see pages 23, 136, and 298)
Students are provided with 1–3 practice problems per chapter with worked-out solutions to test their abilities in solving key problems related to the content of the chapter.

Chapter Review Problems and Self-Test

1. **Calculating Returns**   You bought 400 shares of Metallica Heavy Metal, Inc., at $30 per share. Over the year, you received $.75 per share in dividends. If the stock sold for $33 at the end of the year, what was your dollar return? Your percentage return?

Answers to Self-Test Problems

1. Your dollar return is just your gain or loss in dollars. Here, we receive $.75 in dividends on each of our 400 shares, for a total of $300. In addition, each share rose from $30 to $33, so we make $3 × 400 shares = $1,200. Our total dollar return is thus $300 + $1,200 = $1,500.

   Our percentage return (or just "return" for short) is equal to the $1,500 we made divided by our initial outlay of $30 × 400 shares = $12,000; so $1,500/12,000 = .125 = 12.5%. Equivalently, we could have just noted that each share paid a $.75 dividend and each share gained $3, so the total dollar gain per share was $3.75. As a percentage of the cost of one share ($30), we get $3.75 / 30 = .125 = 12.5%.

Test Your IQ (Investment Quotient) (see pages 138, 299, and 334)
An average of 15 multiple-choice questions are included for each chapter, many of which are taken from past CFA exams. This text is unique in that it presents CFA questions in multiple-choice format—which is how they appear on the actual Level I exam. Answers to theses questions appear in Appendix A.

Test Your Investment Quotient

1. **Securities Regulation**   Which of the following is not a function of the SEC in approving an IPO of a company's common stock shares?

   a. Ensuring that the company is high quality and the stock offering price is fair.
   b. Ensuring full disclosure of the company's financial position.
   c. Ensuring that a prospectus is made available to all interested investors.
   d. Ensuring that the offering does not violate federal securities laws.

Questions and Problems (see pages 26, 140, and 336)   A variety of problems (average of 20 per chapter) are included in each chapter to test students' understanding of the conceptual and problem-solving elements. Each problem is labeled with the subject and the level—core or intermediate. Selected answers appear in Appendix B, and complete solutions are included in the instructor's manual.

Questions and Problems

Core Questions

1. **Calculating Returns**   Suppose you bought 200 shares of stock at an initial price of $42 per share. The stock paid a dividend of $2.40 per share during the following year, and the share price at the end of the year was $31. Compute your total dollar return on this investment. Does your answer change if you keep the stock instead of selling it? Why or why not?

2. **Calculating Yields**   In the previous problem, what is the capital gains yield? The dividend yield? What is the total rate of return on the investment?

Intermediate Questions

11. **Using Returns Distributions**   Based on the historical record, what is the approximate probability that an investment in small stocks will double in value in a single year? How about triple in a single year?

Stock-Trak Exercises (see pages 142, 337, and 572) Unique to this text! This text is the only book that incorporates *Stock-Trak® Portfolio Simulations* exercises. *Stock-Trak®* is one of the most successful trading simulations with over 10,000 college students using trading accounts each semester (see *Supplements* for more information). Go the next step in teaching your students about investment management by encouraging your students to use this product. This section, included in most of the chapters, briefly summarizes topics from the chapter and asks students to perform certain trades as covered in the text.

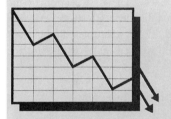
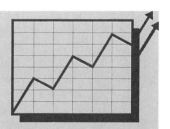

STOCK-TRAK·
Portfolio Simulations

Stock Market Day Trading with Stock-Trak

The Internet has given rise to a new breed of stock market investors—day traders. Day traders buy and sell common stocks within a day and typically close out their positions before the end of the day to avoid carrying a stock position overnight. The most popular trading strategy among day traders is "momentum trading," whereby the day trader tries to identify stocks that have started moving up and will continue to move up through the day. Once such a stock is identified, the day trader buys the stock and tracks its progress through the day. Some time later—perhaps a few minutes, perhaps a few hours—the day trader sells the stock to close out the position before the end of trading that day.

How do you identify stocks with sustainable momentum? Day traders often use sophisticated computer programs to assist their decision processes, but they must ultimately depend on instincts. While most day traders have a difficult time recouping their trading expenses, there are often spectacular successes to inspire the would-be trader. The beauty of a Stock-Trak account is that you can try your hand at day trading without risking your own capital.

To try your hand at day trading using your Stock-Trak account, simultaneously log on to an Internet stock quote server and the Stock-Trak website in the morning, ideally about an hour or two after NYSE trading has started. Note that web browsers support several different sessions at one time and many stock quote servers also provide stock price charts. Next, identify several stocks that are up since the opening of trading that day. Most stock quote servers report intraday stock price statistics, including high and low prices along with an opening price and change in price. Pick two or three stocks and submit an order to Stock-Trak to buy these stocks. Stock-Trak will return a trade confirmation indicating the trade prices for your order. Print the trade confirmation so you don't forget your trade prices. Later in the day, log on to Stock-Trak to close out your position and calculate your profits and losses. Remember, a real day trader will not hold a position overnight. It's easier to sleep that way.

Supplements

We have developed a number of supplements for both teaching and learning to accompany this text:

For Instructors

Instructor's Manual, prepared by Stuart Michelson, University of Central Florida
ISBN 0072312572

We have developed the Instructor's Manual to clearly outline the chapter material, as well as provide extra teaching support to assist new users. The first section of the Instructor's Manual includes an annotated outline of each chapter with suggested websites, references to PowerPoint slides, teaching tips, additional examples, and current events references. The second section contains complete worked-out solutions for the end-of-chapter questions and problems.

Test Bank, prepared by Jeffery A. Manzi, Ohio University
ISBN 0072312548

With almost 1,500 questions, this Test Bank provides questions in true-false and multiple-choice formats and different levels of difficulty to meet any instructor's testing needs.

Computerized Test Bank
ISBN 0072346477

Available in Windows format, this software provides you with the Test Bank in electronic form. The keyword search option lets you browse through the question bank for problems containing a specific word or phrase. Password protection is available for saved tests or for the entire database. Questions can be added, modified, or deleted.

PowerPoint Presentation System, prepared by Stuart Michelson, University of Central Florida
ISBN 0072325860

More than 300 full-color slides of images from the text, lecture outlines, and additional examples and data are available in this product.

Videos
ISBN 0072312564

Irwin/McGraw-Hill has produced a new series of finance videos which are 10-minute case studies on topics such as Financial Markets, Stocks, Bonds, Portfolio Management, Derivatives, and Going Public.

Home Page
www.mhhe.com/cj

Visit the Corrado/Jordan website for a complete look at this text. The On-Line Learning Center (OLC), available to adopters only, contains electronic formats of the supplements as well as additional teaching materials. Or, link to the Finance Resources Access Network (FRAN) page from this site to connect to the F.I.R.E supersite, which contains lots of teaching tips and ideas for all of your courses.

For Students
The Wall Street Journal Edition
ISBN 0072326158

If your instructor ordered this special edition, you will find a reply card bound in the front of the book that entitles you to a 10-week subscription to *The Wall Street Journal*. No additional payment is necessary; the cost of the subscription is included in the price of the book.

Self-Study CD-ROM

Packaged free with every new book purchased from Irwin/McGraw-Hill!

This CD-ROM contains a tutorial program to provide questions written specifically for this text. Students can choose one chapter, or a number of chapters, and the program will select random questions to be answered. Questions were written by Jeffery A. Manzi, Ohio University, and care has been taken to ensure that these questions are not duplicated in the Test Bank. Also included on the CD is the Power Point Presentation Software, and an Options Calculator that helps students perform calculations based on material in Chapter 15.

Ready Notes
ISBN 0072356456

Ready Notes provides a reduced copy of every PowerPoint slide as an inexpensive, but valuable, note-taking system. Ask your Irwin/McGraw-Hill representative about packaging options.

Stock-Trak® Portfolio Simulation

Give your students investment management experience! Irwin/McGraw-Hill has partnered with Stock-Trak® and is providing a free subscription to Stock-Trak® Portfolio Simulations for one semester with the purchase of every *new* copy of *Fundamentals of Investments: Valuation and Management* by Corrado and Jordan. Stock-Trak® gives students $500,000 in play money to allow them to trade stocks, options, futures, bonds, mutual funds, and international stocks—no other simulation offers all these types of securities! Over 600 professors have used this service, and about 10,000 college students each semester participate. Instructors receive reports every week. All trades are done on the web through **www.mhhe.com/cj**. See this site for more information.

Acknowledgments

We have received extensive feedback from reviewers at each step along the way, and we are very grateful to the following dedicated scholars and teachers for their time and expertise:

Charles Appeadu, University of Wisconsin-Madison
Scott Barnhart, Clemson University
Howard W. Bohnen, St. Cloud State University
Paul Bolster, Northeastern University
Joe Brocato, Tarleton State University
John Paul Broussard, Rutgers, The State University of New Jersey
Jorge Omar R. Brusa, University of Arkansas
Carl R. Chen, University of Dayton
Ji Chen, University of Colorado
John Clinebell, University of Northern Colorado

Michael C. Ehrhardt, University of Tennessee, Knoxville
Gay B. Hatfield, University of Mississippi
Thomas M. Krueger, University of Wisconsin, La Crosse
Steven Lifland, High Point University
David Louton, Bryant College
David Loy, Illinois State University
Jeff Manzi, Ohio University
Linda Martin, Arizona State University
Stuart Michelson, University of Central Florida
Edward Miller, University of New Orleans
Lalatendu Misra, University of Texas, San Antonio
M.J. Murray, Winona State University
Samuel H. Penkar, University of Houston
Percy S. Poon, University of Nevada, Las Vegas
Richard W. Taylor, Arkansas State University
Howard Van Auken, Iowa State University
Joe Walker, University of Alabama at Birmingham
John Wingender, Creighton University

We'd like to thank Stuart Michelson, University of Central Florida, for developing the Instructor's Manual and PowerPoint presentation for this text, and Jeff Manzi, Ohio University, for developing the Test Bank and self-study software questions. Authoring supplements for a first edition text is no small feat, and we appreciate their dedication and suggestions throughout this process. We also want to thank Stuart for class-testing the various stages of this text and for providing us with invaluable feedback from his students.

The following University of Kentucky and University of Missouri-Columbia doctoral students did outstanding work on this text: Steve Allen, John Paglia, Scott Beyer, and Kent Ragan; to them fell the unenviable task of technical proofreading, and, in particular, careful checking of each calculation throughout the text and supplements.

We are deeply grateful to the select group of professionals who served as our development team on this edition: Michele Janicek, Development Editor; Randall Adams, Senior Sponsoring Editor, Craig Beytien, Publisher; Mike Junior, Vice President/ Editor-in-Chief; Katie Rose Matthews, Senior Marketing Manager; Jean Lou Hess, Senior Project Manager; Jennifer Hollingsworth, Designer; and Michael McCormick; Production Supervisor. We especially thank Mike Junior for his vision in signing this book, Craig Beytien for his enthusiasm for it, and Michele Janicek for her assistance as we created it. Others at Irwin/McGraw-Hill, to numerous to list here, have improved this book in countless ways.

Throughout the development of this book, we have taken great care to discover and elminate errors. Our goal is to provide the best investments textbook on the market, period. To ensure that future printings and editons are error-free, we gladly offer $10 per arithmetic error to the first person reporting it as a modest token of our appreciation. More than this, we want to know how to make this book better for students and instructors alike. Please write with your suggestions, thoughts, and ideas. You can send comments to: Dr. Charles J. Corrado, c/o Editorial-Finance, Irwin/McGraw-Hill, 1333 Burr Ridge Parkway, Burr Ridge IL, 60521.

Charles J. Corrado

Bradford D. Jordan

Brief Contents

Contents

Chapter 13

Mortgage-Backed Securities 369

Part 4   Options and Futures

Chapter 14

Stock Options 401

Chapter 15

Option Valuation 431

Chapter 16

Futures Contracts 455

Part 5   Portfolio Management

Chapter 17

Diversification and Asset Allocation   487

Chapter 18

**Return, Risk, and the Security Market
Line   517**

Chapter 19

International Finance and Investments   547

Appendixes

Part One

Introduction

1

A Brief History of Risk and Return

Anyone can retire as a millionaire! Consider this: If you invest $2,500 per year while earning 12 percent annual returns, then after 35 years you will have accumulated $1,079,159. But with annual returns of only 8 percent you will have just $430,792. Are these investment returns realistic over a long period of time? Based on the history of financial markets, the answer appears to be yes. For example, over the last 75 years the Standard & Poor's index of large-company common stocks has yielded almost a 13 percent average annual return. ■ The study of investments could begin in many places. After thinking it over, we decided that a brief history lesson is in order, so we start our discussion of risk and return by looking back at what has happened to investors in U.S. financial markets since 1925. In 1931, for example, the stock market lost 43 percent of its value. Just two years later, the market reversed itself and gained 54 percent. In more recent times, the stock market lost about 25 percent of its value on October 19, 1987, alone, and it gained almost 40 percent in 1995. What lessons, if any, should investors learn from such shifts in the stock market? We explore the last seven decades of market history to find out.

The primary goal in this chapter is to see what financial market history can tell us about risk and return. One of the most important things to get out of this discussion is a perspective on the numbers. What is a high return? What is a low return? More generally, what returns should we expect from financial assets such as stocks and bonds, and what are the risks from such investments? Beyond this, we hope that by studying what *did* happen in the past, we will at least gain some insight into what *can* happen in the future.

The history of risk and return is made day by day in global financial markets. The Internet is an excellent source of information on financial markets. Visit our website (at www.mhhe.com/cj) for suggestions on where to find information on recent financial market events.

Not everyone agrees on the value of studying history. On the one hand, there is philosopher George Santayana's famous comment, "Those who do not remember the past are condemned to repeat it." On the other hand, there is industrialist Henry Ford's equally famous comment, "History is more or less bunk." These extremes aside, perhaps everyone would agree with Mark Twain, who observed, with remarkable foresight (and poor grammar), that "October. This is one of the peculiarly dangerous months to speculate in stocks in. The others are July, January, September, April, November, May, March, June, December, August, and February."

Two key observations emerge from a study of financial market history. First, there is a reward for bearing risk, and, at least on average, that reward has been substantial. That's the good news. The bad news is that greater rewards are accompanied by greater risks. The fact that risk and return go together is probably the single most important fact to understand about investments, and it is a point to which we will return many times.

1.1 Returns

We wish to discuss historical returns on different types of financial assets. First, we need to know how to compute the return from an investment. We will consider buying shares of stock in this section, but the basic calculations are the same for any investment.

Dollar Returns

If you buy an asset of any type, your gain (or loss) from that investment is called the *return* on your investment. This return will usually have two components. First, you may receive some cash directly while you own the investment. Second, the value of the asset you purchase may change. In this case, you have a capital gain or capital loss on your investment.[1]

To illustrate, suppose you purchased 100 shares of stock in Harley-Davidson on January 1. At that time, Harley was selling for $37 per share, so your 100 shares cost you $3,700. At the end of the year, you want to see how you did with your investment.

The first thing to consider is that over the year, a company may pay cash dividends to its shareholders. As a stockholder in Harley, you are a part owner of the company, and you are entitled to a portion of any money distributed. So if Harley chooses to pay a dividend, you will receive some cash for every share you own.

---

[1] As a practical matter, what is and what is not a capital gain (or loss) is determined by the Internal Revenue Service. Even so, as is commonly done, we use these terms to refer to a change in value.

In addition to the dividend, the other part of your return is the capital gain or loss on the stock. This part arises from changes in the value of your investment. For example, consider these cash flows:

	Ending Stock Price	
	$40.33	**$34.78**
January 1	$3,700	$3,700
December 31	4,033	3,478
Dividend income	185	185
Capital gain or loss	333	−222

At the beginning of the year, on January 1, the stock is selling for $37 per share, and, as we calculated above, your total outlay for 100 shares is $3,700. Over the year, Harley pays dividends of $1.85 per share. By the end of the year, then, you received dividend income of

$$\text{Dividend income} = \$1.85 \times 100 = \$185$$

Suppose that as of December 31, Harley was selling for $40.33, meaning that the value of your stock increased by $3.33 per share. Your 100 shares are now worth $4,033, so you have a capital gain of

$$\text{Capital gain} = (\$40.33 - \$37) \times 100 = \$333$$

On the other hand, if the price had dropped to, say, $34.78, you would have a capital loss of

$$\text{Capital loss} = (\$34.78 - \$37) \times 100 = -\$222$$

Notice that a capital loss is the same thing as a negative capital gain.

total dollar return
The return on an investment measured in dollars that accounts for all cash flows and capital gains or losses.

The **total dollar return** on your investment is the sum of the dividend and the capital gain:

$$\text{Total dollar return} = \text{Dividend income} + \text{Capital gain (or loss)}$$

In our first example here, the total dollar return is thus given by

$$\text{Total dollar return} = \$185 + \$333 = \$518$$

Overall, between the dividends you received and the increase in the price of the stock, the value of your investment increased from $3,700 to $3,700 + $518 = $4,218.

A common misconception often arises in this context. Suppose you hold on to your Harley-Davidson stock and don't sell it at the end of the year. Should you still consider the capital gain as part of your return? Isn't this only a "paper" gain and not really a cash gain if you don't sell it?

The answer to the first question is a strong yes, and the answer to the second is an equally strong no. The capital gain is every bit as much a part of your return as the dividend, and you should certainly count it as part of your return. The fact that you decide to keep the stock and don't sell (you don't "realize" the gain) is irrelevant because you could have converted it to cash if you had wanted to. Whether you choose to do so is up to you.

After all, if you insist on converting your gain to cash, you could always sell the stock and immediately reinvest by buying the stock back. There is no difference between doing this and just not selling (assuming, of course, that there are no transaction costs or tax consequences from selling the stock). Again, the point is that whether you actually cash out and buy pizzas (or whatever) or reinvest by not selling doesn't affect the return you actually earn.

Percentage Returns

It is usually more convenient to summarize information about returns in percentage terms than in dollar terms, because that way your return doesn't depend on how much you actually invested. With percentage returns the question we want to answer is: How much do we get for each dollar we invest?

To answer this question, let P_t be the price of the stock at the beginning of the year and let D_{t+1} be the dividend paid on the stock during the year. The following cash flows are the same as those shown earlier, except that we have now expressed everything on a per-share basis:

	Ending Stock Price	
	$40.33	**$34.78**
January 1	$37.00	$37.00
December 31	40.33	34.78
Dividend income	1.85	1.85
Capital gain or loss	3.33	−2.22

In our example, the price at the beginning of the year was $37 per share and the dividend paid during the year on each share was $1.85. If we express this dividend as a percentage of the beginning stock price, the result is the *dividend yield:*

$$\text{Dividend yield} = D_{t+1} / P_t$$
$$= \$1.85 / \$37 = .05 = 5\%$$

This says that for each dollar we invested we received 5 cents in dividends.

The second component of our percentage return is the *capital gains yield*. This yield is calculated as the change in the price during the year (the capital gain) divided by the beginning price. With the $40.33 ending price, we get:

$$\text{Capital gains yield} = (P_{t+1} - P_t) / P_t$$
$$= (\$40.33 - \$37) / \$37$$
$$= \$3.33 / \$37 = .09 = 9\%$$

total percent return
The return on an investment measured as a percentage of the originally invested sum that accounts for all cash flows and capital gains or losses.

This 9 percent yield means that for each dollar invested we got 9 cents in capital gains.

Putting it all together, per dollar invested, we get 5 cents in dividends and 9 cents in capital gains for a total of 14 cents. Our **total percent return** is 14 cents on the dollar, or 14 percent. When a return is expressed on a percentage basis, we often refer to it as the *rate of return* on the investment.

To check our calculations, notice that we invested $3,700 and ended up with $4,218. By what percentage did our $3,700 increase? As we saw, we picked up $4,218 − $3,700 = $518. This is an increase of $518 / $3,700, or 14 percent.

Example 1.1   Calculating Percentage Returns

Suppose you buy some stock for $25 per share. After one year, the price is $35 per share. During the year, you received a $2 dividend per share. What is the dividend yield? The capital gains yield? The percentage return? If your total investment was $1,000, how much do you have at the end of the year?

Your $2 dividend per share works out to a dividend yield of

$$\text{Dividend yield} = D_{t+1} / P_t$$
$$= \$2 / \$25$$
$$= 8\%$$

The per-share capital gain is $10, so the capital gains yield is

$$
\begin{aligned}
\text{Capital gains yield} &= (P_{t+1} - P_t) \, / \, P_t \\
&= (\$35 - \$25) \, / \, \$25 \\
&= \$10 \, / \, \$25 \\
&= 40\%
\end{aligned}
$$

The total percentage return is thus 8% + 40% = 48%.

If you had invested $1,000, you would have $1,480 at the end of the year. To check this, note that your $1,000 would have bought you $1,000 / $25 = 40 shares. Your 40 shares would then have paid you a total of 40 × $2 = $80 in cash dividends. Your $10 per share gain would give you a total capital gain of $10 × 40 = $400. Add these together and you get $480, which is a 48 percent total return on your $1,000 investment.

CHECK THIS

1.1a What are the two parts of total return?

1.1b Why are unrealized capital gains or losses included in the calculation of returns?

1.1c What is the difference between a dollar return and a percentage return? Why are percentage returns usually more convenient?

1.2 The Historical Record

We now examine year-to-year historical rates of return on three important categories of financial investments. These returns can be interpreted as what you would have earned if you had invested in portfolios of the following asset categories:

1. Large-capitalization stocks (large-caps). The large-company stock portfolio is the Standard & Poor's index of the largest companies (in terms of total market value of outstanding stock) in the United States. This index is known as the S&P 500, since it contains 500 large companies.

2. Long-term U.S. Treasury bonds. This is a portfolio of U.S. government bonds with a 20-year life remaining until maturity.

3. U.S. Treasury bills. This a portfolio of Treasury bills (T-bills for short) with a three-month investment life.

If you are now not entirely certain what these investments are, don't be overly concerned. We will have much more to say about each in later chapters. For now, just take it as given that these are some of the things that you could have put your money into in years gone by. In addition to the year-to-year returns on these financial instruments, the year-to-year percentage changes in the Consumer Price Index (CPI) are also computed. The CPI is a standard measure of consumer goods price inflation.

A First Look

Before examining the different portfolio returns, we first take a look at the "big picture." Figure 1.1 shows what happened to $1 invested in these three different portfolios at the beginning of 1926 and held over the 72-year period ending in 1997. To fit all the information on a single graph, some modification in scaling is used. As is commonly

Figure 1.1   Investment Returns

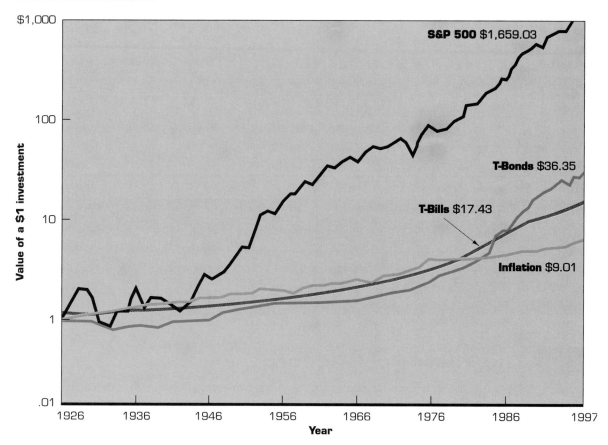

Source: Data from Global Financial Data, reprinted with permission.

done with financial time series, the vertical axis is scaled so that equal distances measure equal percentage (as opposed to dollar) changes in value. Thus, the distance between $10 and $100 is the same as that between $100 and $1,000, since both distances represent the same 900 percent increases.

Looking at Figure 1.1, we see that among these three asset categories the large-cap common stock portfolio did the best. Every dollar invested in the S&P 500 index at the start of 1926 grew to $1,659.03 at the end of 1997. At the other end of the return spectrum, the T-bond portfolio grew to just $36.35, and the T-bill portfolio grew to only $17.43. This bond and bill performance is even less impressive when we consider inflation over this period. As illustrated, the increase in the price level was such that $9.01 was needed in 1997 just to replace the purchasing power of the original $1 in 1926. In other words, an investment of $9.01 in T-bonds (measured in today's dollars) grew to only $36.35 over 72 years.

Given the historical record, why would any investor buy anything other than common stocks? If you look closely at Figure 1.1, you will see the answer—risk. The long-term government bond portfolio grew more slowly than did the stock portfolio, but it also grew much more steadily. The common stocks ended up on top, but as you can see, they grew more erratically much of the time. We examine these differences in volatility more closely later.

| **Figure 1.2** | International Stock Indexes |

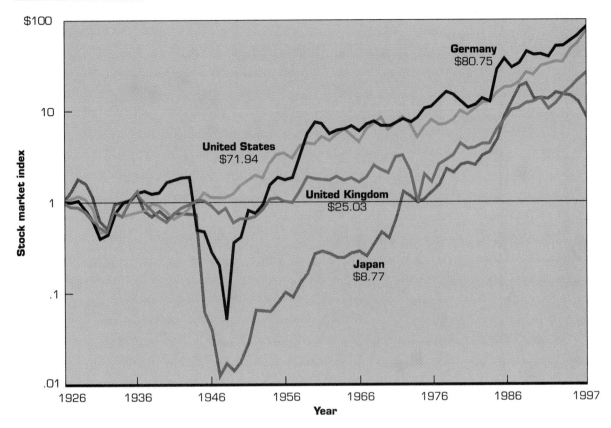

Source: Data from Global Financial Data, reprinted with permission.

A Look Overseas

It is instructive to compare the American financial experience since 1926 with the experience of some major foreign financial markets. Figure 1.2 graphically compares stock market index levels for the United Kingdom (England), Germany, and Japan over the 72-year period 1926 through 1997. Notice that the stock markets in Germany and Japan were devastated at the end of World War II in 1945 and recovered steadily after the war and through most of the postwar era.

If you compare the $71.94 for the United States in Figure 1.2 to the S&P 500 in Figure 1.1, there is an obvious (and very large) difference. The reason for the difference is that, in Figure 1.1, we assume that all dividends received are *reinvested*, meaning that they are used to buy more stock. In contrast, in Figure 1.2, we assume that dividends are not reinvested. Thus, one thing we learn is that whether or not we reinvest can have a big impact on the future value of our portfolio.

A Longer Range Look

The data available on the stock returns before 1925 are not comprehensive, but it is nonetheless possible to trace reasonably accurate returns in U.S. financial markets as far back as 1802. Figure 1.3 shows the values, in 1992, of $1 invested in stocks, long-term bonds, short-term bills, and gold. The CPI is also included for reference.

Figure 1.3   Financial Market History

Total return indexes (1802 – 1997)

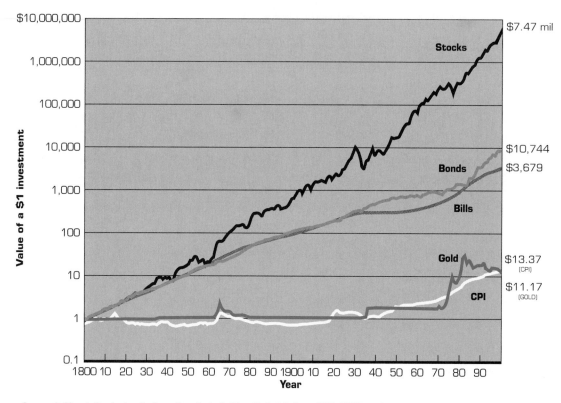

Source: Jeremy J. Siegel, *Stocks for the Long Run,* 2nd ed. (New York: McGraw-Hill, 1998), p. 6.

Inspecting Figure 1.3, we see that $1 invested in stocks grew to an astounding $7.47 million over this 195-year period. During this time, the returns from investing in stocks dwarf those earned on other investments. Notice also in Figure 1.3 that, after almost two centuries, gold has managed to keep up with inflation, but that is about it.

What we see thus far is that there has been a powerful financial incentive for long-term investing. The real moral of the story is this: Get an early start!

A Closer Look

To illustrate the variability of the different investments, Figures 1.4 through 1.6 plot year-to-year percentage returns in the form of vertical bars drawn from the horizontal axis. The height of each bar tells us the return for a particular year. For example, looking at the long-term government bonds (Figure 1.5), we see the largest historical return (44.44 percent) occurred not so long ago (in 1982). This was a good year for bonds. In comparing these charts, notice the differences in the vertical axis scales. With this in mind, you can see how predictably the Treasury bills (Figure 1.6) behaved compared to the S&P 500 index of large-cap stocks (Figure 1.4).

Figure 1.4   S & P 500 Annual Returns

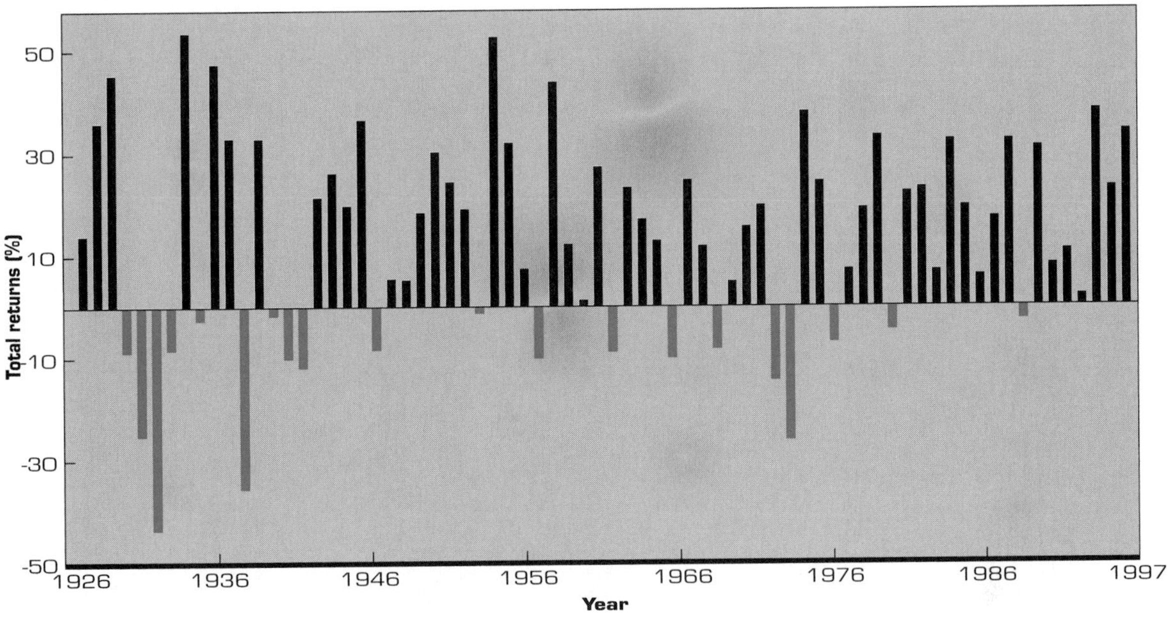

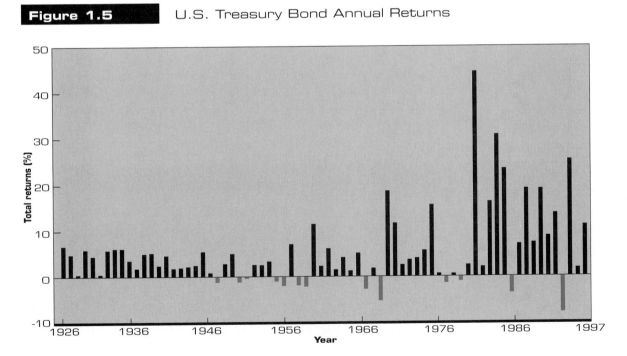

Source: Data from Global Financial Data, reprinted with permission.

Figure 1.5   U.S. Treasury Bond Annual Returns

Source: Data from Global Financial Data, reprinted with permission.

Figure 1.6   U.S. Treasury Bill Annual Returns

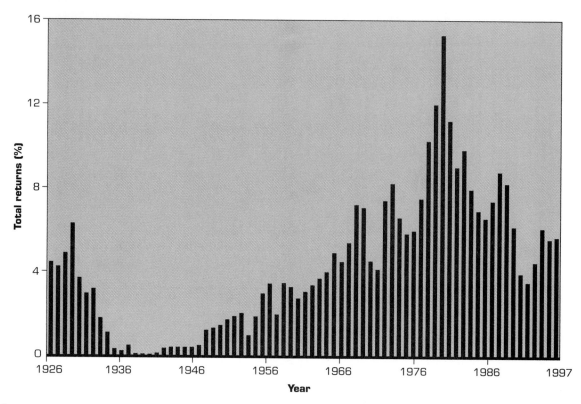

Source: Data from Global Financial Data, reprinted with permission.

The actual year-to-year returns used to draw these bar graphs are displayed in Table 1.1. Looking at this table, we see, for example, that the largest single-year return is an impressive 53.12 percent for the S&P 500 index of large-company stocks in 1933. In contrast, the largest Treasury bill return was merely 15.23 percent (in 1981).

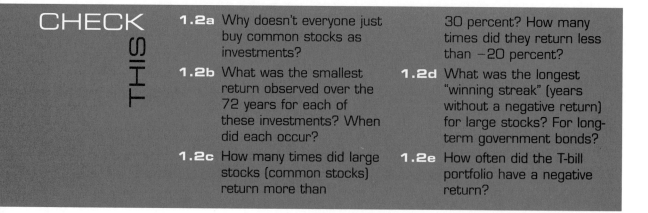

CHECK THIS

1.2a Why doesn't everyone just buy common stocks as investments?

1.2b What was the smallest return observed over the 72 years for each of these investments? When did each occur?

1.2c How many times did large stocks (common stocks) return more than

30 percent? How many times did they return less than −20 percent?

1.2d What was the longest "winning streak" (years without a negative return) for large stocks? For long-term government bonds?

1.2e How often did the T-bill portfolio have a negative return?

Table 1.1 — Annual Returns, 1926–1997

Year	S&P 500	T-Bonds	T-Bills	CPI	Year	S&P 500	T-Bonds	T-Bills	CPI
1926	13.70%	6.50%	4.41%	−1.12%	1962	−8.79%	6.04%	2.80%	1.33%
1927	35.78	4.52	4.21	−2.26	1963	22.72	1.39	3.16	1.64
1928	45.15	0.05	4.87	−1.16	1964	16.43	3.87	3.59	0.97
1929	−8.86	5.77	6.03	0.58	1965	12.38	1.00	3.98	1.92
1930	−25.22	4.18	3.75	−6.40	1966	−10.10	4.79	4.93	3.46
1931	−43.76	0.32	2.62	−9.32	1967	24.04	−2.48	4.49	3.04
1932	−8.40	5.63	2.91	−10.27	1968	11.04	1.57	5.39	4.72
1933	53.12	6.02	1.69	0.76	1969	−8.47	−4.98	6.81	6.20
1934	−2.42	5.94	1.06	1.52	1970	4.00	18.31	6.70	5.57
1935	46.98	3.29	0.26	2.99	1971	14.35	11.49	4.50	3.27
1936	32.33	1.67	0.14	1.45	1972	18.99	2.44	4.06	3.41
1937	−35.68	4.69	0.45	2.86	1973	−14.85	3.43	6.98	8.71
1938	32.26	4.79	0.05	−2.78	1974	−26.58	3.75	8.09	12.34
1939	−1.55	2.26	0.02	0.00	1975	37.42	5.60	6.03	6.94
1940	−10.50	4.31	0.01	0.71	1976	23.76	15.32	5.15	4.86
1941	−12.14	1.54	0.09	9.93	1977	−7.38	0.45	5.28	6.70
1942	20.98	1.80	0.32	9.03	1978	6.54	−1.15	7.23	9.02
1943	25.50	2.01	0.37	2.96	1979	18.59	0.37	10.30	13.29
1944	19.48	2.27	0.38	2.30	1980	32.61	−0.80	12.04	12.52
1945	36.33	5.29	0.38	2.25	1981	−4.97	2.46	15.23	8.92
1946	−8.48	0.54	0.38	18.13	1982	21.67	44.44	11.27	3.83
1947	4.96	−1.02	0.57	8.84	1983	22.57	1.90	8.90	3.79
1948	4.93	2.66	1.04	2.99	1984	6.19	16.00	10.04	3.95
1949	17.76	4.58	1.12	−2.07	1985	31.85	30.67	7.70	3.80
1950	30.03	−0.98	1.21	5.93	1986	18.68	23.13	6.18	1.10
1951	23.88	−0.20	1.54	6.00	1987	5.22	−3.43	5.86	4.43
1952	18.44	2.43	1.74	0.75	1988	16.58	6.83	6.73	4.42
1953	−1.11	2.28	1.95	0.75	1989	31.75	18.81	8.49	4.65
1954	52.43	3.08	0.96	−0.74	1990	−3.13	7.23	7.84	6.11
1955	31.64	−0.73	1.70	0.37	1991	30.53	18.70	5.71	3.06
1956	6.90	−1.72	2.68	2.99	1992	7.62	8.54	3.57	2.90
1957	−10.53	6.82	3.30	2.90	1993	10.07	13.59	3.08	2.75
1958	43.73	−1.72	1.81	1.76	1994	1.27	−7.55	4.15	2.67
1959	12.02	−2.02	3.34	1.73	1995	37.80	25.21	5.64	2.54
1960	0.45	11.21	3.13	1.36	1996	22.74	1.54	5.12	3.32
1961	26.89	2.20	2.35	0.67	1997	33.43	10.97	5.22	1.70

Source: Data from Global Financial Data, reprinted with permission.

1.3   Average Returns: The First Lesson

As you've probably begun to notice, the history of financial market returns in an undigested form is complicated. What we need are simple measures to accurately summarize and describe all these numbers. Accordingly, we discuss how to go about condensing detailed numerical data. We start out by calculating average returns.

Table 1.2	Annual Returns Statistics, 1926–1997			
	Asset Category	Average	Maximum	Minimum
	Large-cap stocks	12.83%	53.12%	−43.76%
	U.S. Treasury bonds	5.41	44.44	−7.55
	U.S. Treasury bills	4.10	15.23	0.01
	Inflation	3.20	18.13	−10.27

Calculating Average Returns

The obvious way to calculate average returns on the different investments in Table 1.1 is to simply add up the yearly returns and divide by 72. The result is the historical average of the individual values. For example, if you add the returns for common stocks for the 72 years, you will get about 923.63 percent. The average annual return is thus 923.63 / 72 = 12.83% You can interpret this 12.83 percent just like any other average. If you picked a year at random from the 72-year history and you had to guess the return in that year, the best guess is 12.83 percent.

Average Returns: The Historical Record

Table 1.2 shows the average returns computed from Table 1.1. These averages don't reflect the impact of inflation. Notice that over this 72-year period the average inflation rate was 3.20 percent per year while the average return on U.S. Treasury bills was 4.10 percent per year. Thus, the average return on Treasury bills exceeded the average rate of inflation by only .90 percent per year! At the other extreme, the return on large-cap common stocks exceeded the rate of inflation by a whopping 12.83% − 3.20% = 9.63%!

Risk Premiums

Now that we have computed some average returns, it seems logical to see how they compare with each other. Based on our discussion above, one such comparison involves government-issued securities. These are free of much of the variability we see in, for example, the stock market.

The government borrows money by issuing debt securities, which come in different forms. The ones we focus on here are Treasury bills. Because these instruments have a very short investment life and because the government can always raise taxes or print money to pay its bills, at least in the short run, there is essentially no risk associated with buying them. Thus, we call the rate of return on such debt the **risk-free rate,** and we will use it as a kind of investing benchmark.

risk-free rate The rate of return on a riskless investment.

A particularly interesting comparison involves the virtually risk-free return on T-bills and the risky return on common stocks. The difference between these two returns can be interpreted as a measure of the **risk premium** on the average risky asset (assuming that the stock of a large U.S. corporation has about average risk compared to all risky assets). We call this the risk premium because it is the additional return we earn by moving from a risk-free investment to a typical risky one, and we interpret it as a reward for bearing risk.

risk premium The extra return on a risky asset over the risk-free rate; the reward for bearing risk.

Risk Premiums: An International Perspective

We've seen that U.S. stock market investors earned significant risk premiums over the last few decades. It is natural to wonder whether this experience is unique to the United States or is a common feature of financial markets worldwide. To gain some perspective on this issue, look back at Figure 1.2 comparing U.S. stock market performance with that of stock markets in England, Germany, and Japan. As in Figure 1.1, what is shown is how the value of a $1 investment made in 1926 performed through the year 1997.

Unlike our previous Figure 1.1, the values in Figure 1.2 do not include dividends, so we are considering only the capital gains portion of stock market returns. In examining Figure 1.2, two things seem apparent. First, investors in all four countries made money, but the amounts differ quite a bit. Surprisingly, although the German stock market was nearly wiped out in World War II, an investment in German stocks is actually worth a little more than a similar U.S. investment. Investors in England lagged behind the United States and Germany, while investors in Japan did much worse.

In fact, the recent Japanese experience provides some insight into how risky stocks can be. Figure 1.7 focuses on the recent performance of the Nikkei 225, a widely followed index of large Japanese stocks. As shown, from 1984 to 1989 the Nikkei rocketed to almost 40,000 from just over 10,000. At its peak, the Tokyo Stock Exchange (TSE) surpassed even the New York Stock Exchange (NYSE) and was the largest market in the world based on the total value of traded stocks. From its peak, however, the Nikkei slid dramatically. By 1998, it had fallen to its lowest level since 1986, thus wiping out more than a decade's gains.

Almost any country, including the United States, has suffered from periods of substantial stock market declines. Nonetheless, the historical evidence from markets around the globe is surprisingly consistent. There does appear to be a risk premium, as over the long run stocks have done better than bonds or bills. But the "over the long run" part of this message is very important, because the long run may be very long indeed!

The First Lesson

From the data in Table 1.2, we can calculate risk premiums for the three different categories of investments. The results are shown in Table 1.3. Notice that the risk premium on T-bills is shown as zero in the table because they are our riskless benchmark. Looking at Table 1.3, we see that the average risk premium earned by the large-cap common stock portfolio is 12.83% − 4.10% = 8.73%. This is a significant reward. The fact that it exists historically is an important observation, and it is the basis for our first lesson: Risky assets, on average, earn a risk premium. Put another way, there is a reward, on average, for bearing risk.

Figure 1.7

Nikkei 225

Source: Reprinted with permission from *The Wall Street Journal,* via Copyright Clearance Center, Inc. © 1998 Dow Jones and Company, Inc. All Rights Reserved Worldwide.

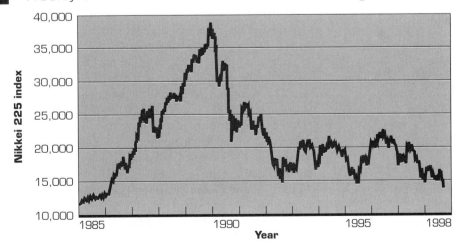

Weekly close of the Nikkei 225-Stock-Average Index

Table 1.3	Risk Premiums, 1926–1997	
	Asset Category	**Average**
	Large-cap stocks	8.73%
	U.S. Treasury bonds	1.31
	U.S. Treasury bills	0.00

Why is this so? Why, for example, is the risk premium for stocks so much larger than the risk premium for bonds? More generally, what determines the relative sizes of the risk premiums for the different assets? These questions speak to the heart of the modern theory of investments, and we will discuss the issues involved many times in the chapters ahead. For now, part of the answer can be found by looking at the historical variability of returns of these different investments. So, to get started, we now turn our attention to measuring variability in returns.

CHECK THIS

1.3a What is a risk premium?

1.3b What was the historical risk premium on common stocks? On U.S. Treasury bonds?

1.3c What is the first lesson from financial market history?

1.4 Return Variability: The Second Lesson

We have already seen that year-to-year returns on common stocks tend to be more volatile than returns on, say, long-term government bonds. We now discuss how to measure this variability so we can begin examining the important subject of risk.

Frequency Distributions and Variability

To get started, we can draw a *frequency distribution* for common stock returns like the one in Figure 1.8. What we have done here is to count the number of times that an annual return on the common stock portfolio falls within each 10 percent range. For example, in Figure 1.8, the height of 11 for the bar within the interval 32 percent to 42 percent means that 11 of the 72 annual returns are in that range. Notice also that the range from 22 percent to 32 percent is the most frequent return interval since the bar in this interval is the highest, representing 16 of 72 returns.

What we need to do now is to actually measure the spread in these returns. We know, for example, that the return on the S&P 500 index of common stocks in a typical year was 12.83 percent. We now want to know by how much the actual return differs from this average in a typical year. In other words, we need a measure of returns volatility. The **variance** and its square root, the **standard deviation,** are the most commonly used measures of volatility. We briefly review how to calculate these next. If you've already studied basic statistics, you should notice that we are simply calculating an ordinary sample variance and standard deviation, just as you may have done many times before.

variance A common measure of volatility.

standard deviation The square root of the variance.

Figure 1.8   S & P 500 Return Frequencies

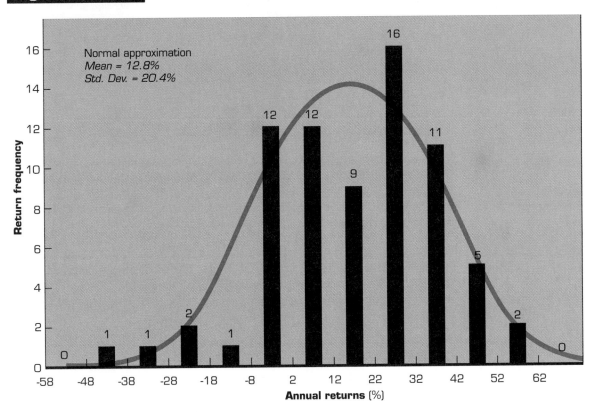

Source: Data from Global Financial Data, reprinted with permission.

The Historical Variance and Standard Deviation

Variance measures the average squared difference between the actual returns and the average return. The bigger this number is, the more the actual returns tend to differ from the average return. To illustrate how we calculate historical variance, suppose a particular investment had returns of 10 percent, 12 percent, 3 percent, and −9 percent over the last four years. The average return is (10% + 12% + 3% − 9%) / 4 = 4%.

Notice that the return is never actually equal to 4 percent. Instead, the first return deviates from the average by 10% − 4% = 6%, the second return deviates from the average by 12% − 4% = 8%, and so on. To compute the variance, we square each of these deviations, add them up, and divide the result by the number of returns less one, or three in this case[2]. These calculations are summarized immediately below.

$$
\begin{array}{rcl}
(10 - 4)^2 & = & 36 \\
(12 - 4)^2 & = & 64 \\
(3 - 4)^2 & = & 1 \\
(-9 - 4)^2 & = & \underline{169} \\
& & 270 \quad \rightarrow \quad \rightarrow \quad 270 \, / \, 3 = 90
\end{array}
$$

---

[2] The reason for dividing by $N - 1$ rather than simply N is based on statistical sampling theory, which is beyond the scope of this book. Just remember that to calculate a variance about a sample average divide the sum of squared deviations from the average by $N - 1$.

To recap, we first calculate the differences between actual returns and their average by subtracting out 4 percent. Second, we square each difference. Third, we sum all squared deviations to get 270. Finally, we divide the sum of the squared deviations by $4 - 1 = 3$.

By these calculations we get $Var(R)$ or σ^2 (read this as "sigma squared"), which is the variance of the return:

$$Var(R) = \sigma^2 = 270 / (4 - 1) = 90$$

The standard deviation is the square root of the variance. So, if $SD(R)$ or σ stands for the standard deviation of return:

$$SD(R) = \sigma = \sqrt{90} = 9.487\%$$

The square root of the variance is used because the variance is measured in "squared" percentages and is hard to interpret. The standard deviation is an ordinary percentage, which here is 9.487 percent.

In general, if we have N historical returns, where N is some number, we can write the historical variance as:

$$Var(R) = [(R_1 - \overline{R})^2 + (R_2 - \overline{R})^2 + \cdots + (R_N - \overline{R})^2] / (N - 1)$$

This formula tells us to do just what we did above: Take each of the N individual returns $(R_1, R_2, \ldots, R_N)$ and subtract the average return, $\overline{R}$; then square the results, and add them all up; finally, divide this total by the number of returns less one $(N - 1)$. The standard deviation is always the square root of $Var(R)$.

Example 1.2   Calculating the Variance and Standard Deviation

Calculate return averages, variances, and standard deviations for S&P 500 large-cap stocks and T-bonds using data for the first five years in Table 1.1, 1926–1930.

First, calculate return averages as follows:

S&P 500 Large-Cap Stocks	T-Bonds
13.70	6.50
35.78	4.52
45.15	0.05
−8.86	5.77
−25.22	4.18
60.55	21.02
Average return: 60.55 / 5 = 12.11	21.02 / 5 = 4.20

Using the averages above, calculate the squared deviations from the average returns and sum the squared deviations as follows:

S&P 500 Large-Cap Stocks		T-Bonds	
$(13.70 - 12.11)^2 =$	2.53	$(6.50 - 4.20)^2 =$	5.29
$(35.78 - 12.11)^2 =$	560.27	$(4.52 - 4.20)^2 =$	0.10
$(45.15 - 12.11)^2 =$	1,091.64	$(0.05 - 4.20)^2 =$	17.22
$(-8.86 - 12.11)^2 =$	439.74	$(5.77 - 4.20)^2 =$	2.46
$(-25.22 - 12.11)^2 =$	1,393.53	$(4.18 - 4.20)^2 =$	0.00
	3,487.71		25.07

Calculate return variances by dividing the sums of squared deviations by four, the number of returns less one.

S&P 500: 3,487.71 / 4 = 871.93   T-bonds: 25.07 / 4 = 6.27

Standard deviations are then calculated as the square root of the variance:

S&P 500: $\sqrt{871.93}$ = 29.53   T-bonds: $\sqrt{6.27}$ = 2.50

Notice that the large-cap stock portfolio had a volatility more than 10 times greater than the T-bond portfolio, which is not unusual during periods of market turbulence.

Table 1.4	Annual Returns Statistics, 1926–1997		
	Asset Category	**Average**	**Standard Deviation**
	Large-cap stocks	12.83%	20.38%
	U.S. Treasury bonds	5.41	8.35
	U.S. Treasury bills	4.10	3.25
	Inflation	3.20	4.52

The Historical Record

Table 1.4 summarizes much of our discussion of financial market history so far. It displays average returns and standard deviations for the three asset category portfolios. Notice that the standard deviation for the stock portfolio (20.38 percent per year) is more than six times larger than the T-bill portfolio's standard deviation (3.25 percent per year).

A useful thing about the distribution shown in Figure 1.8 is that it roughly approximates a normal distribution. Because of this, a good rule of thumb is that the probability that we end up within plus or minus one standard deviation of the average is about 2/3. The probability that we end up within plus or pminus two standard deviations of the average is about 95 percent. Finally, the probability of being more than three standard deviations away from the average is less than 1 percent.[3]

To see why this is useful, notice that Table 1.4 reports that the standard deviation of returns on the large-cap common stocks is 20.38 percent. The average return is 12.83 percent. So the probability that the return in a given year is in the range −7.55 percent to 33.21 percent [12.83% ±1 SD (20.38%)] is about 2/3.

In other words, there is about one chance in three that the return will be *outside* this range. This literally tells you that if you invest in the S&P 500 index of large-company stocks, you should expect to be outside this range in one year out of every three. This reinforces our earlier observations about stock market volatility. However, there is only a 5 percent chance (approximately) that we would end up outside the range −27.93 percent to 53.59 percent [(12.83% ±(2 × 20.38%)].

The Second Lesson

Our observations concerning year-to-year variability in returns are the basis for our second lesson from financial market history. On average, bearing risk is handsomely rewarded, but in a given year, there is a significant chance of a dramatic change in value. Thus our second lesson is: The greater the potential reward, the greater the risk.

---

[3] As many of you recognize, these probabilities are based on the normal distribution. The returns on most types of assets are in fact only roughly normal.

An excellent example of this second lesson is provided by the history of returns on small-capitalization stocks, often called small-caps. A small-cap portfolio of stocks from the smallest size quintile (20 percent) of stocks traded on the New York Stock Exchange (NYSE) earned an average return of 17.21 percent over the 72-year period 1926 through 1997. This average return yields a risk premium of 13.11 percent. Thus, the historical average return and risk premium on a small-cap stock portfolio was almost 5 percent more than the average return and risk premium on the S&P 500 index. However, this extra return came with substantial extra risk; the small-caps return standard deviation was 34.34 percent, or almost double the risk of the S&P 500 portfolio of large-cap stocks.

Example 1.3   Investing in Growth Stocks

As a practical matter, the phrase *growth stock* is frequently a euphemism for small-company stock. Are such investments suitable for "widows and orphans"? Before answering, you should consider historical volatility. For example, from the historical record, what is the approximate probability that you will actually lose 17 percent or more of your money in a single year if you buy stocks from a group of such companies?

The historical average return on a small-cap stock portfolio is 17.21 percent, with an annual standard deviation of 34.34 percent. From our rule of thumb, there is about a 1/3 probability that you will experience a return outside the range −17.13 percent to 51.55 percent (17.21% ± 34.34%).

The odds of being above or below this range are about equal. There is thus about a 1/6 chance (half of 1/3) that you will lose more than 17 percent. So you should expect this to happen once in every six years, on average. Such investments can thus be *very* volatile, and they are not well-suited for those who cannot afford to bear the risk.

CHECK THIS

1.4a In words, how do we calculate a variance? A standard deviation?

1.4b What is the first lesson from financial market history? The second lesson?

1.5 Risk and Return

In previous sections we explored financial market history to see what we could learn about risk and return. In this section we summarize our findings and then conclude our discussion by looking ahead at the subjects we will be examining in later chapters.

The Risk-Return Trade-Off

Figure 1.9 is a way of putting together our findings on risk and return. What it shows is that there is a risk-return trade-off. At one extreme, if we are unwilling to bear any risk at all, but we are willing to forgo the use of our money for a while, then we can earn the risk-free rate. Because the risk-free rate represents compensation for just waiting, it is often called the *time value of money*.

Figure 1.9   Risk-Return Trade-Off

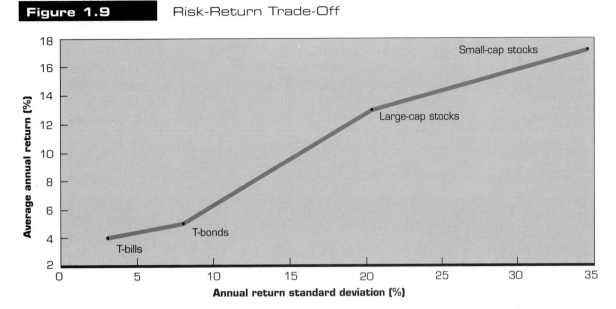

Source: Data from Global Financial Data, reprinted with permission.

If we are willing to bear risk, then we can expect to earn a risk premium, at least on average. Further, the more risk we are willing to bear, the greater is that risk premium. Investment advisers like to say that an investment has a "wait" component and a "worry" component. In our figure, the time value of money is the compensation for waiting, and the risk premium is the compensation for worrying.

There are two important caveats to this discussion. First, risky investments do not *always* pay more than risk-free investments. Indeed, that's precisely what makes them risky. In other words, there is a risk premium *on average*, but, over any particular time interval, there is no guarantee. Second, we've intentionally been a little imprecise about what we mean exactly by risk. As we will discuss in the chapters ahead, not all risks are compensated. Some risks are cheaply and easily avoidable, and there is no expected reward for bearing them. It is only those risks that cannot be easily avoided that are compensated (on average).

A Look Ahead

In the remainder of this text, we focus exclusively on financial assets. An advantage of this approach is that it is limited to four major types: stocks, bonds, options, and futures, in the order that we cover them. This means that we won't be discussing collectibles such as classic automobiles, baseball cards, coins, fine art, or stamps. We also won't be discussing real estate or precious metals such as gold and platinum. It's not that these are unimportant; rather, they are very specialized. So, instead of treating them superficially, we leave a discussion of them for another day (and another book).

As we've indicated, to understand the potential reward from an investment, it is critical to first understand the risk involved. There is an old saying that goes like this: It's easy to make a small fortune investing in _____ (put your favorite investment here)— just start with a large fortune! The moral is that the key to successful investing is to make informed, intelligent decisions about risk. For this reason, we are going to pay particular attention to the things that determine the value of the different assets we discuss and the nature of the associated risks.

One common characteristic that these assets have is that they are bought and sold around the clock and around the world in vast quantities. The way they are traded can be very different, however. We think it is important and interesting to understand exactly what happens when you buy or sell one of these assets, so we will be discussing the different trading mechanisms and the way the different markets function. We will also describe actual buying and selling at various points along the way to show you the steps involved and the results of placing buy and sell orders and having them executed.

GET REAL

This chapter took you through some basic, but important, investment-related calculations. We then walked through the modern history of risk and return, both in the United States and elsewhere. How should you, as an investor or investment manager, put this information to work?

The answer is that you now have a rational, objective basis for thinking about what you stand to make from investing in some important broad asset classes. For the stock market as a whole, as measured by the performance of large-company stocks, you know that you can realistically expect to make 13 percent or so per year on average.

Equally important, you know that you won't make 13 percent in any one year; instead, you'll make more or less. You know that the standard deviation is about 20 percent per year, and you should know what that means in terms of risk. In particular, you need to understand that in one year out of every six, you should expect to lose more than 7 percent (13 percent minus one standard deviation), so this will be a relatively common event. The good news is that in one year out of six, you can realistically expect to earn more than 33 percent (13 percent plus one standard deviation).

The other important, practical thing to understand from this chapter is that a strategy of investing in very low risk assets (such as T-bills) has historically barely kept up with inflation. This might be sufficient for some investors, but if your goal is to do better than that, then you will have to bear some amount of risk to achieve it.

1.6 Summary and Conclusions

This chapter explores financial market history. Such a history lesson is useful because it tells us what to expect in the way of returns from risky assets. We summarized our study of market history with two key lessons:

1. Risky assets, on average, earn a risk premium. There is a reward for bearing risk.

2. The greater the potential reward from a risky investment, the greater is the risk.

When we put these two lessons together, we concluded that there is a risk-return trade-off: The only way to earn a higher return is to take on greater risk.

Key Terms

total dollar return 5   risk premium 14
total percent return 6   variance 16
risk-free rate 14   standard deviation 16

Chapter Review Problems and Self-Test

1. **Calculating Returns**   You bought 400 shares of Metallica Heavy Metal, Inc., at $30 per share. Over the year, you received $.75 per share in dividends. If the stock sold for $33 at the end of the year, what was your dollar return? Your percentage return?

2. **Calculating Returns and Variability**   Using the following returns, calculate the average returns, the variances, and the standard deviations for the following stocks:

Year	Michele, Inc.	Janicek Co.
1	12%	5%
2	−4	−15
3	0	10
4	20	38
5	2	17

Answers to Self-Test Problems

1. Your dollar return is just your gain or loss in dollars. Here, we receive $.75 in dividends on each of our 400 shares, for a total of $300. In addition, each share rose from $30 to $33, so we make $3 × 400 shares = $1,200. Our total dollar return is thus $300 + $1,200 = $1,500.

   Our percentage return (or just "return" for short) is equal to the $1,500 we made divided by our initial outlay of $30 × 400 shares = $12,000; so $1,500/12,000 = .125 = 12.5%. Equivalently, we could have just noted that each share paid a $.75 dividend and each share gained $3, so the total dollar gain per share was $3.75. As a percentage of the cost of one share ($30), we get $3.75 / 30 = .125 = 12.5%.

2. First, calculate return averages as follows:

Michele, Inc.	Janicek Co.
12%	5%
−4	−15
0	10
20	38
2	17
30%	55%

Average return: 30/ 5 = 6%   55/ 5 = 11%

Using the averages above, calculate the squared deviations from the average returns and sum the squared deviations as follows:

Michele, Inc.	Janicek Co.
$(12 - 6)^2 = 36$	$(5 - 11)^2 = 36$
$(-4 - 6)^2 = 100$	$(-15 - 11)^2 = 676$
$(0 - 6)^2 = 36$	$(10 - 11)^2 = 1$
$(20 - 6)^2 = 196$	$(38 - 11)^2 = 729$
$(2 - 6)^2 = 16$	$(17 - 11)^2 = 36$
384	1,478

Calculate return variances by dividing the sums of squared deviations by four, which is the number of returns less one.

$$\text{Michele: } 384 \,/\, 4 = 96 \qquad \text{Janicek: } 1{,}478 \,/\, 4 = 369.5$$

Standard deviations are then calculated as the square root of the variance.

$$\text{Michele: } \sqrt{96} = 9.8\% \qquad \text{Janicek: } \sqrt{369.5} = 19.22\%$$

Test Your Investment Quotient

1. **Stock Returns**   A stock pays a $1.50 dividend and falls in price from $56.25 to $52.75. What is the stockholder's total dollar return?

   a. −$1.50
   b. −$2.00
   c. −$2.50
   d. −$3.00

2. **Stock Returns**   A stock pays a $1 dividend and rises in price from $50 to $53. What is the stockholder's total percentage return?

   a. 8 percent
   b. 4 percent
   c. 5 percent
   d. −2 percent

3. **Prices and Returns**   Over a one-year period, a bond pays 7 percent interest and its price falls from $100 to $98. What is the bondholder's total realized one-year return?

   a. 9 percent
   b. 7 percent
   c. 5 percent
   d. −2 percent

4. **Prices and Returns**   You plan to buy common stock and hold it for one year. You expect to receive both $1.50 in dividends and $26 from the sale of stock at the end of the year. If you wanted to earn a 15 percent return, what is the maximum price you would pay for the stock today? (*1994 CFA Exam*)*

   a. $22.61
   b. $23.91
   c. $24.50
   d. $27.50

5. **Return Components**   The total dollar return on an investment is conventionally said to have two components. What are these two components?

   a. A cash payment and a capital gain or loss
   b. A dollar return and a percentage return
   c. A taxable component and a tax-exempt component
   d. Principal and interest

6. **Investment Returns**   Suppose the value of an investment doubles in a one-year period. In this case, the rate of return on this investment over that one-year period is what amount?

   a. 100 percent even if the gain is not actually realized
   b. 200 percent even if the gain is not actually realized
   c. 100 percent only if the gain is actually realized
   d. 200 percent only if the gain is actually realized

---

* For complete CFA reference, see Appendix B.

7. **Investment Returns** Suppose the value of an investment decreases by half in a one-year period. In this case, the rate of return on this investment over that one-year period is what amount?

   a. −100 percent even if the loss is not actually realized
   b. −50 percent even if the loss is not actually realized
   c. −100 percent only if the loss is actually realized
   d. −50 percent only if the loss is actually realized

8. **Historical Returns** Which of the following asset categories has an annual returns history most closely linked to historical annual rates of inflation?

   a. U.S. Treasury bills
   b. Corporate bonds
   c. Large-company stocks
   d. Small-company stocks

9. **Historical Returns** Based on the annual returns history since 1926, which asset category on average has yielded the highest risk premium?

   a. U.S. government bonds
   b. Corporate bonds
   c. Large-company stocks
   d. Small-company stocks

10. **Financial Markets' Lessons** The first lesson of financial markets history is:

    a. Don't put all your eggs in one basket
    b. Put all your eggs in one basket and watch that basket
    c. Buy low and sell high
    d. Risky assets on average earn a risk premium

11. **Stat 101** Over a four-year period, an investment in T-Rex common stock yields returns of 30 percent, 0 percent, −10 percent, and 20 percent. What is the standard deviation of return for T-Rex stock over this four-year period?

    a. 10 percent
    b. 21.6 percent
    c. 20 percent
    d. 18.3 percent

12. **Stat 101** You calculate an average historical return of 10 percent and a standard deviation of return of 10 percent for an investment in Stonehenge Construction Co. You believe these values represent well the future distribution of returns. Assuming that returns are normally distributed, what is the probability that Stonehenge Construction will yield a negative return?

    a. 17 percent
    b. 33 percent
    c. 50 percent
    d. 20 percent

13. **Stat 101** Given a data series that is normally distributed with a mean of 100 and a standard deviation of 10, about 95 percent of the numbers in the series will fall within which of the following ranges? (*1994 CFA exam*)

    a. 60 to 140
    b. 70 to 130
    c. 80 to 120
    d. 90 to 110

CFA

14. **Stat 101**   For a given set of returns data, in addition to the mean you calculate these three risk measures: range (maximum minus minimum), variance, and standard deviation. Which of the following statements about these three risk measures is correct?

a. The variance is always larger than the standard deviation
b. The mean always lies between the minimum and the maximum
c. The range is always larger than the mean
d. The range is sometimes smaller than the standard deviation

15. **Stat 101**   Which of the following statements about a normal distribution is incorrect?

a. A normal distribution is symmetrically centered on its mean
b. The probability of being within one standard deviation from the mean is about 66 percent
c. The probability of being within two standard deviations from the mean is about 5 percent
d. The probability of a negative value is always one-half.

Questions and Problems

**Core
Questions**

1. **Calculating Returns**   Suppose you bought 200 shares of stock at an initial price of $42 per share. The stock paid a dividend of $2.40 per share during the following year, and the share price at the end of the year was $31. Compute your total dollar return on this investment. Does your answer change if you keep the stock instead of selling it? Why or why not?

2. **Calculating Yields**   In the previous problem, what is the capital gains yield? The dividend yield? What is the total rate of return on the investment?

3. **Calculating Returns**   Rework Problems 1 and 2 assuming that you buy 750 shares of the stock and the ending share price is $60.

4. **Historical Returns**   What is the historical rate of return on each of the following investments? What is the historical risk premium on these investments?

a. Long-term government bonds
b. Treasury bills
c. Common stocks
d. Small stocks

5. **Calculating Average Returns**   The rate of return on Jurassic Jalopies, Inc., stock over the last five years was 25 percent, 17 percent, −22 percent, 29 percent, and 8 percent. Over the same period, the return on Stonehenge Construction Company's stock was 9 percent, 13 percent, 3 percent, 16 percent, and 6 percent. What was the average return on each stock over this period?

6. **Calculating Returns and Variability**   Using the following returns, calculate the average returns, the variances, and the standard deviations for stocks A and B.

Year	A	B
1	14%	22%
2	3	− 5
3	−6	−15
4	11	28
5	9	17

7. **Risk versus Return**   Based on the historical record, rank the following investments in increasing order of risk. Rank the investments in increasing order of average returns. What do you conclude about the relationship between the risk of an investment and the return you expect to earn on it?

a. Common stocks
b. Treasury bills
c. Long-term government bonds
d. Small stocks

8. **Returns and the Bell Curve**   An investment has an expected return of 10 percent per year with a standard deviation of 20 percent. Assuming that the returns on this investment are at least roughly normally distributed, how frequently do you expect to earn between −10 percent and +30 percent?

9. **Returns and the Bell Curve**   An investment has an expected return of 6 percent per year with a standard deviation of 3 percent. Assuming that the returns on this investment are at least roughly normally distributed, how frequently do you expect to lose money?

10. **Using Returns Distributions**   Based on the historical record, if you invest in U.S. Treasury bonds, what is the approximate probability that your return will be less than −2.94 percent in a given year? What range of returns would you expect to see 95 percent of the time? 99 percent of the time?

Intermediate Questions

11. **Using Returns Distributions**   Based on the historical record, what is the approximate probability that an investment in small stocks will double in value in a single year? How about triple in a single year?

12. **More Returns Distributions**   In the previous problem, what is the probability that the return on small stocks will be less than −100 percent in a single year (think about it)? What are the implications for the distribution of returns?

13. **Risk Premiums**   Consider the following common stock and T-bill returns for the period 1980-1986:

Year	Common Stocks	T-Bills
1980	32.6%	12.0%
1981	−5.0	15.2
1982	21.7	11.3
1983	22.6	8.9
1984	6.2	10.0
1985	31.9	7.7
1986	18.7	6.2

a. Calculate the observed risk premium in each year for the common stocks.
b. Calculate the average returns and the average risk premium over this period.
c. Calculate the standard deviation of returns and the standard deviation of the risk premium.
d. Is it possible that the observed risk premium can be negative? Explain how this can happen and what it means.

14. **Inflation and Returns**   Look at Table 1.1 and Figure 1.6. When were T-bill rates at their highest? Why do you think they were so high during this period?

15. **Inflation and Returns**   The returns we have examined are not adjusted for inflation. What do you suppose would happen to our estimated risk premiums if we did account for inflation?

16. **Taxes and Returns**   The returns we have examined are not adjusted for taxes. What do you suppose would happen to our estimated returns and risk premiums if we did account for taxes? What would happen to our volatility measures?

17. **Taxes and Treasury Bills**   As a practical matter, most of the return you earn from investing in Treasury bills is taxed right away as ordinary income. Thus, if you are in a 40 percent tax bracket and you earn 5 percent on a Treasury bill, your aftertax return is only .05 × (1 − .40) = .03, or 3 percent. In other words, 40 percent of your return goes to pay taxes, leaving you with just 3 percent. Once you consider inflation and taxes, how does the long-term return from Treasury bills look?

18. The Long Run   Given your answer to the last question and the discussion in the chapter, why would any rational person do anything other than load up on 100 percent small stocks?

STOCK-TRAK·
Portfolio Simulations

Portfolio Trading Simulations with Stock-Trak

Stock-Trak provides an effective, low-cost way to learn the basics of securities trading on the Internet. With a Stock-Trak account, you can trade stocks, bonds, options, and futures through the Stock-Trak website (www.mhhe.com/cj). Stock-Trak trading is conducted in much the same way as you would trade through your own brokerage account with a broker that supports trading on the Internet. With the Stock-Trak Portfolio Trading Simulation you gain valuable experience trading securities at actual market prices. However, you can't lose real money since Stock-Trak is a simulation.

This textbook contains several sections intended to provide specialized instructions on trading securities through Stock-Trak. We recommend that you start by reading the section "*Trading Common Stocks with Stock-Trak*" at the end of Chapter 2. This section will bring you up to speed on the mechanics of trading common stocks on the Internet. Similar Stock-Trak sections are dispersed throughout the textbook. For example, the section "*Trading Stock Options with Stock-Trak*" at the end of Chapter 14 explains how ticker symbols for stock options must be constructed before submitting an order to trade stock options on the Internet through Stock-Trak. Similarly, the section "*Trading Futures Contracts with Stock-Trak*" at the end of Chapter 16 discusses the intricacies of submitting orders to trade futures contracts. These sections are designed to supplement instructions provided by Stock-Trak in its brochure and at the Stock-Trak website. Remember, you can't lose real money with Stock-Trak, so feel free to experiment!

Stock-Trak Exercises

1. Log on to the Stock-Trak website through www.mhhe.com/cj.

2. While logged on to the Stock-Trak website, review the most current rules and regulations pertaining to Stock-Trak accounts.

3. Explore some of the Internet links to stock market research tools provided by Stock-Trak.

2

Buying and Selling Securities

"First you buy a stock. If it goes up, sell it. If it doesn't go up, don't buy it." You might wish to try Will Rogers's well-known stock market advice, but first you must know the basics of securities trading. Fortunately, trading is a relatively simple task, as attested to by the billions of shares of stocks that trade among investors on a typical, busy day. Essentially, you begin the process by opening a trading account with a brokerage firm and then submitting trading orders. But you should know about some important details beforehand. ■ We hope reading about the history of risk and return in the previous chapter generated some interest in investing on your own. To help you get started, this chapter covers the basics of the investing process. We begin by describing how you go about buying and selling securities such as stocks and bonds. We then outline some of the most important considerations and constraints to keep in mind as you get more involved in the investing process.

2.1   Getting Started

Suppose you have some money that you want to invest. One way to get started is to open an account with a securities broker, such as A.G. Edwards or Merrill Lynch. Such accounts are often called *brokerage* or *trading accounts*. Opening a trading account is straightforward and really much like opening a bank account. You will be asked to supply some basic information about yourself and sign an agreement (often simply called a customer's agreement) that spells out your rights and obligations and those of your broker. You then give your broker a check and instructions on how you want the money invested.

To illustrate, suppose that instead of going to Disneyland, you would rather own part of it. You therefore open an account with $10,000. You instruct your broker to purchase 100 shares of Walt Disney stock and to retain any remaining funds in your account. Your broker will locate a seller and purchase the stock on your behalf. Say shares of stock in Walt Disney Corporation are selling for about $60 per share, so your 100 shares will cost $6,000. In addition, for providing this service, your broker will charge you a commission. How much depends on a number of things, including the type of broker and the size of your order, but on this order, $50 wouldn't be an unusual commission charge. After paying for the stock and paying the commission, you would have $3,950 left in your account. Your broker will hold your stock for you or deliver the shares to you, whichever you wish. At a later date, you can sell your stock by instructing your broker to do so. You would receive the proceeds from the sale, less another commission charge. You can always add money to your account and purchase additional securities, and you can withdraw money from your account or even close it altogether.

In broad terms, this basic explanation is really all there is to it. As we begin to discuss in the next section, however, there is a range of services available to you, and there are important considerations that you need to take into account before you actually begin investing.

Choosing a Broker

The first step in opening an account is choosing a broker. Brokers are typically divided into three groups: full-service brokers, discount brokers, and deep-discount brokers. Table 2.1 lists well-known brokers in each category. What distinguishes the three groups is the level of service they provide and the resulting commissions they charge.

With a deep-discount broker, essentially the only services provided are account maintenance and order execution—that is, buying and selling. You generally deal with a deep-discount broker over the telephone or, increasingly, using a web browser (see the next section on online brokers for a discussion).

At the other extreme, a full-service broker will provide investment advice regarding the types of securities and investment strategies that might be appropriate for you to consider (or avoid). The larger brokerage firms do extensive research on individual companies and securities and maintain lists of recommended (and not recommended) securities. They maintain offices throughout the country, so, depending on where you live, you can actually stop in and speak to the person assigned to your account. A full-service broker will even manage your account for you if you wish.

Discount brokers fall somewhere between the two cases we have discussed so far, offering more investment counseling than the deep-discounters and lower commissions than the full-service brokers. Which type of broker should you choose? It depends on how much advice and service you need or want. If you are the do-it-yourself type, then

Table 2.1	Brokerage Firms and Representative Commissions		
		Commissions ($50 share price)*	
Examples	200 Shares	500 Shares	1,000 Shares
Full-Service Brokers			
A.G. Edwards	$200	$250	$400
Merrill Lynch			
Discount Brokers			
Charles Schwab	$100	$150	$200
Fidelity Brokerage			
Deep-Discount Brokers			
Olde Discount	$60	$100	$125
Quick & Reilly			

*These commissions are approximate and representative only. They do not necessarily correspond to actual rates charged by firms listed in this table.

you may seek out the lowest commissions. If you are not, then a full-service broker might be more suitable. Often investors begin with a full-service broker, then, as they gain experience and confidence, move on to a discount broker.

We should note that the brokerage industry is very competitive, and differences between broker types seem to be blurring. Full-service brokers frequently discount commissions to attract new customers (particularly those with large accounts), and you should not hesitate to ask about commission rates. Similarly, discount brokers have begun to offer securities research and extensive account management services. Basic brokerage services have become almost commodity-like, and, more and more, broker-age firms are competing by offering financial services such as retirement planning, credit cards, and check-writing privileges, to name a few.

Online Brokers

The most important recent change in the brokerage industry is the rapid growth of online brokers, also known as e-brokers or cyberbrokers. With an online broker, you place buy and sell orders over the Internet using a web browser. If you are currently par-ticipating in a portfolio simulation such as Stock-Trak, then you already have a very good idea of how an online account looks and feels.

Before 1995, online accounts essentially did not exist; by 1998, millions of investors were buying and selling securities on-line. Projections suggest that by 2000, more than 10 million online accounts will be active. The industry is growing so rapidly that it is difficult to even count the number of online brokers. By late 1998, the number was approaching 100, but the final tally will surely be much larger.

Online investing has fundamentally changed the discount and deep-discount broker-age industry by slashing costs dramatically. In a typical online trade, no human inter-vention is needed by the broker as the entire process is handled electronically, so oper-ating costs are held to a minimum. As costs have fallen, so have commissions. Even for relatively large trades, online brokers typically charge less than $15 per trade. For budg-et-minded investors and active stock traders, the attraction is clear.

Who are the online brokers? Table 2.2 provides information on some of the larger ones. As the industry evolves, this information changes, so check our website (at www.mhhe.com/cj) for more up-to-date information. Examining the table, you might notice that at least some of these online brokers are actually just branches of large

Table 2.2	Large Online Brokers		
	Broker	**Internet Address**	**Commission for Simple Stock Transaction**
	Charles Schwab	www.schwab.com	$29.95, up to 1,000 shares
	Fidelity Investments	www.fidelity.com	$25, up to 1,000 shares
	DLJdirect	www.dljdirect.com	$20, up to 1,000 shares
	E*Trade	www.etrade.com	$14.95, up to 5,000 shares
	Waterhouse	www.waterhouse.com	$12, up to 5,000 shares
	Ameritrade	www.ameritrade.com	$8, no share limits

discount brokers. Charles Schwab, for example, is both the largest discount broker and the largest online broker.

Competition among online brokers is fierce. Some take a no-frills approach, offering only basic services and very low commission rates. Others, particularly the larger ones, charge a little more but offer a variety of services, including research and various banking services such as check-writing privileges, credit cards, debit cards, and even mortgages. As technology continues to improve and investors become more comfortable using it, online brokerages will almost surely become the dominant form because of their enormous convenience—and the low commission rates.

Security Investors Protection Corporation

Security Investors Protection Corporation (SIPC)
Insurance fund covering investors' brokerage accounts with member firms.

As you are probably aware, when you deposit money in a bank, your account is normally protected (up to $100,000) by the Federal Deposit Insurance Corporation, or FDIC, which is an agency of the U.S. government. However, brokerage firms, even though they are often called investment banks, cannot offer FDIC coverage. Most brokerage firms do belong to the **Security Investors Protection Corporation**, or **SIPC**, which was created in 1970. The SIPC insures your account for up to $500,000 in cash and securities, with a $100,000 cash maximum. Some brokers carry additional insurance beyond SIPC minimums. Unlike the FDIC, the SIPC is not a government agency; it is a private insurance fund supported by the securities industry. However, by government regulations almost all brokerage firms operating in the United States are required to be members of the SIPC.

There is a very important difference between SIPC coverage and FDIC coverage. Up to the maximum coverage, the value of whatever you deposit in a bank is fully guaranteed by the FDIC; you will not lose a cent under any circumstances with FDIC coverage. In contrast, the SIPC insures only that you will receive whatever cash and securities were held for you by your broker in the event of fraud or other failure. The value of any securities, however, is not guaranteed. In other words, you can lose everything in an SIPC-covered account if the value of your securities falls to zero.

Broker–Customer Relations

There are several other important things to keep in mind when dealing with a broker. First, any advice you receive is *not* guaranteed. Far from it—buy and sell recommendations carry the explicit warning that you rely on them at your own risk. Your broker does have a duty to exercise reasonable care in formulating recommendations and not recommend anything grossly unsuitable, but that is essentially the extent of it.

Second, your broker works as your agent and has a legal duty to act in your best interest; however, brokerage firms are in the business of generating brokerage commissions. This fact will probably be spelled out in the account agreement that you sign. There is therefore the potential for a conflict of interest. On rare occasions, a broker is accused of "churning" an account, which refers to extensive trading for the sole purpose of generating commissions. In general, you are responsible for checking your account statements and notifying your broker in the event of any problems, and you should certainly do so.

Finally, in the unlikely event of a significant problem, your account agreement will probably specify very clearly that you must waive your right to sue and/or seek a jury trial. Instead, you agree that any disputes will be settled by arbitration and that arbitration is final and binding. Arbitration is not a legal proceeding and the rules are much less formal. In essence, a panel is appointed by a self-regulatory body of the securities industry to review the case. The panel will be composed of a small number of individuals who are knowledgeable about the securities industry, but a majority of them will not be associated with the industry. The panel makes a finding and, absent extraordinary circumstances, its findings cannot be appealed. The panel does not have to disclose factual findings or legal reasoning.

CHECK THIS

2.1a What are the differences between full-service and deep-discount brokers?

2.1b What is the SIPC? How does SIPC coverage differ from FDIC coverage?

2.2 Brokerage Accounts

The account agreement that you sign has a number of important provisions and details specifying the types of trades that can be made and who can make them. Another important concern is whether the broker will extend credit and the terms under which credit will be extended. We discuss these issues next.

Cash Accounts

cash account A brokerage account in which all transactions are made on a strictly cash basis.

A **cash account** is the simplest arrangement. Securities can be purchased to the extent that sufficient cash is available in the account. If additional purchases are desired, then the needed funds must be promptly supplied.

Margin Accounts

margin account A brokerage account in which, subject to limits, securities can be bought and sold on credit.

call money rate The interest rate brokers pay to borrow bank funds for lending to customer margin accounts.

With a **margin account,** you can, subject to limits, purchase securities on credit using money loaned to you by your broker. Such a purchase is called a *margin purchase.* The interest rate you pay on the money you borrow is based on the broker's **call money rate,** which is, loosely, the rate the broker pays to borrow the money. You pay some amount over the call money rate, called the *spread;* the exact spread depends on your broker and the size of the loan. Suppose the call money rate has been hovering around 7 percent. If a brokerage firm charges a 2.5 percent spread above this rate on loan amounts under $10,000, then you would pay a total of about 9.5 percent. However, this is usually reduced for larger loan amounts. For example, the spread may decline to .75 percent for amounts over $100,000.

There are several important concepts and rules involved in a margin purchase. For concreteness, we focus on stocks in our discussion. The specific margin rules for other investments can be quite different, but the principles and terminology are usually similar.

margin The portion of the value of an investment that is *not* borrowed.

In general, when you purchase securities on credit, some of the money is yours and the rest is borrowed. The amount that is yours is called the **margin.** Margin is usually expressed as a percentage. For example, if you take $7,000 of your own money and borrow an additional $3,000 from your broker, your total investment will be $10,000. Of this $10,000, $7,000 is yours, so the margin is $7,000 / $10,000 = .70, or 70 percent.

It is useful to create an account balance sheet when thinking about margin purchases (and some other issues we'll get to in just a moment). To illustrate, suppose you open a margin account with $5,000. You tell your broker to buy 100 shares of Microsoft. Microsoft is selling for $80 per share, so the total cost will be $8,000. Since you have only $5,000 in the account, you borrow the remaining $3,000. Immediately following the purchase, your account balance sheet would look like this:

Assets		Liabilities and Account Equity	
100 shares of Microsoft	$8,000	Margin loan	$3,000
		Account equity	5,000
Total	$8,000	Total	$8,000

On the left-hand side of this balance sheet we list the account assets, which, in this case, consist of the $8,000 in Microsoft stock you purchased. On the right-hand side we first list the $3,000 loan you took out to partially pay for the stock; this is a liability because, at some point, the loan must be repaid. The difference between the value of the assets held in the account and the loan amount is $5,000. This amount is your *account equity;* that is, the net value of your investment. Notice that your margin is equal to the account equity divided by the value of the stock owned and held in the account: $5,000 / $8,000 = .625, or 62.5 percent.

Example 2.1   The Account Balance Sheet

You want to buy 1,000 shares of Wal-Mart at a price of $24 per share. You put up $18,000 and borrow the rest. What does your account balance sheet look like? What is your margin?

The 1,000 shares of Wal-Mart cost $24,000. You supply $18,000, so you must borrow $6,000. The account balance sheet looks like this:

Assets		Liabilities and Account Equity	
1,000 shares of Wal-mart	$24,000	Margin loan	$ 6,000
		Account equity	18,000
Total	$24,000	Total	$24,000

Your margin is the account equity divided by the value of the stock owned:

$$\text{Margin} = \$18,000 \ / \ \$24,000$$
$$= .75 = 75 \text{ percent}$$

initial margin The minimum margin that must be supplied on a securities purchase.

Initial Margin When you first purchase securities on credit, there is a minimum margin that you must supply. This percentage is called the **initial margin**. The minimum percentage (for stock purchases) is set by the Federal Reserve (the "Fed"), but the exchanges and individual brokerage firms may require higher amounts.

The Fed's power to set initial margin requirements was established in the Securities Exchange Act of 1934. In subsequent years, initial margin requirements ranged from a low of 45 percent to a high of 100 percent. Since 1974, the minimum has been 50 percent (for stock purchases). In other words, if you have $10,000 in cash that is not borrowed, you can borrow up to an additional $10,000 but no more.

We emphasize that these initial margin requirements apply to stocks. In contrast, for the most part, there is little initial margin requirement for government bonds. On the other hand, margin is not allowed at all on certain other types of securities.

Example 2.2 **Calculating Initial Margin**

Suppose you have $6,000 in cash in a trading account with a 50 percent initial margin requirement. What is the largest order you can place (ignoring commissions)? If the initial margin were 60 percent, how would your answer change?

When the initial margin is 50 percent, you must supply half of the total, so $12,000 is the largest order you could place. When the initial margin is 60 percent, your $6,000 must equal 60 percent of the total. In other words, it must be the case that

$$\$6,000 = 0.60 \times \text{Total order}$$
$$\text{Total order} = \$6,000\, /.60$$
$$= \$10,000$$

As this example illustrates, the higher the initial margin required, the less you can borrow.

---

maintenance margin The minimum margin that must be present at all times in a margin account.

margin call A demand for more funds that occurs when the margin in an account drops below the maintenance margin.

Maintenance Margin In addition to the initial margin requirement set by the Fed, brokerage firms and exchanges generally have a **maintenance margin** requirement. For example, the New York Stock Exchange (NYSE) requires a minimum of 25 percent maintenance margin. This amount is the minimum margin required at all times after the purchase.

A typical maintenance margin would be 30 percent. If your margin falls below 30 percent, then you may be subject to a **margin call**, which is a demand by your broker to add to your account, pay off part of the loan, or sell enough securities to bring your margin back up to an acceptable level. If you do not or cannot comply, your securities may be sold. The loan will be repaid out of the proceeds, and any remaining amounts will be credited to your account.

To illustrate, suppose your account has a 50 percent initial margin requirement and the maintenance margin is 30 percent. A particular stock is selling for $50 per share. You have $20,000, and you want to buy as much of this stock as you possibly can. With a 50 percent initial margin, you buy up to $40,000 worth, or 800 shares. The account balance sheet looks like this:

Assets		Liabilities and Account Equity	
800 shares @$50/share	$40,000	Margin loan	$20,000
		Account equity	20,000
Total	$40,000	Total	$40,000

Unfortunately, right after you buy it, the company reveals that it has been artificially inflating earnings for the last three years (this is not good), and the share price falls to $35 per share. What does the account balance sheet look like when this happens? Are you subject to a margin call?

To create the new account balance sheet, we recalculate the total value of the stock. The margin loan stays the same, so the account equity is adjusted as needed:

Assets		Liabilities and Account Equity	
800 shares @$35/share	$28,000	Margin loan	$20,000
		Account equity	8,000
Total	$28,000	Total	$28,000

As shown, the total value of your "position" (i.e., the stock you hold) falls to $28,000, a $12,000 loss. You still owe $20,000 to your broker, so your account equity is $28,000 − $20,000 = $8,000. Your margin is therefore $8,000 / $28,000 = .286, or 28.6 percent. You are below the 30 percent minimum, so you are undermargined and subject to a margin call.

The Effects of Margin   Margin is a form of *financial leverage*. Any time you borrow money to make an investment, the impact is to magnify both your gains and losses, hence the use of the term "leverage." The easiest way to see this is through an example. Imagine that you have $30,000 in an account with a 60 percent initial margin. You now know that you can borrow up to an additional $20,000 and buy $50,000 worth of stock (why?). The call money rate is 5.50 percent; you must pay this rate plus a .50 percent spread. Suppose you buy 1,000 shares of IBM at $50 per share. One year later, IBM is selling for $60 per share. Assuming the call money rate does not change and ignoring dividends, what is your return on this investment?

At the end of the year, your 1,000 shares are worth $60,000. You owe 6 percent interest on the $20,000 you borrowed, or $1,200. If you pay off the loan with interest, you will have $60,000 − $21,200 = $38,800. You started with $30,000 and ended with $38,800, so your net gain is $8,800. In percentage terms, your return was $8,800 / $30,000 = .2933, or 29.33 percent.

How would you have done without the financial leverage created from the margin purchase? In this case, you would have invested just $30,000. At $50 per share, you would have purchased 600 shares. At the end of the year, your 600 shares would be worth $60 apiece, or $36,000 total. Your dollar profit is $6,000, so your percentage return would be $6,000 / $30,000 = .20, or 20 percent. If we compare this to the 29.33 percent that you made above, it's clear that you did substantially better by leveraging.

The downside is that you would do much worse if IBM's stock price fell (or didn't rise very much). For example, if IBM had fallen to $40 a share, you would have lost (check these calculations for practice) $11,200, or 37.33 percent on your margin investment, compared to $6,000, or 20 percent on the unmargined investment. This example illustrates how leveraging an investment through a margin account can cut both ways.

Example 2.3   A Marginal Investment?

A year ago, you bought 300 shares of Ford at $55 per share. You put up the 60 percent initial margin. The call money rate plus the spread you paid was 8 percent. What is your return if the price today is $50? Compare this to the return you would have earned if you had not invested on margin.

Your total investment was 300 shares at $55 per share, or $16,500. You supplied 60 percent, or $9,900, and you borrowed the remaining $6,600. At the end of the year, you owe $6,600 plus 8 percent interest, or $7,128. If the stock sells for $50, then your position is worth $300 \times \$50 = \$15,000$. Deducting the $7,128 leaves $7,872 for you. Since you originally invested $9,900, your dollar loss is $9,900 − $7,872 = $2,028. Your percentage return is $−\$2,028/\$9,900 = −20.48$ percent.

If you had not leveraged your investment, you would have purchased $\$9,900/\$55 = 180$ shares. These would have been worth $180 \times \$50 = \$9,000$. You therefore would have lost $900; your percentage return would have been $−\$900/\$9,900 = −9.09$ percent, compared to the $−20.48$ percent that you lost on your leveraged position.

Example 2.4 **How Low Can It Go?**

In our previous example (Example 2.3), suppose the maintenance margin was 40 percent. At what price per share would you have been subject to a margin call?

To answer, let P^* be the critical price. You own 300 shares, so, at that price, your stock is worth $300 \times P^*$. You borrowed $6,600, so your account equity is equal to the value of your stock less the $6,600 you owe, or $300 \times P^* − \$6,600$. We can summarize this information as follows:

$$\text{Amount borrowed} = \$6,600$$
$$\text{Value of stock} = 300 \times P^*$$
$$\text{Account equity} = 300 \times P^* − \$6,600$$

From our preceding discussion, your percentage margin is your dollar margin (or account equity) divided by the value of the stock:

$$\text{Margin} = \frac{\text{Account equity}}{\text{Value of stock}}$$

$$= \frac{300 \times P^* − \$6,600}{300 \times P^*}$$

Finally, to find the critical price, we will set this margin equal to 40 percent, the maintenance margin, and solve for P^*:

$$.40 = \frac{300 \times P^* − \$6,600}{300 \times P^*}$$
$$.40 \times 300 \times P^* = 300 \times P^* − \$6,600$$
$$P^* = \frac{\$6,600}{180} = \$36.67$$

At any price below $36.67, your margin will be less than 40 percent, and you will be subject to a margin call, so this is the lowest possible price that could be reached before that occurs.

Hypothecation and Street Name Registration

As part of your margin account agreement, you must agree to various conditions. We discuss two of the most important next.

hypothecation
Pledging securities as
collateral against a
loan.

Hypothecation   Any securities you purchase in your margin account will be held by your broker as collateral against the loan made to you. This practice protects the broker because the securities can be sold by the broker if the customer is unwilling or unable to meet a margin call. Putting securities up as collateral against a loan is called **hypothecation.** In fact, a margin agreement is sometimes called a hypothecation agreement. In addition, to borrow the money that it loans to you, your broker will often *re*-hypothecate your securities, meaning that your broker will pledge them as collateral with its lender, normally a bank.

street name An
arrangement under
which a broker is the
registered owner of a
security.

Street Name Registration   Securities in a margin account are normally held in **street name.** This means that the brokerage firm is actually the registered owner. If this were not the case, the brokerage firm could not legally sell the securities should a customer refuse to meet a margin call or otherwise fail to live up to the terms of the margin agreement. With this arrangement, the brokerage firm is the "owner of record," but the account holder is the "beneficial owner."

When a security is held in street name, anything mailed to the security owner, such as an annual report or a dividend check, goes to the brokerage firm. The brokerage firm then passes these on to the account holder. Street name ownership is actually a great convenience to the owner. In fact, because it is usually a free service, even customers with cash accounts generally choose street name ownership. Some of the benefits are:

1. Since the broker holds the security, there is no danger of theft or other loss of the security. This is important because a stolen or lost security cannot be easily or cheaply replaced.

2. Any dividends or interest payments are automatically credited, and they are often credited more quickly (and conveniently) than they would be if the owner received the check in the mail.

3. The broker provides regular account statements showing the value of securities held in the account and any payments received. Also, for tax purposes, the broker will provide all the needed information on a single form at the end of the year, greatly reducing the owner's record-keeping requirements.

Other Account Issues

If you do not wish to manage your account yourself, you can set up an *advisory account*. In this case, you pay someone else to make buy and sell decisions on your behalf. You are responsible for paying any commissions or other costs as well as a management fee.

In a recent innovation, brokerage firms have begun to offer *wrap accounts*. In such an account, you choose a money manager or set of money managers from a group offered by the brokerage firm. All of the costs, commissions, and expenses associated with your account are "wrapped" into a single fee that you pay, hence the name. If you simply authorize your broker to trade for you, then there is no management fee, but you are still responsible for any commissions. This arrangement is termed a *discretionary account*.

Most of the large brokerage firms offer accounts that provide for complete money management, including check-writing privileges, credit cards, and margin loans, especially for larger investors. Such accounts are generally called *asset management accounts*. Often, in such accounts, any uninvested cash is automatically invested to earn interest, and detailed statements are provided on a regular basis to account holders. The terms on these accounts differ from broker to broker, and the services provided are frequently changed in response to competition.

Finally, if you want to buy and sell a broad variety of individual securities, then a brokerage account is almost a requirement. It is true that some companies and other entities (such as the U.S. government) do sell directly to the public, at least at certain times and subject to various restrictions, so you can buy securities directly in some cases. In fact, you could buy and sell through the want ads in your local paper if you were so inclined, but given the modest commissions charged by deep-discount brokers, this hardly seems worth the trouble.

However, you should be aware that if you do not wish to actively buy and sell securities, but you do want to own stocks, bonds, or other financial assets, there is an alternative to a brokerage account: a *mutual fund*. Mutual funds are a means of combining or pooling the funds of a large group of investors. The buy and sell decisions for the resulting pool are then made by a fund manager, who is compensated for the service. Mutual funds have become so important that we will devote an entire chapter to them (Chapter 4) rather than give them short shrift here.

CHECK THIS

2.2a What is the difference between a cash and margin account?

2.2b What is the effect of a margin purchase on gains and losses?

2.2c What is a margin call?

Short Sales

An investor who buys and owns shares of stock is said to be *long in the stock* or to have a *long position*. An investor with a long position will make money if the price of the stock increases and lose money if it goes down. In other words, a long investor hopes that the price will increase.

Now consider a different situation. Suppose you thought, for some reason, that the stock in a particular company was likely to *decrease* in value. You obviously wouldn't want to buy any of it. If you already owned some, you might choose to sell it.

short sale A sale in which the seller does not actually own the security that is sold.

Beyond this, you might decide to engage in a **short sale.** In a short sale, you actually sell a security that you do not own. This is referred to as *shorting the stock*. After the short sale, the investor is said to have a *short position* in the security.

Financial assets of all kinds are sold short, not just shares of stock, and the terms "long" and "short" are universal. However, the mechanics of a short sale differ quite a bit across security types. Even so, regardless of how the short sale is executed, the essence is the same. An investor with a long position benefits from price increases, and, as we will see, an investor with a short position benefits from price decreases. For the sake of illustration, we focus here on shorting shares of stock. Procedures for shorting other types of securities are discussed in later chapters.

Basics of a Short Sale

How can you sell stock you don't own? It is easier than you might think: You borrow the shares of stock from your broker and then you sell them. At some future date, you will buy the same number of shares that you originally borrowed and return them, thereby eliminating the short position. Eliminating the short position is often called *covering the position* or, less commonly, *curing the short*.

You might wonder where your broker will get the stock to loan you. Normally, it will simply come from other margin accounts. Often, when you open a margin account, you are asked to sign a loan-consent agreement, which gives your broker the right to loan shares held in the account. If shares you own are loaned out, you still receive any dividends or other distributions and you can sell the stock if you wish. In other words, the fact that some of your stock may have been loaned out is of little or no consequence as far as you are concerned.

An investor with a short position will profit if the security declines in value. For example, assume that you short 1,000 shares of Liz Claiborne at a price of $10 per share. You receive $10,000 from the sale (more on this in a moment). A month later, the stock is selling for $6 per share. You buy 1,000 shares for $6,000 and return the stock to your broker, thereby covering your position. Because you received $10,000 from the sale and it cost you only $6,000 to cover, you made $4,000.

Conventional Wall Street wisdom states that the way to make money is to "buy low, sell high." With a short sale, we hope to do exactly that, just in opposite order—sell high, buy low. If a short sale strikes you as a little confusing, it might help to think about the everyday use of the terms. Whenever we say that we are "running short" on something, we mean we don't have enough of it. Similarly, when someone says "don't sell me short" they mean don't bet on them not to succeed.

Example 2.5   **The Long and Short of It**

Suppose you short 2,000 shares of GTE at $35 per share. Six months later you cover your short. If GTE is selling for $30 per share at that time, did you make money or lose money? How much? What if you covered at $40?

If you shorted at $35 per share and covered at $30, you originally sold 2,000 shares at $35 and later bought them back at $30, so you made $5 per share, or $10,000. If you covered at $40, you lost $10,000.

Short Sales: Some Details

When you short a stock, you must borrow it from your broker, so there are various requirements you must fulfill. First, there is an initial margin and a maintenance margin. Second, after you sell the borrowed stock, the proceeds from the sale are credited to your account, but you cannot use them. They are, in effect, frozen until you return the stock. Finally, if there are any dividends paid on the stock while you have a short position, you must pay them.

To illustrate, we will again create an account balance sheet. Suppose you want to short 100 shares of Sears when the price is $30 per share. This means you will borrow shares of stock worth a total of $30 × 100 = $3,000. Your broker has a 50 percent initial margin and a 40 percent maintenance margin on short sales.

An important thing to keep in mind with a margin purchase of securities is that margin is calculated as the value of your account equity relative to the value of the securities purchased. With a short sale, margin is calculated as the value of your account equity relative to the value of the securities sold short. Thus, in both cases margin is equal to equity value divided by security value.

In our example here, the initial value of the securities sold short is $3,000 and the initial margin is 50 percent, so you must deposit half of $3,000, or $1,500, in your account at a minimum. With this in mind, after the short sale, your account balance sheet is as follows:

Assets		Liabilities and Account Equity	
Proceeds from sale	$3,000	Short position	$3,000
Initial margin deposit	1,500	Account equity	1,500
Total	$4,500	Total	$4,500

As shown, there are four items on the account balance sheet:

1. *Proceeds from sale.* This is the $3,000 you received when you sold the stock. This amount will remain in your account until you cover your position. Note that you will not earn interest on this amount—it will just sit there as far as you are concerned.

2. *Margin deposit.* This is the 50 percent margin that you had to post. This amount will not change unless there is a margin call. Depending on the circumstances and your particular account agreement, you may earn interest on the initial margin deposit.

3. *Short position.* Because you must eventually buy back the stock and return it, you have a liability. The current cost of eliminating that liability is $3,000.

4. *Account equity.* As always, the account equity is the difference between the total account value ($4,500) and the total liabilities ($3,000).

We now examine two scenarios: (1) the stock price falls to $20 per share, and (2) the stock price rises to $40 per share.

If the stock price falls to $20 per share, then you are still liable for 100 shares, but the cost of those shares is now just $2,000. Your account balance sheet becomes:

Assets		Liabilities and Account Equity	
Proceeds from sale	$3,000	Short position	$2,000
Initial margin deposit	1,500	Account equity	2,500
Total	$4,500	Total	$4,500

Notice that the left-hand side doesn't change. The same $3,000 you originally received is still held, and the $1,500 margin you deposited is still there also. On the right-hand side, the short position is now a $2,000 liability, down from $3,000. Finally, the good news is that the account equity rises by $1,000, so this is your gain. Your margin is equal to account equity divided by the security value (the value of the short position), $2,500 / $2,000 = 1.25, or 125 percent.

However, if the stock price rises to $40, things are not so rosy. Now the 100 shares for which you are liable are worth $4,000:

Assets		Liabilities and Account Equity	
Proceeds from sale	$3,000	Short position	$4,000
Initial margin deposit	1,500	Account equity	500
Total	$4,500	Total	$4,500

Again, the left-hand side doesn't change. The short liability rises by $1,000, and, unfortunately for you, the account equity declines by $1,000, the amount of your loss.

To make matters worse, when the stock price rises to $40, you are severely undermargined. The account equity is $500, but the value of the stock sold short is $4,000. Your margin is $500 / $4,000 = 12.5 percent. Since this is well below the 40 percent maintenance margin, you are subject to a margin call. You have two options: (1) buy back some or all of the stock and return it, or (2) add funds to your account.

Short Interest on Big Board Hits a Record

Short interest on the New York Stock Exchange rose to a record in August 1998, while activity on the American Stock Exchange decreased.

Short interest on the Big Board increased 2.58% to 4,206,357,899 shares on September 15 from a revised 4,100,726,367 shares in mid-August.

On the Amex, the figure fell 0.72% to 204,278,391 shares from a revised 205,759,518 shares in mid-August.

The level of negative sentiment measured by the Big Board's short-interest ratio—sometimes considered a contrarian indicator, as short-interest shares eventually must be purchased—fell to 5.45 from 5.98 in the previous trading period. The short-interest ratio is the number of trading days at the exchange's average daily trading volume required to convert the total short-interest position.

Investors who sell securities "short" borrow stock and sell it, betting that the stock's price will decline and that they will be able to buy the shares back later at a lower price for repayment to the lender. Short interest is the number of shares that haven't been purchased for return to lenders, and as such, is often viewed as an indicator of the degree of negative sentiment among investors in the stocks.

Investors may also rely on short selling for other purposes, including as a hedging strategy related to corporate mergers and acquisitions, to hedge convertible securities and options, or for tax-related purposes.

Average daily Big Board volume was 771,201,550, up from 685,370,716 shares in the previous month. Short positions were calculated for the month including the 21 trading days through September 15.

The next Big Board short-interest report will be published Oct. 22.

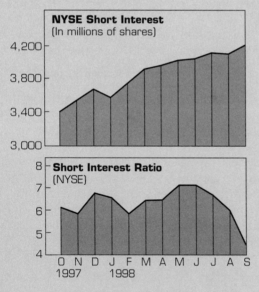

Source: Aaron Lucchetti, "Short Interest on Big Board Hits a Record," *The Wall Street Journal*, September 16, 1998.

Largest Short Positions

Rank	September 15	August 14	Change
NYSE			
1 Walt Disney Hldg	75,350,089	71,732,624	3,617,465
2 AT&T	41,616,230	40,703,168	913,062
3 Wal-Mart Stores	37,758,929	34,422,337	3,336,592
4 Micron Technology	35,620,879	32,536,252	3,084,627
5 Home Depot	33,736,094	30,556,425	3,179,669
6 Columbia/HCA	33,403,803	35,114,881	-1,711,078
7 SBC Comm	33,246,460	32,613,881	632,579
8 Kmart	31,482,473	32,475,896	-993,423
9 Travelers Group	29,221,192	28,154,589	1,066,603
10 Amer Home Prdcts	27,876,265	19,788,931	8,087,334
11 Iomega	27,831,452	28,146,392	-314,940
12 Compaq Computer	27,300,501	30,968,909	-3,668,408
13 Tyco Intl	26,745,408	25,839,632	905,776
14 Mediaone Group	24,835,440	24,832,716	2,724
15 Waste Management	23,991,604	21,460,600	2,531,004
16 Coca-Cola Co.	23,171,781	19,709,453	3,462,328
17 Medpartners	22,807,304	21,123,342	1,683,962
18 Conseco	22,625,304	18,155,934	4,469,370
19 Norwest	21,944,465	16,657,126	5,287,339
20 Bell Atlantic	21,725,506	19,638,936	2,086,570
AMEX			
1 Standard & Prs Dep	27,684,288	22,592,728	5,091,560
2 Trans World Cmmn	10,290,575	11,575,958	-1,285,383
3 Cablevision Sys	9,758,144	9,907,130	-148,986
4 Nabors	9,576,856	9,886,700	-309,844
5 Viacom cl B	8,003,689	8,131,564	-127,875

Example 2.6   A Case of the Shorts

You shorted 5,000 shares of a particular stock at a price of $30 per share. The initial margin is 50 percent, and the maintenance margin is 40 percent. What does your account balance sheet look like following the short?

Following the short, your account becomes:

Assets		**Liabilities and Account Equity**	
Proceeds from sale	$150,000	Short position	$150,000
Initial margin deposit	75,000	Account equity	75,000
Total	$225,000	Total	$225,000

Notice that you shorted $150,000 worth of stock, so, with a 50 percent margin requirement, you deposited $75,000.

Example 2.7   **Margin Calls**

In our previous example (Example 2.6), at what price per share would you be subject to a margin call?

To answer this one, let P^* be the critical price. The short liability then is 5,000 shares at a price of P^*, or $5,000 \times P^*$. The total account value is $225,000, so the account equity is $225,000 - 5,000 \times P^*$. We can summarize this information as follows:

$$\text{Short position} = 5,000 \times P^*$$
$$\text{Account equity} = \$225,000 - 5,000 \times P^*$$

Your margin is the account equity relative to the short liability:

$$\text{Margin} = \frac{\$225,000 - 5,000 \times P^*}{5,000 \times P^*}$$

Finally, to find the critical price, we will set this margin equal to 40 percent, the maintenance margin, and solve for P^*:

$$.40 = \frac{\$225,000 - 5,000 \times P^*}{5,000 \times P^*}$$

$$.40 \times 5,000 \times P^* = \$225,000 - 5,000 \times P^*$$

$$P^* = \frac{\$225,000}{7,000} = \$32.14$$

At any price *above* $32.14, your margin will be less than 40 percent, so you will be subject to a margin call, so this is the highest possible price that could be reached before that occurs.

---

short interest The amount of common stock held in short positions.

At this point you might wonder whether short selling is a common practice among investors. Actually it is quite common and a substantial volume of stock sales are initiated by short sellers. The nearby Investment Updates box on the previous page is a sample *Wall Street Journal* box published weekly reporting **short interest.** Short interest is the amount of common stock held in short positions. As shown, the amount of stock held short for some companies can be several tens of millions of shares, and the total number of shares held short across all companies can be several billion shares.

We conclude our discussion of short sales with an important observation. With a long position, the most you can ever lose is your total investment. In other words, if you buy $10,000 worth of stock, $10,000 is the most you can lose because the worst that can happen is the stock price drops to zero. However, if you short $10,000 in stock, you can lose *much more* than $10,000 because the stock price can keep rising without any particular limit. In fact, as our previous chapter showed, stock prices do tend to rise, at

Time for Investing's Four-Letter Word

What four-letter word should pop into mind when the stock market takes a harrowing nosedive?

No, not those. R-I-S-K.

Risk is the potential for realizing low returns or even losing money, possibly preventing you from meeting important objectives, like sending your kids to the college of their choice or having the retirement lifestyle you crave.

But many financial advisers and other experts say that these days investors aren't taking the idea of risk as seriously as they should, and they are overexposing themselves to stocks.

"The market has been so good for years that investors no longer believe there's risk in investing," says Gary Schatsky, a financial adviser in New York. "And when the market drops hundreds of points and rebounds immediately, that belief is confirmed."

The danger is that when the market declines and stays down for months—as some analysts predict it eventually will—investors won't be able to meet their short-term financial goals. Or, they will panic and sell their investments as their shares are declining in value, which is the worst possible time.

So before the market goes down and stays down, be sure that you understand your tolerance for risk and that your portfolio is designed to match it.

Assessing your risk tolerance, however, can be tricky. You must consider not only how much risk you can *afford* to take but also how much risk you can *stand* to take.

What you can afford depends mainly on your time horizon—how long before you will need the money.

If your investments are targeted for your child's college tuition in three years, for instance, your financial ability to take on risk is low because you may not have time to recover if the value of your portfolio declines. But if you have 10 years before your child heads to college, you can afford to take more risks because you would have plenty of time to ride out dips in the market.

Determining how much risk you can stand—your temperamental tolerance for risk—is more difficult. It isn't quantifiable.

"A variety of behavioral factors come into play," says Richard Bernstein, director of quantitative research at Merrill Lynch & Co. in New York. "If my broker asks me if I want high-risk or low-risk securities, I may say high risk because I don't want to look wimpy."

Similarly, some people will gloss over the less-impressive details of their investing histories, says Ronald Roge, a financial adviser in Bohemia, N.Y. He routinely asks to see copies of his clients' tax returns to get a reliable account of gains or losses.

"The aim is always to find the fine line between greed and fear," he says.

To that end, many financial advisers, brokerage firms and mutual-fund companies have created risk quizzes to help people determine whether they are conservative, moderate or agressive investors. Some firms that offer such quizzes include **Merrill Lynch, T. Rowe Price Associates** Inc., Baltimore, **Zurich Group** Inc.'s Scudder Kemper Investments Inc., New York, and **Vanguard Group** in Malvern, Pa.

"The typical investor may not have ever experienced a negative turn in the stock market. They need to be prepared for that," says Robert Benish, vice president of education programs for Scudder, whose questionnaire is part of a broader investing-education program. "We want to help them understand what risk means to them."

Typically, risk questionnaires include seven to 10 questions about a person's investing experience, financial security, and tendency to make risky or conservative choices.

Some of these risk tests, such as one created by Vanguard (www.vanguard.com), can be found on-line.

The benefit of the questionnaires is that they are an objective resource people can use to get at least a rough idea of their risk tolerance. "It's impossible for someone to assess their risk tolerance alone," says Mr. Bernstein. "I may say I don't like risk, yet will take more risk than the average person."

Many experts warn, however, that the questionnaires should be used simply as a first step to assessing risk tolerance. "They are not precise," says Ron Meier, a certified public accountant who teaches investing-related courses at the College for Financial Planning in Denver, a unit of Apollo Group Inc., Phoenix. "They are good for leading discussions but not for coming up with a final risk score."

The second step, many experts agree, is to ask yourself some difficult questions, such as: How much you can stand to lose over the long term?

"Most people can stand to lose a heck of a lot temporarily," says Mr. Schatsky. The real acid test, he says, is how much of your portfolio's value you can stand to lose over months or years.

Rather than using percentages, think in dollar terms. "When you convert percentages to figures, often you see very different psychological effects," says Richard Wagener, a financial adviser in Columbia, Md. The idea of a 20% decline on, say, a $150,000 portfolio is more abstract than a $30,000 loss, he says.

Source: Karen Hube, "Time for Investing's Four-Letter Word," *The Wall Street Journal*, January 1, 1998.

What's Your Risk Tolerance?

Circle the letter that corresponds to your answer

1. Just 60 days after you put money into an investment, its price falls 20%. Assuming none of the fundamentals have changed, what would you do?

   a. Sell to avoid further worry and try something else
   b. Do nothing and wait for the investment to come back
   c. Buy more. It was a good investment before; now it's a cheap investment, too

2. Now look at the previous question another way. Your investment fell 20%, but it's part of a portfolio being used to meet investment goals with three different time horizons.

2A. What would you do if the goal were five years away?

   a. Sell
   b. Do nothing
   c. Buy more

2B. What would you do if the goal were 15 years away?

   a. Sell
   b. Do nothing
   c. Buy more

2C. What would you do if the goal were 30 years away?

   a. Sell
   b. Do nothing
   c. Buy more

3. The price of your retirement investment jumps 25% a month after you buy it. Again, the fundamentals haven't changed. After you finish gloating, what do you do?

   a. Sell it and lock in your gains
   b. Stay put and hope for more gain
   c. Buy more, it could go higher

4. You're investing for retirement, which is 15 years away. Which would you rather do?

   a. Invest in a money-market fund or guaranteed investment contract, giving up the possibility of major gains, but virtually assuring the safety of your principal
   b. Invest in a 50-50 mix of bond funds and stock funds, in hopes of getting some growth, but also giving yourself some protection in the form of steady income.
   c. Invest in aggressive growth mutual funds whose value will probably fluctuate significantly during the year, but have the potential for impressive gains over five or 10 years

5. You just won a big prize! But which one? It's up to you.

   a. $2,000 in cash
   b. A 50% chance to win $5,000
   c. A 20% chance to win $15,000

6. A good investment opportunity just came along. But you have to borrow money to get in. Would you take out a loan?

   a. Definitely not
   b. Perhaps
   c. Yes

7. Your company is selling stock to its employees. In three years, management plans to take the company public. Until then, you won't be able to sell your shares and you will get no dividends. But your invesetment could multiply as much as 10 times when the company goes public. How much money would you invest?

   a. None
   b. Two months' salary
   c. Four months' salary

To check your score, see the box at the end of the accompanying story.

Source: Scudder Kemper Retirement Services

Scoring Your Risk Tolerance

To score the quiz, add up the number of answers you gave in each category a–c, then multiply as shown to find your score

(a) answers _____ × 1 _____ points
(b) answers _____ × 2 _____ points
(c) answers _____ × 3 _____ points

YOUR SCORE: _____ points

If you scored . . .	You may be a:
9–14 points	Conservative investor
15–21 points	Moderate investor
22–27 points	Aggressive investor

least on average. With this in mind, potential short sellers should remember the following classic bit of Wall Street wisdom: He that sells what isn't his'n, must buy it back or go to prison![1]

2.3a What is a short sale?

2.3b Why might an investor choose to short a stock?

2.3c What is the maximum possible loss on a short sale? Explain.

2.4 Investor Objectives, Constraints, and Strategies

Different investors will have very different investment objectives and strategies. For example, some will be very active, buying and selling frequently; others will be relatively inactive, buying and holding for long periods of time. Some will be willing to bear substantial risk in seeking out returns; for others, safety is a primary concern. In this section, we describe, in general terms, some strategies that are commonly pursued and their relationship to investor constraints and objectives.

In thinking about investor objectives, the most fundamental question is: Why invest at all? For the most part, the only sensible answer is that we invest today to have more tomorrow. In other words, investment is simply deferred consumption; instead of spending today, we choose to wait because we wish to have (or need to have) more to spend later. There is no difference, really, between investing and saving.

Given that we invest now to have more later, the particular investment strategy chosen will depend on, among other things, willingness to bear risk, the time horizon, and taxes. We discuss these and other issues next.

Risk and Return

Probably the most fundamental decision that an investor must make concerns the amount of risk that she is willing to bear. Most investors are *risk-averse,* meaning that, all other things the same, they dislike risk and want to expose themselves to the minimum risk level possible. However, as our previous chapter indicated, larger returns are generally associated with larger risks, so there is a trade-off. In formulating investment objectives, the individual must therefore balance return objectives with risk tolerance.

Attitudes toward risk are strictly personal preferences, and individuals with very similar economic circumstances can have very different degrees of risk aversion. For this reason, the first thing that must be assessed in evaluating the suitability of an investment strategy is risk tolerance. Unfortunately, this is not an easy thing to do. Most individuals have a difficult time articulating in any precise way their attitude toward risk (what's yours?). One reason is that risk is not a simple concept; it is not easily defined or measured. Nevertheless, the nearby Investment Updates box contains an article from *The Wall Street Journal* about risk tolerance that has a short quiz that might help you

---

[1] Of course, the same is true for "she that sells what isn't hers'n"; it just doesn't rhyme as well.

assess your attitude toward risk. When you take the quiz, remember there are no right or wrong answers. Afterwards, score your risk tolerance as shown at the end of the article.

Investor Constraints

In addition to attitude toward risk, an investor's investment strategy will be affected by various constraints. We discuss five of the most common and important constraints next.

Resources   Probably the most obvious constraint, and the one to which many students can most easily relate, is *resources*. Obviously, if you have no money, you cannot invest at all! Beyond that, certain types of investments and investment strategies either explicitly or effectively have minimum requirements. For example, a margin account must normally have a minimum of $2,000 when it is established.

What is the minimum resource level needed? It depends on the investment strategy, and there is no precise answer. Through mutual funds, investments in the stock market can be made for as little as $500 to start, with subsequent investments as small as $100. However, since there are frequently minimum commission levels, account fees, and other costs associated with buying and selling securities, an investor interested in actively trading on her own would probably need more like $5,000 to $50,000.

Horizon   The investment *horizon* refers to the planned life of the investment. For example, individuals frequently save for retirement, where the investment horizon, depending on your age, can be very long. On the other hand, you might be saving to buy a house in the near future, implying a relatively short horizon.

The reason horizon is important is evident in our previous chapter. It is true that stocks outperformed the other investments in the long run, but there were short periods over which they did much worse. Consequently, if you have to pay tuition in 30 days, stocks are probably not the best investment for that money. Thus, in thinking about the riskiness of an investment, one important consideration is when the money will be needed.

Liquidity   For some investors, there is the possibility that an asset will need to be sold quickly. In such cases, the asset's *liquidity* is particularly important. An asset with a high degree of liquidity is one that can be sold quickly without a significant price concession. Such an asset is said to be liquid.

Notice that liquidity has two related dimensions. After all, any asset can be sold quickly and easily if the price is cut sufficiently, so it's not just a question of the ease with which an asset can be sold. Liquidity is difficult to measure precisely, but some assets are clearly much more liquid than others. A good way to think about liquidity is to imagine buying an asset and then immediately reselling it. The less you would lose on this "round-trip" transaction, the more liquid is the asset.

Taxes   Different types of investments are taxed very differently. When we talk about the return on an investment, what is really relevant is the *aftertax* return. As a result, taxes are a vital consideration. Higher tax bracket investors will naturally seek investment strategies with favorable tax treatments while lower tax bracket (or tax-exempt) investors will focus more on pretax returns.

In addition, the way in which an investment is held can affect its tax status. For example, individuals are generally allowed to open individual retirement accounts (IRAs). The returns on an IRA are not taxed until they are withdrawn, so an IRA can grow for decades with no tax payments required. Thus, any investments held in an IRA become tax-deferred.

Special Circumstances   Beyond the general constraints we have discussed, essentially everyone will have some special or unique requirements or opportunities. For example, many companies will match certain types of investments made by employees on a dollar-for-dollar basis (typically up to some maximum per year). In other words, you double your money immediately with complete certainty. Since it is difficult to envision any other investment with such a favorable payoff, such an opportunity should probably be taken even though there may be some undesirable liquidity, tax, or horizon considerations.

A list of possible special circumstances would be essentially endless, so we make no attempt to produce one here. Just to give a few examples, however, the number of dependents and their needs will vary from investor to investor, and the need to provide for dependents will be an important constraint. Some investors want to invest only in companies whose products and activities they consider to be socially or politically suitable, and some investors want to invest primarily in their own community or state. Finally, some investors, such as corporate insiders, face regulatory and legal restrictions on their investing, and others, such as political officeholders, may have to avoid (or at least ethically *should* avoid) some types of investments out of concern for conflicts of interest.

Strategies and Policies

In formulating an investment strategy or policy, the four key areas that must be addressed are investment management, market timing, asset allocation, and security selection. We discuss each of these next.

Investment Management   A basic decision that you and every other investor must make is whether you will manage your investments yourself or hire someone else to do it. At the one extreme, you can open an account with a broker and make all of the buy and sell decisions yourself. At the other extreme, you can invest all of your money in a managed account, such as a wrap account, and make no buy and sell decisions at all.

Often investors partially manage their investments themselves and partially use professional managers. For example, you might divide your money between, say, four different mutual funds. In this case, you have hired four different money managers. However, you decided what types of funds to buy, you chose the particular funds within each type, and you decided how to divide your money between the funds.

It might appear that managing your money by yourself is the cheapest way to go because you save on the management fees. Appearances can be deceiving, however. First of all, you should consider the value of your time. For some, researching investments and making investment decisions is something of a hobby; for many of us, however, it is too time-consuming, and this is a powerful incentive to hire professional management. Also, for some strategies, the costs of doing it yourself can exceed those of hiring someone even after considering fees simply because of the higher commissions and other fees that individual investors frequently pay. For example, it might not be a bad idea for some of your investment to be in real estate, but a small investor will find it very difficult to directly acquire a sound real estate investment at reasonable cost.

An interesting question regarding professional management concerns the possibility of generating superior returns. It would seem logical to argue that by hiring a professional investor to manage your money, you would earn more, at least on average. Surely the pros make better investment decisions than the amateurs! Surprisingly, this isn't necessarily true. We will return to this subject in later chapters, but, for now, we simply note that the possibility of a superior return may not be a compelling reason to prefer professional management.

Market Timing   A second basic investment decision you must make is whether you will try to buy and sell in anticipation of the future direction of the overall market. For example, you might move money into the stock market when you thought it was going to rise, and move money out when you thought it was going to fall. This activity is called **market timing.** Some investors very actively move money around to try to time short-term market movements; others are less active but still try to time longer-term movements. A fully passive strategy is one in which no attempt is made to time the market.

market timing
Buying and selling in anticipation of the overall direction of a market.

Market timing certainly seems like a reasonable thing to do; after all, why leave money in an investment if you expect it to decrease in value? You might be surprised that a common recommendation is that investors *not* try to time the market. As we discuss in more detail in a later chapter, the reason is that successful market timing is, to put it mildly, very difficult. To outperform a completely passive strategy, you must be able to very accurately predict the future; if you make even a small number of bad calls, you will likely never catch up.

Asset Allocation   Another fundamental decision that must be made concerns the distribution of your investment across different types of assets. We saw in Chapter 1 that different asset types—small stocks, large stocks, bonds—have very different risk and return characteristics. In formulating your investment strategy, you must decide what percentage of your money will be placed in each of these broad categories. This decision is called **asset allocation.**

asset allocation The distribution of investment funds among broad classes of assets.

An important asset allocation decision for many investors is how much to invest in common stocks and how much to invest in bonds. There are some basic rules of thumb for this decision, one of the simplest being to split the portfolio into 60 percent stocks and 40 percent bonds. This popular 60–40 mix is generally a reasonable allocation strategy, but you should read the article in the nearby Investment Updates box before you finally decide.

Security Selection   Finally, after deciding who will manage your investment, whether you will try to time the market, and the various asset classes you wish to hold, you must decide which specific securities to buy within each class. This is termed **security selection.**

security selection
Selection of specific securities within a particular class.

For example, you might decide that you want 30 percent of your money in small stocks. This is an asset allocation decision. Next, however, you must decide *which* small stocks to buy. Here again there is an active strategy and a passive strategy. With an

Popular 60-40 Mix Is No Panacea

Why do so many investors hold a mix of 60% stocks and 40% bonds?

As it turns out, there are three main arguments for the 60–40 mix. *But none of them clinch the case.*

It Produces Good Returns in Bad Times

The 1930s and 1940s were a nightmare for investors. In the 1930s, stocks were trounced by deflation. In the 1940s, bonds were battered by inflation. But in both decades, a mix of 60% U.S. stocks and 40% U.S. longer-term government bonds outpaced inflation by a healthy margin.

"What 60–40 has done is kept people whole over an extended period, especially a deflationary period," says Keith Ambachtsheer, a pension consultant in Toronto. "Where 60–40 runs into problems is in the 1970s," when inflation was much higher than in the 1940s. That high inflation not only wreaked havoc on bonds, but also hurt stocks, which were vulnerable because of rich valuations.

It Offers a Decent Mix of Income and Capital Gains

If you are retired and living off your portfolio, you might have been told to buy a 60–40 mix, because you get a moderate amount of income and your portfolio should keep growing along with inflation.

Right now, for instance, stocks yield less than 2%, but bonds kick off around 6%, giving a 60–40 portfolio an overall yield of some 3½%.

Meanwhile, for capital appreciation, you have to rely on your stocks. Over the long haul, these might climb at 7% a year, assuming share price-to-earnings multiples hold steady and earnings per share rise at their historic 7% annual clip. If you have 60% in stocks, that translates into overall portfolio growth of more than 4%, nicely ahead of today's 2% inflation rate.

But in truth, you could keep up with inflation—and generate a much higher yield—by putting far less into stocks and keeping even more in bonds. For retirees, it seems, there is nothing magical about the 60–40 mix.

It Generates the Best Risk-Adjusted Return

Derek Sasveld, a senior consultant with Chicago's Ibbotson Associates, says the theoretical justification for the 60–40 mix came in the mid-1960s. At that time, there was keen interest among some institutional investors in building portfolios that produced good risk-adjusted returns. To find the right mix, they looked at the past 40 years of U.S. stock and bond returns.

"That 60–40 portfolio from 1926 through 1965 was terrific," Mr. Sasveld notes. "The correlation between stocks and bonds at that point was virtually zero."

But times have changed. "Stocks and bonds are now more correlated," Mr. Sasveld says. "People shouldn't think about the 60–40 mix as being a good place to start."

Source: Jonathan Clements, "Not So Magical: Popular 60–40 Mix of Stocks and Bonds Is No Panacea," *The Wall Street Journal*, December 16, 1997.

active strategy, we try to identify those small stocks that we think will do the best in the future; in other words, we try to pick "winners." Investigating particular securities within a broad class in an attempt to identify superior performers is often called *security analysis.*

With a passive security selection strategy, we might just acquire a diverse group of small stocks, perhaps by buying a mutual fund that holds shares in hundreds of small companies (such funds are discussed in detail in Chapter 4).

A useful way to distinguish asset allocation from security selection is to note that asset allocation is essentially a macro-level activity because the focus is on whole markets or classes of assets. Security selection is a much more micro-level activity because the focus is on individual securities.

If we simultaneously consider the active versus passive aspects of asset allocation and security selection, four distinct investment strategies emerge, which we summarize in the following two-by-two table:

	Security Selection	
Asset Allocation	Active	Passive
Active	I	II
Passive	III	IV

With strategy I, we actively move money between asset classes based on our beliefs and expectations about future performance and we also try to pick the best performers in each class. This is a fully active strategy. At the other extreme, strategy IV, we follow a fully passive strategy, neither changing asset allocation very much nor choosing individual securities in an attempt to identify the likely best performers.

With strategy II, we actively vary our holdings by class, but we don't try to choose particular securities within each class. With this strategy, we might move back and forth between short-term government bonds and small stocks in an attempt to time the market. Finally, with strategy III, we don't vary our asset allocations, but we do select individual securities. A diehard stock picker would fall into this category; such an investor holds 100 percent stocks and concentrates solely on buying and selling individual companies.

CHECK THIS

2.4a What does the term "risk-averse" mean?

2.4b What are some of the constraints investors face in making investment decisions?

2.4c What is asset allocation?

2.5 Summary and Conclusions

This chapter explores the investing process. We discuss how to choose a broker and various aspects of broker–customer relations, including hypothecation, street name registration, and arbitration. The use of margin to purchase securities is covered, and the financial leverage effect of a margin purchase is emphasized. We describe short sales in some detail and stress the potentially unlimited losses that can arise from a short position. Finally, we cover some of the constraints faced by investors, and we briefly describe some basic investment strategy considerations, including market timing, asset allocation, and security selection.

GET REAL

This chapter covered the basics of brokerage accounts, some important trade types, and, finally, some big-picture issues regarding investment strategies and objectives. How should you, as an investor or investment manager, put this information to work?

The answer is that you need to open a brokerage account! Investing is like many activities; the best way to learn is by making mistakes. Unfortunately, making mistakes with real money is an expensive way to learn, so we don't recommend trying things like short sales with real money, at least not at first.

Instead, to learn about how to trade and gain some experience with making (and losing) money, you should open a Stock-Trak account (or a similar simulated brokerage account). Take it seriously. Try various trade types and strategies and see how they turn out. The important thing to do is to follow your trades and try to understand why you made or lost money and also why you made or lost the amount you did.

In a similar vein, you should carefully review your account statements to make sure you understand exactly what each item means and how your account equity is calculated.

After you have gained some experience trading "on paper," you should open a real account as soon as you can pull together enough money. Looking back at Chapter 1, you know that it's important to get started early. Once you have a real account, however, it's still a good idea to keep a separate "play money" account to test trading ideas to make sure you really understand them before committing your precious real money.

Key Terms

Security Investors Protection Corporation (SIPC) 34
cash account 35
margin account 35
call money rate 35
margin 36
initial margin 37
maintenance margin 37

margin call 37
hypothecation 40
street name 40
short sale 41
short interest 45
market timing 51
asset allocation 51
security selection 51

Chapter Review Problems and Self-Test

1. **The Account Balance Sheet** Suppose you want to buy 10,000 shares of Intel Corporation at a price of $30 per share. You put up $200,000 and borrow the rest. What does your account balance sheet look like? What is your margin?

2. **Short Sales** Suppose that in the previous problem you shorted 10,000 shares instead of buying. The initial margin is 60 percent. What does the account balance sheet look like following the short?

Answers to Self-Test Problems

1. The 10,000 shares of Intel cost $300,000. You supply $200,000, so you must borrow $100,000. The account balance sheet looks like this:

Assets		Liabilities and Account Equity	
10,000 shares of Intel	$300,000	Margin loan	$100,000
		Account equity	200,000
Total	$300,000	Total	$300,000

Your margin is the account equity divided by the value of the stock owned:

$$\text{Margin} = \$200,000 \, / \, \$300,000$$
$$= .6666 \ldots$$
$$= 67\%$$

2. Following the short, your account is as follows:

Assets		Liabilities and Account Equity	
Proceeds from sale	$300,000	Short position	$300,000
Initial margin deposit	180,000	Account equity	180,000
Total	$480,000	Total	$480,000

Notice that you shorted $300,000 worth of stock, so, with a 60 percent margin requirement, you deposited $180,000.

Test Your Investment Quotient

1. **Brokerage Accounts**   Which of the following agencies provides customer insurance protection for individual brokerage accounts?

   a. Federal Deposit Insurance Corporation (FDIC)
   b. Federal Investor Protection Agency (FIPA)
   c. Securities Investor Protection Corporation (SIPC)
   d. Securities Investor Insurance Agency (SIIA)

2. **Brokerage Accounts**   Which of the following is not a standard provision of a hypothecation agreement?

   a. Right of a broker to lend shares held in street name for a beneficial owner
   b. Right of a broker to pledge shares held in street name as collateral for margin loans
   c. Right of a broker to short sell shares held in street name for a beneficial owner
   d. All of the above are standard provisions of a hypothecation agreement

3. **Leverage**   You deposit $100,000 cash in a brokerage account and purchase $200,000 of stocks on margin by borrowing $100,000 from your broker. Later, the value of your stock holdings falls to $150,000, whereupon you get nervous and close your account. What is the percentage return on your investment?

   a. 0 percent
   b. −25 percent
   c. −50 percent
   d. −75 percent

4. **Leverage**   You deposit $100,000 cash in a brokerage account and short sell $200,000 of stocks. Later, the value of the stocks held short rises to $250,000, whereupon you get nervous and close your account. What is the percentage return on your investment?

   a. 0 percent
   b. −25 percent
   c. −50 percent
   d. −75 percent

5. **Account Margin** You deposit $100,000 cash in a brokerage account and purchase $200,000 of stocks on margin by borrowing $100,000 from your broker. Later, the value of your stock holdings falls to $175,000. What is your account margin in dollars?

   a. $50,000
   b. $75,000
   c. $100,000
   d. $150,000

6. **Account Margin** You deposit $100,000 cash in a brokerage account and purchase $200,000 of stocks on margin by borrowing $100,000 from your broker. Later, the value of your stock holdings falls to $150,000. What is your account margin in percent?

   a. 25 percent
   b. 33 percent
   c. 50 percent
   d. 75 percent

7. **Account Margin** You deposit $100,000 cash in a brokerage account and short sell $200,000 of stocks on margin. Later, the value of the stocks held short rises to $225,000. What is your account margin in dollars?

   a. $50,000
   b. $75,000
   c. $100,000
   d. $150,000

8. **Account Margin** You deposit $100,000 cash in a brokerage account and short sell $200,000 of stocks on margin. Later, the value of the stocks held short rises to $250,000. What is your account margin in percent?

   a. 20 percent
   b. 25 percent
   c. 33 percent
   d. 50 percent

9. **Margin Calls** You deposit $100,000 cash in a brokerage account and purchase $200,000 of stocks on margin by borrowing $100,000 from your broker, who requires maintenance margin of 30 percent. Which of the following is the largest value for your stock holdings for which you will still receive a margin call?

   a. $200,000
   b. $160,000
   c. $140,000
   d. $120,000

10. **Margin Calls** You deposit $100,000 cash in a brokerage account and short sell $200,000 of stocks. Your broker requires maintenance margin of 30 percent. Which of the following is the lowest value for the stocks you are holding short for which you will still receive a margin call?

    a. $260,000
    b. $240,000
    c. $220,000
    d. $200,000

11. **Investment Decisions** Which of the following investment factors, strategies, or tactics is the least relevant to a passive investment policy?

    a. Market timing
    b. Asset allocation
    c. Security selection
    d. Tax status

12. **Investment Decisions** Which of the following investment factors, strategies, or tactics may have little relevance for a passive investment policy?

    a. Market timing
    b. Asset allocation
    c. Security selection
    d. Tax status

13. **Investment Decisions** Which of the following investment strategies or tactics will likely consume the greatest amount of resources, time, effort, and so on, when implementing an active investment policy?

    a. Market timing
    b. Asset allocation
    c. Security selection
    d. Tax strategy

14. **Investment Decisions** Which of the following investment strategies or tactics is likely the most relevant in the decision to short sell a particular stock?

    a. Market timing
    b. Asset allocation
    c. Security selection
    d. Tax strategy

15. **Investment Constraints** Which of the following investment constraints is expected to have the most fundamental impact on the investment decision process for a typical investor?

    a. Investor's tax status
    b. Investor's time horizon
    c. Investor's need for liquidity
    d. Investor's attitude toward risk

Questions and Problems

**Core
Questions**

1. **Margin**   What does it mean to purchase a security on margin? Why might you do it?

2. **Short Sales**   What does it mean to sell a security short? Why might you do it?

3. **Margin Requirements**   What is the reason margin requirements exist?

4. **Allocation versus Selection**   What is the difference between asset allocation and security selection?

5. **Allocation versus Timing**   Are market timing and active asset allocation similar? Why or why not?

6. **Street Name Registration**   Why is street name registration advantageous to investors? Under what circumstances is it required?

7. **Broker–Customer Relations**   Suppose your broker tips you on a hot stock. You invest heavily, but, to your considerable dismay, the stock plummets in value. What recourse do you have against your broker?

8. **Long Profits**   An important difference between a long position in stock and a short position concerns the potential gains and losses. Suppose a stock sells for $18 per share, and you buy 300 shares. What are your potential gains and losses?

9. **Calculating Margin**   Mobil Corporation stock sells for $75 per share, and you've decided to purchase as many shares as you possibly can. You have $7,500 available to invest. What is the maximum number of shares you can buy? Why?

10. **Short Sale Profits**   Suppose you sell short 1,000 shares of a stock at $30 per share. Ignoring borrowing costs and fees, what is the maximum profit you can earn from this investment? What is the potential maximum loss?

Intermediate
Questions

11. **Calculating Margin**   Using the information in problem 9, construct your equity account balance sheet at the time of your purchase. What does your balance sheet look like if the share price rises to $90? What if it falls to $65 per share? What is your margin in both cases?

12. **Calculating Margin**   You've just opened a margin account with $20,000 at your local brokerage firm. You instruct your broker to purchase 600 shares of Apple Computer stock, which currently sells for $50 per share. What is your initial margin? Construct the equity account balance sheet for this position.

13. **Calculating Returns**   In the previous problem, suppose the call money rate is 6 percent and your broker charges you a spread of 1.25 percent over this rate. You hold your Apple stock for six months and sell at a price of $55 per share. The company paid a dividend of $.75 per share the day before you sold your stock. What is your total dollar return from this investment? What is your effective annual rate of return?

14. **Margin Call**   Suppose you purchase 500 shares of IBM stock at $80 per share with an initial cash investment of $24,000. If your broker requires a 30 percent maintenance margin, at what share price will you be subject to a margin call? If you want to keep your position open despite the stock price plunge, what alternatives do you have?

15. **Margin and Leverage**   In the previous problem, suppose the call money rate is 5 percent and you are charged a 1.5 percent premium over this rate. Calculate your return on investment for each of the following share prices one year later. What would your rate of return be in each case if you purchased $24,000 of stock with no margin?
    a. $100
    b. $80
    c. $60

16. **Short Sales**   You believe that Citigroup stock is going to fall and you've decided to sell 2,000 shares short. If the current share price is $50, construct the equity account balance sheet for this trade. Assume the initial margin is 100 percent.

17. **Short Sales**   Repeat the previous problem assuming you short the 2,000 shares on 75 percent margin.

18. **Calculating Short Sale Returns**   You just sold short 1,000 shares of Wetscope, Inc., a fledgling software firm, at $70 per share. You cover your short when the price hits $50 per share one year later. If the company paid $1.00 per share in dividends over this period, what is your rate of return on the investment?

19. **Margin Calls**   You sold short 5,000 shares of stock at a share price of $25 on 60 percent margin. If the maintenance margin for your account is 40 percent, at what share price will you be subject to a margin call?

20. **Liquidity**   The liquidity of an asset directly affects the risk of buying or selling that asset during adverse market conditions. Describe the liquidity risk you face with a short stock position during a market rally, and a long stock position during a market decline.

STOCK-TRAK·
Portfolio Simulations

Trading Common Stocks with Stock-Trak

Stock-Trak allows you to trade common stocks in much the same way you would with an individual brokerage account that supported trading on the Internet. This includes buying, selling, and selling short common stocks trading on the major exchanges—NYSE, AMEX (the American Stock Exchange), and Nasdaq (the National Association of Securities Dealers Automated Quotations). There are a few restrictions, however. For example, Stock-Trak restricts trading to common stocks trading at a price of $5.00 or more per share. Thus many small-company stocks cannot be traded. Stock-Trak also requires that all stock trades be in multiples of 25 shares. You should consult the most recent Stock-Trak rules at the website (www.mhhe.com/cj) for other possible restrictions that might apply.

To trade common stocks with Stock-Trak, you must first know the ticker symbol—a term going back to the era of the ticker tape—of the stock you wish to trade. Stocks trading on NYSE or AMEX have ticker symbols made up from one to three letters. For example, F is the ticker for Ford Motor Company, MU is the ticker for Micron Technology, and TMX is the ticker for TelMex (Teléphonos de México). Nasdaq stocks have four or five letters in their ticker symbols. For example, MSFT is the ticker for Microsoft Corporation, and ADVNA is the symbol for Advanta Corporation.

You should be able to easily find most stock ticker symbols from *The Wall Street Journal*'s NYSE, AMEX, and Nasdaq stock price listings. Tickers can also be found through most Internet stock quote servers. But be careful how you type the company name when requesting a server to look up a ticker symbol. For example, if you simply type "walmart" you will probably not get the desired ticker symbol. But if you type "wal-mart" you will get the ticker WMT for Wal-Mart Stores. After you have found the appropriate ticker symbol, you can submit an order to Stock-Trak.

There are four basic types of stock trades:

1. Buy to open or increase a long position.
2. Sell to close or reduce a long position.
3. Short sell to open or increase a short position.
4. Buy to cover or reduce a short position.

When buying a stock, you take a long position with the hope that the stock price will increase. By selling stock you are closing all or part of a long position. Selling short refers to selling stock shares that you don't own with the hope that you can later buy them back at a lower price. Buying stock shares back to close all or part of a short position is called covering a short position. We will discuss these four types of orders in the sequence of transactions described immediately below.

Suppose you want to buy 1,000 shares of Texas Instruments and short sell 800 shares of Citigroup. These stocks trade on NYSE under the ticker symbols TXN and C, respectively. Your orders might be abbreviated to look like this:

Buy 1,000 TXN

Short 800 C

After execution, you would have a 1,000-share long position in Texas Instruments (TXN) and an 800-share short position in Citigroup (C).

Now, suppose you later want to reduce your long position in TXN to 600 shares and increase your short position in C to 1,200 shares. The necessary orders would be these:

Sell 400 TXN

Short 400 C

After execution, you would have a 600-share long position in Texas Instruments (TXN) and a 1,200-share short position in Citigroup (C).

To close out your long and short positions completely, you would then submit these orders:

Sell 600 TXN

Cover 1,200 C

After execution, you will have closed out both positions completely. Your Stock-Trak account will then reflect any gains or losses on these transactions, including commission costs.

Stock-Trak Exercises

1. Look up stock ticker symbols for these companies: American Express, Delta Air Lines, Exxon, Liz Claiborne, McDonald's, Procter & Gamble, Xerox.

2. Some companies have ticker symbols with only a single letter, for example, the letters B, C, D, F, G, H, K, L, M, N, O, P, R, S, T, U, W, X, Y, and Z are one-letter tickers. What are these companies' names?

3. Can you guess what the company names are for the ticker symbols AAPL, BUD, DIS, FDX, LZB, MAIL, MCIC, PIXR, OSSI, REV, SBUX, TRW, and VO?

4. Log on to the Internet to the NYSE (www.nyse.com) and the Nasdaq-AMEX (www.nasdaq-amex.com) to review the names and ticker symbols of the various companies listed there.

3

Security Types

You invest $5,000 in Yahoo! common stock and just months later sell the shares for $7,500, realizing a 50 percent return. Not bad! At the same time, your neighbor invests $5,000 in Yahoo! stock options, which become worth $25,000 at expiration—a 400 percent return. Yahoo! Clearly there is a big difference between stock shares and stock options. Security type matters! ∎ Our goal in this chapter is to introduce you to some of the different types of securities that are routinely bought and sold in financial markets around the world. As we mentioned in Chapter 1, we will be focusing on financial assets such as bonds, stocks, options, and futures in this book, so these are the securities we briefly describe here. The securities we discuss are covered in much greater detail in the chapters ahead, so we touch on only some of their most essential features in this chapter.

For each of the securities we examine, we ask three questions. First, what is its basic nature and what are its distinguishing characteristics? Second, what are the potential gains and losses from owning it? Third, how are its prices quoted in the financial press?

3.1 Classifying Securities

To begin our overview of security types, we first develop a classification scheme for the different securities. As shown in Table 3.1, financial assets can be grouped into three broad categories, and each of these categories can be further subdivided into a few major subtypes. This classification is not exhaustive, but it covers the major types of financial assets. In the sections that follow, we describe these assets in the order they appear in Table 3.1.

Table 3.1	Classification of Financial Assets	
	Basic Types	**Major Subtypes**
	Interest-bearing	Money market instruments
		Fixed-income securities
	Equities	Common stock
		Preferred stock
	Derivatives	Options
		Futures

When we examine some of these security types in more detail, we will see that the distinctions can become a little blurred, particularly with some recently created financial instruments; as a result, some financial assets are hard to classify. The primary reason is that some instruments are hybrids, meaning that they are combinations of the basic types.

As you may have noticed in our discussion, financial assets, such as bonds and stocks, are often called securities. They are often called financial "instruments" as well. In certain contexts, there are distinctions between these terms, but they are used more or less interchangeably in everyday discussion, so we will stick with common usage.

CHECK THIS

3.1a What are the three basic types of financial assets?

3.1b Why are some financial assets hard to classify?

3.2 Interest-Bearing Assets

Broadly speaking, interest-bearing assets (as the name suggests) pay interest. Some pay interest implicitly and some pay it explicitly, but the common denominator is that the value of these assets depends, at least for the most part, on interest rates. The reason that these assets pay interest is that they all begin life as a loan of some sort, so they are all debt obligations of some issuer.

There are many types of interest-bearing assets. They range from the relatively simple to the astoundingly complex. We discuss some basic types and their features next. The more complex types are discussed in later chapters.

Money Market Instruments

money market instruments Short-term debt obligations of large corporations and governments that mature in a year or less.

For the most part, **money market instruments** are the simplest form of interest-bearing asset. Money market instruments generally have the following two properties:

1. They are essentially IOUs sold by large corporations or governments to borrow money.
2. They mature in less than a year from the time they are sold, meaning that the loan must be repaid within a year.

Most money market instruments trade in very large denominations, and most, but not all, are quite liquid.

The most familiar example of a money market instrument is a Treasury bill, or T-bill for short. Every week, the U.S. Treasury borrows billions of dollars by selling T-bills to the public. Like many (but not all) money market instruments, T-bills are sold on a *discount basis.* This simply means that T-bills are sold at a price that is less than their stated face value. In other words, an investor buys a T-bill at one price and later, when the bill matures, receives the full face value. The difference is the interest earned.

U.S. Treasury bills are the most liquid type of money market instrument—that is, the type with the largest and most active market. Other types of money market instruments traded in active markets include bank certificates of deposit (or CDs) and corporate and municipal money market instruments.

The potential gain from buying a money market instrument is fixed because the owner is promised a fixed future payment. The most important risk is the risk of default, which is the possibility that the borrower will not repay the loan as promised. With a T-bill, there is no possibility of default, so, as we saw in Chapter 1, T-bills are essentially risk-free. In fact, most money market instruments have relatively low risk, but there are exceptions and a few spectacular defaults have occurred in the past.

Prices for different money market instruments are quoted in the financial press in different ways. In fact, usually interest rates are quoted, not prices, so some calculation is necessary to convert rates to prices. The procedures are not complicated, but they involve a fair amount of detail, so we save them for another chapter.

Fixed-Income Securities

fixed-income securities Longer-term debt obligations, often of corporations and governments, that promise to make fixed payments according to a preset schedule.

Fixed-income securities are exactly what the name suggests: securities that promise to make fixed payments according to some preset schedule. The other key characteristic of a fixed-income security is that, like a money market instrument, it begins life as a loan of some sort. Fixed-income securities are therefore debt obligations. They are typically issued by corporations and governments. Unlike money market instruments, fixed-income securities have lives that exceed 12 months at the time they are issued.

The words "note" and "bond" are generic terms for fixed-income securities, but "fixed income" is really more accurate. This term is being used more frequently as securities are increasingly being created that don't fit within traditional note or bond frameworks but are nonetheless fixed-income securities.

Examples of Fixed-Income Securities To give one particularly simple example of a fixed-income security, near the end of every month, the U.S. Treasury sells between $10 billion and $20 billion of two-year notes to the public. If you buy a two-year note when it is issued, you will receive a check every six months for two years for a fixed amount, called the bond's *coupon,* and in two years you will receive the face amount on the note.

Suppose you buy $1 million in face amount of a 6 percent, two-year note. The 6 percent is called the *coupon rate,* and it tells you that you will receive 6 percent of the $1 million face value each year, or $60,000, in two $30,000 semiannual "coupon" payments. In two years, in addition to your final $30,000 coupon payment, you will receive the $1 million face value. The price you would pay for this note depends on market conditions. United States government security prices are discussed in detail in Chapter 12.

Example 3.1 A "Note-Worthy" Investment?

Suppose you buy $100,000 in face amount of a just-issued five-year U.S. Treasury note. If the coupon rate is 5 percent, what will you receive over the next five years if you hold on to your investment?

You will receive 5 percent of $100,000, or $5,000, per year, paid in two semiannual coupons of $2,500. In five years, in addition to the final $2,500 coupon payment, you will receive the $100,000 face amount.

To give a slightly different example, suppose you take out a 48-month car loan. Under the terms of the loan, you promise to make 48 payments of $400 per month. It may not look like it to you, but in taking out this loan, you have issued a fixed-income security to your bank. In fact, your bank may turn around and sell your car loan (perhaps bundled with a large number of others) to an investor. Actually, car loans are not sold all that often, but there is a very active market in student loans, and student loans are routinely bought and sold in huge quantities.

Fixed-Income Price Quotes   Prices for fixed-income securities are quoted in different ways, depending on, among other things, what type of security is being priced. As with money market instruments, there are various details that are very important (and often overlooked), so we will defer an extensive discussion of these price quotes to later chapters. However, just to get an idea of how fixed-income prices look, Figure 3.1 presents an example of *Wall Street Journal* corporate bond quotes.

In Figure 3.1, locate the bond issue labeled "ATT $7\frac{1}{8}$02." This bond was issued by AT&T, the telecommunications giant. The $7\frac{1}{8}$ is the bond's annual coupon rate. If

Figure 3.1

NYSE Bond Trading

NEW YORK EXCHANGE BONDS

Quotations as of 4 p.m. Eastern Time

CORPORATION BONDS

Bonds	Cur Yld.	Vol.	Close	Net Chg.
ATT $4\frac{3}{8}$99	4.4	6	$99\frac{5}{32}$	$+ \frac{7}{32}$
ATT 6s00	6.0	67	$100\frac{1}{8}$	$- \frac{1}{8}$
ATT $5\frac{1}{8}$01	5.2	88	$99\frac{3}{8}$	...
ATT $7\frac{1}{8}$02	6.8	55	$104\frac{3}{4}$	$- \frac{1}{4}$
ATT $6\frac{3}{4}$04	6.3	40	$106\frac{1}{2}$	$- \frac{7}{8}$
ATT 7s05	6.5	146	$107\frac{3}{4}$	$+ \frac{1}{4}$
ATT 8.2s05	7.9	20	$103\frac{7}{8}$	$- 1$
ATT $7\frac{3}{4}$07	6.9	25	113	...
ATT $8\frac{1}{8}$22	7.5	28	108	$+ \frac{1}{8}$
ATT $8\frac{1}{8}$24	7.5	45	$108\frac{3}{8}$	$+ \frac{3}{8}$
ATT $8\frac{5}{8}$31	7.7	16	112	$+ \frac{1}{4}$

you own $1 million in face amount of these bonds, then you will receive $7\frac{1}{8}$ percent (7.125%) per year on the $1 million, or $71,250 per year in two semiannual payments. The 02 tells us that the bond will mature in the year 2002. The next column, labeled "Cur Yld." is the bond's *current yield.* A bond's current yield is its annual coupon divided by its current price; we discuss how to interpret this number in Chapter 9.

The final three columns give us information about trading activity and prices. The column labeled "Vol." is the actual number of bonds that traded that day, 55 in this case. Most corporate bonds have a face value of $1,000 per bond, so 55 bonds represents $55,000 in face value. The next column, labeled "Close," is the closing price for the day. This is simply the last price at which a trade took place that day. Bond prices are quoted as a percentage of face value. In this case, the closing price of $104\frac{3}{4}$ tells that the price was 104.75 percent of face value, or $1,047.50 per bond, assuming a $1,000 face value.

Finally, the column labeled "Net Chg." in Figure 3.1 is the change in the closing price from the previous day's closing price. Here, the $-1/4$ tells us that the closing price of $104\frac{3}{4}$ is down by one-quarter percentage point from the previous closing price, so this bond decreased in value on this day. The format of price quotes in Figure 3.1 is for corporate bonds only. As we will see, other types of bonds, particularly U.S. government bonds, are quoted quite differently.

| **Example 3.2** | **Corporate Bond Quotes** |

In Figure 3.1, which AT&T bond has the longest maturity? Assuming a face value of $1,000 each, how much would you have to pay for 100 of these? Verify that the reported current yield is correct.

The bond with the longest maturity is the ATT $8\frac{5}{8}31$, which matures in 2031. Based on the reported closing price, the price you would pay is 112 percent of face value per bond. Assuming a $1,000 face value, this is $1,120 per bond, or $112,000 for 100 bonds. The current yield is the annual coupon divided by the price, which, in this case, would be $8\frac{5}{8}$ / 112 = 7.7 percent, the number reported.

The potential gains from owning a fixed-income security come in two forms. First, there are the fixed payments promised and the final payment at maturity. In addition, the prices of most fixed-income securities rise when interest rates fall, so there is the possibility of a gain from a favorable movement in rates. An unfavorable change in interest rates will produce a loss.

Another significant risk for many fixed-income securities is the possibility that the issuer will not make the promised payments. This risk depends on the issuer. It doesn't exist for U.S. government bonds, but for many other issuers the possibility is very real. Finally, unlike most money market instruments, fixed-income securities are often quite illiquid, again depending on the issuer and the specific type.

CHECK THIS

3.2a What are the two basic types of interest-bearing assets?

3.2b What are the two basic features of a fixed-income security?

3.3 Equities

Equities are probably the most familiar type of security. They come in two forms: common stock and preferred stock. Of these, common stock is much more important, so we discuss it first.

Common Stock

Common stock represents ownership in a corporation. If you own 100 shares of IBM, for example, then you own about .00002 percent of IBM (IBM has roughly 500 million shares outstanding). It's really that simple. As a part owner, you are entitled to your pro rata share of anything paid out by IBM, and you have the right to vote on important matters regarding IBM. If IBM were to be sold or liquidated, you would receive your share of whatever was left over after all of IBM's debts and other obligations (such as wages) are paid.

The potential benefits from owning common stock come primarily in two forms. First, many companies (but not all) pay cash dividends to their shareholders. However, neither the timing nor the amount of any dividend is guaranteed. At any time, it can be increased, decreased, or omitted altogether. Dividends are paid strictly at the discretion of a company's board of directors, which is elected by shareholders.

The second potential benefit from owning stock is that the value of your stock may rise because share values in general increase or because the future prospects for your particular company improve (or both). The downside is just the reverse; your shares may lose value if either the economy or your particular company falters. As we saw back in Chapter 1, both the potential rewards and the risks from owning common stock have been substantial, particularly shares of stock in smaller companies.

Preferred Stock

The other type of equity security, preferred stock, differs from common stock in several important ways. First, the dividend on a preferred share is usually fixed at some amount and never changed. Further, in the event of liquidation, preferred shares have a particular face value. The reason preferred stock (or preference stock, as it is sometimes termed) is called "preferred" is that a company must pay the fixed dividend on its preferred stock before any dividends can be paid to common shareholders. In other words, preferred shareholders must be paid first.

The dividend on a preferred stock can be omitted at the discretion of the board of directors, so, unlike a debt obligation, there is no legal requirement that the dividend be paid (as long as the common dividend is also skipped). However, some preferred stock is *cumulative,* meaning that any and all skipped dividends must be paid in full (although without interest) before common shareholders can receive a dividend.

Potential gains from owning preferred stock consist of the promised dividend plus any gains from price increases. The potential losses are just the reverse: the dividend may be skipped, and the value of your preferred shares may decline from either market-wide decreases in value or diminished prospects for your particular company's future business (or both).

Preferred stock issues are not rare, but they are much less frequently encountered than common stock issues. Most preferred stock is issued by large companies, particularly banks and, especially, public utilities.

In many ways, preferred stock resembles a fixed-income security; in fact, it is sometimes classified that way. In particular, preferred stocks usually have a fixed payment and a fixed liquidation value. The main difference is that preferred stock is not a debt obligation. Also, for accounting and tax purposes, preferred stock is treated as equity.

Having said this, preferred stock is a good example of why it is sometimes difficult to neatly and precisely classify every security type. To further complicate matters, there are preferred stock issues with dividends that are not fixed, so it seems clear that these are not fixed-income securities, but there are also bond issues that do not make fixed payments and allow the issuer to skip payments under certain circumstances. As we mentioned earlier, these are examples of hybrid securities.

To give a more difficult example, consider a *convertible bond*. Such a bond is an ordinary bond in every way except that it can be exchanged for a fixed number of shares of stock anytime at the bondholder's discretion. Whether this is really a debt or equity instrument is difficult (or even impossible) to say.

Common and Preferred Stock Price Quotes

Unlike fixed-income securities, the price quotes on common and preferred stock are fairly uniform. The part of the stock page from *The Wall Street Journal* seen in Figure 3.2 presents six lines for Chase Manhattan. The first line listed for Chase Manhattan is the common stock; the next five are preferred stock issues. It wouldn't be unusual for a preferred stock-issuing company to have several preferred issues, but for most there would be only one common stock. Also, the only issues listed for a given day were the ones that traded that day; a company may have several preferred issues for which there were no trades, so these would not appear.

In looking at the Chase Manhattan common stock, the first two numbers (labeled "52 Weeks Hi" and "Lo") are the highest and lowest price per share that the stock has sold for over the past 52 weeks. Thus, Chase Manhattan sold for as high as \$77.5625 $\left(77^9/_{16}\right)$ per share and as low as \$40.0625 $\left(40^1/_{16}\right)$ per share. The next piece of information is the company name, often abbreviated, followed by the ticker symbol, which is a unique shorthand symbol assigned to each company. The Chase Manhattan ticker symbol is CMB.

Following the ticker symbol is the dividend, labeled "Div," and the dividend yield, labeled "Yld %." Like most dividend-paying companies, Chase Manhattan pays dividends on a quarterly basis; the dividend number reported here, \$1.44, is actually four times the most recent quarterly dividend. The dividend yield is this annualized dividend divided by the closing price (discussed just below). Next, the price-earnings ratio, or PE, is reported. This ratio, as the name suggests, is equal to the price per share divided by earnings per share. Earnings per share is calculated as the sum of earnings over the last four quarters. We will discuss dividends, dividend yields, and price-earnings ratios in detail in Chapter 6.

Figure 3.2

NYSE Trading

Source: Reprinted from *The Wall Street Journal*, September 23, 1998, with permission via Copyright Clearance Center. Inc © 1998 Dow Jones & Company, Inc. All Rights Reserved Worldwide.

NEW YORK STOCK EXCHANGE COMPOSITE TRANSACTIONS

52 Weeks Hi	Lo	Stock	Sym	Div	Yld %	PE	Vol 100s	Hi	Lo	Close	Net Chg
$77^9/_{16}$	$40^1/_{16}$	ChaseManh	CMB	1.44	3.2	11100	103	$46^7/_{16}$	$43^9/_{16}$	$45^1/_2$	$-\frac{7}{8}$
$28^7/_8$	$24^{15}/_{16}$	ChaseManh pfA		2.63	10.5	...	28	25	$24^{15}/_{16}$	25	...
$28^3/_{16}$	$26^7/_{16}$	ChaseManh pfB		2.44	9.2	...	59	$26^3/_4$	$26^9/_{16}$	$26^9/_{16}$	$-\frac{1}{8}$
$31^9/_{16}$	$29^9/_{16}$	ChaseManh pfC		2.71	9.1	...	67	$29^3/_4$	$29^5/_8$	$29^{11}/_{16}$	$+\frac{1}{16}$
$30^7/_8$	$27^{13}/_{16}$	ChaseManh pfG		2.74	9.7	...	26	$28^3/_8$	$28^1/_4$	$28^3/_8$	$+\frac{1}{8}$
$25^5/_8$	$23^{15}/_{16}$	ChaseManh pfN		1.30e	5.3	...	24	$24^5/_8$	$24^5/_8$	$24^5/_8$	...

The next piece of information, "Vol," is the trading volume for the day, measured in hundreds. Stocks are usually traded in multiples of 100 called "round lots." Anything that is not a multiple of 100 is called an "odd lot." On this particular day, then, 103 round lots, or about 10,300 shares, were traded.

Finally, the last four columns tell us the high price ("Hi") for the day, the low price ("Lo") for the day, the closing price ("Close"), and the change in the closing price from the previous day ("Net Chg"). Chase Manhattan thus traded between a high of $46^7/_{16}$ per share and a low of $43^9/_{16}$ per share. It closed at $45^1/_2$, down 7/8 from the previous trading day.

The information for the five preferred stock issues is interpreted in the same way. For preferred stocks, however, no ticker symbol is given and PE ratios are not reported. The symbol "pf" indicates a preferred issue. When an issuer has more than one preferred issue, a letter is often attached to the pf to uniquely identify a particular issue. Thus, the five Chase Manhattan preferreds have the symbols pfA, pfB, pfC, pfG, and pfN and are called the A-, B-, C-, G-, and N-series.

CHECK THIS

3.3a What are the two types of equity securities?

3.3b Why is preferred stock sometimes classified as a fixed-income security?

Derivatives

primary asset
Security originally sold by a business or government to raise money.

There is a clear distinction between real assets, which are essentially tangible items, and financial assets, which are pieces of paper describing legal claims. Financial assets can be further subdivided into primary and derivative assets. A **primary asset** (sometimes called a *primitive asset*) is a security that was originally sold by a business or government to raise money, and a primary asset represents a claim on the assets of the issuer. Thus, stocks and bonds are primary financial assets.

derivative asset A financial asset that is derived from an existing traded asset rather than issued by a business or government to raise capital. More generally, any financial asset that is not a primary asset.

In contrast, as the name suggests, a **derivative asset** is a financial asset that is derived from an existing primary asset rather than being issued by a business or government to raise capital. As we will see, derivative assets usually represent claims either on other financial assets, such as shares of stock or even other derivative assets, or on the future price of a real asset such as gold. Beyond this, it is difficult to give a general definition of the term "derivative asset" because there are so many different types, and new ones are created almost every day. On the most basic level, however, any financial asset that is not a primary asset is a derivative asset.

To give a simple example of a derivative asset, imagine that you and a friend buy 1,000 shares of a dividend-paying stock, perhaps the Chase Manhattan stock we discussed. You each put up half the money, and you agree to sell your stock in one year. Furthermore, the two of you agree that you will get all the dividends paid while your friend gets all the gains or absorbs all the losses on the 1,000 shares.

This simple arrangement takes a primary asset, shares of Chase Manhattan stock, and creates two derivative assets, the dividend-only shares that you hold and the no-dividend shares held by your friend. Derivative assets such as these actually exist, and there are many variations on this basic theme.

There are two particularly important types of derivative assets, futures and options. Many other types exist, but they can usually be built up from these two basic types, possibly by combining them with other primary assets. Futures are the simpler of the two, so we discuss them first.

Futures Contracts

futures contract
An agreement made today regarding the terms of a trade that will take place later.

In many ways, a futures contract is the simplest of all financial assets. A **futures contract** is just an agreement made today regarding the terms of a trade that will take place later. For example, suppose you know that you will want to buy 100 ounces of gold in six months. One thing you could do is to strike a deal today with a seller in which you promise to pay, say, $400 per ounce in six months for the 100 ounces of gold. In other words, you and the seller agree that six months from now, you will exchange $40,000 for 100 ounces of gold. The agreement that you have created is a futures contract.

With your futures contract, you have locked in the price of gold six months from now. Suppose that gold is actually selling for $450 per ounce in six months. If this occurs, then you benefit from having entered into the futures contract because you have to pay only $400 per ounce. However, if gold is selling for $350, you lose because you are forced to pay $400 per ounce. Thus a futures contract is essentially a bet on the future price of whatever is being bought or sold. Notice that with your futures contract, no money changes hands today.

After entering into the futures contract, what happens if you change your mind in, say, four months, and you want out of the contract? The answer is that you can sell your contract to someone else. You would generally have a gain or a loss when you sell. The contract still has two months to run. If market participants generally believe that gold will be worth more than $400 when the contract matures in two months, then your contract is valuable, and you would have a gain if you sold it. If, on the other hand, market participants think gold will not be worth $400, then you would have a loss on the contract if you sold it because you would have to pay someone else to take it off your hands.

Futures contracts are traded all over the world on many types of assets, and futures contracts can be traced back to ancient civilizations. As we discuss in detail in Chapter 16, there are two broad categories of futures contracts: *financial futures* and *commodity futures.* The difference is that, with financial futures, the underlying asset is intangible, usually a stock index, bonds, or money market instruments. With commodity futures, the underlying asset is a real asset, typically either an agricultural product (such as cattle or wheat) or a natural resource product (such as gold or oil).

Futures Price Quotes

An important feature of traded futures contracts is that they are *standardized,* meaning that one contract calls for the purchase of a specific quantity of the underlying asset. Further, the contract specifies in detail what the underlying asset is and where it is to be delivered. For example, with a wheat contract, one contract specifies that such-and-such a quantity of a particular type of wheat will be delivered at one of a few approved locations on a particular date in exchange for the agreed-upon futures price.

In Figure 3.3 futures price quotations for U.S. Treasury bonds (or "T-bonds" for short) are seen as they appear in *The Wall Street Journal.* Looking at Figure 3.3, we see these are quotes for delivery of T-bonds with a total par, or face, value of $100,000. The letters CBT indicate to us where this contact is traded; in this case, it is the Chicago Board of Trade, the largest futures exchange in the world.

Figure 3.3

Futures Trading

FUTURES PRICES

INTEREST RATE

TREASURY BONDS (CBT)-$100,000; pts. 32nds of 100%

	Open	High	Low	Settle	Change	Lifetime High	Lifetime Low	Open Interest
Dec	130-13	131-16	130-09	131-15	+ 45	131-16	103-13	701,589
Mr99	130-02	131-05	129-30	131-04	+ 45	131-05	103-04	74,643
Sept	129-26	130-03	129-25	130-03	+ 45	130-03	115-11	4,017

Est vol 525,000; vol Tue 321,376; open int 781,064, –9,913.

The first column in Figure 3.3 tells us the delivery date for the bond specified by the contract. For example, the "Dec" indicates that the first contract listed is for T-bond delivery in December. The second is for delivery the following March, and so on. Following the delivery month, we have a series of prices. In order, we have the open price, the high price, the low price, and the settle price. The open price is the price at the start of trading, the high and low are highest and lowest prices for the day, and the settle is the price on the final trade of the day. The "Change" is the change in the settle price from the previous trading day.

The columns labeled "Lifetime High" and "Lifetime Low" refer to the highest and lowest prices over the life of this contract. Finally, the "Open Interest" tells us how many contracts are currently outstanding.

To get a better idea of how futures contracts work, suppose you buy one December contract at the settle price. What you have done is agree to buy T-bonds with a total par value of $100,000 in December at a price of 131-15 per $100 of par value, where the "-15" represents 15/32. Thus 131-15 can also be written as $131^{15}/_{32}$, which represents a price of $131,468.75 per $100,000 face value. No money changes hands today. However, if you take no further action, when December rolls around your T-bond will be delivered, and you must pay for them at that time.

Actually, most futures contracts don't result in delivery. Most buyers and sellers close out their contracts before the delivery date. To close out a contract, you take the opposite side. For example, suppose that with your one T-bond contract, you later decide you no longer wish to be in it. To get out, you simply sell one contract, thereby canceling your position.

Gains and Losses on Futures Contracts

Futures contracts have the potential for enormous gains and losses. To see why, let's consider again buying T-bond contracts based on the settle prices in Figure 3.3. To make matters somewhat more interesting, suppose you buy 20 December contracts at the settle price of $131^{15}/_{32}$ per $100 of par value.

One month later, because of falling inflation, the futures price of T-bonds for December delivery rises five dollars to $136^{15}/_{32}$. This may not seem like a huge increase, but it generates a substantial profit for you. You have locked in a price of $131^{15}/_{32}$ per $100 par value. The price has risen to $136^{15}/_{32}$, so you make a profit of $5 per $100 of par value, or $5,000 per $100,000 face value. With 20 contracts, each of which calls for delivery of $100,000 in face value of T-bonds, you make $20 \times \$5,000 = \$100,000$, so your profit is a tidy $100,000. Of course, if the price had decreased by five dollars, you would have lost $100,000 on your 20-contract position.

Example 3.3 **Future Shock**

Suppose you purchase five Sept 99 contracts at a settle price of $130^{04}/_{32}$. How much will you pay today? Suppose in one month you close your position and the Sept 99 futures price at that time is $125^{20}/_{32}$. Did you make or lose money? How much?

When you purchase the five contracts, you pay nothing today because the transaction is for Sept 99. However, you have agreed to pay $130^{04}/_{32}$ per $100 par value. If, when you close your position in a month, the futures price is $125^{20}/_{32}$, you have a loss of $130^{04}/_{32}$ − $125^{20}/_{32} = 4^{16}/_{32}$ per $100 par value, or $4^{16}/_{32} \times 1,000 = \$4,500$ per contract. Your total loss is thus $4,500 \times 5$ contracts, or $22,500 in all (ouch!).

CHECK THIS

3.4a What is a futures contract?

3.4b What are the general types of futures contracts?

3.4c Explain how you make or lose money on a futures contract.

3.5 Option Contracts

option contract An agreement that gives the owner the right, but not the obligation, to buy or sell a specific asset at a specified price for a set period of time.

An **option contract** is an agreement that gives the owner the right, but not the obligation, to buy or sell (depending on the type of option) a specific asset for a specific price for a specific period of time. The most familiar options are stock options. These are options to buy or sell shares of stock, and they are the focus of our discussion here. Options are a very flexible investment tool, and a great deal is known about them. We present some of the most important concepts here; our detailed coverage begins in Chapter 14.

Option Terminology

call option An option that gives the owner the right, but not the obligation, to buy an asset.

put option An option that gives the owner the right, but not the obligation, to sell an asset.

option premium The price you pay to buy an option.

Options come in two flavors, calls and puts. The owner of a **call option** has the right, but not the obligation, to *buy* an underlying asset at a fixed price for a specified time. The owner of a **put option** has the right, but not the obligation, to *sell* an underlying asset at a fixed price for a specified time.

Options occur frequently in everyday life. Suppose, for example, that you are interested in buying a used car. You and the seller agree that the price will be $3,000. You give the seller $100 to hold the car for one week, meaning that you have one week to come up with the $3,000 purchase price, or else you lose your $100.

This agreement is a call option. You paid the seller $100 for the right, but not the obligation, to buy the car for $3,000. If you change your mind because, for example, you find a better deal elsewhere, you can just walk away. You'll lose your $100, but that is the price you paid for the right, but not the obligation, to buy. The price you pay to purchase an option, the $100 in this example, is called the **option premium**.

strike price The price specified in an option contract at which the underlying asset can be bought (for a call option) or sold (for a put option). Also called the striking price or exercise price.

A few other definitions will be useful. First, the specified price at which the underlying asset can be bought or sold with an option contract is called the **strike price**, the *striking price,* or the *exercise price.* Using an option to buy or sell an asset is called *exercising* the option. The last day on which an option can be exercised is the *expiration date* on the option contract. Finally, an *American option* can be exercised anytime up to and including the expiration date, whereas a *European option* can be exercised only on the expiration date.

Options versus Futures

Our discussion thus far illustrates the two crucial differences between an option contract and a futures contract. The first is that the purchaser of a futures contract is *obligated* to buy the underlying asset at the specified price (and the seller of a futures contract is obligated to sell). The owner of a call option is not obligated to buy, however, unless she wishes to do so; she has the right, but not the obligation.

The second important difference is that when you buy a futures contract, you pay no money (and you receive none if you sell). However, if you buy an option contract, you pay the premium; if you sell an option contract, you receive the premium.

Option Price Quotes

Like futures contracts, most option contracts are standardized. In general, one call option contract, for example, gives the owner the right to buy 100 shares (one round lot) of stock. Similarly, one put option contract gives the owner the right to sell 100 shares.

Figure 3.4 presents *Wall Street Journal* quotes for call and put options on Microsoft common stock. The company identifier, "Micsft," appears in the first column. Just below this identifier is the number $109^{3}/_{16}$ repeated over and over. This is simply the most recent closing price on Microsoft common stock.

Figure 3.4

Options Trading

Source: Reprinted from *The Wall Street Journal,* September 22, 1998, with permission via Copyright Clearance Center, Inc. © 1998 Dow Jones and Company. All Rights Reserved Worldwide.

LISTED OPTIONS QUOTATIONS

Composite volume and close for actively traded equity and LEAPS, or long-term options, with results for the corresponding put or call contract. Volume figures are unofficial. Open interest is total outstanding for all exchanges and reflects previous trading day. Close when possible is shown for the underlying stock on primary market. CB-Chicago Board Options Exchange. AM-American Stock Exchange. PB-Philadelphia Stock Exchange. PC-Pacific Stock Exchange. NY-New York Stock Exchange. XC-Composite. p-Put.

Option/Strike		Exp.	— Call — Vol.	Last	— Put — Vol.	Last
Micsft	75	Oct	...	...	300	$^1/_4$
$109^3/_{16}$	80	Jan	10	$31^1/_8$	535	$1^1/_8$
$109^3/_{16}$	85	Oct	190	$24^1/_4$	210	$^7/_{16}$
$109^3/_{16}$	90	Oct	16	20	275	$^5/_8$
$109^3/_{16}$	90	Apr	1792	26	1600	$4^1/_8$
$109^3/_{16}$	95	Oct	111	$15^1/_2$	3809	$^{13}/_{16}$
$109^3/_{16}$	100	Oct	2063	11	2911	$1^5/_8$
$109^3/_{16}$	100	Jan	317	$15^3/_4$	246	5
$109^3/_{16}$	105	Oct	1074	$7^1/_8$	607	$3^1/_8$
$109^3/_{16}$	105	Nov	10	$9^3/_8$	519	$5^1/_8$
$109^3/_{16}$	105	Jan	112	$12^1/_8$	258	$6^3/_4$
$109^3/_{16}$	110	Oct	4361	$4^5/_8$	117	$4^1/_8$
$109^3/_{16}$	110	Nov	443	$6^7/_8$	8	$6^3/_4$
$109^3/_{16}$	110	Jan	602	10	20	$9^5/_8$
$109^3/_{16}$	115	Oct	4031	$2^1/_4$	60	$8^1/_4$
$109^3/_{16}$	115	Nov	1020	5	80	$9^5/_8$
$109^3/_{16}$	115	Jan	275	$7^7/_8$	22	$11^1/_4$
$109^3/_{16}$	120	Oct	3598	$1^1/_8$	3	$11^1/_4$
$109^3/_{16}$	120	Nov	219	$3^1/_4$	...	$^1/_{120}$
$109^3/_{16}$	120	Jan	208	$5^3/_4$	...	...
$109^3/_{16}$	125	Oct	507	$^7/_{16}$	...	...
$109^3/_{16}$	125	Jan	219	$4^1/_2$	...	...
$109^3/_{16}$	130	Nov	331	$1^1/_4$	...	$^1/_{120}$
$109^3/_{16}$	130	Jan	312	$3^1/_8$	6	$22^1/_8$
$109^3/_{16}$	140	Jan	209	$1^3/_4$	...	...

The second column in Figure 3.4 lists various available strike prices. The third column lists expiration months. So, for example, the Microsoft options listing has strike prices ranging from $75 through $140, and expiration months from October through April.

The fourth and fifth columns give trading volume and premium information about call options. Referring to the second line, the Jan 80 options, we see that 10 contracts were traded and the last (closing) price was 31⅛, or $31.125 per share. Because each contract actually involves 100 shares, the price per contract is $31.125 × 100 = $3,112.5. Finally, the last two columns give the same information for put options.

Suppose you wanted the right to buy 500 shares of Microsoft for $100 sometime between now and January. What would you buy? Based on the information in Figure 3.4, how much would you have to pay?

You want the right to buy, so you want to purchase call options. Since each contract is for 100 shares, and you want the right to buy 500 shares, you need five contracts. The contract you want would be described as the Microsoft January 100 call contract. From Figure 3.4, the option premium for the contract with a $100 strike and a January expiration is 15¾, so one contract would cost $15¾ × 100 = $1,575. The cost for five contracts would therefore be 5 × $1,575 = $7,875.

Example 3.4　　Put Options

Suppose you want the right to sell 200 shares of Microsoft between now and November at a price of $110. In light of the information in Figure 3.4, what contract should you buy? How much will it cost you?

You want the right to sell stock at a fixed price, so you want to buy put options. Specifically, you want to buy two November 110 put contracts. In Figure 3.4, the premium for this contract is given as 6¾. Recalling that this is the premium per share, one contract will cost you $675; so two contracts would be $1,350.

Gains and Losses on Option Contracts

As with futures contracts, option contracts have the potential for large gains and losses. To examine this, let's consider our previous example in which you paid $7,875 for five Microsoft January 100 call contracts. Suppose you hold on to your contracts until January rolls around, and they are just about to expire. What are your gains (or losses) if Microsoft is selling for $130 per share? $90 per share?

If Microsoft is selling for $130 per share, you will profit handsomely. You have the right to buy 500 shares at a price of $100 per share. Since the stock is worth $130, you make $30 per share, or $15,000 in all. So you invested $7,875 and ended up with almost double that in just about four months. Not bad.

If the stock ends up at $90 per share, however, the result is not so pretty. You have the right to buy the stock for $100 when it is selling for $90, so your call options expire worthless. You lose the entire $7,875 you originally invested. In fact, if the stock price is anything less than $100, you lose it all.

Example 3.5　　More on Puts

In Example 3.4, you bought two Microsoft November 110 put contracts for $1,350. Suppose that November arrives, and Microsoft is selling for $90 per share. How did you do? What's the break-even stock price, that is, the price at which you just make enough to cover your $1,350 cost?

Your put contracts give you the right to sell 200 shares of Microsoft at a price of $110 per share. If the stock is worth only $90 per share, your put options are worth $20 per share, or $4,000 in all. To determine the break-even stock price, notice that you paid $6.75 per share for the option, so this is what you must make per share to break even. The break-even stock price is thus $110 − $6.75 = $103.25.

CHECK THIS

3.5a What is a call option? A put option?

3.5b If you buy a call option, what do you hope will happen to the underlying stock? What if you buy a put option?

3.5c What are the two key differences between a futures contract and an option contract?

3.6 Summary and Conclusions

This chapter examines the basic types of financial assets. It discusses three broad classes, interest-bearing assets, equities, and derivative assets. Each of these major groups can be further subdivided. Interest-bearing assets include money market instruments and fixed-income securities. The two major equity types are common stock and preferred stock. The two most important types of derivative assets are options and futures.

For each of the major types of financial assets, we cover three topics. We first describe the basic nature of the asset with an emphasis on what the owner of the asset is entitled to receive. We then illustrate how prices are quoted in the financial press, and we show how to interpret information presented in *The Wall Street Journal*. Finally, we indicate, in fairly broad terms, the potential gains and losses from buying and selling the different assets.

GET REAL

This chapter covered the basics of the four main types of financial assets: stocks, bonds, options, and futures. In addition to discussing basic features, we alerted you to some of the risks associated with these instruments. We particularly stressed the large potential gains and losses possible with derivative assets. How should you, as an investor or investment manager, put this information to work?

Following up on our previous chapter, you need to execute each of the possible transaction types suggested by this chapter in a simulated brokerage account. Your goal is to experience some of the large gains (and losses) to understand them on a personal level. Try to do at least the following:

1. Buy a corporate or government bond.
2. Buy put and call option contracts.
3. Sell put and call contracts.
4. Buy agriculture, natural resource, and financial futures contracts.
5. Sell agriculture, natural resource, and financial futures contracts.

In each case, once you have created the position, be sure to monitor it regularly by checking prices, trading activity, and relevant news using *The Wall Street Journal* or an online information service to understand why it changes in value.

One thing you will discover if you execute these trades is that some of these investments carry relatively low risk and some relatively high risk. Which are which? Under what circumstances is each of these investments appropriate? We will have more to say about these investments later, but you'll get a lot more out of our discussion (and have some fun stories to tell) if you already have some personal experience. As always, it's better to become educated about these things with play money before you commit real money.

Key Terms

money market instrument 65
fixed-income security 65
primary asset 70
derivative asset 70
futures contract 71

option contract 73
call option 73
put option 73
option premium 73
strike price 74

Chapter Review Problems and Self-Test

1. **Corporate Bond Quotes** In Figure 3.1, locate the AT&T bond that matures in the year 2000. What is the coupon rate on this issue? Suppose you purchase $100,000 in face value. How much will this cost? Assuming semiannual payments, what will you receive in coupon payments? Verify the reported current yield.

2. **Call Options** In Figure 3.4, locate the Microsoft January 115 call option. If you buy 10 contracts, how much will you pay? Suppose that in January, just as the option is about to expire, Microsoft is selling for $125 per share. What are your options worth? What is your net profit?

Answers to Self-Test Problems

1. Based on Figure 3.1, the AT&T issue that matures in 2000 (shown as 00) has a 6 percent coupon rate. The price, as a percentage of face value, is 100⅛, or 100.125 percent. If you buy $100,000 in face value, you would thus pay $100,125. You will receive 6 percent of $100,000, or $6,000, in coupon payments every year, paid in two $3,000 semiannual installments. Finally, the current yield is the coupon rate divided by the price, or 6/100.125 = 6.0 percent, the number shown.

2. From Figure 3.4, the January 115 call premium is 7⅞, or $7.875. Because one contract involves 100 shares, the cost of a contract is $787.50, and 10 contacts would cost $7,875. In January, if Microsoft is selling for $125, then you have the right to buy 10 contracts × 100 shares = 1,000 shares at $115. Your contracts are thus worth $125 − $115 = $10 per share, or $10,000 total. Since they cost you $7,875, your net profit is $2,125.

Test Your Investment Quotient

1. **Money Market Securities**   Which of the following is not a common characteristic of money market securities?

   a. Sold on a discount basis
   b. Mature in less than one year
   c. Most important risk is default risk
   d. All of the above are characteristics

2. **Money Market Securities**   Which of the following money market securities is the most liquid?

   a. U.S. Treasury bills
   b. Bank certificates of deposit
   c. Corporate money market debt
   d. Municipality money market debt

3. **Fixed-Income Securities**   On what basis do we normally distinguish money market securities from fixed-income securities?

   a. Issuer
   b. Interest rate
   c. Maturity
   d. Tax status

4. **Fixed-Income Securities**   Your friend told you she just received her semiannual coupon payment on a U.S. Treasury note with a $100,000 face value that pays a 6 percent annual coupon. How much money did she receive from this coupon payment?

   a. $3,000
   b. $6,000
   c. $30,000
   d. $60,000

5. **Common Stock**   A corporation with common stock issued to the public pays dividends

   a. At the discretion of management, who are elected by the shareholders
   b. At the discretion of shareholders, since they own the corporation
   c. At the discretion of the company's board of directors, who are elected by shareholders
   d. At the discretion of the company's board of directors, who are appointed by management

6. **Preferred Stock**   A dividend payment on preferred stock

   a. Can never be omitted if the company is earning a profit
   b. Is automatically omitted if the company realizes a loss from operations
   c. Can be omitted at the discretion of the board of directors
   d. Cannot be omitted at the discretion of the board of directors

7. **Futures Contracts** You buy (go long) five copper futures contracts at 100 cents per pound, where the contract size is 25,000 pounds. At contract maturity, copper is selling for 102 cents per pound. What is your profit (+) or loss (−) on the transaction?

   a. −$2,500
   b. +$2,500
   c. −$25,000
   d. +$25,000

8. **Futures Contracts** You sell (go short) 10 gold futures contracts at $400 per ounce, where the contract size is 100 ounces. At contract maturity, gold is selling for $410 per ounce. What is your profit (+) or loss (−) on the transaction?

   a. −$1,000
   b. +$1,000
   c. −$10,000
   d. +$10,000

9. **Option Contracts** You buy 10 SPX call options with a strike price of 950 at a quoted price of $10. The contract size for SPX options is 100 times the S&P 500 index. At option expiration, the S&P 500 is at 970. What is your net profit on the transaction?

   a. $2,000
   b. $5,000
   c. $10,000
   d. $20,000

10. **Option Contracts** You buy 10 SPX put options with a strike price of 920 at a quoted price of $8. The contract size for SPX options is 100 times the S&P 500 index. At option expiration, the S&P 500 is at 910. What is your net profit on the transaction?

    a. $200
    b. $1,000
    c. $2,000
    d. $10,000

Questions and Problems

**Core
Questions**

1. **Money Market Instruments** What are the distinguishing features of a money market instrument?

2. **Preferred Stock** Why is preferred stock "preferred"?

3. **WSJ Stock Quotes** What is the PE ratio reported for stocks in *The Wall Street Journal?* In particular, how is it computed?

4. **Yields** The current yield on a bond is very similar to what number reported for common and preferred stocks?

5. **Stock Quotations** You found the following stock quote for DRK Enterprises, Inc., in the financial pages of today's newspaper. What was the closing price for this stock that appeared in yesterday's paper? How many round lots of stock were traded yesterday?

52 Weeks		Stock	Sym	Div	Yld %	PE	Vol 100s	Hi	Lo	Close	Net Chg
Hi	Lo										
117	52½	DRK	DRK	3.60	4.6	16	7295	81¾	76	??	−⅜

6. **Stock Quotations** In the previous problem, assume the company has 5 million shares of stock outstanding. What was net income for the most recent four quarters?

7. **Dividend Yields** The following stock quote for Ehrhardt-Daves Corporation (EDC) appeared in the financial press:

| 52 Weeks | | | | | Yld | | Vol | | | | Net |
Hi	Lo	Stock	Sym	Div	%	PE	100s	Hi	Lo	Close	Chg
77	62½	EDC	EDC	??	4.6	26	295	71¾	66	67	-³⁄₈

What was the last quarterly dividend paid for EDC?

8. **Volume Quotations**   Explain how volume is quoted for stocks, corporate bonds, futures, and options.

9. **Futures Contracts**   Changes in what price lead to gains and/or losses in futures contracts?

10. **Futures Contracts**   What is the open interest on a futures contract? What do you think will usually happen to open interest as maturity approaches?

Intermediate Questions

11. **Stock Quotations**   You found the following stock quotes for Gigantus Corporation in today's newspaper. Which preferred stock issue of the company has the largest dividend yield? Which one was the most actively traded yesterday? Which one has traded at the highest dividend yield over the past year?

| 52 Weeks | | | | | Yld | | Vol | | | | Net |
Hi	Lo	Stock	Sym	Div	%	PE	100s	Hi	Lo	Close	Chg
92	50¾	Gigan	GIG	2.50	4.2	22	12690	60¾	60	60	-⅛
13	10½	Gigan pfA		1.20	??	. . .	59	11¾	11½	11⅝	. . .
34	30½	Gigan pfB		3.00	??	. . .	85	32	31½	32	+⅛

12. **Bond Quotations**   Suppose the following bond quote for ISU Corporation appears in the financial pages of today's newspaper. If this bond has a face value of $1,000, what closing price appeared in yesterday's newspaper?

Bonds	Cur Yld	Vol	Close	Net Chg
ISU 7⅞11	8.7	10	??	+½

13. **Bond Quotations**   In the previous problem, in what year does the bond mature? If you currently own 25 of these bonds, how much money will you receive on the next coupon payment date?

14. **Futures Quotations**   The following quotations for the cotton futures trading on the New York Cotton Exchange appear in today's newspaper. How many of the March 1996 contracts are currently open? How many of these contracts should you sell if you wish to hedge 400,000 pounds of cotton for March delivery? If you actually make delivery, how much will you receive?

COTTON (CTN)—50,000 lbs.; cents per lb.

| | Open | High | Low | Settle | Change | Lifetime | | Open |
						High	Low	Interest
Oct95	83.75	85.90	81.16	83.19	+0.85	99.54	58.72	30,129
Dec	85.00	87.30	83.02	85.22	+1.00	99.24	60.19	42,522
Mar96	84.15	86.75	82.35	84.00	+1.25	98.75	61.30	18,752
May	83.42	84.55	82.16	83.68	+0.66	87.67	74.14	8,616
Jul	79.77	80.83	78.48	79.44	+0.39	81.23	75.25	3,456

Est vol 19,000; vol Wed 11,313; open int 103,475, +255.

15. **Futures Quotations**   In the previous problem, approximately how many cotton futures contracts of all maturities were traded yesterday? The day before yesterday?

16. **Using Futures Quotations**   In problem 14, suppose you buy 15 of the December 1995 cotton futures contracts. One month from now, the futures price of this contract is 89.55, and you close out your position. Calculate your dollar profit on this investment.

17. **Options Quotations** Suppose the following stock options quotations for GNR, Inc., appear in today's financial pages. What was the closing share price of the underlying stock? If you wanted to purchase the right to sell 1,500 shares of GNR stock in December at a strike price of $40 per share, how much would this cost you?

Option/Strike		Exp.	Call		Put	
			Vol.	Last	Vol.	Last
GNR	30	Sep	49	9⅞	. . .	. . .
39⅞	35	Sep	228	5	69	¼
39⅞	35	Dec	5	7	. . .	. . .
39⅞	40	Sep	707	1⅜	142	1½
39⅞	40	Oct	598	2⅞	30	2⁷⁄₁₆
39⅞	40	Dec	47	3⅝	25	3⅜
39⅞	45	Sep	645	⁵⁄₁₆	33	5⅛
39⅞	45	Oct	584	1	20	6
39⅞	50	Dec	43	1½	5	13

18. **Options Quotations** In the previous problem, which put contract sells for the lowest price? Which one sells for the highest price? Explain why these respective options trade at such extreme prices.

19. **Using Options Quotations** In problem 17, suppose GNR stock sells for $32 per share in December immediately prior to your options' expiration. What is the rate of return on your investment? What is your rate of return if the stock sells for $42 per share (think about it)? Assume your holding period for this investment is exactly three months.

20. **Options versus Stock** You've located the following option quote for Eric-Cartman, Inc. (ECI):

Option/Strike		Exp.	Call		Put	
			Vol.	Last	Vol.	Last
ECI	10	Sep	29	5⅞	. . .	. . .
20⅛	15	Sep	333	7	69	1¼
20⅛	25	Dec	5	2	. . .	. . .
20⅛	30	Sep	76	1⅜	188	11½
20⅛	35	Oct	89	⅞	. . .	. . .

One of the premiums shown can't possibly be correct. Which one? Why?

4 Mutual Funds

More than 8,000 different mutual funds are available to investors in the United States. Incredibly, this is about the number of different stocks traded on the Nasdaq and the New York Stock Exchange combined. There are funds for aggressive investors and conservative investors, short-term investors and long-term investors. There are bond funds, stock funds, international funds, you-name-it funds. Is there a right fund for you? Let's see!

■ As we discussed in an earlier chapter, if you do not wish to actively buy and sell individual securities on your own, you can invest in stocks, bonds, or other financial assets through a *mutual fund*. Mutual funds are simply a means of combining or pooling the funds of a large group of investors. The buy and sell decisions for the resulting pool are then made by a fund manager, who is compensated for the service provided.

Since mutual funds provide indirect access to financial markets for individual investors, they are a form of financial intermediary. In fact, mutual funds are now the second largest type of intermediary in the United States. Only commercial banks are larger.

Mutual funds have become so important that we devote this entire chapter to them. The number of funds and the different fund types available have grown tremendously in recent years. Indeed, 37 percent of U.S. households held mutual fund assets in 1997, which is up markedly from only 6 percent of U.S. households in 1980.

One of the reasons for the proliferation of mutual funds and fund types is that mutual funds have become, on a very basic level, consumer products. They are created and marketed to the public in ways that are intended to promote buyer appeal. As every business student knows, product differentiation is a basic marketing tactic, and in recent years mutual funds have become increasingly adept at practicing this common marketing technique.

 # Investment Companies and Fund Types

investment company
A business that specializes in pooling funds from individual investors and investing them.

At the most basic level, a company that pools funds obtained from individual investors and invests them is called an **investment company**. In other words, an investment company is a business that specializes in managing financial assets for individual investors. All mutual funds are, in fact, investment companies. As we will see, however, not all investment companies are mutual funds.

In the sections that follow, we will be discussing various aspects of mutual funds and related entities. Figure 4.1 is a big-picture overview of some of the different types of funds and how they are classified. It will serve as a guide for the next several sections. We will define the various terms that appear as we go along.

Open-End versus Closed-End Funds

As Figure 4.1 shows, there are two fundamental types of investment companies, *open-end funds* and *closed-end funds*. The difference is very important. Whenever you invest in a mutual fund, you do so by buying shares in the fund. However, how shares are bought and sold depends on which type of fund you are considering.

Figure 4.1   Fund Types

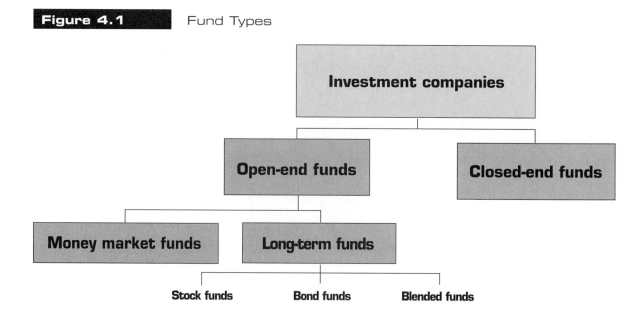

open-end fund An investment company that stands ready to buy and sell shares at any time.

With an **open-end fund**, the fund itself will sell new shares to anyone wishing to buy and will redeem (i.e., buy back) shares from anyone wishing to sell. When an investor wishes to buy open-end fund shares, the fund simply issues them and then invests the money received. When someone wishes to sell open-end fund shares, the fund sells some of its assets and uses the cash to redeem the shares. As a result, with an open-end fund, the number of shares outstanding fluctuates through time.

closed-end fund An investment company with a fixed number of shares that are bought and sold only in the open stock market.

With a **closed-end fund**, the number of shares is fixed and never changes. If you want to buy shares, you must buy them from another investor. Similarly, if you wish to sell shares that you own, you must sell them to another investor.

Thus, the key difference between an open-end fund and a closed-end fund is that, with a closed-end fund, the fund itself does not buy or sell shares. In fact, as we discuss below, shares in closed-end funds are listed on stock exchanges just like ordinary shares of stock, where their shares are bought and sold in the same way. Open-end funds are more popular among individual investors than closed-end funds.

Strictly speaking, the term "mutual fund" actually refers only to an open-end investment company. Thus the phrase "closed-end fund" is a bit of an oxymoron, kind of like jumbo shrimp, and the phrase "open-end mutual fund" is a redundancy, an unnecessary repetition, or restatement. Nonetheless, particularly in recent years, the term "investment company" has all but disappeared from common use, and investment companies are now generically called mutual funds. We will stick with this common terminology whenever it won't lead to confusion.

Net Asset Value

net asset value The value of the assets held by a mutual fund, divided by the number of shares. Abbreviated NAV.

A mutual fund's **net asset value** is an important consideration. Net asset value is calculated by taking the total value of the assets held by the fund and dividing by the number of outstanding shares. For example, suppose a mutual fund has $100 million in assets based on current market values and a total of 5 million shares outstanding. Based on the value of the assets held by the fund, $100 million, each share has a value of $100 million/5 million = $20. This $20 is the fund's net asset value, often abbreviated as NAV.

Example 4.1 **Net Asset Value**

The Fidelity Magellan Fund is the largest mutual fund in the United States with about $88 billion invested (as of early 1999). It has about 680 million shares outstanding. What is its net asset value?

The net asset value is simply the asset value per share, or $88 billion/680 million = $129.

With one important exception, the net asset value of a mutual fund will change essentially every day simply because the value of the assets held by the fund fluctuates. The one exception concerns money market mutual funds, which we discuss in a later section.

As we noted, an open-end fund will generally redeem or buy back shares at any time. The price you will receive for shares you sell is the net asset value. Thus, in our example just above, you could sell your shares back to the fund and receive $20 each. Because the fund stands ready to redeem shares at any time, shares in an open-end fund are always worth their net asset value.

In contrast, because the shares of closed-end funds are bought and sold in the stock markets, their share prices at any point in time may or may not be equal to their net asset values. We examine this issue in more detail in a later section.

CHECK
THIS

4.1a What is an investment company?

4.1b What is the difference between an open-end fund and a closed-end fund?

4.2 Mutual Fund Operations

In this section, we discuss some essentials of mutual fund operations. We focus on how mutual funds are created, marketed, regulated, and taxed. Our discussion here deals primarily with open-end funds, but much of it applies to closed-end funds as well. Further details on closed-end funds are provided in a later section.

Mutual Fund Organization and Creation

A mutual fund is simply a corporation. Like a corporation, a mutual fund is owned by its shareholders. The shareholders elect a board of directors; the board of directors is responsible for hiring a manager to oversee the fund's operations. Although mutual funds often belong to a larger "family" of funds, every fund is a separate company owned by its shareholders.

Most mutual funds are created by investment advisory firms, which are businesses that specialize in managing mutual funds. Investment advisory firms are also called mutual fund companies. Increasingly, such firms have additional operations such as discount brokerages and other financial services.

There are hundreds of investment advisory firms in the United States. The largest, and probably best known, is Fidelity Investments, with over 220 mutual funds, $500 billion in assets under management, and 36 million shareholder accounts. Dreyfus, Franklin, and Vanguard are some other well-known examples. Many brokerage firms, such as Merrill Lynch and Charles Schwab, also have large investment advisory operations.

Investment advisory firms create mutual funds simply because they wish to manage them to earn fees. A typical management fee might be .75 percent of the total assets in the fund per year. A fund with $200 million in assets would not be especially large but could nonetheless generate management fees of about $1.5 million per year. Thus, there is a significant economic incentive to create funds and attract investors to them.

For example, a company like Fidelity might one day decide that there is a demand for a fund that buys stock in companies that grow and process citrus fruits. Fidelity could form a mutual fund that specializes in such companies and call it something like the Fidelity Lemon Fund.[1] A fund manager would be appointed, and shares in the fund would be offered to the public. As shares are sold, the money received is invested. If the fund is a success, a large amount of money will be attracted and Fidelity would benefit from the fees it earns. If the fund is not a success, the board can vote to liquidate it and return shareholders' money or merge it with another fund.

---

[1] Fidelity would probably come up with a better name.

As our hypothetical example illustrates, an investment advisory firm such as Fidelity can (and often will) create new funds from time to time. Through time, this process leads to a family of funds all managed by the same advisory firm. Each fund in the family will have its own fund manager, but the advisory firm will generally handle the record keeping, marketing, and much of the research that underlies the fund's investment decisions.

In principle, the directors of a mutual fund in a particular family, acting on behalf of the fund shareholders, could vote to fire the investment advisory firm and hire a different one. As a practical matter, this rarely, if ever, occurs. At least part of the reason is that the directors are originally appointed by the fund's founder, and they are routinely reelected. Unhappy shareholders generally "vote with their feet"—that is, sell their shares and invest elsewhere.

Taxation of Investment Companies

As long as an investment company meets certain rules set by the Internal Revenue Service, it is treated as a "regulated investment company" for tax purposes. This is important because a regulated investment company does not pay taxes on its investment income. Instead, the fund passes through all realized investment income to fund shareholders, who then pay taxes on these distributions as though they owned the securities directly. Essentially, the fund simply acts as a conduit, funneling gains and losses to fund owners.

To qualify as a regulated investment company, the fund must follow three basic rules. The first rule is that it must in fact be an investment company holding almost all of its assets as investments in stocks, bonds, and other securities. The second rule limits the fund to using no more than five percent of its assets when acquiring a particular security. This is a diversification rule. The third rule is that the fund must pass through all realized investment income to fund shareholders as soon as it is realized.

The Fund Prospectus and Annual Report

Mutual funds are required by law to produce a document known as a *prospectus*. The prospectus must be supplied to any investor wishing to purchase shares. Mutual funds must also provide an annual report to their shareholders. The annual report and the prospectus, which are sometimes combined, contain financial statements along with specific information concerning the fund's expenses, gains and losses, holdings, objectives, and management. We discuss many of these items in the next few sections.

CHECK THIS

4.2a How do mutual funds usually get started?

4.2b How are mutual funds taxed?

4.3 Mutual Fund Costs and Fees

All mutual funds have various expenses that are paid by the fund's shareholders. These expenses can vary considerably from fund to fund, however, and one of the most important considerations in evaluating a fund is its expense structure. All else the same, lower expenses are preferred, of course, but, as we discuss, matters are not quite that cut and dried.

Types of Expenses and Fees

There are basically four types of expenses or fees associated with buying and owning mutual fund shares:

1. Sales charges or "loads."
2. 12b-1 fees.
3. Management fees.
4. Trading costs.

We discuss each of these in turn.

front-end load A
sales charge levied on
purchases of shares
in some mutual funds.

Sales Charges   Many mutual funds charge a fee whenever shares are purchased. These fees are generally called **front-end loads**. Funds that charge loads are called *load funds*. Funds that have no such charges are called *no-load funds*.

When you purchase shares in a load fund, you pay a price in excess of the net asset value, called the *offering price*. The difference between the offering price and the net asset value is the *load*. Shares in no-load funds are sold at net asset value.

Front-end loads can range as high as 8.5 percent, but 5 percent or so would be more typical. Some funds, with front-end loads in the 2 percent to 3 percent range, are described as *low-load funds*.

Front-end loads are expressed as a percentage of the offering price, not the net asset value. For example, suppose a load fund has an offering price of $100 and a net asset value of $98. The front-end load is $2, which, as a percentage of the $100 offering price, is $2/$100 = 2 percent. The way front-end loads are calculated understates the load slightly. In our example here, you are paying $100 for something worth only $98, so the load is really $2/$98 = 2.04 percent.

Example 4.2   Front-End Loads

On January 20, 1995, according to *The Wall Street Journal,* the Common Sense Growth fund had a net asset value of $13.91. The offering price was $15.20. Is this a load fund? What is the front-end load?

Since the offering price, which is the price you must pay to purchase shares, exceeds the net asset value, this is definitely a load fund. The load can be calculated by taking the difference between the offering price and the net asset value, $1.29, and dividing by the $15.20 offering price. The result is a hefty front-end load of 8.5 percent.

Some funds have "back-end" loads, which are charges levied on redemptions. These loads are often called *contingent deferred sales charges* and abbreviated CDSC. The CDSC usually declines through time. It might start out at 6 percent for shares held less than one year, then drop to 3 percent for shares held for two years, and disappear altogether on shares held for three or more years.

12b-1 fees Named
for SEC Rule 12b-1,
which allows funds to
spend up to 1 percent
of fund assets
annually to cover
distribution and
marketing costs.

12b-1 Fees   So-called **12b-1 fees** are named for the Securities and Exchange Commission (SEC) rule that permits them. Mutual funds are allowed to use a portion of the fund's assets to cover distribution and marketing costs. Funds that market directly to the public may use 12b-1 fees to pay for advertising and direct mailing costs. Funds that rely on brokers and other sales force personnel often use 12b-1 fees to provide compensation for their services. The total amount of these fees could be .75 percent to 1.0 percent of the fund's assets per year.

Frequently, 12b-1 fees are used in conjunction with a CDSC. Such funds will often have no front-end load, but they effectively make it up through these other costs. Such funds may look like no-load funds, but they are really disguised load funds. Mutual funds with no front-end or back-end loads and no or minimal 12b-1 fees are often called "pure" no-load funds to distinguish them from the "not-so-pure" funds that may have no loads but still charge hefty 12b-1 fees.

Management Fees   We briefly discussed management fees in an earlier section. Fees are usually based first on the size of the fund. Beyond this, there is often an incentive provision that increases the fee if the fund outperforms some benchmark, often the S&P 500 (this index is discussed in Chapter 1). Management fees generally range from .25 percent to 1.0 percent of total funds assets every year.

turnover A measure of how much trading a fund does, calculated as the lesser of total purchases or sales during a year divided by average daily assets.

Trading Costs   Mutual funds have brokerage expenses from trading just like individuals do. As a result, mutual funds that do a lot of trading will have relatively high trading costs.

Trading costs can be difficult to get a handle on because they are not reported directly. However, in the prospectus, funds are required to report something known as **turnover**. A fund's turnover is a measure of how much trading a fund does. It is calculated as the lesser of a fund's total purchases or sales during a year, divided by average daily assets.[2]

Example 4.3   Turnover

Suppose a fund had average daily assets of $50 million during 1998. It bought $80 million worth of stock and sold $70 million during the year. What is its turnover?

The lesser of purchases or sales is $70 million, and average daily assets are $50 million. Turnover is thus $70/$50 = 1.4 times.

A fund with a turnover of 1.0 has, in effect, sold off its entire portfolio and replaced it once during the year. Similarly, a turnover of .50 indicates that, loosely speaking, the fund replaced half of its holdings during the year. All else the same, a higher turnover indicates more frequent trading and higher trading costs.

Expense Reporting

Mutual funds are required to report expenses in a fairly standardized way in the prospectus. The exact format varies, but the information reported is generally the same. There are three parts to an expense statement. Figure 4.2 shows this information as it was reported for the Fidelity Retirement Growth Fund for the year 1998.

The first part of the statement shows shareholder transaction expenses, which are generally loads and deferred sales charges. As indicated, for this fund, there is no front-end load either on shares purchased or on dividends received that are reinvested in the fund (it's common for mutual fund shareholders to simply reinvest any dividends received from the fund). The second item shows that there is no CDSC. The third item, labeled "exchange fee," refers to exchanging shares in this mutual fund for shares in another Fidelity fund. There is no charge for this; some funds levy a small fee.

---

[2] Purchases and sales for a fund are usually different because of purchases and redemptions of fund shares by shareholders. For example, if a fund is growing, purchases will exceed sales.

Figure 4.2

Mutual Fund
Expenses

Fidelity

Retirement Growth

Fund

Prospectus

Expenses

Expenses

Shareholder transaction expenses are charges you pay when you buy or sell shares of a fund.

Maximum sales charge on purchases and reinvested dividends	None
Deferred sales charge on redemptions	None
Exchange fee	None

Annual fund operating expenses

are paid out of the fund's assets. The fund pays a management fee that varies based on its performance. It also incurs other expenses for services such as maintaining shareholder records and furnishing shareholder statements and fund reports. The fund's expenses are factored into its share price or dividends and are not charged directly to shareholder accounts.

The following are projections based on historical expenses and are calculated as a percentage of average net assets.

Management fee	.40%
12b-1 fee	None
Other expenses	.22%
Total fund operating expenses	.62%

Examples: Let's say, hypothetically, that the fund's annual return is 5% and that its operating expenses are exactly as just described. For every $10,000 you invested, here's how much you would pay in total expenses if you close your account after the number of years indicated:

After 1 year	$63
After 3 years	$199
After 5 years	$346
After 10 years	$774

These examples illustrate the effect of expenses, but are not meant to suggest actual or expected costs or returns, all of which may vary.

The second part of the statement, "Annual fund operating expenses," includes the management and 12b-1 fees. This fund's management fee was .40 percent of assets. There was no 12b-1 fee. The other expenses include things like legal, accounting, and

"Soft Dollars" Makes Comparing Fund Costs Hard

Savvy investors have learned that mutual funds with lean expenses can produce better returns. But can you find out what a fund's expenses really are?

Probably not, because fund managers can, and do, hide much of their actual costs by paying for research, computers, stock-quote systems and even phone calls and newspaper subscriptions with so-called soft dollars instead of cash.

It works like this: Say a fund manager needs a new laptop computer. Instead of buying the laptop and putting it down as a fund expense, the manager pays a slightly higher-than-necessary commission to a stock-broker—hence the term soft dollars—and the broker buys the laptop for him. Or, the fund manager might buy the computer himself and send the bill to the broker. In general, a fund's expenses cover management fees and general operating costs, but not commissions.

The more a fund manager can use soft dollars to pay expenses, the less expensive it appears that it is to run the fund—because soft dollars aren't included in calculating a fund's annual expenses. The consumer reading a prospectus is none the wiser.

Consumers can find out how much fund advisers pay in total commissions by requesting a "statement of additional information" from the fund. But that statement doesn't break out soft dollars. So a reader can't tell how much higher the commissions are than they would have been in the absence of soft-dollar dealings.

Raising Trading Costs

Soft dollars can also result in higher trading costs for the fund. That can occur if a fund group's trading desk improperly steers stock and bond trades to certain soft-dollar brokers despite higher commissions charged by those brokers.

Despite their resemblance to kickbacks, soft dollars are legal in most instances. And they are nothing new. They originated way back when the Securities and Exchange Commission required brokerage firms to charge customers fixed commission rates. Soft dollars became a popular incentive for brokers to offer customers, and when the SEC deregulated commissions in 1975, it allowed the practice to continue.

A 1993 survey by Greenwich Associates, a consulting firm in Greenwich, Conn., found that 30% of commissions paid by investment firms were paid in "soft dollars."

reporting costs along with director fees. At .22 percent of assets, these costs are not trivial. The sum of these three items is the fund's total operating expense expressed as a percentage of assets, .62 percent in this case. To put this in perspective, this fund has about $5 billion in assets, so operating costs were $31 million, of which about $20 million was paid to the fund manager.

The third part of the expense report gives a hypothetical example showing the total expense you would pay over time per $10,000 invested. The example is strictly hypothetical, however, and is only a rough guide. As shown here, your costs would amount to $774 after 10 years per $10,000 invested. This third part of the expense statement is not all that useful, really. What matters for this fund is that expenses appear to run about 1 percent per year, so that is what you pay.

One thing to watch out for is that funds may have 12b-1 plans but may choose not to spend anything in a particular year. Similarly, the fund manager can choose to rebate some of the management fee in a particular year (especially if the fund has done poorly). These actions create a low expense figure for a given year, but this does not mean that expenses won't be higher in the future.

Another caveat concerns certain practices in the mutual fund business (and elsewhere in the securities industry) involving so-called soft dollars. These are essentially hidden costs, and, as our Investment Updates box describes, can make it difficult to compare fund expenses from one fund to the next.

Why Pay Loads and Fees?

Given that pure no-load funds exist, you might wonder why anyone would buy load funds or funds with substantial CDSC or 12b-1 fees. It is becoming increasingly difficult to give a good answer to this question. At one time, there simply weren't many no-load funds, and those that existed weren't widely known. Today, there are many good no-load funds, and competition among funds is forcing many funds to lower or do away with loads and other fees.

Having said this, there are basically two reasons that you might want to consider a load fund or a fund with above-average fees. First, you may simply want a fund run by a particular manager. A good example of this is the Fidelity Magellan Fund we mentioned earlier. For much of its life, it was run by Peter Lynch, who is widely regarded as one of the most successful managers in the history of the business. The Magellan Fund was (and is) a load fund, leaving you no choice but to pay the load to obtain Lynch's expertise.

The other reason to consider paying a load is that you want a specialized type of fund. For example, you might be interested in investing in a fund that invests only in a particular foreign country such as Brazil. We'll discuss such specialty funds in a later section, but for now we note that there is little competition among specialty funds, and as a result loads and fees tend to be higher.

CHECK THIS

4.3a What is the difference between a load fund and a no-load fund?

4.3b What are 12b-1 fees?

4.4 Short-Term Funds

Mutual funds are usually divided into two major groups, short-term funds and long-term funds. Short-term funds are collectively known as *money market mutual funds.* Long-term funds essentially include everything that is not a money market fund. We discuss long-term funds in our next section; here we focus on money market funds.

Money Market Mutual Funds

money market mutual fund A mutual fund specializing in money market instruments.

As the name suggests, **money market mutual funds**, or MMMFs, specialize in money market instruments. As we described in Chapter 3, these are short-term debt obligations issued by governments and corporations. Money market funds were introduced in the early 1970s and have grown tremendously. By 1999, about 1,000 money market funds managed more than $1.4 trillion in assets for 35 million investors. All money market funds are open-end funds.

Most money market funds invest in high-quality, low-risk instruments with maturities of less than 90 days. As a result, they have relatively little risk. However, some buy riskier assets or have longer maturities than others, so they do not all carry equally low risk. For example, some buy only very short-term U.S. government securities and are therefore essentially risk-free. Others buy mostly securities issued by corporations which entail some risk. We discuss the different types of money market instruments and their relative risks in Chapter 9.

Money Market Fund Accounting   A unique feature of money market funds is that their net asset values are always $1 per share. This is purely an accounting gimmick, however. A money market fund simply sets the number of shares equal to the fund's assets. In other words, if the fund has $100 million in assets, then it has 100 million shares. As the fund earns interest on its investments, the fund owners are simply given more shares.

The reason money market mutual funds always maintain a $1 net asset value is to make them resemble bank accounts. As long as a money market fund invests in very safe, interest-bearing, short-maturity assets, its net asset value will not drop below $1 per share. However, there is no guarantee that this will not happen, and the term "breaking the buck" is used to describe dropping below $1 in net asset value. This is a very rare occurrence, but, in 1994, several large money market funds experienced substantial losses because they purchased relatively risky derivative assets and broke the buck, so it definitely can happen.

Taxes and Money Market Funds   Money market funds are either taxable or tax-exempt. Taxable funds are more common; of the $1.5 trillion in total money market fund assets in 1999, taxable funds accounted for about 84 percent. As the name suggests, the difference in the two fund types lies in their tax treatment. As a general rule, interest earned on state and local government (or "municipal") securities is exempt from federal income tax. Nontaxable money market funds therefore buy only these types of tax-exempt securities.

Some tax-exempt funds go even further. Interest paid by one state is often subject to state taxes in another. Some tax-exempt funds therefore buy only securities issued by a single state. For residents of that state, the interest earned is free of both federal and state taxes. For beleaguered New York City residents, there are even "triple-tax-free" funds that invest only in New York City obligations, thereby allowing residents to escape federal, state, and local income taxes on the interest received.

Because of their favorable tax treatment, tax-exempt money market instruments have much lower interest rates, or *yields*.[3] For example, in early 1999, taxable money funds offered about 4.6 percent interest, whereas tax-exempt funds offered only 2.8 percent interest. Which is better depends on your individual tax bracket. If you're in a 40 percent bracket, then the taxable fund is paying only $4.6\% \times (1 - .40) = 2.76\%$ on an aftertax basis, so you're slightly better off with the tax-exempt fund.

Example 4.4   **Taxes and Money Market Fund Yields**

In our discussion just above, suppose you were in a 25 percent tax bracket. Which type of fund is more attractive?

On an aftertax basis, the taxable fund is offering $4.6\% \times (1 - .25) = 3.45\%$, so the taxable fund is more attractive.

Money Market Deposit Accounts

Most banks offer what are called "money market" deposit accounts, or MMDAs, which are much like money market mutual funds. For example, both money market funds and money market accounts generally have limited check-writing privileges.

---

[3] We discuss how yields on money market instruments are calculated in Chapter 9.

There is a very important distinction between such a bank-offered money market account and a money market fund, however. A bank money market account is a bank deposit and offers FDIC protection, whereas a money market fund does not. A money market fund will generally offer SIPC protection, but this is not a perfect substitute. Confusingly, some banks offer both money market accounts and, through a separate, affiliated entity, money market funds.

CHECK THIS

4.4a What is a money market mutual fund? What are the two types?

4.4b How do money market mutual funds maintain a constant net asset value?

4.5 Long-Term Funds

There are many different types of long-term funds. Historically, mutual funds were classified as stock, bond, or income funds. As a part of the rapid growth in mutual funds, however, it is becoming increasingly difficult to place all funds into these three categories. Also, providers of mutual fund information do not use the same classification schemes.

Mutual funds have different goals, and a fund's objective is the major determinant of the fund type. All mutual funds must state the fund's objective in the prospectus. For example, the Fidelity Retirement Growth Fund we discussed earlier states in its prospectus:

> The fund seeks capital appreciation by investing substantially in common stocks. In pursuit of its goal, the fund has the flexibility to invest in large or small domestic or foreign companies. The fund does not place any emphasis on income.

Thus this fund invests in different types of stocks with the goal of capital appreciation without regard to dividend income. This is clearly a stock fund, and it would further be classified as a "capital appreciation" fund or "aggressive growth" fund, depending on whose classification scheme is used.

Mutual fund objectives are an important consideration; unfortunately, the truth is they frequently are too vague to provide useful information. For example, a very common objective reads like this: "The Big Bucks Fund seeks capital appreciation, income, and capital preservation." Translation: The fund seeks to (1) increase the value of its shares, (2) generate income for its shareholders, and (3) not lose money. Well, don't we all! More to the point, funds with very similar-sounding objectives can have very different portfolios and, consequently, very different risks. As a result, it is a mistake to look only at a fund's stated objective: Actual portfolio holdings speak louder than prospectus promises.

In our next section, we discuss information available on mutual funds, focusing on *The Wall Street Journal,* which uses a mutual fund classification scheme from Lipper Analytical Services, Inc., a major provider of mutual fund information. A brief description of the Lipper categories is given in Figure 4.3. For the sake of consistency, we generally follow this classification in discussing fund types. Thus the four major categories we discuss are stock funds, taxable bond funds, municipal bond funds, and combined stock and bond funds.

Stock Funds

Stock funds exist in great variety. We consider nine separate general types and some subtypes. We also consider some new varieties that don't fit in any category.

Capital Appreciation versus Income   The first four types of stock funds trade off capital appreciation and dividend income.

1. *Capital appreciation.* As in our example just above, these funds seek maximum capital appreciation. They generally invest in whatever companies have, in the opinion of the fund manager, the best prospects for share price appreciation without regard to dividends, company size, or, for some funds, country. Often this means investing in unproven companies or perceived out-of-favor companies.

2. *Growth.* These funds also seek capital appreciation, but they tend to invest in larger, more established companies. Such funds may be somewhat less volatile as a result. Dividends are not an important consideration.

3. *Growth and income.* Capital appreciation is still the main goal, but at least part of the focus is on dividend-paying companies.

4. *Equity income.* These funds focus almost exclusively on stocks with relatively high dividend yields, thereby maximizing the current income on the portfolio.

Figure 4.3

Mutual Fund Objectives

Source: Reprinted by permission from *The Wall Street Journal*, September 28, 1998, © 1998 Dow Jones & Company, Inc. All Rights Reserved Worldwide.

MUTUAL FUND OBJECTIVES

Categories compiled by The Wall Street Journal, based on classifications by Lipper Analytical Services Inc.

STOCK FUNDS

Capital Appreciation (CP): Seeks rapid capital growth, often through high portfolio turnover.
Growth (GR): Invests in companies expecting higher than average revenue and earnings growth.
Growth & Income (GI): Pursues both price and dividend growth. Category includes S&P 500 index funds.
Equity Income (EI): Tends to favor stock with the highest dividends.
Small Cap (SC): Stocks of lesser-known, small companies.
MidCap (MC): Shares of middle-sized companies.
Sector (SE): Health/Biotechnology; Natural Resources; Environmental; Science & Technology; Specialty & Miscellaneous; Utility; Financial Services; Real Estate; Gold Oriented funds.
Global Stock (GL): Includes small company global. Can invest in U.S.
International Stock (IL) (non-U.S.): International; European region; Pacific region; Pacific Ex-Japan; Japanese; Latin American; Canadian; Emerging Markets; International small cap.

TAXABLE BOND FUNDS

Short-Term (SB): Ultrashort obligation and short, short-intermediate investment grade corporate debt.
Short-Term U.S. (SG): Short-term U.S. Treasury; Short, short-intermediate U.S. government funds.
Intermediate (IB): Investment grade corporate debt of up to 10-year maturity.
Intermediate U.S. (IG): U.S. Treasury and government agency debt.
Long-Term (AB): Corporate A-rated; Corporate BBB-rated.
Long-Term U.S. (LG): U.S. Treasury; U.S. government; zero coupon.
General U.S. Taxable (GT): Can invest in different types of bonds.
High-Yield Taxable (HC): High-yield, high-risk bonds.
Mortgage (MG): Ginnie Mae and general mortgage; Adjustable-Rate Mortgage.
World (WB): Short world multi-market; short world single-market; global income; International Income; Emerging-Markets debt.

MUNICIPAL BOND FUNDS

Short-Term Muni (SM): Short, short-intermediate municipal debt; Short-intermediate term California; Single states short-intermediate municipal debt.
Intermediate Muni (IM): Intermediate-term municipal debt including single-state funds.
General Muni (GM): A variety of municipal debt.
Single-State Municipal (SS): Funds that invest in debt of individual states.
High Yield Municipal (HM): High yield low credit quality.
Insured (NM): California insured, New York Insured, all other insured.

STOCK & BOND FUNDS

Stock/Bond Blend (MP): Multi-purpose funds such as Balanced; convertible securities; income; flexible income; flexible portfolio; global flexible and other multi-purpose funds that invest in both stocks and bonds.

Among these four fund types, the greater the emphasis on growth, the greater the risk, at least as a general matter. Again, however, these are only rough classifications. Equity income funds, for example, frequently invest heavily in public utility stocks; such stocks had heavy losses in the first part of the 1990s.

Company Size–Based Funds   These next two fund types focus on companies in a particular size range.

1. *Small company.* As the name suggests, these funds focus on stocks in small companies, where "small" refers to the total market value of the stock. Such funds are often called "small-cap" funds, where "cap" is short for total market value or capitalization. In Chapter 1, we saw that small stocks have traditionally performed very well, at least over the long run, hence the demand for funds that specialize in such stocks. With small-company mutual funds, what constitutes small is variable, ranging from perhaps $10 million up to $1 billion or so in total market value, and some funds specialize in smaller companies than others. Since most small companies don't pay dividends, these funds necessarily emphasize capital appreciation.

2. *Midcap.* These funds usually specialize in stocks that are too small to be in the S&P 500 index but too large to be considered small stocks.

International Funds   The next two fund groups invest internationally. Research has shown that diversifying internationally can significantly improve the risk-return trade-off for investors, and international funds have been among the most rapidly growing. However, that growth slowed sharply in the late 1990s.

1. *Global.* These funds have substantial international holdings but also maintain significant investments in U.S. stocks.

2. *International.* These funds are like global funds, except they focus on non-U.S. equities.

Among international funds, some specialize in specific regions of the world, such as Europe, the Pacific Rim, or South America. Others specialize in individual countries. Today, there is at least one mutual fund specializing in essentially every country in the world that has a stock market, however small.

International funds that specialize in countries with small or recently established stock markets are often called *emerging markets funds.* Almost all single-country funds, and especially emerging markets funds, are not well-diversified and have historically been extremely volatile.

Many funds that are not classified as international funds may actually have substantial overseas investments, so this is one thing to watch out for. For example, as of the end of 1993, the Templeton Capital Accumulator Fund, which was classified as a growth fund, had 80 percent of its portfolio invested internationally.

Sector Funds   Sector funds specialize in specific sectors of the economy and often focus on particular industries or particular commodities. There are far too many different types to list here. There are funds that only buy software companies, and funds that only buy hardware companies. There are funds that specialize in natural gas producers, oil producers, and precious metals producers. In fact, essentially every major industry in the U.S. economy is covered by at least one fund.

One thing to notice about sector funds is that, like single-country funds, they are obviously not well-diversified. Every year, many of the best performing mutual funds (in terms of total return) are sector funds simply because whatever sector of the economy is hottest will generally have the largest stock price increases. Funds specializing in that sector will do well. In the same vein, and for the same reason, the worst performing funds are also almost always some type of sector fund. When it comes to mutual funds, past performance is almost always an unreliable guide to future performance; nowhere is this more true than with sector funds.

Other Fund Types and Issues Three other types of stock funds that don't fit easily into one of the above categories bear discussing: *index funds,* so-called *social conscience funds,* and *tax-managed funds.*

1. *Index funds.* Index funds simply hold the stocks that make up a particular index in the same relative proportions as the index. The most important index funds are S&P 500 funds, which are intended to track the performance of the S&P 500, the large stock index we discuss in Chapter 1. By their nature, index funds are passively managed, meaning that the fund manager trades only as necessary to match the index. Such funds are appealing in part because they are generally characterized by low turnover and low operating expenses. Another reason index funds have grown rapidly is that there is considerable debate over whether mutual fund managers can consistently beat the averages. If they can't, the argument runs, why pay loads and management fees when it's cheaper just to buy the averages by indexing? We discuss this issue in more detail later.

2. *Social conscience funds.* These funds are a relatively new creation. They invest only in companies whose products, policies, or politics are viewed as socially desirable. The specific social objectives range from environmental issues to personnel policies. As the accompanying Investment Updates box shows, the Parnassus Fund is a well-known example, avoiding the alcoholic beverage, tobacco, gambling, weapons, and nuclear power industries. Of course, consensus on what is socially desirable or responsible is hard to find. In fact, there are so-called sin funds (and sector funds) that specialize in these very industries!

3. *Tax-managed funds.* Taxable mutual funds are generally managed without regard for the tax liabilities of fund owners. Fund managers focus on (and are frequently rewarded based on) total pretax returns. However, recent research has shown that some fairly simple strategies can greatly improve the aftertax returns to shareholders and that focusing just on pretax returns is not a good idea for taxable investors. Tax-managed funds try to hold down turnover to minimize realized capital gains, and they try to match realized gains with realized losses. Such strategies work particularly well for index funds. For example, the Schwab 1000 Fund is a fund that tracks the Russell 1000 Index, a widely followed 1,000-stock index. However, the fund will deviate from strictly following the index to a certain extent to avoid realizing taxable gains, and, as a result, the fund holds turnover to a minimum. Fund shareholders have largely escaped taxes as a result. We predict funds promoting such strategies will become increasingly common as investors become more aware of the tax consequences of fund ownership.

Taxable and Municipal Bond Funds

Most bond funds invest in domestic corporate and government securities, although some invest in foreign government and non-U.S. corporate bonds as well. As we will see, there are a relatively small number of bond fund types.

There are basically five characteristics that distinguish bond funds:

1. Maturity range. Different funds hold bonds of different maturities, ranging from quite short (2 years) to quite long (25–30 years).
2. Credit quality. Some bonds are much safer than others in terms of the possibility of default. United States government bonds have no default risk, while so-called junk bonds have significant default risk.
3. Taxability. Municipal bond funds buy only bonds that are free from federal income tax. Taxable funds buy only taxable issues.
4. Type of bond. Some funds specialize in particular types of fixed-income instruments such as mortgages.
5. Country. Most bond funds buy only domestic issues, but some buy foreign company and government issues.

Short-Term and Intermediate-Term Funds   As the names suggest, these two fund types focus on bonds in a specific maturity range. Short-term maturities are generally considered to be less than five years. Intermediate-term would be less than 10 years. There are both taxable and municipal bond funds with these maturity targets.

One thing to be careful of with these types of funds is that the credit quality of the issues can vary from fund to fund. One fund could hold very risky intermediate-term bonds, while another might hold only U.S. government issues with similar maturities.

General Funds   For both taxable and municipal bonds, this category is kind of a catch-all. Funds in this category simply don't specialize in any particular way. Our warning just above concerning varied credit quality applies here. Maturities can differ substantially as well.

High-Yield Funds   High-yield municipal and taxable funds specialize in low-credit quality issues. Such issues have higher yields because of their greater risks. As a result, high-yield bond funds can be quite volatile.

Mortgage Funds   A number of funds specialize in so-called mortgage-backed securities such as GNMA (Government National Mortgage Association, referred to as "Ginnie Mae") issues. We discuss this important type of security in detail in Chapter 13. There are no municipal mortgage-backed securities (yet), so these are all taxable bond funds.

World Funds   A relatively limited number of taxable funds invest worldwide. Some specialize in only government issues; others buy a variety of non-U.S. issues. These are all taxable funds.

Insured Funds   This is a type of municipal bond fund. Municipal bond issuers frequently purchase insurance that guarantees the bond's payments will be made. Such bonds have very little possibility of default, so some funds specialize in them.

Parnassus Fund

A Saintly Stock Picker Names Angels to Ascend 48% in '95

Jerry Dodson, 51, dean of socially responsible investing (defined below), is not your typical tree-hugging stock picker. In November, for example, the manager of the $150 million Parnassus Fund in San Francisco (3.5% load, 800-999-3505) voted for California Gov. Pete Wilson because the incumbent Republican took a stronger pro-business stance than Democratic challenger Kathleen Brown. Moreover, Dodson, unlike most of his fund's peers, particularly the 13 politically correct ones, has trounced the market over the past three years. For that period, his fund returned 94%, triple the 32% earned by the S&P 500 index and the 30% average for socially responsible stock funds overall. What about disappointing 1994? At last count, Parnassus was up 8%, vs. no change for the S&P 500 and the do-gooders' 3% decline.

Why aren't the other altruistic funds so enriching? They tend to buy inherently pricey growth stocks "that happen to be good corporate citizens," says Dodson, a Harvard M.B.A. who founded Parnassus 10 years ago and now heads its team of four analysts. "We're strict value investors who wait until these companies encounter a sudden—but temporary—setback that effectively wrings much of the risk out of the stock."

Sister Mary's Answered Prayer

It's easy to see why Jerry Dodson's "socially responsible" Parnassus Fund is a popular investment for charities and other nonprofits—source of 15% of the fund's $150 million in assets. "Our investment universe is about 200 companies that are ethical, respect the environment, treat employees well and are sensitive to their communities," says Dodson. "Moroever, none is involved in alcohol, tobacco, gambling, weapons contracting and nuclear power." Those saintly traits certainly appealed to Sister Mary Bernadette McNulty, treasurer of the Sisters of St. Joseph of Orange, a 250-member order that runs eight hospitals in California. In late 1990, with the Dow mired at 2600 (down 10% from its then record peak before Iraq kidnapped Kuwait in August of that year), she says the group gamely socked 20% of its portfolio into Parnassus. The payoff? At last count the sisters' initial stake had risen in value nearly 2.5 times, or 30% a year, vs. the Dow's corresponding 12% annual return. "Jerry is by far the top performer among the seven investment managers we employ," she adds.

Source: "Parnassus Fund" pp. 149, 152, from the January 1995 issue of MONEY.

Single-State Municipal Funds   Earlier we discussed how some money market funds specialize in issues from a single state. The same is true for some bond funds. Such funds are especially important in large states such as California and high-tax states. Confusingly, this classification refers only to long-term funds. Short and intermediate single-state funds are classified with other maturity-based municipal funds.

Stock and Bond Funds

This last major fund group includes a variety of funds. The only common feature is that these funds don't invest exclusively in either stocks or bonds. For this reason, they are often called "blended" or "hybrid" funds. We discuss a few of the main types.

Balanced Funds   Balanced funds maintain a relatively fixed split between stocks and bonds. They emphasize relatively safe, high-quality investments. Such funds provide a kind of "one-stop" shopping for fund investors, particularly smaller investors, because they diversify into both stocks and bonds.

Asset Allocation Funds   Two types of funds carry this label. The first is an extended version of a balanced fund. Such a fund holds relatively fixed proportional investments in stocks, bonds, money market instruments, and perhaps real estate or some other investment class. The target proportions may be updated or modified periodically.

The other type of asset allocation fund is often called a *flexible portfolio fund.* Here, the fund manager may hold up to 100 percent stocks, bonds, or money market instruments, depending on her views about the likely performance of these investments. These funds essentially try to time the market, guessing which general type of investment will do well (or least poorly) over the months ahead.

Convertible Funds   Some bonds are convertible, meaning they can be swapped for a fixed number of shares of stock at the option of the bondholder. Some mutual funds specialize in these bonds.

Income Funds   An income fund emphasizes generating dividend and coupon income on its investments, so it would hold a variety of dividend-paying common and preferred stocks and bonds of various maturities.

CHECK THIS

4.5a What are the three major types of long-term fund? Give several examples of each and describe their investment policies.

4.5b What do single-state municipal funds, single-

country stock funds, and sector stock funds have in common?

4.5c What are the distinguishing characteristics of a bond fund?

4.6 Mutual Fund Performance

We close our discussion of open-end mutual funds by looking at some of the performance information reported in the financial press. We then discuss the usefulness of such information for selecting mutual funds.

Mutual Fund Performance Information

Mutual fund performance is very closely tracked by a number of organizations. Financial publications of all types periodically provide mutual fund data, and many provide lists of recommended funds. We examine *Wall Street Journal* information in this section, but by no means is this the only source or the most comprehensive.[4] However, *The Wall Street Journal* is a particularly timely source because it reports mutual fund year-to-date returns on a daily basis, and it provides a summary of average investment performance by fund category on a regular basis. The information we consider here applies only to open-end funds.

Figure 4.4 reproduces "Performance Yardsticks," a feature appearing in the *Journal* each Friday. This table compares the recent investment performance of 32 fund categories, including 16 equity funds, 9 taxable bond funds, 5 municipal bond funds, gold funds, and balanced stock and bond funds.

---

[4] For more detailed information, publications from companies such as Morningstar, Weisenberger, and Value Line are often available in the library. Of course, a mutual fund's prospectus and annual report contain a great deal of information as well.

Figure 4.4

Mutual Fund
Performance

Source: Reprinted by
permission of *The Wall Street
Journal,* October 22, 1998
via Copyright Clearance
Center, Inc. © 1998 Dow
Jones and Company, Inc. All
Rights Reserved Worldwide.

Performance Yardsticks

How Fund Categories Stack Up

INVESTMENT OBJECTIVE	YEAR-TO-DATE	FOUR WEEKS	ONE YEAR	3 YRS (annualized)	5 YRS (annualized)
Capital Appreciation	− 2.11%	− 0.67%	− 7.47%	+ 11.25%	+ 10.98%
Growth	+ 4.46	+ 1.26	+ 1.34	+ 17.21	+ 15.74
Small-Cap Stock	− 16.43	− 1.74	− 21.68	+ 7.59	+ 9.35
Mid-Cap Stock	− 7.81	− 1.22	− 12.14	+ 9.84	+ 10.82
Growth & Income	+ 4.15	+ 2.79	+ 3.50	+ 19.16	+ 16.57
Equity Income	+ 2.13	+ 2.43	+ 3.07	+ 17.62	+ 15.06
Global (inc U.S.)	+ 0.13	+ 1.87	− 4.93	+ 10.13	+ 9.95
International (non U.S.)	+ 1.80	+ 2.62	− 4.93	+ 6.86	+ 6.47
European Region	+ 8.88	+ 0.68	+ 6.61	+ 16.96	+ 14.28
Latin America	− 37.69	+ 7.54	− 46.38	+ 0.28	− 4.81
Pacific Region	− 15.92	+10.31	− 28.49	− 14.15	− 7.95
Emerging Markets	− 33.07	+ 3.46	− 44.62	− 11.12	− 8.11
Science & Technology	+ 9.08	− 0.51	− 4.52	+ 10.49	+ 16.05
Health & Biotech	+ 5.27	− 2.28	+ 0.49	+ 16.97	+ 18.32
Natural Resources	− 19.75	+ 1.31	− 32.12	+ 5.12	+ 4.37
Gold	− 10.70	− 1.09	− 35.88	− 17.90	− 11.47
Utility	+ 7.20	+ 1.76	+ 15.74	+ 16.25	+ 11.50
Balanced	+ 4.47	+ 1.31	+ 4.69	+ 13.98	+ 12.06
Intermediate Corp. Debt	+ 6.83	− 0.21	+ 9.25	+ 7.30	+ 6.13
Intermediate Govt	+ 7.47	+ 0.07	+ 10.01	+ 7.23	+ 5.86
Long-Term Govt	+ 7.79	− 0.30	+ 11.40	+ 7.45	+ 6.13
High-Yield Taxable	− 6.56	− 3.34	− 6.42	+ 6.71	+ 6.73
Mortgage Bond	+ 4.94	− 0.16	+ 6.84	+ 6.70	+ 5.74
Short-Term US	+ 6.17	+ 0.42	+ 7.80	+ 6.32	+ 5.27
Long-Term	+ 5.05	− 0.69	+ 7.38	+ 7.19	+ 6.26
General US Taxable	− 1.31	− 0.84	− 1.22	+ 6.79	+ 5.73
World Income	+ 1.00	+ 2.32	+ 0.79	+ 6.79	+ 5.02
Short-Term Muni	+ 4.07	+ 0.50	+ 5.50	+ 4.77	+ 4.29
Intermed.-Term Muni	+ 4.99	+ 0.49	+ 7.61	+ 6.04	+ 5.11
General L-T Muni	+ 5.04	+ 0.23	+ 8.60	+ 7.10	+ 5.47
High-Yield Muni	+ 4.84	+ 0.13	+ 7.98	+ 7.38	+ 6.01
Insured Muni	+ 5.17	+ 0.38	+ 8.70	+ 6.90	+ 5.38

ON A TOTAL RETURN BASIS

Figure 4.5 is a small section of the mutual fund price quotations reported in *The Wall Street Journal* daily. All of the funds listed in Figure 4.5 belong to the very large family of funds managed by Fidelity Investments. An arrow points to one particular fund, the Blue Chip Growth Fund (abbreviated BluCh). After the name of the fund, the next thing listed is the net asset value, or NAV, as of the close of trading. Here we see that Blue Chip closed at a price of $42.76. Next we have the change in the NAV from the previous day, revealing that the Blue Chip Fund gained 50 cents per share. Finally, the last column reports the fund's year-to-date performance, up 14.4 percent in this case.

In Figure 4.5, notice that a number of funds have the small letter "r" immediately after their names. This indicates that a redemption charge may apply. For the funds

Figure 4.5

Fidelity
Investments
Funds

Source: Reprinted by
permission of *The Wall Street
Journal,* October 22, 1998
via Copyright Clearance
Center, Inc. © 1998 Dow
Jones and Company, Inc. All
Rights Reserved Worldwide.

Blue Chip Fund →

Name	NAV	Net Chg	YTD %ret	Name	NAV	Net Chg	YTD %ret
Fidelity Invest:				Fidelity Invest:			
AMgrIn	12.45	+0.01	+ 5.8	France r	14.45	+0.13	+15.1
A Mgr	18.67	+0.09	+ 4.2	GNMA	10.89	−0.01	+ 5.2
AMgrGr	19.23	+0.13	+ 4.1	Germany r	14.25	−0.07	+11.9
Balanc	15.08	+0.10	+ 9.6	GloBal	15.55	+0.06	+ 7.6
BluCh	42.76	+0.50	+14.4	Govtinc	10.22	−0.02	+ 7.9
Canad r	12.56	+0.05	−24.0	GroCo	46.07	+0.70	+ 7.4
CapAp	18.58	+0.27	− 4.1	GroInc	40.51	+0.21	+11.7
Cpinc r	8.91	+0.10	− 5.0	Highinc r	11.32	+0.08	− 5.5
CngS	336.73	−0.66	+11.1	HKChna	9.61	−0.03	−12.8
Contra	49.96	+0.54	+ 7.3	IntBd	10.33	−0.01	+ 6.7
Controll	8.88	+0.15	NS	IntGov	9.98	−0.01	+ 7.2
CnvSc	17.26	+0.35	+ 1.3	IntGr	19.24	+0.06	− 2.3
Destl	25.83	...	+ 9.3	IntlBnd	9.06	+0.03	+ 4.5
Destll	14.93	...	+ 8.3	IntVal	12.07	+0.01	− 0.3
DisEq	26.99	+0.19	+ 4.4	InvGB	7.40	−0.01	+ 6.5
DivIntl	16.78	−0.02	+ 4.0	Japan r	10.27	−0.21	+ 2.5
DivGth	25.60	+0.16	+19.6	JpnSmCo r	6.04	−0.11	+ 9.4
EmGr r	26.81	+0.43	+13.3	LargeCap	14.31	+0.19	+15.0
EmrMkt r	6.55	+0.06	−31.8	LatinAm r	10.94	+0.30	−36.5
Eq Inc	52.31	+0.23	+ 2.2	LowP r	20.87	+0.15	− 9.1
EQII	28.66	+0.18	+ 8.7	MagIn	102.83	+1.02	+10.8
Europ r	31.83	+0.12	+ 6.3	MidCap	15.16	+0.15	− 2.9
ErCapAp r	15.81	+0.08	+ 7.7	MtgSec	11.03	...	+ 5.1
Exch	226.34	+1.50	+ 7.6	NewMkt r	8.94	+0.06	−24.4
Export	16.67	+0.24	+ 2.6	NewMill	22.64	+0.55	+ 2.4
Fidel	31.75	+0.29	+12.0	Nordic	15.66	+0.01	+10.1
Fifty	13.89	+0.24	− 4.8	OTC	34.10	+0.41	+ 9.7

listed here, this most commonly occurs with the single-country funds such as Canada,
France, Germany, and Japan.

How Useful Are Fund Performance Ratings?

If you look at the three-year and five-year returns reported in Figure 4.4, you might
wonder why anyone would buy a fund in a category other than those with the highest returns. Well, the lessons learned in Chapter 1 suggest the answer that these historical returns do not consider the riskiness of the various fund categories. For
example, if the market has done well, the best ranked funds may simply be the riskiest funds, since the riskiest funds normally perform the best in a rising market. In a
market downturn, however, these best ranked funds are most likely to become the
worst ranked funds, since the riskiest funds normally perform the worst in a falling
market.

These problems with performance measures deal with the evaluation of historical
performance. However, there is an even more fundamental criterion. Ultimately, we
don't care about historical performance; we care about *future* performance. Whether
historical performance is useful in predicting future performance is the subject of ongo-
ing debate.

CHECK THIS

4.6a Which mutual fund in
Figure 4.5 had the best
year-to-date return? The
worst?

4.6b What are some of the
problems with comparing
historical performance
numbers?

4.7 Closed-End Funds

It is probably fitting that we close our mutual fund chapter with a discussion of closed-end funds. As we will see, such funds have some unusual aspects.

Closed-End Funds Performance Information

As we described above, the major difference between a closed-end fund and an open-end fund is that closed-end funds don't buy and sell shares. Instead, there is a fixed number of shares in the fund, and these shares are bought and sold on the open market. About 500 closed-end funds have their shares traded on U.S. stock exchanges, which is far fewer than the roughly 8,000 open-end mutual funds available to investors.

Figure 4.6 shows some NYSE quotes from *The Wall Street Journal.* An arrow points to the Mexico Fund, a closed-end single-country fund. Such funds are one of the more common closed-end fund types. Single-state municipal bond funds are another common type (see, for example, listings beginning with "Nuveen" in the *Journal*).

In Figure 4.6, notice how the listing for the Mexico Fund is almost indistinguishable from the common stock listing for Micron Technology immediately below it. The first tipoff that it is a fund and not a stock is the letters "Fd" at the end of the fund's name indicating the abbreviation for a "fund." Another tipoff is that no PE ratio is reported, although the same is true for many stocks with PE ratios that are not meaningful.

The Closed-End Fund Discount Mystery

Wall Street has many unsolved puzzles, and one of the most famous and enduring has to do with prices of shares in closed-end funds. As we noted earlier, shares in closed-end funds trade in the marketplace. As a result, share prices can differ from net asset values. In fact, most closed-end funds sell at a discount relative to their net asset values, and the discount is sometimes substantial.

For example, suppose a closed-end fund owns $100 million worth of stock. It has 10 million shares outstanding, so the NAV is clearly $10. It would not be at all unusual, however, for the share price to be only $9, indicating a 10 percent discount. What is puzzling about this discount is that you can apparently buy $10 worth of stock for only $9!

Figure 4.6

The Mexico Fund (MXF)

Source: Reprinted by permission from *The Wall Street Journal,* October 22, 1998, © 1998 Dow Jones & Company, Inc. All Rights Reserved Worldwide.

52 Weeks Hi	Lo	Stock	Sym	Div	Yld %	PE	Vol 100s	Hi	Lo	Close	Net Chg
22⁵/₈	17³/₈	Mestek	MCC	...	...	11	13	18¹/₈	18¹/₈	18¹/₈	...
26¹/₈	25¹/₄	MetEdCap p/A		2.25	8.8	...	7	25¹¹/₁₆	25¹¹/₁₆	25¹¹/₁₆	+ ¹/₈
17³/₈	10⁵/₈	MetPro	MPR	.30l	2.5	12	112	12¹/₄	12	12¹/₈	+ ¹/₈
20¹/₈	6⁹/₁₆	Mtls USA	MUI		...	12	577	10¹/₁₆	9⁵/₈	9³/₄	+ ³/₁₆
27	7¹/₈	MtroGldwnMyr	MGM		...	dd	1667	9⁵/₈	8⁵/₈	8¹⁵/₁₆	−¹³/₁₆
10¹/₈	6¹/₄	Metrogas	MGS	.90e	11.0	...	11	8⁵/₈	8³/₁₆	8³/₁₆	...
22⁷/₈	14	MetlrToledo	MTD		...	...	769	22³/₈	20¹/₂	21⁷/₈	+ 1³/₈
11¹/₁₆	4⁵/₁₆	MexEqIncoFd	MXE	3.56e	55.3	...	673	6¹/₂	6¹/₈	6⁷/₁₆	+ ⁵/₁₆
22¹/₈	7⁵/₁₆	MexicoFd	MXF	.83e	7.3	...	5800	11⁷/₁₆	10¹³/₁₆	11⁷/₁₆	+ ⁷/₁₆
38¹⁵/₁₆	20¹/₈	MicronTch	MU		...	dd	24238	34¹¹/₁₆	33³/₈	34¹¹/₁₆	+¹¹/₁₆
29⁷/₈	22³/₄	MidAmApt	MAA	2.20	9.0	24	353	24³/₈	24	24³/₈	+ ¹/₁₆
27	23¹/₄	MidAmApt pfA		2.37	9.8	...	8	24¹/₄	24	24¹/₁₆	− ³/₁₆
25¹/₄	23	MidAmApt pfC		.59p	...	...	51	23⁷/₈	23¹/₈	23⁷/₈	+ ⁷/₁₆
16³/₄	4⁷/₁₆	MidAtlMed	MME		...	dd	3935	6⁹/₁₆	6¹/₁₆	6¹/₂	+ ⁷/₁₆
15	11	MidAtlRltyTr	MRR	1.00	7.7	18	17	13⁵/₁₆	13¹/₁₆	13¹/₁₆	...
26⁷/₁₆	17	MidAmEngy	MEC	1.20	4.6	18	2545	26¹/₈	25³/₈	25⁷/₈	+ ¹/₁₆
26³/₄	25	MidAmEngy QUPS A		2.00	7.7	...	63	25¹⁵/₁₆	25⁵/₈	25¹⁵/₁₆	+ ¹/₈
26⁷/₈	14³/₄	Midas	MDS	.04e	.2	...	263	26¹/₄	26	26¹/₄	...

Rebound Candidates for '95

Closed-end funds are piling up in Wall Street's discount bin.

How they got there is a painful story for investors. But now that they're languishing, some closed-end funds could be positioned for a revival in 1995, analysts say.

In 1994, the 537 closed-end funds—the publicly traded equivalent of mutual funds—saw their average "discounts" widen to levels unseen in four years. A discount happens when the price of a closed-end fund, typically traded on the New York Stock Exchange, drops below the value of the fund's actual stockholdings. (In contrast, when a fund's price races ahead of its actual value, it's considered to trade at a "premium.")

"This is the time to buy closed-ends. This is where you make your money," declares Ron Olin, president of Deep Discount Advisors, an Asheville, N.C., money manager specializing in closed-end funds.

Which is not to say that investors should run out and buy any old closed-end fund that's trading at a discount. Many got that way for a good reason. ("Some funds are cheap because they stink," says one analyst.) But the overall group does appear to have been overly punished. And, just as with common stocks, it's often good to buy when things look worst.

"Discounts can often be a pretty good contrarian market indicator," says Colin Mathews, analyst at Morningstar Closed-End Funds newsletter in Chicago.

Mr. Mathews notes that if you bought closed-end funds in mid-1990, the last time the sector was this battered, "You would have done extremely well. Conversely, if you saw the premiums at the end of 1993, particularly among emerging-markets funds like the Latin America funds, and pulled out, you would have gotten out at the top."

Source: William Power, "Offer Rebound Candidates for '95," *The Wall Street Journal*, January 6, 1995. © 1995 Dow Jones & Company, Inc. All Rights Reserved Worldwide.

Wall Street's Discount Store

Closed-End Discounts Widen . . .

Average monthly premium or discount of closed-end funds

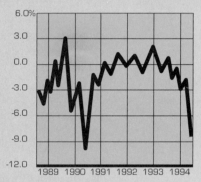

Source: Morningstar Closed-End Funds.

Led by Asian Funds

Funds with largest difference between recent discount and average historical discount.*

Fund	Recent Premium or Discount	Percentage Points Below Avg.
Korea	+5.5%	−40.7
Taiwan	−9.3	−34.0
Thai	−21.8	−32.7
Spain	−9.2	−19.8
Gemini II Inc.	+12.2	−18.8
NAIC Growth	−17.0	−18.2
Germany	−15.5	−17.2
Colonial Muni	−11.2	−16.5
Convertible Holdings	+5.9	−16.2
Blackrock Strategic	−13.7	−15.9

*Dates as of Dec. 15, 1994.

To make matters even more perplexing, the typical discount fluctuates over time. As the accompanying Investment Updates box explains, sometimes the discount is very wide; at other times, it almost disappears. Despite a great deal of research, the closed-end fund discount phenomenon remains largely unexplained.

Because of the discount available on closed-end funds, it is often argued that funds with the largest discounts are attractive investments. The problem with this argument is that it assumes that the discount will narrow or disappear. Unfortunately, this may or may not happen; the discount might get even wider.

Sometimes, although not often, the average closed-end fund sells at a premium, implying that investors are willing to pay more than the NAV for shares. This case is not quite as perplexing; however; after all, investors in load funds do the same thing. The reasons we discussed for paying loads might apply to these cases.

One last comment on closed-end funds seems appropriate. When a closed-end fund is first created, its shares are offered for sale to the public. For example, a closed-end fund might raise $50 million by selling 5 million shares to the public at $10 per share (the original offer price is almost always $10), which is the fund's NAV.

If you pay $10, then you are very likely to shortly discover two unpleasant facts. First, the fund promoter will be paid, say, 7 percent of the proceeds right off the top, or about $3.5 million (this will be disclosed in the prospectus). This fee will come out of the fund, leaving a total value of $46.5 million and a NAV of $9.30. Further, as we have seen, the shares will probably trade at a discount relative to NAV in the market, so you would lose another piece of your investment almost immediately. In short, newly offered closed-end funds are generally very poor investments.

CHECK THIS

4.7a What is the closed-end fund puzzle?

4.7b Why are newly offered closed-end funds often a poor investment?

4.8 Summary and Conclusions

We have covered many aspects of mutual fund investing in this chapter. We have seen that there are thousands of mutual funds and dozens of types. A few of the more important distinctions we made can be summarized as follows:

1. Some funds are open-end and some are closed-end. Open-end funds stand ready to buy or sell shares. Closed-end funds do not; instead, their shares trade on the stock exchanges.

2. Some open-end funds have front-end loads, meaning that there is a fee tacked on to the fund's net asset value when you buy. Other funds are no-load. Various costs and fees exist, including back-end loads and 12b-1 fees.

3. Funds have very different objectives and, as a result, very different risk and return potentials. Furthermore, funds with similar-sounding objectives can, in fact, be quite different. It is important to consider a fund's actual holdings and investment policies, not just read its stated objective.

4. Mutual fund information is widely available, but performance information should be used with caution. The best performing funds are often the ones with the greatest risks or the ones that just happened to be in the right investment at the right time.

GET
REAL

This chapter covered the essentials of mutual funds. How should you, as an investor or investment manager, put this information to work?

The first thing to do is to start looking at mutual fund prospectuses. These are written to be accessible to novice investors (or, at least, they are *supposed* to be written that way). The best way to begin exploring is to visit websites. Almost any large mutual fund company will have extensive online information available. Links to some of the better known families are available at our web page. It is important to look at different funds within a given family and also to look across families. Compare growth funds to growth funds, for example. This adventure will give you some of the real-life background you need to select the types of funds most suitable for you or someone else.

Once you have examined prospectuses on different funds, it's time to invest. Beginning with your simulated account, pick a few funds, invest, and observe the outcomes. Open-end mutual funds are probably the place most of you will begin investing real dollars. An initial purchase can be made with a relatively small amount, perhaps $500, and subsequent purchases can be made in amounts of as little as $50.

Most important of all, most employers now provide employees with retirement plans. The way these work is that, typically, your employer will make a contribution to a mutual fund you select (often from a fairly limited set). Your employer may even match or more than match a contribution you make. Such plans may be the only retirement benefit offered, but they can be an extraordinary opportunity for those who take full advantage of them by getting the largest possible match and then investing in a suitable fund. It's an important choice, so the more knowledge you have regarding mutual funds, the better your outcome is likely to be.

Key Terms

investment company 84
open-end fund 85
closed-end fund 85
net asset value 85

front-end load 88
12b-1 fees 88
turnover 89
money market mutual fund 92

Chapter Review Problems and Self-Test

1. **Front-End Loads**   The Madura HiGro Fund has a net asset value of $50 per share. It charges a 3 percent load. How much will you pay for 100 shares?

2. **Turnover**   The Starks Income Fund's average daily total assets were $100 million for the year just completed. Its stock purchases for the year were $20 million, while its sales were $12.5 million. What was its turnover?

Answers to Self-Test Problems

1. You will pay 100 times the offering price. Since the load is computed as a percentage of the offering price, we can compute the offering price as follows:

$$\text{Net asset value} = (1 - \text{Front-end load}) \times \text{Offering price}$$

In other words, the NAV is 97 percent of the offering price. Since the NAV is $50, the offering price is $50/.97 = $51.55. You will pay $5,155 in all, of which $155 is a load.

2. Turnover is the lesser of purchases or sales divided by average daily assets. In this case, sales are smaller at $12.5, so turnover is $12.5/$100 = .125 times.

Test Your Investment Quotient

1. **Mutual Fund Investing** Which of the following is the least likely advantage of mutual fund investing?

   a. Diversification
   b. Professional management
   c. Convenience
   d. Mutual fund returns are normally higher than market average returns

2. **Open-End Funds** An open-end mutual fund is owned by which of the following?

   a. An investment company
   b. An investment advisory firm
   c. A "family of funds" mutual fund company
   d. Its shareholders

3. **Closed-End Funds** Which of the following is most true of a closed-end investment company?

   a. The fund's share price is usually greater than net asset value.
   b. The fund's share price is set equal to net asset value.
   c. Fund shares outstanding vary with purchases and redemptions by shareholders.
   d. Fund shares outstanding are fixed at the issue date.

4. **Closed-End Funds** A closed end fund is owned by which of the following?

   a. An investment company
   b. An investment advisory firm
   c. A "family of funds" mutual fund company
   d. Its shareholders

5. **Investment Advisory Firms** Which of the following is not true about the typical relationship between a mutual fund and an investment advisory firm? The investment advisory firm

   a. Owns the mutual fund
   b. Manages the mutual fund's assets
   c. Manages shareholder purchase and redemption operations
   d. Receives a management fee for services rendered

6. **Fund Types** Which mutual fund type is most likely to own stocks paying the highest dividend yields?

   a. Capital appreciation fund
   b. Equity income fund
   c. Growth and income fund
   d. Growth fund

7. **Fund Types** Which mutual fund type is most likely to own stocks paying the lowest dividend yields?

   a. Capital appreciation fund
   b. Equity income fund
   c. Growth and income fund
   d. Growth fund

8. **Fund Types**   Which mutual fund type will most likely incur the greatest tax liability for its investors?

   a. Index fund
   b. Municipal bond fund
   c. Income fund
   d. Growth fund

9. **Fund Types**   Which mutual fund type will most likely incur the smallest tax liability for its investors?

   a. Index fund
   b. Municipal bond fund
   c. Income fund
   d. Growth fund

10. **Fund Types**   Which mutual fund type will most likely incur the greatest overall risk levels for its investors?

    a. Large-cap index fund
    b. Insured municipal bond fund
    c. Money market mutual fund
    d. Small-cap growth fund

11. **Fund Types**   Which mutual fund type will most likely incur the smallest overall risk levels for its investors?

    a. Large-cap index fund
    b. Insured municipal bond fund
    c. Money market mutual fund
    d. Small-cap growth fund

12. **Mutual Fund Fees**   Which of the following mutual fund fees is assessed on an annual basis?

    a. 12b-1 fees
    b. Front-end load
    c. Back-end load
    d. Contingent deferred sales charge (CDSC)

13. **Mutual Fund Fees**   Which of the following mutual fund fees will most likely be the biggest expense for a long-term fund investor?

    a. 12b-1 fees
    b. Front-end load
    c. Back-end load
    d. Contingent deferred sales charge (CDSC)

14. **Mutual Fund Fees**   Over a five-year period and accounting for the time value of money, which of the following mutual fund fees produces the biggest expense?

    a. 1 percent annual 12b-1 fees
    b. 5 percent front-end load
    c. 5 percent back-end load
    d. 5 percent contingent deferred sales charge (CDSC)

15. **Mutual Fund Fees**   Which of the following mutual fund fees and expenses is the most difficult for investors to assess?

    a. Sales charges or "loads"
    b. 12b-1 fees
    c. Management fees
    d. Trading costs

Questions and Problems

**Core
Questions**

1. **Fund Ownership** Who actually owns a mutual fund? Who runs it?

2. **Loads** Given that no-load funds are widely available, why would a rational investor pay a front-end load? More generally, why don't fund investors always seek out funds with the lowest loads, management fees, and other fees?

3. **Money Market Funds** Is it true that the NAV of a money market mutual fund never changes? How is this possible?

4. **Money Market Deposits Accounts** What is the difference between a money market deposit account and a money market mutual fund? Which is riskier?

5. **Net Asset Value** The World Income Appreciation Fund has current assets with a market value of $2.5 billion and has 75 million shares outstanding. What is the net asset value (NAV) for this mutual fund?

6. **Front-End Loads** Suppose the mutual fund in the previous problem has a current market price quotation of $36.03. Is this a load fund? If so, calculate the front-end load.

7. **Calculating NAV** The ANZUS Growth and Equity Fund is a "low-load" fund. The current offer price quotation for this mutual fund is $56.00, and the front-end load is 2.5 percent. What is the NAV? If there are 12.5 million shares outstanding, what is the current market value of assets owned by the ANZUS fund?

8. **Fund Goals** What is a capital appreciation fund? An equity income fund? Which is likely to be riskier? Why?

9. **Money Market Funds** The Johnson Liquid Assets Money Market Mutual Fund has a NAV of $1 per share. During 1999, the assets held by this fund appreciated by 6.9 percent. If you had invested $25,000 in this fund at the start of the year, how many shares would you own at the end of the year? What will the NAV of this fund be at the end of 1999 Why?

10. **Open versus Closed-End Funds** If you were concerned about the liquidity of mutual fund shares that you held, would you rather hold shares in a closed-end or open-end fund? Why?

Use the following mutual fund entry from The Wall Street Journal *to answer the next two questions:*

| Hankey | r | 10.25 | +.10 | + 3.5 |

11. **Mutual Fund Information** What is this fund's NAV? What was the NAV yesterday? If you buy 100 shares, assuming this is a no-load fund, what will it cost you?

12. **Mutual Fund Performance** What does the +3.5 tell us about the Hankey fund?

**Intermediate
Questions**

13. **Calculating Turnover** A sector fund specializing in commercial bank stocks had average daily assets of $1.2 billion in 1999. This fund sold $650 million worth of stock during the year, and its turnover ratio was .45. How much stock did this mutual fund purchase during the year?

14. **Calculating Fees** In the previous problem, suppose the annual operating expense ratio for the mutual fund in 1999 is 1.25 percent, and the management fee is .85 percent. How much money did the fund's management earn during 1995? If the fund doesn't charge any 12b-1 fees, how much were miscellaneous and administrative expenses during the year?

15. **Calculating Fees** You purchased 2,000 shares in the New Pacific Growth Fund on January 2, 1999, at an offering price of $18.75 per share. The front-end load for this fund is 6 percent, and the back-end load for redemptions within one year is 3 percent. The underlying assets in this mutual fund appreciate (including reinvested dividends) by 18 percent during 1995, and you sell back your shares at the end of the year. If the operating expense ratio for the New Pacific Fund is 1.35 percent, what is your total return from this investment? What do you conclude about the impact of fees in evaluating mutual fund performance?

16. **Calculating Fees**   Suppose in the previous problem that the mutual fund has no front-end load or back-end load. Further suppose that the operating expense ratio for the fund is .85 percent. What is your return on investment now?

17. **Taxes and MMMFs**   Suppose you're evaluating three alternative MMMF investments. The first fund buys a diversified portfolio of municipal securities from across the country and yields 4.8 percent. The second fund buys only taxable, short-term commercial paper and yields 7.5 percent. The third fund specializes in the municipal debt from the state of New Jersey and yields 4.5 percent. If you are a New Jersey resident, your federal tax bracket is 35 percent, and your state tax bracket is 8 percent, which of these three MMMFs offers you the highest aftertax yield?

18. **Taxes and MMMFs**   In the previous problem, which MMMF offers you the highest yield if you are a resident of Texas, which has no state income tax?

19. **Closed-End Funds**   The Argentina Fund has $275 million in assets and sells at a 12.5 percent discount to NAV. If the quoted share price for this closed-end fund is $8.75, how many shares are outstanding? If you purchase 1,000 shares of this fund, what will the total shares outstanding be now?

20. **Closed-End Fund Discounts**   Suppose you purchase 5,000 shares of a closed-end mutual fund at its initial public offering; the offer price is $10 per share. The offering prospectus discloses that the fund promoter gets a 9 percent fee from the offering. If this fund sells at a 10 percent discount to NAV the day after the initial public offering, what is the value of your investment?

STOCK-TRAK·
Portfolio Simulations

Trading Mutual Funds with Stock-Trak

Stock-Trak allows you to trade mutual funds as simply as it allows you to trade common stocks. There are some restrictions: You cannot use margin to buy mutual fund shares and fund shares cannot be sold short. You should consult the most recent rules at the Stock-Trak website (www.stocktrak.com) for other restrictions that might apply.

To trade mutual funds with Stock-Trak, you must know the ticker symbol of the fund whose shares you wish to buy or sell. Unfortunately, you cannot find mutual fund ticker symbols in *The Wall Street Journal.* Mutual fund ticker symbols can be conveniently obtained through many quote servers on the Internet, for example, the Yahoo Internet quote server (quote.yahoo.com). You simply type the name of the mutual fund into the symbol look-up function and submit it to the quote server. After you have the ticker symbol for the fund of interest, you can use it just like a stock ticker to get a price quote from the quote server.

Mutual fund ticker symbols normally comprise five letters, where the last letter is an X. For example, FMAGX is the ticker for the Fidelity Magellan Fund, VFINX is the ticker for the Vanguard Index Trust 500 Fund, and SNXFX is the ticker for the Schwab 1000 Equity Fund.

When buying mutual fund shares, you take a long position, hoping the fund's share price will increase. Suppose you want to invest $10,000 in the Kemper Small Capital Value Fund, which has the ticker symbol KDSAX. You submit your order as "buy $10,000 KDSAX." Later, suppose you want to sell $4,000 in KDSAX shares. You submit this order as "sell $4,000 KDSAX."

Stock-Trak Exercise

1. Look up stock ticker symbols for these mutual funds: Templeton Foreign Equity Fund, Strong Growth Fund, and T. Rowe Price Blue Chip Growth Fund.

Part Two

Stock Markets

5 The Stock Market

On May **17, 1792,** a group of commodity brokers met and signed the now famous Buttonwood Tree Agreement, thereby establishing the forerunner of what soon became the New York Stock Exchange. Today, the NYSE is the world's largest and best known stock exchange. In 1998, the NYSE transacted more than $7 trillion in stock trades representing over 150 billion shares. Established in 1971, and less well known, Nasdaq executes trades for a similar number of stock shares. Together, the NYSE and Nasdaq account for the majority of stock trading in the United States. ■ With this chapter, we begin in earnest our study of stock markets. This chapter presents a "big picture" overview of who owns stocks, how a stock exchange works, and how to read and understand stock market information reported in the financial press. A good place to start is by looking at stock ownership.

5.1 Who Owns Stocks?

If you invest in common stock, you will find yourself in generally good company. More than one in every three adult Americans owns stock shares directly or owns them indirectly through a defined contribution pension fund or stock mutual fund. Interestingly, only about 38 percent of all stockholders in 1992 had brokerage accounts, attesting to the importance of mutual funds and defined contribution pension funds. Stock ownership has become increasingly democratic in recent decades. For example, in 1962 the wealthiest 2.5 percent of American households owned 75 percent of all publicly traded stock. In contrast, by 1992 the wealthiest 18 percent of households owned less than 50 percent of all publicly traded stock.[1]

While the number of individual investors owning stock has increased in recent decades, the proportion of all outstanding stock shares held directly by all individuals has actually declined. For example, individual investors held about 50 percent of the then $3.2 trillion total value of all publicly traded U.S. stocks in 1992, down from 84 percent in 1965. However, these percentages exclude mutual funds, which in 1992 held almost 9 percent of all U.S. stocks.

Since most (but not all) stock mutual fund shares are owned by individual investors, it is appropriate to add in mutual fund shares held by individuals. With this adjustment, individuals held about 56 percent of all U.S. stocks in 1992. The remaining 44 percent of all stock shares was held predominantly by institutional investors, like pension funds or insurance companies, along with a relatively small portion held by foreign investors.

Many individuals also hold a substantial investment in the stock market indirectly through one or more financial institutions, such as pension funds and insurance companies. It is very likely that now, or in the near future, you will participate in a pension plan sponsored by your employer. Indeed, pension funds are the dominant type of institutional investor. In 1992, pension funds held $4.4 trillion of funds invested in stocks, bonds, real estate, and other assets. The next three largest categories of institutional investors were insurance companies with $1.6 trillion, investment firms such as mutual funds with $1.4 trillion, and bank trusts with $.9 trillion. While most of this total of over $8 trillion of institutional funds was invested in real estate, bonds, and other assets, about $1.5 trillion was invested in common stocks. As we said, you are in generally good company.

CHECK THIS

5.1a Do individuals own a significant portion of publicly traded common stocks in the United States?

5.1b Has the proportion of publicly traded common stocks in the United States held by individuals changed through time?

5.1c Has ownership of publicly traded common stocks in the United States become more or less concentrated among wealthy individuals in recent decades?

---

[1] *Shareownership 1995,* New York Stock Exchange.

5.2 The Primary and Secondary Stock Markets

primary market The market in which new securities are originally sold to investors.

secondary market The market in which previously issued securities trade among investors.

The stock market consists of a **primary market** and a **secondary market**. In the primary, or new-issue market, shares of stock are first brought to the market and sold to investors. In the secondary market, existing shares are traded among investors.

In the primary market, companies issue new securities to raise money. In the secondary market, investors are constantly appraising the values of companies by buying and selling shares previously issued by these companies. We next discuss the operation of the primary market for common stocks, and then we turn our attention to the secondary market for stocks.

The Primary Market for Common Stock

initial public offering (IPO) An initial public offer occurs when a company offers stock for sale to the public for the first time.

The primary market for common stock is how new securities are first brought to market. It is best known as the market for **initial public offerings (IPOs)**. An IPO occurs when a company offers stock for sale to the public for the first time. Typically, the company is small and growing, and it needs to raise capital for further expansion.

To illustrate how an IPO occurs, suppose that several years ago you started a software company. Your company was initially set up as a privately held corporation with 100,000 shares of stock, all sold for one dollar per share. The reason your company is privately held is that shares were not offered for sale to the general public. Instead, you bought 50,000 shares for yourself and sold the remaining 50,000 shares to a few supportive friends and relatives.

Fortunately, your company has prospered beyond all expectations. However, company growth is now hampered by a lack of capital. At an informal stockholders' meeting, it is agreed to take the company public. Not really knowing how to do this, you consult your accountant, who recommends an **investment banking firm**. An investment banking firm, among other things, specializes in arranging financing for companies by finding investors to buy newly issued securities.

investment banking firm A firm specializing in arranging financing for companies.

After lengthy negotiations, including an examination of your company's current financial condition and plans for future growth, your investment banker suggests an issue of 4 million shares of common stock. Two million shares will be distributed to the original stockholders (you and your original investors) in exchange for their old shares. These 2 million shares distributed to the original stockholders ensure that effective control of the corporation will remain in their hands.

underwrite To assume the risk of buying newly issued securities from a company and reselling them to investors.

After much haggling, your investment banker agrees to **underwrite** the stock issue by purchasing the other 2 million shares from your company for $10 per share. The net effect of this transaction is that you have sold half the company to the underwriter for $20 million. The proceeds from the sale will allow your company to construct its own headquarters building and double its staff of programmers and sales consultants.

Your investment banker will not keep the 2 million shares but instead will resell them in the primary market. She thinks the stock can probably be sold for $12 per share in an IPO. The difference between the $12 the underwriter sells the stock for and the $10 per share you received is called the *underwriter spread* and is a basic part of the underwriter's compensation.

fixed commitment
Underwriting arrangement in which the investment banker guarantees the firm a fixed amount for its securities.

best effort
Arrangement in which the investment banker does not guarantee the firm a fixed amount for its securities.

Securities and Exchange Commission (SEC)
Federal regulatory agency charged with enforcing U.S. securities laws and regulations.

prospectus
Document prepared as part of a security offering detailing a company's financial position, its operations, and investment plans for the future.

red herring A preliminary prospectus not yet approved by the SEC.

This agreement, under which the underwriter pays the firm a fixed amount, is called a **fixed commitment**. With a fixed (or firm) commitment, the underwriter assumes the risk that investors cannot be persuaded to buy the stock at a price above $10 per share. The other major type of arrangement, called a **best effort**, is just that. Here, the investment banker promises to get the best price possible but does not guarantee the company a specific amount. Strictly speaking, a best-effort arrangement is therefore *not* underwritten, but the phrase "best-effort underwriting" is often used nonetheless.

As is common with an IPO, some restrictions are imposed on you as part of the underwriting contract. Most important, you and the other original stockholders agree not to sell any of your personal stockholdings for one year after the underwriting. This ties most of your wealth to the company's success and makes selling the stock to investors a more credible undertaking by the underwriter. Essentially, investors are assured that you will be working hard to expand the company and increase its earnings.

After the underwriting terms are decided, much of your time will be devoted to the mechanics of the offering. In particular, before shares can be sold to the public, the issue must obtain an approved registration with the **Securities and Exchange Commission (SEC)**. The SEC is the federal regulatory agency charged with regulating U.S. securities markets.

SEC regulations governing IPOs are especially strict. To gain SEC approval, you must prepare a **prospectus**, normally with the help of outside accounting, auditing, and legal experts. The prospectus contains a detailed account of your company's financial position, its operations, and investment plans for the future. Once the prospectus is prepared, it is submitted to the SEC for approval. The SEC makes no judgment about the quality of your company or the value of your stock. Instead, it only checks to make sure that various rules regarding full disclosure and other issues have been satisfied.

While awaiting SEC approval, your investment banker will circulate a preliminary prospectus among investors to generate interest in the stock offering. This document is commonly called a **red herring** because the cover page is stamped in red ink, indicating that final approval for the stock issue has not yet been obtained. The preliminary prospectus is essentially complete except for the final offering price and a few other pieces of information. These are not set because market conditions might change while SEC approval is being sought. Upon obtaining SEC approval, the prospectus will be updated and completed, and your underwriter can begin selling your company's shares to investors.

Along the way, the underwriter will usually place announcements in newspapers indicating how to obtain a prospectus. Because of their appearance, these announcements are known as *tombstones,* and they are a familiar sight in the financial press. A sample tombstone as it appeared in *The Wall Street Journal* is shown in Figure 5.1.

As Figure 5.1 shows, a typical tombstone states the name of the company, some information about the stock issue being sold, and the underwriters for the issue. All but very small issues generally involve more than one underwriter, and the names of the participating underwriters are usually listed at the bottom of the tombstone. Those listed first are the "lead" underwriters, who are primarily responsible for managing the issue process.

Initial public stock offerings vary in size a great deal. The 2 million share issue for your hypothetical software company discussed above is a fairly small issue. The largest public offering in the United States was the 1998 sale of shares in Conoco, an oil

Figure 5.1   IPO Tombstone

This announcement is neither an offer to sell nor a solicitation of an offer to buy any of these Securities. The offer is made only by the Prospectus.

3,450,000 Shares

Class A Common Stock

Price $69 a Share

Copies of the Prospectus may be obtained in any State from only such of the undersigned as may legally offer these Securities in compliance with the securities laws of such State.

MORGAN STANLEY DEAN WITTER

BT ALEX.BROWN
Incorporated

CREDIT SUISSE FIRST BOSTON

HAMBRECHT & QUIST

MERRILL LYNCH & CO.

October 23, 1998

NTT DoCoMo, Conoco Enliven Market for IPOs

Huge initial public offerings for a Japanese telecommunications giant and for Conoco, Inc. have drawn investors back into the battered market for new stocks. But analysts expect demand for most IPOs to remain spotty.

Japanese mobile-telecommunications company NTT Mobile Communications Network, Inc., known as NTT DoCoMo, started trading on the Tokyo Stock Exchange last night after completing the largest IPO in world history, an $18 billion initial global offering led by Goldman, Sachs & Co. and Nikko Securities.

And this morning, DuPont Co.'s oil subsidiary Conoco is scheduled to start trading as the largest U.S. IPO. The offering for the Houston company was priced at $23 a share last night; about $4.4 billion in Conoco shares were sold in the IPO led by Morgan Stanley Dean Witter & Co., eclipsing the previous U.S. IPO record set by Lucent Technologies, Inc. in 1996.

But while the large deals show investors still have an appetite for stocks, analysts warn that buyers aren't eager to throw money at any new public company, most of which are small and young. Both Conoco and DoCoMo developed profitable businesses over years as subsidiaries of larger, established companies, and therefore they were seen differently. Indeed, if the IPO market is open, it is only "for big-cap, relatively prosaic companies," says Richard L. Kauffman, head of global-equity capital markets for Morgan Stanley Dean Witter.

Some analysts maintain that IPOs are shifting in the current market environment from a tool for small "growth" companies to the domain of large-cap conglomerates looking to shed businesses. Since June, more than 80% of the money raised through IPOs went to larger companies, up substantially from 29% in the first five months of the year, says New York data provider CommScan.

The Largest IPOs. U.S. only (excluding closed-end funds), by global proceeds raised at the time of offering

COMPANY	DATE	VALUE (billions)
Conoco	Today	$4.40*
Lucent Technologies	April '96	3.03
Allstate	June '93	2.12
Assoc. First Capital	May '96	1.94
Consolidated Rail	March '87	1.65
USEC	July '98	1.43
Pacific Telesis	Dec. '93	1.38
Republic Services	June '98	1.32
Henley Group	May '86	1.28
Lyondell Petrochem	Jan. '89	1.20
Coca-Cola Ent.	Nov. '86	1.18
Nabisco Holdings	Jan. '95	1.10

*Yesterday's pricing
Source: Securities Data Co.

subsidiary of DuPont. The new shares were offered at $23 per share to create a $4.4 billion public offering. The nearby Investment Updates box contains *The Wall Street Journal* news story for the issue announcement, which includes a list of the largest IPOs in recent years.

The Secondary Market for Common Stock

In the secondary market for common stock, investors buy and sell shares with other investors. If you think of the primary market as the new-car showroom at an automotive dealer, where cars are first sold to the public, then the secondary market is just the used-car lot.

Secondary market stock trading among investors is directed through three channels. An investor may trade:

1. Directly with other investors.
2. Indirectly through a broker who arranges transactions for others.
3. Directly with a dealer who buys and sells securities from inventory.

As we discussed in Chapter 2, for individual investors, almost all common stock transactions are made through a broker. However, large institutional investors, such as pension funds and mutual funds, trade through both brokers and dealers, and also trade directly with other institutional investors.

Dealers and Brokers

dealer A trader who buys and sells securities from inventory.

broker An intermediary who arranges security transactions among investors.

bid price The price a dealer is willing to pay.

ask price The price at which a dealer is willing to sell. Also called the *offer* or *offering* price.

spread The difference between the bid and ask prices.

Since most securities transactions involve dealers and brokers, it is important that you understand exactly what these terms mean. A **dealer** maintains an inventory and stands ready to buy and sell at any time. By contrast, a **broker** brings buyers and sellers together but does not maintain an inventory. Thus, when we speak of used-car dealers and real estate brokers, we recognize that the used-car dealer maintains an inventory, whereas the real estate broker normally does not.

In the securities markets, a dealer stands ready to buy securities from investors wishing to sell them and sell securities to investors wishing to buy them. An important part of the dealer function involves maintaining an inventory to accommodate temporary buy and sell order imbalances. The price a dealer is willing to pay is called the **bid price**. The price at which a dealer will sell is called the **ask price** (sometimes called the offered or offering price). The difference between the bid and ask prices is called the **spread**.

A dealer attempts to profit by selling securities at a higher price than the average price paid for them. Of course, this is a goal for all investors, but the distinguishing characteristic of securities dealers is that they hold securities in inventory only until the first opportunity to resell them. Essentially, trading from inventory is their business.

Dealers exist in all areas of the economy of course, not just in the stock markets. For example, your local university bookstore is both a primary- and secondary-market textbook dealer. If you buy a new book, then this is a primary-market transaction. If you buy a used book, this is a secondary-market transaction, and you pay the store's ask price. If you sell the book back, you receive the store's bid price, typically half the ask price. The bookstore's spread is the difference between the bid and ask prices.

In contrast, a securities broker arranges transactions between investors, matching investors wishing to buy securities with investors wishing to sell securities. Brokers may match investors with other investors, investors with dealers, and sometimes even dealers with dealers. The distinctive characteristic of security brokers is that they do not buy or sell securities for their own account. Facilitating trades by others is their business.

Most common stock trading is directed through an organized stock exchange or a trading network. Whether a stock exchange or a trading network, the goal is to match investors wishing to buy stocks with investors wishing to sell stocks. The largest, most active organized stock exchange in the United States is the New York Stock Exchange (NYSE). Second and third in size are the Chicago Stock Exchange (CHX) and the American Stock Exchange (AMEX), respectively. These are followed by four regional exchanges: the Boston Stock Exchange (BSE), the Cincinnati Stock Exchange (CSE), (which is actually located in Chicago!), the Pacific Stock Exchange (PSE) in Los Angeles, and the Philadelphia Stock Exchange (PHLX). The major competitor to the organized stock exchanges is the vast trading network known as Nasdaq. In 1998, Nasdaq and the AMEX merged to form a single company, but the two organizations retained their original features. We next discuss the organization of the NYSE, and then we turn to a discussion of Nasdaq.

CHECK THIS

5.2a Is an IPO a primary- or secondary-market transaction?

5.2b Which is bigger, the bid price or the ask price? Why?

5.2c What is the difference between a securities broker and a securities dealer?

5.3 The New York Stock Exchange

The New York Stock Exchange (NYSE, pronounced "Ny-see"), popularly known as the Big Board, celebrated its bicentennial in 1992. It has occupied its current building on Wall Street since the turn of the century, and today it is a not-for-profit New York State corporation. You may be surprised to read that a stock exchange could be a not-for-profit corporation. Actually, this is not unusual since a stock exchange is owned by its members and exists only to provide facilities for exchange members to conduct business. In this capacity, the NYSE operates as a cooperative on a not-for-profit basis. However, NYSE *members* conducting business on the exchange generally represent securities firms and brokerage companies that all most definitely operate on a for-profit basis.

NYSE Membership

NYSE member The owner of a seat on the NYSE.

The NYSE has 1,366 exchange **members**, who are said to own "seats" on the exchange. Technically, a seat is the personal property of the individual purchasing it. Typically, however, the individual who is the registered owner of a seat is an employee of a securities firm such as Merrill Lynch. The securities firm has actually paid for the seat and is effectively the owner. The firm is said to be a member organization (or member firm), and some member organizations own numerous seats on the exchange in this way.

Exchange seat owners can buy and sell securities on the exchange floor without paying commissions. For this and other reasons, exchange seats are valuable assets and are regularly bought and sold. Interestingly, prior to 1986, the highest seat price paid was $625,000 just before the 1929 market crash. Since then, the lowest seat price paid was $55,000 in 1977. As it turns out, that was a very good price for the buyer. In 1999, the price of a seat on the NYSE was about $2 million. It could be even higher by the time you read this.

In addition to paying the price of a seat, a prospective NYSE member must be sponsored by two current members and possess a clean record with regard to security laws violations or felony convictions of any kind. However, it is not necessary to actually own a seat to trade commission-free on the exchange floor, since seats can be leased. Leasing is common and about half of all NYSE seats are leased. Even if you only wish to lease a seat on the exchange, you must pass the same close scrutiny as someone wishing to buy a seat.

Exchange members elect 24 members of a 27-member board of directors. The three additional board members—the chairman of the board, the executive vice chairman, and the president—are *ex officio* members selected by the Board. *"Ex officio"* means that they are members of the board of directors by virtue of their positions as appointed professional managers of the exchange. While the board sets exchange policy, actual management is performed by a professional staff. Technically, NYSE members collectively own the exchange, but the NYSE is organized to insulate professional staff from undue pressure from exchange members.

Types of Members

commission brokers
Agents who execute customer orders to buy and sell stock transmitted to the exchange floor. Typically, they are employees of NYSE member firms.

The largest number of NYSE members are registered as **commission brokers**. The business of a commission broker is to execute customer orders to buy and sell stocks. A commission broker's primary responsibility to customers is to get the best possible prices for their orders. Their number varies, but about 500 NYSE members are commission brokers.

NYSE commission brokers typically are employees of brokerage companies that are NYSE member firms. Member firms operating as brokerage companies accept customer orders to buy and sell securities and relay these orders to their commission brokers for execution. Member firm activities represent the most vital functions of the NYSE, simply because their business is the original reason the exchange exists.

specialist NYSE member acting as a dealer on the exchange floor. Often called a *market maker*.

Second in number of NYSE members are **specialists**, so named because each acts as an assigned dealer for a small set of securities. With a few exceptions, each security listed for trading on the NYSE is assigned to a single specialist. Specialists are also called *market makers* because they are obligated to maintain a fair and orderly market for the securities assigned to them.

As market makers, specialists post bid prices and ask prices for securities assigned to them. The bid price is the price at which a specialist is obligated to buy a security from a seller, and an ask price is the price at which a specialist is obligated to sell a security to a buyer. As we have discussed elsewhere, the difference between the bid price and the ask price is called the bid-ask spread, or simply the spread.

Specialists make a market by standing ready to buy at bid prices and sell at ask prices when there is a temporary disparity between the flow of buy and sell orders for a security. In this capacity, they act as dealers for their own accounts. In so doing, they provide liquidity to the market. Their function is vital, since the work of commission brokers would be quite difficult without the specialists. As we discuss in the next section, specialists also act as brokers.

About 400 NYSE members are specialists. In 1998, all NYSE specialists belonged to one of 30 specialist firms. However, almost half of all NYSE trading is concentrated in stocks managed by the three largest specialist firms. These three largest specialist firms, the number of stocks for which they act as specialists, and their percentage of NYSE trading volume are shown immediately below.

Specialist Firm	Number of Stocks	Dollar Volume (%)
LaBranche/Wagner Stott	442	21.8%
JJC Spec./Merrill Lynch	340	13.2
Spear, Leeds, & Kellogg	286	13.6

floor brokers NYSE members who execute orders for commission brokers on a fee basis. Sometimes called *two-dollar brokers*.

Third in number of exchange members are **floor brokers**. Floor brokers are often used by commission brokers when they are too busy to handle certain orders themselves.

SuperDOT system
Electronic NYSE
system allowing orders
to be transmitted
directly to specialists
for immediate
execution.

floor traders NYSE
members who trade
for their own
accounts, trying to
anticipate and profit
from temporary price
fluctuations.

Instead, they will delegate some orders to floor brokers for execution. Floor brokers are sometimes called two-dollar brokers, a name earned at a time when the standard fee for their service was only two dollars. Today the fee is variable, and certainly higher than two dollars. Floor brokers do well when stock trading volume is high, but with low volume they may be inactive for lengthy periods.

In recent years, floor brokers have become less important on the exchange floor because of the efficient **SuperDOT system** (the "DOT" stands for designated order turnaround), which allows orders to be transmitted electronically directly to the specialist. SuperDOT trading now accounts for a substantial percentage of all trading on the NYSE, particularly on small orders.

Finally, a small number of NYSE members are **floor traders**, who independently trade for their own accounts. Floor traders try to anticipate temporary price fluctuations and profit from them by buying low and selling high. In recent decades, the number of floor traders has declined substantially, suggesting that it has become increasingly difficult to profit from short-term trading on the exchange floor.

NYSE-Listed Stocks

A company is said to be "listed" on the NYSE if its stock is traded there. In late 1998, stocks from 3,090 companies were listed on the "Big Board," as the NYSE is sometimes called, representing 237 billion shares with a market value of $9 trillion. This total includes many large companies so well known that we easily recognize them by their initials—for example, IBM, AT&T, GE, and GM. This total also includes many companies that are not so readily recognized. For example, relatively few would instantly recognize AEP as American Electric Power, but AEX might be recognized as American Express.

Companies that wish to have their stock listed for trading on the Big Board must apply for the privilege. If the application is approved, the company must pay an initial listing fee. In 1998, this fee was $36,800, plus a per-share charge that ranged from $14,750 per million shares for the first 2 million shares, to $1,900 for each million shares above 300 million. In addition to an initial listing fee, the NYSE assesses an annual listing fee. In 1998, the annual listing fee was $1,650 per million for the first 2 million shares and $830 for each additional million shares. Thus, a small company with 2 million shares outstanding would pay an initial listing fee of $66,300, plus annual listing fees of $3,300.

The NYSE has minimum requirements for companies wishing to apply for listing on the Big Board. Although the requirements might change from time to time, the normal minimum requirements in effect in 1998 included:

1. The company's total number of shareholders must be at least 2,200, and stock trading in the previous six months must have been at least 100,000 shares a month on average.

2. At least 1.1 million stock shares must be held in public hands.

3. Publicly held shares must have at least $40 million in market value.

4. The company must have annual earnings of $2.5 million before taxes in the most recent year and $2 million pretax earnings in each of the preceding two years.

5. The company must have net tangible assets of $40 million.

In practice, most companies with stock listed on the NYSE easily exceed these minimum listing requirements.

CHECK THIS

5.3a What are the four types of members of the New York Stock Exchange?

5.3b Which NYSE member type is the most numerous? Which type is the second most numerous?

5.3c NYSE provides more details on listing requirements at its website (www.nyse.com).

5.4 Operation of the New York Stock Exchange

Now that we have a basic idea of how the NYSE is organized and who the major players are, we turn to the question of how trading actually takes place. Fundamentally, the business of the NYSE is to attract and process *order flow*—the flow of customer orders to buy and sell stocks. Customers of the NYSE are the millions of individual investors and tens of thousands of institutional investors who place their orders to buy and sell NYSE-listed stock shares with member-firm brokerage operations.

The NYSE has been quite successful in attracting order flow. In 1998, the average stock trading volume on the NYSE was close to 700 million shares per day. About one-third of all NYSE stock trading volume is attributable to individual investors, and almost half is derived from institutional investors. The remainder represents NYSE-member trading, which is largely attributed to specialists acting as market makers.

NYSE Floor Activity

Quite likely you have seen film footage of the NYSE trading floor on television, or you may have visited the NYSE and viewed exchange floor activity from the gallery (it's worth the trip). Either way, you saw a big room, about the size of a small basketball gym. This big room is called "the big room." There are two other, smaller rooms that you normally don't see. One is called "the garage" because that is literally what it was before it was taken over for securities trading, and the other is called the "blue room" because, well, the room is painted blue.

On the floor of the exchange are a number of stations, each with a roughly figure-eight shape. These stations have multiple counters with numerous computer terminal screens above and on the sides. People operate behind and in front of the counters in relatively stationary positions.

Other people move around on the exchange floor, frequently returning to the many telephone booths positioned along exchange walls. In all, you may have been reminded of worker ants moving around an ant colony. It is natural to wonder: What are all those people doing down there (and why are so many wearing funny-looking coats)?

As an overview of exchange floor activity, here is a quick look at what goes on. Each of the counters at the figure-eight shaped stations is a **specialist's post**. Specialists normally operate in front of their posts to monitor and manage trading in the stocks assigned to them. Clerical employees working for the specialists operate behind the counters. Moving from the many telephone booths out to the exchange floor and back

specialist's post
Fixed place on the exchange floor where the specialist operates.

again are swarms of commission brokers, receiving relayed customer orders, walking out to specialist posts where the orders can be executed, and returning to confirm order executions and receive new customer orders.

To better understand activity on the NYSE trading floor, imagine yourself as a commission broker. Your phone clerk has just handed you an order to sell 3,000 shares of VO (the ticker symbol for Seagrams common stock) for a customer of the brokerage company that employs you. The order is a **market order**, meaning that the customer wants to sell the stock at the best possible price as soon as possible. You immediately walk (running violates exchange rules) to the specialist's post where VO stock is traded.

Upon approaching the specialist's post where VO is traded, you check the terminal screen for information on the current market price for VO stock. The screen reveals that the last executed trade for VO was at $70\frac{5}{8}$, and that the specialist is bidding $70\frac{1}{2}$ per share. You could immediately sell to the specialist at $70\frac{1}{2}$, but that would be too easy.

Instead, as the customer's representative, you are obligated to get the best possible price. It is your job to "work" the order, and your job depends on providing satisfactory order execution service. So you look around for another broker who represents a customer who wants to buy VO stock. Luckily, you quickly find another broker at the specialist's post with a market order to buy 3,000 shares of VO. Noticing that the dealer is asking $70\frac{3}{4}$ per share, you both agree to execute your orders with each other at a price of $70\frac{5}{8}$. This price, exactly halfway between the specialist's bid and ask prices, saves each of your customers $\$\frac{1}{8} \times 3,000 = \$375$ compared to the specialist's prices.

In a trade of this type, in which one commission broker buys from another, the specialist acts only as a broker assisting in matching buy orders and sell orders. On an actively traded stock, there can be many commission brokers buying and selling. In such cases, trading is said to occur "in the crowd." Thus, the specialist functions as a broker as long as there are buyers and sellers available. The specialist steps in as a dealer only when necessary to fill an order that would otherwise go unfilled.

In reality, not all orders are executed so easily. For example, suppose you are unable to quickly find another broker with an order to buy 3,000 shares of VO. Since you have a market order, you may have no choice but to sell to the specialist at the bid price of $70\frac{1}{2}$. In this case, the need to execute an order quickly takes priority, and the specialist provides the necessary liquidity to allow immediate order execution.

In this situation, the specialist is often able to help commission brokers by agreeing to "stop" the stock. By stopping stock for a sell order, the specialist agrees to try to help you get a better price while also guaranteeing a minimum price. For your sell order, the specialist might guarantee a minimum price of $70\frac{1}{2}$ but try to get a better price, say, $70\frac{5}{8}$. So agreed, you leave the order with the specialist. If the next offer to buy VO is at a price of $70\frac{5}{8}$, the specialist will fill your order at that price. But if no better offer appears forthcoming, the specialist will execute the order at the guaranteed price of $70\frac{1}{2}$—if necessary, from the specialist's own inventory.

Stopping stock is also a goodwill gesture. The NYSE places great emphasis on the quality of performance by specialists, which is evaluated regularly through surveys of commission brokers' satisfaction. Specialists are expected to assist brokers in getting the best prices for customer orders, to provide liquidity to the market, and to maintain an orderly market for all securities assigned to them. Stopping stock helps accomplish these objectives.

market order A customer order to buy or sell securities marked for immediate execution at the current market price.

Special Order Types

limit order Customer order to buy or sell securities with a specified "limit" price. The order can be executed only at the limit price or a better price.

Many orders are transmitted to the NYSE floor as **limit orders**. A limit order is an order to buy or sell stock, where the customer specifies a maximum price he is willing to pay in the case of a buy order, or a minimum price he will accept in the case of a sell order. For example, suppose that as a NYSE commission broker, you receive a limit order to sell 3,000 shares of VO stock at 70¾. This means that the customer is not willing to accept any price below 70¾ per share, even if it means missing the trade.

One strategy for handling limit orders is to hold the order and frequently check for potential buyers at the specialist post for VO stock. However, this is unnecessary because you can leave a limit order with the specialist. As a service to brokers, NYSE specialists display unfilled limit orders on the terminal screens at their posts for all approaching brokers to see. If another broker wants to buy VO at 70¾, the specialist will execute the sale for you. This service saves considerable time and energy for busy commission brokers. Indeed, monitoring and executing unfilled limit orders is a very important function of the NYSE specialist.

stop order Customer order to buy or sell securities when a preset "stop" price is reached.

A **stop order** may appear similar to a limit order, but there is an important difference. With a stop order, the customer specifies a "stop" price. This stop price serves as a trigger point. No trade can occur until the stock price reaches this stop price. When the stock price reaches the stop price, the stop order is immediately converted into a market order. Since the order is now a market order, the customer may get a price that is better or worse than the stop price. Thus, the stop price only serves as a trigger point for conversion into a market order. Unlike a limit price, the stop price places no limit on the price at which a trade can occur. Once converted to a market order, the trade is executed just like any other market order.

As an example of a stop order, suppose that you receive a customer's stop order to sell 3,000 shares of VO stock at a stop price of 71½. This means that the customer does not want the order executed until the stock price reaches 71½ per share, at which time the order is immediately converted to a market order. As a market order, the broker may then execute at the best price available, which may or may not be 71½ per share. The stop order in this example is called a *stop-gain order*, because the stop price that triggers a market order to sell is *above* the current stock price.

Another, and more common type of stop order, is the *stop-loss order*. A stop-loss order is an order to sell shares if the stock price reaches a stop price *below* the current stock price. For example, suppose that you receive a customer's stop order to sell 3,000 shares of VO stock at a stop price of 69½. This means that the customer does not want the order executed until the stock price reaches 69½ per share, at which time the order is immediately converted into a market order. As a market order, you may then execute at the best price available, which may or may not be 69½ per share. Notice that a stop order is completely different from the specialist's stopping the stock, discussed earlier.

In addition to the stop-loss and stop-gain orders just described, there are two more basic stop order types. These are *start-gain* and *start-loss orders,* which are stop orders to *buy* stock shares when the stock price reaches the preset stop price. For example, suppose you receive a customer's stop order to buy 2,500 shares of VO stock at a stop price of 72. Since the market is at 70½ bid and 70¾ ask, this is a start-gain order because the stop price is *above* the current market price. Likewise, if you receive a stop order to buy VO stock at a stop price of 68, this is a start-loss order because the stop price is *below* the current market price. Table 5.1 summarizes the characteristics of limit and stop orders.

Table 5.1	Stock Market Order Types	
Order Type	**Buy**	**Sell**
Market order	Buy at best price available for immediate execution.	Sell at best price available for immediate execution.
Limit order	Buy at best price available, but not more than the preset limit price. Forgo purchase if limit is not met.	Sell at best price available, but not less than the preset limit price. Forgo sale if limit is not met.
Stop orders	Start gain: convert to a market order to buy when the stock price crosses the stop price from below. Start loss: convert to a market order to . buy when the stock price crosses the stop price from above.	Stop gain: convert to a market order to sell when the stock price crosses the stop price from below. Stop loss: convert to a market order to sell when the stock price crosses the stop price from above.
Stop-limit orders	Start-limit gain: convert to a limit order to buy when the stock price crosses the stop price from below. Start-limit loss: convert to a limit order to buy when the stock price crosses the stop price from above.	Stop-limit gain: convert to a limit order to sell when the stock price crosses the stop price from below. Stop-limit loss: convert to a limit order to sell when the stock price crosses the stop price from above.

A limit price can be attached to a stop order to create a *stop-limit order.* This is different from a simple stop order in that once the stock price reaches the preset stop price the order is converted into a limit order. By contrast, a simple stop order is converted into a market order. For example, suppose you receive a customer's stop order to buy 2,500 shares of VO stock at a stop price of $71\frac{1}{2}$ with a limit of 72. When the stock price reaches $71\frac{1}{2}$, the order is converted into a limit order with a limit price of 72. At this point, the limit order is just like any other limit order.

Another type of order that requires special attention is the *short-sale order.* As explained in Chapter 2, a short sale involves borrowing stock shares and then selling the borrowed shares in the hope of buying them back later at a lower price. Short-sale loans are normally arranged through the customer's broker. New York Stock Exchange rules require that when shares are sold as part of a short-sale transaction, the order must be marked as a short-sale transaction when it is transmitted to the NYSE floor.

NYSE uptick rule
Rule for short sales requiring that before a short sale can be executed, the last price change must be an uptick.

Sell orders marked as short sales are subject to the **NYSE uptick rule**. According to the NYSE uptick rule, a short sale can be executed only if the last price change was an uptick. For example, suppose the last two trades were executed at $55\frac{1}{2}$ and then $55\frac{5}{8}$. The last price change was an uptick of 1/8, and a short sale can be executed at a price of $55\frac{5}{8}$ or higher. Alternatively, suppose the last two trades were executed at $55\frac{1}{2}$ and $55\frac{1}{4}$, where the last price change was two downticks of 1/8. In this case, a short sale can be executed only at a price of $55\frac{3}{8}$ or higher. For this latter case, the short sale can itself generate the uptick and be the next trade at $55\frac{3}{8}$ or higher.

The NYSE enacted the uptick rule to make it more difficult for speculators to drive down a stock's price by repeated short sales. Interestingly, the uptick rule is a NYSE rule only and does not necessarily apply to short-sale transactions executed elsewhere. Since many NYSE-listed stocks are now traded elsewhere, the uptick rule is less of a constraint than it once was. The Nasdaq has recently instituted a similar rule.

Finally, colored coats are worn by many of the people on the floor of the exchange. The color of the coat indicates the person's job or position. Clerks, runners, visitors, exchange officials, and so on, wear particular colors to identify themselves. Also, since things can get a little hectic on a busy day with the result that good clothing may not last long, the cheap coats offer some protection. Nevertheless, many specialists and floor brokers wear a good business suit every day simply out of habit and pride.

CHECK THIS

5.4a What are the four main types of orders to buy and sell common stocks?

5.4b What do specialists do?

5.4c What is a limit order? How do limit and stop orders differ?

5.5 Nasdaq

In terms of total dollar volume of trading, the second largest stock market in the United States is Nasdaq (say "Naz-dak"). In fact, in terms of companies listed and, on many days recently, number of shares traded, Nasdaq is bigger than the NYSE. The somewhat odd name is derived from the acronym NASDAQ, which stands for National Association of Securities Dealers Automated Quotations system. But Nasdaq is now a name in its own right and the all-capitals acronym should no longer be used.

Nasdaq Operations

Introduced in 1971, the Nasdaq market is a computer network of securities dealers who disseminate timely security price quotes to Nasdaq subscribers. These dealers act as market makers for securities listed on Nasdaq. As market makers, Nasdaq dealers post bid and ask prices at which they accept sell and buy orders, respectively. With each price quote, they also post the number of stock shares that they obligate themselves to trade at their quoted prices.

Like NYSE specialists, Nasdaq market makers trade on an inventory basis, that is, using their inventory as a buffer to absorb buy and sell order imbalances. Unlike the NYSE specialist system, Nasdaq features multiple market makers for actively traded stocks. Thus, there are two key differences between the NYSE and Nasdaq:

1. Nasdaq is a computer network and has no physical location where trading takes place.

2. Nasdaq has a multiple market maker system rather than a specialist system.

over-the-counter (OTC) market
Securities market in which trading is almost exclusively done through dealers who buy and sell for their own inventories.

Traditionally, a securities market largely characterized by dealers who buy and sell securities for their own inventories is called an **over-the-counter (OTC) market**. Consequently, Nasdaq is often referred to as an OTC market. However, in their efforts to promote a distinct image, Nasdaq officials prefer that the term OTC not be used when referring to the Nasdaq market. Nevertheless, old habits die hard, and many people still refer to Nasdaq as an OTC market.

In July 1998, more than 5,983 security issues from 5,354 companies were listed on the Nasdaq system, with an average of about a dozen market makers for each security. Through the years, the Nasdaq multiple-dealer system has experienced strong growth. In the first six months of 1994, Nasdaq trading volume averaged 299 million shares per day—an amount that exceeded daily average NYSE share volume for the first time. Only three years later, in 1997, Nasdaq trading volume averaged 646 million shares per day. However, because Nasdaq predominantly handles smaller-stock transactions, its dollar volume of trading is less than NYSE dollar volume. In 1997, the dollar value of all Nasdaq securities trading was $4.5 trillion versus $5.8 trillion for the NYSE. Nevertheless, Nasdaq is a growing and formidable competitor to the NYSE.

Nasdaq is managed by the National Association of Securities Dealers (NASD). Currently, every broker or dealer in the United States that conducts a securities business with the public is required by law to be a member of the NASD. In 1997, the NASD had 534,989 registered representatives associated with 5,553 member firms operating through 60,151 branch offices around the world. To become an NASD-registered representative, you must be sponsored by an NASD member firm, pass a thorough background investigation, and pass an examination demonstrating that you have a comprehensive knowledge of the rules and regulations of NASD as well as a general knowledge of securities matters. As a registered representative, you are allowed to act as a securities broker with customers—a position that normally requires frequent access to Nasdaq.

The Nasdaq System

The Nasdaq network operates with three levels of information access. Level 1 terminals are designed to provide registered representatives with a timely, accurate source of price quotations for their clients. Bid and ask prices available on Level 1 terminals are median quotes from all registered market makers for a particular security.

Level 2 terminals connect market makers with brokers and other dealers and allow subscribers to view price quotes from all Nasdaq market makers. In particular, they have access to **inside quotes**, which are the highest bid quotes and the lowest asked quotes for a Nasdaq-listed security. Access to inside quotes is necessary to get the best prices for member firm customers. Level 3 terminals are for the use of market makers only. These terminals allow Nasdaq dealers to enter or change their price quote information.

inside quotes Highest bid quotes and the lowest ask quotes offered by dealers for a security.

The Nasdaq National Market (NNM) was introduced by NASD in 1982 as a further enhancement to an already successful Nasdaq system. When introduced, it was called the National Market System (NMS). Only the most actively traded securities are listed on the Nasdaq National Market. An important feature of the NNM is its last-trade reporting system, which allows Nasdaq subscribers to check the price and size of the last transaction for any security listed on the NNM. This last-trade information is listed in addition to dealer price quotes. In 1997, more than 4,300 Nasdaq securities were listed on the Nasdaq National Market, with an average of over 12 market makers per NNM security.

The success of the Nasdaq National Market as a competitor to NYSE and other organized exchanges can be judged by its ability to attract stock listings by companies that traditionally might have chosen to be listed on the NYSE. Such well-known companies as Microsoft, MCI Worldcom, Apple Computer, Intel, Liz Claiborne, Yahoo!, and Starbucks list their securities on Nasdaq.

5.5a How does Nasdaq differ from the NYSE?

5.5b What are the different levels of access to the Nasdaq network?

5.5c The Nasdaq website (www.nasdaq.com) provides a wealth of information about Nasdaq's activities.

NYSE and Nasdaq Competitors

third market Off-exchange market for securities listed on an organized exchange.

The NYSE and Nasdaq face strong competition in the market for order execution services from securities trading firms operating in the **third market**. The phrase "third market" refers to trading in exchange-listed securities that occurs off the exchange on which the security is listed. For example, a substantial volume of NYSE-listed stock trading is executed through independent securities trading firms.

One well-known example of third-market trading is the securities trading firm of Bernard L. Madoff Investment Securities. In 1992, Madoff Securities executed a daily average of $740 million in trading volume of NYSE-listed stocks, which then represented about 9 percent of all NYSE trading volume. Independent trading firms like Madoff Securities lure a large volume of trades away from the New York Stock Exchange by paying a small commission, say, a penny a share, to brokerage firms that direct customer orders to them for execution. This practice is called "paying for order flow" and is controversial. Nevertheless, the SEC permits it.

fourth market Market for exchange-listed securities in which investors trade directly with other investors, usually through a computer network.

Nasdaq and NYSE also face substantial competition from the **fourth market**. The term "fourth market" refers to direct trading of exchange-listed securities among investors. A good example of fourth-market trading activity is Instinet, an electronic trading network that facilitates trading among its subscribers.

Instinet subscribers are typically institutional investors and securities trading firms that wish to bypass Nasdaq and NYSE and trade directly with each other. Essentially, Instinet allows subscribers to trade securities at prices inside dealer bid-ask spreads. This means that they can buy securities at prices lower than dealer-asked prices and sell securities at prices higher than dealer-bid prices.

In recent years, Instinet has grown to account for about one-fifth of all trading in Nasdaq-listed stocks. The chief advantage of Instinet is a significant reduction in trading costs. A secondary advantage of Instinet is that it allows institutions to trade with anonymity. Nasdaq has a similar system called SelectNet. However, SelectNet has not been as popular as Instinet, largely because only Nasdaq brokers and dealers can subscribe to SelectNet, and because SelectNet does not ensure trader anonymity.

The third and fourth markets are not the only NYSE and Nasdaq competitors. Regional exchanges also attract substantial trading volume away from NYSE and Nasdaq. For example, over 2,000 stock issues are dually listed on NYSE and either on Nasdaq or at least one regional exchange.

CHECK
THIS

5.6a What is the third market
for securities?

5.6b What is the fourth market
for securities?

5.7 Stock Market Information

Many newspapers publish current price information for a selection of stocks. In the United States, the newspaper best known for reporting stock price information is *The Wall Street Journal.* Investors interested in an overview of stock market activity refer to daily summaries. Among other things, these summaries contain information regarding several stock market indexes. Immediately below, we describe the most important stock market indexes.

The Dow Jones Industrial Average

The most widely followed barometer of day-to-day stock market activity is the Dow Jones Industrial Average (DJIA), often called the "Dow" for short. The DJIA is an index of the stock prices of 30 large companies representative of American industry. There are two more specialized Dow Jones averages, a utilities average and a transportation average. We will focus on the industrial average. Figure 5.2 reproduces a chart of the DJIA from "The Dow Jones Averages" column, which is published every day in *The Wall Street Journal.*

Figure 5.2 shows daily high, low, and closing prices for the DJIA from July through December 1998. As indicated in the upper right-hand corner, the vertical bars in the chart indicate the range of index high and low values on each trading day. The tick mark on the right side of each day's bar marks the closing value of the index on that day. We therefore see that, based on closing prices, the Dow reached a high of about 9,350 in mid-July and then fell to about 7,500 in late August, for a substantial decrease. (This was a scary time to be in the market!) Later the market recovered to reach a new high in late November, followed by another dip and rise before year's end.

Although the Dow is the most familiar stock market index, there are a number of other widely followed indexes. In fact, as we begin to discuss next, the Dow is not the most representative index by any means, and the way it is computed presents various problems that can make it difficult to interpret.

Stock Market Indexes

The "Dow Jones Averages" column is informative, but a serious market watcher may be interested in more detail regarding recent stock market activity. A more comprehensive view of stock market trading is contained in the "Stock Market Data Bank." Figure 5.3 is an excerpt from a "Stock Market Data Bank" column, which is published daily in *The Wall Street Journal.*

The excerpt we examine here, "Major Indexes," reports information about a variety of stock market indexes. The first two columns report high and low index values observed during the previous 365 days. The third column lists the names of all reported indexes. Columns four through six report the daily high, low, and close for each index.

Figure 5.2

Dow Jones
Industrials
Average

Source: *The Wall Street Journal,* October 1998. Reprinted by permission of Dow Jones & Company, Inc. via Copyright Clearance Center, Inc. © 1998 Dow Jones & Company, Inc. All Rights Reserved Worldwide.

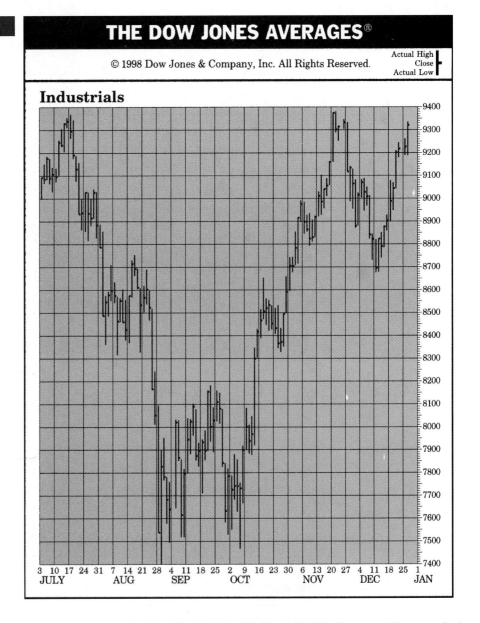

THE DOW JONES AVERAGES®

Columns seven and eight, labeled "Net Chg" and "% Chg," report daily numerical and percentage changes for each index. The next two columns, labeled "12-Mo Chg" and "% Chg," list numerical and percentage changes for each index over the previous 365 days. The last two columns, labeled "From 12/31" and "% Chg," list numerical and percentage changes for each index since the end of the last calendar year.

As shown in Figure 5.3, in addition to the Dow Jones averages, the Stock Market Data Bank also reports information for a number of other stock market indexes. Of the non–Dow Jones indexes shown, by far the best known and most widely followed is the Standard & Poor's Index of 500 stocks, commonly abbreviated as the S&P 500, or often just the S&P. We have seen this index before. In Chapter 1, we used it as a benchmark to track the performance of large common stocks for the last seven decades.

Figure 5.3

Stock Market Major Indexes

Source: *The Wall Street Journal,* October 13, 1998. Reprinted by permission of Dow Jones & Company, Inc. via copyright Clearance Center, Inc. © 1998 Dow Jones & Company, Inc. All Rights Reserved Worldwide.

STOCK MARKET DATA BANK — 10/13/98

MAJOR INDEXES

†12-MO HIGH	†12-MO LOW		DAILY HIGH	DAILY LOW	CLOSE	NET CHG	% CHG	†12-MO CHG	% CHG	FROM 12/31	% CHG
DOW JONES AVERAGES											
9337.97	7161.15	30 Industrials	8009.97	7884.59	7938.14	−63.33	− 0.79	−158.15	− 1.95	+ 29.89	+ 0.38
3686.02	2345.00	20 Transportation	2469.31	2417.22	2420.60	−48.23	− 1.95	−897.09	−27.04	−835.90	−25.67
320.51	237.44	15 Utilities	305.59	300.32	x305.56	+ 5.04	+ 1.68	+ 63.46	+26.21	+ 32.49	+11.90
2960.79	2358.51	65 Composite	2501.16	2464.88	x2480.61	−13.51	− 0.54	−125.24	− 4.81	−126.76	− 4.86
1123.85	833.91	DJ Global—US	940.54	927.92	934.42	− 4.19	− 0.45	+ 15.42	+ 1.68	+ 12.08	+ 1.31
NEW YORK STOCK EXCHANGE											
600.75	463.21	Composite	494.53	488.90	492.14	− 0.81	− 0.16	− 16.43	− 3.23	− 19.05	− 3.73
736.35	576.81	Industrials	617.60	609.16	612.92	− 3.38	− 0.55	− 24.10	− 3.78	− 17.46	− 2.77
398.77	288.27	Utilities	381.29	375.56	381.26	+ 5.70	+ 1.52	+ 74.67	+24.36	+ 46.07	+13.74
537.19	351.13	Transportation	375.78	364.23	366.33	− 8.78	− 2.34	−108.32	−22.82	− 99.92	−21.43
599.15	399.19	Finance	431.70	423.70	427.21	+ 1.82	+ 0.43	− 59.51	−12.23	− 68.75	−13.86
STANDARD & POOR'S INDEXES											
1186.75	876.99	500 Index	1000.78	987.55	994.80	− 2.91	− 0.29	+ 24.52	+ 2.53	+ 24.37	+ 2.51
1380.57	1019.09	Industrials	1198.15	1180.71	1189.70	− 6.97	− 0 58	+ 57.72	+ 5.10	+ 68.32	+ 6.09
267.38	202.07	Utilities	254.36	249.83	254.36	+ 4.53	+ 1.81	+ 47.01	+22.67	+ 18.55	+ 7.87
380.67	275.93	400 MidCap	290.51	286.18	287.14	− 3.37	− 1.16	− 51.56	−15.22	− 46.23	−13.87
206.18	128.70	600 SmallCap	135.36	133.51	133.61	− 1.75	− 1.29	− 58.47	−30.44	− 47.55	−26.25
251.95	189.63	1500 Index	209.56	206.84	208.24	− 0.82	− 0.39	− 1.38	− 0.66	− 0.56	− 0.27
NASDAQ STOCK MARKET											
2014.25	1419.12	Composite	1547.05	1504.70	1509.45	−36.63	− 2.37	−223.34	−12.89	− 60.90	− 3.88
1465.89	938.99	Nasdaq 100	1244.84	1198.55	1206.90	− 6.50	− 2.94	+ 75.47	+ 6.67	+216.10	+21.81
1408.56	882.40	Industrials	941.06	927.34	927.53	−14.84	− 1.57	−475.58	−33.89	−293.50	−24.04
1945.34	1346.58	Insurance	1425.11	1410.70	1414.23	− 8.68	− 0.61	−426.16	−23.16	−383.72	−21.34
2297.71	1486.32	Banks	1614.95	1590.36	1592.97	−16.08	− 1.00	−358.48	−18.37	−490.25	−23.53
921.60	584.92	Computer	759.87	732.40	738.27	−24.86	− 3.26	+ 17.62	+ 2.45	+119.61	+19.33
460.92	279.66	Telecommunications	339.72	332.50	332.50	− 7.71	− 2.27	+ 24.92	+ 8.10	+ 25.90	+ 8.45
OTHERS											
753.67	563.75	Amex Composite	581.61	576.70	577.86	− 3.15	− 0.54	−136.93	−19.16	−106.75	−15.59
620.15	465.43	Russell 1000	516.40	509.88	513.40	− 1.91	− 0.37	+ 0.26	+ 0.05	− 0.39	− 0.08
491.41	310.28	Russell 2000	325.69	320.33	320.33	− 5.29	− 1.62	−143.64	−30.96	−116.69	−26.70
647.54	494.91	Russell 3000	531.92	525.16	528.49	− 2.46	− 0.46	− 17.25	− 3.16	− 14.56	− 2.68
508.39	346.66	Value—Line (geom.)	360.56	356.20	357.32	− 3.24	− 0.90	−118.10	−24.84	− 97.03	−21.36
11106.10	8537.05	Wilshire 5000	...	...	8960.41	−52.94	− 0 59	−442.81	− 4.71	−337.78	− 3.63

† Based on comparable trading day In preceding year.

If you were to scrutinize the various indexes in Figure 5.3, you would quickly find that there are essentially four differences between them: (1) the market covered; (2) the types of stocks included; (3) how many stocks are included; and (4) how the index is calculated.

The first three of these differences are straightforward. Some indexes listed in Figure 5.3, such as the Dow Jones Utilities, focus on specific industries. Others, such as the Nasdaq Composite, focus on particular markets. Some have a small number of stocks; others, such as the Wilshire 5000, have a huge number (5,000 in this case).

price-weighted index
Stock market index in which stocks are held in proportion to their share price.

How stock market indexes are computed is not quite so straightforward, but it is important to understand. There are two major types of stock market index: price-weighted and value-weighted. With a **price-weighted index**, stocks are held in the index in proportion to their share prices. With a **value-weighted index**, stocks are held in proportion to their total company market values.

value-weighted index
Stock market index in which stocks are held in proportion to their total company market value.

The best way to understand the difference between price and value weighting is to consider an example. To keep things relatively simple, we suppose that there are only two companies in the entire market. We have the following information about their shares outstanding, share prices, and total market values:

	Shares Outstanding	Price per Share		Total Market Value	
		Beginning of Year	End of Year	Beginning of Year	End of Year
Company A	50 million	$10	$14	$500 million	$700 million
Company B	1 million	$50	$40	$ 50 million	$ 40 million

As shown, Company A has a lower share price but many more shares outstanding. Ignoring dividends, notice that Company A's stock price rose by 40 percent ($10 to $14) while Company B's stock price fell by 20 percent ($50 to $40).

The question we want to answer here is simply: How did the market do for the year? There are several ways we could answer this question. We could first focus on what happened to the average share price. The average share price was ($10 + $50)/2 = $30 at the beginning of the year, and ($14 + $40)/2 = $27 at the end, so the average share price fell. If we take the average share price as our index, then our index fell from 30 to 27, for a change of −3 points. Since the index began at 30, this is a −3/30 = −10% decrease. We might therefore say that the market was "off" by 10 percent.

This is an example of a price-weighted index. Because Company B's stock price is five times bigger than Company A's, it carries five times as much weight in the index. This explains why the index was down even though Company A's stock gained 40 percent whereas Company B's stock only lost 20 percent. The Dow Jones indexes are priced weighted.

Alternatively, instead of focusing on the price of a typical share, we could look at what happened to the total value of a typical company. Here we notice that the average total value, in millions, rose from ($500 + $50)/2 = $275 to ($700 + $40)/2 = $370. If we take average total company value as our index, then our index rose from 275 to 370, a 35 percent *increase.*

This is an example of a value-weighted index. The influence a company has in this case depends on its overall change in total market value, not just its stock price change. Because Company A has a much larger total value, it carries a much larger weight in the index. With the exception of the Dow Jones indexes, most of the other indexes in Figure 5.3, including the Standard & Poor's, are value weighted.

Now we have a problem. One index tells us the market was down by 10 percent, while the other tells us it was up by 35 percent. Which one is correct? The answer seems fairly obvious. The total value of the market as a whole grew from $550 million to $740 million, so the market as a whole increased in value. Put differently, investors as a whole owned stock worth $550 million at the beginning of the year and $740 million at the end of the year. So, on the whole, stock market investors earned 35 percent, even though the average share price went down.

This example shows that a price-weighted index is often misleading as an indicator of total market value. The basic flaw in a price-weighted index is that the effect a company has on the index depends on the price of a single share. However, the price of a single share is only part of the story. Unless the number of shares is also considered, the time impact on the overall market isn't known, and a distorted picture can emerge.

Example 5.1   Caution: Indexes under Construction

Suppose there are only two stocks in the market and the following information is given:

	Shares Outstanding	Price per Share Beginning of Year	Price per Share End of Year
Quark Co.	10 million	$10	$11
Bashir, Inc.	20 million	$20	$25

Construct price- and value-weighted indexes and calculate the percentage changes in each.

The average share price rose from $15 to $18, or $3, so the price-weighted index would be up by 3/15 = 20 percent. Average total market value, in millions, rose from $250 to $305, so the value-weighted index rose by 55/250 = 22 percent.

More on Price-Weighted Indexes

Earlier we indicated that the Dow Jones averages are price weighted. Given this, you may wonder why the Dow Jones Industrial Average has such a high value when the stock prices used to calculate the average are much smaller. To answer this question, we must explain one last detail about price-weighted indexes.

The extra detail concerns the effects of stock splits on price-weighted indexes. For example, in a 2-for-1 stock split, all current shareholders receive two new shares in exchange for each old share that they own. However, the total value of the company does not change because it is still the same company after the stock split. There are just twice as many shares, each worth half as much.

A stock split has no effect on a value-weighted index since the total value of the company does not change. But it can have a dramatic effect on a price-weighted index. To see this, consider what happens to the price-weighted and value-weighted indexes we created above when Company B enacts a 2-for-1 stock split. Based on beginning prices, with a 2-for-1 split, Company B's shares fall to $25. The price-weighted index falls to (10 + 25)/2 = 17.50 from 30, even though nothing really happened.

For a price-weighted index, the problem of stock splits can be addressed by adjusting the divisor each time a split occurs. Once again, an example is the best way to illustrate. In the case stated just above, suppose we wanted the index value to stay at 30 even though B's price per share fell to $25 as a result of the split. The only way to accomplish this is to add together the new stock prices and divide by something less than 2.

This new number is called the *index divisor,* and it is adjusted as needed to remove the effect of stock splits. To find the new divisor in our case, the stock prices are $25 and $10, and we want the index to equal 30. We solve for the new divisor, d, as follows:

$$\text{Index level} = \frac{\text{Sum of stock prices}}{\text{Divisor}}$$

$$30 = \frac{25 + 10}{d}$$

$$d = \frac{35}{30} = 1.16666......$$

The new divisor is thus approximately 1.17.

Adjusting the divisor takes care of the problem in one sense, but it creates another problem. Since we are no longer dividing the sum of the share prices by the number of companies in the index, we can no longer interpret the change in the index as the change in price of an average share.

Example 5.2   Adjusting the Divisor

Take a look back at Example 5.1. Suppose that Bashir splits 5-for-1. Based on beginning information, what is the new divisor?

Following a 5-for-1 split, Bashir's share price will fall from $20 to $4. With no adjustment to the divisor, the price-weighted index would drop from 15 to $(10 + 4)/2 = 7$. To keep the index at its old level of 15, we need to solve for a new divisor such that $(10 + 4)/d = 15$. In this case, the new divisor would be $14/15 = .93333 \ldots$, illustrating that the divisor can drop below 1.0.

The Dow Jones Divisors

The method we described of adjusting the divisor on a price-weighted index for stock splits is the method used to adjust the Dow Jones averages. Through time, with repeated adjustments for stock splits, the divisor becomes smaller and smaller. For example, in October 1998 the divisor on the DJIA was a nice, precise .24275214. Since there are 30 stocks in the index, the divisor on the DJIA would be 30 if it were never adjusted, so it has declined substantially. The other Dow Jones averages have similarly odd values.

Figure 5.4 is an example of the "Dow Jones Averages Hour by Hour" table appearing in *The Wall Street Journal*. This table reports hourly changes in the Dow Jones averages during the five most recent trading days. It also reports current divisors for the Dow Jones averages—Industrials, Transportation, Utilities, and Composite. In Figure 5.4, the actual high (and low) values are exactly what the name suggests—the highest (and lowest) values observed. The theoretical high (low) is computed using the highest (lowest) stock prices reached during the day for each of the stocks in the index. If all stocks in an index reached their highest (lowest) prices at the same time, the actual and theoretical index values would be the same.

Given its shortcomings, you might wonder why the financial press continues to report the Dow Jones averages. The reason is tradition; the Dow Jones averages have been around for more than 100 years, and each new generation of investors becomes accustomed to its quirks.

index staleness
Condition that occurs when an index does not reflect all current price information because some of the stocks in the index have not traded recently.

So which index is the best? The most popular alternative to the DJIA is the value-weighted S&P 500. You might further wonder, however, why this popular index limits itself to 500 stocks. The answer is timeliness and accuracy. Almost all stocks in the S&P 500 index trade every day, and therefore accurate daily updates of market prices are available each day. Stocks that do not trade every day can cause **index staleness**. Index staleness occurs when an index does not reflect all current price information because some of the stocks in the index have not traded recently. Also, as a practical matter, the largest 500 companies account for an overwhelming portion of the value of the overall stock market.

Figure 5.4

Hourly Dow
Jones Averages

Source: *The Wall Street
Journal,* © 1998 Dow Jones
& Company, Inc. All Rights
Reserved Worldwide.

The Dow Jones Averages Hour by Hour

Following are the Dow Jones averages of INDUSTRIAL, TRANSPORTATION and UTILITY stocks.

DATE	OPEN	10 AM	11 AM	12 NOON	1 PM	2 PM	3 PM	CLOSE	CHG	%	HIGH*	LOW*	HIGH*	LOW*
											(THEORETICAL)		(ACTUAL)	
30 INDUSTRIALS: (divisor: 0.24275214)														
Oct 13	8002.50	7996.58	7981.91	7970.32	7972.90	7937.62	7905.18	7938.14	− 63.33	− 0.79	8093.90	7805.29	8009.97	7884.59
Oct 12	7900.55	8015.63	8056.57	8074.85	8040.87	8013.32	8042.67	8001.47	+101.95	+ 1.29	8162.65	7931.19	8084.64 a7900.55
Oct 9	7734.74	7774.39	7670.38	7746.84	7809.66	7819.19	7884.84	7899.52	+167.61	+ 2.17	7976.76	7628.15	7917.28	7666.51
Oct 8	7734.48	7629.18	7621.46	7492.98	7530.06	7500.96	7647.98	7731.91	− 9.78	− 0.13	7822.02	7399.78	7756.37	7467.49
Oct 7	7745.18	7782.63	7791.13	7749.93	7782.89	7766.92	7683.25	7741.69	− 1.29	− 0.02	7913.94	7558.89	7858.32	7629.18
20 TRANSPORTATION COS.: (divisor: 0.25918163)														
											(THEORETICAL)		(ACTUAL)	
Oct 13	2466.42	2447.85	2446.40	2451.23	2447.37	2441.58	2420.12	2420.60	− 48.23	− 1.95	2493.18	2385.15	2469.31	2417.22
Oct 12	2430.73	2481.37	2488.36	2484.86	2483.06	2465.81	2463.89	2468.83	+ 39.31	+ 1.62	2530.56	2429.28	2502.11	2430.73
Oct 9	2348.14	2380.33	2345.12	2361.76	2397.57	2405.65	2415.29	2429.52	+ 84.52	+ 3.60	2469.55	2319.80	2436.03	2344.04
Oct 8	2447.85	2330.89	2338.25	2286.04	2293.52	2298.10	2336.68	2345.00	−102.85	− 4.20	2395.04	2260.24 a2447.85	2282.18
Oct 7	2533.46	2519.23	2519.59	2491.01	2493.79	2488.84	2459.18	2447.85	− 85.61	− 3.18	2555.40	2410.95	2536.59	2433.74
15 UTILITIES: (divisor: 2.0859524)														
											(THEORETICAL)		(ACTUAL)	
Oct 13	300.38	304.21	302.98	302.32	302.20	302.89	302.62	305.56	+ 5.04	+ 1.68	307.83	299.44	305.59	300.32
Oct 12	311.64	306.54	302.95	303.19	301.57	300.76	300.85	300.52	− 10.94	− 3.51	311.37	298.04 a311.79	299.92
Oct 9	320.51	316.97	313.11	312.36	311.76	311.34	311.10	311.46	− 9.05	− 2.82	320.45	308.25	320.57	310.59
Oct 8	319.25	316.40	318.71	315.83	318.56	317.75	318.65	320.51	+ 1.38	+ 0.43	322.60	312.93	320.51	315.74
Oct 7	317.48	321.53	319.07	318.14	318.98	317.21	317.06	319.13	+ 1.65	+ 0.52	323.65	313.86	322.21	315.23
65 STOCKS COMPOSITE AVERAGE: (divisor: 1.2866769)														
											(THEORETICAL)		(ACTUAL)	
Oct 13	2493.26	2494.85	2489.94	2487.61	2487.12	2480.71	2469.54	2480.61	− 13.51	− 0.54	2528.32	2438.50	2501.16	2464.88
Oct 12	2484.94	2508.93	2512.29	2515.42	2506.07	2496.23	2501.43	2494.12	+ 9.42	+ 0.38	2554.55	2468.86	2519.33	2484.94
Oct 9	2451.35	2460.02	2426.89	2443.94	2461.79	2464.49	2478.57	2484.70	+ 33.98	+ 1.39	2521.90	2406.20	2488.48	2426.16
Oct 8	2471.05	2421.26	2425.70	2386.14	2399.16	2393.28	2430.29	2450.72	− 20.33	− 0.82	2481.20	2358.69	2471.05	2383.76
Oct 7	2485.65	2497.13	2494.68	2479.89	2487.68	2480.91	2459.10	2471.05	− 14.81	− 0.60	2532.54	2420.58	2512.92	2443.87

*a–Actual high or low exceeds theoretical value due to computational method. q–Actual. r–Revised.

CHECK THIS

5.7a What is the difference between price- and value-weighting in the construction of stock market indexes? Give an example of a well-known index of each type.

5.7b Which is better, price- or value-weighting? Why?

5.7c Which stock market index is likely to contain the greater degree of index staleness, the S&P 500 or the Wilshire 5000 index?

5.8 Summary and Conclusions

This chapter introduced you to stock markets. We discussed who owns stocks, how the stock exchanges operate, and how stock market indexes are constructed and interpreted. Along the way we saw that:

1. Individual investors, directly or through mutual funds, own over half of all traded stocks. The rest are owned mostly by financial institutions such as pension funds and insurance companies.

2. The stock market is composed of a primary market, where stock shares are first sold, and a secondary market, where investors trade shares among themselves. In the primary market, companies raise money for investment projects.

Investment bankers specialize in arranging financing for companies in the primary market. Investment bankers often act as underwriters, buying newly issued stock from the company and then reselling the stock to the public. The primary market is best known as the market for initial public offerings (IPOs).

3. In the secondary market, investors trade securities with other investors. Secondary market transactions are directed through three channels: directly with other investors, indirectly through a broker, or directly with a dealer. We saw that a broker matches buyers and sellers; a dealer buys and sells out of inventory.

4. Most common stock trading is directed through an organized stock exchange or through a trading network. The largest organized stock exchange in the United States is the New York Stock Exchange (NYSE). Popularly known as the Big Board, NYSE is owned by its members. There are four major types of NYSE members: commission brokers, specialists, floor brokers, and floor traders. We discussed the role of each in the functioning of the exchange.

5. The second largest stock market in the United States is Nasdaq. Nasdaq is a computer network of securities dealers, who act as market makers for securities listed on Nasdaq.

6. The NYSE and Nasdaq face strong competition from securities trading firms operating in the third and fourth markets. The third market refers to off-exchange trading of exchange-listed securities by securities firms. The fourth market refers to direct trading among investors. The regional stock exchanges also attract substantial trading volume away from NYSE and Nasdaq.

7. The most widely followed barometer of day-to-day stock market activity is the Dow Jones Industrial Average (DJIA). The DJIA is an index of the stock prices of 30 large companies representative of American industry. Other indexes are also common. Among these, the best known is the Standard & Poor's Index of 500 stocks, abbreviated as the S&P 500. We described how these indexes are computed, with particular attention to some of the problems encountered.

GET REAL

This chapter covered the operations and organization of the major stock markets. It also covered some of the most important order types and the construction of stock market indexes. How should you, as an investor or investment manager, put this information to work?

First, as in some previous chapters, you need to submit as many as possible of the different order types suggested by this chapter in a simulated brokerage account (note that not all simulated brokerage accounts allow all trade types). Your goal is to gain experience with the different order types and what they mean and accomplish for you as an investor or investment manager.

In each case, once you have placed the order, be sure to monitor the price of the stock in question to see if any of your orders should be executed. When an order is executed, compare the result to the stop or limit price to see how you did.

The second thing to do is to start observing the different indexes and learning how they are computed, what's in them, and what they are intended to cover. For example, the Nasdaq 100 is made up of the largest Nasdaq stocks. Is this index broadly representative of big stocks in general? Of Nasdaq stocks in general? Why is the Russell 2000 index widely followed (note that it *doesn't* contain 2,000 big stocks)?

Key Terms

primary market 115
secondary market 115
initial public offering (IPO) 115
investment banking firm 115
underwrite 115
fixed commitment 116
best effort 116
Securities and Exchange Commission (SEC) 116
prospectus 116
red herring 116
dealer 119
broker 119
bid price 119
ask price 119
spread 119
NYSE member 120
commission broker 121

specialist 121
floor brokers 121
SuperDOT system 122
floor traders 122
specialist's post 123
market order 124
limit order 125
stop order 125
NYSE uptick rule 126
over-the-counter (OTC) market 127
inside quotes 128
third market 129
fourth market 129
price-weighted index 132
value-weighted index 132
index staleness 135

Chapter Review Problems and Self-Test

1. **Index Construction**   Suppose there are only two stocks in the market and the following information is given:

	Shares Outstanding	Price per Share	
		Beginning of Year	**End of Year**
Ally Co.	100 million	$ 60	$ 66
McBeal, Inc.	400 million	$120	$100

Construct price- and value-weighted indexes and calculate the percentage changes in each.

2. **Stock Splits**   In the previous problem, suppose that McBeal splits 3-for-1. Based on beginning information, what is the new divisor?

Answers to Self-Test Problems

1. The average share price at the beginning of the year is ($60 + $120)/2 = $90. At the end of the year, the average price is $83. Thus, the average price declined by $7 from $90, a percentage drop of −$7/$90 = −7.78%. Total market cap at the beginning of the year is $60 × 100 million + $120 × 400 million = $54 billion. It falls to $46.6 billion, a decline of $7.4 billion. The percentage decline is −$7.4 billion/$54 billion = −13.7%, or almost twice as much as the price-weighted index.

2. Following a 3-for-1 split, McBeal's share price falls from $120 to $40. To keep the price-weighted index at its old level of 90, we need a new divisor such that $(60 + 40)/d = 90$. In this case, the new divisor would be $100/90 = 1.1111$.

Test Your Investment Quotient

1. **Securities Regulation**   Which of the following is not a function of the SEC in approving an IPO of a company's common stock shares?

   a. Ensuring that the company is high quality and the stock offering price is fair.
   b. Ensuring full disclosure of the company's financial position.
   c. Ensuring that a prospectus is made available to all interested investors.
   d. Ensuring that the offering does not violate federal securities laws.

2. **New York Stock Exchange**   The largest number of NYSE members are registered as:

   a. Stockholders
   b. Commission brokers
   c. Specialists
   d. Floor traders

3. **New York Stock Exchange**   The second largest number of NYSE members are registered as:

   a. Stockholders
   b. Commission brokers
   c. Specialists
   d. Floor traders

4. **New York Stock Exchange**   Specialists on the NYSE typically are:

   a. Independent dealers.
   b. Representatives of the major stock brokerage firms.
   c. Appointed by the SEC.
   d. Associated with one of about 40 specialist firms.

5. **New York Stock Exchange**   Which of the following activities are *not* conducted by specialists on the NYSE? (*1991 CFA exam*)

   a. Acting as dealers for their own accounts.
   b. Monitoring compliance with margin requirements.
   c. Providing liquidity to the market.
   d. Monitoring and executing unfilled limit orders.

6. **Stock Markets**   Which of the following is a common feature of both the Nasdaq National Market and the New York Stock Exchange?

   a. The New York City location for operations.
   b. The reliance on commission brokers for efficient order execution.
   c. The use of dealers to ensure liquidity.
   d. The number of market makers per individual stock issue.

7. **Stock Markets**   What is a securities market characterized by dealers who buy and sell securities for their own inventories traditionally called? (*1991 CFA exam*)

   a. A primary market.
   b. A secondary market.
   c. An over-the-counter market.
   d. An institutional market.

8. **Stock Markets**   What is the over-the-counter market for exchange-listed securities called? (*1991 CFA exam*)

   a. Third market
   b. Fourth market
   c. After-market
   d. Block market

9. **Stock Trading**   An institutional investor wishing to sell a very large block of stock, say, 10,000 shares or more, is most likely to get the best price in which market?

   a. The primary market
   b. The secondary market
   c. The third market
   d. The fourth market

10. **Stock Trading**   You wish to sell short shares of GM common stock traded on the NYSE. If the last two transactions were at $43\frac{1}{8}$ followed by $43\frac{1}{4}$, the next transaction can be a short sale only at a price of:

   a. $43\frac{1}{8}$ or higher

   b. $43\frac{1}{4}$ or higher

   c. $43\frac{1}{4}$ or lower

   d. $43\frac{1}{8}$ or lower

11. **Stock Indexes**   Which one of the following statements regarding the Dow Jones Industrial Average is false?

   a. The DJIA contains 30 well-known large-company stocks.
   b. The DJIA is affected equally by dollar changes in low- and high-priced stocks.
   c. The DJIA is affected equally by percentage changes in low- and high-priced stocks.
   d. The DJIA divisor must be adjusted for stock splits.

12. **Stock Indexes**   If the market prices of each of the 30 stocks in the Dow Jones Industrial Average all change by the same percentage amount during a given day, which stock will have the greatest impact on the DJIA? (*1991 CFA exam*)

   a. The one whose stock trades at the highest dollar price per share.
   b. The one whose total equity has the highest market value.
   c. The one having the greatest amount of equity in its capital structure.
   d. The one having the lowest volatility.

13. **Stock Indexes**   In calculating the Standard & Poor's stock price indexes, how are adjustments for stock splits made? (*1990 CFA exam*)

   a. By adjusting the divisor.
   b. Automatically, due to the manner in which the index is calculated.
   c. By adjusting the numerator.
   d. Quarterly, on the last trading day of each quarter.

14. **Stock Indexes**   Which of the following indexes includes the largest number of actively traded stocks? (*1990 CFA exam*)

   a. The Nasdaq Composite Index.
   b. The NYSE Composite Index.
   c. The Wilshire 5000 Index.
   d. The Value Line Composite Index

Questions and Problems

Core Questions

1. **Primary and Secondary Markets**   If you were to visit your local Chevrolet retailer, there is both a primary and a secondary market in action. Explain. Is the Chevy retailer a dealer or a broker?

2. **Specialists**   On the NYSE, does a specialist act as a dealer or a broker? Or both?

3. **Stops and Limits**   If an investor wants to buy a stock at a price that is less than its current price, what are the relative advantages and disadvantage of a stop order as compared to a limit order?

4. **Stop That!**   What is a stop-loss order? Why might it be used? Is it sure to stop a loss?

5. **Order Types**   Suppose Microsoft is currently trading at $100. You want to buy it if it reaches $120. What type of order should you submit?

6. **Order Types**　Suppose Dell is currently trading at $65. You think that if it reaches $70, it will continue to climb, so you want to buy it if and when it gets there. Should you submit a limit order to buy at $70?

7. **Stop-Limit Orders**　What is a stop-limit order? How many prices do you have to specify?

8. **Upticks**　What is the uptick rule? Where does it apply? Why does it exist?

9. **Nasdaq Quotes**　With regard to the Nasdaq, what are inside quotes?

10. **Index Composition**　There are basically four factors that differentiate stock market indexes. What are they? Comment on each.

11. **Index Composition**　Is it necessarily true that, all else the same, an index with more stocks is better? What is the issue here?

**Intermediate
Questions**

12. **Index Construction**　Suppose there are only two stocks in the market and the following information is given:

	Shares Outstanding	Price per Share	
		Beginning of Year	End of Year
Black Co.	200 million	$30	$ 39
Scholes, Inc.	50 million	$80	$140

Construct price- and value-weighted indexes and calculate the percentage changes in each.

13. **Price-Weighted Indexes**　We have seen that the Dow indexes are adjusted for stock splits by changing the divisor. Why is this necessary? Can you think of another way to adjust for splits?

14. **Price-Weighted Indexes**　Suppose the following three defense stocks are to be combined into a stock index in January 1998 (perhaps a portfolio manager believes these stocks are an appropriate benchmark for his or her performance):

	Shares (millions)	Price		
		1/1/98	1/1/99	1/1/00
Douglas McDonnell	150	$60	$75	$60
Dynamics General	750	20	25	40
International Rockwell	300	40	35	35

a. Calculate the initial value of the index if a price-weighting scheme is used.
b. What is the rate of return on this index for the year ending December 31, 1998? For the year ending December 31, 1999?
c. What is the total return on this index over the two-year period 1998 and 1999?

15. **Price-Weighted Indexes**　In the previous problem, suppose that Douglas McDonnell shareholders approve a 5-for-1 stock split on January 1, 1999. What is the new divisor for the index? Calculate the rate of return on the index for the year ending December 31, 1999, if Douglas McDonnell's share price on January 1, 2000, is $12 per share. What is the total two-year return on the index now?

16. **Equally Weighted Indexes**　In addition to price-weighted and value-weighted indexes, an equally weighted index is one in which the index value is computed from the average rate of return of the stocks comprising the index. Equally weighted indexes are frequently used by financial researchers to measure portfolio performance.

a. Using the information in problem 14, compute the rate of return on an equally weighted index of the three defense stocks for the year ending December 31, 1998.
b. If the index value is set to 100 on January 1, 1998, what will the index value be on January 1, 2000? What is the rate of return on the index for 1999?
c. Compute the total two-year return on this index.

17. **Value-Weighted Indexes**   Repeat problem 14 if a value-weighted index is used. Assume the index is scaled by a factor of 10 million; that is, if the average firm's market value is $5 billion, the index would be quoted as 500.

18. **Value-Weighted Indexes**   In the previous problem, will your answers change if Douglas McDonnell stock splits? Why or why not?

19. **Interpreting Index Values**   Suppose you want to replicate the performance of several stock indexes, some of which are price weighted, others value weighted, and still others equally weighted. Describe the investment strategy you need for each of the index types. Are any of the three strategies passive, in that no portfolio rebalancing need be performed to perfectly replicate the index (assuming no stock splits or cash distributions)? Which of the three strategies do you think is most often followed by small investors? Which strategy is the most difficult to implement?

STOCK-TRAK·
Portfolio Simulations

Stock Market Day Trading with Stock-Trak

The Internet has given rise to a new breed of stock market investors—day traders. Day traders buy and sell common stocks within a day and typically close out their positions before the end of the day to avoid carrying a stock position overnight. The most popular trading strategy among day traders is "momentum trading," whereby the day trader tries to identify stocks that have started moving up and will continue to move up through the day. Once such a stock is identified, the day trader buys the stock and tracks its progress through the day. Some time later—perhaps a few minutes, perhaps a few hours—the day trader sells the stock to close out the position before the end of trading that day.

How do you identify stocks with sustainable momentum? Day traders often use sophisticated computer programs to assist their decision processes, but they must ultimately depend on instincts. While most day traders have a difficult time recouping their trading expenses, there are often spectacular successes to inspire the would-be trader. The beauty of a Stock-Trak account is that you can try your hand at day trading without risking your own capital.

To try your hand at day trading using your Stock-Trak account, simultaneously log on to an Internet stock quote server and the Stock-Trak website in the morning, ideally about an hour or two after NYSE trading has started. Note that web browsers support several different sessions at one time and many stock quote servers also provide stock price charts. Next, identify several stocks that are up since the opening of trading that day. Most stock quote servers report intraday stock price statistics, including high and low prices along with an opening price and change in price. Pick two or three stocks and submit an order to Stock-Trak to buy these stocks. Stock-Trak will return a trade confirmation indicating the trade prices for your order. Print the trade confirmation so you don't forget your trade prices. Later in the day, log on to Stock-Trak to close out your position and calculate your profits and losses. Remember, a real day trader will not hold a position overnight. It's easier to sleep that way.

Stock-Trak Exercise

1. If it's a rainy day and you're bored, log on to Stock-Trak and a stock quote server and stay logged on for several hours. Indulge yourself with frequent buying and selling based on your instincts. Try to set a pace of executing at least five or six trades an hour. Be careful—day trading can be addictive and you might forget to go to your investments class.

6

Common Stock Valuation

A fundamental assertion of finance holds that a security's value is based on the present value of its future cash flows. Accordingly, common stock valuation attempts the difficult task of predicting the future. Consider that the average dividend yield for large-company stocks is about 2 percent. This implies that the present value of dividends to be paid over the next 10 years constitutes only a fraction of the stock price. Thus, most of the value of a typical stock is derived from dividends to be paid more than 10 years away! ■ As a stock market investor, not only must you decide which stocks to buy and which stocks to sell, but you must also decide when to buy them and when to sell them. In the words of a well-known Kenny Rogers song, "You gotta know when to hold 'em, and know when to fold 'em." This task requires a careful appraisal of intrinsic economic value. In this chapter, we examine several methods commonly used by financial analysts to assess the economic value of common stocks. These methods are grouped into two categories: dividend discount models and price ratio models. After studying these models, we provide an analysis of a real company to illustrate the use of the methods discussed in this chapter.

6.1 Security Analysis: Be Careful Out There

It may seem odd that we start our discussion with an admonition to be careful, but in this case, we think it is a good idea. The methods we discuss in this chapter are examples of those used by many investors and security analysts to assist in making buy and sell decisions for individual stocks. The basic idea is to identify both "undervalued" or "cheap" stocks to buy and "overvalued" or "rich" stocks to sell. In practice, however, many stocks that look cheap may in fact be correctly priced for reasons not immediately apparent to the analyst. Indeed, the hallmark of a good analyst is a cautious attitude and a willingness to probe further and deeper before committing to a final investment recommendation.

fundamental analysis Examination of a firm's accounting statements and other financial and economic information to assess the economic value of a company's stock.

The type of security analysis we describe in this chapter falls under the heading of **fundamental analysis**. Numbers such as a company's earnings per share, cash flow, book equity value, and sales are often called *fundamentals* because they describe, on a basic level, a specific firm's operations and profits (or lack of profits).

Fundamental analysis represents the examination of these and other accounting statement–based company data used to assess the value of a company's stock. Information regarding such things as management quality, products, and product markets is often examined as well.

Our cautionary note is based on the skepticism these techniques should engender, at least when applied simplistically. As our later chapter on market efficiency explains, there is good reason to believe that too-simple techniques that rely on widely available information are not likely to yield systematically superior investment results. In fact, they could lead to unnecessarily risky investment decisions. This is especially true for ordinary investors (like most of us) who do not have timely access to the information that a professional security analyst working for a major securities firm would possess.

As a result, our goal here is not to teach you how to "pick" stocks with a promise that you will become rich. Certainly, one chapter in an investments text is not likely to be sufficient to acquire that level of investment savvy. Instead, an appreciation of the techniques in this chapter is important simply because buy and sell recommendations made by securities firms are frequently couched in the terms we introduce here. Much of the discussion of individual companies in the financial press relies on these concepts as well, so some background is necessary just to interpret much commonly presented investment information. In essence, you must learn both the lingo and the concepts of security analysis.

CHECK THIS

6.1a What is fundamental analysis?

6.1b What is a "rich" stock? What is a "cheap" stock?

The Dividend Discount Model

A fundamental principle of finance holds that the economic value of a security is properly measured by the sum of its future cash flows, where the cash flows are adjusted for risk and the time value of money. For example, suppose a risky security will pay either $100 or $200 with equal probability one year from today. The expected future payoff is $150 = ($100 + $200) / 2, and the security's value today is the $150 expected future value discounted for a one-year waiting period.

If the appropriate discount rate for this security is, say, 5 percent, then the present value of the expected future cash flow is $150 / 1.05 = $142.86. If instead the appropriate discount rate is 15 percent, then the present value is $150 / 1.15 = $130.43. As this example illustrates, the choice of a discount rate can have a substantial impact on an assessment of security value.

dividend discount model (DDM)
Method of estimating the value of a share of stock as the present value of all expected future dividend payments.

A popular model used to value common stock is the **dividend discount model**, or **DDM**. The dividend discount model values a share of stock as the sum of all expected future dividend payments, where the dividends are adjusted for risk and the time value of money.

For example, suppose a company pays a dividend at the end of each year. Let $D(t)$ denote a dividend to be paid t years from now, and let $V(0)$ represent the present value of the future dividend stream. Also, let k denote the appropriate risk-adjusted discount rate. Using the dividend discount model, the present value of a share of this company's stock is measured as this sum of discounted future dividends:

$$V(0) = \frac{D(1)}{(1 + k)} + \frac{D(2)}{(1 + k)^2} + \frac{D(3)}{(1 + k)^3} + \cdots + \frac{D(T)}{(1 + k)^T} \qquad \textbf{6.1}$$

This expression for present value assumes that the last dividend is paid T years from now, where the value of T depends on the specific valuation problem considered. Thus, if $T = 3$ years and $D(1) = D(2) = D(3) = \$100$, the present value, $V(0)$, is stated as

$$V(0) = \frac{\$100}{(1 + k)} + \frac{\$100}{(1 + k)^2} + \frac{\$100}{(1 + k)^3}$$

If the discount rate is $k = 10$ percent, then a quick calculation yields $V(0) = \$248.69$, so the stock price should be about $250 per share.

Example 6.1   Using the DDM

Suppose again that a stock pays three annual dividends of $100 per year and the discount rate is $k = 15$ percent. In this case, what is the present value $V(0)$ of the stock?

With a 15 percent discount rate, we have

$$V(0) = \frac{\$100}{(1.15)} + \frac{\$100}{(1.15)^2} + \frac{\$100}{(1.15)^3}$$

Check that the answer is $V(0) = \$228.32$.

Example 6.2   **More DDM**

Suppose instead that the stock pays three annual dividends of $10, $20, and $30 in years 1, 2, and 3, respectively, and the discount rate is $k = 10$ percent. What is the present value $V(0)$ of the stock?

In this case, we have

$$V(0) = \frac{\$10}{(1.10)} + \frac{\$20}{(1.10)^2} + \frac{\$30}{(1.10)^3}$$

Check that the answer is $V(0) = \$48.16$.

Constant Dividend Growth Rate Model

constant growth rate model A version of the dividend discount model that assumes a constant dividend growth rate.

For many applications, the dividend discount model is simplified substantially by assuming that dividends will grow at a constant growth rate. This is called a **constant growth rate model**. Letting a constant growth rate be denoted by g, then successive annual dividends are stated as $D(t + 1) = D(t)(1 + g)$.

For example, suppose the next dividend is $D(1) = \$100$, and the dividend growth rate is $g = 10$ percent. This growth rate yields a second annual dividend of $D(2) = \$100 \times 1.10 = \$110$, and a third annual dividend of $D(3) = \$100 \times 1.10 \times 1.10 = \$100 \times (1.10)^2 = \$121$. If the discount rate is $k = 12$ percent, the present value of these three sequential dividend payments is the sum of their separate present values:

$$V(0) = \frac{\$100}{(1.12)} + \frac{\$110}{(1.12)^2} + \frac{\$121}{(1.12)^3}$$

$$= \$263.10$$

If the number of dividends to be paid is large, calculating the present value of each dividend separately is tedious and possibly prone to error. Fortunately, if the growth rate is constant, some simplified expressions are available to handle certain special cases. For example, suppose a stock will pay annual dividends over the next T years and these dividends will grow at a constant growth rate g and be discounted at the rate k. The current dividend is $D(0)$, the next dividend is $D(1) = D(0)(1 + g)$, the following dividend is $D(2) = D(1)(1 + g)$, and so forth. The present value of the next T dividends, that is, $D(1)$ through $D(T)$, can be calculated using this relatively simple formula:

$$V(0) = \frac{D(0)(1 + g)}{k - g}\left[1 - \left(\frac{1 + g}{1 + k}\right)^T\right] \qquad g \neq k \qquad \qquad \textbf{6.2}$$

Notice that this expression requires that the growth rate and the discount rate not be equal to each other, that is, $k \neq g$, since this requires division by zero. Actually, when the growth rate is equal to the discount rate, that is, $k = g$, the effects of growth and discounting cancel exactly, and the present value $V(0)$ is simply the number of payments T times the current dividend $D(0)$:

$$V(0) = T \times D(0) \qquad g = k$$

As a numerical illustration of the constant growth rate model, suppose that the growth rate is $g = 8$ percent, the discount rate is $k = 10$ percent, the number of future annual dividends is $T = 20$ years, and the current dividend is $D(0) = \$10$. In this case, a present value calculation yields this amount:

$$V(0) = \frac{\$10(1.08)}{.10 - .08} \left[1 - \left(\frac{1.08}{1.10} \right)^{20} \right]$$

$$= \$165.88$$

Example 6.3   **Using the Constant Growth Model**

Suppose that the dividend growth rate is 10 percent, the discount rate is 8 percent, there are 20 years of dividends to be paid, and the current dividend is $10. What is the value of the stock based on the constant growth model?

Plugging in the relevant numbers, we have

$$V(0) = \frac{\$10(1.10)}{.08 - .10} \left[1 - \left(\frac{1.10}{1.08} \right)^{20} \right]$$

$$= \$243.86$$

Thus the price should be $V(0) = \$243.86$.

Constant Perpetual Growth

A particularly simple form of the dividend discount model occurs in the case where a firm will pay dividends that grow at the constant rate g forever. This case is called the **constant perpetual growth model**. In the constant perpetual growth model, present values are calculated using this relatively simple formula:

constant perpetual growth model A version of the dividend discount model in which dividends grow forever at a constant rate, and the growth rate is strictly less than the discount rate.

$$V(0) = \frac{D(0)(1 + g)}{k - g} \qquad g < k \qquad \textbf{6.3}$$

Since $D(0)(1 + g) = D(1)$, we could also write the constant perpetual growth model as

$$V(0) = \frac{D(1)}{k - g} \qquad g < k \qquad \textbf{6.4}$$

Either way, we have a very simple, and very widely used, expression for the value of a share of stock based on future dividend payments.

Notice that the constant perpetual growth model requires that the growth rate be strictly less than the discount rate, that is, $g < k$. It looks like the share value would be negative if this were not true. Actually, the formula is simply not valid in this case. The reason is that a perpetual dividend growth rate greater than a discount rate implies an *infinite* value because the present value of the dividends keeps getting bigger and bigger. Since no security can have infinite value, the requirement that $g < k$ simply makes good economic sense.

To illustrate the constant perpetual growth model, suppose that the growth rate is $g = 4$ percent, the discount rate is $k = 9$ percent, and the current dividend is $D(0) = \$10$. In this case, a simple calculation yields

$$V(0) = \frac{\$10(1.04)}{.09 - .04} = \$208$$

Example 6.4   Using the Constant Perpetual Growth Model

Suppose dividends for a particular company are projected to grow at 5 percent forever. If the discount rate is 15 percent and the current dividend is $10, what is the value of the stock?

$$V(0) = \frac{\$10(1.05)}{.15 - .05} = \$105$$

As shown, the stock should sell for $105.

Applications of the Constant Perpetual Growth Model

In practice, the simplicity of the constant perpetual growth model makes it the most popular dividend discount model. Certainly, the model satisfies Einstein's famous dictum: "Simplify as much as possible, but no more." However, experienced financial analysts are keenly aware that the constant perpetual growth model can be usefully applied only to companies with a history of relatively stable earnings and dividend growth expected to continue into the distant future.

A standard example of an industry for which the constant perpetual growth model can often be usefully applied is the electric utility industry. Consider the first company in the Dow Jones Utilities, American Electric Power, which is traded on the New York Stock Exchange under the ticker symbol AEP. At midyear 1997, AEP's annual dividend was $2.40; thus we set $D(0) = \$2.40$.

To use the constant perpetual growth model, we also need a discount rate and a growth rate. An old quick and dirty rule of thumb for a risk-adjusted discount rate for electric utility companies is the yield to maturity on 20-year maturity U.S. Treasury bonds, plus 2 percent. At the time this example was written, the yield on 20-year maturity T-bonds was about 6.75 percent. Adding 2 percent, we get a discount rate of $k = 8.75$ percent.

At midyear 1997, AEP had not increased its dividend for several years. However, a future growth rate of 0.0 percent for AEP might be unduly pessimistic, since income and cash flow grew at a rate of 3.4 percent over the prior five years. Furthermore, the median dividend growth rate for the electric utility industry was 1.8 percent. Thus, a rate of, say, 2 percent might be more realistic as an estimate of future growth.

Putting it all together, we have $k = 8.75$ percent, $g = 2.0$ percent, and $D(0) = \$2.40$. Using these numbers, we obtain this estimate for the value of a share of AEP stock:

$$V(0) = \frac{\$2.40(1.02)}{.0875 - .02} = \$36.27$$

This estimate is less than the midyear 1997 AEP stock price of $43, possibly suggesting that AEP stock was overvalued.

We emphasize the word "possibly" here because we made several assumptions in the process of coming up with this estimate. A change in any of these assumptions could easily lead us to a different conclusion. We will return to this point several times in future discussions.

Example 6.5   Valuing Detroit Ed

In 1997, the utility company Detroit Edison (ticker DTE) paid a $2.08 dividend. Using $D(0) = \$2.08$, $k = 8.75$ percent, and $g = 2.0$ percent, calculate a present value estimate for DTE. Compare this with the 1997 DTE stock price of $29.

Plugging in the relevant numbers, we immediately have

$$V(0) = \frac{\$2.08(1.02)}{.0875 - .02} = \$31.43$$

We see that our estimated price is a little higher than the $29 stock price.

The Sustainable Growth Rate

sustainable growth rate A dividend growth rate that can be sustained by a company's earnings.

retained earnings Earnings retained within the firm to finance growth.

payout ratio Proportion of earnings paid out as dividends.

retention ratio Proportion of earnings retained for reinvestment.

In using the constant perpetual growth model, it is necessary to come up with an estimate of g, the growth rate in dividends. In our previous examples, we touched on two ways to do this: (1) using the company's historical average growth rate, or (2) using an industry median or average growth rate. We now describe using a third way, known as the **sustainable growth rate**, which involves using a company's earnings to estimate g.

As we have discussed, a limitation of the constant perpetual growth model is that it should be applied only to companies with stable dividend and earnings growth. Essentially, a company's earnings can be paid out as dividends to its stockholders or kept as **retained earnings** within the firm to finance future growth. The proportion of earnings paid to stockholders as dividends is called the **payout ratio**. The proportion of earnings retained for reinvestment is called the **retention ratio**.

If we let D stand for dividends and EPS stand for earnings per share, then the payout ratio is simply D/EPS. Since anything not paid out is retained, the retention ratio is just one minus the payout ratio. For example, if a company's current dividend is $4 per share, and its earnings per share are currently $10, then the payout ratio is $4 / $10 = .40, or 40 percent, and the retention ratio is $1 - .40 = .60$, or 60 percent.

A firm's sustainable growth rate is equal to its return on equity (ROE) times its retention ratio:[1]

$$\text{Sustainable growth rate} = \text{ROE} \times \text{Retention ratio} \qquad \textbf{6.5}$$

$$= \text{ROE} \times (1 - \text{Payout ratio})$$

Return on equity is commonly computed using an accounting-based performance measure and is calculated as a firm's net income divided by stockholders' equity:

$$\text{Return on equity (ROE)} = \text{Net income / Equity} \qquad \textbf{6.6}$$

Example 6.6 Calculating Sustainable Growth

At midyear 1997, American Electric Power (AEP) had a return on equity of ROE = 12.5 percent, earnings per share of EPS = $3.09, and a per-share dividend of $D(0) = \$2.40$. What was AEP's retention ratio? Its sustainable growth rate?

AEP's dividend payout was $2.40 / $3.09 = .777, or 77.7 percent. Its retention ratio was thus $1 - .777 = .223$, or 22.3 percent. Finally, the AEP's sustainable growth rate was .223 × 12.5% = 2.79%.

---

[1] Strictly speaking, this formula is correct only if ROE is calculated using beginning-of-period stockholder's equity. If ending figures are used, then the precise formula is ROE × Retention ratio / [1 − (ROE × Retention ratio)]. However, the error from not using the precise formula is usually small, so most analysts do not bother with it.

Example 6.7   **Valuing American Electric Power (AEP)**

Using AEP's sustainable growth rate of 2.79 percent (see Example 6.6) as an estimate of perpetual dividend growth and its current dividend of $2.40, what is the value of AEP's stock assuming a discount rate of 8.75 percent?

If we plug the various numbers into the perpetual growth model, we obtain a value of $41.39 = $2.40(1.0279) / (.0875 − .0279). This is fairly close to AEP's midyear 1997 stock price of $43, suggesting that AEP stock was probably correctly valued, at least on the basis of a 2.79 percent sustainable growth rate for future dividends.

Example 6.8   **Valuing Detroit Ed (DTE)**

In 1997, DTE had a return on equity of ROE = 7.9 percent, earnings per share of EPS = $1.87, and a per-share dividend of $D(0)$ = $2.08. Assuming an 8.75 percent discount rate, what is the value of DTE's stock?

DTE's payout ratio was $2.08 / $1.87 = 1.112. Thus, DTE's retention ratio was 1 − 1.112 = −.112, or −11.2 percent. DTE's sustainable growth rate was −.112 × 7.9% = −.00885, or −.885%. Finally, using the constant growth model, we obtain a value of $2.08(.99115) / [.0875 − (−.0085)] = $21.47. This is much less than DTE's 1997 stock price of $29, suggesting that DTE's stock is perhaps overvalued, or, more likely, that a −.885 percent growth rate underestimates DTE's future dividend growth.

As illustrated by Example 6.8, a common problem with sustainable growth rates is that they are sensitive to year-to-year fluctuations in earnings. As a result, security analysts routinely adjust sustainable growth rate estimates to smooth out the effects of earnings variations. Unfortunately, there is no universally standard method to adjust a sustainable growth rate, and analysts depend a great deal on personal experience and their own subjective judgment.

CHECK THIS

6.2a Compare the dividend discount model, the constant growth model, and the constant perpetual growth model. How are they alike? How do they differ?

6.2b What is a sustainable growth rate? How is it calculated?

6.3   The Two-Stage Dividend Growth Model

In the previous section, we examined dividend discount models based on a single growth rate. You may have already thought that a single growth rate is often unrealistic, since companies experience temporary periods of unusually high or low growth, with growth eventually converging to an industry average or an economywide average. In such cases as these, financial analysts frequently use a **two-stage dividend growth model**.

two-stage dividend growth model
Dividend model that assumes a firm will temporarily grow at a rate different from its long-term growth rate.

A two-stage dividend growth model assumes that a firm will initially grow at a rate g_1 during a first stage of growth lasting T years, and thereafter grow at a rate g_2 during a perpetual second stage of growth. The present value formula for the two-stage dividend growth model is stated as follows:

$$V(0) = \frac{D(0)(1 + g_1)}{k - g_1}\left[1 - \left(\frac{1 + g_1}{1 + k}\right)^T\right] + \left(\frac{1 + g_1}{1 + k}\right)^T \frac{D(0)(1 + g_2)}{k - g_2} \qquad 6.7$$

At first glance, this expression looks a little complicated. However, it simplifies if we look at its two distinct parts individually. The first term on the right-hand side measures the present value of the first T dividends and is the same expression we used earlier for the constant growth model. The second term then measures the present value of all subsequent dividends.

Using the formula is mostly a matter of "plug and chug" with a calculator. For example, suppose a firm has a current dividend of $2, and dividends are expected to grow at the rate $g_1 = 20$ percent for $T = 5$ years, and thereafter grow at the rate $g_2 = 5$ percent. With a discount rate of $k = 12$ percent, the present value $V(0)$ is calculated as

$$V(0) = \frac{\$2(1.20)}{.12 - .20}\left[1 - \left(\frac{1.20}{1.12}\right)^5\right] + \left(\frac{1.20}{1.12}\right)^5 \frac{\$2(1.05)}{.12 - .05}$$

$$= \$12.36 + \$42.36$$

$$= \$54.72$$

In this calculation, the total present value of $54.72 is the sum of a $12.36 present value for the first five dividends plus a $42.36 present value for all subsequent dividends.

Example 6.9   Using the Two-Stage Model

Suppose a firm has a current dividend of $D(0) = \$5$, which is expected to "shrink" at the rate $g_1 = -10$ percent for $T = 5$ years and thereafter grow at the rate $g_2 = 4$ percent. With a discount rate of $k = 10$ percent, what is the value of the stock?

Using the two-stage model, present value, $V(0)$, is calculated as

$$V(0) = \frac{\$5(.90)}{.10 - (-.10)}\left[1 - \left(\frac{.90}{1.10}\right)^5\right] + \left(\frac{.90}{1.10}\right)^5 \frac{\$5(1.04)}{.10 - .04}$$

$$= \$14.25 + \$31.78$$

$$= \$46.03$$

The total present value of $46.03 is the sum of a $14.25 present value of the first five dividends plus a $31.78 present value of all subsequent dividends.

The two-stage growth formula requires that the second-stage growth rate be strictly less than the discount rate, that is, $g_2 < k$. However, the first-stage growth rate g_1 can be greater, smaller, or equal to the discount rate. In the special case where the first-stage growth rate is equal to the discount rate, that is, $g_1 = k$, the two-stage formula reduces to this form:

$$V(0) = D(0) \times T + \frac{D(0)(1 + g_2)}{k - g_2}$$

You may notice with satisfaction that this two-stage formula is much simpler than the general two-stage formula. However, a first-stage growth rate is rarely exactly equal to a risk-adjusted discount rate, so this simplified formula sees little use.

Example 6.10 Valuing American Express

American Express is a stock in the Dow Jones Industrial Average that trades on the New York Stock Exchange under the ticker symbol AXP. At midyear 1997, AXP's previous five-year growth rate was 19.6 percent and analysts were forecasting a 13.2 percent long-term growth rate. Suppose AXP grows at a 19.6 percent rate for another five years, and thereafter grows at a 13.2 percent rate. What value would we place on AXP by assuming a 14.5 percent discount rate? AXP's 1997 dividend was $.92.

Plugging in all the relevant numbers into a two-stage present value calculation yields

$$V(0) = \frac{\$.92(1.196)}{.145 - .196}\left[1 - \left(\frac{1.196}{1.145}\right)^5\right] + \left(\frac{1.196}{1.145}\right)^5 \frac{\$.92(1.132)}{.145 - .132}$$

$$= \$5.25 + \$99.61$$

$$= \$104.86$$

This present value estimate is somewhat higher than American Express's $80 midyear 1997 stock price, suggesting that AXP might be undervalued or that these growth rate estimates are overly optimistic.

Example 6.11 Have a Pepsi?

PepsiCo, Inc. stock trades on the New York Stock Exchange under the ticker symbol PEP. At midyear 1997, analysts forecasted a long-term 12.0 percent growth rate for PepsiCo, although its recent five-year growth was only 1.2 percent. Suppose PEP grows at a 1.2 percent rate for five years, and thereafter grows at a 12.0 percent rate. Assuming a 16.0 percent discount rate, what value would you place on PEP? The 1997 dividend was $.47.

Once again, we round up all the relevant numbers and plug them in:

$$V(0) = \frac{\$.47(1.012)}{.16 - .012}\left[1 - \left(\frac{1.012}{1.16}\right)^5\right] + \left(\frac{1.012}{1.16}\right)^5 \frac{\$.47(1.12)}{.16 - .12}$$

$$= \$1.59 + \$6.65$$

$$= \$8.24$$

This present value is grossly lower than PepsiCo's 1997 stock price of $37.50, suggesting that something is probably wrong with our analysis. Since the discount rate is greater than the first-stage growth rate used above, we should try to use the constant perpetual growth model. The constant perpetual growth formula yields this present value calculation:

$$V(0) = \frac{\$.47(1.12)}{.16 - .12}$$

$$= \$13.16$$

This is still far below PepsiCo's actual $37.50 stock price. The lesson of this example is that the dividend discount model does not always work well. Analysts know this—so should you!

As a practical matter, most stocks with a first-stage growth rate greater than a discount rate do not pay dividends and therefore cannot be evaluated using a dividend discount model. Nevertheless, as our next example shows, there are some high-growth companies that pay regular dividends.

Example 6.12 Stride-Rite Corp.

Stride-Rite trades under the ticker symbol SRR. At midyear 1997, analysts forecasted a 30 percent growth rate for Stride-Rite. Suppose SRR grows at this rate for five years, and thereafter grows at a sector average 9.4 percent rate. Assuming a 13.9 percent discount rate, and beginning with SRR's 1997 dividend of $.20, what is your estimate of SRR's value?

A two-stage present value calculation yields

$$V(0) = \frac{\$.20(1.30)}{.139 - .30}\left[1 - \left(\frac{1.30}{1.139}\right)^5\right] + \left[\frac{1.30}{1.139}\right]^5 \frac{\$.20(1.094)}{.139 - .094}$$

$$= \$1.51 + \$9.42$$

$$= \$10.93$$

This present value estimate is lower than Stride-Rite's 1997 stock price of $13.06, suggesting that SRR might be overvalued.

Discount Rates for Dividend Discount Models

You may wonder where the discount rates used in the preceding examples come from. The answer is that they come from the *capital asset pricing model* (CAPM). Although a detailed discussion of the CAPM is deferred to a later chapter, we can here point out that based on the CAPM, the discount rate for a stock can be estimated using this formula:

Discount rate = U.S. T-bill rate + (Stock beta × Stock market risk premium) **6.8**

The components of this formula, as we use it here, are defined as follows:

U.S. T-bill rate:	Return on 90-day U.S. T-bills
Stock beta:	Risk relative to an average stock
Stock market risk premium:	Risk premium for an average stock

The basic intuition for this approach can be traced back to Chapter 1. There we saw that the return we expect to earn on a risky asset had two parts, a "wait" component and a "worry" component. We labeled the wait component as the *time value of money,* and we noted that it can be measured as the return we earn from an essentially riskless investment. Here we use the return on a 90-day Treasury bill as the riskless return.

We called the worry component the *risk premium,* and we noted that the greater the risk, the greater the risk premium. Depending on the exact period studied, the risk premium for the market as a whole over the past 70 or so years has averaged about 8.6 percent. This 8.6 percent can be interpreted as the risk premium for bearing an average amount of stock market risk, and we use it as the stock market risk premium.

beta Measure of a stock's risk relative to the stock market average.

Finally, when we look at a particular stock, we recognize that it may be more or less risky than an average stock. A stock's **beta** is a measure of a single stock's risk relative to an average stock, and we discuss beta at length in a later chapter. For now, it suffices to know that the market average beta is 1.0. A beta of 1.5 indicates that a stock has 50 percent more risk than average, so its risk premium is 50 percent higher. A beta of .50 indicates that a stock is 50 percent less sensitive than average to market volatility, and has a smaller risk premium.

When this chapter was written, the Treasury bill rate was 5 percent. Taking it as given for now, the stock beta for PepsiCo of 1.28 yields an estimated discount rate of

5% + (1.28 × 8.6%) = 16.0%. Similarly, the stock beta for American Express of 1.11 yields the discount rate 5% + (1.11 × 8.6%) = 14.5%. For the remainder of this chapter, we use discount rates calculated according to this CAPM formula.

Example 6.13 Stride-Rite's Beta

Look back at Example 6.12. What beta did we use to determine the appropriate discount rate for Stride-Rite? How do you interpret this beta?

Again assuming a T-bill rate of 5 percent and stock market risk premium of 8.6 percent, we have

$$13.9\% = 5\% + \text{Stock beta} \times 8.6\%$$

thus

$$\text{Stock beta} = \frac{13.9\% - 5\%}{8.6\%} = 1.035$$

Since Stride-Rite's beta is greater than 1.0, it had greater risk than an average stock—specifically, 3.5 percent more.

Observations on Dividend Discount Models

We have examined two dividend discount models: the constant perpetual growth model and the two-stage dividend growth model. Each model has advantages and disadvantages. Certainly, the main advantage of the constant perpetual growth model is that it is simple to compute. However, it has several disadvantages: (1) it is not usable for firms not paying dividends, (2) it is not usable when a growth rate is greater than a discount rate, (3) it is sensitive to the choice of growth rate and discount rate, (4) discount rates and growth rates may be difficult to estimate accurately, and (5) constant perpetual growth is often an unrealistic assumption.

The two-stage dividend growth model offers several improvements: (1) it is more realistic, since it accounts for low, high, or zero growth in the first stage, followed by constant long-term growth in the second stage, and (2) it is usable when a first-stage growth rate is greater than a discount rate. However, the two-stage model is also sensitive to the choice of discount rate and growth rates, and it is not useful for companies that don't pay dividends.

Financial analysts readily acknowledge the limitations of dividend discount models. Consequently, they also turn to other valuation methods to expand their analyses. In the next section, we discuss some popular stock valuation methods based on price ratios.

CHECK THIS

6.3a What are the three parts of a CAPM-determined discount rate?

6.3b Under what circumstances is a two-stage dividend discount model appropriate?

Price Ratio Analysis

Price ratios are widely used by financial analysts, more so even than dividend discount models. Of course, all valuation methods try to accomplish the same thing, which is to appraise the economic value of a company's stock. However, analysts readily agree that no single method can adequately handle this task on all occasions. In this section, we therefore examine several of the most popular price ratio methods and provide examples of their use in financial analysis.

Price-Earnings Ratios

price-earnings (P/E) ratio Current stock price divided by annual earnings per share (EPS).

earnings yield Inverse of the P/E ratio: earnings divided by price (E/P).

The most popular price ratio used to assess the value of common stock is a company's **price-earnings ratio**, abbreviated as **P/E ratio.** In fact, as we saw in Chapter 3, P/E ratios are reported in the financial press every day. As we discussed, a price-earnings ratio is calculated as the ratio of a firm's current stock price divided by its annual earnings per share (EPS).

The inverse of a P/E ratio is called an **earnings yield**, and it is measured as earnings per share divided by a current stock price (E/P). Clearly, an earnings yield and a price-earnings ratio are simply two ways to measure the same thing. In practice, earnings yields are less commonly stated and used than P/E ratios.

Since most companies report earnings each quarter, annual earnings per share can be calculated either as the most recent quarterly earnings per share times four or as the sum of the last four quarterly earnings per share figures. Most analysts prefer the first method of multiplying the latest quarterly earnings per share value times four. However, some published data sources, including *The Wall Street Journal,* report annual earnings per share as the sum of the last four quarters' figures. The difference is usually small, but it can sometimes be a source of confusion.

growth stocks A term often used to describe high-P/E stocks.

Financial analysts often refer to high-P/E stocks as **growth stocks**. To see why, notice that a P/E ratio is measured as a *current* stock price over *current* earnings per share. Now, consider two companies with the same current earnings per share, where one company is a high-growth company and the other is a low-growth company. Which company do you think should have a higher stock price, the high-growth company or the low-growth company?

This question is a no-brainer. All else equal, we would be surprised if the high-growth company did not have a higher stock price, and therefore a higher P/E ratio. In general, companies with higher expected earnings growth will have higher P/E ratios, which is why high-P/E stocks are often referred to as growth stocks.

To give an example, Starbucks Corporation is a specialty coffee retailer with a history of aggressive sales growth. Its stock trades on the Nasdaq under the ticker symbol SBUX. At midyear 1997, SBUX stock traded at $38 per share with earnings per share of EPS = $.48, it therefore had a P/E ratio of $38 / $.48 = 79.2. By contrast, the median P/E ratio for retail food stores was 24.4. SBUX paid no dividends and reinvested all earnings. Because of its strong growth and high P/E ratio, SBUX would be regarded as a growth stock.

value stocks A term often used to describe low-P/E stocks.

The reasons high-P/E stocks are called growth stocks seems obvious enough; however, in a seeming defiance of logic, low-P/E stocks are often referred to as **value stocks**. The reason is that low-P/E stocks are often viewed as "cheap" relative to *current* earnings. (Notice again the emphasis on "current.") This suggests that these stocks may represent good investment values, and hence the term value stocks.

For example, at midyear 1997, Chrysler Corporation stock traded for $37 per share with earnings per share of EPS = $4.30. Its P/E ratio of 8.6 was far below the median automotive industry P/E ratio of 16.4. Because of its low P/E ratio, Chrysler might be regarded as a value stock.

Having said all this, we want to emphasize that the terms "growth stock" and "value stock" are mostly just commonly-used labels. Of course, only time will tell whether a high-P/E stock turns out to actually be a high-growth stock, or whether a low-P/E stock is really a good value.

Price-Cash Flow Ratios

price-cash flow (P/CF) ratio Current stock price divided by current cash flow per share.

Instead of price-earnings (P/E) ratios, many analysts prefer to look at price-cash flow (P/CF) ratios. A **price-cash flow (P/CF) ratio** is measured as a company's current stock price divided by its current annual cash flow per share. Like earnings, cash flow is normally reported quarterly and most analysts multiply the last quarterly cash flow figure by four to obtain annual cash flow. Again, like earnings, many published data sources report annual cash flow as a sum of the latest four quarterly cash flows.

cash flow In the context of the price-cash flow ratio, usually taken to be net income plus depreciation.

There are a variety of definitions of **cash flow**. In this context, the most common measure is simply calculated as net income plus depreciation, so this is the one we use here. In the next chapter, we examine in detail how cash flow is calculated in a firm's financial statements. Cash flow is usually reported in a firm's financial statements and labeled as cash flow from operations (or operating cash flow).

The difference between earnings and cash flow is often confusing, largely because of the way that standard accounting practice defines net income. Essentially, net income is measured as revenues minus expenses. Obviously, this is logical. However, not all expenses are actually cash expenses. The most important exception is depreciation.

When a firm acquires a long-lived asset such as a new factory facility, standard accounting practice does not deduct the cost of the factory all at once, even though it is actually paid for all at once. Instead, the cost is deducted over time. These deductions do not represent actual cash payments, however. The actual cash payment occurred when the factory was purchased. At this point you may be a little confused about why the difference is important, but hang in there for a few more paragraphs.

Most analysts agree that in examining a company's financial performance, cash flow can be more informative than net income. To see why, consider the hypothetical example of two identical companies: Twiddle-Dee Co. and Twiddle-Dum Co. Suppose that both companies have the same constant revenues and expenses in each year over a three-year period. These constant revenues and cash expenses (excluding depreciation) yield the same constant annual cash flows, and they are stated as follows:

	Twiddle-Dee	**Twiddle-Dum**
Revenues	$5,000	$5,000
Cash expenses	− 3,000	− 3,000
Cash flow	$2,000	$2,000

Thus, both companies have the same $2,000 cash flow in each of the three years of this hypothetical example.

Next, suppose that both companies incur total depreciation of $3,000 spread out over the three-year period. Standard accounting practice sometimes allows a manager to choose among several depreciation schedules. Twiddle-Dee Co. chooses straight-line depreciation and Twiddle-Dum Co. chooses accelerated depreciation. These two depreciation schedules are tabulated below:

	Twiddle-Dee	Twiddle-Dum
Year 1	$1,000	$1,500
Year 2	1,000	1,000
Year 3	1,000	500
Total	$3,000	$3,000

Note that total depreciation over the three-year period is the same for both companies. However, Twiddle-Dee Co. has the same $1,000 depreciation in each year, while Twiddle-Dum Co. has accelerated depreciation of $1,500 in the first year, $1,000 in the second year, and $500 depreciation in the third year.

Now, let's look at the resulting annual cash flows and net income figures for the two companies, recalling that in each year, Cash flow = Net income + Depreciation:

	Twiddle-Dee		Twiddle-Dum	
	Cash Flow	Net Income	Cash Flow	Net Income
Year 1	$2,000	$1,000	$2,000	$ 500
Year 2	2,000	1,000	2,000	1,000
Year 3	2,000	1,000	2,000	1,500
Total	$6,000	$3,000	$6,000	$3,000

Note that Twiddle-Dum Co.'s net income is lower in the first year and higher in the third year than Twiddle-Dee Co.'s net income. This is purely a result of Twiddle-Dum Co.'s accelerated depreciation schedule, and has nothing to do with Twiddle-Dum Co.'s actual profitability. However, an inexperienced analyst observing Twiddle-Dum Co.'s rapidly rising annual earnings figures might incorrectly label Twiddle-Dum as a growth company. An experienced analyst would observe that there was no cash flow growth to support this naive conclusion.

Financial analysts typically use both price-earnings ratios and price-cash flow ratios. They point out that when a company's earnings per share is not significantly larger than its cash flow per share (CFPS), this is a signal, at least potentially, of good-quality earnings. The term "quality" means that the accounting earnings mostly reflect actual cash flow, not just accounting numbers. When earnings and cash flow are far from each other, this may be a signal of poor quality earnings.

Going back to some earlier examples, at midyear 1997, Starbucks Corporation had cash flow per share of CFPS = $1.19, yielding a P/CF ratio of 31.9. Notice that SBUX cash flow per share was over twice its earnings per share of $.48, suggesting good quality earnings. At midyear 1997, Chrysler Corporation had a cash flow per share of CFPS = $8, yielding a P/CF ratio of 4.6. This was somewhat lower than Chrysler's P/E ratio of 8.6, suggesting that Chrysler had good-quality earnings.

Price-Sales Ratios

price-sales (P/S) ratio Current stock price divided by annual sales per share.

An alternative view of a company's performance is provided by its **price-sales (P/S) ratio**. A price-sales ratio is calculated as the current price of a company's stock divided by its current annual sales revenue per share. A price-sales ratio focuses on a company's ability to generate sales growth. Essentially, a high P/S ratio would suggest high sales growth, while a low P/S ratio might indicate sluggish sales growth.

Book Value Rarely Required Reading Now

Money managers are closing the book on book value.

Bargain-hunting investors used to pay a lot of attention to book value, namely a company's assets minus its liabilities. But now even die-hard fans concede that this measure of a company's worth has lost much of its meaning because of new accounting rules, share buybacks, and write-offs.

"I was a big proponent of book value," says Richard Fontaine, a Towson, Md., stock-picker with $270 million under management. "But it's very difficult to use it as a yardstick anymore. The distortions have gotten so big that it's got rid of most of the value."

For value investors, who favor beaten-down stocks that are cheap compared with corporate assets, book value used to provide an easy way to find bargains. All you had to do was compare a company's stock price with its book value on a per-share basis, which can be calculated using the balance sheet in a company's annual report. Value investors would often be drawn to companies whose shares were trading near or below book value.

These days, however, few stocks are at such depressed levels. According to the Leuthold Group, a Minneapolis research firm, the companies in the Standard & Poor's 400-stock index are trading at an astounding 3.1 times book value, higher even than at the 1987 stock market peak. Part of the reason is lofty stock prices. But also important has been the shrinking book value of many companies.

"Book-value measurements have gone through so many changes as to be almost meaningless," says Wayne Nordberg, partner in charge of equity investments at New York's Lord Abbett & Co. "We look at it. But it doesn't occupy the same position in our analytical process as it did five or 10 years ago."

Why was book value considered so important? It reflects the amount of money invested in a company through issuing stock and retained earnings. If a company's shares are below book value, they are in effect trading for less than the capital invested in the firm.

For investors anxious to find cheap stocks, that may be an appetizing prospect. Unfortunately, book value is more than simply the sum of equity capital raised and earnings retained.

Mr. Nordberg says many companies have seen their book values shrink sharply because of share

---

For example, at midyear 1997, Starbucks Corporation had a price-sales ratio of 3.7, compared to the median food store P/S ratio of .7. This is consistent with our other price ratios indicating that Starbucks is a growth company. Of course, only time will tell how much growth Starbucks will actually realize. In contrast, at midyear 1997, Chrysler Corporation had a price-sales ratio of .4, which was the same as the automotive industry median P/S ratio of .4. This indicates that Chrysler's sales revenue might only be expected to grow at the industry average rate.

Price-Book Ratios

price-book (P/B) ratio Market value of a company's common stock divided by its book (or accounting) value of equity.

A very basic price ratio for a company is its **price-book (P/B) ratio**, sometimes called the market-book ratio. A price-book ratio is measured as the market value of a company's outstanding common stock divided by its book value of equity.

Price-book ratios are appealing because book values represent, in principle, historical cost. The stock price is an indicator of current value, so a price-book ratio simply measures what the equity is worth today relative to what it cost. A ratio bigger than 1.0 indicates that the firm has been successful in creating value for its stockholders. A ratio smaller than 1.0 indicates that the company is actually worth less than it cost.

This interpretation of price-book ratio seems simple enough, but the truth is that because of varied and changing accounting standards, book values are difficult to interpret. For this and other reasons, price-book ratios may not have as much information value as they once did. The nearby Investment Updates box contains an article reprinted from *The Wall Street Journal* discussing well-known problems associated with the use of book values in financial analysis.

repurchases, write-offs caused by corporate restructurings and the adoption of a new accounting rule that requires the setup of a reserve to cover retiree health benefits. Many money managers believe these items sometimes artificially depress a company's book value.

Last year, for instance, General Motors' book value shrank to $8.47 a share from $42.89, in large part because of new accounting rules regarding retiree benefits. At Dayton Hudson, book value fell between year-end 1986 and year-end 1989, as the retailer bought large chunks of its own stock. In recent years, International Business Machines' book value has shriveled as the computer giant took write-offs to cover its restructuring.

As individual companies have taken hits to their book value, the stock market has started to appear increasingly expensive based on price-to-book multiples. The trend prompted Goldman Sachs's market strategist Abby Cohen to issue a report saying "investors should not conclude that market valuation has worsened."

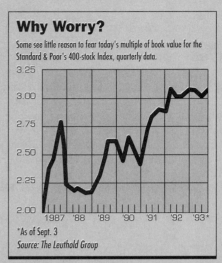

Why Worry?

Some see little reason to fear today's multiple of book value for the Standard & Poor's 400-stock Index, quarterly data.

*As of Sept. 3
Source: The Leuthold Group

Source: Jonathan Clements, "Book Value Rarely Required Reading Now," *The Wall Street Journal*, September 10, 1993. Reprinted by permission of Dow Jones, Inc., via Copyright Clearance Center, Inc. © 1993 Dow Jones & Company, Inc. All Rights Reserved Worldwide.

Applications of Price Ratio Analysis

Price-earnings ratios, price-cash flow ratios, and price-sales ratios are commonly used to calculate estimates of expected future stock prices. This is done by multiplying a historical average price ratio by an expected future value for the price-ratio denominator variable. For example, Table 6.1 summarizes such a price ratio analysis for Intel Corporation (INTC) based on midyear 1997 information.

In Table 6.1, the current value row contains midyear 1997 values for earnings per share, cash flow per share, and sales per share (SPS). The five-year average ratio row contains five-year average P/E, P/CF, and P/S ratios, and the growth rate row contains five-year historical average EPS, CFPS, and SPS growth rates.

The expected price row contains expected stock prices one year hence. The basic idea is this. Since Intel has had an average P/E ratio of 13.5, we will assume that Intel's stock price will be 13.5 times its earnings one year from now. To estimate

Table 6.1	Price Ratio Analysis for Intel Corporation (INTC) Midyear 1997 Stock Price: $89.88		
	Earnings (P/E)	Cash Flow (P/CF)	Sales (P/S)
Current value per share	$3.49	$4.62	$12.67
Five-year average price ratio	13.5	9.6	3.0
Growth rate	42.7%	39.6%	34.3%
Expected stock price	$67.23	$61.92	$51.05

Flaws in Market Gauges

Even before last week's impressive rally, the stock market was outrageously expensive. At least that's what some key market yardsticks show.

But hold on to your sell orders. Many investment experts reckon the fault lies not with the market, but with the measuring sticks. In particular, these experts see serious shortcomings in three popular stock-market gauges: the price-to-book value ratio, dividend yield, and the price-to-earnings multiple.

The three standard measures "are all flawed in some way," says Frazier Evans, senior economist at Colonial Group, the Boston mutual-fund company. "You have to look under the surface. I'd say that the market is not as expensive as it looks."

Dwindling Dividends

Consider, for instance, the market's dividend yield. The companies in the Standard & Poor's 500-stock index are paying annual dividends amounting to 2.8% of their current stock prices. That's well below the historical average dividend yield of 4.7% and not far above the all-time low of 2.64%, which was hit in 1987, just before that year's stock-market crash.

A danger signal? Maybe not. The reason is that corporations seem to be paying out far less of their earnings as dividends these days. Instead, companies are using profits to expand their businesses and buy their own shares—actions designed to boost stock prices.

The shift should please most investors. Because dividend income is taxed more heavily than capital gains, shareholders benefit more if returns come in the form of higher stock prices, rather than big dividends.

The dividend-yield gauge also is being thrown out of whack by other factors, says Arnold Kaufman, editor of Standard & Poor's Outlook, a weekly newsletter. For instance, "dividends are being held down by the special problems of large dividend-paying industry groups, such as telephones, utilities, and drugs," he says.

Effect on Book Value

At first blush, the market's price-to-book value also suggests shares are richly priced. Bargain hunters often look for stocks that are trading below book value, which is the difference between a company's assets and its liabilities expressed on a per-share basis.

But these days, precious few stocks trade below book value. Indeed, Mr. Kaufman figures stocks on average are trading at more than three times book value, compared with just 1.2 times book in the late 1970s.

But once again, the measuring gauge may be faulty. Book value has been distorted by share repurchases, special charges due to corporate restructurings, and the adoption of a new accounting rule concerning retiree health benefits. "Price-to-book value has lost a lot of its usefulness," Mr. Kaufman concludes.

What about price-to-earnings multiples? Right now, the market is trading at about 15 times expected 1995 earnings, a tad above the historical average. "There are fewer problems with P/E ratios than with the other two measures," says Kathleen Crowley, a senior vice president with Chicago's Stratford Advisory Group.

Even so, earnings multiples also can mislead. In recent years, reported earnings have been depressed by special charges. In addition, experts say the market's earnings multiple shouldn't be viewed in isolation, but instead should be considered in the context of items like interest rates and inflation.

Source: Jonathan Clements, "Flaws in Market Gauges," *The Wall Street Journal*, September 7, 1995. Reprinted by permission of Dow Jones, Inc., via Copyright Clearance Center, Inc. © 1995 Dow Jones & Company, Inc. All Rights Reserved Worldwide.

Intel's earnings one year from now, we note that Intel's earnings have typically grown at a rate of 42.7 percent per year. If earnings continue to grow at this rate, then next year's earnings will be equal to this year's earnings multiplied by 1.427. Putting it all together, we have:

$$\text{Expected price} = \text{Historical P/E ratio} \times \text{Projected EPS}$$

$$= \text{Historical P/E ratio} \times \text{Current EPS} \times (1 + \text{Historical EPS growth rate})$$

$$= 13.5 \times \$3.49 \times 1.427$$

$$= \$67.23$$

The same procedure is used to calculate an expected price based on cash flow per share:

$$\text{Expected price} = \text{P/CF ratio} \times \text{CFPS} \times (1 + \text{Cash flow growth rate})$$
$$= 9.6 \times \$4.62 \times 1.396$$
$$= \$61.92$$

Finally, an expected price based on sales per share is calculated as

$$\text{Expected price} = \text{P/S ratio} \times \text{SPS} \times (1 + \text{Sales growth rate})$$
$$= 3.0 \times \$12.67 \times 1.343$$
$$= \$51.05$$

Notice that each price ratio method yields a different expected future price. This is normal. Since each method uses different information, each makes a different prediction. As Mark Twain once remarked: "Prediction is difficult, especially about the future." We agree, especially since Intel's stock price was trading in the $90–$100 range in the second half of 1997, despite the fact that price ratio analysis suggested that Intel stock was overvalued.

An interesting and informative *Wall Street Journal* article discussing the limitations of price ratios in financial analysis is reproduced in the nearby Investment Updates box.

Example 6.14 Going to Disneyland

Table 6.2 contains some information about Walt Disney Corporation. Calculate expected share prices using each of the three price ratio approaches we have discussed.

Table 6.2	**Price Ratio Analysis for Walt Disney Corporation (DIS)** **Midyear 1997 Stock Price: $79.31**		
	Earnings (P/E)	**Cash Flow (P/CF)**	**Sales (P/S)**
Current value per share	$2.66	$9.92	$32.21
Five-year average price ratio	35.2	10.3	2.4
Growth rate	10.4%	25.4%	25.1%

Using the P/E approach, we come up with the following estimate of the price of Walt Disney stock in one year:

$$\text{Expected price} = \text{Average P/E} \times \text{Current EPS} \times (1 + \text{Growth rate})$$
$$= 35.2 \times \$2.66 \times 1.104$$
$$= \$103.37$$

Check that the price-cash flow and price-sales approaches give estimates of $128.13 and $96.71, respectively. All of these prices suggest that Disney is potentially undervalued.

CHECK THIS

6.4a Why are high-P/E stocks sometimes called growth stocks?

6.4b Why might an analyst prefer a price-cash flow ratio to a price-earnings ratio?

6.5 An Analysis of the McGraw-Hill Company

Stock market investors have available to them many sources of information about the financial performance of companies with publicly traded stock shares. Indeed, the sheer volume of information available can often be overwhelming. For this reason, several sources publish reference summaries for individual companies.

One well-known example is the *Value Line Investment Survey,* a published reference with frequent updates. *Value Line* provides what many investors consider to be the best one-page company summaries available. Current updates to the *Value Line Investment Survey* are available at most stock brokerage offices and many public libraries. Figure 6.1 presents a partial one-page summary for the McGraw-Hill Corporation published by *Value Line* in late 1998. We will make frequent reference to information found in the *Value Line* summary in the following discussion of McGraw-Hill common stock.

As shown in the title bar of Figure 6.1, McGraw-Hill stock trades on the New York Stock Exchange (NYSE) under the ticker symbol MHP. When this survey went to press, McGraw-Hill's stock price was $82, with a P/E ratio of 24.8. *Value Line* calculates a P/E ratio as the most recent stock price divided by the latest six months' earnings per share plus earnings per share estimated for the next six months. McGraw-Hill's relative P/E ratio of 1.49 is obtained by dividing its current P/E by the median P/E ratio of all stocks under review by *Value Line*. The dividend yield of 2.0 percent is calculated by dividing estimated dividends for the coming year by the current stock price.

At this point, as you look over *Value Line*'s summary in Figure 6.1, you realize that *Value Line* has packed a considerable amount of information onto a single page. We acknowledge the efficiency of the *Value Line* one-page surveys by not trying to cover all items on the entire page. Most items are well-explained in Figure 6.2, which contains a complete sample page (see pp. 167–168). However, some items in Figure 6.1 differ from those in Figure 6.2 reflecting changes made by *Value Line*. In the following discussion, we refer only to information needed to illustrate the analytic methods discussed previously in this chapter.

Our first task is to estimate a discount rate for McGraw-Hill. *Value Line* reports a beta of .90 for McGraw-Hill. Using a then-current Treasury bill rate of 4 percent and an historical stock market risk premium of 8.73 percent, we obtain a discount rate estimate for McGraw-Hill using the CAPM of $4\% + (.90 \times 8.73\%) = 11.86\%$.

Our next task is to calculate a sustainable growth rate. *Value Line* reports projected 1998 earnings per share of $3.30 and dividends per share of $1.56. *Value Line* also reports a 1998 return on equity of ROE = 21.5 percent (reported as "Return on Shr. Equity"), which implies a retention ratio of $1 - \$1.56/\$3.30 = 52.7\%$. Putting these together yields a sustainable growth rate of $.527 \times 21.5\% = 11.33\%$.

Finally, with a discount rate and sustainable growth rate we can calculate a present value for McGraw-Hill stock. Using a constant perpetual growth model with the 1998 dividend of $D(0) = \$1.56$ (calculated as four times the most recent quarterly dividend) a discount rate of $k = 11.86$ percent, and a growth rate of $g = 11.33$ percent, we calculate this present value of expected future dividends for McGraw-Hill stock:

$$V(0) = \frac{\$1.56(1.1133)}{.1186 - .1133}$$

$$= \$327.69$$

This present value of $327.69 is grossly higher than McGraw-Hill's $82 stock price, suggesting that the constant growth rate model is inappropriate for this company.

Value Line also reports annual growth rates for sales, cash flow, earnings, dividends, and book value in the box labeled "Annual Rates." These include historical 5-year and 10-year growth rates, along with expected growth rates for the next 3–5 years provided by *Value Line* analysts. These growth rates could also be used as a basis for present value calculations, and different answers would result.

We next turn to a price ratio analysis for McGraw-Hill. We will estimate expected future stock prices using five-year average price ratios that we will calculate along with expected growth rates supplied by *Value Line* analysts. The *Value Line* survey

Figure 6.1	Value Line Analysis Sheet

McGRAW-HILL NYSE-MHP — RECENT PRICE **82** — P/E RATIO **24.8** (Trailing: 26.5 / Median: 18.0) — RELATIVE P/E RATIO **1.49** — DIV'D YLD **2.0%** — VALUE LINE **1827**

TIMELINESS 3 Raised 7/25/97
SAFETY 1 Raised 6/4/93
TECHNICAL 3 Lowered 11/14/97
BETA .90 (1.00 = Market)

2001-03 PROJECTIONS

	Price	Gain	Ann'l Total Return
High	115	(+40%)	11%
Low	95	(+15%)	6%

Insider Decisions

	O	N	D	J	F	M	A	M	J
to Buy	0	0	0	0	0	0	0	1	0
Options	2	2	1	0	0	0	3	2	1
to Sell	0	0	0	0	0	1	0	1	1

Institutional Decisions

	3Q1997	4Q1997	1Q1998
to Buy	135	157	152
to Sell	135	123	165
Hld's(000)	71545	70541	69471

Percent shares traded: 12.0 / 8.0 / 4.0

LEGENDS
— 11.0 x "Cash Flow" p sh
.... Relative Price Strength
2-for-1 split 4/96
Options: Yes
Shaded area indicates recession

High: 42.3 38.0 43.1 30.6 32.4 33.3 37.6 38.6 43.8 49.3 75.4 87.0
Low: 21.5 23.4 19.9 24.9 26.5 27.6 31.3 31.8 37.3 44.9 68.5

Target Price Range 2001 2002 2003

% TOT. RETURN 7/98

	THIS STOCK	VL ARITH. INDEX
1 yr.	23.4	6.4
3 yr.	130.7	64.2
5 yr.	190.0	112.8

1982	1983	1984	1985	1986	1987	1988	1989	1990	1991	1992	1993	1994	1995	1996	1997	1998	1999	© VALUE LINE PUB., INC.	01-03
11.97	12.91	13.93	14.79	15.61	18.16	18.72	18.37	19.81	19.81	20.87	22.22	27.79	29.31	30.89	35.66	38.35	41.50	Sales per sh A	52.55
1.35	1.54	1.70	1.89	2.03	2.31	2.41	2.41	2.45	2.01	2.08	2.30	4.36	4.58	4.91	5.89	6.15	6.75	"Cash Flow" per sh	9.00
1.10	1.26	1.43	1.46	1.52	1.56	1.73	1.70	1.70	1.52	1.57	1.75	2.05	2.28	2.50	2.91	3.30	3.75	Earnings per sh B	5.75
.47	.54	.62	.70	.76	.84	.92	1.00	1.08	1.10	1.12	1.14	1.16	1.20	1.32	1.44	1.56	1.68	Div'ds Decl'd per sh C■	2.10
.42	.49	.50	.48	.42	.54	.46	.60	.98	.52	.57	.50	.78	.59	.64	.79	1.55	.85	Cap'l Spending per sh	.85
5.42	6.14	6.93	7.70	8.52	8.56	7.50	9.04	9.50	9.75	10.18	9.25	8.33	9.19	10.34	13.68	14.48	15.55	Book Value per sh D	25.90
99.73	100.32	100.65	100.80	101.00	96.44	97.12	97.37	97.85	98.09	98.27	98.83	99.34	100.14	99.53	99.10	97.50	96.90	Common Shs Outst'g E	95.15
12.7	17.6	14.4	15.7	18.5	21.1	17.4	20.4	14.8	18.6	19.1	18.2	16.9	16.7	17.7	20.6	Bold figures are Value Line estimates		Avg Ann'l P/E Ratio	18.0
1.40	1.49	1.34	1.27	1.25	1.41	1.44	1.54	1.10	1.19	1.16	1.08	1.11	1.12	1.11	1.19			Relative P/E Ratio	1.30
3.4%	2.4%	3.0%	3.1%	2.7%	2.6%	3.1%	2.9%	4.1%	3.9%	3.7%	3.6%	3.4%	3.2%	3.0%	2.4%			Avg Ann'l Div'd Yield	2.0%

CAPITAL STRUCTURE as of 6/30/98
Total Debt $735.1 mill. Due in 5 Yrs $77.4 mill.
LT Debt $606.9 mill. LT Interest $48.0 mill.
(L-T int. earned: 11.0x; total int. coverage: 10.0x)
(30% of Cap'l)
Leases, Uncapitalized Annual rentals $35.1 mill.

Pension Liability None

Pfd Stock None
Common Stock 99,300,000 shs. (70% of Cap'l)
outstanding at 8/12/98.
MARKET CAP: $8.1 billion (Large Cap)

CURRENT POSITION ($MILL)	1996	1997	6/30/98
Cash Assets	3.4	4.8	32.6
Receivables	879.5	972.4	926.0
Inventory (FIFO)	273.2	290.5	362.5
Other	193.5	196.7	181.2
Current Assets	1349.6	1464.4	1502.3
Accts Payable	241.7	295.2	255.3
Debt Due	24.5	77.4	128.2
Other	952.5	833.6	860.2
Current Liab.	1218.7	1206.2	1243.7

ANNUAL RATES of change (per sh)	Past 10 Yrs.	Past 5 Yrs.	Est'd '95-'97 to '01-'03
Sales	7.0%	9.5%	8.5%
"Cash Flow"	9.5%	18.5%	8.5%
Earnings	5.5%	9.5%	12.5%
Dividends	5.5%	3.5%	7.5%
Book Value	4.5%	5.5%	11.5%

1818.0	1789.0	1938.6	1943.0	2050.5	2195.5	2760.9	2935.3	3074.7	3534.1	3740	4020	Sales ($mill)	5000
18.7%	19.1%	20.2%	16.4%	16.4%	15.8%	21.9%	21.6%	21.5%	22.0%	22.0%	22.0%	Operating Margin	23.0%
66.2	68.9	66.8	48.9	51.3	54.9	230.0	231.4	238.6	293.5	275	285	Depreciation ($mill)	305
167.4	165.3	172.5	148.0	153.2	172.2	203.1	227.1	250.1	290.7	325	370	Net Profit ($mill)	550
40.4%	42.1%	43.0%	42.7%	42.7%	41.8%	41.2%	41.2%	36.8%	38.3%	38.5%	38.0%	Income Tax Rate	38.0%
9.2%	9.2%	8.9%	7.6%	7.5%	7.8%	7.4%	7.7%	8.1%	8.2%	8.7%	9.2%	Net Profit Margin	11.0%
157.4	47.2	116.4	123.6	70.3	62.9	116.1	193.3	130.9	258.2	260	260	Working Cap'l ($mill)	325
1.9	377.6	507.6	437.3	358.7	757.6	657.5	557.4	556.9	607.0	650	600	Long-Term Debt ($mill)	600
922.8	880.2	954.3	999.0	908.8	823.0	913.1	1035.1	1361.1	1434.7	1515	1675	Shr. Equity ($mill) D	2465
18.1%	14.2%	13.4%	11.6%	13.2%	11.8%	14.4%	15.9%	14.2%	15.4%	16.0%	17.5%	Return on Total Cap'l	18.5%
18.1%	18.8%	18.1%	14.8%	16.9%	20.9%	22.2%	21.9%	18.4%	20.3%	21.5%	22.0%	Return on Shr. Equity	22.5%
8.5%	7.5%	7.0%	4.1%	4.8%	7.3%	9.7%	10.4%	8.7%	10.3%	11.5%	12.5%	Retained to Com Eq	14.0%
53%	60%	61%	72%	71%	65%	56%	53%	53%	49%	47%	44%	All Div'ds to Net Prof	37%

BUSINESS: The McGraw-Hill Companies, Inc. is a multimedia information provider. Publishes textbooks, technical and popular books, periodicals (*Business Week, Aviation Week, ENR,* et al). Entered Macmillan/McGraw-Hill School Publish. joint venture in '89; purchased remaining 50% in 10/93. Markets info. svcs. for the financial and construc. fields (*Standard & Poor's, J.J. Kenny, F.W. Dodge, Data Resources, Platt's*). Owns 4 TV stations. Labor costs: est'd 33% of sales. 1997 deprec. rate: 13%. Has 14,000 emplys.; 7,370 stkhldrs. Offcrs. & Dirctrs. own 3% of shares (3/98 Proxy). Chairman: Joseph L. Dionne. President and C.E.O.: Harold McGraw III. Incorp.: New York. Address: 1221 Avenue of the Americas, New York, NY 10020. Tel.: 212-512-2000.

Source: *Value Line,* August 28, 1998.

Figure 6.2   Value Line Analysis Chart

Callout numbers around the chart: 1, 2, 3, 4, 5, 6, 7, 8, 9, 10 (left side); 11, 12, 13, 14, 15, 16, 17, 18, 19 (top); 20, 21, 22, 23, 24, 25, 26, 27 (right side).

COCA-COLA NYSE-KO

RECENT PRICE	68	P/E RATIO	40.0	Trailing: 43.9 / Median: 23.0	RELATIVE P/E RATIO	2.22	DIV'D YLD	0.9%	VALUE LINE

TIMELINESS 2 Above Average (Relative Price Perform- ance Next 12 Mos.)

SAFETY 1 Highest (Scale: 1 Highest to 5 Lowest)

BETA 1.15 (1.00 = Market)

2000-02 PROJECTIONS

	Price	Gain	Ann'l Total Return
High	80	(+20%)	5%
Low	65	(-5%)	Nil

Insider Decisions

	S	O	N	D	J	F	M	A	M
to Buy	0	0	1	0	1	1	0	0	0
Options	0	3	1	1	2	0	0	2	1
to Sell	0	0	0	0	1	1	0	0	0

Institutional Decisions

	3Q'96	4Q'96	1Q'97
to Buy	298	308	279
to Sell	416	431	471
Hld's(000)	189283	176806	211108

Percent shares traded: 6.0 / 4.0 / 2.0

High/Low per year:
	5.6 3.2	6.6 3.6	5.7 4.4	10.1 5.4	12.3 8.2	20.4 10.7	22.7 17.8	22.5 18.8	26.7 19.4	40.2 24.4	54.3 36.1	72.6 51.1

Target Price Range 2000 2001 2002

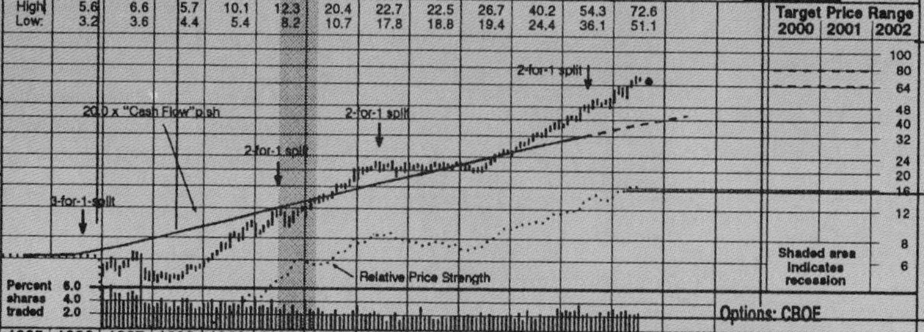

Scale: 100, 80, 64, 48, 40, 32, 24, 20, 16, 12, 8, 6

20.0 x "Cash Flow" p'sh

2-for-1 split

2-for-1 split

3-for-1 split

Relative Price Strength

Shaded area indicates recession

Options: CBOE

1981	1982	1983	1984	1985	1986	1987	1988	1989	1990	1991	1992	1993	1994	1995	1996	1997	1998	© VALUE LINE PUB., INC.	00-02
1.98	1.92	2.09	2.35	2.56	2.81	2.57	2.94	3.33	3.83	4.35	5.00	5.38	6.34	7.19	7.48	7.90	8.90	Sales per sh A	12.60
.20	.20	.22	.25	.28	.31	.36	.43	.50	.60	.71	.84	.98	1.16	1.37	1.60	1.90	2.20	"Cash Flow" per sh	3.15
.15	.16	.17	.20	.22	.26	.30	.36	.42	.51	.61	.72	.84	.99	1.19	1.40	1.70	1.95	Earnings per sh B	2.85
.10	.10	.11	.12	.12	.13	.14	.15	.17	.20	.24	.28	.34	.39	.44	.50	.56	.62	Div'ds Decl'd per sh ■ C	.86
.11	.10	.12	.11	.16	.12	.10	.14	.17	.22	.30	.41	.31	.34	.37	.40	.45	.50	Cap'l Spending per sh	.65
.77	.85	.89	.88	.96	1.14	1.08	1.07	1.18	1.41	1.67	1.49	1.77	2.05	2.15	2.48	3.10	3.80	Book Value per sh D	6.50
2967.0	3257.8	3272.5	3139.8	3087.9	3080.1	2978.8	2838.3	2696.1	2673.0	2657.9	2613.7	2594.9	2551.9	2504.6	2481.0	2445.0	2410.0	Common Shs Outst'g E	2300.0
9.6	9.6	12.6	12.2	13.6	17.3	18.0	13.9	17.8	20.4	24.4	28.7	25.1	22.5	26.8	32.8	Bold figures are Value Line estimates		Avg Ann'l P/E Ratio	25.0
1.17	1.06	1.07	1.14	1.10	1.17	1.20	1.15	1.35	1.52	1.56	1.74	1.48	1.48	1.79	2.07			Relative P/E Ratio	1.80
6.7%	6.5%	5.2%	4.8%	4.2%	2.9%	2.6%	3.0%	2.3%	1.9%	1.6%	1.4%	1.6%	1.7%	1.4%	1.1%			Avg Ann'l Div'd Yield	1.2%

CAPITAL STRUCTURE as of 3/31/97

Total Debt $3788.0 mill.
LT Debt $949.0 mill.   LT interest $62.0 mill.
(Total interest coverage: 17x)
(13% of Cap'l)

Pension Liability None

Pfd Stock None

Common Stock 2,477,234,641 shs.
(87% of Cap'l)

CURRENT POSITION ($MIL.)

	1995	1996	3/31/97
Cash Assets	1315.0	1658.0	2237.0
Receivables	1695.0	1164.10	1697.0
Inventory (Avg Cst)	1117.0	952.0	1051.0
Other	1323.0	1659.0	1355.0
Current Assets	5450.0	5910.0	6340.0
Accts Payable	2894.0	2972.0	3104.0
Debt Due	2923.0	3397.0	2839.0
Other	1531.0	1037.0	1367.0
Current Liab.	7348.0	7406.0	7310.0

ANNUAL RATES of change (per sh)

	Past 10 Yrs.	Past 5 Yrs.	Est'd '94-'96 to '00-'02
Sales	10.5%	13.0%	10.5%
"Cash Flow"	17.0%	18.0%	15.0%
Earnings	18.0%	18.5%	15.5%
Dividends	13.5%	17.0%	12.0%
Book Value	8.5%	9.5%	10.5%

Cal-endar	QUARTERLY SALES ($ mil.) Mar.31	Jun.30	Sep.30	Dec.31	Full Year
1994	3352	4342	4461	4017	16172
1995	3854	4936	4895	4333	18018
1996	4194	5253	4656	4443	18546
1997	4138	5075	5164	4962	19325
1998	4525	5800	5625	5450	21400

Cal-endar	EARNINGS PER SHARE B Mar.31	Jun.30	Sep.30	Dec.31	Full Year
1994	.20	.30	.28	.21	.99
1995	.25	.36	.32	.26	1.19
1996	.28	.42	.39	.31	1.40
1997	.40	.53	.43	.34	1.70
1998	.45	.58	.50	.42	1.95

Cal-endar	QUARTERLY DIVIDENDS PAID C ■ Mar.31	Jun.30	Sep.30	Dec.31	Full Year
1993	--	.085	.085	.17	.34
1994	--	.098	.098	.195	.39
1995	--	.11	.11	.22	.44
1996	--	.125	.125	.25	.50
1997	--	.14	.14		

7658.3	8337.8	8965.8	10236	11572	13074	13957	16172	18018	18546	19325	21400	Sales ($mil)	29000
19.8%	21.2%	21.3%	21.4%	22.3%	23.7%	24.8%	25.5%	25.2%	23.7%	29.0%	30.0%	Operating Margin	31.0%
153.5	169.8	183.8	243.9	261.4	321.9	360.0	411.0	454.0	479.0	485	515	Depreciation ($mill)	650
916.1	1044.7	1192.8	1381.9	1618.0	1883.8	2188.0	2554.0	2986.0	3492.0	4175	4730	Net Profit ($mill)	6600
35.0%	34.0%	32.4%	31.4%	32.1%	31.4%	31.3%	31.5%	31.0%	24.0%	31.0%	31.0%	Income Tax Rate	31.0%
12.0%	12.5%	13.3%	13.5%	14.0%	14.4%	15.7%	15.8%	16.6%	18.8%	21.6%	22.1%	Net Profit Margin	22.8%
17.7	376.5	d54.4	d153.7	26.6	d1056	d737.0	d972.0	d1898	d1496	d1100	d650	Working Cap'l ($mill)	1100
803.4	761.1	548.7	535.9	985.3	1120.1	1428.0	1426.0	1141.0	1116.0	1165	1215	Long-Term Debt ($mill)	1265
3223.8	3345.3	3485.5	3849.2	4425.8	3888.4	4584.0	5235.0	5392.0	6156.0	7560	9100	Net Worth ($mill)	14580
23.6%	28.2%	30.2%	32.2%	30.6%	38.4%	37.7%	39.3%	46.5%	48.5%	49.0%	47.0%	% Earned Total Cap'l	42.5%
28.4%	31.2%	34.2%	35.9%	36.6%	48.4%	47.7%	48.8%	55.4%	56.7%	55.0%	52.0%	% Earned Net Worth	45.5%
15.3%	19.8%	22.0%	22.0%	22.1%	29.5%	28.5%	29.6%	34.8%	36.5%	37.0%	35.5%	% Retained to Com Eq	31.5%
46%	42%	41%	40%	40%	39%	40%	39%	37%	36%	33%	32%	% All Div'ds to Net Prof	30%

BUSINESS: The Coca-Cola Company is the world's largest soft drink company. Distributes major brands (*Coca-Cola, Sprite, Fanta, TAB*, etc.) through bottlers throughout the world. Foreign (non-U.S.) operations accounted for 67% of net sales and 79% of profits in 1996. Food division, world's largest distributor of juice products (*Minute Maid, Five Alive, Hi-C*, etc.). Coca-Cola Enterprises, 45%-

owned soft drink bottler. Advertising costs, 7.7% of sales. Has approximately 26,000 employees; 225,000 stockholders. Berkshire Hathaway owns 8.1% of stock (1997 Proxy). 1996 dep. rate: 8.6%. Estimated plant age: 4 years. Chairman and Chief Executive Officer: Roberto C. Goizueta. Incorporated: Delaware. Address: One Coca-Cola Plaza, Atlanta, Georgia 30313. Tel.: 404-676-2121.

Coca-Cola's earnings moved up sharply again in first half of 1997, although sales actually fell. The decline in the top line was the result of the sale in 1996 of previously consolidated bottling operations in France, Belgium, and east Germany and a stronger U.S. dollar. Worldwide gallon shipments of concentrates were up 8% for the six months, and there were selective price increases. Profit margins improved as concentrate sales accounted for a larger portion of the business, and there were sizable gains ($0.16 a share after taxes) from the sale of bottlers in the United Kingdom and the Philippines. (Coca-Cola has a long-term strategy of taking equity positions in bottlers that need capital and then sometime later usually selling those positions when a bottler gets stronger; since this is done on a regular basis, the company considers any gains to be part of normal operating income, and we have treated it the same way.) With fewer shares outstanding, share earnings were up 31%. **Revenues and profit growth should be strong for the rest of this year and in 1998,** although the increase next year will

probably be somewhat less than in this year since capital gains are likely to be smaller. In the U.S., the core brands are all doing well, and we expect that to continue. Two new products, *Surge* and *Citra* look promising, and *Barq's, Powerade, Fruitopia*, and *Nestea* should have higher sales. Rapid growth is expected again overseas, where Coke is the dominant soft drink brand in most markets. Demand has been increasing particularly fast in East Central Europe, China, India, and, recently, the Middle East. **The company's goal is to increase profits 15%-20% a year,** and we think it will be successful in doing that in the coming 3 to 5 years. Worldwide demand for soft drinks will continue to grow, and Coke has the infrastructure, financial strength, and marketing skills to take advantage of it. **Coke shares continue to be ranked to outperform the market in the coming six to 12 months,** but, because the price has risen so much and the price/earnings ratio is so high, we look for only modest appreciation, at best, out 3 to 5 years. *Stephen Sanborn, CFA   August 15, 1997*

(A) Includes Columbia Pictures: 7/82-12/86. (B) Based on average shares outstanding. Next earnings report due late Oct. Excludes special gains: '81, 2¢; '86, 8¢; disc. op. gains

(loss): '83, (1¢); '85, 2¢; '89, 2¢; nonrec. gain (loss): '89, 36¢; '92, (8¢). (C) Next div'd meeting about Oct. 16. Goes ex Sept. 11. Div'd payment dates: April 1, July 1, Oct. 1, Dec. 15. ■

Div'd reinvestment plan avail. (D) Incl. intangibles. In '96: $753.0 mill., 30¢/sh. (E) In millions, adj. for stock splits.

Company's Financial Strength	A++
Stock's Price Stability	85
Price Growth Persistence	90
Earnings Predictability	100

To subscribe call 1-800-833-0046.

Factual material is obtained from sources believed to be reliable, but the publisher is not responsible for any errors or omissions contained herein. For the confidential use of subscribers. Reprinting, copying, and distribution by permission only. Copyright 1997 by Value Line Publishing, Inc. ® Reg. TM—Value Line, Inc.

Source: *Value Line,* "How To Invest in Common Stocks: A Guide to Using the Value Line Investment Survey," 1998.

Callout Explanations

1. Here is the core of Value Line's advice—the rank for Timeliness; the rank for Safety; Beta—the stock's sensitivity to fluctuations of the market as a whole.

2. The projected average annual return—based on estimated three- to five-year price appreciation plus dividend income.

3. The record of insider decisions—decisions by officers and directors to buy or sell as reported to the SEC one month or more after execution.

4. A record of the decisions taken by the biggest institutions (over $28 billion in equity holdings)—including banks, insurance companies, mutual funds—to buy or sell during the past three quarters and the total number of shares bought or sold.

5. The capital structure as of recent date showing the percentage of capital in long-term debt (13%) and in common stock (87%); the number of times that total interest charges were earned (17 as of August 1997).

6. Current position—current assets and current liabilities, the components of working capital.

7. Annual rates of change (on a per-share basis). Actual past, estimated future.

8. Quarterly earnings are shown on a per-share basis (estimates in bold type), quarterly sales on a gross basis.

9. Quarterly dividends paid are actual payments. The total of dividends paid in four quarters may not equal the figure shown in the annual series on dividends declared. (Sometimes a dividend declared at the end of the year will be paid in the first quarter of the following year).

10. Footnotes explain a number of things, such as the way earnings are reported, whether "fully diluted," on a "primary" basis, or on an "average shares outstanding" basis.

11. The stock's highest and lowest price of the year.

12. The Value Line—reported earnings plus depreciation ("cash flow") multiplied by a number selected to correlate the stock's three- to five-year projected target price with "cash flow" projected out to 1997–98.

13. Monthly price ranges of the stock—plotted on a ratio (logarithmic) grid to show percentage changes in true proportion. For example, a ratio chart equalizes the move of a $10 stock that rises to $11 with that of a $100 stock that rises to $110. Both have advanced 10 percent and over the same space on a ratio grid.

14. Recent price—nine days prior to delivery date.

15. P/E ratio—the most recent price divided by the latest six months' earnings per share plus earnings estimated for the next six months.

16. P/E median—a rounded average of four middle values of the range of average annual price/earnings ratios over the past 10 years.

17. Relative P/E ratio—the stock's current P/E divided by the median P/E for all stocks under Value Line review.

18. Dividend yield—cash dividends estimated to be declared in the next 12 months divided by the recent price.

19. Options patch—indicates listed options are available on the stock and on what exchange they are most actively traded.

20. The three- to five-year target price range, estimated. The range is placed in proper position on the price chart and is shown numerically in the "2000-02 Projections" box on the left side of the price chart.

21. Relative price strength describes the stock's past price performance relative to the Value Line Composite Average of 1,700 stocks. The Timeliness rank usually predicts the future direction of this line.

22. The number of shares traded monthly as a percentage of the total outstanding.

23. Statistical milestones that reveal significant long-term trends. The statistics are presented in two ways: 1) the upper series records results on a per-share basis; 2) the lower records results on a gross basis. Note that the statistics for the current year are estimated, as are the figures for the average of the years 2000–2002. The estimate would be revised, if necessary, should future evidence require. The weekly *Summary & Index* would promptly call attention to such revisions.

24. A condensed summary of the business, significant shareholders, and the company's address and telephone number.

25. A 400-word report on recent developments and prospects—issued once every three months on a preset schedule.

26. The date of delivery to the subscribers. The survey is mailed on a schedule that aims for delivery to every subscriber on Friday afternoon.

27. Value Line's Indexes of Financial Strength, Price Stability, Price Growth Persistence, and Earnings Predictability.

page reports annual average price-earnings ratios, but it does not report average price-cash flow ratios or average price-sales ratios. In this case, a quick way to calculate an average P/CF ratio is to multiply an average P/E ratio by the ratio of earnings per share over cash flow per share: P/CF = P/E × EPS/CFPS.

For example, McGraw-Hill's 1997 average P/E was 20.6, EPS was $2.91, and CFPS was $5.89. Thus a quick calculation of McGraw-Hill's 1997 average P/CF ratio is 20.6 × 2.91/5.89 = 10.18. Similarly, the 1997 average P/S ratio is 20.6 × 2.91/35.66 = 1.68. Average price ratio calculations for P/CF ratios and P/S ratios for the years 1993 through 1997 are provided in Table 6.3, along with five-year averages for each price ratio. Be sure that you understand where all the numbers come from.

The five-year average price ratios calculated in Table 6.3 are used in the price ratio analysis in Table 6.4. The expected growth rates for earnings, cash flow, and sales provided by *Value Line* analysts are used to calculate expected stock prices for McGraw-Hill one year hence. For reference, the three formulas used to calculate expected prices are restated here:

$$\text{Expected price} = \text{P/E ratio} \times \text{EPS} \times (1 + \text{Earnings growth rate})$$

$$\text{Expected price} = \text{P/CF ratio} \times \text{CFPS} \times (1 + \text{Cash flow growth rate})$$

$$\text{Expected price} = \text{P/S ratio} \times \text{SPS} \times (1 + \text{Sales growth rate})$$

We can now summarize our analysis by listing the stock prices obtained by the methods described in this chapter, along with the model used to derive them:

Dividend discount model:	$327.69
Price-earnings model:	$66.90
Price-cash flow model:	$65.79
Price-sales model:	$59.09

These price ratio methods suggest that McGraw-Hill stock might be overvalued at its then-current price of $82. Thus, we might cautiously conclude that McGraw-Hill stock is overvalued. However, only time will tell if this is so. It could simply be the case that the market is anticipating strong sales for this textbook, which is published by McGraw Hill.

Table 6.3

Price Ratio Calculations for McGraw-Hill Company

	1993	1994	1995	1996	1997	Average
EPS	$1.75	$2.05	$2.28	$2.50	$2.91	$2.30
P/E	18.20	16.90	16.70	17.70	20.60	18.02
CFPS	$2.30	$4.36	$4.58	$4.91	$5.89	$4.41
P/CFPS	13.85	7.95	8.31	9.01	10.18	9.86
SPS	$22.22	$27.79	$29.31	$30.89	$35.66	$29.17
P/SPS	1.43	1.25	1.30	1.43	1.68	1.42

Table 6.4

Price Ratio Analysis for McGraw-Hill (MHP)
Late 1998 Stock Price: $82

	Earnings (P/E)	Cash Flow (P/CF)	Sales (P/S)
Current value per share	$3.30	$6.15	$38.35
Five-year average price ratio	18.02	9.86	1.42
Growth rate	12.50%	8.50%	8.50%
Expected stock price	$66.90	$65.79	$59.09

CHECK THIS

6.5a Locate *Value Line*'s projected growth rate in dividends. How does it compare to the sustainable growth rate we estimated?

Reevaluate the stock price using the constant perpetual dividend model and this growth rate.

6.6 Summary and Conclusions

In this chapter, we examined several methods of fundamental analysis used by financial analysts to value common stocks. These methods belong to two categories: dividend discount models and price ratio models. We saw that:

1. Dividend discount models value common stock as the sum of all expected future dividend payments, where the dividends are adjusted for risk and the time value of money.

2. The dividend discount model is often simplified by assuming that dividends will grow at a constant growth rate. A particularly simple form of the dividend discount model is the case in which dividends grow at a constant perpetual growth rate. The simplicity of the constant perpetual growth model makes it the most popular dividend discount model. However, it should be applied only to companies with stable earnings and dividend growth.

3. Dividend models require an estimate of future growth. We described the sustainable growth rate, which is measured as a firm's return on equity times its retention ratio, and illustrated its use.

4. Companies often experience temporary periods of unusually high or low growth, where growth eventually converges to an industry average. In such cases, analysts frequently use a two-stage dividend growth model.

5. Price ratios are widely used by financial analysts. The most popular price ratio is a company's price-earnings ratio. A P/E ratio is calculated as the ratio of a firm's stock price divided by its earnings per share (EPS).

6. Financial analysts often refer to high-P/E stocks as growth stocks and low-P/E stocks as value stocks. In general, companies with high expected earnings growth will have high P/E ratios, which is why high-P/E stocks are referred to as growth stocks. Low-P/E stocks are referred to as value stocks because they are viewed as cheap relative to current earnings.

7. Instead of price-earnings ratios, many analysts prefer to look at price-cash flow (P/CF) ratios. A price-cash flow ratio is measured as a company's stock price divided by its cash flow. Most analysts agree that cash flow can provide more information than net income about a company's financial performance.

8. An alternative view of a company's performance is provided by its price-sales (P/S) ratio. A price-sales ratio is calculated as the price of a company's stock divided by its annual sales revenue per share. A price-sales ratio focuses on a company's ability to generate sales growth. A high P/S ratio suggests high sales growth, while a low P/S ratio suggests low sales growth.

9. A basic price ratio for a company is its price-book (P/B) ratio. A price-book ratio is measured as the market value of a company's outstanding common stock divided by its book value of equity. A high P/B ratio suggests that a company is potentially expensive, while a low P/B value suggests that a company may be cheap.

10. A common procedure using price-earnings ratios, price-cash flow ratios, and price-sales ratios is to calculate estimates of expected future stock prices. However, each price ratio method yields a different expected future stock price. Since each method uses different information, each makes a different prediction.

GET REAL

This chapter introduced you to some of the basics of common stock valuation and fundamental analysis. It focused on two important tools used by stock analysts in the real world to assess whether a particular stock is "rich" or "cheap": dividend discount models and price ratio analysis. How should you, as an investor or investment manager, put this information to use?

The answer is you need to pick some stocks and get to work! As we discussed in the chapter, experience and judgment are needed in using these models, and the only way to obtain these is through practice. Try to identify a few stocks that look cheap and buy them in a simulated brokerage account such as Stock-Trak. At the same time, find a few that look rich and short them.

As time passes, your analyses may prove to be correct or incorrect, but the only way to get started is to apply the tools and witness the outcomes. If your cheap stocks get cheaper, try to understand what you missed. It may be that you are correct, but not enough time has passed. There is an old bit of Wall Street wisdom that goes like this: If you thought stock in Company X was cheap at $40 a share, you've got to love it if the price falls to $20!

Similarly, if your rich stocks get richer, should you hold your position or fold? You may be correct, in which case patience will be rewarded. Of course, with a short position, the penalty for being incorrect is potentially unlimited!

The other thing to do is to start studying P/E ratios. Scan *The Wall Street Journal* (or a similar source of market information) and look at the range of P/Es. What's a low P/E? What's a high one? Do they really correspond to what you would call growth and value stocks? Once again, you should pick a few of each type and invest in them to learn more about value versus growth investing.

Key Terms

fundamental analysis 146
dividend discount model (DDM) 147
constant growth rate model 148
constant perpetual growth model 149
sustainable growth rate 151
retained earnings 151
payout ratio 151
retention ratio 151
two-stage dividend growth model 152

beta 155
price-earnings (P/E) ratio 157
earnings yield 157
growth stocks 157
value stocks 157
price-cash flow (P/CF) ratio 158
cash flow 158
price-sales (P/S) ratio 159
price-book (P/B) ratio 160

Chapter Review Problems and Self-Test

1. **The Perpetual Growth Model** Suppose dividends for a particular company are projected to grow at 6 percent forever. If the discount rate is 16 percent and the current dividend is $2, what is the value of the stock?

2. **The Two-Stage Growth Model** Suppose the Titanic Ice Cube Co.'s dividend grows at a 20 percent rate for the next three years. Thereafter, it grows at a 12 percent rate. What value would we place on Titanic assuming a 15 percent discount rate? Titanic's most recent dividend was $3.

3. **Price Ratio Analysis** The table below contains some information about the Jordan Air Co. Provide expected share prices using each of the three price ratio approaches we have discussed.

Price Ratio Analysis for Jordan Air
Current stock price: $40

	Earnings (P/E)	Cash Flow (P/CF)	Sales (P/S)
Current value per share	$2.00	$6.00	$30.00
Five-year average price ratio	25	7	1.5
Growth rate	10%	16%	14%

Answers to Self-Test Problems

1. Plugging the relevant numbers into the constant perpetual growth formula results in

$$V(0) = \frac{\$2(1.06)}{.16 - .06} = \$21.20$$

As shown, the stock should sell for $21.20.

2. Plugging all the relevant numbers into the two-stage formula gets us

$$V(0) = \frac{\$3(1.20)}{.15 - .20}\left[1 - \left(\frac{1.20}{1.15}\right)^3\right] + \left(\frac{1.20}{1.15}\right)^3 \frac{\$3(1.12)}{.15 - .12}$$

$$= \$9.81 + \$127.25$$

$$= \$137.06$$

Thus, the stock should go for about $137.

3. Using the P/E approach, we come up with the following estimate of the price of Jordan Air in one year:

$$\text{Estimated price} = \text{Average P/E} \times \text{Current EPS} \times (1 + \text{Growth rate})$$

$$= 25 \times \$2 \times 1.10$$

$$= \$55$$

Using the P/CF approach, we get:

$$\text{Estimated price} = \text{Average P/CF} \times \text{Current CFPS} \times (1 + \text{Growth rate})$$

$$= 7 \times \$6 \times 1.16$$

$$= \$48.72$$

Finally, using the P/S approach, we get:

$$\text{Estimated price} = \text{Average P/S} \times \text{Current SPS} \times (1 + \text{Growth rate})$$

$$= 1.5 \times \$30 \times 1.14$$

$$= \$51.30$$

Test Your Investment Quotient

1. **Sustainable Growth**   A company has a return on equity of ROE = 20 percent, and, from earnings per share of EPS = $5, it pays a $2 dividend. What is the company's sustainable growth rate?

    a. 8 percent
    b. 10 percent
    c. 12 percent
    d. 20 percent

2. **Sustainable Growth**   If the return on equity for a firm is 15 percent and the retention ratio is 40 percent, the sustainable growth rate of earnings and dividends is which of the following? (*1994 CFA exam*)

    a. 6 percent
    b. 9 percent
    c. 15 percent
    d. 40 percent

3. **Dividend Discount Model**   Suppose a security pays a current dividend of $5 and all future dividends will grow at a rate of 8 percent per year forever. Assuming the appropriate discount rate is 12 percent, what is the value of this security?

    a. $135
    b. $270
    c. $13.50
    d. $1,350

4. **Dividend Discount Model**   The constant-growth dividend discount model will not produce a finite value if the dividend growth rate is which of the following? (*1994 CFA exam*)

    a. Above its historical average.
    b. Above the required rate of return.
    c. Below its historical average.
    d. Below the required rate of return.

5. **Dividend Discount Model**   In applying the constant-growth dividend discount model, a stock's intrinsic value will do which of the following when the required rate of return is lowered? (*1994 CFA exam*)

    a. Decrease.
    b. Increase.
    c. Remain unchanged.
    d. Decrease or increase, depending on other factors.

6. **Dividend Discount Model**   The constant-growth dividend discount model would typically be most appropriate for valuing the stock of which of the following? (*1994 CFA exam*)

    a. A new venture expected to retain all earnings for several years.
    b. A rapidly growing company.
    c. A moderate growth, mature company.
    d. A company with valuable assets not yet generating profits.

7. **Dividend Discount Model**   A stock has a required return of 15 percent, a constant growth rate of 10 percent, and a dividend payout ratio of 50 percent. What should the stock's P/E ratio be? (*1994 CFA exam*)

    a. 3.0
    b. 4.5
    c. 9.0
    d. 11.0

8. **CAPM Discount Rate** If the U.S. Treasury bill rate is 5 percent and the stock market risk premium is 8 percent, then the CAPM discount rate for a security with a beta of 1.25 is

   a. 12 percent
   b. 13 percent
   c. 14.25 percent
   d. 15 percent

9. **CAPM Discount Rate** If the U.S. Treasury bill rate is 5 percent and the stock market risk premium is 8 percent, then the CAPM discount rate for a security with a beta of .75 is

   a. 6 percent
   b. 8 percent
   c. 11 percent
   d. 13 percent

10. **Dividend Discount Model** A stock will not pay dividends until three years from now. The dividend then will be $2.00 per share, the dividend payout ratio will be 40 percent, and return on equity will be 15 percent. If the required rate of return is 12 percent, which of the following is closest to the value of the stock? (*1994 CFA exam*)

    a. $27
    b. $33
    c. $53
    d. $67

11. **Dividend Discount Model** Assume that at the end of the next year, Company A will pay a $2.00 dividend per share, an increase from the current dividend of $1.50 per share. After that, the dividend is expected to increase at a constant rate of 5 percent. If you require a 12 percent return on the stock, what is the value of the stock? (*1991 CFA exam*)

    a. $28.57
    b. $28.79
    c. $30.00
    d. $31.78

12. **Dividend Discount Model** A share of stock will pay a dividend of $1.00 one year from now, with dividend growth of 5 percent thereafter. In the context of a dividend discount model, the stock is correctly priced at $10 today. According to the constant dividend growth model, if the required return is 15 percent, what should the value of the stock be two years from now? (*1994 CFA exam*)

    a. $11.03
    b. $12.10
    c. $13.23
    d. $14.40

13. **Cash Flow** Which of the following best defines cash flow?

    a. Net income plus depreciation.
    b. Net income minus depreciation.
    c. Net income plus taxes minus depreciation.
    d. Net income plus taxes divided by depreciation.

14. **Price Ratios** Two similar companies have the same price-sales and price-earnings ratios. However, Company A has a lower price-cash flow ratio than Company B. This most likely simply indicates that

    a. A has lower quality earnings than B.
    b. A has lower quality cash flow than B.
    c. A uses straight-line depreciation, while B uses accelerated depreciation.
    d. A uses accelerated depreciation, while B uses straight-line depreciation.

15. Price Ratios   Two similar companies acquire substantial new production facilities, which they both will depreciate over a 10-year period. However, Company A uses accelerated depreciation while Company B uses straight-line depreciation. In the first year that the assets are depreciated, which of the following is most likely to occur?

a. A's P/CF ratio will be higher than B's.
b. A's P/CF ratio will be lower than B's.
c. A's P/E ratio will be higher than B's.
d. A's P/E ratio will be lower than B's.

Questions and Problems

**Core
Questions**

1. Dividend Discount Model   What is the basic principle behind dividend discount models?

2. P/E Ratios   Why do growth stocks tend to have higher P/E ratios than value stocks?

3. Earnings Yields   What is the earnings yield on a stock?

4. Cash Flow   In computing the price-cash flow ratio, how is cash flow per share usually measured?

5. Dividend Valuation   CJ Industries will pay a regular dividend of $3.50 per share for each of the next three years. At the end of the three years, the company will also pay out a $40 per share liquidating dividend, and the company will cease operations. If the discount rate is 9 percent, what is the current value of the company's stock?

6. Dividend Valuation   In the previous problem, suppose the current share price is $50. If all other information remains the same, what must the liquidating dividend be?

7. Dividend Discount Model   Trust Bankers just paid an annual dividend of $2 per share. The expected dividend growth rate is 5 percent, the discount rate is 10 percent, and the dividends will last for 5 more years. What is the value of the stock? What if the dividends last for 10 more years? 30 years? 100 years?

8. Dividend Discount Model   Apple Grove, Inc., will pay dividends for the next 10 years. The expected dividend growth rate for this firm is 8 percent, the discount rate is 15 percent, and the stock currently sells for $25 per share. How much must the most recent dividend payment have been?

9. Dividend Growth Model   Suppose that Kojak, Inc., just paid a dividend of $3.75 per share. The company will continue to pay dividends for the next 20 years and then go out of business. If the discount rate is 12 percent per year, what is the value of stock for a dividend growth rate of 20 percent? 12 percent? 6 percent? 0 percent? −5 percent?

10. Perpetual Dividend Growth   Atlantis Seafood Company stock currently sells for $70 per share. The company is expected to pay a dividend of $4 per share next year, and analysts project that dividends should increase at 4 percent per year for the indefinite future. What must the relevant discount rate be for Atlantis stock?

11. Perpetual Dividend Growth   Xytex Products just paid a dividend of $1.25 per share, and the stock currently sells for $25. If the discount rate is 15 percent, what is the dividend growth rate?

12. Perpetual Dividend Growth   Sturgis Light & Power increases its dividend 5 percent per year every year. This utility is valued using a discount rate of 8 percent, and the stock currently sells for $85 per share. If you buy a share of stock today and hold on to it for at least three years, what do you expect the value of your dividend check to be three years from today?

13. Sustainable Growth   Johnson Products earned $12.50 per share last year and paid a $5 per share dividend. If ROE was 20 percent, what is the sustainable growth rate?

14. **Sustainable Growth**   Caterwallar stock has a sustainable growth rate of 5 percent, ROE of 20 percent, and dividends per share of $3.00. If the P/E ratio is 15, what is the value of a share of stock?

**Intermediate
Questions**

15. **Multiple Growth Rates**   Netscrape Communications does not currently pay a dividend. You expect the company to begin paying a $3 per share dividend in five years, and you expect dividends to grow perpetually at 12 percent per year thereafter. If the discount rate is 15 percent, how much is the stock currently worth?

16. **Multiple Growth Rates**   PerfectlySoft Corp. is experiencing rapid growth. Dividends are expected to grow at 30 percent per year during the next three years, 20 percent over the following year, and then 6 percent per year thereafter indefinitely. The required return on this stock is 15 percent, and the stock currently sells for $42.50 per share. What is the projected dividend for the coming year?

17. **Multiple Growth Rates**   Callaway Corporation is expected to pay the following dividends over the next four years: $2.25, $4.00, $3.00, $1.00. Afterwards, the company pledges to maintain a constant 8 percent growth rate in dividends forever. If the required return on the stock is 16 percent, what is the current share price?

18. **Multiple Growth Rates**   My Money, Inc., just paid a dividend of $2.50 per share on its stock. The growth rate in dividends is expected to be a constant 6.5 percent per year indefinitely. Investors require a 20 percent return on the stock for the first three years, then a 15 percent return for the next three years, and then a 10 percent return thereafter. What is the current share price for My Money?

19. **Price Ratio Analysis**   Given the information below, compute the expected share price at the end of 2000 using price ratio analysis.

	1994	1995	1996	1997	1998	1999
Price	$28	$35	$32	$44	$48	$50
EPS	2.00	2.25	2.30	3.15	3.45	3.75
CFPS	8.00	8.75	8.25	10.00	11.00	11.40
SPS	50	58	55	72	80	86

20. **Dividend Growth Analysis**   In the previous problem, suppose dividends per share over this same period were $.75, $.80, $.80, $1.00, $1.10, and $1.20, respectively. Compute the expected share price for 2000 by the perpetual dividend growth method. Assume the market risk premium is 8.5 percent, Treasury bills yield 5 percent, and the projected beta of this firm is 1.10.

STOCK-TRAK
Portfolio Simulations

Dogs of the Dow Stock Trading with Stock-Trak

A popular investment strategy that many investment advisers recommend to their clients is the so-called "dogs of the Dow" strategy. Under this strategy, an investor ranks the 30 stocks in the Dow Jones Industrial Average according to their dividend yields. The investor then buys the five Dow stocks with the highest dividend yields. Six months or a year later, the five stocks in the DJIA with the highest dividend yields are again identified and the investor switches funds into these stocks. This strategy has gained a reputation for often outperforming the entire 30-stock Dow average.

If you would like to try the dogs of the Dow strategy with your Stock-Trak account, obtain the names of the 30 stocks in the DJIA from *The Wall Street Journal*. Next, find these stocks in *The Wall Street Journal* stock price listings and record their dividend yields. Identify the five Dow stocks with the highest dividend yields and, just for fun, also record the five Dow stocks with the lowest dividend yields. You might try investing all your Stock-Trak funds in the high-dividend Dow stocks, following a pure dogs of the Dow strategy. Alternatively, you can invest half your funds in the low-dividend Dow stocks and the other half in the high-dividend Dow stocks and then compare them to determine which dividend strategy performs best.

Value versus Growth Stock Trading with Stock-Trak

Portfolio managers often pursue investment strategies based on either value stocks or growth stocks. With Stock-Trak you can try these strategies yourself. Look through *The Wall Street Journal* stock price listings, and identify several low-P/E stocks and several high-P/E stocks. Try to find P/E ratios below 10 for the low-P/E stocks and P/E ratios greater than 40 for the high-P/E stocks. Use the low-P/E stocks to form a *value* portfolio and the high-P/E stocks to form a *growth* portfolio.

Using your Stock-Trak account, you can try several strategies based on your value and growth portfolios. You can invest all your Stock-Trak funds in the value portfolio or you can invest all your funds in the growth portfolio. Alternatively, you can invest half your funds in each of the value and growth portfolios and compare the returns to determine which strategy performs best.

Stock-Trak Exercises

1. In a more sophisticated version of the dogs of the Dow strategy, you buy the high-dividend Dow stocks and short sell the low-dividend Dow stocks. This strategy requires a little more effort but the results might be a little more interesting.

2. A similarly sophisticated strategy can be based on value stocks versus growth stocks. If you believe value stocks will outperform growth stocks, then you buy low-P/E stocks and short sell high-P/E stocks. But if you believe growth stocks will outperform value stocks, then you buy high-P/E stocks and short sell low-P/E stocks.

7

Earnings and Cash Flow Analysis

Cash flow is a company's lifeblood, and for a healthy company, the primary source of cash flow is earnings. Little wonder that security analysts are obsessed with both, since their goal is to predict future earnings and cash flow. An analyst who predicts accurately has a head start in knowing which stocks will go up and which stocks will go down. ■ In the previous chapter, we examined some important concepts of stock analysis and valuation. Here we probe deeper into the topic of common stock valuation through an analysis of earnings and cash flow. In particular, we focus on earnings and cash flow forecasting. This chapter will acquaint you with financial accounting concepts necessary to understand basic financial statements and perform earnings and cash flow analysis using these financial statements. You may not become an expert analyst—this requires experience. But you will have a grasp of the fundamentals, which is a good start.

Unfortunately, most investors have difficulty reading financial statements and instead rely on various secondary sources of financial information. Of course, this is good for those involved with publishing secondary financial information.

Bear in mind, however, that no one is paid well just for reading such sources of financial information. By reading this chapter, you take an important step toward becoming financial statement literate, and an extra course in financial accounting is also helpful. But ultimately you learn to read financial statements by reading financial statements! Like a good game of golf or tennis, financial statement reading skills require practice. If you have an aptitude for it, financial statement analysis is a skill worth mastering. Good analysts are paid well, but good analysis is expected in return. Maybe you too can become one of the few, the proud—a financial analyst.

7.1 Sources of Financial Information

Good financial analysis begins with good financial information. An excellent primary source of financial information about any company is its annual report to stockholders. Most companies expend considerable resources preparing and distributing annual reports. In addition to their stockholders, companies also make annual reports available to anyone requesting a copy. A convenient way to request copies of annual reports from several companies simultaneously is to use the annual reports service provided by *The Wall Street Journal*. If you open the *Journal* to its daily stock price reports, you will see a shamrock symbol ♣ next to entries for many individual stocks. The shamrock indicates that the company will send annual reports to readers who request them through *The Wall Street Journal*. Requests can be submitted by telephone or by fax.

The Internet is a convenient source of financial information about many companies. For example, the New York Stock Exchange website (www.nyse.com) provides a directory of websites for companies whose stock trades on the exchange. The content of company websites varies greatly, but many provide recent quarterly or annual financial reports.

In addition to company annual reports, a wealth of primary financial information is available to investors through the Securities and Exchange Commission. The SEC requires corporations with publicly traded securities to prepare and submit financial statements on a regular basis. When received, these documents are made available for immediate public access through the SEC's Electronic Data Gathering and Retrieval (EDGAR) archives. The **EDGAR** archives are accessible free of charge through the Internet (www.sec.gov) and are an excellent source of timely financial information.

EDGAR Electronic archive of company filings with the SEC.

The most important EDGAR document is the annual **10K** report, often simply called the "10K." Companies are required to submit an EDGAR-compatible 10K file to the SEC at the end of each fiscal year. They are also required to file quarterly updates, called 10Qs. The **10Q** is a mini-10K filed each quarter, except when the 10K is filed. Every 10K and 10Q report contains three important financial statements: a balance sheet, an income statement, and a cash flow statement. You must be familiar with these three financial statements to analyze company earnings and cash flow.

10K Annual company report filed with the SEC.

10Q Quarterly updates of 10K reports filed with the SEC.

7.2 Financial Statements

Financial statements reveal the hard facts about a company's operating and financial performance. This is why the SEC requires timely dissemination of financial statements to the public. It's also why security analysts spend considerable time poring over a firm's financial statements before making an investment recommendation. A firm's balance sheet, income statement, and cash flow statement are essential reading for securi-

balance sheet
Accounting statement that provides a snapshot view of a company's assets and liabilities on a particular date.

income statement
Summary statement of a firm's revenues and expenses over a specific accounting period, usually a quarter or a year.

cash flow statement
Analysis of a firm's sources and uses of cash over the accounting period, summarizing operating, investing, and financing cash flows.

ty analysts. Each of these interrelated statements offers a distinct perspective. The **balance sheet** provides a snapshot view of a company's assets and liabilities on a particular date. The **income statement** measures operating performance over an accounting period, usually a quarter or a year, and summarizes company revenues and expenses. The **cash flow statement** reports how cash was generated and where it was used over the accounting period. Understanding the format and contents of these three financial statements is a prerequisite for understanding earnings and cash flow analysis.

We begin by considering the basic structure and general format of financial statements through a descriptive analysis of the balance sheet, income statement, and cash flow statement of a hypothetical intergalactic company—the Borg Corporation.

The Balance Sheet

Table 7.1 presents year-end 2535 and 2536 balance sheets for Borg Corporation. The format of these balance sheets is typical of that contained in company annual reports distributed to stockholders and 10K filings with the SEC. Get used to the accounting practice of specifying subtraction with parentheses and calculating subtotals while moving down a column of numbers. For example, Borg's 2536 fixed assets section is reproduced below, with the left numerical column following standard accounting notation and the right numerical column following standard arithmetic notation:

Fixed Assets	Accounting Style	Numeric Style
Plant facilities	$35,000	$35,000
Production equipment	20,000	+20,000
Administrative facilities	15,000	+15,000
Patents	10,000	+10,000
Accumulated depreciation	(20,000)	−20,000
Total fixed assets	$60,000	$60,000

Common to both numerical columns, an underline indicates that the numbers listed above should be summed. However, accounting notation omits the plus "+" sign and subtraction is indicated by parentheses "( )" instead of the more familiar minus "−" sign. Referring to Table 7.1, notice that total fixed assets is a subtotal used to calculate total assets, which is indicated by a double underline. With these conventions in mind, let us look over these sample balance sheets and try to become familiar with their format and contents.

asset Anything a company owns that has value.

The Borg Corporation balance sheet has four major **asset** categories: current assets, fixed assets, investments, and other assets. Current assets are cash or items that will be converted to cash or be used within a year. For example, inventory will be sold, accounts receivable will be collected, and materials and supplies will be used within a year. Cash is, or course, the quintessential current asset. Fixed assets have an expected life longer than one year and are used in normal business operations. Fixed assets may be tangible or intangible. Property, plant, and equipment are the most common tangible fixed assets. Rights, patents, and licenses are common intangible assets. Except for land, all fixed assets normally depreciate in value over time. Investments include various securities held for investment purposes. Goodwill measures the premium paid over market value to acquire an asset. For example, a company may pay $50 per share for

Table 7.1	BORG CORPORATION Balance Sheets, 2536 and 2535		
		Year 2536	**Year 2535**
Current assets			
	Cash	$ 2,000	$ 1,356
	Accounts receivable	1,200	1,200
	Prepaid expenses	500	500
	Materials and supplies	300	300
	Inventory	6,000	6,000
	Total current assets	$ 10,000	$ 9,356
Fixed assets			
	Plant facilities	$ 35,000	$35,000
	Production equipment	20,000	20,000
	Administrative facilities	15,000	15,000
	Patents	10,000	10,000
	Accumulated depreciation	(20,000)	(17,000)
	Total fixed assets	$ 60,000	$63,000
Investments			
	Cardassian Mining		
	7% Preferred stock	$ 10,000	$10,000
	Klingon Enterprises		
	Common stock	10,000	
	Goodwill	5,000	
	Total investments	$ 25,000	$10,000
Other assets		5,000	5,000
Total assets		$100,000	$87,356
Current liabilities			
	Short-term debt	$ 10,000	$10,000
	Accounts payable	2,000	2,000
	Leasing obligations	3,000	3,000
	Total current liabilities	$ 15,000	$15,000
Long-term debt		$ 30,000	$20,000
Other liabilities		5,000	5,000
Total liabilities		$ 50,000	$40,000
Stockholder equity			
	Paid-in capital	$ 10,000	$10,000
	Retained earnings	40,000	37,356
	Total stockholder equity	$ 50,000	$47,356
Total liabilities and equity		$100,000	$87,356
	Shares outstanding	2,000	2,000
	Year-end stock price	$40	$36

stock with a market price of $40 per share when acquiring a very large block of stock. Other assets include miscellaneous items not readily fitting into any of the other asset categories. The sum of these four categories of assets is the firm's total assets.

Table 7.2

BORG CORPORATION
Condensed Balance Sheet

Cash	$ 2,000	Current liabilities	$ 15,000
Operating assets	8,000	Long-term debt	30,000
Fixed assets	60,000	Other liabilities	5,000
Investments	25,000		
Other assets	5,000	Stockholder equity	50,000
Total assets	$100,000	Total liabilities and equity	$100,000

liability A firm's
financial obligation.

The Borg balance sheet has three major **liability** categories: current liabilities, long-term debt, and other liabilities. Current liabilities normally require payment or other action within a one-year period. These include accounts payable and accrued taxes. Long-term debt includes notes, bonds, or other loans with a maturity longer than one year. Other liabilities include miscellaneous items not belonging to any other liability category.

equity An ownership
interest in the
company.

Stockholder **equity** is the difference between total assets and total liabilities. It includes paid-in capital, which is the amount received by the company from issuing common stock, and retained earnings, which represent accumulated income not paid out as dividends but instead used to finance company growth.

A fundamental accounting identity for balance sheets states that assets are equal to liabilities plus equity:

$$\text{Assets} = \text{Liabilities} + \text{Equity}. \qquad \textbf{7.1}$$

This identity implies that the balance sheet always "balances" because the left side is always equal in value to the right side. If an imbalance occurs when a balance sheet is created, then an accounting error has been made and needs to be corrected.

Financial analysts often find it useful to condense a balance sheet down to its principal categories. This has the desirable effect of simplifying further analysis while still revealing the basic structure of the company's assets and liabilities. How much a balance sheet can be condensed and still be useful is a subjective judgment of the analyst. When making this decision, recall Albert Einstein's famous dictum: "Simplify as much as possible, but no more."

Table 7.2 is a condensed version of Borg's balance sheet that still preserves its basic structure. Notice that the current assets rows are reduced to two components, cash and operating assets. We separate cash from operating assets for a good reason. Later, we show that net cash increase from the cash flow statement is used to adjust cash on the balance sheet. This adjustment is more clearly illustrated by first separating current assets into cash and operating assets.

CHECK THIS

7.2a What are some examples of current assets?

7.2b What are some examples of fixed assets?

7.2c What are some examples of current liabilities?

7.2d Which accounts in Figure 7.1 show changes between 2535 and 2536 balance sheets?

The Income Statement

Table 7.3 is a condensed income statement for Borg Corporation. The left column follows standard accounting notation and the right column follows familiar arithmetic notation. Of course, the right column would not appear in an actual financial statement and is included here for convenience only. This income statement reports revenues and expenses for the corporation over a one-year accounting period. Examine it carefully and be sure you are familiar with its top-down structure.

The income statement begins with net sales, from which cost of goods sold (COGS) is subtracted to yield gross profit. Cost of goods sold represents direct costs of production and sales; that is, costs that vary directly with the level of production and sales. Next, operating expenses are subtracted from gross profit to yield operating **income**. Operating expenses are indirect costs of administration and marketing; that is, costs that do not vary directly with production and sales.

income The difference between a company's revenues and expenses, used to pay dividends to stockholders or kept as retained earnings within the company to finance future growth.

In addition to operating income from its own business operations, Borg Corporation has investment income from preferred stock dividends. Adding this investment income and then subtracting interest expense on debt yields pretax income. Finally, subtracting income taxes from pretax income yields net income. Net income is often referred to as the "bottom line" because it is normally the last line of the income statement. In this example, however, we have added dividends and retained earnings information, items that often appear in a separate financial statement. To avoid a separate statement, we here show that Borg Corporation paid dividends during the year. The sum of dividends and retained earnings is equal to net income:

$$\text{Net income} = \text{Dividends} + \text{Retained earnings} \qquad \textbf{7.2}$$

The footnote to Table 7.3 explains that only 20 percent of preferred stock dividends are taxable. This feature of the federal tax code allows a company to exclude 80 percent of dividends received from another company from federal income tax.[1] In this case, Borg receives $700 in dividends from Cardassian Mining and pays taxes on only $140 (20 percent) of this amount. Assuming a 40 percent tax rate, the actual tax amount is $56 = 40\% \times \$140$.

Table 7.3

BORG CORPORATION
Condensed Income Statement

Net sales	$90,000	$90,000
Cost of goods sold	(70,000)	−70,000
Gross profit	$20,000	$20,000
Operating expenses	(13,000)	−13,000
Operating income	$ 7,000	$ 7,000
Investment income	700	+700
Interest expense	(2,000)	−2,000
Pretax income	$ 5,700	$ 5,700
Income taxes[a]	(2,056)	−2,056
Net income	$ 3,644	$ 3,644
Dividends	(1,000)	−1,000
Retained earnings	$ 2,644	$ 2,644

[a] A tax rate of 40 percent is applied to the total of operating income less interest expense plus the taxable 20 percent portion of preferred stock dividends: $7,000 − \$2,000 + 20\% \times 7\% \times \$10,000 = \$5,140$ and $40\% \times \$5,140 = \$2,056$.

---

[1] Actually, the exclusion is either 70 or 80 percent depending on how much of another company's stock is held.

CHECK
THIS

7.2e What is cost of goods sold (COGS)?

7.2f What is the difference between gross profit and operating income?

7.2g What is the difference between net income and pretax income?

7.2h What is meant by retained earnings?

The Cash Flow Statement

The cash flow statement reports where a company generated cash and where cash was used over a specific accounting period. The cash flow statement assigns all cash flows to one of three categories: operating cash flows, investment cash flows, or financing cash flows.

Table 7.4 is a condensed cash flow statement for Borg Corporation. (This is the last appearance of both accounting and arithmetic notation.) The cash flow statement begins with net income, which is the principal accounting measure of earnings for a corporation. However, net income and **cash flow** are not the same and often deviate greatly from each other. A primary reason why income differs from cash flow is that income contains **noncash items**. For example, depreciation is a noncash expense that must be added to net income when calculating cash flow. Adjusting net income for noncash items yields **operating cash flow**.

Operating cash flow is the first of three cash flow categories reported in the cash flow statement. The second and third categories are investment cash flow and financing cash flow. **Investment cash flow** includes any purchases or sales of fixed assets and investments. For example, Borg's purchase of Klingon Enterprises common stock reported in footnote a is an investment cash flow. **Financing cash flow** includes any funds raised by an issuance of securities or expended by a repurchase of outstanding securities. In this example, Borg's $10,000 debt issue and $1,000 dividend payout reported in footnote b are examples of financing cash flows.

Standard accounting practice specifies that dividend payments to stockholders are financing cash flows, whereas interest payments to bondholders are operating cash flows. One reason is that dividend payments are discretionary, while interest payments are mandatory. Also, interest payments are tax-deductible expenses, but dividend payouts are not tax deductible. In any case, interest payments are cash expenses reported on the income statement. Since they are cash expenses, they do not appear in the cash flow statement to reconcile the difference between income and cash flow.

cash flow Income realized in cash form.

noncash items Income and expense items not realized in cash form.

operating cash flow Cash generated by a firm's normal business operations.

investment cash flow Cash flow resulting from purchases and sales of fixed assets and investments.

financing cash flow Cash flow originating from the issuance or repurchase of securities and the payment of dividends.

Table 7.4

BORG CORPORATION
Condensed Cash Flow Statement

Net income	$ 3,644	$3,644
Depreciation	3,000	+3,000
Operating cash flow	$ 6,644	$6,644
Investment cash flow[a]	(15,000)	−15,000
Financing cash flow[b]	9,000	+9,000
Net cash increase	$ 644	$ 644

[a] December 2536 purchase of 50 percent interest in Klingon Enterprises for $15,000 (including $5,000 goodwill).

[b] Issue of $10,000 par value 8 percent coupon bonds, less a $1,000 dividend payout.

The sum of operating cash flow, investment cash flow, and financing cash flow yields the net change in the firm's cash. This change is the "bottom line" of the cash flow statement and reveals how much cash flowed into or out of the company's cash account during an accounting period.

CHECK THIS

7.2i	What is the difference between net income and operating cash flow?	cash flow and a financing cash flow?
7.2j	What are some noncash items used to calculate operating cash flow?	**7.2l** What is meant by net increase in cash?
7.2k	What is the difference between an investment	**7.2m** Can you explain why a cash item like interest expense does not appear on the cash flow statement?

Performance Ratios and Price Ratios

Annual reports and 10Ks normally contain various items of supplemental information about the company. For example, certain profitability ratios may be reported to assist interpretation of the company's operating efficiency. For Borg Corporation, some standard profitability ratios are calculated as follows.

Ratio	Formula	Calculation
Gross margin	$\dfrac{\text{Gross profit}}{\text{Net sales}}$	$\dfrac{\$20{,}000}{\$90{,}000} = 22.22\%$
Operating margin	$\dfrac{\text{Operating income}}{\text{Net sales}}$	$\dfrac{\$7{,}000}{\$90{,}000} = 7.78\%$
Return on assets (ROA)	$\dfrac{\text{Net income}}{\text{Total assets}}$	$\dfrac{\$3{,}644}{\$100{,}000} = 3.64\%$
Return on equity (ROE)	$\dfrac{\text{Net income}}{\text{Stockholder equity}}$	$\dfrac{\$3{,}644}{\$50{,}000} = 7.29\%$

return on assets (ROA) Net income stated as a percentage of total assets.

return on equity (ROE) Net income stated as a percentage of stockholder equity.

Notice that **return on assets (ROA)** and **return on equity (ROE)** are calculated using current year-end values for total assets and stockholder equity. It could be argued that prior-year values should be used for these calculations. However, standard practice calls for the use of current year-end values.

Annual reports and 10Ks may also report per-share calculations of book value, earnings, and operating cash flow, respectively. Per-share calculations require the number of common stock shares outstanding. Borg's balance sheet reports 2,000 shares of common stock outstanding. Thus, for Borg Corporation, these per-share values are calculated as follows:

Ratio	Formula	Calculation
Book value per share (BVPS)	$\dfrac{\text{Stockholder equity}}{\text{Shares outstanding}}$	$\dfrac{\$50{,}000}{2{,}000} = \$25$
Earnings per share (EPS)	$\dfrac{\text{Net income}}{\text{Shares outstanding}}$	$\dfrac{\$3{,}644}{2{,}000} = \$1.82$
Cash flow per share (CFPS)	$\dfrac{\text{Operating cash flow}}{\text{Shares outstanding}}$	$\dfrac{\$6{,}644}{2{,}000} = \$3.32$

Notice that cash flow per share (CFPS) is calculated using operating cash flow—*not* the bottom line on the cash flow statement! Most of the time when you hear the term "cash flow," it refers to operating cash flow.

Recall that in the previous chapter, we made extensive use of price ratios to analyze stock values. Using per-share values calculated immediately above, and Borg's year-end stock price of $40 per share, we get the following price ratios:

Ratio	Formula	Calculation
Price-book (P/B)	$\dfrac{\text{Stock price}}{\text{BVPS}}$	$\dfrac{\$40}{\$25} = 1.6$
Price-earnings (P/E)	$\dfrac{\text{Stock price}}{\text{EPS}}$	$\dfrac{\$40}{\$1.82} = 22$
Price-cash flow (P/CF)	$\dfrac{\text{Stock price}}{\text{CFPS}}$	$\dfrac{\$40}{\$3.32} = 12$

We use these price ratios later when assessing the potential impact of a sales campaign on Borg Corporation's future stock price.

CHECK THIS

7.2n What is the difference between gross margin and operating margin?

7.2o What is the difference between return on assets and return on equity?

7.2p What is the difference between earnings per share and cash flow per share?

7.2q How is cash flow per share calculated?

7.3 Financial Statement Forecasting

pro forma financial statements
Statements prepared using certain assumptions about future income, cash flow, and other items. Pro forma literally means according to prescribed form.

In December 2536, Borg publicly announced the completed acquisition of a 50 percent financial interest in Ferengi Traders. However, half the acquired shares do not carry voting rights, so the acquisition is treated as a simple investment on the balance sheet. The stated purpose of the acquisition was to expand sales outlets. Complementing the acquisition, Borg also announced plans for a marketing campaign to increase next year's net sales to a targeted $120,000.

As a Borg analyst, you must examine the potential impact of these actions. You immediately contact Borg management to inquire about the details of the acquisition and the marketing campaign. Armed with this additional information, you decide to construct **pro forma financial statements** for Borg Corporation for the year 2537. You also decide to formulate your analysis by considering two scenarios: an optimistic sales scenario and a pessimistic sales scenario. Under the optimistic scenario, the marketing campaign is successful and targeted net sales of $120,000 are realized with an assumed cost of goods sold of $90,000. Under the pessimistic scenario, only $100,000 of net sales are realized with a cost of goods sold of $80,000. Operating expenses will be $17,000 under both scenarios, reflecting the costs of the marketing campaign. The appropriate sequence for your analysis is to construct pro forma income statements, then pro forma cash flow statements, followed by pro forma balance sheets.

The Pro Forma Income Statement

Table 7.5 contains side-by-side pro forma income statements for Borg Corporation corresponding to optimistic and pessimistic sales scenarios in the coming year. These begin with the assumed net sales and cost of goods sold values for both scenarios. They then proceed with the standard top-down calculations of income where several calculation methods and additional assumptions are explained in footnotes. The optimistic sales scenario produces a net income of $8,264, of which $1,000 is paid as dividends and $7,264 is kept as retained earnings. Under the pessimistic sales scenario net income is only $764, with $1,000 of dividends and −$236 of retained earnings.

Footnote a explains that investment income is $2,200 under optimistic sales and $700 under pessimistic sales. This reflects constant preferred stock dividends of $700 and assumed noncash investment income from Ferengi Traders of $1,500 under optimistic sales and $0 under pessimistic sales. The difference in scenario investment incomes stems from the fact that Ferengi is involved with the sales campaign.

Footnote c explains that taxes are paid on operating income less interest expense plus the taxable portion of preferred stock dividends. Notice that Borg's noncash investment income from Ferengi Traders is not taxed because Ferengi paid no dividends. In this situation, Borg records the value of its investment in Ferengi as its share of Ferengi's stockholder equity value. Thus, when Ferengi adds retained earnings to its equity value,

Table 7.5	BORG CORPORATION Pro Forma Income Statements		
		Optimistic	**Pessimistic**
Net sales		$120,000	$100,000
Cost of goods sold		(90,000)	(80,000)
Gross profit		$ 30,000	$ 20,000
Operating expenses		(17,000)	(17,000)
Operating income		$ 13,000	$ 3,000
Investment income[a]		2,200	700
Interest expense[b]		(2,800)	(2,800)
Pretax income		$ 12,400	$ 900
Income taxes[c]		(4,136)	(136)
Net income		$ 8,264	$ 764
Dividends[d]		$ 1,000	$ 1,000
Retained earnings		$ 7,264	$ (236)

[a] Preferred stock dividends of $700 plus $1,500 noncash investment income from Ferengi Traders under optimistic sales results and $0 under pessimistic sales results, i.e., $700 + $1,500 = $2,200.

[b] Prior-year interest expense of $2,000 plus payment of 8 percent coupons on the December 2536 debt issue of $10,000, i.e., $2,000 + 8% × $10,000 = $2,800.

[c] Tax rate of 40% applied to the sum of operating income less interest expense plus the 20 percent taxable portion of preferred stock dividends, i.e., ($13,000 − $2,800 + 20% × 7% × $10,000) × 40% = $4,136.

[d] Assumes no change in dividends from prior year.

Borg records its share of the addition as noncash income and changes the balance sheet value of its investment in Ferengi accordingly. The next step of your analysis is construction of pro forma cash flow statements.

CHECK THIS

7.3a Create a pro forma income statement for Borg Corporation corresponding to pessimistic

sales results assuming noncash investment losses of $1,000.

The Pro Forma Cash Flow Statement

Table 7.6 contains side-by-side pro forma cash flow statements for Borg Corporation under optimistic and pessimistic sales scenarios. Under the optimistic sales scenario the net cash increase is $6,964; under the pessimistic scenario the net cash change −$36. The net cash increase is applied to adjust the cash account on the pro forma balance sheet. This adjustment is now more convenient since you separated cash from operating assets in Borg's condensed balance sheet.

Footnote a explains that goodwill amortization is $200 per year based on a 25-year amortization schedule. This amortization is applied to the $5,000 of goodwill on Borg's prior-year balance sheet associated with its purchase of a 50 percent stake in Ferengi Traders. Footnote b explains that operating assets are assumed to increase by $2,000 under optimistic sales and $3,000 under pessimistic sales. These increases are realistic since a sales campaign will surely require additional inventory. The increase is bigger under pessimistic sales because more inventory goes unsold. Your next step is to create the pro forma balance sheet for Borg Corporation.

Table 7.6

BORG CORPORATION
Pro Forma Cash Flow Statements

	Optimistic	Pessimistic
Net income	$ 8,264	$ 764
Depreciation/amortization[a]	3,200	3,200
Increase in operating assets[b]	(2,000)	(3,000)
Noncash investment income	(1,500)	(0)
Operating cash flow	$ 7,964	$ 964
Investment cash flow[c]	$ 0	$ 0
Financing cash flow[d]	$(1,000)	$(1,000)
Net cash increase	$ 6,964	$ (36)

[a] Assumes the same $3,000 depreciation as in the prior year and annual goodwill amortization of $200 based on a 25-year amortization schedule.

[b] Assumes an increase in operating assets of $2,000 under optimistic sales and $3,000 under pessimistic sales.

[c] Assumes no new investments.

[d] Assumes no change in dividend payouts.

CHECK THIS

7.3b Create a pro forma cash flow statement for Borg Corporation under pessimistic sales results assuming noncash investment losses of $1,000.

The Pro Forma Balance Sheet

Table 7.7 contains side-by-side pro forma balance sheets for Borg Corporation as they might result from optimistic and pessimistic sales scenarios. This balance sheet is created by starting with the prior-year condensed balance sheet and then making the following adjustments consistent with the pro forma income statements and cash flow statements:

1. Cash of $2,000 is adjusted by a net cash increase of $6,964 under the optimistic sales scenario and −$36 under the pessimistic sales scenario.

2. Current assets of $8,000 are increased by $2,000 under the optimistic sales scenario and increased by $3,000 under the pessimistic sales scenario.

3. Fixed assets of $60,000 are adjusted by depreciation of $3,000, which is the same under both sales scenarios.

4. Investments of $25,000 are increased by the assumed noncash investment income from Ferengi Traders of $1,500 under optimistic sales and $0 under pessimistic sales, less $200 of goodwill amortization. As noted earlier, the difference by scenario is based on the fact that Ferengi is involved with the sales campaign.

5. Equity of $50,000 is adjusted for retained earnings of $7,264 under optimistic sales and −$236 under pessimistic sales.

All other accounts remain unchanged, which is a simplifying assumption made to focus attention on the immediate impact of the sales campaign.

CHECK THIS

7.3c Create a pro forma balance sheet for Borg under a pessimistic sales scenario assuming noncash investment losses of $1,000.

Projected Profitability and Price Ratios

In addition to preparing pro forma financial statements, you also decide to calculate projected profitability ratios and per-share values under optimistic and pessimistic sales scenarios. These are reported immediately below and compared with their original year-end values.

Table 7.7

BORG CORPORATION
Pro Forma Balance Sheets

	Optimistic	Pessimistic
Cash[a]	$ 8,964	$ 1,964
Operating assets[b]	10,000	11,000
Fixed assets[c]	57,000	57,000
Investments[d]	26,300	24,800
Other assets	5,000	5,000
Total assets	$107,264	$99,764
Current liabilities	$ 15,000	$15,000
Long-term debt	30,000	30,000
Other liabilities	5,000	5,000
Stockholder equity[e]	57,264	49,764
Total liabilities and equity	$107,264	$99,764

[a] Prior-year cash of $2,000 plus $6,964 (optimistic) and −$36 (pessimistic) net cash increase from the pro forma cash flow statement.

[b] Prior-year operating assets of $8,000 plus an additional $2,000 under optimistic sales and $3,000 under pessimistic sales.

[c] Prior-year fixed assets of $60,000 less the assumed $3,000 depreciation.

[d] Prior-year investments of $25,000 plus noncash investment income of $1,500 under optimistic sales only less $200 goodwill amortization.

[e] Prior-year equity of $50,000 plus $7,264 (optimistic) and −$236 (pessimistic) retained earnings from the pro forma income statement.

	Original	Optimistic	Pessimistic
Gross margin	22.22%	25%	20%
Operating margin	7.78%	10.83%	3%
Return on assets (ROA)	3.64%	7.70%	.77%
Return on equity (ROE)	7.29%	14.43%	1.54%
Book value per share (BVPS)	$25	$28.63	$24.88
Earnings per share (EPS)	$1.82	$4.13	$.38
Cash flow per share (CFPS)	$3.32	$3.98	$.48

One common method of analysis is to calculate projected stock prices under optimistic and pessimistic sales scenarios using prior-period price ratios and projected per-share values from pro forma financial statements. Similar procedures were performed in the previous chapter using prior-period average price ratios and per-share values based on growth rate projections. For Borg Corporation, you decide to take year-end 2536 price ratios and multiply each ratio by its corresponding pro forma per-share value. The results of these projected stock price calculations are shown immediately below.

	Projected Stock Prices	
	Optimistic	Pessimistic
BVPS × P/B	$45.81	$39.81
EPS × P/E	$90.86	$ 8.36
CFPS × P/CF	$47.76	$ 5.76

These projected stock prices reflect widely varying degrees of sensitivity to optimistic and pessimistic sales scenario outcomes. For example, projected prices based on EPS and CFPS are especially sensitive to which scenario is realized. On the other hand, projected stock prices based on BVPS are far less sensitive to scenario realization.

Which projected stock price is correct? Well, it clearly depends on which sales scenario is realized and which price ratio the financial markets will actually use to value Borg Corporation's stock. This is where experience and breadth of knowledge count immensely. Of course no one can make perfectly accurate predictions, but the analyst's job is to expertly assess the situation and make an investment recommendation supported by reasonable facts and investigation. But some analysts are better than others. Like professional baseball players, professional stock analysts with better batting averages can do very well financially.

Adolph Coors Company Case Study

After carefully reading the analysis of Borg Corporation, you should have a reasonably clear picture of how earnings and cash flow analyses might proceed using pro forma financial statements. To further illustrate the use of pro forma financial statements in earnings and cash flow analysis, this section presents an analysis based on the 1995 financial statements for Adolph Coors Company. Using data for a real company provides a real challenge.

This section begins with a review of Coors 1995 financial statements. We then proceed to analyze the effects on earnings and cash flow that might result from product sales either rising or falling by 10 percent. The analysis is similar to that for Borg Corporation, but there are a few important differences. Amounts shown are in thousands of dollars (except earnings per share).

Adolph Coors 1995 condensed balance sheet is shown in Table 7.8, where all numbers are scaled to represent thousands of dollars. This balance sheet shows that at year-end 1995 Coors had $1.39 billion of total assets and $695 million of stockholder equity. In Table 7.9, the Adolph Coors 1995 condensed income statement, the bottom line reveals that Coors earned $43 million in net income from $1,675 million in net sales. From these values, we calculate Adolph Coors's return on assets as 3.1 percent and return on equity as 6.2 percent. Also, with 38.17 million shares outstanding, Coors realized 1995 earnings per share of $1.13. Finally, based on Coors 1995 year-end stock price of $23.25, we obtain a price-book ratio of 1.28 and a price-earnings ratio of 20.58.

The operating cash flow section of Adolph Coors condensed 1995 cash flow statement (Table 7.10) shows that in 1995 deferred taxes increased and losses were realized on property sales. Also, operating assets increased while current liabilities decreased. The investing cash flow section reveals net purchases of properties and other assets. The financing cash flow section shows that cash was raised by issuing more long-term debt than was redeemed, but cash was expended by buying more stock shares than were sold. Finally, notice the adjustment to net cash flow due to the effects of foreign currency translation. This is a commonly encountered item for companies with assets denominated in foreign currencies. The adjustment reflects revaluations due to changes in exchange rates. However, the exact method of adjustment is not important here. The bottom line of the cash flow statement is that Coors realized a 1995 operating cash flow of $90.1 million, with cash flow per share of $2.36 and a price-cash flow ratio of 9.85.

We now move on to what-if analyses of earnings and cash flow. Specifically, what might happen to earnings and cash flow if product sales increased or decreased by 10 percent? To perform this analysis, we proceed through the same sequence of operations as before. That is, we first create a pro forma income statement, then a pro forma cash flow statement, and finally a pro forma balance sheet.

Table 7.8

ADOLPH COORS COMPANY
1995 Balance Sheet
($ in 000)

Cash and cash equivalents	$ 32,386
Operating assets	330,134
Property, plant, equipment	887,409
Goodwill	26,470
Other assets	110,458
Total assets	$1,386,857
Current liabilities	$ 323,663
Long-term debt	195,000
Other liabilities	173,178
Total liabilities	$ 691,841
Paid-in capital	$ 43,726
Retained earnings	651,290
Total shareholder equity	$ 695,016
Total liabilities and equity	$1,386,857

Table 7.9

ADOLPH COORS COMPANY
1995 Income Statement
($ in 000)

Net sales	$1,675,379
Cost of goods sold	(1,091,763)
Gross profit	$ 583,616
Operating expenses	(503,688)
Operating income	$ 79,928
Other income	3,868
Net interest expense	(10,518)
Pretax income	$ 73,278
Income tax	30,100
Net income	$ 43,178
Earnings per share	$1.13
Shares outstanding (000)	38,170

Pro forma income statements corresponding to a 10 percent increase and a 10 percent decrease in net sales and cost of goods sold for Coors are shown in Table 7.11. For convenience, italics indicate items for which constant 1995 values are used. The ±10 percent changes in net sales and cost of goods sold cause gross profit to increase and decrease by 10 percent also. However, since operating expenses are assumed to be a constant 1995 value across the two sales scenarios, operating income varies considerably. Carrying forward 1995 other income and net interest expense yields pretax incomes that vary significantly across sales scenarios. By assuming the same average tax rate as in 1995, we obtain net income values across both sales scenarios. Then, letting 1995 dividends continue unchanged, we get positive and negative pro forma retained earnings values. These retained earnings values from the pro forma income statement will be used to adjust cumulative retained earnings on the pro forma balance sheet. But first we take these pro forma net income values as starting points to create pro forma cash flow statements.

Table 7.10

ADOLPH COORS COMPANY
1995 Cash Flow Statement
($ in 000)

Net income	$ 43,178
Depreciation and amortization	122,830
Loss on sale of properties	1,274
Change in deferred taxes	(1,744)
Changes in operating assets	(19,122)
Changes in current liabilities	(56,319)
Operating cash flow	$ 90,097
Net additions to properties	$(101,349)
Changes in other assets	(14,823)
Investing cash flow	($ 116,172)
Issuance/redemption of long-term debt	$ 56,000
Issuance/purchase of stock	(5,819)
Dividends paid	(19,066)
Other financing	(116)
Financing cash flow	$ 30,999
Net cash increase	$ 4,924
Net cash increase after foreign currency translation adjustment	$ 5,218

Table 7.11

ADOLPH COORS COMPANY
Pro Forma 1996 Income Statements
($ in 000, except earnings per share)

	+10% Sales Growth	−10% Sales Growth
Net sales	$1,842,917)	$1,507,841)
Cost of goods sold[a]	(1,200,939	(982,587
Gross profit	$ 641,978)	$ 525,254)
*Operating expenses**	(503,688	(503,688
Operating income	$ 138,290	$ 21,566
Other income	3,868)	3,868)
Net interest expense	(10,518	(10,518
Pretax income	$ 131,640)	$ 14,916)
Income tax[b]	(53,972	(6,116
Net income	$ 77,668	$8,800
Dividends	$ 19,066	$ 19,066
Retained earnings	$ 58,602	($10,266)
Earnings per share	$2.03	$.23
Shares outstanding	38,170	38,170

[a] Assumes a constant 1995 gross margin, which implies that cost of goods sold changes by the same ±10% as net sales.

[b] Assumes a constant 1995 average tax rate of 41 percent.

*Italics indicate items with constant 1995 values.

Pro forma cash flow statements for Coors appear in Table 7.12, where italics indicate that constant 1995 values are used. These statements begin with pro forma net income values, to which we add back constant 1995 depreciation and amortization expenses and also adjust for constant 1995 changes in operating assets and current liabilities. This yields operating cash flows across both sales scenarios. Since our intention is to isolate the impacts of changes in net sales, we set investment cash flow equal to zero in both sales

Table 7.12	ADOLPH COORS COMPANY Pro Forma Cash Flow Statements ($ in OOO)		

	+10% Sales Growth	−10% Sales Growth
Net income	$ 77,668	$ 8,800
Depreciation/amortization*	122,830	122,830
Changes in operating assets	(19,122)	(19,122)
Changes in current liabilities	(56,319)	(56,319)
Operating cash flow	$125,057	$ 56,189
Investment cash flow[a]	0	0
Financing cash flow[b]	(19,066)	(19,066)
Net cash increase	$105,991	$ 37,123

[a] Assumes zero investment cash flows.

[b] Assumes a zero change in shares outstanding, long-term debt, and other financing, but constant 1995 dividends of $19,066.

*Italics indicate items with constant 1995 values.

scenarios. Similarly, for financing cash flows, we set the change in long-term debt to zero. Then, summing operating, investment, and financing cash flows yields net cash increases for the two sales scenarios. Since currency translation effects are unrelated to sales, we exclude them from our analysis. Now, we move on to the pro forma balance sheets.

To create Coors pro forma balance sheets, as in Table 7.13, the first two steps should be:

1. Adjust retained earnings on the balance sheet with retained earnings from the income statement.

2. Adjust cash on the balance sheet with net cash increase from the cash flow statement.

Since retained earnings and the net cash increase are not equal, at this point the balance sheets will not balance. However, all items making up the difference between retained earnings and the net cash increase appear on the cash flow statement. Therefore, all subsequent adjustments will come from the cash flow statement. In this example, two adjustments are needed.

First, property, plant, and equipment and goodwill accounts must be adjusted to reflect depreciation and amortization. For realistic detail, notice that constant 1995 depreciation and amortization of $122,830 is allocated in 1996 as $2,647 of amortization (10 percent of 1995 goodwill) and $120,183 of depreciation as follows.

1995 Property, plant, and equipment	$ 887,409
1996 Depreciation	(120,183)
1996 Property, plant, and equipment	$ 767,226

1995 Goodwill	$ 26,470
1996 Amortization	(2,647)
1996 Goodwill	$ 23,823

Since depreciation and amortization are part of the difference between retained earnings and net cash flow, these adjustments move the balance sheet closer to balancing. Second, the operating assets line is increased by $19,122 and current liabilities decreased by $56,319. This brings the balance sheet to a complete balance.

To complete the analysis of Adolph Coors, projected profitability ratios and per-share values under increased and decreased sales scenarios are reported immediately below and compared with their original year-end 1995 values.

Table 7.13	ADOLPH COORS COMPANY

ADOLPH COORS COMPANY
Pro Forma Balance Sheet
($ in 000)

	+10% Sales Growth	−10% Sales Growth
Cash	$ 138,377	$ 69,509
Operating assets[a]	349,256	349,256
Property, plant, and equipment[b]	767,226	767,226
Goodwill	23,823	23,823
*Other assets**	110,458	110,458
Total assets	$1,389,140	$1,320,272
Current liabilities[c]	$ 267,344	$ 267,344
Long-term debt	195,000	195,000
Other liabilities	173,178	173,178
Total liabilities	$ 635,522	$ 635,522
Paid-in capital	$ 43,726	$ 43,726
Retained earnings	709,892	641,024
Total shareholder equity	$ 753,618	$ 684,750
Total liabilities and equity	$1,389,140	$1,320,272

[a] 1995 operating assets of $330,134 plus an increase of $19,122.

[b] Depreciation and amortization of $122,830 is allocated as $2,647 of amortization (10 percent of 1995 goodwill) and $120,183 of depreciation.

[c] 1995 current liabilities of $323,663 less $56,319.

*Italics indicate items with constant 1995 values.

	Original	+10 Percent	−10 Percent
Gross margin	34.83%	34.83%	34.83%
Operating margin	4.77%	7.50%	1.43%
Return on assets (ROA)	3.11%	5.59%	.67%
Return on equity (ROE)	6.21%	10.31%	1.29%
Book value per share (BVPS)	$18.21	$19.74	$17.94
Earnings per share (EPS)	$ 1.13	$ 2.03	$ .23
Cash flow per share (CFPS)	$ 2.36	$ 3.28	$ 1.47

For Adolph Coors Company, taking year-end 1995 price ratios and multiplying each ratio by its corresponding projected 1996 per-share value results in the following projected stock price calculations:

	Projected Stock Prices	
	+10 Percent	−10 Percent
BVPS × P/B	$25.27	$22.96
EPS × P/E	$41.78	$ 4.73
CFPS × P/CF	$32.31	$14.48

These projected stock prices reflect widely varying degrees of sensitivity to sales scenario outcomes. Earnings per share and cash flow per share are especially sensitive to which scenario is realized, while book value per share is less sensitive to scenario realization.

7.5 Summary and Conclusions

This chapter focuses on earnings and cash flow analysis using financial statement information. Several important aspects of financial statements and their use were covered. These are summarized as follows:

1. A primary source of financial information is a company's annual report. In addition, the annual 10K report and the quarterly 10Q updates filed with the SEC are available from the EDGAR archives.

2. Three financial statements are essential reading for securities analysts: the balance sheet, the income statement, and the cash flow statement.

3. The balance sheet has three sections: assets, which are used to generate earnings; liabilities, which are financial obligations; and equity, representing ownership claims. A fundamental accounting identity for balance sheets states that assets are equal to liabilities plus equity:

$$\text{Assets} = \text{Liabilities} + \text{Equity}$$

4. The balance sheet has four major asset categories: current assets, fixed assets, investments, and other assets.

5. The balance sheet has three major liability categories: current liabilities, long-term debt, and other liabilities

6. The income statement reports revenues and expenses. Income is used to pay dividends or retained to finance future growth. Net income is the "bottom line" for a company.

7. The cash flow statement reports how cash was generated and where it was used. The cash flow statement assigns all cash flows to one of three categories: operating cash flow, investment cash flow, or financing cash flow. The sum of operating cash flow, investment cash flow, and financing cash flow yields the net cash increase.

8. Profitability ratios based on financial statement information are often reported to assist interpretation of a company's operating efficiency. Some standard profitability ratios are calculated as follows:

$$\text{Gross margin} = \frac{\text{Gross profit}}{\text{Net sales}}$$

$$\text{Operating margin} = \frac{\text{Operating income}}{\text{Net sales}}$$

$$\text{Return on assets (ROA)} = \frac{\text{Net income}}{\text{Total assets}}$$

$$\text{Return on equity (ROE)} = \frac{\text{Net income}}{\text{Stockholder equity}}$$

9. Annual reports and 10Ks may also report per-share calculations of book value, earnings, and operating cash flow, respectively. These per-share values are calculated as follows:

$$\text{Book value per share (BVPS)} = \frac{\text{Stockholder equity}}{\text{Shares outstanding}}$$

$$\text{Earnings per share (EPS)} = \frac{\text{Net income}}{\text{Shares outstanding}}$$

$$\text{Cash flow per share (CFPS)} = \frac{\text{Operating cash flow}}{\text{Shares outstanding}}$$

Dividing the common stock price by the preceding per-share values, we get the following price ratios:

$$\text{Price-book ratio (P/B)} = \frac{\text{Stock price}}{\text{BVPS}}$$

$$\text{Price-earnings ratio (P/E)} = \frac{\text{Stock price}}{\text{EPS}}$$

$$\text{Price-cash flow ratio (P/CF)} = \frac{\text{Stock price}}{\text{CFPS}}$$

10. One common method of analysis is to calculate projected stock prices using prior-period price ratios and projected per-share values from pro forma financial statements. These projected stock prices are calculated as follows:

$$\text{BVPS} \times \text{P/B} = \text{Projected price based on pro forma book value}$$
$$\text{EPS} \times \text{P/E} = \text{Projected price based on pro forma earnings}$$
$$\text{CFPS} \times \text{P/CF} = \text{Projected price based on pro forma cash flow}$$

GET REAL

This chapter builds on the preceding chapter by going deeper into earnings and cash flow, two of the most important tools of fundamental analysis. It focuses on using financial statement information to develop pro forma numbers to use in stock valuation. How should you, as an investor or investment manager, put this information to work?

The answer is you need to get your fingers dirty! Financial statement information is easy to get, either on the web through EDGAR (or any number of other sources) or through the mail, using, for example, *The Wall Street Journal*'s statement service. As with all forms of financial analysis, the only way to gain experience is through practice. Nowhere is that more true than the examination of financial statements. The only way to learn to read with an expert eye is to study a large number of them.

To get started, pick a stock that you like, perhaps because it appears cheap based on our last chapter, and examine its financial statements. Follow this chapter's Coors analysis to do this. When you are finished, you will have created your own pro forma statements, and you will have an idea of the possible range of values for the stock price next year. Does the stock still look cheap?

As you read a company's financial statements, an important exercise is to try to understand what each number really represents. Why is it there? Is it a cash or market value? Or is it just an accounting number (like depreciation)? Financial analysts spend a great deal of time "adjusting" the numbers on financial statements, trying to make them correspond more closely to current market conditions than to historical costs.

Key Terms

Chapter Review Problems and Self-Test

1. **Margin Calculations**   Use the following income statement for McGwire-Sosa Lumber Co. to calculate gross and operating margins.

McGWIRE-SOSA LUMBER
1999 Income Statement

Net sales	$4,000
Cost of goods sold	(3,200)
Gross profit	$ 800
Operating expenses	(200)
Operating income	$ 600
Other income	40
Net interest expense	(60)
Pretax income	$ 580
Income tax	232
Net income	$ 348
Earnings per share	$1.74
Recent price	$38.28

2. **Return Calculations**   Use the following balance sheet for McGwire-Sosa Lumber Co. along with the income statement in the previous problem to calculate return on assets and return on equity.

McGWIRE-SOSA LUMBER
1999 Balance Sheet

Cash and cash equivalents	$ 200
Operating assets	200
Property, plant, and equipment	1,580
Other assets	108
Total assets	$2,088
Current liabilities	$ 370
Long-term debt	306
Other liabilities	20
Total liabilities	$ 696
Paid-in capital	$ 300
Retained earnings	1,092
Total shareholder equity	$1,392
Total liabilities and equity	$2,088

3. **Pro Forma Income Statements**   Prepare a pro forma income statement for McGwire-Sosa Lumber Co. assuming a 5 percent increase in sales. Based only on the pro forma income statement, what is the projected stock price? (Hint: what is the price-earnings ratio?)

Answers to Self-Test Problems

1. Gross margin is $800/$4,000 = 20%.
   Operating margin is $600/$4,000 = 15%.

2. Return on asssets is $348/$2,088 = 16.67%
   Return on equity is $348/$1,392 = 25%.

3. With 5 percent sales growth, sales will rise to $4,200 from $4,000. The pro forma income statement follows. A constant gross margin is assumed, implying that cost of goods sold will also rise by 5 percent. A constant tax rate of 40 percent is used. Items in italics are carried over unchanged.

McGWIRE-SOSA LUMBER
Pro Forma 2000 Income Statement

Net sales	$4,200
Cost of goods sold	(3,360)
Gross profit	$ 840
Operating expenses	(200)
Operating income	$ 640
Other income	40
Net interest expense	(60)
Pretax income	$ 620
Income tax	248
Net income	$ 372
Earnings per share	$1.86

To get a projected stock price, notice that the price-earnings ratio was $38.28/$1.74 = 22. Using this ratio as a benchmark, the pro forma earnings of $1.86 imply a stock price of 22 × $1.86 = $40.92.

Test Your Investment Quotient

1. **Cash Flow**   Cash flow per share is calculated as
   a. Net cash flow / Shares outstanding
   b. Operating cash flow / Shares outstanding
   c. Investing cash flow / Shares outstanding
   d. Financing cash flow / Shares outstanding

2. **Cash Flow**   Which of the following is not an adjustment to net income used to obtain operating cash flow?
   a. Changes in operating assets.
   b. Changes in current liabilities.
   c. Loss on sale of assets.
   d. Dividends paid.

3. **Financial Ratios**   Which of the following profitability ratios is incorrect?
   a. Gross margin = Gross profit / Cost of goods sold.
   b. Operating margin = Operating income / Net sales.
   c. Return on assets = Net income / Total assets.
   d. Return on equity = Net income / Stockholder equity.

4. **Financial Ratios** Which of the following per-share ratios is incorrect?

   a. Book value per share = Total assets / Shares outstanding.
   b. Earnings per share = Net income / Shares outstanding.
   c. Cash flow per share = Operating cash flow / Shares outstanding.
   d. Dividends per share = Dividends paid / Shares outstanding.

5. **Stock Repurchase** A company repurchase of common stock outstanding has which of the following effects?

   a. A decrease in shares outstanding.
   b. An increase in stockholder equity.
   c. A decrease in paid-in capital.
   d. A positive investment cash flow.

Use the following information to answer the next four questions:

Net income:	$8
Depreciation/amortization:	2
Repurchase of outstanding common stock:	5
Issuance of new debt:	9
Sale of property:	6
Purchase of equipment:	7
Dividend payments:	2

6. **Cash Flow Analysis** Operating cash flow is

   a. $10
   b. $8
   c. $6
   d. $15

7. **Cash Flow Analysis** Investing cash flow is

   a. $1
   b. $(1)
   c. $6
   d. $(6)

8. **Cash Flow Analysis** Financing cash flow is

   a. $4
   b. $(4)
   c. $2
   d. $(2)

9. **Cash Flow Analysis** Net cash increase is

   a. $9
   b. $10
   c. $11
   d. $12

Use the following financial data to answer the next three questions:

Cash payments for interest:	$ (12)
Retirement of common stock:	(32)
Cash payments to merchandise suppliers:	(85)
Purchase of land:	(8)
Sale of equipment:	30
Payments of dividends:	(37)
Cash payment for salaries:	(35)
Cash collection from customers:	260
Purchase of equipment:	(40)

10. **Cash Flow Analysis**   Cash flows from operating activities are (*1994 CFA exam*)
   a. $91
   b. $128
   c. $140
   d. $175

11. **Cash Flow Analysis**   Cash flows from investing activities are (*1994 CFA exam*)
   a. $(67)
   b. $(48)
   c. $(18)
   d. $(10)

12. **Cash Flow Analysis**   Cash flows from financing activities are (*1994 CFA exam*)
   a. $(81)
   b. $(69)
   c. $(49)
   d. $(37)

13. **Cash Flow Analysis**   A firm has net sales of $3,000, cash expenses (including taxes) of $1,400, and depreciation of $500. If accounts receivable increase over the period by $400, cash flow from operations equals (*1994 CFA exam*)
   a. $1,200
   b. $1,600
   c. $1,700
   d. $2,100

14. **Cash Flow Analysis**   A firm using straight-line depreciation reports gross investment in fixed assets of $80 million, accumulated depreciation of $45 million, and annual depreciation expense of $5 million. The approximate average age of fixed assets is (*1994 CFA exam*)
   a. 7 years
   b. 9 years
   c. 15 years
   d. 16 years

15. **Preferred Dividends**   What proportion of preferred stock dividends received by a corporation is normally exempt from federal income taxation?
   a. 25 percent
   b. 50 percent
   c. 80 percent
   d. 100 percent

Questions and Problems

**Core
Questions**

1. **10K and 10Q**   What are the 10K and 10Q reports? Who are they filed by? What do they contain? Who are they filed with? What is the easiest way to retrieve one?

2. **Financial Statements**   In very broad terms, what is the difference between an income statement and a balance sheet?

3. **Current Events**   What makes current assets and liabilities "current?" Are operating assets "current?"

4. **Income and EPS**   What is the relationship between net income and earnings per share (EPS)?

5. **Noncash Items**   Why do we say depreciation is a "noncash item?"

6. **Cash Flow**   What are the three sections on a standard cash flow statement?

7. **Operating Cash Flow**   In the context of the standard cash flow statement, what is operating cash flow?

8. **Pro Formas**   What is a pro forma financial statement?

9. **Retained Earnings** What is the difference between the "retained earnings" number on the income statement and the balance sheet?

10. **Gross!** What is the difference between gross margin and operating margin? What do they tell us? Generally speaking, are larger or smaller values better?

11. **More Gross** Which is larger, gross margin or operating margin? Can either be negative? Can both?

12. **Dividends and Taxes** Are dividends paid a tax-deductible expense to the paying company? Suppose a company receives dividends from another. How are these taxed?

Intermediate Questions

13. **Cash Flows** The bottom line on a standard cash flow statement is calculated how? What exactly does it represent?

14. **Cash Flow** Cash flow per share is a commonly evaluated number. How is it conventionally computed?

15. **Retained Earnings** Take a look at the balance sheet for Coors (Table 7.8). On it, retained earnings are about $651 million. How do you interpret this amount? Does it mean that Coors has $651 million in cash available to spend?

Use the following financial statement information to answer the next five questions. Amounts are in thousands of dollars (except number of shares and price per share):

DIXIE CHICKENS
2000 Balance Sheet
($ in 000)

Cash and cash equivalents	$ 100
Operating assets	300
Property, plant, and equipment	800
Other assets	40
Total assets	$1,240
Current liabilities	$ 100
Long-term debt	400
Other liabilities	20
Total liabilities	$ 520
Paid-in capital	$ 30
Retained earnings	690
Total shareholder equity	$ 720
Total liabilities and equity	$1,240

DIXIE CHICKENS
2000 Income Statement
($ in 000)

Net sales	$2,480
Cost of goods sold	(1,660)
Gross profit	$ 820
Operating expenses	(600)
Operating income	$ 220
Other income	90
Net interest expense	(70)
Pretax income	$ 240
Income tax	(96)
Net income	$ 144
Earnings per share	$1.20
Shares outstanding	120,000
Recent price	$24

DIXIE CHICKENS
2000 Cash Flow Statement

Net income	$ 144
Depreciation and amortization	100
Changes in operating assets	(50)
Changes in current liabilities	40
Operating cash flow	$ 234)
Net additions to properties	$ (200)
Changes in other assets	(40)
Investment cash flow	$(240)
Issuance/redemption of long-term debt	94
Dividends paid	(72)
Financing cash flow	$ 22
Net cash increase	$ 16

16. **Calculating Margins**   Calculate the gross and operating margins for Dixie Chickens.

17. **Calculating Profitability Measures**   Calculate ROA and ROE for Dixie Chickens. How do you interpret these ratios?

18. **Calculating Per-Share Measures**   Calculate the price-book, price-earnings, and price-cash flow ratios for Dixie Chickens.

19. **Pro Forma Financial Statements**   Following the Coors example in the chapter, prepare a pro forma income statement, balance sheet, and cash flow statement for Dixie Chickens assuming a 10 percent increase in sales.

20. **Projected Share Prices**   Based on the previous two questions, what is the projected stock price assuming a 10 percent increase in sales?

8

Stock Price Behavior and Market Efficiency

"One of the funny things about the stock market is that every time one man buys, another sells, and both think they are astute."

William Feather

"There are two times in a man's life when he shouldn't speculate: When he can't afford it, and when he can."

Mark Twain

Our discussion of investments in this chapter ranges from the most controversial issues, to the most intriguing, to the most baffling. We begin with bull markets, bear markets, and market psychology. We then move into the question of whether you, or indeed anyone, can consistently "beat the market." Finally, we close the chapter by describing market phenomena that sound more like carnival side shows, such as "the amazing January effect."

8.1 Technical Analysis

technical analysis
Techniques for predicting market direction based on (1) historical price and volume behavior, and (2) investor sentiment.

In our previous two chapters, we discussed fundamental analysis. We saw that fundamental analysis focuses mostly on company financial information. There is a completely different, and controversial, approach to stock market analysis called **technical analysis**. Technical analysis boils down to an attempt to predict the direction of future stock price movements based on two major types of information: (1) historical price and volume behavior and (2) investor sentiment.

Technical analysis techniques are centuries old, and their number is enormous. Many, many books on the subject have been written. For this reason, we only touch on the subject and introduce some of its key ideas in the next few sections. Although we focus on the use of technical analysis in the stock market, you should be aware that it is very widely used in the commodity markets, and most comments or discussion here apply to those markets as well.

As you probably know, investors with a positive outlook on the market are often called "bulls," and a rising market is called a bull market. Pessimistic investors are called "bears," and a falling market is called a bear market (just remember that bear markets are hard to bear). Technical analysts essentially search for bullish or bearish signals, meaning positive or negative indicators about stock prices or market direction.

Dow Theory

Dow theory Method for predicting market direction that relies on the Dow Industrial and the Dow Transportation averages.

Dow theory is a method of analyzing and interpreting stock market movements that dates back to the turn of the century. The theory is named after Charles Dow, a cofounder of the Dow Jones Company and an editor of the Dow Jones–owned newspaper, *The Wall Street Journal.*

The essence of Dow theory is that there are, at all times, three forces at work in the stock market: (1) a primary direction or trend, (2) a secondary reaction or trend, and (3) daily fluctuations. According to the theory, the primary direction is either bullish (up) or bearish (down), and it reflects the long-run direction of the market.

However, the market can, for limited periods of time, depart from its primary direction. These departures are called secondary reactions or trends and may last for several weeks or months. These are eliminated by *corrections,* which are reversions back to the primary direction. Daily fluctuations are essentially noise and are of no real importance.

The basic purpose of the Dow theory is to signal changes in the primary direction. To do this, two stock market averages, the Dow Jones Industrial Average (DJIA) and the Dow Jones Transportation Average (DJTA), are monitored. If one of these departs from the primary trend, the movement is viewed as secondary. However, if a departure in one is followed by a departure in the other, then this is viewed as a *confirmation* that the primary trend has changed. The Dow theory was, at one time, very well known and widely followed. It is less popular today, but its basic principles underlie more contemporary approaches to technical analysis.

Support and Resistance Levels

support level Price or level below which a stock or the market as a whole is unlikely to go.

A key concept in technical analysis is the identification of support and resistance levels. A **support level** is a price or level below which a stock or the market as a whole is unlikely to go. A **resistance level** is a price or level above which a stock or the market as a whole is unlikely to rise.

resistance level
Price or level above which a stock or the market as a whole is unlikely to rise.

The idea behind these levels is straightforward. As a stock's price (or the market as a whole) falls, it reaches a point where investors increasingly believe that it can fall no further—the point at which it "bottoms out." Essentially, buying by bargain-hungry investors ("bottom feeders") picks up at that point, thereby "supporting" the price. A resistance level is the same thing in the opposite direction. As a stock (or the market) rises, it eventually "tops out" and investor selling picks up. This selling is often referred to as "profit taking."

Resistance and support areas are usually viewed as psychological barriers. As the DJIA approaches levels with three zeroes, such as 12,000, talk of "psychologically important" barriers picks up in the financial press. A "breakout" occurs when a stock (or the market) passes through either a support or a resistance level. A breakout is usually interpreted to mean that the price or level will continue in that direction. As this discussion illustrates, there is much colorful language used under the heading of technical analysis. We will see many more examples just ahead.

Technical Indicators

Technical analysts rely on a variety of so-called technical indicators to forecast the direction of the market. Every day, *The Wall Street Journal* publishes a variety of such indicators in the "Stock Market Data Bank" section. An excerpt of the "Diaries" section appears in Figure 8.1.

Much, but not all, of the information presented is self-explanatory. The first item listed in Figure 8.1 is the number of "issues traded." This number fluctuates because, on any given day, there may be no trading in certain issues. In the following lines, we see the number of price "advances," the number of price "declines," and the number of "unchanged" prices. Also listed are the number of stock prices reaching "new highs" and "new lows."

One popular technical indicator is called the "advance/decline line." This line shows, for some period, the cumulative difference between advancing issues and declining issues. For example, suppose we had the following information for a particular trading week:

Advance / Decline Line Calculation

Weekday	Issues Advancing	Issues Declining	Difference	Cumulative
Monday	1,015	1,200	−185	−185
Tuesday	900	1,312	−412	−597
Wednesday	1,100	1,108	−8	−605
Thursday	1,250	1,000	+250	−355
Friday	1,100	1,080	+20	−335

In the table just above, notice how we take the difference between the number of issues advancing and declining on each day and then cumulate the difference through time. For example, on Monday, 185 more issues declined than advanced. On Tuesday, 412 more issues declined than advanced. Over the two days, the cumulative advance/decline is thus −185 + −412 = −597.

This cumulative advance/decline, once plotted, is the advance/decline line. A negative advance/decline line would be considered a bearish signal, but an up direction is a positive sign. The advance/decline line is often used to measure market "breadth." If the market is going up, for example, then technical analysts view it as a good sign if the advance is widespread as measured by advancing versus declining issues, rather than being concentrated in a small number of issues.

Figure 8.1

Market Diaries

Source: *The Wall Street Journal,* November 19, 1998. Reprinted by permission of Dow Jones, Inc., via Copyright Clearance Center, Inc. © 1998 Dow Jones & Company, Inc. All Rights Reserved Worldwide.

STOCK MARKET DATA BANK   11/19/98

DIARIES

NYSE	THUR	WED	WK AGO
Issues traded	3, 530	3, 547	3, 527
Advances	1, 714	1, 514	1, 350
Declines	1, 267	1, 545	1, 681
Unchanged	549	488	496
New highs	75	50	42
New lows	31	33	23
zAdv vol (000)	372, 453	353, 132	a271, 110
zDecl vol (000)	253, 705	269, 123	a393, 562
zTotal vol (000)	669, 388	650, 509	660, 248
Closing tick	+ 479	+ 476	+ 428
Closing Arms (trin)	0.92	.75	1.17
zBlock trades	14, 058	12, 783	13, 397
NASDAQ			
Issues traded	5, 352	5, 352	5, 359
Advances	2, 119	2, 044	1, 788
Declines	1, 848	1, 935	2, 219
Unchanged	1, 385	1, 373	1, 352
New highs	89	57	40
New lows	31	41	32
Adv vol (000)	567, 991	564, 106	381, 060
Decl vol (000)	369, 686	296, 121	385, 220
Total vol (000)	981, 677	899, 113	804, 298
Block trades	12, 360	11, 141	9, 655
AMEX			
Issues traded	740	728	724
Advances	261	270	248
Declines	304	289	311
Unchanged	175	169	165
New highs	11	9	9
New lows	15	12	14
zAdv vol (000)	17, 289	14, 100	9, 879
zDecl vol (000)	7, 905	7, 836	12, 389
zTotal vol (000)	27, 861	25, 279	24, 510
Comp vol (000)	37, 682	36, 468	32, 889
zBlock trades	n.a.	486	451

The next three lines in Figure 8.1 deal with trading volume. These lines, titled "zAdv vol," "zDecl vol," and "zTotal vol." represent trading volume for advancing issues, declining issues, and all issues, respectively. The "z" here and elsewhere indicates that the information reported is for the NYSE only or AMEX. Also, the sum of "zAdv vol" and "zDecl vol" does not equal "zTotal vol" because of volume in issues with unchanged prices. For a technical analyst, heavy volume is generally viewed as a bullish signal of buyer interest. This is particularly true if more issues are up than down and if there are a lot of new highs to go along.

The final three numbers are also of interest to technicians. The first, labeled "Closing tick," is the difference between the number of shares that closed on an uptick and those that closed on a downtick. From our discussion of the NYSE short sale rule in Chapter 5, you know that an uptick occurs when the last price change was positive; a downtick is just the reverse. The tick gives an indication of where the market was heading as it closed.

The entry labeled "Closing Arms (trin)" is the ratio of average trading volume in declining issues to average trading volume in advancing issues. It is calculated as follows:

$$\text{Trin} = \frac{\text{Declining volume / Declines}}{\text{Advancing volume / Advances}} \qquad \textbf{8.1}$$

The ratio is named after its inventor, Richard Arms; it is often called the "trin," which is an acronym for "tr(end) in(dicator)." Values greater than 1.0 are considered bearish because the indication is that declining shares had heavier volume.

The final piece of information in Figure 8.1, "zBlock trades," refers to trades in excess of 10,000 shares. At one time, such trades were taken to be indicators of buying or selling by large institutional investors. However, today such trades are routine, and it is difficult to see how this information is particularly useful.

Charting

Technical analysts rely heavily on charts showing recent market activity in terms of either prices or, less commonly, volume. In fact, technical analysis is sometimes called "charting," and technical analysts are often called "chartists." There are many types of charts, but the basic idea is that by studying charts of past market prices (or other information), the chartist identifies particular patterns that signal the direction of a stock or the market as a whole.

We will briefly describe four charting techniques—relative strength charts, moving average charts, hi-lo-close and candlestick charts, and point-and-figure charts—just to give you an idea of some common types.

Relative Strength Charts

relative strength
A measure of the performance of one investment relative to another.

Relative strength charts illustrate the performance of one company, industry, or market relative to another. If you look back at the *Value Line* exhibit in Chapter 6, you will see a plot labeled "relative strength." Very commonly, such plots are created to analyze how a stock has done relative to its industry or the market as a whole.

To illustrate how such plots are constructed, suppose that on some particular day, we invest equal amounts, say $100, in both Ford and GM (the amount does not matter, what matters is that the original investment is the same for both). On every subsequent day, we take the ratio of the value of our Ford investment to the value of our GM investment, and we plot it. A ratio bigger than 1.0 indicates that, on a relative basis, Ford has outperformed GM, and vice versa. Thus, a value of 1.20 indicates that Ford has done 20 percent better than GM over the period studied. Notice that if both stocks are down, a ratio bigger than 1.0 indicates that Ford is down by less than GM.

Example 8.1   Relative Strength

Consider the following series of monthly stock prices for two hypothetical companies:

Month	Stock A	Stock B
1	$25	$50
2	24	48
3	22	45
4	22	40
5	20	39
6	19	38

On a relative basis, how has stock A done compared to stock B?

To answer, suppose we had purchased four shares of A and two shares of B for an investment of $100 in each. We can calculate the value of our investment in each month and then take the ratio of A to B as follows:

Investment Value

Month	Stock A (4 shares)	Stock B (2 shares)	Relative Strength
1	$100	$100	1.00
2	96	96	1.00
3	88	90	0.98
4	88	80	1.10
5	80	78	1.03
6	76	76	1.00

What we see is that over the first four months both stocks were down, but A outperformed B by 10 percent. However, after six months the two had done equally well (or equally poorly).

Moving Average Charts

moving average An average daily price or index level, calculated using a fixed number of previous days' prices or levels, updated each day.

Technical analysts frequently study **moving average** charts. Such charts are used in an attempt to identify short- and long-term trends, often along the lines suggested by Dow theory. The way we construct a 30-day moving average stock price, for example, is to take the prices from the previous 30 trading days and average them. We do this for every day, so that the average "moves" in the sense that each day we update the average by dropping the oldest day and adding the most recent day. Such an average has the effect of smoothing out day-to-day fluctuations.

For example, it is common to compare 30-day moving averages to 200-day moving averages. The 200-day average might be thought of as indicative of the long-run trend, while the 30-day average would be the short-run trend. If the 200-day average was rising while the 30-day average was falling, the indication might be that price declines are expected in the short term, but the long-term outlook is favorable. Alternatively, the indication might be that there is a danger of a change in the long-term trend.

Example 8.2   A Moving Experience

Using the stock prices in Example 8.1, construct three-month moving averages for both stocks.

In the table that follows, we repeat the stock prices and then provide the requested moving averages. Notice that the first two months do not have a moving average figure. Why?

	Stock Prices		**Moving Averages**	
Month	Stock A	Stock B	Stock A	Stock B
1	$25	$50		
2	24	48		
3	22	45	$23.67	$47.67
4	22	40	22.67	44.33
5	20	39	21.33	41.33
6	19	38	20.33	??.??

To give an example of these calculations, to get the month 5 average for stock A, we take the three most recent prices—$20, $22, and $22—and average them: (20 + 22 + 22) / 3 = 21.33. Supply the missing number. (Hint: its square root is about 6.245!)

Hi-Lo-Close and Candlestick Charts

hi-lo-close chart Plot of high, low, and closing prices.

A **hi-lo-close chart** is a bar chart showing, for each day, the high price, the low price, and the closing price. We have already seen such a chart in Chapter 5, where these values were plotted for the Dow Jones Industrial Averages. Technical analysts study such charts, looking for particular patterns. We describe some patterns in a section just below.

Candlestick charts have been used in Japan to chart rice prices for several centuries, but they have only recently become popular in the United States.[1] A **candlestick**

candlestick chart Plot of high, low, open, and closing prices that shows whether the closing price was above or below the opening price.

chart is an extended version of a hi-lo-close chart that provides a compact way of plotting the high, low, open, and closing prices through time while also showing whether the opening price was above or below the closing price. The name stems from the fact that the resulting figure looks like a candlestick with a wick at both ends. Most spreadsheet packages for personal computers can automatically generate both hi-lo-close and candlestick charts. Candlestick charts are sometimes called hi-lo-close-open charts, abbreviated HLCO.

Figure 8.2 illustrates the basics of candlestick charting. As shown, the body of the candlestick is defined by the opening and closing prices. If the closing price is higher than the opening, the body is clear or white; otherwise, it is black. Extending above and below the body are the upper and lower shadows, which are defined by the high and low prices for the day.

To a candlestick chartist, the length of the body, the length of the shadows, and the color of the candle are all important. Plots of candlesticks are used to foretell future market or stock price movements. For example, a series of white candles is a bullish signal; a series of black candles is a bearish signal.

Figure 8.2

Candlestick Making

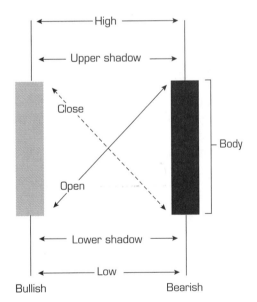

The longer the body, the more bullish or bearish the implication may be.

---

[1] This discussion relies, in part, on Chapter 6 of *The Handbook of Technical Analysis,* Darrell R. Jobman, ed. (Chicago: Probus Publishing, 1995).

Example 8.3 **Candlesticks**

On November 17, 1998, the DJIA opened at 9010.99 and closed at 8986.28. The high and low were 9158.26 and 8870.42. Describe the candlestick that would be created with this data.

The body of the candle would be black because the closing price is below the open. It would be 9010.99 − 8986.28 = 24.71 points in height. The upper shadow would be long since the high price for the day is 9158.26 − 9010.99 = 147.27 points above the body. The lower shadow would extend 8986.28 − 8870.42 = 115.86 points below the body.

Certain patterns, some with quite exotic-sounding names, are especially meaningful to the candlestick chartist. We consider just a very few examples in Figure 8.3. The leftmost candlesticks in Figure 8.3 show a "dark cloud cover." Here a white candle with a long body is followed by a long-bodied black candle. When this occurs during a general uptrend, the possibility of a slowing or reversal in the uptrend is suggested. The middle candlesticks in Figure 8.3 show a "bearish engulfing pattern." Here the market opened higher than the previous day's close, but closed lower than the previous day's open. In the context of an uptrend, this would be considered a bearish indicator. Finally, the rightmost candles in Figure 8.3 show a "harami" (Japanese for "pregnant") pattern. The body of the second day's candle lies inside that of the first day's. To a candlestick chartist, the harami signals market uncertainty and the possibility of a change in trend.

Point-and-Figure Charts

point-and-figure chart Technical analysis chart showing only major price moves and their direction.

Point-and-figure charts are a way of showing only major price moves and their direction. Because minor, or "sideways," moves are ignored, some chartists feel that point-and-figure charts provide a better indication of important trends. This type of charting is much easier to illustrate than explain, so Table 8.1 contains 24 days of stock prices that we will use to construct the point-and-figure chart in Table 8.2.

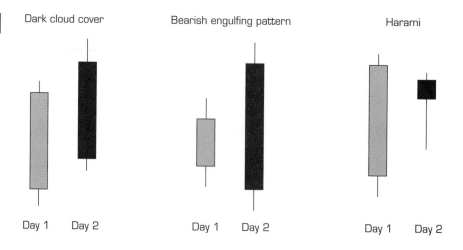

Figure 8.3

Candlestick Formations

Dark cloud cover   Bearish engulfing pattern   Harami

Day 1   Day 2   Day 1   Day 2   Day 1   Day 2

Table 8.1	Stock Price Information					
Date	**Price**	**Date**	**Price**	**Date**	**Price**	
July 2	$50	July 13	$55	July 25	55	
July 3	51	July 16	56	July 26	56	X
July 5	52 X	July 17	54 O	July 27	58	X
July 6	51	July 18	54	July 30	60	X
July 9	54 X	July 19	54	July 31	54	O
July 10	54	July 20	53	August 1	55	
July 11	56 X	July 23	52 O	August 2	52	O
July 12	55	July 24	54 X	August 3	50	O

Table 8.2	Point-and-Figure Chart			
60			X	
58			X	
56	X		X	
54	X	O	X	O
52	X	O		O
50				O

To build a point-and-figure chart, we have to decide what constitutes a "major" move. We will use $2 here, but the size is up to the user. In Table 8.1, the stock price starts at $50. We take no action until it moves up or down by at least $2. Here, it moves to $52 on July 5, and, as shown in the table, we mark an upmove with an "X." In looking at Table 8.2, notice that we put an "X" in the first column at $52. We take no further action until the stock price moves up or down by another $2. When it hits $54, and then $56, we mark these prices with an X in Table 8.1, and we put X's in the first column of Table 8.2 in the boxes corresponding to $54 and $56.

After we reach $56, the next $2 move is down to $54. We mark this with an "O" in Table 8.1. Because the price has moved in a new direction, we start a new column in Table 8.2, marking an O in the second column at $54. From here, we just keep on going, marking every $2 move as an X or an O, depending on its direction, and then coding it in Table 8.2. A new column starts every time there is a change in direction.

As shown in the more detailed point-and-figure chart in Figure 8.4, buy and sell signals are created when new highs (buy) or new lows (sell) are reached. A lateral series of price reversals, indicating periods of indecisiveness in the market, is called a *congestion area*.

Chart Formations

Once a chart is drawn, technical analysts examine it for various formations or pattern types in an attempt to predict stock price or market direction. There are many such formations, and we cover only one example here. Figure 8.5 shows a stylized example of one particularly well-known formation, the head-and-shoulders. Although it sounds like a dandruff shampoo, it is, in the eyes of the technical analyst, a decisively bearish indicator. When the stock price "pierces the neckline" after the right shoulder is finished, it's time to sell, or so a technical analyst would suggest.

Figure 8.4   Point-and-Figure Chart

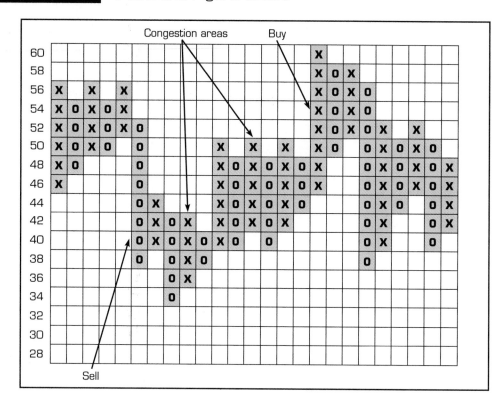

The head-and-shoulders formation in Figure 8.5 is quite clear, but real data rarely produce such a neat picture. In reality, whether a particular pattern is present or not seems to be mostly in the eye of the chartist. Technical analysts agree that chart interpretation is more a subjective art than an objective science. This subjectivity is one reason that technical analysis is viewed by many with skepticism. We will discuss some additional problems with technical analysis shortly.

There is one other thing to note under the heading of predicting market direction. Although we are not trained technical analysts, we are able to predict the direction of the stock market with about 70 percent accuracy. Don't be impressed; we just say "up" every time. (The market indeed goes up about 70 percent of the time.)

Other Technical Indicators

We close our discussion of technical analysis by describing a few additional technical indicators. The "odd-lot" indicator looks at whether odd-lot purchases (purchases of fewer than 100 shares) are up or down. One argument is that odd-lot purchases represent the activities of smaller, unsophisticated investors, so when they start buying, it's time to sell. This is a good example of a "contrarian" indicator. In contrast, some argue that since short selling is a fairly sophisticated tactic, increases in short selling are a negative signal.

Some indicators can seem a little silly. For example, there is the "hemline" indicator. The claim here is that hemlines tend to rise in good times, so rising hemlines indicate a rising market. One of the most famous (or fatuous, depending on how you look

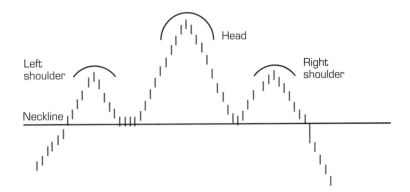

Figure 8.5

Head-and-Shoulders Formation

at it) indicators is the Super Bowl indicator, which forecasts the direction of the market based on whether the National Football Conference or the American Football Conference wins. A win by the National Football Conference is bullish. This probably strikes you as absurd, so you might be surprised to learn that for the period 1967–1988, this indicator forecast the direction of the stock market with more than 90 percent accuracy!

CHECK THIS

8.1a What is technical analysis?

8.1b What is the difference between a hi-lo-close

chart and a point-and-figure chart?

8.1c What does a candlestick chart show?

8.2 Market Efficiency

market efficiency
Relation between stock prices and information available to investors indicating whether it is possible to "beat the market"; if a market is efficient, it is not possible, except by luck.

efficiency market hypothesis (EMH)
Theory asserting that, as a practical matter, the major financial markets reflect all relevant information at a given time.

Now we come to what is probably the most controversial and intriguing issue in investments, **market efficiency**. The debate regarding market efficiency has raged for several decades now, and it shows little sign of abating. The central issue is simple enough: Can you, or can anyone, consistently "beat the market?"

We will give a little more precise definition below, but, in essence, if the answer to this question is "no," then the market is said to be efficient. The **efficient markets hypothesis (EMH)** asserts that, as a practical matter, the organized financial markets, particularly the NYSE, are efficient. This is the core controversy.

In the sections that follow, we discuss the issues surrounding the EMH. We focus on the stock markets because that is where the debate (and the research) has concentrated. However, the same principles and arguments would exist in any of the organized financial markets.

What Does "Beat the Market" Mean?

Good question. As we discussed in Chapter 1 and elsewhere, there is a risk-return trade-off. On average at least, we expect riskier investments to have larger returns than less risky investments. So the fact that an investment appears to have a high or low return doesn't tell us much. We need to know if the return was high or low relative to the risk involved.

excess return A return in excess of that earned by other investments having the same risk.

Instead, to determine if an investment is superior, we need to compare **excess returns**. The excess return on an investment is the difference between what that investment earned and what other investments with the same risk earned. A positive excess return means that an investment has outperformed other investments of the same risk. Thus *consistently earning a positive excess return* is what we mean by "beating the market."

Forms of Market Efficiency

Now that we have a little more precise notion of what it means to beat the market, we can be a little more precise about market efficiency. A market is efficient *with respect to some particular information* if that information is not useful in earning a positive excess return. Notice the emphasis we place on "with respect to some particular information."

For example, it seems unlikely that knowledge of Shaquille O'Neal's low free-throw shooting percentage would be of any use in beating the market. If so, we would say that the market is efficient with respect to the information in O'Neal's free throw percentage. On the other hand, if you have prior knowledge concerning impending takeover offers, you could most definitely use that information to earn a positive excess return. Thus, the market is not efficient with regard to this information. We hasten to add that such information is probably "insider" information, and insider trading is illegal (in the United States, at least). Using it might well earn you a jail cell and a stiff financial penalty.

Thus, the question of whether a market is efficient is meaningful only relative to some type of information. Put differently, if you are asked whether a particular market is efficient, you should always reply, "With respect to what information?" Three general types of information are particularly interesting in this context, and it is traditional to define three forms of market efficiency: weak, semistrong, and strong.

weak-form efficient market A market in which past prices and volume figures are of no use in beating the market.

A **weak-form efficient market** is one in which the information reflected in past prices and volume figures is of no value in beating the market. You probably realize immediately what is controversial about this. If past prices and volume are of no use, then technical analysis is of no use whatsoever. You might as well read tea leaves as stock price charts if the market is weak-form efficient.

semistrong-form efficient market A market in which publicly available information is of no use in beating the market.

In a **semistrong-form efficient market** publicly available information of any and all kinds is of no use in beating the market. If a market is semistrong-form efficient, then the fundamental analysis techniques we described in our previous chapter are useless. Also, notice that past prices and volume data are publicly available information, so if a market is semistrong-form efficient, it is also weak-form efficient.

The implications of semistrong-form efficiency are, at a minimum, semistaggering. What it literally means is that nothing in the library, for example, is of any value in earning a positive excess return. How about a firm's financial statements? Useless. Information in the financial press? Worthless. This book? Sad to say, if the market is semistrong-form efficient, there is nothing in this book that will be of any use in beating the market. You can probably imagine that this form of market efficiency is hotly disputed.

strong-form efficient market A market in which information of any kind, public or private, is of no use in beating the market.

Finally, in a **strong-form efficient market** no information of any kind, public or private, is useful in beating the market. Notice that if a market is strong-form efficient, it is necessarily weak- and semistrong-form efficient as well. Ignoring the issue of legality, it is clear that nonpublic inside information of many types would enable you to earn essentially unlimited returns, so this case is not particularly interesting. Instead the debate focuses on the first two forms.

Why Would a Market Be Efficient?

The driving force toward market efficiency is simply competition and the profit motive. Investors constantly try to identify superior performing investments. Using the most advanced information processing tools available, investors and security analysts constantly appraise stock values, buying those that look even slightly undervalued and selling those that look even slightly overvalued. This constant appraisal and buying and selling activity, and the research that backs it all up, act to ensure that prices never differ much from their efficient market price.

To give you an idea of how strong the incentive is to identify superior investments, consider a large mutual fund such as the Fidelity Magellan Fund. As we mentioned in Chapter 5, this is the largest equity fund in the United States, with over $70 billion under management (as of mid-1999). Suppose Fidelity was able through its research to improve the performance of this fund by 20 basis points (recall that a basis point is 1 percent of 1 percent, i.e., .0001) for one year only. How much would this one-time 20–basis point improvement be worth?

The answer is .002 × $70 billion, or $140 million. Thus Fidelity would be willing to spend up to $140 million to boost the performance of this one fund by as little as 1/5 of 1 percent for a single year only. As this example shows, even relatively small performance enhancements are worth tremendous amounts of money, and thereby create the incentive to unearth relevant information and use it.

Because of this incentive, the fundamental characteristic of an efficient market is that prices are correct in the sense that they fully reflect relevant information. If and when new information comes to light, prices may change, and they may change by a lot. It just depends on the new information. However, in an efficient market, right here, right now, price is a consensus opinion of value, where that consensus is based on the information and intellect of hundreds of thousands, or even millions, of investors around the world.

Are Financial Markets Efficient?

Financial markets are the most extensively documented of all human endeavors. Mountains of financial market data are collected and reported every day. These data, and stock market data in particular, have been analyzed and reanalyzed and then reanalyzed some more to address market efficiency.

You would think that with all this analysis going on, we would know whether markets are efficient, but we really don't. Instead, what we seem to have, at least in the minds of some researchers, is a growing realization that beyond a point, we just can't tell.

For example, it is not difficult to program a computer to test trading strategies that are based solely on historic prices and volume figures. Many such strategies have been tested, and the bulk of the evidence indicates that such strategies are not useful as a realistic matter. The implication is that technical analysis does not work.

However, a technical analyst would protest that a computer program is just a beginning. The technical analyst would say that other, nonquantifiable information and analysis are also needed. This is the subjective element we discussed earlier, and, since it cannot even be articulated, it cannot be programmed in a computer to test, so the debate goes on.

More generally, there are four basic reasons why market efficiency is so difficult to test:

1. The risk-adjustment problem.
2. The relevant information problem.
3. The dumb luck problem.
4. The data snooping problem.

We will briefly discuss each in turn.

The first issue, the risk adjustment problem, is the most straightforward to understand. Earlier, we noted that beating the market means consistently earning a positive excess return. To determine whether an investment has a positive excess return, we have to adjust for its risk. As we will discuss in a later chapter, the truth is that we are not even certain exactly what we mean by risk, much less how to precisely measure it and adjust for it. Thus, what appears to be a positive excess return may just be the result of a faulty risk adjustment procedure.

The second issue, the relevant information problem, is even more troublesome. Remember that market efficiency is meaningful only relative to some particular information. As we look back in time and try to assess whether some particular behavior was inefficient, we have to recognize that we cannot possibly know all the information that may have been underlying that behavior.

For example, suppose we see that 10 years ago the price of a stock shot up by 100 percent over a short period of time and then subsequently collapsed (it happens). We dig through all the historical information we can find, but we can find no reason for this behavior. What can we conclude? Nothing, really. For all we know, a rumor existed of a takeover that never materialized, and, relative to this information, the price behavior was perfectly efficient.

In general, there is no way to tell whether we have all the relevant information. Without *all* the relevant information, we cannot tell if some observed price behavior is inefficient. Put differently, any price behavior, no matter how bizarre, could probably be efficient, and therefore explainable, with respect to *some* information.

The third problem has to do with evaluating investors and money managers. One type of evidence frequently cited to prove that markets can be beaten is the enviable track record of certain legendary investors. For example, in 1999, Warren Buffett was the second wealthiest person in the United States; he made his $30+ billion dollar fortune primarily from shrewd stock market investing over many years. *The Wall Street Journal* article reproduced in the nearby Investment Updates box gives some information on the track record of Warren Buffett and other investment superstars.

The argument presented in the Investment Updates box is that, since at least some investors seem to be able to beat the market, it must be the case that there are inefficiencies. Is this correct? Maybe yes, maybe no. You may be familiar with the following expression: "If you put 1,000 monkeys in front of 1,000 typewriters for 1,000 years, one of them will produce an entire Shakespeare play." It is equally true that if you put thousands of monkeys to work picking stocks for a portfolio, you would find that some monkeys appear to be amazingly talented and rack up extraordinary gains. As you surely recognize, however, this is just due to random chance.

Now we don't mean to be insulting by comparing monkeys to money managers (some of our best friends are monkeys), but it is true that if we track the performance of thousands of money managers over some period of time, some managers will accumulate remarkable track records and a lot of publicity. Are they good or are they lucky? If we could track them for many decades, we might be able to tell, but for the most part, money managers are not around long enough for us to accumulate enough data.

Who's Number One?

Is Warren Buffett the greatest investor of all time? That question can never be settled, any more than baseball fans can settle the question of whether Babe Ruth was greater than Hank Aaron. But a good case can be made for Mr. Buffett.

The table lists a few of the most successful investors in history. A couple of them—George Soros and Peter Lynch—show higher compound average annual returns than Mr. Buffett's. But that doesn't truly settle the debate.

Mr. Lynch, for example, compiled a sparkling 29% annual return as manager of the Fidelity Magellan Fund. At first blush, that seems to top Mr. Buffett's 27% annual return. However, during the 13-year stretch when Mr. Lynch was burning up the track, Mr. Buffett did even better: up 39% a year, according to Morningstar, Inc.

Mr. Soros, manager of Quantum Fund, also has a higher annual return than Mr. Buffett. But Mr. Buffett has maintained his performance for a longer time. Also, notes Edward Macheski, a money manager in Chatham, N.Y., Mr. Buffett racked up his king-sized returns without much use of leverage, or debt, to magnify investment results. Hedge funds, such as those run by Mr. Soros, Michael Steinhardt, and Julian Robertson, often use heavy leverage.

The Buffett record shown in the table is a composite. From 1957 to 1969, his main investment vehicle was Buffett Partnership Ltd. In 1965, the partnership acquired a controlling interest in Berkshire, which became Mr. Buffett's main vehicle in 1970.

Source: John R. Dorfman, "Who's Number One?" *The Wall Street Journal*, August 18, 1995. Reprinted by permission of Dow Jones, Inc., via Copyright Clearance Center, Inc. © 1995 Dow Jones & Company, Inc. All Rights Reserved Worldwide.

A Pantheon of Great Investors
Financial professionals consider these people among the greatest investors of all time. Even in this select group, Warren Buffett stands out.

Name	Main Affiliation	Estimated Returns*	Comments
Warren Buffett	Berkshire Hathaway	Up 27% a year since 1957	Wants to invest in "wonderful businesses." Favorite holding period: forever.
Benjamin Graham	Graham-Newman	Up 17% a year, 1929–1956	Considered the father of value investing. Liked stocks that are cheap relative to earnings or book value.
John Maynard Keynes	National Mutual Life Assurance Society (Britain)	Up most years during treacherous 1930s markets	Famous economist was also an avid and serious investor. Posted big losses but even bigger gains.
Peter Lynch	Fidelity Magellan Fund	Up 29% a year, May 1977–May 1990	Bought dozens of stocks in industries he favored. Workaholic until his surprise "retirement."
Julian Robertson	Tiger Fund	Up 27% a year since September 1980	Names hedge funds after big cats—"Tiger," "Puma," "Jaguar." Big player in Latin America, Japan, etc.
George Soros	Quantum Fund	Up 34% a year since 1969	Huge bets on international currencies and bonds; uses major leverage.
Michael Steinhardt	Steinhardt Partners	Up 21% a year since 1968	Hunch player, bold trader in both U.S. and foreign markets.
John Templeton	Templeton Growth Fund	Up 18% a year, November 1954–March 1987	Bargain hunter worldwide; a pioneer of international investing

*Estimated compound annual returns, after fees. With certain funds, publicly available results for foreign clients are used to approximate results for U.S. clients.

Source: Morningstar Inc.; U.S. Offshore Funds Directory; "Benjamin Graham on Value Investing" by Jane Lowe, *Wall Street Journal* research.

Bull Market Is Trampling Investment

Rules are made to be broken, at least as far as today's stock market is concerned.

The remarkable bull market in stocks that carried the Dow Jones Industrial Average temporarily over 9000 for the first time Friday has made mincemeat of not just valuation relics like dividend yield; many other favorite investment rules are also losing their reliability. (The average, at one point up 43.85 to 9030.49, failed to close above the milestone, ending the day down 3.23, at 8983.41.)

Vernon Winters, chief investment officer of Mellon Private Asset Management in Boston, says, "Certain techniques and rules of thumb may work for a period of time but they generally aren't going to stand the test of time. With the technology available today, if there is some simple formula that someone is espousing for making money, it will probably be arbitraged away fairly quickly."

There are good, fundamental reasons why rules that once worked may no longer. Richard Bernstein, head of quantitative research at Merrill Lynch, tracks 40 stock selection styles and finds one style tends to outperform for three to five years before sinking back. But the winning style is a function of the profit cycle, not the popularity of the style, he maintains.

Whoever is right, it's certainly getting harder to find reliable ways to beat the market. Consider the "Dogs of the Dow." A portfolio of the 10 highest-yielding of the 30 stocks in the Dow industrials—normally the average's underperformers, or dogs—selected at the beginning of every year outperformed the overall average in all but five of the 23 years from 1971 to 1993.

That track record proved irresistible. Since 1991, the assets in Merrill Lynch's unit investment trust dedicated to the strategy have ballooned to $10 billion from $50 million. Alas, the Dogs have since lost their winning ways. They have underperformed in three of the four years from 1994 to 1997. In the first quarter of this year, the dogs rose 7.3%, lagging behind the industrials' 11.7%, according to Merrill. "The dollars flowing into the strategy have perhaps arbitraged away the potential for superior performance," says Mr. Winters.

Our final problem has to do with what is known as "data snooping." Instead of monkeys at typewriters, think now of 1,000 untenured assistant professors of finance with 1,000 computers all studying the same data, looking for inefficiencies. Apparent patterns will surely be found.

In fact, researchers *have* discovered extremely simple patterns that, at least historically, have been quite successful and very hard to explain (we discuss some of these in the next section). These discoveries raise another problem: ghosts in the data. If we look long enough and hard enough at any data, we are bound to find some apparent patterns by sheer chance, but are they real? The nearby Investment Updates box discusses several examples of investment strategies that worked well in the past but no longer appear to provide superior returns.

Notwithstanding the four problems we have discussed, based on the last 20 to 30 years of scientific research, three generalities about market efficiency seem in order. First, short-term stock price and market movements appear to be very difficult, or even impossible, to predict with any accuracy, at least with any objective method of which we are aware. Second, the market reacts quickly and sharply to new information, and the vast majority of studies of the impact of new information find little or no evidence that the market underreacts or overreacts to new information in a way that can be profitably exploited. Third, if the stock market can be beaten, the way to do it is at least not *obvious,* so the implication is that the market is not grossly inefficient.

Some Implications of Market Efficiency

To the extent that you think a market is efficient, there are some important investment implications. Going back to Chapter 2, we saw that the investment process can be viewed as having two parts: asset allocation and security selection. Even if all markets

Rules of the Past

Mike Kochmann, director of marketing and trading for defined asset funds at Merrill Lynch, counters that the Dogs of the Dow is "a value strategy . . . that will show its real strength in choppy or down markets."

Other rules have predicted small stocks are the place to be. But they've been crushed by the big-cap juggernaut of recent years. For example, small stocks should outperform when the dollar is strong because large multinationals take a hit to their foreign currency–denominated sales and profits. Last year, the dollar rose 10% against a basket of foreign currencies. Yet Prudential Securities calculated that the fourth-quarter profits of companies with capitalization of $50 billion and over were up 13.1% from a year earlier, while the profits of companies with capitalization between $500 million and $1 billion rose just 1.5%. Last year, the S&P 500 rose 31% while the Russell 2000 index of smaller capitalization stocks advanced 21%.

Remember the January effect? Donald Keim, a finance professor at the Wharton School of Business, found in a landmark study that small stocks outperformed large ones in the first weeks of every year but two between 1926 and the mid-1970s. One explanation was that illiquid (or hard-to-trade) small stocks would be depressed by investors' tax-related year-end selling, only to bounce back early in the new year. But small stocks have underperformed each January for the past five years, according to Prudential, leading some to dub it the "January defect." One explanation is that fund managers buy up small stocks in December in anticipation of the effect.

Prof. Keim says the effect can still be found if measured as he originally did, but it has weakened. But even when it did exist, it was almost impossible to exploit because the underlying small stocks were so illiquid that trading costs would eat up most or all of the profit, he says.

Source: Greg Ip, "Bull Market Is Trampling Investment Rules of the Past," *The Wall Street Journal*, April 6, 1998. Reprinted with permission via Copyright Clearance Center, Inc. © 1998 Dow Jones & Company, Inc.

are efficient, asset allocation is still important because the way you divide your money between the various types of investments will strongly influence your overall risk-return relation.

However, if markets are efficient, then security selection is less important, and you do not have to worry too much about overpaying or underpaying for any particular security. In fact, if markets are efficient, you would probably be better off just buying a large basket of stocks and following a passive investment strategy. Your main goal would be to hold your costs to a minimum while maintaining a broadly diversified portfolio. We discussed index funds, which exist for just this purpose, in Chapter 4.

In broader terms, if markets are efficient, then little role exists for professional money managers. You should not pay load fees to buy mutual fund shares, and you should shop for low management fees. You should not work with full-service brokers, and so on. From the standpoint of an investor, it's a commodity-type market.

If markets are efficient, there is one other thing that you should not do: You should not try to time the market. Recall that market timing amounts to moving money in and out of the market based on your expectations of future market direction. All you accomplish with an efficient market is to guarantee that you will, on average, underperform the market.

In fact, market efficiency aside, market timing is hard to recommend. Historically, most of the gains earned in the stock market have tended to occur over relatively short periods of time. If you miss even a single one of these short market runups, you will likely never catch up. Put differently, successful market timing requires phenomenal accuracy to be of any benefit, and anything less than that will, based on the historic record, result in underperforming the market.

CHECK THIS

8.2a What does it mean to "beat the market"?

8.2b What are the forms of market efficiency?

8.2c Why is market efficiency difficult to evaluate?

8.3 Stock Price Behavior and Market Efficiency

This section concludes our discussion of market efficiency. We first discuss some aspects of stock price behavior that are both baffling and hard to reconcile with market efficiency. We then examine the track records of investment professionals and find results that are both baffling and hard to reconcile with anything *other* than market efficiency.

The Day-of-the-Week Effect

In the stock market, which day of the week has, on average, the biggest return? The question might strike you as a little ridiculous; after all, what would make one day different from any other on average? On further reflection, though, you might realize that one day is different: Monday.

When we calculate a daily return for the stock market, we take the percentage change in closing prices from one trading day to the next. For every day except Monday this is a 24-hour period. However, since the markets are closed on the weekends, the average return on Monday is based on the percentage change from Friday's close to Monday's close, a 72-hour period. Thus, the average Monday return would be computed over a three-day period, not just a one-day period. We therefore conclude that Monday should have the highest average return; in fact, Monday's average return should be three times as large.

Given this reasoning, it may come as a surprise to you to learn that Monday has the *lowest* average return! In fact, Monday is the only day with a *negative* average return. This is the **day-of-the-week effect**. Table 8.3 shows the average return by day of the week for the S&P 500 for the period July 1962 through December 1994.

The negative return on Monday is quite significant, both in a statistical sense and in an economic sense. This day-of-the-week effect does not appear to be a fluke; it exists in other markets, such as the bond market, and it exists in stock markets outside the United States. It has eluded explanation since it was first carefully documented in the early 1980s, and it continues to do so as this is written.

Critics of the EMH point to this strange behavior as evidence of market inefficiency. The problem with this criticism is that while the behavior is odd, how it can be used to earn a positive excess return is not clear, so whether it points to inefficiency is hard to say.

day-of-the-week effect The tendency for Monday to have a negative average return.

The Amazing January Effect

We saw in Chapter 1 that small common stocks have significantly outdistanced large common stocks over the last seven decades. Beginning in the early 1980s, researchers reported that the difference was too large even to be explained by differences in risk. In other words, small stocks appeared to earn positive excess returns.

Table 8.3	Average Daily S & P 500 Returns by Day of the Week, Dividends Not Included				
Weekday:	Monday	Tuesday	Wednesday	Thursday	Friday
Average return:	−.078%	.035%	.098%	.026%	.063%

Further research found that, in fact, a substantial percentage of the return on small stocks has historically occurred early in the month of January, particularly in the few days surrounding the turn of the year. Even closer research documents that this peculiar phenomenon is more pronounced for stocks that have experienced significant declines in value, or "losers."

Thus, we have the famous "small-stock-in-January-especially-around-the-turn-of-the-year-for-losers effect," or SSIJEATTOTYFL for short. For obvious reasons, this

January effect
Tendency for small stocks to have large returns in January.

phenomenon is usually just dubbed the **January effect**. To give you an idea of how big this effect is, we have first plotted average returns by month going back to 1925 for the S&P 500 in Figure 8.6A. As shown, the average return per month has been just under 1 percent.

In Figure 8.6A, there is nothing remarkable about January; the largest average monthly return occurred in July; the lowest in September. From a statistical standpoint, there is nothing too exceptional about these large stock returns. After all, some month has to be highest, and some month has to be the lowest.

| Figure 8.6A | S & P 500 Average Monthly Returns |

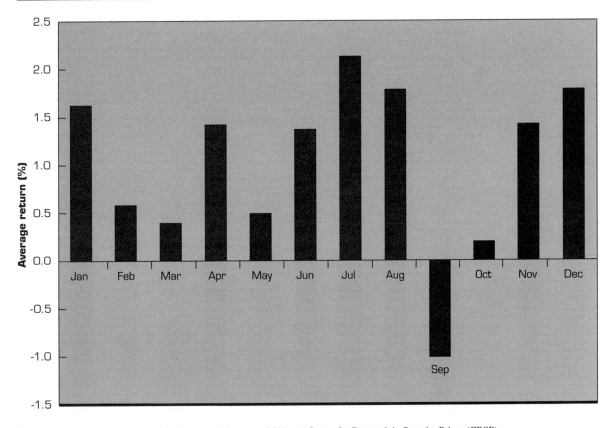

Source: Author calculations using data from the University of Chicago Center for Research in Security Prices (CRSP).

Figure 8.6B, however, shows average returns by month for small stocks (notice the difference in vertical axis scaling between Figures 8.6A and 8.6B). The month of January definitely jumps out. Over the 70 years covered, small stocks have gained, on average, almost 7 percent in the month of January alone! Comparing, Figures 8.6A and 8.6B, we see that outside the month of January, and to a smaller extent, February, small stocks have not done especially well relative to the S&P 500.

The January effect appears to exist in most major markets around the world, so it's not unique to the United States (it's actually more pronounced in some other markets). It also exists in some markets other than the stock markets. Critics of market efficiency point to enormous gains to be had from simply investing in January and ask: How can an efficient market have such unusual behavior? Why don't investors take advantage of this opportunity and thereby drive it out of existence?

Unlike the day-of-the-week effect, the January effect is at least partially understood. There are two factors that are thought to be important. The first is tax-loss selling. Investors have a strong tax incentive to sell stocks that have gone down in value to realize the loss for tax purposes. This leads to a pattern of selling near the end of the year and buying after the turn of the year. In large stocks, this activity wouldn't have much effect, but in the smaller stocks it could. Or so the argument runs.

The tax-loss selling argument is plausible. One study, for example, examined whether the January effect existed in the United States before there was an income tax (yes,

Figure 8.6B   Small Stocks' Average Monthly Returns

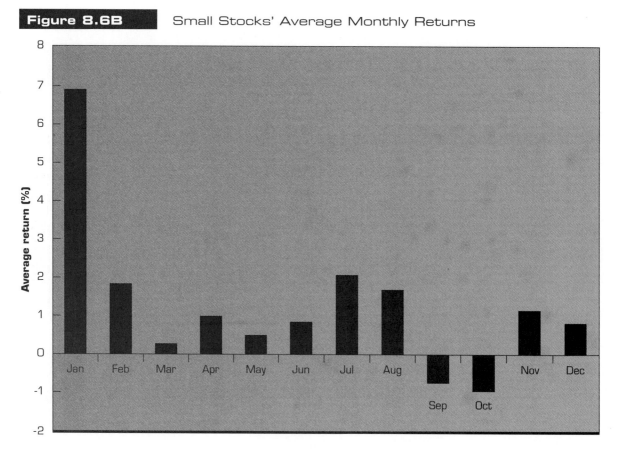

Source: Author calculations using data from the University of Chicago Center for Research in Security Prices (CRSP).

Virginia, there was such a time) and found no January effect. However, the January effect has been found in other countries that didn't (or don't) have calendar tax years or didn't (or don't) have capital gains taxes. However, foreign investors in those markets (such as U.S. investors) did (or do). So, debate continues about the tax-loss selling explanation.

The second factor has to do with institutional investors. The argument here has several pieces, but the gist of it is that these large investors compensate portfolio managers based on their performance over the calendar year. Portfolio managers therefore pile into small stocks at the beginning of the year because of their growth potential, bidding up prices. Over the course of the year, they shed the stocks that do poorly because they don't want to be seen as having a bunch of "losers" in their portfolios (this is called "window dressing"). Also, because performance is typically measured relative to the S&P 500, portfolio managers who begin to lag because of losses in small stocks have an incentive to move into the S&P to make sure they don't end up too far behind. Managers who are well ahead late in the year have an incentive to move into the S&P to preserve their leads (this is called "bonus lock-in").

There is a lot more that could be said about the January effect, but we will leave it here. In evaluating this oddity, keep in mind that, unlike the day-of-the-week effect, the January effect does not even exist for the market as a whole, so, in "big-picture" terms, it is not all that important. Also, it doesn't happen every year, so attempts to exploit it will occasionally suffer substantial losses.

The day-of-the-week and January effects are examples of calendar effects. There are others. For example, there is a general "turn-of-the-month" effect: stock market returns are highest around the turn of every month. There are noncalendar anomalies as well. For example, the market does worse on cloudy days than sunny days. Rather than continuing with a laundry list of anomalies, however much fun they might provide, we will instead turn to what was arguably the most spectacular event in market history—the crash of 1987.

The October 1987 Crash

It used to be that when we spoke of "Black Monday" and "the Crash," we meant October 29, 1929. On that day alone, the market lost about 13 percent of its value on heavy trading of 16.4 million shares. As the DJIA fell more than 30 points to 230, investors lost over $10 billion.

Then along came October 19, 1987, which we *now* call Black Monday. It was indeed a dark and stormy day on Wall Street; the market lost over 20 percent of its value on a record volume of 600 million shares traded. The Dow plummeted 500 points to 1,700, leaving investors with about $500 billion in losses that day. To put this decline in perspective, before October 1987, the Dow had never fallen by more than 100 points, and more than 300 million shares had never traded on a single day.[2]

What happened? It's not exactly ancient history, but, here again, debate rages (you're probably getting tired of hearing that). One faction says that irrational investors had bid up stock prices to ridiculous levels until Black Monday, when the bubble popped, leading to panic selling as investors headed for the exits.

The other faction says that before October 19, markets were volatile, volume was heavy, and some ominous signs about the economy were filtering in. On October 14–16, the market fell by over 10 percent, the largest three-day drop since May 1940 when German troops broke through French lines near the start of World War II. To top

---

[2] We thank Jay R. Ritter of the University of Florida for supplying us with some of this information.

it all off, market values had risen sharply because of a dramatic increase in takeover activity, but Congress was in session (meaning that nobody's money was safe) and was actively considering antitakeover legislation.

Another factor is that beginning a few years before the crash, large investors had developed techniques known as *program trading* for very rapidly selling enormous quantities of stock following a market decline. These techniques were still largely untested because the market had been strong for years. However, on Friday, October 16, the Dow fell by 108 points on heavy volume. When the market opened on Monday, sell orders came pouring in at a pace never before seen. In fact, these program trades were (and are) blamed for much of what happened.

About the only thing we know for certain about the crash is that the exchanges suffered a meltdown. The NYSE simply could not handle the volume. Posting of prices was delayed by hours, so investors had no idea what their positions were worth. The specialists couldn't handle the order flow, and some specialists actually began selling. Nasdaq basically went off-line as it became impossible to get through to market makers. It has been alleged that many quit answering the phone.

On the two days following the crash, prices *rose* by about 14 percent, one of the biggest short-term gains ever. Prices remained volatile for some time, but, as antitakeover talk died down, the market recovered.

NYSE circuit breakers Rules that kick in to slow or stop trading when the DJIA declines by more than a preset amount in a trading session.

As a result of the crash, changes have occurred. Upgrades have made it possible to handle much heavier trading volume, for example. One of the most interesting changes was the introduction of the **NYSE circuit breakers**. Different circuit breakers are triggered if the DJIA drops by 10, 20, or 30 percent. These 10, 20, and 30 percent decline levels, respectively, in the DJIA will result in the following actions:

1. A 10 percent drop in the DJIA will halt trading for one hour if the decline occurs before 2 P.M.; for 30 minutes if before 2:30 P.M.; and have no effect between 2:30 and 4 P.M.

2. A 20 percent drop will halt trading for two hours if the decline occurs before 1 P.M.; for one hour if before 2 P.M.; and for the remainder of the day if between 2 and 4 P.M.

3. A 30 percent drop will halt trading for the remainder of the day regardless of when the decline occurs.

These specific circuit breaker trigger levels were implemented in October 1998. Because circuit breakers are designed to slow a market decline, they are often called "speed bumps." Naturally, how well they work is a matter of debate.

One of the most remarkable things about the crash is how little impact it seems to have had. If you look back to Chapter 1, you'll see that the market was actually up slightly in 1987. The postcrash period has been one of the better times to be in the market, and the crash increasingly looks like a blip in one of the greatest bull markets U.S. investors have ever seen. One thing seems clearly true: October is the cruelest month for market investors. Indeed, two years after the crash, on October 13, 1989, a mini-crash occurred as the Dow fell 190 points in the afternoon following the collapse of a proposed buyout of United Airlines.

Performance of Professional Money Managers

By now you're probably wondering how anyone could think that markets are efficient. Before you make up your mind, there's one last "anomaly" that we need to tell you about. It has to do with the performance of professional money managers, a subject we touched on briefly in Chapter 4.

Starting with managers as a group, Figure 8.7 shows, for 1971 through 1993, the percentage of general equity mutual funds (GEFs) that were outperformed by the Wilshire 5000 index. As shown, out of 23 years, the *index* won 15 times.

Figure 8.8 shows the cumulative performance of the Wilshire 5000 index versus the average general equity mutual fund and the median equity pension fund. The pros lagged badly over this period. The managed money earned slightly under 11 percent per year, whereas the unmanaged index earned 12 percent per year. Notice that a 1 percent margin over a 22-year period is substantial.

Figures 8.7 and 8.8 raise a difficult question for security analysts and other investment professionals. If markets are inefficient, and tools like fundamental analysis are valuable, why don't mutual fund and pension fund managers do better? Why can't they even beat the averages? Why do they actually *lag* the averages?

The performance of professional money managers is especially troublesome when we consider the enormous resources at their disposal and the substantial survivor bias that exists. The survivor bias comes into being because managers and funds that do especially poorly disappear. If it were possible to beat the market, then this Darwinian process of elimination should lead to a situation in which the survivors, as a group, are capable of doing it.

It is sometimes thought that while professional managers as a group tend to lag the market indexes, some managers are consistently better. There is evidence indicating that some managers are better than other managers, but even this evidence is fairly weak, particularly for recent years. There is little evidence of consistent ability by anyone to beat the averages.

To give an example, we briefly discussed the usefulness of mutual fund rankings in Chapter 4. The most widely read investment magazine, *Forbes,* publishes extensive mutual fund information. In 1995, it published its 40th annual mutual fund survey, which included rankings of 1,801 mutual funds. As *Forbes* has done every year since 1975, it produced a short "honor role" of mutual funds. These are funds judged by *Forbes* as the overall top performers in up and down markets. How useful is this advice?

To answer, suppose that you, as an investor, had followed *Forbes*'s advice since 1975 and purchased the honor role funds every year. How would you have done? Over the 16-year period 1975–1990, you would have earned an average annual return of 13.38 percent.

Figure 8.7

Equity Funds vs. Wilshire 5000

Source: John C. Bogle, *Bogle on Mutual Funds: New Perspective for the Intelligent Investor* (New York: Irwin Professional Publishing), 1994.

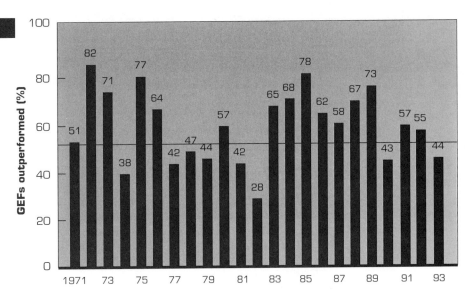

Figure 8.8

Equity Funds
vs. Wilshire
5000

Source: John C. Bogle, *Bogle on Mutual Funds: New Perspective for the Intelligent Investor* (New York: Irwin Professional Publishing), 1994.

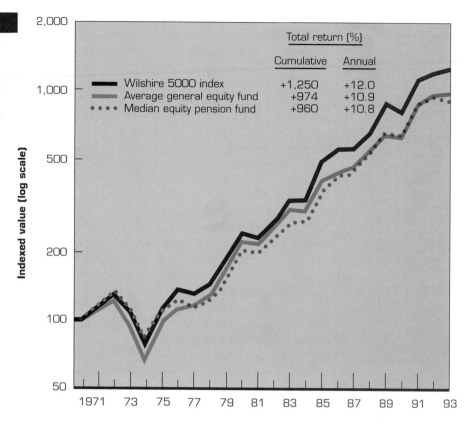

Not bad, but if you had purchased the S&P 500 instead, you would have earned 14.86 percent! Furthermore, in the second half of the 16 years, the *Forbes* funds earned an average of 10.46 percent while the S&P averaged 16.43 percent.[3] Finally, the 13.38 percent earned by the *Forbes* honor role does *not* include load fees, so your actual return would have been worse.

CHECK THIS

8.3a What are the day-of-the-week and January effects?

8.3b Why is the performance of professional money managers puzzling?

8.4 Summary and Conclusions

In this chapter, we examined technical analysis, market efficiency, and stock price behavior. We saw that:

---

[3] The figures are from Table VIII in Burton G. Malkiel, "Returns from Investing in Mutual Funds 1971–1991," *Journal of Finance* 50, June 1995.

1. Technical analysts rely on past price and volume figures to predict the future. They use various indicators and rely heavily on the interpretation of different types of charts.

2. Beating the market means consistently earning a positive excess return. A positive excess return is a return above that earned by investments of the same risk.

3. If it is not possible to beat the market using a particular type of information, we say that the market is efficient with respect to that information.

4. If markets are weak-form efficient, past price and volume figures are of no use in earning a positive excess return, implying that technical analysis would be of little or no value. If markets are semistrong-form efficient, no public information is of use in earning a positive excess return, implying that fundamental analysis would be of no value. Strong-form efficiency implies that no information, public or private, would be of any use.

5. Market efficiency is difficult to test. We examined four reasons: (1) the risk-adjustment problem, (2) the relevant information problem, (3) the dumb luck problem, and (4) the data snooping problem.

6. Stock prices have exhibited peculiar, difficult to explain, behavior. We discussed the day-of-the-week effect, the January effect, and the crash of 1987 as examples.

7. Despite their tremendous resources, experience, opportunities, and incentives, and despite the patterns and other oddities that have existed historically in the stock market, professional money managers have been unable to consistently beat the market. This is true both for professionals as a group and for individuals. This one fact, more than anything else, seems to suggest that markets are generally rather efficient.

GET REAL

This chapter covered technical analysis and market efficiency. In it, we raised a significant question. Can you, or indeed anyone, consistently beat the market? In other words, is the market efficient? This is a question that every investor needs to think about because it has direct, practical implications for investing and portfolio management.

If you think the market is relatively efficient, then your investment strategy should focus on minimizing costs and taxes. Asset allocation is your primary concern, and you will still need to establish the risk level you are comfortable with. But beyond this, you should be a buy-and-hold investor, transacting only when absolutely necessary. Investments such as low-cost, low-turnover mutual funds make a lot of sense. Tools for analyzing the market, particularly the tools of technical analysis, are irrelevant at best. Thus, in some ways, the appropriate investment strategy is kind of boring, but it's the one that will pay off over the long haul in an efficient market.

In contrast, if you think the market is not particularly efficient, then you've got to be a security picker. You also have to decide what tools—technical analysis, fundamental analysis, or both—will be the ones you use. This is also true if you are in the money management business; you have to decide which specific stocks or bonds to hold.

In the end, the only way to find out if you've got what it takes to beat the market is to try, and the best way to try is with a simulated brokerage account such as Stock-Trak. Be honest with yourself: You think you can beat the market; most novice investors do. Some change their minds and some don't. As to which tools to use, try some technical analysis and see if it works for you. If it does, great. If not, well, there are other tools at your disposal.

Key Terms

technical analysis 208	market efficiency 217
Dow theory 208	efficient market hypothesis (EMH) 217
support level 208	excess return 218
resistance level 209	weak-form efficient market 218
relative strength 211	semistrong-form efficient market 218
moving average 212	strong-form efficient market 218
hi-lo-close chart 213	day-of-the-week effect 224
candlestick chart 213	January effect 225
point-and-figure chart 214	NYSE circuit breaker 228

Chapter Review Problems and Self-Test

1. **It's All Relative**   Consider the following series of monthly stock prices for two companies:

Week	Phat Co	GRRL Power
1	$10	$80
2	12	82
3	16	80
4	15	84
5	14	85
6	12	88

On a relative basis, how has Phat done compared to GRRL Power?

2. **Moving Averages**   Using the prices from the previous problem, calculate the three-month moving average prices for both companies.

Answers to Self-Test Problems

1. Suppose we had purchased eight shares of Phat and one share of GRRL Power. We can calculate the value of our investment in each month and then take the ratio of Phat to GRRL Power as follows:

	Investment Value		
Week	Phat Co. (8 shares)	GRRL Power (1 share)	Relative Strength
1	$ 80	$80	1.00
2	96	82	1.17
3	128	80	1.60
4	120	84	1.43
5	112	85	1.32
6	96	88	1.09

Phat Co. has significantly outperformed GRRL Power over much of this period; however, after six weeks, the margin has fallen to about 9 percent from as high as 60 percent.

2. The moving averages must be calculated relative to the share price; also note that results can't be computed for the first two weeks because of insufficient data.

Week	Phat Co.	Phat Co. Moving Average	GRRL Power	GRRL Power Moving Average
1	$10	—	$80	—
2	12	—	82	—
3	16	$12.67	80	$80.67
4	15	14.33	84	82.00
5	14	15.00	85	83.00
6	12	13.67	88	85.67

Test Your Investment Quotient

1. **Technical Analysis**   Which of the following is a basic assumption of technical analysis in contrast to fundamental analysis? (*1994 CFA exam*)

   a. Financial statements provide information crucial in valuing a stock.
   b. A stock's market price will approach its intrinsic value over time.
   c. Aggregate supply and demand for goods and services are key determinants of stock value.
   d. Security prices move in patterns, which repeat over long periods.

2. **Technical Analysis**   Which of the following is least likely to be of interest to a technical analyst?

   a. A 15-day moving average of trading volume.
   b. A relative strength analysis of stock price momentum.
   c. Company earnings and cash flow growth.
   d. A daily history of the ratio of advancing issues over declining issues.

3. **Dow Theory**   Dow theory asserts that there are three forces at work in the stock market at any time. Which of the following is not one of these Dow theory forces?

   a. Daily price fluctuations.
   b. A secondary reaction or trend.
   c. A primary direction or trend.
   d. Reversals or overreactions.

4. **Technical Indicators**   The advance/decline line is typically used to

   a. Measure psychological barriers.
   b. Measure market breadth.
   c. Assess bull market sentiment.
   d. Assess bear market sentiment.

5. **Technical Indicators**   The Closing Arms (trin, or trend indicator) ratio is the ratio of

   a. Average trading volumes in declining issues to advancing issues.
   b. Average trading volumes in advancing issues to declining issues.
   c. The number of advancing issues to the number of declining issues.
   d. The number of declining issues to the number of advancing issues.

6. **Technical Indicators**   Resistance and support areas for a stock market index are viewed as technical indicators of

   a. Economic barriers
   b. Psychological barriers
   c. Circuit breakers
   d. Holding patterns

7. **Technical Charts** Which of the following pieces of information cannot be observed in a daily candlestick chart covering a several-month period?

   a. Daily high and low prices.
   b. Weekly high and low prices.
   c. Daily opening and closing prices.
   d. Daily opening and closing trading volume.

8. **Technical Charts** Which of the following pieces of information cannot be observed in a point-and-figure chart covering a several-month period?

   a. Amount of time elapsed during a major price trend.
   b. Number of major price upmoves.
   c. Number of major price downmoves.
   d. Number of major price moves forming a trend.

9. **Efficient Markets Hypothesis** After lengthy trial and error, you discover a trading system that would have doubled the value of your investment every six months if applied over the last three years. Which of the following problems makes it difficult to conclude that this is an example of market inefficiency?

   a. Risk-adjustment problem
   b. Relevant information problem
   c. Dumb luck problem
   d. Data snooping problem

10. **Efficient Markets Hypothesis** Using only publicly available financial information to select stocks for your portfolio, over the past three years your portfolio has outperformed the S&P 500 index by an average of 15 percent per year. Which of the following problems makes it difficult to conclude that this is an example of market inefficiency?

    a. Risk-adjustment problem
    b. Relevant information problem
    c. Dumb luck problem
    d. Data snooping problem

11. **Efficient Markets Hypothesis** In discussions of financial market efficiency, which of the following is not one of the stylized forms of market efficiency?

    a. Strong form
    b. Semistrong form
    c. Weak form
    d. Economic form

12. **Beating the Market** Which of the follow is not considered a problem when evaluating the ability of a trading system to "beat the market?"

    a. Risk-adjustment problem
    b. Relevant information problem
    c. Data measurement problem
    d. Data snooping problem

13. **Calendar Anomalies** Which day of the week, on average, has had the lowest stock market returns as measured by the S&P 500 index?

    a. Monday
    b. Tuesday
    c. Thursday
    d. Friday

14. **Calendar Anomalies**   Which month of the year, on average, has had the highest stock market returns as measured by a small-stock portfolio?

   a. January
   b. March
   c. June
   d. December

15. **Circuit Breakers**   Which of the following intraday changes in the Dow Jones Industrials Average (DJIA) will trigger a circuit breaker halting NYSE trading for one hour?

   a. 10 percent drop before 2 P.M.
   b. 10 percent drop after 2 P.M.
   c. 10 percent rise before 2 P.M.
   d. 10 percent rise after 2 P.M.

Questions and Problems

Core Questions

1. **Dow Theory**   In the context of Dow theory, what are the three forces at work at all times? Which is the most important?

2. **Technical Analysis**   To a technical analyst, what are support and resistance areas?

3. **Dow Theory**   In the context of Dow theory, what are corrections and confirmations?

4. **Bad Breadth?**   On a particular day, the stock market as a whole is up; however, losers outnumber gainers by 2,000 to 1,600. What might a technical analyst conclude?

5. **A Call to Arms**   How is the Arms ratio computed? What is it designed to capture?

6. **Advance/Decline Lines**   Use the data below to construct the advance/decline line for the stock market. Volume figures are in thousands of shares.

	Advancing	Adv. Vol.	Declining	Dec. Vol.
Monday	1,685	225,000	840	66,000
Tuesday	1,720	164,000	1,000	115,000
Wednesday	560	59,000	2,025	265,000
Thursday	880	100,000	1,625	145,000
Friday	1,550	185,000	950	105,000

7. **Calculating Arms Ratio**   Using the data in the previous problem, construct the Arms ratio on each of the five trading days.

8. **Relative Strength Trends**   The table below shows end-of-month stock prices for Coca-Cola and Pepsi over a six-month period. Construct the relative strength indicator over this period for Coca-Cola stock relative to Pepsi.

Month	Coca-Cola	Pepsi
1	$40	$25
2	45	28
3	48	32
4	44	33
5	49	35
6	55	36

9. **Moving Average Indicators**   Using the data in the previous problem, calculate the three-month moving average for Coca-Cola and Pepsi stock.

10. **January**   With regard to the January effect, what is the role that institutional investors are thought to play?

11. **Candlesticks**   Suppose that on a particular day the S&P 500 opened at 431.30, closed at 439.50, and the high and low for the day were 447.20 and 430.00, respectively. Describe how you would construct a candlestick plot for these data.

12. **Bad Timing?**   A key concern in technical analysis such as the Dow theory is to identify turning points in market direction and thereby time the market. What are the implications of market efficiency for market timing?

13. **Point-and-Figure Plots**   Daily closing prices for U.S. Surgical, Inc., are shown below for a six-week period. If you consider a major move to be $3, construct the point-and-figure chart for U.S. Surgical stock over this time period.

	M	T	W	R	F
Week 1:	80	79	78	75	72
Week 2:	70	66	60	62	63
Week 3:	64	64	62	59	55
Week 4:	58	62	60	57	58
Week 5:	57	62	69	70	70
Week 6:	72	70	63	69	69

14. **Point-and-Figure Plots**   Point-and-figure plots differ from high-low-close and candlestick charts in one important way. What is it? Why might a point-and-figure chart be more informative?

15. **Efficient Markets**   A stock market analyst is able to identify mispriced stocks by comparing the average price for the last 10 days to the average price for the last 60 days. If this is true, what do you know about the market?

16. **Efficient Markets**   Critically evaluate the following statement: "Playing the stock market is like gambling. Such speculative investing has no social value, other than the pleasure people get from this form of gambling."

17. **Misconceptions about Efficient Markets**   There are several celebrated investors and stock pickers who have recorded huge returns on their investments over the past two decades. Is the success of these particular investors an invalidation of an efficient stock market? Explain.

18. **Interpreting Efficient Markets**   For each of the following scenarios, discuss whether profit opportunities exist from trading in the stock of the firm under the conditions that (1) the market is not weak-form efficient, (2) the market is weak-form but not semistrong-form efficient, (3) the market is semistrong-form but not strong-form efficient, and (4) the market is strong-form efficient.

   a. The stock price has risen steadily each day for the past 30 days.

   b. The financial statements for a company were released three days ago, and you believe you've uncovered some anomalies in the company's inventory and cost control reporting techniques that are understating the firm's true liquidity strength.

   c. You observe that the senior management of a company has been buying a lot of the company's stock on the open market over the past week.

   d. Your next-door neighbor, who happens to be a computer analyst at the local steel plant, casually mentions that a German steel conglomerate hinted yesterday that it might try to acquire the local firm in a hostile takeover.

19. **Dow Theory** Why do you think the industrial and transportation averages are the two that underlie Dow theory?

20. **Performance of the Pros** In the mid- to late 1990s, the performance of the pros was unusually poor—on the order of 90 percent of all equity mutual funds underperformed a passively managed index fund. How does this bear on the issue of market efficiency?

STOCK-TRAK·
Portfolio Simulations

Beating the Market with Stock-Trak

A personal Stock-Trak account provides an excellent opportunity for you to try your favorite strategy to beat the market without putting your personal funds at risk. The material in this chapter suggests several strategies. For example, Charles Dow originally intended Dow theory as a method to analyze movements of the overall stock market. However, the basic tenets of Dow theory can also be usefully applied to individual stocks. Essentially, this involves distinguishing genuine price trends from background noise. Since your investment horizon with a Stock-Trak account is probably no longer than a few months, you will want to identify secondary trends expected to last from only a few weeks to a few months. Beginning with about a dozen stock price charts, cull out three or four with the most distinguishable short-term price trends. If a stock has an upward price trend, you should buy that stock. If a stock has a downward price trend, then you should short sell the stock.

In examining price charts for various stocks, you will observe many other types of patterns. Support and resistance levels are examples of simple, yet intriguing patterns. Suppose you discover a stock price bumping up against a resistance ceiling and you conclude that a breakout appears imminent, then you should buy the stock.

There are many other patterns that you might look for. Indeed, technical analysis is based largely on the detection of patterns that might repeat themselves in the near future. Remember, however, that technical analysis is part science and part art. You can learn the science by reading books, but you can absorb the art only through experience. If there is some special strategy that you want to experiment with, do it risk-free with your Stock-Trak account. No matter what happens, you will probably learn something useful from the experience.

Stock-Trak Exercises

1. You will need to peruse a number of different stock price charts before you can identify distinct trends or support and resistance levels. Fortunately, a number of Internet quote servers allow access to individual stock price charts. One popular example is the Yahoo quote server (quote.yahoo.com), but there are many others.

2. Identify two stocks with upward price trends and two stocks with downward price trends. Buy the first two stocks and short sell the second two stocks. This strategy focuses on identifying price trends while reducing the risk of an overall market movement that might simultaneously affect all four stocks in your portfolio.

3. Identify two stocks bumping up against a resistance ceiling and another two stocks bumping down against a support floor. Buy the first two stocks and short sell the second two stocks. This strategy focuses on capturing price breakouts while maintaining a market-neutral portfolio.

Part Three

Interest Rates and Bond Markets

9 Interest Rates

One truism of commerce holds that time is money, but how much time is how much money? Interest is a rental payment for money, and an interest rate tells us how much money for how much time. But there are many interest rates, each corresponding to a particular money market. Interest rates state money prices in each of these markets. ■ This chapter is the first dealing specifically with interest-bearing assets. As we discussed in Chapter 3, there are two basic types of interest-bearing assets, money market instruments and fixed-income securities. For both types of assets, interest rates are a key determinant of asset values. Furthermore, since there are well over $20 trillion in interest-bearing assets outstanding, interest rates play a pivotal role in financial markets and the economy.

Because interest rates are one of the most closely watched financial market indicators, we devote this entire chapter to them. We first discuss the many different interest rates that are commonly reported in the financial press, along with some of the different ways interest rates are calculated and quoted. We then go on to describe the basic determinants and separable components of interest rates.

9.1 Interest Rate History and Money Market Rates

Recall from Chapter 3 that money market instruments are debt obligations that have a maturity of less than one year at the time they are originally issued. Each business day, *The Wall Street Journal* publishes a list of current interest rates for several categories of money market securities in its "Money Rates" report. We will discuss each of these interest rates and the securities they represent immediately below. First, however, we take a quick look at the history of interest rates.

Interest Rate History

In Chapter 1, we saw how looking back at the history of returns on various types of investments gave us a useful perspective on rates of return. Similar insights are available from interest rate history. For example, at midyear 1999, short-term interest rates were about 4.5 percent and long-term rates were about 6 percent. We might ask, "Are these rates unusually high or low?" To find out, we examine Figure 9.1, which graphically illustrates almost 200 years of interest rates in the United States.

Two interest rates are plotted in Figure 9.1, one for bills and one for bonds. Both rates are based on U.S. Treasury securities, or close substitutes. We discuss bills and bonds in detail in this chapter and the next chapter. For now, it is enough to know that bills are short term and bonds are long term, so what is plotted in Figure 9.1 are short- and long-term interest rates.

Probably the most striking feature in Figure 9.1 is the fact that the highest interest rates in U.S. history occurred in the not-too-distant past. Rates began rising sharply in the 1970s, and then peaked at extraordinary levels in the early 1980s. They have generally declined since then. The other striking aspect of U.S. interest rate history is the very low short-term interest rates that prevailed from the 1930s to the 1960s. This was the result, in large part, of deliberate actions by the Federal

Figure 9.1   Interest Rate History (U.S. Interest Rates, 1800–1992)

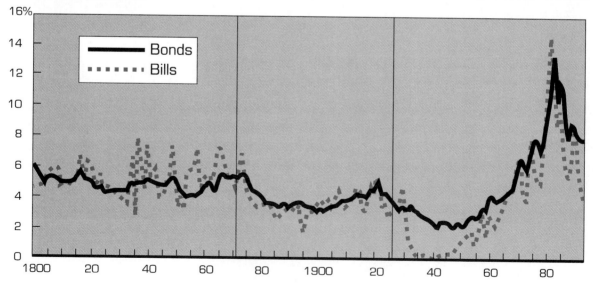

Source: Jeremy Siegel, "Stocks for the Long Run," The McGraw-Hill Companies, © 1998.

Reserve Board to keep short-term rates low—a policy that ultimately proved unsustainable and even disastrous. Much was learned by the experience, however, and now the Fed is more concerned with controlling inflation.

With long-term rates close to 6 percent as this chapter is written, many market observers have commented that these interest rate levels are extraordinarily low. Based on the history of interest rates illustrated in Figure 9.1, however, 6 percent may be low relative to the last 25 years, but it is not at all low compared to rates during the 170-year period from 1800 to 1970. Indeed, long-term rates would have to fall to 4 percent or lower to be considered low by historical standards (but don't hold your breath).

Money Market Rates

prime rate The basic interest rate on short-term loans that the largest commercial banks charge to their most creditworthy corporate customers.

Figure 9.2 reproduces a *Wall Street Journal* "Money Rates" report of interest rates for the most important money market instruments. A commonly quoted interest rate is the **prime rate**. The prime rate is a key short-term interest rate since it is the basic interest rate that large commercial banks charge on short-term loans to their most creditworthy corporate customers. The prime rate is well-known as a **bellwether rate** of bank lending to business.

bellwether rate Interest rate that serves as a leader or as a leading indicator of future trends, e.g., interest rates as a bellwether of inflation.

Loan rates to corporations with less than the highest credit rating are often quoted as the prime rate plus a premium, where the premium depends on the credit quality of the borrower. For example, a medium-sized corporation with a good credit rating might be charged the prime rate plus 1.5 percent for a short-term bank loan. Besides a prime rate for the United States, the "Money Rates" report also lists foreign prime rates for Canada, Germany, Japan, Switzerland, and Great Britain.

Federal funds rate Interest rate that banks charge each other for overnight loans of $1 million or more.

The **Federal funds rate** (or just "Fed funds") is a fundamental interest rate for commercial bank activity. The Fed funds rate is the interest rate that banks charge each other for overnight loans of $1 million or more. This interbank rate is set by continuous bidding among banks, where banks wishing to lend funds quote "offer rates" (rates at which they are willing to lend), and banks wishing to borrow funds quote "bid rates" (rates they are willing to pay). Notice that four different rates are stated: *high* is the

---

Figure 9.2

Money Market Interest Rates

Source: *The Wall Street Journal*, November 18, 1998. Reprinted by permission of Dow Jones, Inc., via Copyright Clearance Center, Inc., © 1998 Dow Jones and Company, Inc. All Rights Reserved Worldwide.

MONEY RATES

November 17, 1998

The key U.S. and foreign annual interest rates below are a guide to general levels but don't always represent actual transactions.

PRIME RATE: 8.00% (effective 11/16/98). The base rate on corporate loans posted by at least 75% of the nation's 30 largest banks.

DISCOUNT RATE: 4.50% (effective 11/17/98). The charge on loans to depository institutions by the Federal Reserve Banks.

FEDERAL FUNDS: 5 1/4% high, 3 1/2% low, 4 1/4% near closing bid, 4 3/8% offered. Reserves traded among commercial banks for overnight use in amounts of $1 million or more. Source: Prebon Yamane (U.S.A.) Inc.

CALL MONEY: 6.75% (effective 11/15/98). The charge on loans to brokers on stock exchange collateral. Source: Telerate.

COMMERCIAL PAPER placed directly by General Electric Capital Corp.: 5.16% 30 to 32 days; 5.14% 30 days; 5.10% 31 to 55 days; 5.32% 56 to 63 days; 5.22% 64 to 92 days; 5.10% 93 to 125 days; 5.03% 126 to 153 days; 4.94% 154 to 190 days; 4.80% 191 to 270 days.

COMMERCIAL PAPER: High-grade unsecured notes sold through dealers by major corporations: 4.85% 30 days; 5.15% 60 days; 5.05% 90 days.

CERTIFICATES OF DEPOSIT: 4.80% one month; 4.90% two months; 4.99% three months; 5.12% six months; 4.96% one year. Average of top rates paid by major New York banks on primary new issues of negotiable C.D.s, usually on amounts of $1 million and more. The minimum unit is $100,000. Typical rates in the secondary market: 5.17% one month; 5.29% three months; 5.07% six months.

BANKERS ACCEPTANCES: 4.85% 30 days; 5.10% 60 days; 5.03% 90 days; 4.95% 120 days; 4.90% 150 days; 4.85% 180 days. Offered rates of negotiable, bank-backed business credit instruments typically financing an import order.

LONDON LATE EURODOLLARS: 5 3/16% - 5 1/16% one month; 5 7/16% - 5 5/16% two months; 5 11/32% - 5 7/32% three months; 5 5/16% - 5 3/16% four months; 5 3/16% - 5 1/16% five months; 5 5/32% - 5 1/32% six months.

LONDON INTERBANK OFFERED RATES (LIBOR): 5.26391% one month; 5.39907% three months; 5.18906% six months; 5.06125% one year. British Bankers' Association average of Interbank offered rates for dollar deposits in the London market based on quotations at 16 major banks. Effective rate for contracts entered into two days from date appearing at top of this column.

FOREIGN PRIME RATES: Canada 7.00%; Germany 3.64%; Japan 1.500%; Switzerland 3.250%; Britain 6.75%. These rate indications aren't directly comparable; lending practices vary widely by location.

TREASURY BILLS: Results of the Monday, November 16, 1998, auction of short-term U.S. government bills, sold at a discount from face value in units of $10,000 to $1 million: 4.40% 13 weeks; 4.43% 26 weeks.

FEDERAL HOME LOAN MORTGAGE CORP. (Freddie Mac): Posted yields on 30-year mortgage commitments. Delivery within 30 days 6.75%, 60 days 6.80%, standard conventional fixed-rate mortgages; 5.625%, 2% rate capped one-year adjustable rate mortgages. Source: Telerate.

FEDERAL NATIONAL MORTGAGE ASSOCIATION (Fannie Mae): Posted yields of 30-year mortgage commitments (priced at par) for delivery within 30 days 6.74%, 60 days 6.78%, standard conventional fixed-rate mortgages; 5.65%, 6/2 rate capped one-year adjustable rate mortgages. Source: Telerate.

MERRILL LYNCH READY ASSETS TRUST: 4.69%. Annualized average rate of return after expenses for the past 30 days; not a forecast of future returns.

highest rate offered and *low* is the lowest rate bid during a day's trading; *near closing bid* is a bid rate to borrow and *near closing offered* is an offered rate to lend near the end of the day's trading.

discount rate The interest rate that the Fed offers to commercial banks for overnight reserve loans.

The Federal Reserve's **discount rate** is another pivotal interest rate for commercial banks. The discount rate is the interest rate that the Fed offers to commercial banks for overnight reserve loans. You might recall from your Money and Banking class that banks are required to maintain reserves equal to some fraction of their deposit liabilities. When a bank cannot supply sufficient reserves from internal sources, it must borrow reserves from other banks through the Federal funds market. Therefore, the Fed discount rate and the Fed funds rate are closely linked. The Fed funds rate is normally slightly higher than the Federal Reserve's discount rate.

The Federal Reserve Bank is the central bank of the United States. It is charged with the responsibility of managing interest rates and the money supply to control inflation and promote stable economic growth. The discount rate is a basic tool of monetary policy for the Federal Reserve Bank. An announced change in the discount rate is often interpreted as a signal of the Federal Reserve's intentions regarding future monetary policy. For example, by increasing the discount rate, the Federal Reserve may be signaling that it intends to pursue a tight-money policy, most likely to control budding inflationary pressures. Similarly, by decreasing the discount rate, the Federal Reserve may be signaling an intent to pursue a loose-money policy to stimulate economic activity. Of course, many times a discount rate change is simply a case of the Federal Reserve catching up to financial market conditions rather than leading them. Indeed, the Federal Reserve often acts like the lead goose, who, upon looking back and seeing the flock heading in another direction, quickly flies over to resume its position as "leader" of the flock.

call money rate The interest rate brokerage firms pay for call money loans, which are bank loans to brokerage firms. This rate is used as the basis for customer rates on margin loans.

The next interest rate reported is the **call money rate**, or simply the call rate. "Call money" refers to loans from banks to security brokerage firms, and the call rate is the interest rate that brokerage firms pay on call money loans. As we discussed in Chapter 2, brokers use funds raised through call money loans to make margin loans to customers to finance leveraged stock and bond purchases. The call money rate is the basic rate that brokers use to set interest rates on customer call money loans. Brokers typically charge their customers the call money rate plus a premium, where the broker and the customer may negotiate the premium. For example, a broker may charge a customer the basic call money rate plus 1 percent for a margin loan to purchase common stock.

commercial paper Short-term, unsecured debt issued by the largest corporations.

Commercial paper is short-term, unsecured debt issued by the largest corporations. The commercial paper market is dominated by financial corporations, such as banks and insurance companies, or financial subsidiaries of large corporations. As shown in Figure 9.2, a leading commercial paper rate is the rate that General Electric Capital Corporation (the finance arm of General Electric) pays on short-term debt issues. This commercial paper rate is a benchmark for this market because General Electric Capital is one of the largest single issuers of commercial paper. Most other corporations issuing commercial paper will pay a slightly higher interest rate than this benchmark rate. Commercial paper is a popular investment vehicle for portfolio managers and corporate treasurers with excess funds on hand that they wish to invest on a short-term basis.

certificate of deposit (CD) Large-denomination deposits of $100,000 or more at commercial banks for a specified term.

Certificates of deposit, or **CDs,** represent large-denomination deposits of $100,000 or more at commercial banks for a specified term. The interest rate paid on CDs usually varies according to the term of the deposit. For example, a one-year CD may pay a higher interest rate than a six-month CD, which in turn may pay a higher interest rate than a three-month CD.

Large-denomination certificates of deposit are generally negotiable instruments, meaning that they can be bought and sold among investors. Consequently, they are often called negotiable certificates of deposits, or negotiable CDs. Negotiable CDs can be bought and sold through a broker. The large-denomination CDs described here should not be confused with the small-denomination CDs that banks offer retail customers. These small-denomination CDs are simply bank time deposits. They normally pay a lower interest rate than large-denomination CDs and are not negotiable instruments.

banker's acceptance
A postdated check on which a bank has guaranteed payment; commonly used to finance international trade transactions.

A **banker's acceptance** is essentially a postdated check upon which a commercial bank has guaranteed payment. Banker's acceptances are normally used to finance international trade transactions. For example, as an importer, you wish to purchase computer components from a company in Singapore and to pay for the goods three months after delivery, so you write a postdated check. You and the exporter agree, however, that once the goods are shipped, your bank will guarantee payment on the date specified on the check.

After your goods are shipped, the exporter presents the relevant documentation, and, if all is in order, your bank stamps the word *ACCEPTED* on your check. At this point your bank has created an acceptance, which means it has promised to pay the acceptance's face value (the amount of the check) at maturity (the date on the check). The exporter can then hold on to the acceptance or sell it in the money market. The banker's acceptance rate published in "Money Rates" is the interest rate for acceptances issued by the largest commercial banks.

London Eurodollars
Certificates of deposit denominated in U.S. dollars at commercial banks in London.

London Eurodollars are certificates of deposit denominated in U.S. dollars at commercial banks in London. Eurodollar rates are interest rates paid for large-denomination deposits. Eurodollar CDs are negotiable and are traded in a large, very active Eurodollar money market. The "Money Rates" report lists Eurodollar rates for various maturities obtained from transactions occurring late in the day.

London Interbank Offered Rate (LIBOR) Interest rate that international banks charge one another for overnight Eurodollar loans.

The **London Interbank Offered Rate (LIBOR)** is the interest rate offered by London commercial banks for dollar deposits from other banks. The LIBOR rate is perhaps the most frequently cited rate used to represent the London money market. Bank lending rates are often stated as LIBOR plus a premium, where the premium is negotiated between the bank and its customer. For example, a corporation may be quoted a loan rate from a London bank at LIBOR plus 2 percent.

U.S. Treasury bill (T-bill) A short-term U.S. government debt instrument issued by the U.S. Treasury.

U.S. Treasury bills, or just **T-bills,** represent short-term U.S. government debt issued through the U.S. Treasury. The Treasury bill market is the largest market for short-term debt securities in the world. As such, the Treasury bill market leads all other credit markets in determining the general level of short-term interest rates. "Money Rates" reports Treasury bill interest rates set during the most recent weekly Treasury bill auction. Interest rates determined at each Treasury bill auction are closely watched by professional money managers throughout the world.

The Federal Home Loan Mortgage Corporation (FHLMC), commonly called "Freddie Mac," and the Federal National Mortgage Association (FNMA), commonly called "Fannie Mae," are government-sponsored agencies that purchase large blocks of home mortgages and combine them into mortgage pools, where each pool may represent several tens of millions of dollars of home mortgages. We will discuss mortgage pools in depth in Chapter 13. The interest rates reported in "Money Rates" are an indicator of rates on newly-created home mortgages. Since home mortgages are long-term obligations, these are not actually money market rates. However, with several trillion dollars of mortgages outstanding, the mortgage market has a considerable influence on money market activity.

The Merrill Lynch Ready Assets Trust is a money market fund for customer accounts with the brokerage firm of Merrill Lynch. Recall from Chapter 4 that money market funds are mutual funds that invest in money market instruments. The interest rate reported in the "Money Rates" report is an average of interest rates paid on fund accounts over the previous month.

In its daily "Credit Markets" column, *The Wall Street Journal* reports the most recent developments in the various markets for interest-bearing assets. A sample "Credit Markets" report is shown later, in an Investment Updates box. A recurring feature of this section are charts of information regarding current interest rates and interest rates over the most recent several-month period. Figure 9.3 presents sample chart boxes from the "Credit Markets" column.

Figure 9.3

Interest Rates

Source: Reprinted by permission of Dow Jones, Inc., via Copyright Clearance Center, Inc. © 1998 Dow Jones and Company, Inc. All Rights Reserved Worldwide.

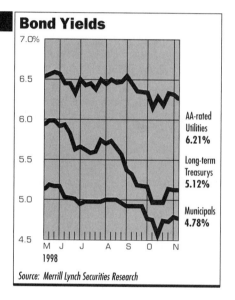

Bond Yields

AA-rated Utilities **6.21%**

Long-term Treasurys **5.12%**

Municipals **4.78%**

Source: Merrill Lynch Securities Research

Key Interest Rates

Annualized interest rates on certain investments as reported by the Federal Reserve Board on a weekly-average basis

	Week Ended:	
	Nov. 20, 1998	Nov. 13, 1998
Treasury bills (90 day)-a	4.35	4.44
Commrcl paper (Non-Finl., 90 day)-a	5.04	5.13
Commrcl paper (Finl., 90 day)-a	5.13	5.24
Certfs of Deposit (Resale, 3 month)	5.21	5.31
Certfs of Deposit (Resale, 6 month)	5.05	5.11
Federal funds (Overnight)-b	4.89	4.80
Eurodollars (90 day)-b	5.20	5.30
Treasury bills (one year)-c	4.54	4.52
Treasury notes (two year)-c	4.62	4.52
Treasury notes (three year)-c	4.60	4.57
Treasury notes (five year)-c	4.59	4.51
Treasury notes (ten year)-c	4.85	4.82
Treasury bonds (30 year)-c	5.26	5.27

a—Discounted rates. b—Week ended Wednesday, Nov. 18, 1998 and Wednesday, Nov. 11, 1998. c—Yields, adjusted for constant maturity.

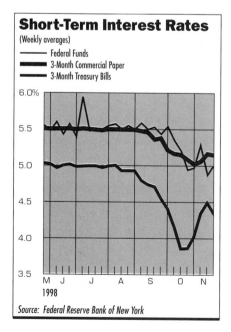

Short-Term Interest Rates

(Weekly averages)

— Federal Funds
— 3-Month Commercial Paper
— 3-Month Treasury Bills

Source: Federal Reserve Bank of New York

Consumer Savings Rates

Money Market Deposits–a	2.36%
Interest Checking–a	1.10%
Six-month Certificates–a	4.16%
One-year Certificates–a	4.27%
Thirty-month Certificates–a	4.34%
Five-year certificates–a	4.47%
U.S. Savings EE Bonds–b	4.60%
U.S. Savings I-Bonds–b,c	5.05%

a–Average rate paid yesterday by 100 large banks and thrifts in the 10 largest metropolitan areas as compiled by Bank Rate Monitor.
b–Three-month interest penalty if redeemed before 5 years.
c–For I-Bonds bought in September and October 1998; applies for the first six months after issue.

The "Bond Yields" chart in Figure 9.3 is published each Monday. It graphs recent yields for AA-rated (medium-high credit quality) utility company bonds, long-term Treasury bonds, and municipal bonds. The "Key Interest Rates" chart in Figure 9.3 is published each Tuesday. This chart lists current interest rates for the major money market instruments along with interest rates for U.S. Treasury notes and bonds (which we discuss in a subsequent section). The "Short-Term Interest Rates" chart in Figure 9.3 is published each Thursday. It displays weekly averages of the Federal funds rate, the three-month commercial paper rate, and the three-month Treasury bill rate over the most recent several months. The "Consumer Savings Rates" box in Figure 9.3D is also published each Thursday. This box lists prevailing interest rates for money market deposits, bank certificates of deposits, and U.S. Savings bonds.

CHECK THIS

9.1a Which money market interest rates are most important to commercial banks?

9.1b Which money market interest rates are most important to nonbank corporations?

9.2 Money Market Prices and Rates

pure discount security An interest-bearing asset that makes a single payment of face value at maturity with no payments before maturity.

Money market securities typically make a single payment of face value at maturity and make no payments before maturity. Such securities are called **pure discount securities** because they sell at a discount relative to their face value. In this section, we discuss the relationship between the price of a money market instrument and the interest rate quoted on it.

One of the things you will notice in this section is that there are several different ways market participants quote interest rates. This presents a problem when we wish to compare rates on different investments. But before we can do this, we must put them on a common footing.

After going through the various interest rate conventions and conversions needed to compare them, you might wonder why everybody doesn't just agree to compute interest rates and prices in some uniform way. Well perhaps they should, but they definitely do not. As a result, we must review some of the various procedures actually used in money markets. We hope you come to recognize that the calculations are neither mysterious nor even especially difficult, although they are rooted in centuries-old procedures and may sometimes be tedious. However, given the billions of dollars of securities traded every day based on these numbers, it is important to understand them.

One other thing to notice is that the word "yield" appears frequently. For now, you can take it as given that the yield on an interest-bearing asset is simply a measure of the interest rate being offered by the asset. We will discuss the topic of yields in greater detail in the next chapter.

Bank Discount Rate Quotes

bank discount basis A method for quoting interest rates on money market instruments.

Interest rates for some key money market securities, including Treasury bills and banker's acceptances, are quoted on a **bank discount basis**, or simply discount basis. An interest rate quoted on a discount basis is often called a discount yield. If we are given an interest rate quoted on a bank discount basis for a particular money market instrument, then we calculate the price of that instrument as follows:

$$\text{Current price} = \text{Face value} \times \left(1 - \frac{\text{Days to maturity}}{360} \times \text{Discount yield}\right) \quad \textbf{9.1}$$

The term "discount yield" here simply refers to the quoted interest rate. It should not be confused with the Federal Reserve's discount rate discussed earlier.

To give an example, suppose a banker's acceptance has a face value of $1 million that will be paid in 90 days. If the interest rate, quoted on a discount basis, is 5 percent, what is the current price of the acceptance?

As the following calculation shows, a discount yield of 5 percent and maturity of 90 days gives a current price of $987,500.

$$\$987,500 = \$1,000,000 \times \left(1 - \frac{90}{360} \times .05\right)$$

The difference between the face value of $1 million and the price of $987,500 is $12,500 and is called the "discount." This discount is the interest earned over the 90-day period until the acceptance matures.

Notice that the formula used to calculate the acceptance price assumes a 360-day business year. This practice dates back to a time when calculations were performed manually. Assuming a 360-day business year, with exactly four 90-day quarters rather than a true 365-day calendar year, made manual discount calculations simpler and less subject to error. Consequently, if $1 million is discounted over a full calendar year of 365 days using a bank discount yield of 5 percent and an assumed 360-day business year, the resulting price of $949,305.56 is calculated as follows:

$$\$949,305.56 = \$1,000,000 \times \left(1 - \frac{365}{360} \times .05\right)$$

Example 9.1   Money Market Prices

The rate on a particular money market instrument, quoted on a discount basis, is 6 percent. The instrument has a face value of $100,000 and will mature in 71 days. What is its price? What if it had 51 days to maturity?

Using the bank discount basis formula, we have

$$\text{Current price} = \text{Face value} \times \left(1 - \frac{\text{Days to maturity}}{360} \times \text{Discount rate}\right)$$

$$\$98,816.67 = \$100,000 \times \left(1 - \frac{71}{360} \times .06\right)$$

Check for yourself that the price in the second case of a 51-day maturity is $99,150.

Treasury Bill Quotes

The Wall Street Journal reports current interest rates on U.S. Treasury bills each business day. Figure 9.4 reproduces a "Treasury Bills" interest rate report. The maturity of each bill issue is stated in month-day-year format, followed by the number of days remaining until the bill matures. The two columns following the days to maturity give the bid and asked discounts for each bill issue. The bid discount is used by Treasury bill dealers to state what they are willing to pay for a Treasury bill, and the asked discount is used to state what price a dealer will accept to sell a Treasury bill. The next column shows the change in the asked discount from the previous day.

Figure 9.4

U.S. Treasury Bills

Source: Reprinted by permission of Dow Jones, Inc. via Copyright Clearance Center, Inc., © 1998 Dow Jones and Company, Inc. All Rights Reserved Worldwide.

TREASURY BILLS

Maturity	Days to Mat.	Bid	Asked	Chg.	Ask Yld	Maturity	Days to Mat.	Bid	Asked	Chg.	Ask Yld
Dec 03 '98	3	3.31	3.23	−0.04	3.28	Mar 25 '99	115	4.38	4.36	....	4.48
Dec 10 '98	10	4.41	4.33	−0.14	4.40	Apr 01 '99	122	4.43	4.41	−0.01	4.54
Dec 17 '98	17	4.32	4.24	+0.02	4.31	Apr 08 '99	129	4.43	4.41	....	4.54
Dec 24 '98	24	4.34	4.26	−0.04	4.33	Apr 15 '99	136	4.41	4.39	−0.04	4.53
Dec 31 '98	31	4.33	4.29	−0.03	4.37	Apr 22 '99	143	4.45	4.43	−0.01	4.51
Jan 07 '99	38	4.18	4.14	−0.04	4.22	Apr 29 '99	150	4.45	4.43	....	4.58
Jan 14 '99	45	4.18	4.14	−0.07	4.22	May 06 '99	157	4.42	4.40	−0.03	4.55
Jan 21 '99	52	4.50	4.46	−0.05	4.55	May 13 '99	164	4.42	4.40	−0.02	4.55
Jan 28 '99	59	4.35	4.31	−0.07	4.40	May 20 '99	171	4.43	4.41	−0.02	4.57
Feb 04 '99	66	4.43	4.41	−0.02	4.51	May 27 '99	178	4.46	4.45	−0.02	4.61
Feb 11 '99	73	4.41	4.39	−0.05	4.49	Jun 03 '99	185	4.43	4.42	....	4.58
Feb 18 '99	80	4.41	4.39	−0.05	4.49	Jun 24 '99	206	4.38	4.36	−0.05	4.52
Feb 25 '99	87	4.42	4.41	−0.03	4.52	Jul 22 '99	234	4.44	4.42	+0.01	4.59
Mar 04 '99	94	4.42	4.40	−0.03	4.51	Aug 19 '99	262	4.45	4.43	+0.01	4.61
Mar 04 '99	94	4.47	4.46	....	4.58	Sep 16 '99	290	4.42	4.40	+0.01	4.59
Mar 11 '99	101	4.36	4.34	−0.03	4.45	Oct 14 '99	318	4.42	4.40	+0.03	4.60
Mar 18 '99	108	4.36	4.34	−0.03	4.46	Nov 12 '99	347	4.38	4.37	+0.03	4.58

For example, consider a bill issue with 154 days to maturity, with a bid discount rate of 5.44 percent and an asked discount rate of 5.42 percent. For a $1 million face value Treasury bill, the corresponding bid and asked prices can be calculated by using the discounts shown along with our bank discount basis pricing formula. For example, the bid price would be

$$\text{Bid price} = \$976,728.89 = \$1,000,000 \times \left(1 - \frac{154}{360} \times .0544\right)$$

Check that the ask price would be $976,814.44.

Example 9.2   T-Bill Prices

Suppose you wanted to buy a T-bill with 280 days to maturity and a face value of $5,000,000. How much would you have to pay if the asked discount is 5.49 percent?

Since you are buying, you must pay the asked price. To calculate the asked price, we use the asked discount in the bank discount basis formula:

$$\text{Asked price} = \$4,786,500 = \$5,000,000 \times \left(1 - \frac{280}{360} \times .0549\right)$$

Calculate a bid price for this T-bill assuming a bid discount of 5.54 percent. Notice that the asked price is higher than the bid price even though the asked discount is lower than the bid discount. The reason is that a bigger discount produces a lower price.

The last column in Figure 9.4 lists the asked yield ("Ask Yld") for each Treasury bill issue. It is important to realize that the asked yield is *not* quoted on a discount basis. Instead, it is a "bond equivalent yield." Unlike a discount rate, a bond equivalent yield assumes a 365-day calendar year. Bond equivalent yields are principally used to compare yields on Treasury bills with yields on other money market instruments as well as Treasury bonds and other bonds (we discuss these long-term yields in the next chapter).

Bank Discount Yields versus Bond Equivalent Yields

A bank discount yield is converted to a bond equivalent yield using the following formula:

$$\text{Bond equivalent yield} = \frac{365 \times \text{Discount yield}}{360 - \text{Days to maturity} \times \text{Discount yield}} \qquad \textbf{9.2}$$

This conversion formula is correct for maturities of six months or less. Calculation of bond equivalent yields for maturities greater than six months is more complicated, and we will not discuss it here (This is why many investments books cut off their tables of T-bill rates at 180 days!)

For example, suppose the asked discount rate on a T-bill with 170 days to maturity is 3.22 percent. What is the bond equivalent yield? Plugging into the conversion formula, a 3.22 percent discount is converted into a bond equivalent yield as follows:

$$3.315\% = \frac{365 \times .0322}{360 - 170 \times .0322}$$

The bond equivalent yield is thus 3.315 percent.

Example 9.3   Bond Equivalent Yields

Suppose a T-bill has 45 days to maturity and an asked discount of 5 percent. What is the bond equivalent yield?

Using the bond equivalent yield conversion formula, we have

$$5.101\% = \frac{365 \times .05}{360 - 45 \times .05}$$

The bond equivalent yield is thus 5.101 percent.

One common cause of confusion about bond equivalent yield calculations is the way that leap years are handled. The rule is that we must use 366 days if February 29 occurs within the next 12 months. For example, 2000 will be a leap year. So, beginning on March 1, 1999, we must use 366 days in Equation 9.2. Then beginning on March 1, 2000, we must revert back to using 365 days.

Example 9.4   Back to the Future: Leap Year Bond Equivalent Yields

Calculate the asked yield (bond equivalent yield) for a T-bill price quoted in December 1999 with 119 days to maturity and an asked discount of 5.41 percent.

Since the 12-month period following the date of the price quote includes February 29, we must use 366 days. Plugging this into the conversion formula, we get:

$$5.60\% = \frac{366 \times .0541}{360 - 119 \times .0541}$$

This 5.60 percent is the ask yield stated as a bond equivalent yield.

We can calculate a Treasury bill asked price using the asked yield, which is a bond equivalent yield, as follows:

$$\text{Bill price} = \frac{\text{Face value}}{1 + \text{Bond equivalent yield} \times \text{Days to maturity}/365} \qquad \textbf{9.3}$$

For example, just above we calculated the 3.315 percent bond equivalent yield on a T-bill with 170 days to maturity and a 3.22 percent asked discount rate. If we calculate its price using this bond equivalent yield, we get

$$\$983,892 = \frac{\$1,000,000}{1 + .03515 \times 170/365}$$

Check that, ignoring a small rounding error, you get the same price using the bank discount formula.

One other potentially confusing issue can come up. If you examine the days to maturity reported by the *Journal,* you will notice that they seem to be consistently off by a day or two. There are two reasons for this. First, quotes published in *The Wall Street Journal* on, say, a Wednesday refer to T-bill prices and rates quoted on Tuesday, the day before. Second, published quoted prices assume "skip-day" settlement, which means the quoted prices are for delivery and payment in two business days. Days to maturity published in *The Wall Street Journal* are measured relative to this skip-settlement day. But just in case you're not completely confused yet, T-bill settlement no longer operates on a skip-day basis. Rather, T-bill settlement actually operates on a "next-day" basis, meaning that prices are quoted for delivery the following business day. So why does the *Journal* continue to use skip-day settlement? The answer is simply tradition.

Bond Equivalent Yields, APRs, and EARs

Money market rates not quoted on a discount basis are generally quoted on a "simple" interest basis. Simple interest rates are calculated just like the annual percentage rate (APR) on a consumer loan. So, for the most part, money market rates are either bank discount rates or APRs. For example, CD rates are APRs.

In fact, the bond equivalent yield on a T-bill with less than six months to maturity is also an APR. As a result, like any APR, it understates the true interest rate, which is usually called the *effective annual rate,* or EAR. In the context of the money market, EARs are sometimes referred to as effective annual yields, effective yields, or annualized yields. Whatever it is called, to find out what a T-bill, or any other money market instrument, is *really* going to pay you, yet another conversion is needed. We will get to the needed conversion in a moment.

First, however, recall that an APR is equal to the interest rate per period multiplied by the number of periods in a year. For example, if the rate on a car loan is 1 percent per month, then the APR is $1\% \times 12 = 12\%$. In general, if we let m be the number of periods in a year, an APR is converted to an EAR as follows:

$$1 + EAR = \left(1 + \frac{APR}{m}\right)^m \qquad \textbf{9.4}$$

For example, on our 12 percent APR car loan, the EAR can be determined by

$$1 + EAR = \left(1 + \frac{.12}{12}\right)^{12}$$

$$= 1.01^{12}$$

$$= 1.126825$$

$$EAR = 12.6825\%$$

Thus, the rate on the car loan is really 12.6825 percent per year.

Example 9.5   APRs and EARs

A typical credit card may quote an APR of 18 percent. On closer inspection, you will find that the rate is actually 1.5 percent per month. What annual interest rate are you *really* paying on such a credit card?

With 12 periods in a year, an APR of 18 percent is converted to an EAR as follows:

$$1 + EAR = \left(1 + \frac{.18}{12}\right)^{12}$$

$$= 1.015^{12}$$

$$= 1.1956$$

$$EAR = 19.56\%$$

Thus, the rate on this credit card is really 19.56 percent per year.

Now, to see that the bond equivalent yield on a T-bill is just an APR, we can first calculate the price on the bill we considered earlier (3.22 percent asked discount, 170 days to maturity). Using the bank discount formula, the asked price, for $1 million in face value, is

$$\text{Asked price} = \$984{,}794 = \$1{,}000{,}000 \times \left(1 - \frac{170}{360} \times .0322\right)$$

The discount is $15,206. Thus on this 170-day investment, you earn $15,206 in interest on an investment of $984,794. On a percentage basis, you earned

$$1.544\% = \frac{\$15{,}206}{\$984{,}794}$$

In a 365-day year, there are 365/170 = 2.147 periods of 170-day length. So if we multiply what you earned over the 170-day period by the number of 170-day periods in a year, we get

$$3.315\% = 2.147 \times 1.544\%$$

This is precisely the bond equivalent yield we calculated earlier.

Finally, for this T-bill we can calculate the EAR using this 3.315 percent:

$$1 + EAR = \left(1 + \frac{.03315}{2.147}\right)^{2.147}$$

$$= 1.03344$$

$$EAR = 3.344\%$$

In the end, we have three different rates for this simple T-bill. The last one, the EAR, finally tells us what we really want to know: What are we actually going to earn?

Example 9.6   Discounts, APRs, and EARs

A money market instrument with 60 days to maturity has a quoted ask price of 99, meaning $99 per $100 face value. What are the banker's discount yield, the bond equivalent yield, and the effective annual return?

First, to get the discount yield, we have to use the bank discount formula and solve for the discount yield:

$$\$99 = \$100 \times \left(1 - \frac{60}{360} \times \text{Discount yield}\right)$$

With a little algebra, we see that the discount yield is 6 percent.

We convert this to a bond equivalent yield as follows:

$$6.145\% = \frac{365 \times .06}{360 - 60 \times .06}$$

The bond equivalent yield is thus 6.145 percent.

Finally, to get the EAR, note that there are 6.0833 sixty-day periods in a year, so

$$1 + EAR = \left(1 + \frac{.06145}{6.0833}\right)^{6.0833}$$

$$= 1.06305$$

$$EAR = 6.305\%$$

This example illustrates the general result that the discount rate is lower than the bond equivalent yield, which in turn is less than the EAR.

CHECK THIS

9.2a What are the three different types of interest rate quotes that are important for money market instruments?

9.2b How are T-bill rates quoted? How are CD rates quoted?

9.2c Of the three different types of interest rate quotes, which is the largest? Which is the smallest? Which is the most relevant?

9.3 Rates and Yields on Fixed-Income Securities

Thus far we have focused on short-term interest rates, where "short-term" means one year or less. Of course, these are not the only interest rates we are interested in, so we now begin to discuss longer term rates by looking at fixed-income securities. To keep this discussion to a manageable length, we defer the details of how some longer term rates are computed to Chapter 10.

Fixed-income securities include long-term debt contracts from a wide variety of issuers. The largest single category of fixed-income securities is debt issued by the U.S. government. The second largest category of fixed-income securities is mortgage debt issued to finance real estate purchases. The two other large categories of fixed-income securities are debt issued by corporations and debt issued by municipal governments. Each of these categories represents more than a trillion dollars of outstanding debt. Corporate bonds are covered in detail in Chapter 11 and municipal government bonds are covered in Chapter 12.

Credit Markets

Bonds Decline as Fed Lowers Rates

Bond investors spent weeks debating whether the Federal Reserve would cut interest rates at its November meeting. But when the Fed finally confirmed market expectations and cut interest rates yesterday, bonds barely moved and the market remained torn over whether more rate cuts will materialize.

Many bond traders and investors had predicted that the Fed would cut rates at either the November or December meetings to ensure that recent improvements in the liquidity and tone of various credit markets wouldn't dissipate.

As a result, the decision to cut the federal-fund rate—the rate at which banks lend to each other—a quarter-point to 4.75%, and the largely symbolic discount rate—at which the Fed itself lends to banks—a quarter-point to 4.5%, helped risky bonds retain recent strength, but didn't give the overall market much of a lift.

By the end of the day, the bellwether 30-year Treasury bond fell 5/32, or $1.563 for a bond with a $1,000 face value, to 99 6/32. The bond's yield, which moves in the opposite direction of its price, rose to 5.296%. The long bond rallied to a high of 100 4/32 after the announcement, adding to modest early gains, but profit-taking sent prices lower by the day's finish.

Prices of two-year notes, which usually provide a good indication of the market's sentiment about future rate cuts, were up 2/32 before the rate cut, and jumped 7/32 immediately after the decision. These securities ended the day unchanged, yielding 4.56%.

Source: Gregory Zuckerman, "Bonds Decline as Fed Lowers Rates," *The Wall Street Journal*, September 18, 1998. Reprinted by permission of Dow Jones, Inc., via Copyright Clearance Center, Inc.© 1998 Dow Jones & Company, Inc. All Rights Reserved Worldwide.

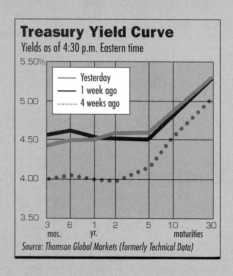

Treasury Yield Curve

Yields as of 4:30 p.m. Eastern time

— Yesterday
— 1 week ago
••••••• 4 weeks ago

Source: Thomson Global Markets (formerly Technical Data)

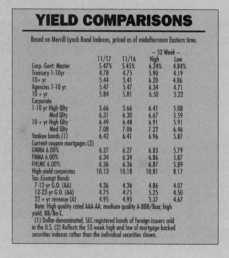

YIELD COMPARISONS

Based on Merrill Lynch Bond Indexes, priced as of midafternoon Eastern time.

	11/17	11/16	52 Week High	52 Week Low
Corp.-Govt. Master	5.47%	5.45%	6.24%	4.84%
Treasury 1-10yr	4.78	4.75	5.90	4.19
10+ yr	5.44	5.41	6.20	4.86
Agencies 1-10 yr	5.47	5.47	6.34	4.71
10 + yr	5.84	5.81	6.50	5.22
Corporate				
1-10 yr High Qlty	5.66	5.66	6.41	5.08
Med Qlty	6.31	6.30	6.67	5.59
10 + yr High Qlty	6.49	6.48	6.91	5.91
Med Qlty	7.08	7.06	7.22	6.46
Yankee bonds (1)	6.42	6.41	6.96	5.87
Current-coupon mortgages (2)				
GNMA 6.00%	6.27	6.27	6.83	5.79
FNMA 6.00%	6.34	6.34	6.86	5.87
FHLMC 6.00%	6.36	6.36	6.87	5.89
High-yield corporates	10.13	10.18	10.81	8.17
Tax-Exempt Bonds				
7-12-yr G.O. (AA)	4.36	4.36	4.86	4.07
12-22-yr G.O. (AA)	4.75	4.75	5.25	4.50
22 + yr revenue (A)	4.95	4.95	5.37	4.67

Note: High quality rated AAA-AA; medium quality A-BBB/Baa; high yield, BB/Ba-C.
(1) Dollar-denominated, SEC-registered bonds of foreign issuers sold in the U.S. (2) Reflects the 52-week high and low of mortgage-backed securities indexes rather than the individual securities shown.

Because of its sheer size, the leading world market for debt securities is the market for U.S. Treasury securities. Interest rates for U.S. Treasury debt are closely watched throughout the world, and daily reports can be found in most major newspapers. *The Wall Street Journal* provides a daily summary of activity in the U.S. Treasury market in its "Credit Markets" column, as seen in the nearby Investment Updates box.

The Treasury Yield Curve

Treasury yield curve
A graph of Treasury yields plotted against maturities.

Every day, the "Credit Markets" column contains a graphical display of a current **Treasury yield curve**, which is a plot of Treasury yields against maturities. Yields are measured along the vertical axis and maturities are measured along the horizontal axis.

The light grey line represents the most current yield curve, while the background lines represent recent yield curves. Thus, the "Treasury Yield Curve" box illustrates both where Treasury interest rates are now and where they were recently.

The Treasury yield curve is fundamental to bond market analysis because it represents the interest rates that financial markets are charging to the world's largest debtor with the world's highest credit rating—the U.S. government. In essence, the Treasury yield curve represents interest rates for default-free lending across the maturity spectrum. As such, almost all other domestic interest rates are determined with respect to U.S. Treasury interest rates.

Rates on Other Fixed-Income Investments

The "Yield Comparisons" table immediately below the Treasury yield curve in the box gives interest rates based on bond market indexes constructed by the securities firm Merrill Lynch. Both current interest rates and the highest and lowest interest rates over the previous 52-week period are reported for a number of bond indexes. These bond market indexes provide yield information on many different types of bonds. Since we will be discussing these in much more detail in the next several chapters, we touch on them only briefly here.

The first two indexes represent U.S. Treasury securities with 1- to 10-year maturities and 10- to 30-year maturities. The longest maturity securities issued by the Treasury are 30-year maturity bonds. The next two indexes represent U.S. government agency debt with 1- to 10-year maturities, and debt with more than 10 years to maturity. A variety of government agencies borrow money in financial markets. The Tennessee Valley Authority (TVA) is an example.

In recent years, U.S. government agencies have issued debt with maturities as long as 50 years. U.S. government agency debt does not carry the same credit guarantee as U.S. Treasury debt, and therefore interest rates on agency debt reflect a premium over interest rates on Treasury debt. Also, agency securities are often subject to state taxes, whereas Treasury securities are not.

The next four indexes represent debt issued by domestic corporations according to their maturity and credit rating. Notice that corporate debt with a high credit quality pays a higher interest rate than U.S. government agency debt, which in turn pays a higher interest rate than U.S. Treasury debt. As expected, medium credit quality corporate debt pays a higher interest rate than high credit quality corporate debt.

"Yankee bonds" are issued by foreign corporations for sale in the United States. These bonds are denominated in U.S. dollars so investors do not have to worry that changing foreign exchange rates will affect debt values.

As we noted previously, the Federal Home Loan Mortgage Corporation (FHLMC), or Freddie Mac, and the Federal National Mortgage Association (FNMA), or Fannie Mae, are government-sponsored agencies that repackage home mortgages into mortgage pools, where each pool represents several tens of millions of dollars of home mortgages. A third agency, the Government National Mortgage Association (GNMA), better known as "Ginnie Mae," is also an active mortgage repackager. The interest rates reported for these agencies correspond to indexes constructed from many mortgage pools.

"High-yield corporates" refers to corporate bonds with above-average default risk. These bonds are usually avoided by conservative investors, but they may be attractive to investors who understand and are willing to accept the risks involved. Because of their much higher credit risk, the interest rates for these bonds are significantly higher than those for even medium-quality corporate bonds.

"New tax-exempts" are bonds issued by municipal governments. Coupon interest payments on most municipal bonds are exempt from federal income taxes, and they are often exempt from state income taxes as well. The tax-exempt interest rates reported in the "Yield Comparisons" table are based on indexes for high-quality municipal bonds corresponding to 10-year maturity and 20-year maturity general obligation bonds (GOs) and 30-year maturity revenue bonds.

General obligation bonds are secured by the general taxing power of the issuing municipality. Revenue bonds are secured by revenues generated from specific projects, for example, toll roads, airports, or user fees for services. As shown, because of their tax-exempt status, interest rates on high-quality municipal bonds are lower than interest rates on comparable U.S. Treasury securities.

CHECK THIS

9.3a What is the yield curve? Why is it important?

9.3b Why are corporate bond yields higher than Treasury bond yields?

9.3c Why are municipal bond yields lower than Treasury bond yields?

9.4 The Term Structure of Interest Rates

term structure of interest rates
Relationship between time to maturity and interest rates for default-free, pure discount instruments.

The yield curve tells us the relationship between Treasury bond yields and time to maturity. The **term structure of interest rates** (or just "term structure") is a similar, but not identical, relationship. Recall that a pure discount instrument has a single payment of face value at maturity with no other payments until then. Treasury bonds are *not* pure discount instruments because they pay coupons every six months. Pure discount instruments with more than a year to maturity are often called "zero coupon bonds," or just "zeroes," because they are, in effect, bonds with a zero coupon rate.

The term structure of interest rates is the relationship between time to maturity and interest rates for default-free, pure discount instruments. So, the difference between the yield curve and the term structure is that the yield curve is based on coupon bonds, whereas the term structure is based on pure discount instruments. The term structure is sometimes called the "zero coupon yield curve" to distinguish it from the Treasury yield curve.

Treasury STRIPS

U.S. Treasury STRIPS Pure discount securities created by stripping coupons and principal payments of Treasury notes and bonds. Stands for Separate Trading of Registered Interest and Principal of Securities.

Until about 1987, the term structure of interest rates was not directly observable simply because default-free, pure discount instruments with maturities greater than one year did not exist or reliable data on them were not available. Today, however, the term structure of interest rates can be easily seen by examining yields on **U.S. Treasury STRIPS**.

STRIPS are pure discount instruments created by "stripping" the coupons and principal payments of U.S. Treasury notes and bonds into separate parts and then selling the parts separately. The term STRIPS stands for Separate Trading of Registered Interest and Principal of Securities. For example, a Treasury note with 10 years to maturity will make 20 semiannual coupon payments during its life and will also make a principal payment at maturity. This note can therefore be stripped into 21 separate parts, and each part can be bought and sold separately. The Treasury allows notes and bonds with 10 years or more to maturity (at the time they are issued) to be stripped. Currently, this means that 10-year notes and 30-year bonds can be stripped.[1]

Figure 9.5 is a sample "U.S. Treasury STRIPS" daily report of individual STRIPS prices and yields as it appeared in *The Wall Street Journal.* The first column of Figure 9.5 gives the maturity of each STRIPS listed. The second column reports whether the STRIPS were created from a coupon payment or a principal payment. There are three possible symbols in column 2: *ci* stands for coupon interest, *np* stands for note principal, and *bp* stands for bond principal. The next two columns contain bid and asked

Figure 9.5   Treasury STRIPS

U.S. TREASURY STRIPS

Mat.	Type	Bid	Asked	Chg	Ask Yld
Feb 99	ci	99:01	99:01	+ 1	4.70
Feb 99	np	99:02	99:02	+ 1	4.59
May 99	ci	97:28	97:29	+ 1	4.72
May 99	np	97:28	97:28	+ 1	4.76
Aug 99	ci	96:24	96:25	+ 1	4.69
Aug 99	np	96:24	96:24	+ 1	4.72
Nov 99	ci	95:21	95:22	+ 1	4.67
Nov 99	np	95:21	95:21	+ 1	4.69
Feb 00	ci	94:17	94:18	+ 1	4.70
Feb 00	np	94:17	94:18	+ 1	4.70
May 00	ci	93:14	93:15	+ 1	4.70
May 00	np	93:14	93:15	+ 1	4.70
Aug 00	ci	92:12	92:13	+ 2	4.69
Aug 00	np	92:11	92:12	+ 2	4.70
Nov 00	ci	91:10	91:11	+ 2	4.68
Nov 00	np	91:10	91:11	+ 2	4.69
Feb 01	ci	90:08	90:09	+ 3	4.69
Feb 01	np	90:07	90:09	+ 3	4.70
May 01	ci	89:06	89:07	+ 3	4.70
May 01	np	89:06	89:07	+ 3	4.70
Aug 01	ci	88:04	88:06	+ 3	4.70
Aug 01	np	88:03	88:04	+ 3	4.72
Nov 01	ci	87:01	87:03	+ 4	4.73
Nov 01	np	87:00	87:02	+ 4	4.74
Feb 02	ci	86:00	86:02	+ 3	4.74
May 02	ci	84:30	85:00	+ 3	4.76
May 02	np	84:26	84:28	+ 3	4.80
Aug 02	ci	83:30	83:31	+ 3	4.76
Aug 02	np	83:28	83:30	+ 3	4.78
Nov 02	ci	83:27	83:31	+ 4	4.47
Feb 03	ci	81:30	82:01	+ 4	4.76
Feb 03	np	81:30	82:01	+ 4	4.76
May 03	ci	80:29	81:00	+ 4	4.78
Aug 03	ci	80:03	80:06	+ 4	4.74
Aug 03	np	80:09	80:12	+ 4	7.69
Nov 03	ci	79:00	79:04	+ 4	4.78
Feb 04	ci	78:01	78:05	+ 3	4.79
Feb 04	np	78:18	78:22	+ 3	4.66
May 04	ci	77:00	77:04	+ 3	4.82
May 04	np	77:09	77:13	+ 3	4.75
Aug 04	ci	76:11	76:16	+ 3	4.75
Aug 04	np	76:11	76:16	+ 3	4.75
Nov 04	ci	75:02	75:06	+ 3	4.85
Nov 04	bp	74:29	75:01	+ 2	4.88
Nov 04	np	75:06	75:10	+ 3	4.82
Feb 05	ci	74:02	74:07	+ 3	4.86
Feb 05	np	74:10	74:14	+ 3	4.81
May 05	ci	73:03	73:07	+ 4	4.89
May 05	bp	72:31	73:03	+ 2	4.91
May 05	np	73:21	73:25	+ 4	4.76
Aug 05	ci	72:07	72:12	+ 4	4.88
Aug 05	bp	72:02	72:06	+ 4	4.92
Aug 05	np	72:27	73:00	+ 4	4.75
Nov 05	ci	71:12	71:16	+ 4	4.88
Nov 05	np	72:09	72:14	+ 4	4.69
Feb 06	ci	70:10	70:15	+ 4	4.92
Feb 06	bp	70:23	70:28	+ 4	4.84
Feb 06	np	71:03	71:08	+ 4	4.76
May 06	ci	69:14	69:19	+ 4	4.92

Mat.	Type	Bid	Asked	Chg	Ask Yld
Aug 06	ci	68:25	68:30	+ 4	4.89
Nov 06	ci	68:01	68:07	+ 4	4.87
Feb 07	ci	66:24	66:29	+ 4	4.95
May 07	ci	65:30	66:03	+ 4	4.95
Aug 07	ci	65:07	65:13	+ 4	4.94
Nov 07	ci	64:20	64:25	+ 4	4.91
Feb 08	ci	63:05	63:10	+ 5	5.03
May 08	ci	62:09	62:14	+ 5	5.04
Aug 08	ci	61:20	61:26	+ 5	5.02
Nov 08	ci	60:19	60:25	+ 5	5.07
Feb 09	ci	59:15	59:21	+ 5	5.13
May 09	ci	58:19	58:24	+ 5	5.15
Aug 09	ci	57:22	57:28	+ 5	5.17
Nov 09	ci	56:29	57:02	+ 6	5.18
Nov 09	bp	56:12	56:17	+ 5	5.27
Feb 10	ci	55:31	56:05	+ 7	5.22
May 10	ci	55:03	55:09	+ 7	5.24
Aug 10	ci	54:09	54:15	+ 7	5.26
Nov 10	ci	53:14	53:20	+ 7	5.28
Feb 11	ci	52:20	52:26	+ 2	5.30
May 11	ci	51:26	52:00	+ 2	5.32
Aug 11	ci	51:00	51:06	+ 2	5.34
Nov 11	ci	50:06	50:12	+ 2	5.36
Feb 12	ci	49:14	49:20	+ 1	5.38
May 12	ci	48:22	48:28	+ 1	5.39
Aug 12	ci	47:30	48:04	+ 2	5.41
Nov 12	ci	47:07	47:14	+ 3	5.42
Feb 13	ci	46:16	46:22	+ 4	5.43
May 13	ci	45:25	45:31	+ 4	5.45
Aug 13	ci	45:02	45:08	+ 4	5.46
Nov 13	ci	44:12	44:18	+ 4	5.48
Feb 14	ci	43:23	43:29	+ 4	5.49
May 14	ci	43:02	43:08	+ 4	5.50
Aug 14	ci	42:13	42:19	+ 4	5.51
Nov 14	ci	41:24	41:31	+ 4	5.52
Feb 15	ci	41:05	41:11	+ 6	5.51
Feb 15	bp	43:13	43:19	+ 6	5.19
May 15	ci	40:17	40:23	+ 6	5.53
Aug 15	ci	39:29	40:04	+ 6	5.54
Aug 15	bp	41:13	41:19	+ 6	5.32
Nov 15	ci	39:10	39:16	+ 6	5.55
Nov 15	bp	40:07	40:14	+ 6	5.41
Feb 16	ci	38:23	38:29	+ 6	5.56
Feb 16	bp	39:08	39:15	+ 6	5.48
May 16	ci	38:05	38:11	+ 6	5.51
May 16	bp	38:18	38:24	+ 6	5.51
Aug 16	ci	37:19	37:26	+ 6	5.57
Nov 16	ci	37:02	37:08	+ 6	5.58
Nov 16	bp	37:08	37:14	+ 6	5.55
Feb 17	ci	36:13	36:20	+ 6	5.60
May 17	ci	35:30	36:04	+ 6	5.59
May 17	bp	36:02	36:08	+ 6	5.57
Aug 17	bp	35:13	35:19	+ 6	5.60
Aug 17	ci	35:18	35:24	+ 6	5.58
Nov 17	ci	34:29	35:04	+ 6	5.60
Feb 18	ci	34:11	34:17	+ 5	5.61
May 18	ci	33:28	34:02	+ 5	5.61
May 18	bp	33:30	34:04	+ 5	5.60
Aug 18	ci	33:18	33:25	+ 5	5.59

Mat.	Type	Bid	Asked	Chg	Ask Yld
Nov 18	ci	32:30	33:04	+ 5	5.61
Nov 18	bp	33:00	33:06	+ 5	5.60
Feb 19	ci	32:14	32:21	+ 5	5.62
Feb 19	bp	32:17	32:23	+ 5	5.61
May 19	ci	32:00	32:06	+ 5	5.62
Aug 19	ci	31:17	31:23	+ 5	5.62
Aug 19	bp	31:20	31:26	+ 5	5.61
Nov 19	ci	31:03	31:09	+ 5	5.62
Feb 20	ci	30:22	30:28	+ 5	5.62
Feb 20	bp	30:25	30:31	+ 5	5.60
May 20	ci	30:08	30:14	+ 5	5.62
May 20	bp	30:11	30:17	+ 5	5.61
Aug 20	ci	29:27	30:01	+ 5	5.62
Aug 20	bp	29:30	30:04	+ 5	5.61
Nov 20	ci	29:13	29:19	+ 5	5.62
Feb 21	ci	29:02	29:08	+ 5	5.61
Feb 21	bp	29:07	29:13	+ 5	5.59
May 21	ci	28:23	28:29	+ 5	5.61
May 21	bp	28:25	28:31	+ 5	5.60
Aug 21	ci	28:11	28:17	+ 5	5.60
Aug 21	bp	28:14	28:21	+ 5	5.58
Nov 21	ci	28:00	28:06	+ 5	5.59
Nov 21	bp	28:04	28:10	+ 5	5.57
Feb 22	ci	27:21	27:27	+ 5	5.59
May 22	ci	27:11	27:17	+ 5	5.58
Aug 22	ci	27:01	27:07	+ 5	5.57
Aug 22	bp	27:07	27:13	+ 5	5.54
Nov 22	ci	26:23	26:29	+ 5	5.56
Nov 22	bp	26:27	27:01	+ 5	5.54
Feb 23	ci	26:13	26:19	+ 5	5.55
Feb 23	bp	26:20	26:26	+ 5	5.51
May 23	ci	26:02	26:08	+ 5	5.55
Aug 23	ci	25:22	25:28	+ 5	5.55
Aug 23	bp	26:06	26:12	+ 5	5.47
Nov 23	ci	25:12	25:18	+ 5	5.54
Feb 24	ci	25:05	25:10	+ 5	5.52
May 24	ci	24:27	25:01	+ 5	5.52
Aug 24	ci	24:17	24:23	+ 5	5.51
Nov 24	ci	24:10	24:16	+ 5	5.49
Nov 24	bp	24:14	24:20	+ 5	5.47
Feb 25	ci	24:02	24:08	+ 5	5.48
Feb 25	bp	24:07	24:13	+ 5	5.46
May 25	ci	23:25	23:31	+ 5	5.47
Aug 25	ci	23:18	23:24	+ 5	5.46
Aug 25	bp	23:18	23:24	+ 5	5.46
Nov 25	ci	23:07	23:13	+ 5	5.46
Feb 26	ci	22:26	23:00	+ 5	5.48
Feb 26	bp	23:09	23:15	+ 5	5.40
May 26	ci	22:17	22:23	+ 5	5.47
Aug 26	ci	22:08	22:14	+ 5	5.47
Aug 26	bp	22:12	22:18	+ 5	5.45
Nov 26	ci	22:01	22:07	+ 5	5.46
Nov 26	bp	22:04	22:10	+ 5	5.44
Feb 27	ci	21:30	22:03	+ 5	5.42
Feb 27	bp	22:00	22:05	+ 5	5.41
May 27	ci	21:17	21:23	+ 5	5.44
Aug 27	ci	21:18	21:24	+ 5	5.39
Aug 27	bp	21:23	21:28	+ 7	5.36
Nov 27	ci	21:28	22:02	+ 5	5.29
Nov 27	bp	21:29	22:03	+ 5	5.28

[1] Although four 20-year bond issues eligible for stripping still exist, 20-year maturity bonds are no longer issued.

prices for each STRIPS. As always, the bid price is a quote of what dealers were willing to pay to buy the STRIPS, and the asked price is a quote of what dealers were willing to accept to sell the STRIPS.

STRIPS prices are stated as a price per $100 of face value. For example, consider a coupon interest STRIPS with an asked price quoted of 74:08. This means that the price per $100 face value is $74.25, since the 08 to the right of the colon in the stated price 74:08 stands for thirty-seconds of a dollar. Thus 74:08 stands for $74 \frac{8}{32}$. The next-to-the-last column in Figure 9.5 reports the change in the asked price quote from the previous day. Price changes are also stated in thirty-seconds of a dollar. Thus, $+ 1$ means $+ 1/32$ of a dollar, or $+ 3.125$ cents per $100 face value.

Why are STRIPS prices quoted in thirty-seconds? For the same reason that stocks are quoted in sixteenths: Nobody really knows. That's the way they have been quoted historically, and the tradition continues. Why don't traders go to decimal quotes? They probably will someday, but don't hold your breath.

The last column in Figure 9.5 lists asked yields, which are yields on the STRIPS based on their asked price quotes. Notice that there is a different asked yield, or interest rate, for each maturity. This tells us that interest rates determined in financial markets generally differ according to the maturity of a security.

Yields for U.S. Treasury STRIPS

An asked yield for a U.S. Treasury STRIP is an APR (APRs were discussed earlier in this chapter). It is calculated as two times the true semiannual rate. Calculation of the yield on a STRIPS is a standard time value of money calculation. The price today of the STRIPS is the *present value;* the face value received at maturity is the *future value.* As you probably know, the relationship between present values and futures values is

$$\text{Present value} = \frac{\text{Future value}}{(1 + r)^N}$$

In this equation, r is the rate per period and N is the number of periods. Notice that a period is not necessarily one year long.[2] For Treasury STRIPS, the number of periods is two times the number of years to maturity, here denoted by $2M,$ and the interest rate is the yield to maturity (YTM) divided by 2:

$$\text{STRIPS price} = \frac{\text{Face value}}{(1 + \text{YTM}/2)^{2M}} \qquad \textbf{9.5}$$

Consider a STRIPS with an asked price of 42:23, a reported yield of 6.40, and 13.5 years to maturity. The actual semiannual rate is $6.40\% / 2 = 3.20\%$. Also, 13.5 years to maturity converts to 2×13.5, or 27 semiannual periods. To check that the reported price is correct given the reported yield, we plug in future value, rate per period, and number of periods:

$$\text{STRIPS price} = \frac{\$100}{(1 + .032)^{27}}$$

$$= 42:23$$

The price shown is rounded to the nearest thirty-second.

---

[2] Any financial calculator can perform these calculations, but we will work them the hard way for the benefit of those who don't have financial calculators.

If we need to go the other way and calculate the asked yield on a STRIPS given its price, we can rearrange the basic present value equation to solve it for r:

$$r = \left(\frac{\text{Future value}}{\text{Present value}}\right)^{\frac{1}{N}}$$

Here for STRIPS, $N = 2M$ is the number of semiannual periods and $r = YTM/2$ is the semiannual interest rate.

$$YTM = 2 \times \left(\frac{\text{Face value}}{\text{STRIPS price}}\right)^{\frac{1}{2M}} \qquad \textbf{9.6}$$

Consider a STRIPS maturing in six years with an asked price of 73:01. Its yield to maturity of 5.30724 percent as calculated immediately below becomes 5.31 percent after rounding to two decimal places.

$$5.30724\% = 2 \times \left[\left(\frac{100}{73.03125}\right)^{\frac{1}{12}} - 1\right]$$

As another example, consider a STRIPS maturing in 20 years with an asked price of 26:06. As calculated immediately below, its yield to maturity of 6.8129 percent becomes 6.81 percent after rounding to two decimal places.

$$6.8129\% = 2 \times \left[\left(\frac{100}{26.1875}\right)^{\frac{1}{40}} - 1\right]$$

CHECK THIS

9.4a What is the yield to maturity (YTM) of a STRIP maturing in five years if its asked price quote is 77:24?

9.4b What is the YTM of a STRIPS maturing in 15 years if its asked price quote is 38:26?

9.4c What is the YTM of a STRIPS maturing in 25 years if its asked price quote is 18:21?

9.5 Nominal versus Real Interest Rates

nominal interest rates Interest rates as they are normally observed and quoted, with no adjustment for inflation.

There is a fundamental distinction between *nominal* and *real* interest rates. **Nominal interest rates** are interest rates as we ordinarily observe them, for example, as they are reported in *The Wall Street Journal*. Thus, all the money market rates we discussed earlier in this chapter and the STRIPS yields we discussed just above are nominal rates.

Real Interest Rates

real interest rates Interest rates adjusted for the effect of inflation, calculated as the nominal rate less the rate of inflation.

Real interest rates are nominal rates adjusted for the effects of price inflation. To obtain a real interest rate, simply subtract an inflation rate from a nominal interest rate:

$$\text{Real interest rate} = \text{Nominal interest rate} - \text{Inflation rate} \qquad \textbf{9.7}$$

The real interest rate is so-called because it measures the real change in the purchasing power of an investment. For example, if the nominal interest rate for a one-year certificate of deposit is 7 percent, then a one-year deposit of $100,000 will grow to $107,000. But if the inflation rate over the same year is 4 percent, you would need $104,000 after one year passes to buy what cost $100,000 today. Thus, the real increase in purchasing power for your investment is only $3,000 and therefore the real interest rate is only 3 percent.

Figure 9.6 displays real interest rates based on annual rates of return on U.S. Treasury bills and inflation rates over the 43-year period, 1950 through 1992. As shown in Figure 9.6, following a negative spike at the beginning of the Korean War in 1950, real interest rates for Treasury bills were generally positive until the Organization of Petroleum-Exporting Countries' (OPEC) oil embargo in 1973. After this, real rates were generally negative until the Federal Reserve Board initiated a tight-money policy to fight an inflationary spiral in the late 1970s. The tight-money policy caused the 1980s to begin with historically high real interest rates. Throughout the 1980s, real Treasury bill rates were falling as inflation subsided. During this 43-year period the average real Treasury bill interest rate was slightly less than 1 percent.

The Fisher Hypothesis

Fisher hypothesis
Assertion that the general level of nominal interest rates follows the general level of inflation.

The relationship between nominal interest rates and the rate of inflation is often couched in terms of the *Fisher hypothesis,* which is named for the famous economist Irving Fisher, who formally proposed it in 1930. The **Fisher hypothesis** simply asserts that the general level of nominal interest rates follows the general level of inflation.

According to the Fisher hypothesis, interest rates are on average higher than the rate of inflation. Therefore, it logically follows that short-term interest rates reflect current inflation, while long-term interest rates reflect investor expectations of future inflation. Figure 9.7 graphs nominal interest rates and inflation rates used to create Figure 9.6. Notice that when inflation rates were high, Treasury bill returns tended to be high also, as predicted by the Fisher hypothesis.

Figure 9.6   Real T-Bill Rates

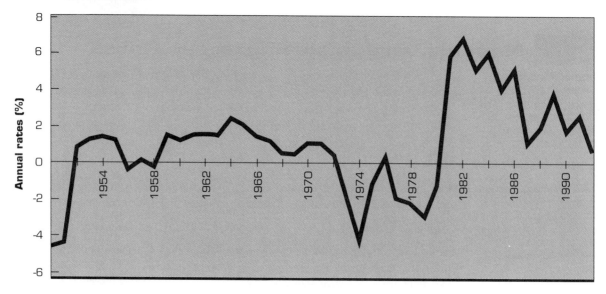

Source: Federal Reserve Board of Governors and Global Financial Data.

Figure 9.7 Inflation Rates and T-Bill Rates

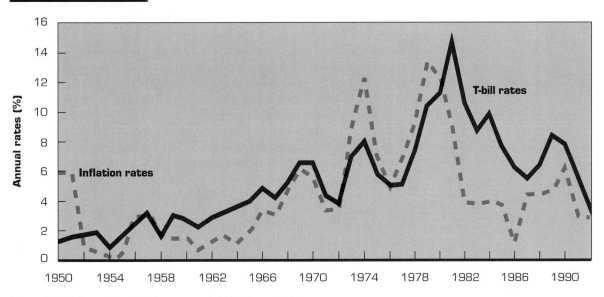

Source: Federal Reserve Board of Governors and Global Financial Data.

9.6 Traditional Theories of the Term Structure

Yield curves have been studied by financial economists for well over a century. During this period a number of different theories have been proposed to explain why yield curves may be upward sloping at one point in time and then downward sloping or flat at another point in time. We discuss three of the most popular traditional theories of the term structure in this section. We then present a modern perspective on the term structure in the following section.

Expectations Theory

expectations theory
The term structure of interest rates is a reflection of financial market beliefs regarding future interest rates.

According to the **expectations theory** of the term structure of interest rates, the shape of a yield curve expresses financial market expectations regarding future interest rates. Essentially, an upward-sloping yield curve predicts an increase in interest rates, and a downward-sloping yield curve predicts a decrease in interest rates. A flat yield curve expresses the sentiment that interest rates are not expected to change in the near future.

Expectations and Forward Rates   The basic principles of the expectations theory can be explained with a two-period example. Let r_1 stand for the current market interest rate on a one-year investment, and let r_2 be the current market interest rate on a two-year investment. Also, let $r_{1,1}$ be the market interest rate on a one-year investment that will be available in one year. Of course, this rate is not known today.

For a two-year investment, you have two strategies available. First, you can invest for two years at the rate r_2. In this case, $1 invested today will become $\$(1 + r_2)^2$ in two years. For example, if $r_2 = 10$ percent, you would have $\$1 \times (1.10)^2 = \$1.21$ in two years for every dollar you invest.

Alternatively, you can invest for one year at the rate r_1, and, at the end of one year, you can reinvest the proceeds at the rate $r_{1,1}$. In this case, $1 invested today will become $\$(1 + r_1)(1 + r_{1,1})$ in two years. For example, suppose $r_1 = 10$ percent and, after a year passes, it turns out that $r_{1,1} = 8$ percent. Then you would end up with $\$1 \times 1.10 \times 1.08 = \$1.188$. Alternatively, suppose that after a year passes it turns out that $r_{1,1} = 12$ percent; then you would have $\$1 \times 1.10 \times 1.12 = \$1.232$. Notice that this second strategy entails some uncertainty since the next year's interest rate, $r_{1,1}$, is not known when you originally select your investment strategy.

The expectations theory of the term structure of interest rates asserts that, on average, the two-year investment proceeds, $\$(1 + r_2)^2$ and $\$(1 + r_1)(1 + r_{1,1})$, will be equal. In fact, we can obtain what is known as the implied **forward rate**, $f_{1,1}$, by setting the two total proceeds equal to each other:

forward rate An expected future interest rate implied by current interest rates.

$$(1 + r_2)^2 = (1 + r_1)(1 + f_{1,1})$$

Solving for the forward rate, $f_{1,1}$, we see that

$$f_{1,1} = \frac{(1 + r_2)^2}{1 + r_1} - 1$$

Notice that this forward interest rate is simply a future interest rate implied by current interest rates.

According to expectations theory, the forward rate $f_{1,1}$ is an accurate predictor of the rate $r_{1,1}$ to be realized one year in the future. Thus, if $r_2 = 10$ percent and $r_1 = 8$ percent, then $f_{1,1} = 12$ percent, approximately, which predicts that the one-year interest rate will increase from its current value of 10 percent to 12 percent. Alternatively, if $r_2 = 10$ percent and $r_1 = 12$ percent, then $f_{1,1} = 8$ percent, approximately, which predicts that the one-year interest rate will decrease from its current value of 10 percent to 8 percent.

In general, if $r_2 > r_1$, such that the term structure is upward sloping, then expectations theory predicts an interest rate increase. Similarly, if $r_2 < r_1$, indicating a downward-sloping term structure, then expectations theory predicts an interest rate decrease. Thus, the slope of the term structures points in the predicted direction of future interest rate changes.

Example 9.7   Looking Forward

Suppose the yield on a two-year STRIPS is 7 percent and the yield on a one-year STRIPS is 6 percent. Based on the expectations theory, what will the yield on a one-year STRIPS be one year from now?

According to the expectations theory, the implied forward rate is an accurate predictor of what the interest rate will be. Thus, solving for the forward rate, we have

$$(1 + r_2)^2 = (1 + r_1)(1 + f_{1,1})$$

$$(1 + .07)^2 = (1 + .06)(1 + f_{1,1})$$

and the forward rate is

$$f_{1,1} = \frac{1.07^2}{1.06} - 1 = 8.00943\%$$

Based on the expectations theory, the rate next year will be about 8 percent. Notice that this is higher than the current rate, as we would predict since the term structure is upward sloping.

Expectations Theory and the Fisher Hypothesis   The expectations theory is closely related to the Fisher hypothesis we discussed earlier. The relationship between the expectations theory of interest rates and the Fisher hypothesis is stated as follows. If expected future inflation is higher than current inflation, then we are likely to see an upward-sloping term structure where long-term interest rates are higher than short-term interest rates. Similarly, if future inflation is expected to be lower than its current level, we would then be likely to see a downward-sloping term structure where long rates are lower than short rates.

In other words, taken together, the expectations theory and the Fisher hypothesis assert that an upward-sloping term structure tells us that the market expects that nominal interest rates and inflation are likely to be higher in the future.

Maturity Preference Theory

Another traditional theory of the term structure asserts that lenders prefer to lend short-term to avoid tying up funds for long periods of time. In other words, they have a preference for shorter maturities. At the same time, borrowers prefer to borrow long-term to lock in secure financing for long periods of time.

maturity preference theory Long-term interest rates contain a maturity premium necessary to induce lenders into making longer term loans.

According to the **maturity preference theory**, then, borrowers have to pay a higher rate to borrow long-term rather than short-term to essentially bribe lenders into loaning funds for longer maturities. The extra interest is called a *maturity premium*.[3]

The Fisher hypothesis, maturity preference theory, and expectations theory can coexist without problem. For example, suppose the shape of a yield curve is basically determined by expected future interest rates according to expectations theory. But where do expected future interest rates come from? According to the Fisher hypothesis, expectations regarding future interest rates are based on expected future rates of inflation. Thus, expectations theory and the Fisher hypothesis mesh quite nicely.

Furthermore, a basic yield curve determined by inflationary expectations could also accommodate maturity preference theory. All we need to do is add a maturity premium to longer term interest rates. In this view, long-term, default-free interest rates have three components: a real rate, an anticipated future inflation rate, and a maturity premium.

---

[3] Traditionally, maturity preference theory has been known as "liquidity" preference theory and the maturity premium was termed a "liquidity" premium. However, as we discussed in Chapter 2, the term "liquidity" is universally used to indicate the relative ease with which an asset can be sold. Also, the term "liquidity premium" now has a different meaning. To avoid confusion and to make this theory more consistent with modern views of liquidity, interest rates, and the term structure, we have adopted the more descriptive name of maturity premium.

Market Segmentation Theory

market segmentation theory
Debt markets are segmented by maturity, with the result that interest rates for various maturities are determined separately in each segment.

An alternative theory of the term structure of interest rates is the **market segmentation theory**, which asserts that debt markets are segmented according to the various maturities of debt instruments available for investment. By this theory, each maturity represents a separate, distinct market. For example, one group of lenders and borrowers may prefer to lend and borrow using securities with a maturity of 10 years, while another group may prefer to lend and borrow using securities with a maturity of 5 years. Segmentation theory simply states that interest rates corresponding to each maturity are determined separately by supply and demand conditions in each market segment.

Another theory of the term structure, known as the *preferred habitat theory,* is essentially a compromise between market segmentation and maturity preference. In the preferred habitat theory, as in the market segmentation theory, different investors have different preferred maturities. The difference is that they can be induced to move to less preferred maturities by a higher interest rate. In the maturity preference theory, the preferred habitat is always toward shorter maturities rather than longer maturities.

CHECK THIS

9.6a According to the expectations theory, what does an upward-sloping term structure indicate?

9.6b What basic assertion does maturity preference theory make about investor preferences? If this assertion is correct, how does it affect the term structure of interest rates?

9.7 Determinants of Nominal Interest Rates: A Modern Perspective

Our understanding of the term structure of interest rates has increased significantly in the last few decades. Also, the evolution of fixed-income markets has shown us that, at least to some extent, traditional theories discussed in our previous section may be inadequate to explain the term structure. We discuss some problems with these theories next and then move on to a modern perspective.

Problems with Traditional Theories

To illustrate some problems with traditional theories, we could examine the behavior of the term structure in the last two decades. What we would find is that the term structure is almost always upward sloping. But contrary to the expectations hypothesis, interest rates have not always risen. Furthermore, as we saw with STRIPS term structure, it is often the case that the term structure turns down at very long maturities. According to the expectations hypothesis, market participants apparently expect rates to rise for 20 or so years and then decline. This seems to be stretching things a bit.

In terms of maturity preference, the world's biggest borrower, the U.S. government, borrows much more heavily short term than long term. Furthermore, many of the biggest buyers of fixed-income securities, such as pension funds, have a strong preference for *long* maturities. It is hard to square these facts with the behavioral assumptions underlying the maturity preference theory.

Finally, in terms of market segmentation, the U.S. government borrows at all maturities. Many institutional investors, such as mutual funds, are more than willing to move maturities to obtain more favorable rates. At the same time, there are bond trading operations that do nothing other than buy and sell various maturity issues to exploit even very small perceived premiums. In short, in the modern fixed-income market, market segmentation does not seem to be a powerful force.

Modern Term Structure Theory

Going back to Chapter 1, we saw that long-term government bonds had higher returns, on average, than short-term T-bills. They had substantially more risk as well. In other words, there appears to be a risk-return trade-off for default-free bonds as well, and long-term bonds appear to have a risk premium.

Notice that this risk premium doesn't result from the possibility of default since it exists on default-free U.S. government debt. Instead, it exists because longer term bond prices are more volatile than shorter term prices. As we discuss in detail in the next chapter, the reason is that for a given change in interest rates, long-term bond prices change more than short-term bonds. Put differently, long-term bond prices are much more sensitive to interest rate changes than short-term bonds. This is called *interest rate risk,* and the risk premium on longer term bonds is called the *interest rate risk premium.*

The interest rate risk premium carried by long-term bonds leads us to a modern reinterpretation of the maturity preference hypothesis. All other things the same, investors do prefer short-term bonds to long-term bonds. The reason is simply that short-term bonds are less risky. As a result, long-term bonds have to offer higher yields to compensate investors for the extra interest rate risk.

Putting it together, the modern view of the term structure suggests that nominal interest rates on default-free securities can be stated as follows:

$$NI = RI + IP + RP \qquad\qquad \textbf{9.8}$$

where NI = Nominal interest rate
     RI = Real interest rate
     IP = Inflation premium
    RP = Interest rate risk premium

In this decomposition, the real rate of interest is assumed to be the same for all securities, and, on average, the real interest rate is positive, as predicted by the Fisher hypothesis.

As we discussed above, the inflation premium (IP) reflects investor expectations of future price inflation. The inflation premium may be different for securities with different maturities because expected inflation may be different over different future horizons. For example, the expected average rate of inflation over the next two years may be different from the expected average rate of inflation over the next five years.

In addition to the real rate and the inflation premium, nominal rates reflect an interest rate risk premium (RP) which increases with the maturity of the security being considered. As a result, if interest rates are expected to remain constant through time, the term structure would have a positive slope. This is consistent with maturity preference theory. Indeed, for zero coupon bonds the interest rate risk premium and the maturity premium are the same thing.

The separate effects of the inflation premium and the interest rate risk premium are difficult to distinguish. For example, the yields for U.S. Treasury STRIPS in Figure 9.5 reveal a substantial yield premium for long-maturity STRIPS over short-term STRIPS. This yield premium for long-maturity STRIPS reflects the combined effects of the inflation premium and the risk premium. However, it is unclear how much of the total premium is caused by an inflation premium and how much is due to a risk premium.

Liquidity and Default Risk

Thus far we have examined the components of interest rates on default-free, highly liquid securities such as Treasury STRIPS. We now expand our coverage to securities that are either less liquid, not default-free, or both, to present a more detailed decomposition of nominal interest rates. When we are finished, what we will see is that nominal interest rates for individual securities can be decomposed into five basic components as follows:

$$NI = RI + IP + RP + LP + DP \qquad \textbf{9.9}$$

where NI = Nominal interest rate
RI = Real interest rate
IP = Inflation premium
RP = Interest rate risk premium
LP = Liquidity premium
DP = Default premium

We have already discussed the first three components of the nominal interest rate. We now consider the two new ones on our list, the default and liquidity premiums.

The *liquidity premium* (LP) is a reflection of the fact that two otherwise identical securities may have very different degrees of liquidity. All else the same, the one with less liquidity would have to offer a higher yield as compensation.

The fifth and final component of a nominal interest rate is a *default premium* (DP). Investors demand a default premium to assume the risk of holding a security that might default on its promised payments. Naturally, the greater is the risk of default for a particular bond issue, the larger is the default premium required by investors. The topic of default risk is discussed in detail for corporate bonds in Chapter 11 and municipal bonds in Chapter 12.

9.8 Summary and Conclusions

The time value of money is arguably the most important principle of finance. Interest rates are a convenient way to measure and state the time value of money. Furthermore, understanding interest rates is essential for understanding money market and fixed-income securities. In this chapter, we covered a number of topics relating to interest rates, including:

1. Important short-term money market rates include the prime rate, the Federal funds rate, and the Federal Reserve's discount rate. The prime rate is a bellwether of bank lending to business, while the Federal funds rate and the Federal Reserve's discount rate are indicators of the availability of money and credit within the banking system.

2. A Treasury yield curve graphs the relationship between yields on U.S. Treasury securities and their maturities. The Treasury yield curve is fundamental to bond market analysis because it represents the interest rates that financial markets are charging to the world's largest debtor with the world's highest credit rating—the U.S. government.

3. The term structure of interest rates is the fundamental relationship between time to maturity and interest rates for default-free, pure discount instruments such as U.S. Treasury STRIPS.

4. A number of different theories—including the expectations theory, the maturity preference theory, and the market segmentation theory—have been proposed to explain why the term structure of interest rates and yield curves may be upward sloping at one point in time and then downward sloping or flat at another time. In a modern view of the term structure, yields on default-free, pure discount bonds are determined by the real rate of interest, expectations of future inflation, and an interest rate risk premium.

5. Interest rates have five basic components: the real rate, an inflation premium, an interest rate risk premium, a liquidity premium, and a default premium. U.S. Treasury securities are free of default risk and are very liquid, so the last two components are absent from such instruments. For other issues, however, these components are very important.

GET REAL

This chapter covered the essentials of interest rates. How should you, as an investor or investment manager, put this information to work?

The best thing to do is to buy a variety of the instruments we discuss in the chapter. STRIPS, in particular, are an important class of investment both for institutional and individual investors. To gain some practical experience with the risks and rewards from STRIPS investing, you should invest equal dollar amounts in several different STRIPS with different maturities. Pick short-term (a few years), intermediate-term (10 or so years) and long-term (25 years or longer), for example. Once you make the investments, monitor the yields and prices. You will observe that the different maturity STRIPS will behave quite differently; understanding why this is so is fundamental to fixed-income investing.

A good way to study some of the money market instruments we discuss in this chapter is to examine the actual holdings of money market mutual funds (MMMFs). At the same time, it is a good idea to read an MMMF's prospectus, which provides details of the types of investments the fund can make. What you will see is that some MMMFs can buy only a limited number of these instruments, whereas others have much broader investing options. Your goal in this is to gain an understanding of the risks of the different types of money market instruments and the factors that lead some funds to invest in certain types and others to avoid them.

Key Terms

prime rate 243
bellwether rate 243
Federal funds rate 243
discount rate 244
call money rate 244
commercial paper 244
certificate of deposit (CD) 244
banker's acceptance 245
London Eurodollars 245
London Interbank Offered Rate (LIBOR) 245
U.S. Treasury bill (T-bill) 245

pure discount security 247
bank discount basis 247
Treasury yield curve 254
term structure of interest rates 256
U.S. Treasury STRIPS 256
nominal interest rates 259
real interest rates 259
Fisher hypothesis 260
expectations theory 261
forward rate 262
maturity preference theory 263
market segmentation theory 264

Chapter Review Problems and Self-Test

1. **Money Market Prices**   The rate on a particular money market instrument, quoted on a discount basis, is 5 percent. The instrument has a face value of $100,000 and will mature in 40 days. What is its price?

2. **Bond Equivalent Yields**   Suppose a T-bill has 75 days to maturity and an asked discount of 4 percent. What is the bond equivalent yield?

Answers to Self-Test Problems

1. Using the bank discount basis formula, we have

$$\text{Current price} = \text{Face value} \times \left(1 - \frac{\text{Days to maturity}}{360} \times \text{Discount rate}\right)$$

$$\$99{,}444.44 = \$100{,}000 \times \left(1 - \frac{40}{360} \times .05\right)$$

You would pay $99,444.44.

2. Using the bond equivalent yield conversion formula, we have

$$4.09\% = \frac{365 \times .04}{360 - 75 \times .04}$$

The bond equivalent yield is thus 4.09 percent.

Test Your Investment Quotient

1. **Interest Rates**   Which of the following interest rates is a bellwether (leading indicator) rate of bank lending to business?

   a. Unsecured business loan rate.
   b. Prime rate.
   c. Commercial paper rate.
   d. Banker's acceptance rate.

2. **Interest Rates**   Among the following interest rates, which is normally the highest rate?

   a. Commercial paper rate.
   b. U.S. Treasury bill rate.
   c. Federal funds rate.
   d. Federal Reserve discount rate.

3. **T-Bill Yields**   A U.S. Treasury bill with 180 days to maturity has a discount yield of 5 percent and a face value of $100,000. What is its current price?

   a. $97,500
   b. $95,000
   c. $92,500
   d. $90,000

4. **T-Bill Yields**   A 30-day U.S. Treasury bill is selling at a 12 percent yield on a discount basis. Which of the following is its approximate bond equivalent yield? (*1988 CFA exam*)

   a. 6.0 percent
   b. 11.7 percent
   c. 12.0 percent
   d. 12.3 percent

5. **Effective Annual Rates** A credit card company states an annual percentage rate (APR) of 12 percent, which is actually a rate of 1 percent per month. What is the EAR?

   a. 12 percent
   b. 12.68 percent
   c. 13.08 percent
   d. 13.76 percent

6. **STRIPS Yields** A U.S. Treasury STRIPS maturing in 10 years has a current price of $502.57 for $1,000 of face value. What is the yield to maturity of this STRIPS?

   a. 7.0 percent
   b. 7.12 percent
   c. 8.0 percent
   d. 8.12 percent

7. **Bond Yields** An analyst finds that the semiannual interest rate that equates the present value of the bond's cash flow to its current market price is 3.85 percent. Consider the following possible alternatives: (*1991 CFA exam*)

   i. The bond equivalent yield on this security is 7.70 percent.
   ii. The effective annual yield on the bond is 7.85 percent.
   iii. The bond's yield to maturity is 7.70 percent.
   iv. The bond's horizon return is 8.35 percent.

   Which of these alternatives are true?

   a. i and ii only.
   b. ii, iii, and iv only.
   c. i, ii, and iii only.
   d. iii only.

8. **Yield Curves** Assuming that the yield curve and term structure are both upward sloping at all maturities, which of the following debt instruments will have the highest interest rate as measured by its yield to maturity?

   a. 20-year maturity U.S. Treasury STRIPS.
   b. 20-year maturity U.S. Treasury bond.
   c. 20-year maturity municipal bond.
   d. 10-year maturity U.S. Treasury note.

9. **Fisher Hypothesis** The Fisher hypothesis essentially asserts which of the following?

   a. Nominal interest rates follow inflation.
   b. Real interest rates follow inflation.
   c. Inflation follows real interest rates.
   d. Inflation follows nominal interest rates.

10. **Term Structure Theory** Which one of the following statements about the term structure of interest rates is true? (*1993 CFA exam*)

    a. The expectations hypothesis indicates a flat yield curve if anticipated future short-term rates exceed current short-term rates.
    b. The expectations hypothesis contends that the long-term rate is equal to the anticipated short-term rate.
    c. The liquidity premium theory indicates that, all else being equal, longer maturities will have lower yields.
    d. The market segmentation theory contends that borrowers and lenders prefer particular segments of the yield curve.

11. **Term Structure Theory** Which one of the following is not an explanation of the relationship between a bond's interest rate and its term to maturity? (*1988 CFA exam*)

    a. Default (credit) risk hypothesis.
    b. Expectations hypothesis.
    c. Liquidity preference hypothesis.
    d. Segmentation hypothesis.

12. **Term Structure Theory**   Which theory explains the shape of the yield curve by considering the relative demands for various maturities? (*1989 CFA exam*)

    a. Relative strength theory
    b. Segmentation theory
    c. Unbiased expectations theory
    d. Liquidity premium theory

13. **Term Structure Theory**   The concepts of spot and forward rates are most closely associated with which one of the following explanations of the term structure of interest rates? (*1992 CFA exam*)

    a. Expectations hypothesis
    b. Liquidity premium theory
    c. Preferred habitat hypothesis
    d. Segmented market theory

14. **Forward Rates**   The current one-year interest rate is 6 percent and the current two-year interest rate is 7 percent. What is the implied forward rate for next year's one-year rate?

    a. 9 percent
    b. 8 percent
    c. 7 percent
    d. 6 percent

15. **Forward Rates**   The six-month Treasury bill spot rate is 4.0 percent, and the one-year Treasury bill spot rate is 5.0 percent. The implied six-month forward rate six months from now is which of the following? (*1994 CFA exam*)

    a. 3.0 percent
    b. 4.5 percent
    c. 5.5 percent
    d. 5.9 percent

Questions and Problems

Core Questions

1. **Interest Rate History**   Based on the history of interest rates, what is the range of short-term rates that have occurred in the United States? The range of long-term rates? What is a typical value for each?

2. **Discount Securities**   What are pure discount securities? Give two examples.

3. **Fed Funds versus the Discount Rate**   Compare and contrast the Fed funds rate and the discount rate. Which do you think is more volatile? Which market do you think is more active? Why?

4. **Commercial Paper**   Compare and contrast commercial paper and Treasury bills. Which would typically offer a higher interest rate? Why?

5. **LIBOR**   What is LIBOR? Why is it important?

6. **Zeroes**   What is a zero coupon bond? How does it differ from a pure discount security?

7. **Bank Discount Rates**   Why do you suppose rates on some money market instruments are quoted on a bank discount basis? (Hint: Why use a 360-day year?)

8. **STRIPS**   With regard to STRIPS, what do "ci," "np," and "bp" represent?

9. **Nominal and Real Rates**   When we observe interest rates in the financial press, do we see nominal or real rates? Which are more relevant to investors?

10. **Munis versus Treasuries**   Which would have a higher yield, a municipal bond or a Treasury bond of the same maturity?

11. **Treasury Bill Prices** How much would you pay for a U.S. Treasury bill with 89 days to maturity quoted at a discount yield of 5.50 percent? Assume a $1 million face value.

12. **Treasury Bill Prices** In the previous problem, what is the bond-equivalent yield?

13. **Money Market Prices** The treasurer of a large corporation wants to invest $10 million in excess short-term cash in a particular money market investment. The prospectus quotes the instrument at a true yield of 6.10 percent; that is, the EAR for this investment is 6.10 percent. However, the treasurer wants to know the money market yield on this instrument to make it comparable to the T-bills and CDs she has already bought. If the term of the instrument is 120 days, what are the bond-equivalent and discount yields on this investment?

Use the following information to answer the next six questions:

U.S. Treasury STRIPS, close of business, February 15, 2000:

Maturity	Price	Maturity	Price
Feb01	95:10	Feb04	79:03
Feb02	90:05	Feb05	74:07
Feb03	84:29	Feb06	69:16

14. **Zero Coupon Bonds** Calculate the quoted yield for each of the six STRIPS given in the table above. Does the market expect interest rates to go up or down in the future?

15. **Zero Coupon Bonds** What is the yield of the two-year STRIP expressed as an EAR?

16. **Forward Interest Rates** According to the pure expectations theory of interest rates, how much do you expect to pay for a one-year STRIPS on February 15, 2001? What is the corresponding implied forward rate? How does your answer compare to the current yield on a one-year STRIPS? What does this tell you about the relationship between implied forward rates, the shape of the zero-coupon yield curve, and market expectations about future spot interest rates?

17. **Forward Interest Rates** According to the pure expectations theory of interest rates, how much do you expect to pay for a five-year STRIPS on February 15, 2001? How much do you expect to pay for a two-year STRIPS on February 15, 2003?

18. **Forward Interest Rates** This problem is a little harder. Suppose the term structure is set according to pure expectations and the maturity preference theory. To be specific, investors require no compensation for holding investments with a maturity of one year, but they demand a premium of .30 percent for holding investments with a maturity of two years. Given this information, how much would you pay for a one-year STRIPS on February 15, 2001? What is the corresponding implied forward rate? Compare your answer to the solutions you found in Problem 16. What does this tell you about the effect of a maturity premium on implied forward rates?

19. **Bond Price Changes** Suppose the (quoted) yield on each of the six STRIPS increases by .25 percent. Calculate the percentage change in price for the one-year, three-year, and six-year STRIPS. Which one has the largest price change? Now suppose that the quoted price on each STRIPS decreases by 16/32. Calculate the percentage change in (quoted) yield for the one-year, three-year, and six-year STRIPS. Which one has the largest yield change? What do your answers tell you about the relationship between prices, yields, and maturity for discount bonds?

20. **Inflation and Returns** You observe that the current interest rate on short-term U.S. Treasury bills is 5 percent. You also read in the newspaper that the GDP deflator, which is a common macroeconomic indicator used by market analysts to gauge the inflation rate, currently implies that inflation is 3.5 percent. Given this information, what is the approximate real rate of interest on short-term Treasury bills? Is it likely that your answer would change if you used some alternative measure for the inflation rate, such as the CPI? What does this tell you about the observability and accuracy of real interest rates compared to nominal interest rates?

STOCK-TRAK·
Portfolio Simulations

Trading Interest Rates with Stock-Trak

Your Stock-Trak account allows you to trade on changes in interest rates by buying and selling securities whose values depend on interest rates. U.S. Treasury STRIPS are the simplest instruments used to trade interest rates, since specific STRIPS are available for trading short-term, intermediate-term, or long-term interest rates. Stock-Trak supports trading in about a dozen different STRIPS issues. A current list of STRIPS available for Stock-Trak trading is found on our website in the Stock-Trak Section. (www.mhhe.com/cj).

Suppose you believe that long-term interest rates will fall over the next few weeks. This will cause long-maturity STRIPS prices to rise, so the appropriate trading strategy is to buy long-maturity STRIPS now and sell them later, after they rise in value. For example, you wish to buy STRIPS maturing in 2024. The Stock-Trak ticker symbol for these STRIPS is B-ST24. Each STRIPS has a face value of $1,000 and a current price that depends on its yield to maturity. For example, a STRIPS maturing in 24 years with a 6 percent yield has a price of $242. A yield change of 50 basis points to 5.5 percent will increase the price to $271.94. This represents a trading profit of $29.94 for each STRIPS you bought. Thus, if you bought 100 STRIPS, your total profit would be $2,994.

Stock-Trak Exercises

1. Read several recent "Credit Markets" sections in *The Wall Street Journal* and attempt to deduce which direction long-term interest rates will move during the next few weeks. If you think interest rates will go down, then buy the longest maturity STRIPS available through Stock-Trak. After several weeks, close out your position and assess your success in forecasting interest rate changes.

2. To try more advanced interest rate trading strategies, you will need to master the basics of trading futures contracts on interest rate–sensitive securities. If your interest is piqued, then peer ahead to the end of Chapter 16 for a discussion of trading interest rate futures contracts with Stock-Trak.

10 Bond Prices and Yields

Interest **rates go up** and bond prices go down. But which bonds go up the most and which go up the least? Interest rates go down and bond prices go up. But which bonds go down the most and which go down the least? For bond portfolio managers, these are very important questions about interest rate risk. An understanding of interest rate risk rests on an understanding of the relationship between bond prices and yields. ■ In the preceding chapter on interest rates, we introduced the subject of bond yields. As we promised there, we now return to this subject and discuss bond prices and yields in some detail. We first describe how bond yields are determined and how they are interpreted. We then go on to examine what happens to bond prices as yields change. Finally, once we have a good understanding of the relation between bond prices and yields, we examine some of the fundamental tools of bond risk analysis used by fixed-income portfolio managers.

10.1 Bond Basics

A bond essentially is a security that offers the investor a series of fixed interest payments during its life, along with a fixed payment of principal when it matures. So long as the bond issuer does not default, the schedule of payments does not change. When originally issued, bonds normally have maturities ranging from 2 years to 30 years, but bonds with maturities of 50 or 100 years also exist. Bonds issued with maturities of less than 10 years are usually called notes. A very small number of bond issues have no stated maturity, and these are referred to as perpetuities or consols.

Straight Bonds

The most common type of bond is the so-called straight bond. By definition, a straight bond is an IOU that obligates the issuer to pay to the bondholder a fixed sum of money at the bond's maturity along with constant, periodic interest payments during the life of the bond. The fixed sum paid at maturity is referred to as bond principal, par value, stated value, or face value. The periodic interest payments are called coupons. Perhaps the best example of straight bonds are U.S. Treasury bonds issued by the federal government to finance the national debt. However, business corporations and municipal governments also routinely issue debt in the form of straight bonds.

In addition to a straight bond component, many bonds have additional special features. These features are sometimes designed to enhance a bond's appeal to investors. For example, convertible bonds have a conversion feature that grants bondholders the right to convert their bonds into shares of common stock of the issuing corporation. As another example, "putable" bonds have a put feature that grants bondholders the right to sell their bonds back to the issuer at a special put price.

These and other special features are attached to many bond issues, but we defer discussion of special bond features until later chapters. For now, it is only important to know that when a bond is issued with one or more special features, strictly speaking it is no longer a straight bond. However, bonds with attached special features will normally have a straight bond component, namely, the periodic coupon payments and fixed principal payment at maturity. For this reason, straight bonds are important as the basic unit of bond analysis.

The prototypical example of a straight bond pays a series of constant semiannual coupons, along with a face value of $1,000 payable at maturity. This example is used in this chapter because it is common and realistic. For example, most corporate bonds are sold with a face value of $1,000 per bond, and most bonds (in the United States at least) pay constant semiannual coupons.

Coupon Rate and Current Yield

A familiarity with bond yield measures is important for understanding the financial characteristics of bonds. As we briefly discussed in Chapter 3, two basic yield measures for a bond are its coupon rate and current yield.

coupon rate A bond's annual coupon divided by its price. Also called *coupon yield* or *nominal yield*.

A bond's **coupon rate** is defined as its annual coupon amount divided by its par value, or, in other words, its annual coupon expressed as a percentage of face value:

$$\text{Coupon rate} = \frac{\text{Annual coupon}}{\text{Par value}} \qquad \textbf{10.1}$$

For example, suppose a $1,000 par value bond pays semiannual coupons of $40. The annual coupon is then $80, and stated as a percentage of par value the bond's coupon rate is $80 / $1,000 = 8%. A coupon rate is often referred to as the *coupon yield* or the *nominal yield*. Notice that the word "nominal" here has nothing to do with inflation.

current yield A bond's annual coupon divided by its market price.

A bond's **current yield** is its annual coupon payment divided by its current market price:

$$\text{Current yield} = \frac{\text{Annual coupon}}{\text{Bond price}} \qquad \textbf{10.2}$$

For example, suppose a $1,000 par value bond paying an $80 annual coupon has a price of $1,032.25. The current yield is $80 / $1,032.25 = 7.75%. Similarly, a price of $969.75 implies a current yield of $80 / $969.75 = 8.25%. Notice that whenever there is a change in the bond's price, the coupon rate remains constant. However, a bond's current yield is inversely related to its price, and it changes whenever the bond's price changes.

CHECK THIS

10.1a What is a straight bond?

10.1b What is a bond's coupon rate? Its current yield?

10.2 Straight Bond Prices and Yield to Maturity

yield to maturity (YTM) The discount rate that equates a bond's price with the present value of its future cash flows. Also called *promised yield* or just *yield.*

The single most important yield measure for a bond is its **yield to maturity**, commonly abbreviated as **YTM**. By definition, a bond's yield to maturity is the discount rate that equates the bond's price with the computed present value of its future cash flows. A bond's yield to maturity is sometimes called its *promised yield,* but, more commonly, the yield to maturity of a bond is simply referred to as its *yield.* In general, if the term "yield" is being used with no qualification, it means yield to maturity.

Straight Bond Prices

For straight bonds, the following standard formula is used to calculate a bond's price given its yield:

$$\text{Bond price} = \frac{C}{YTM}\left[1 - \frac{1}{(1 + YTM/2)^{2M}}\right] + \frac{FV}{(1 + YTM/2)^{2M}} \qquad \textbf{10.3}$$

where

C = Annual coupon, the sum of two semiannual coupons
FV = Face value
M = Maturity in years
YTM = Yield to maturity

In this formula, the coupon used is the annual coupon, which is the sum of the two semiannual coupons. As discussed in our previous chapter for U.S. Treasury STRIPS, the yield on a bond is an annual percentage rate (APR), calculated as twice the true semiannual yield. As a result, the yield on a bond somewhat understates its effective annual rate (EAR).

The straight bond pricing formula has two separate components. The first component is the present value of all the coupon payments. Since the coupons are fixed and paid on a regular basis, you may recognize that they form an ordinary annuity, and the first piece of the bond pricing formula is a standard calculation for the present value of an annuity. The other component represents the present value of the principal payment at maturity, and it is a standard calculation for the present value of a single lump sum.

Calculating bond prices is mostly "plug and chug" with a calculator. In fact, a good financial calculator or spreadsheet should have this formula built into it. In addition, a Treasury Notes and Bonds calculator software program is included on the self-study CD-ROM that is included with this text. In any case, we will work through a few examples the long way just to illustrate the calculations.

Suppose a bond has a $1,000 face value, 20 years to maturity, an 8 percent coupon rate, and a yield of 9 percent. What's the price? Using the straight bond pricing formula, the price of this bond is calculated as follows:

1. Present value of semiannual coupons:

$$\frac{\$80}{.09}\left[1 - \frac{1}{(1.045)^{40}}\right] = \$736.06337$$

2. Present value of $1,000 principal:

$$\frac{\$1,000}{(1.045)^{40}} = \$171.92871$$

The price of the bond is the sum of the present values of coupons and principal:

$$\text{Bond price} = \$736.06 + \$171.93 = \$907.99$$

So, this bond sells for $907.99.

Example 10.1 Calculating Straight Bond Prices

Suppose a bond has 20 years to maturity and a coupon rate of 8 percent. The bond's yield to maturity is 7 percent. What's the price?

In this case, the coupon rate is 8 percent and the face value is $1,000, so the annual coupon is $80. The bond's price is calculated as follows:

1. Present value of semiannual coupons:

$$\frac{\$80}{.07}\left[1 - \frac{1}{(1.035)^{40}}\right] = \$854.20289$$

2. Present value of $1,000 principal:

$$\frac{\$1,000}{(1.035)^{40}} = \$252.57247$$

The bond's price is the sum of coupon and principal present values:

$$\text{Bond price} = \$854.20 + \$252.57 = \$1,106.77$$

This bond sells for $1,106.77.

Premium and Discount Bonds

Bonds are commonly distinguished according to whether they are selling at par value or at a discount or premium relative to par value. These three relative price descriptions—premium, discount, and par bonds—are defined as follows:

1. **Premium bonds:** Bonds with a price greater than par value are said to be selling at a premium. The yield to maturity of a premium bond is less than its coupon rate.

2. **Discount bonds:** Bonds with a price less than par value are said to be selling at a discount. The yield to maturity of a discount bond is greater than its coupon rate.

3. **Par bonds:** Bonds with a price equal to par value are said to be selling at par. The yield to maturity of a par bond is equal to its coupon rate.

The important thing to notice is that whether a bond sells at a premium or discount depends on the relation between its coupon rate and its yield. If the coupon rate exceeds the yield, then the bond will sell at a premium. If the coupon is less than the yield, the bond will sell at a discount.

Example 10.2 Premium and Discount Bonds

Consider a bond with eight years to maturity and a 7 percent coupon rate. If its yield to maturity is 9 percent, does this bond sell at a premium or discount? Verify your answer by calculating the bond's price.

Since the coupon rate is smaller than the yield, this is a discount bond. Check that its price is $887.66.

The relationship between bond prices and bond maturities for premium and discount bonds is graphically illustrated in Figure 10.1 for bonds with an 8 percent coupon rate. The vertical axis measures bond prices and the horizontal axis measures bond maturities.

Figure 10.1 also describes the paths of premium and discount bond prices as their maturities shorten with the passage of time, assuming no changes in yield to maturity. As shown, the time paths of premium and discount bond prices follow smooth curves. Over time, the price of a premium bond declines and the price of a discount bond rises. At maturity, the price of each bond converges to its par value.

Figure 10.1 illustrates the general result that, for discount bonds, holding the coupon rate and yield to maturity constant, the longer the term to maturity of the bond the greater is the discount from par value. For premium bonds, holding the coupon rate and yield to maturity constant, the longer the term to maturity of the bond the greater is the premium over par value.

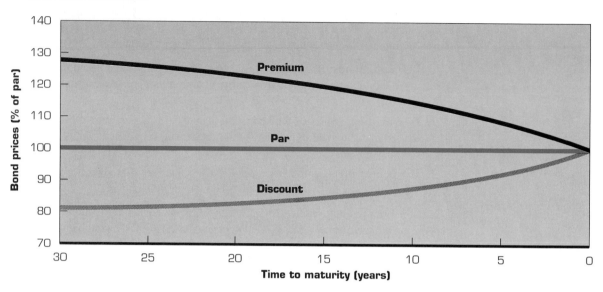

Figure 10.1　　Premium, Par, and Discount Bond Prices

Example 10.3 Premium Bonds

Consider two bonds, both with a 9 percent coupon rate and the same yield to maturity of 7 percent, but with different maturities of 5 and 10 years. Which has the higher price? Verify your answer by calculating the prices.

First, since both bonds have a 9 percent coupon and a 7 percent yield, both bonds sell at a premium. Based on what we know, the one with the longer maturity will have a higher price. We can check these conclusions by calculating the prices as follows:

5-year maturity premium bond price:

$$\frac{\$90}{.07}\left[1 - \frac{1}{(1.035)^{10}}\right] + \frac{\$1,000}{(1.035)^{10}} = \$1,083.17$$

10-year maturity premium bond price:

$$\frac{\$90}{.07}\left[1 - \frac{1}{(1.035)^{20}}\right] + \frac{\$1,000}{(1.035)^{20}} = \$1,142.12$$

Notice that the longer maturity premium bond has a higher price, as we predicted.

Example 10.4 Discount Bonds

Now consider two bonds, both with a 9 percent coupon rate and the same yield to maturity of 11 percent, but with different maturities of 5 and 10 years. Which has the higher price? Verify your answer by calculating prices.

These are both discount bonds. (Why?) The one with the shorter maturity will have a higher price. To check, the prices can be calculated as follows:

5-year maturity discount bond price:

$$\frac{\$90}{.11}\left[1 - \frac{1}{(1.055)^{10}}\right] + \frac{\$1,000}{(1.055)^{10}} = \$924.62$$

10-year maturity discount bond price:

$$\frac{\$90}{.11}\left[1 - \frac{1}{(1.055)^{20}}\right] + \frac{\$1,000}{(1.055)^{20}} = \$880.50$$

In this case, the shorter maturity discount bond has the higher price.

Relationships among Yield Measures

We have discussed three different bond rates or yields in this chapter—the coupon rate, the current rate, and the yield to maturity. We've seen the relationship between coupon rates and yields for discount and premium bonds. We can extend this to include current yields by simply noting that the current yield is always between the coupon rate and the yield to maturity (unless the bond is selling at par, in which case all three are equal).

Putting together our observations about yield measures, we have the following:

Premium bonds: **Coupon rate > Current yield > Yield to maturity**

Discount bonds: **Coupon rate < Current yield < Yield to maturity**

Par value bonds: **Coupon rate = Current yield = Yield to maturity**

Thus, when a premium bond and a discount bond both have the same yield to maturity, the premium bond has a higher current yield than the discount bond. However, as shown in Figure 10.1, the advantage of a high current yield for a premium bond is offset by the fact that the price of a premium bond must ultimately fall to its face value when the bond matures. Similarly, the disadvantage of a low current yield for a discount bond is offset by the fact that the price of a discount bond must ultimately rise to its face value at maturity. For these reasons, current yield is not a reliable guide to what an actual yield will be.

CHECK THIS

10.2a A straight bond's price has two components. What are they?

10.2b What do you call a bond that sells for more than its face value?

10.2c What is the relationship between a bond's price and its term to maturity when the bond's coupon rate is equal to its yield to maturity?

10.2d Does current yield more strongly overstate yield to maturity for long-maturity or short-maturity premium bonds?

10.3 More on Yields

In the previous section, we focused on finding a straight bond's price given its yield. In this section, we reverse direction to find a bond's yield given its price. We then discuss the relationship among the various yield measures we have seen. We finish the section with some additional yield calculations.

Calculating Yields

To calculate a bond's yield given its price, we use the same straight bond formula used above. The only way to find the yield is by trial and error. Financial calculators and spreadsheets do it this way at very high speed.

To illustrate, suppose we have a 6 percent bond with 10 years to maturity. Its price is 90, meaning 90 percent of face value. Assuming a $1,000 face value, the price is $900 and the coupon is $60 per year. What's the yield?

To find out, all we can do is try different yields until we come across the one that produces a price of $900. However, we can speed things up quite a bit by making an educated guess using what we know about bond prices and yields. We know the yield on this bond is greater than its 6 percent coupon rate because it is a discount bond. So let's first try 8 percent in the straight bond pricing formula:

$$\frac{\$60}{.08}\left[1 - \frac{1}{(1.04)^{20}}\right] + \frac{\$1,000}{(1.04)^{20}} = \$864.10$$

The price with an 8 percent yield is $864.10, which is somewhat less than the $900 price, but not too far off.

To finish, we need to ask whether the 8 percent we used was too high or too low. We know that the higher the yield, the lower is the price, thus 8 percent is a little too high. So let's try 7.5 percent:

$$\frac{\$60}{.075}\left[1 - \frac{1}{(1.0375)^{20}}\right] + \frac{\$1,000}{(1.0375)^{20}} = \$895.78$$

Now we're very close. We're still a little too high on the yield (since the price is a little low). If you try 7.4 percent, you'll see that the resulting price is $902.29, so the yield is between 7.4 and 7.5 percent (it's actually 7.435 percent). Of course, these calculations are done much faster using a calculator like the Treasury Notes and Bonds software calculator included with this textbook.

Example 10.5 Calculating YTM

Suppose a bond has eight years to maturity, a price of 110, and a coupon rate of 8 percent. What is its yield?

This is a premium bond, so its yield is less than the 8 percent coupon. If we try 6 percent, we get (check this) $1,125.61. The yield is therefore a little bigger than 6 percent. If we try 6.5 percent, we get (check this) $1,092.43, so the answer is slightly less than 6.5 percent. Check that 6.4 percent is almost exact (the exact yield is 6.3843 percent).

Yield to Call

callable bond A bond is callable if the issuer can buy it back before it matures.

call price The price the issuer of a callable bond must pay to buy it back.

call protection period The period during which a callable bond cannot be called. Also called a *call deferment period.*

The discussion in this chapter so far has assumed that a bond will have an actual maturity equal to its originally stated maturity. However, this is not always so since most bonds are **callable bonds**. When a bond issue is callable, the issuer can buy back outstanding bonds before the bonds mature. In exchange, bondholders receive a special **call price**, which is often equal to face value, although it may be slightly higher. When a call price is equal to face value, the bond is said to be *callable at par.*

Bonds are called at the convenience of the issuer, and a call usually occurs after a fall in market interest rates allows issuers to refinance outstanding debt with new bonds paying lower coupons. However, an issuer's call privilege is often restricted so that outstanding bonds cannot be called until the end of a specified **call protection period**, also termed a *call deferment period.* As a typical example, a bond issued with a 20-year maturity may be sold to investors subject to the restriction that it is callable anytime after an initial five-year call protection period.

yield to call (YTC)
Measure of return that assumes a bond will be redeemed at the earliest call date.

If a bond is callable, its yield to maturity may no longer be a useful number. Instead, the **yield to call**, commonly abbreviated **YTC**, may be more meaningful. Yield to call is a yield measure that assumes a bond issue will be called at its earliest possible call date.

We calculate a bond's yield to call using the straight bond pricing formula we have been using with two changes. First, instead of time to maturity, we use time to the first possible call date. Second, instead of face value, we use the call price. The resulting formula is thus

$$\text{Callable bond price} = \frac{C}{YTC}\left[1 - \frac{1}{(1 + YTC/2)^{2T}}\right] + \frac{CP}{(1 + YTC/2)^{2T}} \qquad \textbf{10.4}$$

where
C = Constant annual coupon
CP = Call price of the bond
T = Time in years until earliest possible call date
YTC = Yield to call assuming semiannual coupons

Calculating a yield to call requires the same trial-and-error procedure as calculating a yield to maturity. Most financial calculators will either handle the calculation directly or can be tricked into it by just changing the face value to the call price and the time to maturity to time to call.

To give a trial-and-error example, suppose a 20-year bond has a coupon of 8 percent, a price of 98, and is callable in 10 years. The call price is 105. What are its yield to maturity and yield to call?

Based on our earlier discussion, we know the yield to maturity is slightly bigger than the coupon rate. (Why?) After some calculation, we find it to be 8.2 percent.

To find the bond's yield to call, we pretend it has a face value of 105 instead of 100 ($1,050 versus $1,000) and will mature in 10 years. With these two changes, the procedure is exactly the same. We can try 8.5 percent, for example:

$$\frac{\$80}{.085}\left[1 - \frac{1}{(1.0425)^{20}}\right] + \frac{\$1,050}{(1.0425)^{20}} = \$988.51$$

Since this $988.51 is a little too high, the yield to call is slightly bigger than 8.5 percent. If we try 8.6, we find that the price is $981.83, so the yield to call is about 8.6 percent (it's 8.6276 percent). Again, the calculations are faster using a calculator like the Treasury Notes and Bonds software calculator included with this textbook.

A natural question comes up in this context. Which is bigger, the yield to maturity or the yield to call? The answer depends on the call price. However, if the bond is callable at par (as many are), then, for a premium bond, the yield to maturity is greater. For a discount bond, the reverse is true.

Example 10.6 Yield to Call

An 8.5 percent, 30-year bond is callable at par in 10 years. If the price is 105, which is bigger, the yield to call or maturity?

Since this is a premium bond callable at par, the yield to maturity is bigger. We can verify this by calculating both yields. Check that the yield to maturity is 8.06 percent, whereas the yield to call is 7.77 percent.

Interest Rate Risk and Malkiel's Theorems

interest rate risk The possibility that changes in interest rates will result in losses in a bond's value.

Bond yields are essentially interest rates, and, like interest rates, they fluctuate through time. When interest rates change, bond prices change. This is called **interest rate risk**. The term "interest rate risk" refers to the possibility of losses on a bond from changes in interest rates.

Promised Yield and Realized Yield

The terms *yield to maturity* and *promised yield* both seem to imply that the yield originally stated when a bond is purchased is what you will actually earn if you hold the bond until it matures. Actually, this is not generally correct. The return or yield you actually earn on a bond is called the **realized yield**, and an originally stated yield to maturity is almost never exactly equal to the realized yield.

realized yield The yield actually earned or "realized" on a bond.

The reason a realized yield will almost always differ from a promised yield is that interest rates fluctuate, causing bond prices to rise or fall. One consequence is that if a bond is sold before maturity, its price may be higher or lower than originally anticipated, and, as a result, the actually realized yield will be different from the promised yield.

Another important reason why realized yields generally differ from promised yields relates to the bond's coupons. We will get to this in the next section. For now, you should know that, for the most part, a bond's realized yield will equal its promised yield only if its yield doesn't change at all over the life of the bond, an unlikely event.

Interest Rate Risk and Maturity

While changing interest rates systematically affect all bond prices, it is important to realize that the impact of changing interest rates is not the same for all bonds. Some bonds are more sensitive to interest rate changes than others. To illustrate, Figure 10.2 shows how two bonds with different maturities can have different price sensitivities to changes in bond yields.

In Figure 10.2, bond prices are measured on the vertical axis and bond yields are measured on the horizontal axis. Both bonds have the same 8 percent coupon rate, but one bond has a 5-year maturity while the other bond has a 20-year maturity. Both bonds display the inverse relationship between bond prices and bond yields. Since both bonds have the same 8 percent coupon rate, and both sell for par, their yields are 8 percent.

However, when bond yields are greater than 8 percent, the 20-year maturity bond has a lower price than the 5-year maturity bond. In contrast, when bond yields are less than 8 percent, the 20-year maturity bond has a higher price than the 5-year maturity bond.

Figure 10.2 Bond Prices and Yields

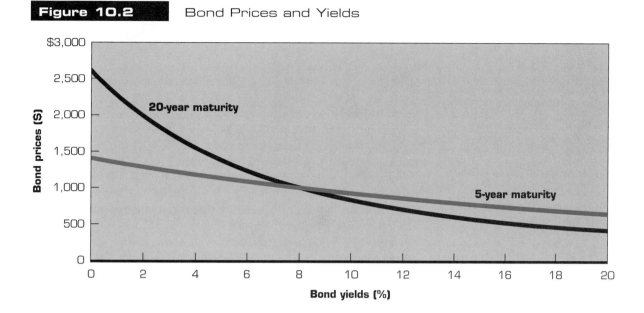

Essentially, falling yields cause both bond prices to rise, but the longer maturity bond experiences a larger price increase than the shorter maturity bond. Similarly, rising yields cause both bond prices to fall, but the price of the longer maturity bond falls by more than the price of the shorter maturity bond.

Malkiel's Theorems

The effect illustrated in Figure 10.2, along with some other important relationships among bond prices, maturities, coupon rates, and yields, is succinctly described by Burton Malkiel's five bond price theorems.[1] These five theorems are:

1. Bond prices and bond yields move in opposite directions. As a bond's yield increases, its price decreases. Conversely, as a bond's yield decreases, its price increases.

2. For a given change in a bond's yield to maturity, the longer the term to maturity of the bond, the greater will be the magnitude of the change in the bond's price.

3. For a given change in a bond's yield to maturity, the size of the change in the bond's price increases at a diminishing rate as the bond's term to maturity lengthens.

4. For a given change in a bond's yield to maturity, the absolute magnitude of the resulting change in the bond's price is inversely related to the bond's coupon rate.

5. For a given absolute change in a bond's yield to maturity, the magnitude of the price increase caused by a decrease in yield is greater than the price decrease caused by an increase in yield.

---

[1] Burton C. Malkiel, "Expectations, Bond Prices, and the Term Structure of Interest Rates," *Quarterly Journal of Economics,* May 1962, pp. 197–218.

The first, second, and fourth of these theorems are the simplest and most important. The first one says that bond prices and yields move in opposite directions. The second one says that longer term bonds are more sensitive to changes in yields than shorter term bonds. The fourth one says that lower coupon bonds are more sensitive to changes in yields than higher coupon bonds.

The third theorem says that a bond's sensitivity to interest rate changes increases as its maturity grows, but at a diminishing rate. In other words, a 10-year bond is much more sensitive to changes in yield than a 1-year bond. However, a 30-year bond is only slightly more sensitive than a 20-year bond. Finally, the fifth theorem says essentially that the loss you would suffer from, say, a 1 percent increase in yields is less than the gain you would enjoy from a 1 percent decrease in yields.

Table 10.1 illustrates the first three of these theorems by providing prices for 8 percent coupon bonds with maturities of 5, 10, and 20 years and yields to maturity of 7 percent and 9 percent. Be sure to check these for practice. As the first theorem says, bond prices are lower when yields are higher (9 percent versus 7 percent). As the second theorem indicates, the differences in bond prices between yields of 7 percent and 9 percent are greater for bonds with a longer term to maturity. However, as the third theorem states, the effect increases at a diminishing rate as the maturity lengthens. To see this, notice that $136.10 is 67.7 percent larger than $81.14, while $198.79 is only 46.1 percent larger than $136.10.

To illustrate the last two theorems, we present prices for 20-year maturity bonds with coupon rates and yields to maturity of 6 percent, 8 percent, and 10 percent (again, calculate these for practice) in Table 10.2. To illustrate the fourth theorem, compare the loss on the 6 percent and the 8 percent bonds as yields move from 8 percent to 10 percent. The 6 percent bond loses ($656.82 − $802.07) / $802.07 = −18.1%. The 8 percent bond loses ($828.41 − $1,000)/$1,000 = −17.2%, showing that the bond with the lower coupon is more sensitive to a change in yields. You can (and should) verify that the same is true for a yield increase.

Finally, to illustrate the fifth theorem, take a look at the 8 percent coupon bond in Table 10.2. As yields decrease by 2 percent from 8 percent to 6 percent, its price climbs by $231.15. As yields rise by 2 percent, the bond's price falls by $171.59.

As we have discussed, bond maturity is an important factor determining the sensitivity of a bond's price to changes in interest rates. However, bond maturity is an incomplete measure of bond price sensitivity to yield changes. For example, we have seen that

Table 10.1 — **Bond Prices and Yields**

		Time to Maturity		
Yields		5 Years	10 Years	20 Years
7%		$1,041.58	$1,071.06	$1,106.78
9%		960.44	934.96	907.99
Price difference	$	81.14	$ 136.10	$ 198.79

Table 10.2 — **Twenty-Year Bond Prices and Yields**

	Coupon Rates		
Yields	6 Percent	8 Percent	10 Percent
6%	$1,000.00	$1,231.15	$1,462.30
8%	802.07	1,000.00	1,197.93
10%	656.82	828.41	1,000.00

a bond's coupon rate is also important. An improved measure of interest rate risk for bonds that accounts both for differences in maturity and differences in coupon rates is our next subject.

CHECK THIS

10.4a True or false: A bond price's sensitivity to interest rate changes increases at an increasing rate as maturity lengthens.

10.4b Which is more sensitive to an interest rate shift: a low-coupon bond or a high-coupon bond?

10.5 Duration

duration A widely used measure of a bond's sensitivity to changes in bond yields.

To account for differences in interest rate risk across bonds with different coupon rates and maturities, the concept of **duration** is widely applied. As we will explore in some detail, duration measures a bond's sensitivity to interest rate changes. The idea behind duration was first presented by Frederick Macaulay in an early study of U.S. financial markets.[2] Today, duration is a very widely used measure of a bond's price sensitivity to changes in bond yields.

Macaulay Duration

There are several duration measures. The original version is called *Macaulay duration*. The usefulness of Macaulay duration stems from the fact that it satisfies the following approximate relationship between percentage changes in bond prices and changes in bond yields:

$$\text{Percentage change in bond price} \approx \text{Duration} \times \frac{\text{Change in } YTM}{(1 + YTM/2)} \qquad \textbf{10.5}$$

As a consequence, two bonds with the same duration, but not necessarily the same maturity, have approximately the same price sensitivity to a change in bond yields. This approximation is quite accurate for relatively small changes in yields, but it becomes less accurate when large changes are considered.

To see how we use this result, suppose a bond has a Macaulay duration of six years, and its yield decreases from 10 percent to 9.5 percent. The resulting percentage change in the price of the bond is calculated as follows:

$$6 \times \frac{.10 - .095}{1.05} \approx 2.86\%$$

Thus, the bond's price rises by 2.86 percent in response to a yield decrease of 50 basis points.

---

[2] Frederick Macaulay, *Some Theoretical Problems Suggested by the Movements of Interest Rates, Bond Yields, and Stock Prices in the United States since 1856* (New York: National Bureau of Economic Research, 1938).

Example 10.7 Macaulay Duration

A bond has a Macaulay duration of 11 years, and its yield increases from 8 percent to 8.5 percent. What will happen to the price of the bond?

The resulting percentage change in the price of the bond can be calculated as follows:

$$11 \times \frac{.08 - .085}{1.04} \approx -5.29\%$$

The bond's price declines by approximately 5.29 percent in response to a 50 basis point increase in yields.

Modified Duration

Some analysts prefer to use a variation of Macaulay's duration called *modified duration*. The relationship between Macaulay duration and modified duration for bonds paying semiannual coupons is simply

$$\text{Modified duration} = \frac{\text{Macaulay duration}}{(1 + YTM/2)} \qquad \textbf{10.6}$$

As a result, based on modified duration, the approximate relationship between percentage changes in bond prices and changes in bond yields is just

$$\text{Percentage change in bond price} = \text{Modified duration} \times \text{Change in } YTM \qquad \textbf{10.7}$$

In other words, to calculate the percentage change in the bond's price, we just multiply the modified duration by the change in yields.

Example 10.8 Modified Duration

A bond has a Macaulay duration of 8.5 years and a yield to maturity of 9 percent. What is its modified duration?

The bond's modified duration is calculated as follows:

$$\frac{8.5}{1.045} = 8.134$$

Notice that we divided the yield by 2 to get the semiannual yield.

Example 10.9 Modified Duration

A bond has a modified duration of seven years. Suppose its yield increases from 8 percent to 8.5 percent. What happens to its price?

We can very easily determine the resulting percentage change in the price of the bond using its modified duration:

$$7 \times (.08 - .085) \approx -3.5\%$$

The bond's price declines by about 3.5 percent.

Calculating Macaulay's Duration

Macaulay's duration is often described as a bond's *effective maturity*. For this reason, duration values are conventionally stated in years. The first fundamental principle for calculating the duration of a bond concerns the duration of a zero coupon bond. Specifically, the duration of a zero coupon bond is equal to its maturity. Thus, on a pure discount instrument, such as the U.S. Treasury STRIPS we discussed in Chapter 9, no calculation is necessary to come up with Macaulay duration.

The second fundamental principle for calculating duration concerns the duration of a coupon bond with multiple cash flows. The duration of a coupon bond is a weighted average of individual maturities of all the bond's separate cash flows. The weights attached to the maturity of each cash flow are proportionate to the present values of each cash flow.

A sample duration calculation for a bond with three years until maturity is illustrated in Table 10.3 The bond sells at par value. It has an 8 percent coupon rate and an 8 percent yield to maturity.

As shown in Table 10.3, calculating a bond's duration can be laborious—especially if the bond has a large number of separate cash flows. Fortunately, relatively simple formulas are available for many of the important cases. For example, if a bond is selling for par value, its duration can be calculated easily using the following formula:

$$\text{Par value bond duration} = \frac{(1 + YTM/2)}{YTM}\left[1 - \frac{1}{(1 + YTM/2)^{2M}}\right] \qquad \textbf{10.8}$$

where

M = Bond maturity in years
YTM = Yield to maturity assuming semiannual coupons

Table 10.3

Calculating Bond Duration

Years	Cash Flow	Discount Factor	Present Value	Years × Present Value ÷ Bond Price
0.5	$ 40	.96154	$ 38.4615	.0192 years
1	40	.92456	36.9822	.0370
1.5	40	.88900	35.5599	.0533
2	40	.85480	34.1922	.0684
2.5	40	.82193	32.8771	.0822
3	1040	.79031	821.9271	2.4658
			$1,000.00	2.7259 years
			Bond price	Bond duration

Example 10.10 Duration for a Par Value Bond

Suppose a par value bond has a 6 percent coupon and 10 years to maturity. What is its duration?

Since the bond sells for par, its yield is equal to its coupon rate, 6 percent. Plugging this into the par value bond duration formula, we have

$$\text{Par value bond duration} = \frac{(1 + .06/2)}{.06}\left[1 - \frac{1}{(1 + .06/2)^{20}}\right]$$

After a little work on a calculator, we find that the duration is 7.66 years.

The par value bond duration formula (Equation 10.8) is useful for calculating the duration of a bond that is actually selling at par value. Unfortunately, the general formula for bonds not necessarily selling at par value is somewhat more complicated. The general duration formula for a bond paying constant semiannual coupons is

$$\text{Duration} = \frac{1 + YTM/2}{YTM} - \frac{(1 + YTM/2) + M(C - YTM)}{YTM + C[(1 + YTM/2)^{2M} - 1]} \qquad \textbf{10.9}$$

where

C = Constant annual coupon rate
M = Bond maturity in years
YTM = Yield to maturity assuming semiannual coupons

Although somewhat tedious for manual calculations, this formula is used in many computer programs that calculate bond durations. For example, the Treasury Notes and Bonds calculator program included with this book uses this duration formula. Some popular personal computer spreadsheet packages also have a built-in function to perform this calculation.

Example 10.11 Duration for a Discount Bond

A bond has a yield to maturity of 7 percent. It matures in 12 years. Its coupon rate is 6 percent. What is its modified duration?

We first must calculate the Macaulay duration using the unpleasant-looking formula just above. We finish by converting the Macaulay duration to modified duration. Plugging into the duration formula, we have

$$\text{Duration} = \frac{1 + .07/2}{.07} - \frac{(1 + .07/2) + 12(.06 - .07)}{.07 + .06[(1 + .07/2)^{24} - 1]}$$

$$= \frac{1.035}{.07} - \frac{1.035 + 12(-.01)}{.07 + .06(1.035^{24} - 1)}$$

After a little button pushing, we find that the duration is 8.56 years. Finally, converting to modified duration, we find that the modified duration is equal to 8.56/1.035 = 8.27 years.

Properties of Duration

Macaulay duration has a number of important properties. For straight bonds, the basic properties of Macaulay duration can be summarized as follows:

1. All else the same, the longer a bond's maturity, the longer is its duration.
2. All else the same, a bond's duration increases at a decreasing rate as maturity lengthens.
3. All else the same, the higher a bond's coupon, the shorter is its duration.
4. All else the same, a higher yield to maturity implies a shorter duration, and a lower yield to maturity implies a longer duration.

As we saw earlier, a zero coupon bond has a duration equal to its maturity. The duration on a bond with coupons is always less than its maturity. Because of the second principle, durations much longer than 10 or 15 years are rarely seen. There is an exception to some of these principles that involves very long maturity bonds selling at a very steep discount. This exception rarely occurs in practice, so these principles are generally correct.

A graphical illustration of the relationship between duration and maturity is presented in Figure 10.3, where duration is measured on the vertical axis and maturity is measured on the horizontal axis. In Figure 10.3, the yield to maturity for all bonds is 10 percent. Bonds with coupon rates of 0 percent, 5 percent, 10 percent, and 15 percent are presented. As the figure shows, the duration of a zero coupon bond rises step for step with maturity. For the coupon bonds, however, the duration initially moves closely with maturity, as our first duration principle suggests, but, consistent with the second principle, the lines begin to flatten out after four or five years. Also, consistent with our third principle, the lower coupon bonds have higher durations.

Figure 10.3   Bond Duration and Maturity

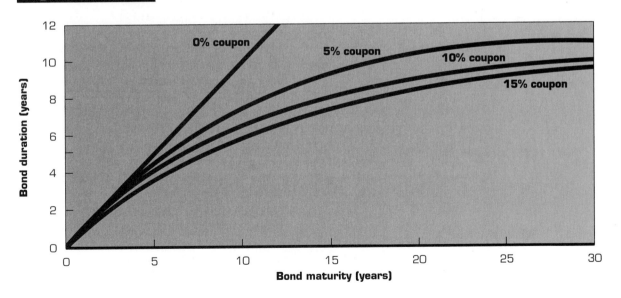

CHECK

THIS

10.5a What does duration measure?

10.5b What is the duration of a zero coupon bond?

10.5c What happens to a bond's duration as its maturity grows?

10.6 Dedicated Portfolios and Reinvestment Risk

Duration has another property that makes it a vital tool in bond portfolio management. To explore this subject, we first need to introduce two important concepts, dedicated portfolios and reinvestment risk.

Dedicated Portfolios

dedicated portfolio A bond portfolio created to prepare for a future cash outlay.

Bond portfolios are often created for the purpose of preparing for a future liability payment or other cash outlay. A portfolio formed for such a specific purpose is called a **dedicated portfolio**. When the future liability payment of a dedicated portfolio is due on a known date, that date is commonly called the portfolio's *target date*.

Pension funds provide a good example of dedicated portfolio management. A pension fund normally knows years in advance the amount of benefit payments it must make to its beneficiaries. The fund then purchases bonds in the amount needed to prepare for these payments.

To illustrate, suppose the Safety First pension fund estimates that it must pay benefits of about $100 million in five years. Using semiannual discounting, and assuming that bonds currently yield 8 percent, the present value of Safety First's future liability is calculated as follows:

$$\frac{\$100,000,000}{(1.04)^{10}} \approx \$67,556,417$$

This amount, about $67.5 million, represents the investment necessary for Safety First to construct a dedicated bond portfolio to fund a future liability of $100 million.

Next, suppose the Safety First pension fund creates a dedicated portfolio by investing exactly $67.5 million in bonds selling at par value with a coupon rate of 8 percent to prepare for the $100 million payout in 5 years. The Safety First fund decides to follow a maturity matching strategy whereby it invests only in bonds with maturities that match the portfolio's five-year target date.

Since Safety First is investing $67.5 million in bonds that pay an 8 percent annual coupon, the fund receives $5.4 million in coupons each year, along with $67.5 million of principal at the bonds' five-year maturity. As the coupons come in, Safety First reinvests them. If all coupons are reinvested at an 8 percent yield, the fund's portfolio will grow to about $99.916 million on its target date. This is the future value of $67.5 million compounded at 4 percent semiannually for five years:

$$\$67.5 \text{ million} \times (1.04)^{10} \approx \$100 \text{ million}$$

This amount is also equal to the future value of all coupons reinvested at 8 percent, plus the $67.5 million of bond principal received at maturity. To see this, we calculate the future value of the coupons (using the standard formula for the future value of an annuity) and then add the $67.5 million:

$$\frac{\$5.4 \text{ million}}{.08} [(1.04)^{10} - 1] + \$67.5 \text{ million} \approx \$100 \text{ million}$$

Thus, as long as the annual coupons are reinvested at 8 percent, Safety First's bond fund will grow to the amount needed.

Reinvestment Risk

As we have seen, the bond investment strategy of the Safety First pension fund will be successful if all coupons received during the life of the investment can be reinvested at a constant 8 percent yield. However, in reality, yields at which coupons can be reinvested are uncertain, and a target date surplus or shortfall is therefore likely to occur.

reinvestment rate risk The uncertainty about future or target date portfolio value that results from the need to reinvest bond coupons at yields not known in advance.

The uncertainty about future or target date portfolio value that results from the need to reinvest bond coupons at yields that cannot be predicted in advance is called **reinvestment rate risk**. Thus, the uncertain portfolio value on the target date represents reinvestment risk. In general, more distant target dates entail greater uncertainty and reinvestment risk.

To examine the impact of reinvestment risk, we continue with the example of the Safety First pension fund's dedicated bond portfolio. We will consider two cases, one in which all bond coupons are reinvested at a higher 9 percent yield, and one in which all coupons are reinvested at a lower 7 percent yield. In this case, the payment of the fixed $67.5 million principal plus the future value of the 10 semiannual coupons compounded at an uncertain rate, either 9 percent or 7 percent, comprises the total five-year target date portfolio value.

For 9 percent and 7 percent yields, these target date portfolio values are calculated as follows:

$$\frac{\$5.4 \text{ million}}{.09} [(1.045)^{10} - 1] + \$67.5 \text{ million} = \$100.678 \text{ million}$$

and

$$\frac{\$5.4 \text{ million}}{.07} [(1.035)^{10} - 1] + \$67.5 \text{ million} = \$99.175 \text{ million}$$

As shown, a target date portfolio value of $100.678 million is realized through a 9 percent reinvestment rate, and a value of $99.175 million is realized by a 7 percent reinvestment rate. The difference between these two amounts, about $1.5 million, represents reinvestment risk.

As this example illustrates, a maturity matching strategy for a dedicated bond portfolio entails substantial reinvestment risk. Indeed, this example understates a pension fund's total reinvestment risk since it considers only a single target date. In reality, pension funds have a series of target dates, and a shortfall at one target date typically coincides with shortfalls at other target dates as well.

A simple solution for reinvestment risk is to purchase zero coupon bonds that pay a fixed principal at a maturity chosen to match a dedicated portfolio's target date. Since there are no coupons to reinvest, there is no reinvestment risk! However, a zero coupon bond strategy has its drawbacks. As a practical matter, U.S. Treasury STRIPS are the only zero coupon bonds issued in sufficient quantity to even begin to satisfy the dedicated portfolio needs of pension funds, insurance companies, and other institutional investors. However, U.S. Treasury securities have lower yields than even the highest quality corporate bonds. A yield difference of only .25 percent between Treasury securities and corporate bonds can make a substantial difference in the initial cost of a dedicated bond portfolio.

For example, suppose that Treasury STRIPS have a yield of 7.75 percent. Using semiannual compounding, the present value of these zero coupon bonds providing a principal payment of $100 million at a five-year maturity is calculated as follows:

$$\frac{\$100 \text{ million}}{(1.03875)^{10}} \approx \$68.374 \text{ million}$$

This cost of $68.374 million based on a 7.75 percent yield is significantly higher than the previously stated cost of $67.556 million based on an 8 percent yield. From the perspective of the Safety First pension fund, this represents a hefty premium to pay to eliminate reinvestment risk. Fortunately, as we discuss in the next section, other methods are available at lower cost.

CHECK THIS

10.6a What is a dedicated portfolio?

10.6b What is reinvestment rate risk?

10.7 Immunization

immunization
Constructing a portfolio to minimize the uncertainty surrounding its target date value.

Constructing a dedicated portfolio to minimize the uncertainty in its target date value is called **immunization**. In this section, we show how duration can be used to immunize a bond portfolio against reinvestment risk.

Price Risk versus Reinvestment Rate Risk

price risk The risk that bond prices will decrease which arises in dedicated portfolios when the target date value of a bond or bond portfolio is not known with certainty.

To understand how immunization is accomplished, suppose you own a bond with eight years to maturity. However, your target date is actually just six years from now. If interest rates rise, are you happy or unhappy?

Your initial reaction is probably "unhappy" because you know that as interest rates rise, bond values fall. However, things are not so simple. Clearly, if interest rates rise, then, in six years, your bond will be worth less than it would have been at a lower rate. This is called **price risk**. However, it is also true that you will be able to reinvest the coupons you receive at a higher interest rate. As a result, your reinvested coupons will be worth more. In fact, the net effect of an interest rate increase might be to make you *better* off.

As our simple example illustrates, for a dedicated portfolio, interest rate changes have two effects. Interest rate increases act to decrease bond prices (price risk) but increase the future value of reinvested coupons (reinvestment rate risk). In the other direction, interest rate decreases act to increase bond values but decrease the future value of reinvested coupons. The key observation is that these two effects—price risk and reinvestment rate risk—tend to offset each other.

You might wonder if it is possible to engineer a portfolio in which these two effects offset each other more or less precisely. As we illustrate next, the answer is most definitely yes.

Immunization by Duration Matching

The key to immunizing a dedicated portfolio is to match its duration to its target date. If this is done, then the impacts of price and reinvestment rate risk will almost exactly offset, and interest rate changes will have a minimal impact on the target date value of the portfolio. In fact, immunization is often simply referred to as duration matching.

To see how a duration matching strategy can be applied to reduce target date uncertainty, suppose the Safety First pension fund initially purchases $67.5 million of par value bonds paying 8 percent coupons with a maturity of 6.2 years. From the par value duration formula we discussed earlier, a maturity of 6.2 years corresponds to a duration of 5 years. Thus, the duration of Safety First's dedicated bond portfolio is now matched to its five-year portfolio target date.

Suppose that immediately after the bonds are purchased, a one-time shock causes bond yields to either jump up to 10 percent or jump down to 6 percent. As a result, all coupons are reinvested at either a 10 percent yield or a 6 percent yield, depending on which way rates jump.

This example is illustrated in Figure 10.4, where the left vertical axis measures initial bond portfolio values, and the right vertical axis measures bond portfolio values realized by holding the portfolio until the bonds mature in 6.2 years. The horizontal axis measures the passage of time from initial investment to bond maturity. The positively sloped lines plot bond portfolio values through time for bond yields that have jumped to either 10 percent or 6 percent immediately after the initial investment of $67.5 million in par value 8 percent coupon bonds. This example assumes that after their initial jump, bond yields remain unchanged.

As shown in Figure 10.4, the initial jump in yields causes the value of Safety First's bond portfolio to jump in the opposite direction. If yields increase, bond prices fall but coupons are reinvested at a higher interest rate, thereby leading to a higher portfolio

Figure 10.4 Bond Price and Reinvestment Rate Risk

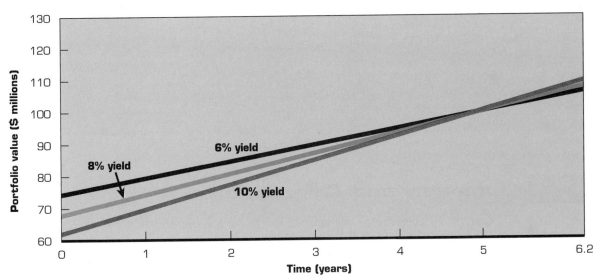

value at maturity. In contrast, if yields decrease, bond prices rise but a lower reinvestment rate reduces the value of the portfolio at maturity.

However, what is remarkable is that regardless of whether yields rise or fall, there is almost no difference in Safety First's portfolio value at the duration-matched five-year target date. Thus, the immunization strategy of matching the duration of Safety First's dedicated portfolio to its portfolio target date has almost entirely eliminated reinvestment risk.

Dynamic Immunization

The example of the Safety First pension fund immunizing a dedicated bond portfolio by a duration matching strategy assumed that the bond portfolio was subject to a single yield shock. In reality, bond yields change constantly. Therefore, successful immunization requires that a dedicated portfolio be rebalanced frequently to maintain a portfolio duration equal to the portfolio's target date.

For example, by purchasing bonds with a maturity of 6.2 years, the Safety First pension fund had matched the duration of the dedicated portfolio to the fund's 5-year target date. One year later, however, the target date is four years away, and bonds with a duration of four years are required to maintain a duration matching strategy. Assuming interest rates haven't changed, the par value duration formula shows that a maturity of 4.7 years corresponds to a duration of 4 years. Thus, to maintain a duration-matched target date, the Safety First fund must sell its originally purchased bonds now with a maturity of 5.2 years and replace them with bonds having a maturity of 4.7 years.

dynamic immunization

Periodic rebalancing of a dedicated bond portfolio to maintain a duration that matches the target maturity date.

The strategy of periodically rebalancing a dedicated bond portfolio to maintain a portfolio duration matched to a specific target date is called **dynamic immunization**. The advantage of dynamic immunization is that reinvestment risk caused by continually changing bond yields is greatly reduced. The drawback of dynamic immunization is that each portfolio rebalancing incurs management and transaction costs. Therefore, portfolios should not be rebalanced too frequently. In practice, rebalancing on an intermittent basis, say, each quarter, is a reasonable compromise between the costs of rebalancing and the benefits of dynamic immunization.

CHECK THIS

10.7a What are the two effects on the target date value of a dedicated portfolio of a shift in yields? Explain why they tend to offset.

10.7b How can a dedicated portfolio be immunized against shifts in yields?

10.7c Why is rebalancing necessary to maintain immunization?

10.8 Summary and Conclusions

This chapter covers the basics of bonds, bond yields, duration, and immunization. In this chapter we saw that:

1. Bonds are commonly distinguished according to whether they are selling at par value or at a discount or premium relative to par value. Bonds with a price greater than par value are said to be selling at a premium; bonds with a price less than par value are said to be selling at a discount.

2. There are three different yield measures: coupon yield or rate, current yield, and yield to maturity. Each is calculated using a specific equation, and which is the biggest or smallest depends on whether the bond is selling at a discount or premium.

3. Important relationships among bond prices, maturities, coupon rates, and yields are described by Malkiel's five bond price theorems.

4. A stated yield to maturity is almost never equal to an actually realized yield because yields are subject to bond price risk and coupon reinvestment rate risk. Bond price risk is the risk that a bond sold before maturity must be sold at a price different from the price predicted by an originally stated yield to maturity. Coupon reinvestment risk is the risk that bond coupons must be reinvested at yields different from an originally stated yield to maturity.

5. To account for differences in interest rate risk across bonds with different coupon rates and maturities, the concept of duration is widely applied. Duration is a direct measure of a bond's price sensitivity to changes in bond yields.

6. Bond portfolios are often created for the purpose of preparing for a future liability payment. Portfolios formed for such a specific purpose are called dedicated portfolios. When the future liability payment of a dedicated portfolio is due on a known date, that date is called the portfolio's target date.

7. Minimizing the uncertainty of the value of a dedicated portfolio's future target date value is called immunization. A strategy of matching a bond portfolio's duration to the target maturity date accomplishes this goal.

GET REAL

This chapter covered bond basics. How should you, as an investor or investment manager, put this information to work?

Now that you've been exposed to basic facts about bonds, their prices, and their yields, the next thing to do is to examine some real bonds and see how the various principles we have discussed work out in the real world. The easiest way to do this is to buy some bonds and then observe the behavior of their prices and yields as time goes by. The best place to start is Treasury bonds because they are, for the most part, fairly generic straight bonds.

With a simulated brokerage account (such as Stock-Trak), try putting equal (or approximately equal) dollar amounts into two Treasury bonds with the same maturity but different coupons. This position will let you see the impact of coupon rates on price volatility. Similarly, buy two bonds (in approximately equal dollar amounts) with very different maturities but the same (or nearly the same) coupon rates. You'll see firsthand how maturity plays a key role in the riskiness of bond investing.

While you're at it, calculate the durations of the bonds you buy. As their yields fluctuate, check that the percentage change in price is very close to what your calculated duration suggests it should be.

Key Terms

coupon rate 276
current yield 277
yield to maturity (YTM) 277
callable bond 282
call price 282
call protection period 282
yield to call (YTC) 283
interest rate risk 284

realized yield 284
duration 287
dedicated portfolio 292
reinvestment rate risk 293
immunization 294
price risk 294
dynamic immunization 296

Chapter Review Problems and Self-Test

1. **Straight Bond Prices**   Suppose a bond has 10 years to maturity and a coupon rate of 6 percent. The bond's yield to maturity is 8 percent. What's the price?

2. **Premium Bonds**   Suppose we have two bonds, both with a 6 percent coupon rate and the same yield to maturity of 4 percent, but with different maturities of 5 and 15 years. Which has the higher price? Verify your answer by calculating the prices.

3. **Macaulay Duration**   A bond has a Macaulay duration of nine years, and its yield increases from 6 percent to 6.25 percent. What will happen to the price of the bond?

Answers to Self-Test Problems

1. Here, the coupon rate is 6 percent and the face value is $1,000, so the annual coupon is $60. The bond's price is calculated as follows:

Present value of semiannual coupons:

$$\frac{\$60}{.08}\left[1 - \frac{1}{(1.04)^{20}}\right] = \$407.70979$$

Present value of $1,000 principal:

$$\frac{\$1,000}{(1.04)^{20}} = \$456.38695$$

The bond's price is the sum of coupon and principal present values:

$$\text{Bond price} = \$407.71 + \$456.39 = \$864.10$$

2. Because both bonds have a 6 percent coupon and a 4 percent yield, both bonds sell at a premium, and the one with the longer maturity will have a higher price. We can verify these conclusions by calculating the prices as follows:

5-year maturity premium bond price:

$$\frac{\$60}{.04}\left[1 - \frac{1}{(1.02)^{10}}\right] + \frac{\$1,000}{(1.02)^{10}} = \$1,089.83$$

15-year maturity premium bond price:

$$\frac{\$60}{.04}\left[1 - \frac{1}{(1.02)^{30}}\right] + \frac{\$1,000}{(1.02)^{30}} = \$1,223.96$$

Notice that the longer maturity premium bond has a higher price, just as we thought.

3. The resulting percentage change in the price of the bond can be calculated as follows:

$$9 \times \frac{.06 - .0625}{1.03} \approx -2.18\%$$

The bond's price declines by approximately 2.18 percent in response to a 25 basis point increase in yields.

Test Your Investment Quotient

1. **Yield to Maturity**   The yield to maturity on a bond is: (*1993 CFA exam*)

    a. Below the coupon rate when the bond sells at a discount and above the coupon rate when the bond sells at a premium.
    b. The interest rate that makes the present value of the payments equal to the bond price.
    c. Based on the assumption that all future payments received are reinvested at the coupon rate.
    d. Based on the assumption that all future payments received are reinvested at future market rates.

2. **Bond Yields**   In which one of the following cases is the bond selling at a discount? (*1989 CFA exam*)

    a. Coupon rate is greater than current yield, which is greater than yield to maturity.
    b. Coupon rate, current yield, and yield to maturity are all the same.
    c. Coupon rate is less than current yield, which is less than yield to maturity.
    d. Coupon rate is less than current yield, which is greater than yield to maturity.

3. **Bond Yields**   When are yield to maturity and current yield on a bond equal? (*1992 CFA exam*)

    a. When market interest rates begin to level off.
    b. If the bond sells at a price in excess of its par value.
    c. When the expected holding period is greater than one year.
    d. If the coupon and market interest rate are equal.

4. **Bond Prices**   Consider a five-year bond with a 10 percent coupon that is presently trading at a yield to maturity of 8 percent. If market interest rates do not change, one year from now the price of this bond: (*1991 CFA exam*)

    a. Will be higher.
    b. Will be lower.
    c. Will be the same.
    d. Cannot be determined.

5. **Bond Prices**   Using semiannual compounding, what would the price of a 15-year zero coupon bond that has a par value of $1,000 and a required return of 8 percent be? (*1991 CFA exam*)

    a. $308
    b. $315
    c. $464
    d. $555

6. **Duration**   Another term for bond duration is: (*1992 CFA exam*)

    a. Actual maturity
    b. Effective maturity
    c. Calculated maturity
    d. Near-term maturity

7. **Duration**   Which statement is true for the Macaulay duration of a zero coupon bond? (*1994 CFA exam*)

    a. It is equal to the bond's maturity in years.
    b. It is equal to one-half the bond's maturity in years.
    c. It is equal to the bond's maturity in years divided by its yield to maturity.
    d. It cannot be calculated because of the lack of coupons.

8. **Duration**   Which one of the following bonds has the shortest duration? (*1988 CFA exam*)

   a. Zero coupon, 10-year maturity.
   b. Zero coupon, 13-year maturity.
   c. 8 percent coupon, 10-year maturity.
   d. 8 percent coupon, 13-year maturity.

9. **Duration**   Identify the bond that has the longest duration (no calculations necessary). (*1990 CFA exam*)

   a. 20-year maturity with an 8 percent coupon.
   b. 20-year maturity with a 12 percent coupon.
   c. 15-year maturity with a 0 percent coupon.
   d. 10-year maturity with a 15 percent coupon.

10. **Duration**   Which bond has the longest duration? (*1992 CFA exam*)

    a. 8-year maturity, 6 percent coupon.
    b. 8-year maturity, 11 percent coupon.
    c. 15-year maturity, 6 percent coupon.
    d. 15-year maturity, 11 percent coupon.

11. **Duration**   The duration of a bond normally increases with an increase in: (*1991 CFA exam*)

    a. Term to maturity.
    b. Yield to maturity.
    c. Coupon rate.
    d. All of the above.

12. **Duration**   When interest rates decline, what happens to the duration of a 30-year bond selling at a premium? (*1992 CFA exam*)

    a. It increases.
    b. It decreases.
    c. It remains the same.
    d. It increases at first, then declines.

13. **Duration**   An 8 percent, 20-year corporate bond is priced to yield 9 percent. The Macaulay duration for this bond is 8.85 years. Given this information, how many years is the bond's modified duration? (*1992 CFA exam*)

    a. 8.12
    b. 8.47
    c. 8.51
    d. 9.25

14. **Using Duration**   A nine-year bond has a yield to maturity of 10 percent and a modified duration of 6.54 years. If the market yield changes by 50 basis points, what is the change in the bond's price? (*1992 CFA exam*)

    a. 3.27 percent
    b. 3.66 percent
    c. 6.54 percent
    d. 7.21 percent

15. **Using Duration**   A 6 percent coupon bond paying interest semiannually has a modified duration of 10 years, sells for $800, and is priced at a yield to maturity (YTM) of 8 percent. If the YTM increases to 9 percent, the predicted change in price, using the duration concept, decreases by which of the following amounts? (*1994 CFA exam*)

    a. $76.56
    b. $76.92
    c. $77.67
    d. $80.00

Questions and Problems

Core Questions

1. **Bond Prices** What are premium, discount, and par bonds?

2. **Bond Features** In the United States, what is the normal face value for a corporate and U.S. government bond? How are coupons calculated? How often are coupons paid?

3. **Coupon Rates and Current Yields** What are the coupon rate and current yield on a bond? What happens to these if a bond's price rises?

4. **Interest Rate Risk** What is interest rate risk? What are the roles of a bond's coupon and maturity in determining its level of interest rate risk?

5. **Bond Yields** For a premium bond, which is greater, the coupon rate or the yield to maturity? Why? For a discount bond? Why?

6. **Bond Yields** What is the difference between a bond's promised yield and its realized yield? Which is more relevant? When we calculate a bond's yield to maturity, which of these are we calculating?

7. **Interpreting Bond Yields** Is the yield to maturity (YTM) on a bond the same thing as the required return? Is YTM the same thing as the coupon rate? Suppose that today a 10 percent coupon bond sells at par. Two years from now, the required return on the same bond is 8 percent. What is the coupon rate on the bond now? The YTM?

8. **Interpreting Bond Yields** Suppose you buy a 9 percent coupon, 15-year bond today when it's first issued. If interest rates suddenly rise to 15 percent, what happens to the value of your bond? Why?

9. **Bond Prices** CIR Inc. has 7 percent coupon bonds on the market that have 11 years left to maturity. If the YTM on these bonds is 8.5 percent, what is the current bond price?

10. **Bond Yields** Trincor Company bonds have a coupon rate of 10.25 percent, 14 years to maturity, and a current price of $1,225. What is the YTM? The current yield?

Intermediate Questions

11. **Coupon Rates** Dunbar Corporation has bonds on the market with 10.5 years to maturity, a YTM of 10 percent, and a current price of $860. What must the coupon rate be on Dunbar's bonds?

12. **Bond Prices** Jane's Pizzeria issued 10-year bonds *one year ago* at a coupon rate of 8.75 percent. If the YTM on these bonds is 7.25 percent, what is the current bond price?

13. **Bond Yields** Jerry's Spaghetti Factory issued 12-year bonds *two years ago* at a coupon rate of 9.5 percent. If these bonds currently sell for 96 percent of par value, what is the YTM?

14. **Bond Prices versus Yields** (*a*) What is the relationship between the price of a bond and its YTM? (*b*) Explain why some bonds sell at a premium to par value, and other bonds sell at a discount. What do you know about the relationship between the coupon rate and the YTM for premium bonds? What about discount bonds? For bonds selling at par value? (*c*) What is the relationship between the current yield and YTM for premium bonds? For discount bonds? For bonds selling at par value?

15. **Yield to Call** For callable bonds, the financial press generally reports either the yield to maturity or the yield to call. Often yield to call is reported for premium bonds, and yield to maturity is reported for discount bonds. What is the reasoning behind this convention?

16. **Bond Price Movements** Bond X is a premium bond with a 9 percent coupon, a YTM of 7 percent, and 15 years to maturity. Bond Y is a discount bond with a 6 percent coupon, a YTM of 9 percent, and also 15 years to maturity. If interest rates remain unchanged, what do you expect the price of these bonds to be 1 year from now? In 5 years? In 10 years? In 14 years? In 15 years? What's going on here?

17. **Interest Rate Risk** Both bond A and bond B have 8 percent coupons and are priced at par value. Bond A has 2 years to maturity, while bond B has 15 years to maturity. If interest rates suddenly rise by 2 percent, what is the percentage change in price of bond A? Of bond B? If rates were to suddenly fall by 2 percent instead, what would the percentage change in price of bond A be now? Of bond B? Illustrate your answers by graphing bond prices versus YTM. What does this problem tell you about the interest rate risk of longer term bonds?

18. **Interest Rate Risk**   Bond J is a 4 percent coupon bond. Bond K is a 10 percent coupon bond. Both bonds have 10 years to maturity and have a YTM of 9 percent. If interest rates suddenly rise by 2 percent, what is the percentage price change of these bonds? What if rates suddenly fall by 2 percent instead? What does this problem tell you about the interest rate risk of lower coupon bonds?

19. **Finding the Bond Maturity**   ABC Co. has 10 percent coupon bonds with a YTM of 8.5 percent. The current yield on these bonds is 9.01 percent. How many years do these bonds have left until they mature?

20. **Finding the Maturity**   You've just found a 10 percent coupon bond on the market that sells for par value. What is the maturity on this bond?

21. **Realized Yields**   Suppose you buy a 10 percent coupon bond today for $1,100. The bond has 10 years to maturity. What rate of return do you expect to earn on your investment? Two years from now, the YTM on your bond has declined by 2.5 percent, and you decide to sell. What price will your bond sell for? What is the realized yield on your investment? Compare this yield to the YTM when you first bought the bond. Why are they different?

22. **Yield to Call**   XYZ Company has a 9 percent callable bond outstanding on the market with 12 years to maturity, call protection for the next 5 years, and a call premium of $100. What is the yield to call for this bond if the current price is 120 percent of par value?

23. **Calculating Duration**   What is the Macaulay duration of an 8 percent coupon bond with three years to maturity and a current price of $937.10? What is the modified duration?

24. **Using Duration**   In the previous problem, suppose the yield on the bond suddenly decreases by 2 percent. Use duration to estimate the new price of the bond. Compare your answer to the new bond price calculated from the usual bond pricing formula. What do your results tell you about the accuracy of duration?

 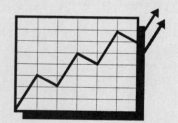

STOCK-TRAK·
Portfolio Simulations

Using Duration when Trading Interest Rates with Stock-Trak

Duration is an effective measure of interest rate risk and can be usefully applied to strategies for trading interest rates. In the preceding chapter, we recommended using U.S. Treasury STRIPS as a vehicle for trading interest rates with Stock-Trak. In this chapter, we pointed out that the duration of a STRIPS is equal to its maturity and therefore requires no special calculations. This implies this simple relationship between STRIPS price changes and STRIPS yield changes:

$$\text{Percentage change in STRIPS price} \approx - \text{STRIPS maturity} \times \frac{\text{Change in } YTM}{(1 + YTM/2)}$$

Suppose you are holding 20-year STRIPS with a yield of 6 percent and believe that the yield on these STRIPS could fall by 50 basis points over the next few weeks. If this occurs, it will cause 20-year STRIPS prices to rise by about 9.7 percent. But if instead the yield rose by 50 basis points, it would cause 20-year STRIPS prices to fall by about 9. 7 percent.

Stock-Trak Exercise

1. Buy a STRIPS security and record its price, maturity, and yield. After a week or two, calculate the percentage change in price and change in yield for your STRIPS. Plug in the original yield, change in yield, and maturity into the right-hand side of the above equation to compute the predicted percentage change in the STRIPS price. How closely does this predicted percentage change in the STRIPS price compare with the actual percentage change in the STRIPS price?

11 Corporate Bonds

A corporation issues bonds intending to meet all required payments of interest and repayment of principal. Investors buy bonds believing that the corporation intends to fulfill its debt obligation in a timely manner. Although defaults can and do occur, the market for corporate bonds exists only because corporations are able to convince investors of their original intent to avoid default. Reaching this state of trust is not a trivial process, and it normally requires elaborate contractual arrangements. ■ Almost all corporations issue notes and bonds to raise money to finance investment projects. Indeed, for many corporations, the value of notes and bonds outstanding can exceed the value of common stock shares outstanding. Nevertheless, most investors do not think of corporate bonds when they think about investing. This is because corporate bonds represent specialized investment instruments that are usually bought by financial institutions like insurance companies and pension funds. For professional money managers at these institutions, a knowledge of corporate bonds is absolutely essential. This chapter introduces you to the specialized knowledge that these money managers possess.

11.1 Corporate Bond Basics

Corporate bonds represent the debt of a corporation owed to its bondholders. More specifically, a corporate bond is a security issued by a corporation that represents a promise to pay to its bondholders a fixed sum of money at a future maturity date, along with periodic payments of interest. The fixed sum paid at maturity is the bond's *principal,* also called its par or face value. The periodic interest payments are called *coupons.*

From an investor's point of view, corporate bonds represent an investment distinct from common stock. The three most fundamental differences are these:

1. Common stock represents an ownership claim on the corporation, whereas bonds represent a creditor's claim on the corporation.

2. Promised cash flows—that is, coupons and principal—to be paid to bondholders are stated in advance when the bond is issued. By contrast, the amount and timing of dividends paid to common stockholders may change at any time.

3. Most corporate bonds are issued as callable bonds, which means that the bond issuer has the right to buy back outstanding bonds before the maturity date of the bond issue. When a bond issue is called, coupon payments stop and the bondholders are forced to surrender their bonds to the issuer in exchange for the cash payment of a specified call price. By contrast, common stock is almost never callable.

The corporate bond market is large, with several trillion dollars of corporate bonds outstanding in the United States. The sheer size of the corporate bond market prompts an important inquiry: Who owns corporate bonds and why? The answer is that most corporate bond investors belong to only a few distinct categories. The single largest group of corporate bond investors is life insurance companies, which hold about a third of all outstanding corporate bonds. Remaining ownership shares are roughly equally balanced among individual investors, pension funds, banks, and foreign investors.

The pattern of corporate bond ownership is largely explained by the fact that corporate bonds provide a source of predictable cash flows. While individual bonds occasionally default on their promised cash payments, large institutional investors can diversify away most default risk by including a large number of different bond issues in their portfolios. For this reason, life insurance companies and pension funds find that corporate bonds are a natural investment vehicle to provide for future payments of retirement and death benefits, since both the timing and amount of these benefit payments can be matched with bond cash flows. These institutions can eliminate much of their financial risk by matching the timing of cash flows received from a bond portfolio to the timing of cash flows needed to make benefit payments—a strategy called cash flow matching. For this reason, life insurance companies and pension funds together own more than half of all outstanding corporate bonds. For similar reasons, individual investors might own corporate bonds as a source of steady cash income. However, since individual investors cannot easily diversify default risk, they should normally invest only in bonds with higher credit quality.

Every corporate bond issue has a specific set of issue terms associated with it. The issue terms associated with any particular bond can range from a relatively simple arrangement, where the bond is little more than an IOU of the corporation, to a com-

plain vanilla bonds
Bonds issued with a relatively standard set of features.

plex contract specifying in great detail what the issuer can and cannot do with respect to its obligations to bondholders. Bonds issued with a standard, relatively simple set of features are popularly called **plain vanilla bonds**.

As an illustration of a plain vanilla corporate debt issue, Table 11.1 summarizes the issue terms for a note issue by Software Iz Us, the software company you took public in Chapter 5. Referring to Table 11.1, we see that the Software Iz Us notes were issued in December 1998 and mature five years later in December 2003. Each individual note has a face value denomination of $1,000. Since the total issue amount is $20 million, the entire issue contains 20,000 notes. Each note pays a $100 annual coupon, which is equal to 10 percent of its face value. The annual coupon is split between two semiannual $50 payments made each June and December. Based on the original offer price of 100, which means 100 percent of the $1,000 face value, the notes have a yield to maturity of 10 percent. The notes are not callable, which means that the debt may not be paid off before maturity.

unsecured debt
Bonds, notes, or other debt issued with no specific collateral pledged as security for the bond issue.

The Software Iz Us notes are **unsecured debt**, which means that no specific collateral has been pledged as security for the notes. In the event that the issuer defaults on its promised payments, the noteholders may take legal action to acquire sufficient assets of the company to settle their claims as creditors.

When issued, the Software Iz Us notes were not reviewed by a rating agency like Moody's or Standard & Poor's. Thus, the notes are unrated. If the notes were to be assigned a credit rating, they would probably be rated as "junk grade." The term "junk," commonly used for high-risk debt issues, is unduly pejorative. After all, your company must repay the debt. However, the high-risk character of the software industry portends an above-average probability that your company may have difficulty paying off the debt in a timely manner.

Reflecting their below-average credit quality, the Software Iz Us notes were not issued to the general public. Instead, the notes were privately placed with two insurance companies. Such private placements are common among relatively small debt issues. Private placements will be discussed in greater detail later in this chapter.

11.2 Types of Corporate Bonds

debentures
Unsecured bonds issued by a corporation.

Debentures are the most frequently issued type of corporate bond. Debenture bonds represent an unsecured debt of a corporation. Debenture bondholders have a legal claim as general creditors of the corporation. In the event of a default by the issuing corpora-

Table 11.1	Software Iz Us Five-Year Note Issue	
Issue amount	$20 million	Note issue total face value is $20 million
Issue date	12/15/98	Notes offered to the public in December 1998
Maturity date	12/31/03	Remaining principal due December 31, 2003
Face value	$1,000	Face value denomination is $1,000 per note
Coupon interest	$100 per annum	Annual coupons are $100 per note
Coupon dates	6/30, 12/31	Coupons are paid semiannually
Offering price	100	Offer price is 100 percent of face value
Yield to maturity	10%	Based on stated offer price
Call provision	Not callable	Notes may not be paid off before maturity
Security	None	Notes are unsecured
Rating	Not rated	Privately placed note issue

tion, the bondholders' claim extends to all corporate assets. However, they may have to share this claim with other creditors who have an equal legal claim or yield to creditors with a higher legal claim.

In addition to debentures, there are three other basic types of corporate bonds: mortgage bonds, collateral trust bonds, and equipment trust certificates. **Mortgage bonds** represent debt issued with a lien on specific property, usually real estate, pledged as security for the bonds. A mortgage lien gives bondholders the legal right to foreclose property pledged by the issuer to satisfy an unpaid debt obligation. However, in actual practice, foreclosure and sale of mortgaged property following a default may not be the most desirable strategy for bondholders. Instead, it is common for a corporation in financial distress to reorganize itself and negotiate a new debt contract with bondholders. In these negotiations, a mortgage lien can be an important bargaining tool for the trustee representing the bondholders.

Collateral trust bonds are characterized by a pledge of financial assets as security for the bond issue. Collateral trust bonds are commonly issued by holding companies, which may pledge the stocks, bonds, or other securities issued by their subsidiaries as collateral for their own bond issue. The legal arrangement for pledging collateral securities is similar to that for a mortgage lien. In the event of an issuer's default on contractual obligations to bondholders, the bondholders have a legal right to foreclose on collateralized securities in the amount necessary to settle an outstanding debt obligation.

Equipment trust certificates represent debt issued by a trustee to purchase heavy industrial equipment that is leased and used by railroads, airlines, and other companies with a demand for heavy equipment. Under this financial arrangement, investors purchase equipment trust certificates and the proceeds from this sale are used to purchase equipment. Formal ownership of the equipment remains with a trustee appointed to represent the certificate holders. The trustee then leases the equipment to a company. In return, the company promises to make a series of scheduled lease payments over a specified leasing period. The trustee collects the lease payments and distributes all revenues, less expenses, as dividends to the certificate holders. These distributions are conventionally called dividends because they are generated as income from a trust. The lease arrangement usually ends after a specified number of years when the leasing company makes a final lease payment and may take possession of the used equipment. From the certificate holders' point of view, this financial arrangement is superior to a mortgage lien since they actually own the equipment during the leasing period. Thus, if the leasing corporation defaults, the equipment can be sold without the effort and expense of a formal foreclosure process. Since the underlying equipment for this type of financing is typically built according to an industry standard, the equipment can usually be quickly sold or leased to another company in the same line of business.

Figure 11.1 is a *Wall Street Journal* bond announcement for an aircraft equipment trust for Northwest Airlines. Notice that the $243 million issue is split into two parts: $177 million of senior notes paying 8.26 percent interest and $66 million of subordinated notes paying 9.36 percent interest. The senior notes have a first claim on the aircraft in the event of a default by the airline, while the subordinated notes have a secondary claim. In the event of a default, investment losses for the trust will primarily be absorbed by the subordinated noteholders. For this reason the subordinated notes are riskier, and therefore pay a higher interest rate. Of course, if no default actually occurs, it would turn out that the subordinated notes were actually a better investment. However, there is no way of knowing this in advance.

---

mortgage bond Debt secured with a property lien.

collateral trust bond Debt secured with financial collateral.

equipment trust certificate Shares in a trust with income from a lease contract.

Figure 11.1 Equipment Trust Notes Issue

March 11, 1994

$243,000,000

NWA Trust No. 1

$177,000,000 8.26% Class A Senior Aircraft Notes
$66,000,000 9.36% Class B Subordinated Aircraft Notes

The 8.26% Class A Senior Aircraft Notes and the 9.36% Class B Subordinated Aircraft Notes are secured by, among other things, a security interest in certain aircraft sold by Northwest Airlines, Inc. ("Northwest") to an owner trust for a purchase price of $443 million and the lease relating to such Aircraft, including the right to receive amounts payable by Northwest under such lease. The Noteholders also have the benefit of a liquidity facility, initially provided by General Electric Capital Corporation, to support certain payments of interest on the Notes.

Lehman Brothers　　　　BT Securities Corporation

11.2a Given that a bond issue is one of the four basic types discussed in this section, how would the specific bond type affect the credit quality of the bond?

11.2b Why might some bond types be more or less risky with respect to the risk of default?

11.2c Given that a default has occurred, why might the trustee's job of representing the financial interests of the bondholders be easier for some bond types than for others?

11.3 Bond Indentures

A bond indenture is a formal written agreement between the corporation and the bondholders. It is an important legal document that spells out in detail the mutual rights and obligations of the corporation and the bondholders with respect to the bond issue. Indenture contracts are often quite long, sometimes several hundred pages, and make for very tedious reading. In fact, very few bond investors ever read the original indenture but instead might refer to an **indenture summary** provided in the **prospectus** that was circulated when the bond issue was originally sold to the public. Alternatively, a summary of the most important features of an indenture is published by debt rating agencies.

indenture summary
Description of the contractual terms of a new bond issue included in a bond's prospectus.

The Trust Indenture Act of 1939 requires that any bond issue subject to regulation by the Securities and Exchange Commission (SEC), which includes most corporate bond and note issues sold to the general public, must have a trustee appointed to represent the interests of the bondholders. Also, all responsibilities of a duly appointed trustee must be specified in detail in the indenture. Some corporations maintain a blanket or open-ended indenture that applies to all currently outstanding bonds and any new bonds that are issued, while other corporations write a new indenture contract for each new bond issue sold to the public.

prospectus
Document prepared as part of a security offering detailing information about a company's financial position, its operations, and investment plans.

Descriptions of the most important provisions frequently specified in a bond indenture agreement are presented next.

Bond Seniority Provisions

A corporation may have several different bond issues outstanding; these issues normally can be differentiated according to the seniority of their claims on the firm's assets. Seniority usually is specified in the indenture contract.

Consider a corporation with two outstanding bond issues: (1) a mortgage bond issue with certain real estate assets pledged as security and (2) a debenture bond issue with no specific assets pledged as security. In this case, the mortgage bond issue has a senior claim on the pledged assets but no specific claim on other corporate assets. The debenture bond has a claim on all corporate assets not specifically pledged as security for the mortgage bond, but it would have only a residual claim on assets pledged as security for the mortgage bond issue. This residual claim would apply only after all obligations to the mortgage bondholders have been satisfied.

senior debentures
Bonds that have a higher claim on the firm's assets than other bonds.

subordinated debentures Bonds that have a claim on the firm's assets after those with a higher claim have been satisfied.

negative pledge clause Bond indenture provision that prohibits new debt from being issued with seniority over an existing issue.

bond refunding
Process of calling an outstanding bond issue and refinancing it by a new bond issue.

As another example, suppose a corporation has two outstanding debenture issues. In this case, seniority is normally assigned to the bonds first issued by the corporation. The bonds issued earliest have a senior claim on the pledged assets and are called **senior debentures**. The bonds issued later have a junior or subordinate claim, and are called **subordinated debentures**.

The seniority of an existing debt issue is usually protected by a **negative pledge clause** in the bond indenture. A negative pledge clause prohibits a new issue of debt with seniority over a currently outstanding issue. However, it may allow a new debt issue to share equally in the seniority of an existing issue. A negative pledge clause is part of the indenture agreement of most senior debenture bonds.

Call Provisions

Most corporate bond issues have a call provision allowing the issuer to buy back all or part of its outstanding bonds at a specified call price sometime before the bonds mature. The most frequent motive for a corporation to call outstanding bonds is to take advantage of a general fall in market interest rates. Lower interest rates allow the corporation to replace currently outstanding high-coupon bonds with a new issue of bonds paying lower coupons. Replacing existing bonds with new bonds is called **bond refunding**.

From an investor's point of view, a call provision has a distinct disadvantage. For example, suppose an investor is currently holding bonds paying 10 percent coupons. Further suppose that, after a fall in market interest rates, the corporation is able to issue new bonds that only pay 8 percent coupons. By calling existing 10 percent coupon bonds, the issuer forces bondholders to surrender their bonds in exchange for the call price. But this happens at a time when the bondholders can reinvest funds only at lower interest rates. If instead the bonds were noncallable, the bondholders would continue to receive the original 10 percent coupons. For this reason, callable bonds are less attractive to investors than noncallable bonds. Consequently, a callable bond will sell at a lower price than a comparable noncallable bond.

Despite their lower prices, corporations generally prefer to issue callable bonds. However, to reduce the price gap between callable and noncallable bonds issuers typically allow the indenture contract to specify certain restrictions on their ability to call an outstanding bond issue. Three features are commonly used to restrict an issuer's call privilege:

1. Callable bonds usually have a *deferred call provision* which provides a *call protection period* during which a bond issue cannot be called. For example, a bond may be call-protected for a period of five years after its issue date.

2. A call price often includes a *call premium* over par value. A standard arrangement stipulates a call premium equal to one-year's coupon payments for a call occurring at the earliest possible call date. Over time, the call premium is gradually reduced until it is eliminated entirely. After some future date, the bonds become callable at par value.

3. Some indentures specifically prohibit an issuer from calling outstanding bonds for the purpose of refunding at a lower coupon rate but still allow a call for other reasons. This *refunding provision* prevents the corporation from calling an outstanding bond issue solely as a response to falling market interest rates. However, the corporation can still pay off its bond debt ahead of schedule by using funds acquired from, say, earnings, or funds obtained from the sale of newly issued common stock.

CHECK
THIS

11.3a After a call protection
period has elapsed, why
is the call price an

effective ceiling on the
market price of a
callable bond?

Graphical Analysis of Callable Bond Prices

After a bond's call protection period has elapsed, a rational investor would be unwilling to pay much more than the call price for the bond since the issuer might call the bond at any time and pay only the call price for the bond. Consequently, a bond's call price serves as an effective ceiling on its market price. It is important for bond investors to understand how the existence of a price ceiling for callable bonds alters the standard price-yield relationship for bonds.

The relationship between interest rates and prices for comparable callable and noncallable bonds is illustrated in Figure 11.2. In this example, the vertical axis measures bond prices and the horizontal axis measures bond yields. In this two-bond example, both bonds pay an 8 percent coupon and are alike in all respects except that one of the bonds is callable any time at par value.

As shown, the noncallable bond has the standard *convex price-yield relationship,* where the price-yield curve is bowed toward the origin. When the price-yield curve is bowed to the origin this is called *positive convexity.* In contrast, the callable bond has a convex or bowed price-yield relationship in the region of high yields, but is bowed away from the origin in the region of low yields. This is called *negative con-*

Figure 11.2   Callable and Noncallable Bonds

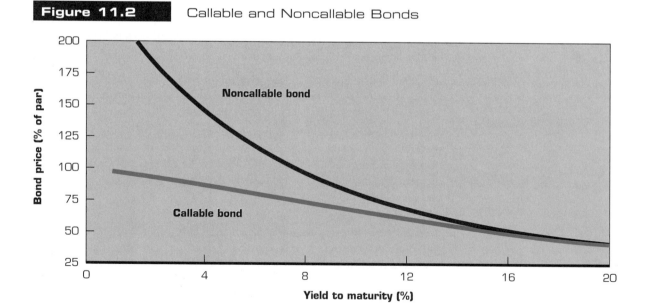

vexity. The important lesson here is that no matter how low market interest rates might fall, the maximum price of an unprotected callable bond is generally bounded above by its call price.

Put Provisions

put bonds A bond that can be sold back to the issuer at a prespecified price on any of a sequence of prespecified dates. Also called *extendible bonds.*

A bond issue with a put provision grants bondholders the right to sell their bonds back to the issuer at a special *put price,* normally set at par value. These so-called **put bonds** are "putable" on each of a series of designated *put dates.* These are often scheduled to occur annually but sometimes occur at more frequent intervals. At each put date, the bondholder decides whether to sell the bond back to the issuer or continue to hold the bond until the next put date. For this reason, put bonds are often called *extendible bonds* because the bondholder has the option of extending the maturity of the bond at each put date.

Notice that by granting bondholders an option to sell their bonds back to the corporation at par value the put feature provides an effective floor on the market price of the bond. Thus, the put feature offers protection to bondholders from rising interest rates and the associated fall in bond prices.

A put feature also helps protect bondholders from acts of the corporation that might cause a deterioration of the bond's credit quality. However, this protection is not granted without a cost to bond investors, since a putable bond will command a higher market price than a comparable nonputable bond.

CHECK THIS

11.3b Using Figure 11.2 as a guide, what would the price-yield relationship look like for a non-callable bond putable at par value?

11.3c Under what conditions would a put feature not yield an effective floor for the market price of a put bond? (Hint: Think about default risk.)

Bond-to-Stock Conversion Provisions

convertible bonds Bonds that holders can exchange for common stock according to a prespecified conversion ratio.

Some bonds have a valuable bond-to-stock conversion feature. These bonds are called convertible bonds. **Convertible bonds** grant bondholders the right to exchange each bond for a designated number of common stock shares of the issuing firm. To avoid confusion in a discussion of convertible bonds, it is important to understand some basic terminology.

1. The number of common stock shares acquired in exchange for each converted bond is called the *conversion ratio:*

   Conversion ratio = Number of stock shares acquired by conversion

2. The par value of a convertible bond divided by its conversion ratio is called the bond's *conversion price:*

$$\text{Conversion price} = \frac{\text{Bond par value}}{\text{Conversion ratio}}$$

3. The market price per share of common stock acquired by conversion times the bond's conversion ratio is called the bond's *conversion value:*

$$\text{Conversion value} = \text{Price per share of stock} \times \text{Conversion ratio}$$

For example, suppose a convertible bond with a par value of $1,000 can be converted into 20 shares of the issuing firm's common stock. In this case, the conversion price is $1,000 / 20 = $50. Continuing this example, suppose the firm's common stock has a market price of $40 per share, then the conversion value of a single bond is 20 × $40 = $800.

Figure 11.3 is *The Wall Street Journal* announcement of an issue of convertible subordinated notes by Advanced Micro Devices (AMD). The notes pay a 6 percent coupon rate and mature in 2005. The conversion price for this note issue is $37 per share, which implies a conversion ratio of 27.027 shares of common stock for each $1,000 face value note.

From an investor's perspective, the conversion privilege of convertible bonds has the distinct advantage that bondholders can receive a share of any increase in common stock value. However, the conversion option has a price. A corporation can sell convertible bonds at par value with a coupon rate substantially less than the coupon rate of comparable nonconvertible bonds. This forgone coupon interest represents the price of the bond's conversion option.

When convertible bonds are originally issued, their conversion ratio is customarily set to yield a conversion value 10 percent to 20 percent less than par value. For example, suppose the common stock of a company has a price of $30 per share and the company issues convertible bonds with a par value of $1,000 per bond. To set the original conversion value at $900 per bond, the company would set a conversion ratio of 30 stock shares per bond. Thereafter, the conversion ratio is fixed, but each bond's conversion value becomes linked to the firm's stock price, which may rise or fall in value. The price of a convertible bond reflects the conversion value of the bond. In general, the higher the conversion value the higher is the bond price, and vice versa.

Investing in convertible bonds is more complicated than owning nonconvertible bonds, because the conversion privilege presents convertible bondholders with an important timing decision. When is the best time to exercise a bond's conversion option and exchange the bond for shares of common stock? The answer is that investors should normally postpone conversion as long as possible, because while they hold the bonds they continue to receive coupon payments. After converting to common stock they lose all subsequent coupons. In general, unless the total dividend payments on stock acquired by conversion are somewhat greater than the forgone bond coupon payments, investors should hold on to their convertible bonds to continue to receive coupon payments.

The rational decision of convertible bondholders to postpone conversion as long as possible is limited, however, since convertible bonds are almost always callable. Firms customarily call outstanding convertible bonds when their conversion value has risen by 10 percent to 15 percent above bond par value, although there are many exceptions to this rule. When a convertible bond issue is called by the issuer, bondholders are forced to make an immediate decision whether to convert to common stock shares or accept a cash payment of the call price. Fortunately, the decision is simple—convertible bondholders should choose whichever is more valuable, the call price or the conversion value.

Figure 11.3 Convertible Notes Issue

This announcement is neither an offer to sell, nor a solicitation of an offer to buy, any of these securities.
The offer is made only by the Prospectus and related Prospectus Supplement.

June 24, 1998

$517,500,000

AMD⌐

Advanced Micro Devices, Inc.

6% Convertible Subordinated Notes due 2005

The 6% Convertible Subordinated Notes due 2005 (the "Notes") will be convertible at the option of the holder into shares of common stock, par value $.01 per share (the "Common Stock"), of Advanced Micro Devices, Inc. (the "Company") at any time at or prior to maturity, unless previously redeemed or repurchased, at a conversion price of $37.00 per share (equivalent to a conversion rate of 27.027 shares per $1,000 principal amount of Notes), subject to adjustment in certain events.

Price 100%

Copies of the Prospectus and related Prospectus Supplement may be obtained in any State from such of the undersigned as may legally offer these securities in compliance with the securities laws of such State.

Donaldson, Lufkin & Jenrette
Securities Corporation

Salomon Smith Barney

Source: Reprinted with permission from Dow Jones & Company, Inc., via Copyright Clearance Center, Inc., © 1998 Dow Jones & Company, Inc. All Rights Reserved Worldwide.

CHECK
THIS

11.3d Describe the conversion
decision that convertible
bondholders must make

when the bonds
mature.

Graphical Analysis of Convertible Bond Prices

The price of a convertible bond is closely linked to the value of the underlying common stock shares that can be acquired by conversion. A higher stock price implies a higher bond price, and conversely a lower stock price yields a lower bond price.

The relationship between the price of a convertible bond and the price of the firm's common stock is depicted in Figure 11.4. In this example, the convertible bond's price is measured on the vertical axis and the stock price is measured along the horizontal axis. The straight, upward-sloping line is the bond's conversion value; the slope of the line is the conversion ratio. The horizontal line represents the price of a comparable nonconvertible bond with the same coupon rate, maturity, and credit quality.

in-the-money bond A
convertible bond
whose conversion
value is greater than
its call price.

A convertible bond is said to be an **in-the-money bond** when its conversion value is greater than its call price. If an in-the-money convertible bond is called, rational bondholders will convert their bonds into common stock. When the conversion value is less than the call price, a convertible bond is said to be *out of the money*. If an out-of-the-money bond is called, rational bondholders will accept the call price and forgo the conversion option. In practice, however, convertible bonds are seldom called when they are out of the money.

Figure 11.4   Convertible Bond Prices

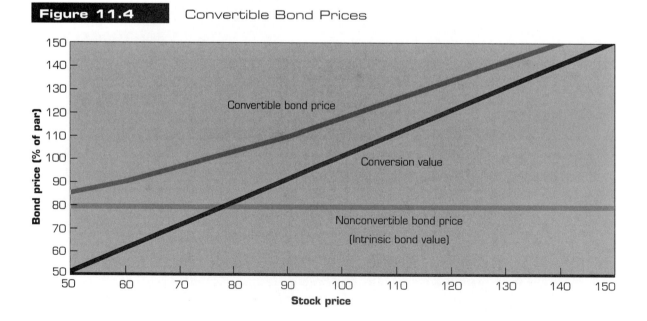

The curved line in Figure 11.4 shows the relationship between a convertible bond's price and the underlying stock price. As shown, there are two lower bounds on the value of a convertible bond. First, a convertible bond's price can never fall below its **intrinsic bond value,** also comonly called its *investment value* or *straight bond value*. This value is what the bond would be worth if it was not convertible, but otherwise identical in terms of coupon, maturity, and credit quality. Second, a convertible bond can never sell for less than its *conversion value* because, if it did, investors could simply buy the bond and convert, thereby realizing an immediate, riskless profit.

Thus, the *floor value* of a convertibnle bond is its intrinsic bond value or its conversion value, whichever is larger. As shown in Figure 11.4, however, a convertible bond will generally sell for more than this floor value. This extra is the amount that investors are willing to pay for the right, but not the obligation, to convert the bond at a future date at a potentially much higher stock price.

An interesting variation of a bond-to-stock conversion feature occurs when the company issuing the bonds is different from the company whose stock is acquired by the conversion. In this case, the bonds are called **exchangeable bonds**. Figure 11.5 presents a *Wall Street Journal* announcement of an issue of exchangeable subordinated debentures by the McKesson Corporation. These debentures are exchangeable for common stock shares of Armor All Products Corporation. McKesson is a retail distributor and Armor All markets consumer chemical products. Exchangeable bonds, while not unusual, are less common than convertible bonds.

intrinsic bond value
The price below which a convertible bond cannot fall, equal to the value of a comparable nonconvertible bond. Also called *investment value*.

exchangeable bonds
Bonds that can be converted into common stock shares of a company other than the issuer's.

CHECK THIS

11.3e For nonconvertible bonds, the call price is a ceiling on the market price of the bond. Why might the call price not be an effective ceiling on the price of a convertible bond?

Bond Maturity and Principal Payment Provisions

term bonds Bonds issued with a single maturity date.

Term bonds represent the most common corporate bond maturity structure. A term bond issue has a single maturity date. On this date, all outstanding bond principal must be paid off. The indenture contract for a term bond issue normally stipulates the creation of a *sinking fund,* that is, an account established to repay bondholders through a series of **fractional redemptions** before the bond reaches maturity. Thus, at maturity, only a fraction of the original bond issue will still be outstanding. Sinking fund provisions are discussed in more detail later.

serial bonds Bonds issued with a regular sequence of maturity dates.

An alternative maturity structure is provided by **serial bonds**, where a fraction of an entire bond issue is scheduled to mature in each year over a specified period. Essentially, a serial bond issue represents a collection of subissues with sequential maturities. As an example, a serial bond issue may stipulate that one-tenth of an entire bond issue must be redeemed in each year over a 10-year period, with the last fraction redeemed at maturity. Serial bonds generally do not have a call provision, whereas term bonds usually do have a call provision.

Figure 11.5 Exchangeable Debentures Issue

This announcement is neither an offer to sell nor a solicitation of an offer to buy any of these Securities. The offer is made only by the Prospectus.

$180,000,000

McKesson Corporation

4½% Exchangeable Subordinated Debentures Due 2004

Exchangeable for Shares of Common Stock of
Armor All Products Corporation

Interest Payable March 1 and September 1

Price 100% and Accrued Interest, if any

Copies of the Prospectus may be obtained in any State from only such of the undersigned as may legally offer these Securities in compliance with the securities laws of such State.

MORGAN STANLEY & CO.
Incorporated

MONTGOMERY SECURITIES

MONNESS, CRESPI, HARDT & CO. INC.   **WHEAT FIRST BUTCHER & SINGER**
Capital Markets

March 17, 1994

Disney Amazes Investors with Sale of 100-Year Bonds

The corporate race to lock in low credit costs hit a fever pitch as Walt Disney Co. began marketing the first 100-year bonds to be sold by any borrower since 1954.

Bond traders were stunned to hear that the entertainment concern is expecting to sell $150 million of 100-year bonds at a yield of only about 7.5%, barely 0.95 percentage points above 30-year U.S. Treasury bonds.

"It's crazy," said William Gross, head of fixed-income investments at Pacific Investment Management Co. Noting the ups and down of the entertainment industry, he said: "Look at the path of Coney Island over the last 50 years and see what happens to amusement parks."

"Obviously we're going through a phase in the market where everyone is pushing the envelope where they can," said Glenn Murphy, chief investment officer of Travelers Asset Management, Inc. The Disney issue will turn out to be a "historic artifact, a curiosity," he said.

Disney's bond issue may not really be around for a century. It can be called away from investors by the company after 30 years. But demand for the issue is said to be brisk and there is even some talk that the offering size might be increased.

The 100-year buyers are expected to be the usual flock of pension funds, insurers, and financial advisers, according to Mark Seigel, head of corporate underwriting at Morgan Stanley & Co., which will lead the underwriting. Merrill Lynch & Co. will co-manage the deal.

While 100-year bonds are rare, they seem a fitting climax to a recent flurry of very long-dated corporate bonds. So far this year, five companies have sold 50-year bonds for a total of $1.13 billion. Last year one company sold 50-year bonds, and before that, none had sold such long-dated securities in decades.

Demand for such long-dated bond issues has grown in recent months because investors, sick of measly returns, are becoming more willing to shoulder greater risks in return for higher yields, even marginally higher ones as in the case of the Disney bonds.

Source: Thomas T. Vogel, Jr., "Disney Amazes Investors with Sale of 100-Year Bonds," *The Wall Street Journal*, July 21, 1993. Reprinted by permission of Dow Jones & Company, Inc., via Copyright Clearance Center, Inc. © 1993 Dow Jones & Company, Inc. All Rights Reserved Worldwide.

When originally issued, most corporate bonds have maturities of 30 years or less. However, in recent years some companies have issued bonds with 40- and 50-year maturities. In 1993, Walt Disney Company made headlines in the financial press when it sold $300 million of 100-year maturity bonds. This bond issue became popularly known as "Sleeping Beauty Bonds," after the classic Disney movie. However, the prince might arrive early for these bonds since they are callable after 30 years. Nevertheless, this was the first time since 1954 that 100-year bonds were sold by any borrower in the United States. Only days later, however, Coca-Cola issued $150 million of 100-year maturity bonds. Both the Disney and Coke bond issues locked in the unusually low interest rates prevailing in 1993. *Wall Street Journal* articles covering the Disney and Coke century bond issues are reproduced in the accompanying Investment Updates boxes.

Sinking Fund Provisions

sinking fund An account used to provide for scheduled redemptions of outstanding bonds.

The indentures of most term bonds include a **sinking fund** provision that requires the corporation to make periodic payments into a trustee-managed account. Account reserves are then used to provide for scheduled redemptions of outstanding bonds. The existence of a sinking fund is an important consideration for bond investors mainly for two reasons:

1. A sinking fund provides a degree of security to bondholders, since payments into the sinking fund can be used only to pay outstanding obligations to bondholders.

2. A sinking fund provision requires fractional bond issue redemptions according to a preset schedule. Therefore, some bondholders will be repaid their invested principal before the stated maturity for their bonds whether they want repayment or not.

As part of a *scheduled sinking fund redemption,* some bondholders may be forced to surrender their bonds in exchange for cash payment of a special *sinking fund call price.* For this reason, not all bondholders may be able to hold their bonds until maturity, even though the entire bond issue has not been called according to a general call provision. For example, the indenture for a 25-year maturity bond issue may require that one-twentieth of the bond issue be retired annually, beginning immediately after an initial 5-year call protection period.

Typically, when a redemption is due, the sinking fund trustee will select bonds by lottery. Selected bonds are then called, and the affected bondholders receive the call price, which for sinking fund redemptions is usually par value. However, the issuer normally has a valuable option to buy back the required number of bonds in the open market and deliver them to the sinking fund trustee instead of delivering the cash required for a par value redemption. Issuers naturally prefer to exercise this option when bonds can be repurchased in the open market at less than par value.

CHECK THIS

11.3f For bond investors, what are some of the advantages and disadvantages of a sinking fund provision?

Coupon Payment Provisions

Coupon rates are stated on an annual basis. For example, an 8 percent coupon rate indicates that the issuer promises to pay 8 percent of a bond's face value to the bondholder each year. However, splitting an annual coupon into two semiannual payments is an almost universal practice in the United States. An exact schedule of coupon payment dates is specified in the bond indenture when the bonds are originally issued.

If a company suspends payment of coupon interest, it is said to be in default. Default is a serious matter. In general, bondholders have an unconditional right to the timely payment of interest and principal. They also have a right to bring legal action to enforce such payments. Upon suspension of coupon payments, the bondholders could, for example, demand an acceleration of principal repayment along with all past-due interest. However, a corporation in financial distress has a right to seek protection in bankruptcy court from inflexible demands by bondholders. As a practical matter, it is often in the best interests of both the bondholders and the corporation to negotiate a new debt contract. Indeed, bankruptcy courts normally encourage a settlement that minimizes any intervention on their part.

11.4 Protective Covenants

protective covenants
Restrictions in a bond indenture designed to protect bondholders.

In addition to the provisions already discussed, a bond indenture is likely to contain a number of **protective covenants**. These agreements are designed to protect bondholders by restricting the actions of a corporation that might cause a deterioration in the credit quality of a bond issue. Protective covenants can be classified into two types: negative covenants and positive, or affirmative, covenants.

A *negative covenant* is a "thou shalt not" for the corporation. Here are some examples of negative covenants that might be found in an indenture agreement:

1. The firm cannot pay dividends to stockholders in excess of what is allowed by a formula based on the firm's earnings.

2. The firm cannot issue new bonds that are senior to currently outstanding bonds. Also, the amount of a new bond issue cannot exceed an amount specified by a formula based on the firm's net worth.

3. The firm cannot refund an existing bond issue with new bonds paying a lower coupon rate than the currently outstanding bond issue it would replace.

4. The firm cannot buy bonds issued by other companies, nor can it guarantee the debt of any other company.

A *positive covenant* is a "thou shalt." It specifies things that a corporation must do, or conditions that it must abide by. Here are some common examples of positive covenants:

1. Proceeds from the sale of assets must be used either to acquire other assets of equal value or to redeem outstanding bonds.

2. In the event of a merger, acquisition, or spinoff, the firm must give bondholders the right to redeem their bonds at par value.

3. The firm must maintain the good condition of all assets pledged as security for an outstanding bond issue.

4. The firm must periodically supply audited financial information to bondholders.

CHECK
THIS

11.4a Why would a corporation voluntarily include protective covenants in its bond indenture contract?

Event Risk

event risk The possibility that the issuing corporation will experience a significant change in its bond credit quality.

Protective covenants in a bond indenture help shield bondholders from event risk. **Event risk** is broadly defined as the possibility that some structural or financial change to the corporation will cause a significant deterioration in the credit quality of a bond issue, thereby causing the affected bonds to lose substantial market value.

A classic example of event risk, and what could happen to bondholders without adequate covenant protection, is provided by an incident involving Marriott Corporation, best known for its chain of hotels and resorts. In October 1992, Marriott announced its intention to spin off part of the company. The spinoff, called Host Marriott, would acquire most of the parent company's debt and its poorly performing real estate holdings. The parent, Marriott International, would be left relatively debt-free with possession of most of the better performing properties, including its hotel management division.

On the announcement date, the affected Marriott bonds fell in value by about 30 percent, reflecting severe concern about the impact of the spinoff on the credit quality of the bonds. On the same day, Marriott stock rose in value by about 30 percent, reflecting a large wealth transfer from bondholders to stockholders. A subsequent bondholder legal challenge was unsuccessful. Standard & Poor's later announced that it was formally revising its credit ratings on Marriott bonds to recognize the impact of the spinoff. (Credit ratings are discussed in detail in a later section.) Debt remaining with Marriott International would have an investment-grade rating, while bonds assigned to Host Marriott would have junk bond status. *The Wall Street Journal* report covering the story is reproduced in the nearby Investment Updates box.

CHECK   11.5a   What are some possible protective covenants that would have protected Marriott bondholders from the adverse impact of the spinoff. . . .

 Bonds without Indentures

private placement A new bond issue sold to one or more parties in private transactions not available to the public.

The Trust Indenture Act of 1939 does not require an indenture when a bond issue is not sold to the general public. For example, the bonds may be sold only to one or more financial institutions in what is called a **private placement**. Private placements are exempt from registration requirements with the SEC. Nevertheless, even privately placed debt issues often have a formal indenture contract.

When a corporation issues debt without an indenture, it makes an unconditional promise to pay interest and principal according to a simple debt contract. Debt issued without an indenture is basically a simple IOU of the corporation. Bond analysts sometimes reserve the designation "bonds" to mean corporate debt subject to an indenture and refer to corporate debt not subject to an indenture as "notes." However, it is more common to distinguish between bonds and notes on the basis of maturity, where bonds designate relatively long maturities, say, 10 years or longer, and notes designate maturities less than 10 years. Both definitions overlap since most long-term debt is issued subject to an indenture, and most privately placed short-term debt is issued as a simple IOU. In between, however, privately placed intermediate-maturity debt may or may not

Marriott to Split, Making 2 Firms

Marriott Corp. shareholders approved a plan to split the company into a real-estate concern, with most of Marriott's debt, and a high-growth hotel-management company.

The split, approved by 85% of the shares voted, was the main issue at Marriott's annual meeting Friday. Under the plan, which is expected to take effect in September, stockholders will receive a share of Marriott International, Inc., the hotel-management operation, for each Marriott share they own. Then Marriott Corp. will be renamed Host Marriott Corp., an entity that will operate the real-estate side of the business.

The plan stunned bondholders when it was announced in October. They argued that the financial support of their debt was being undermined, and a suit by some of the bondholders is still pending.

Marriott shares have risen 60% since the plan's announcement. In New York Stock Exchange trading Friday, Marriott closed at $27.785, up 12.5 cents. The stock has traded as low as $15.50 in the past year.

The Marriott family controls more than 25% of the 100.8 million shares outstanding as of Jan. 1.

Marriott's directors set a distribution date for the split dividend of Sept. 10 for shares of record Sept. 1.

J. W. Marriott, 61 years old and currently chairman and president of the company, will be chairman, president and chief executive officer of Marriott International, while his brother, Richard E. Marriott, 54, will be chairman of Host Marriott. Richard Marriott is currently vice chairman and executive vice president of the company.

In addition to the bondholders' lawsuit seeking to block the reorganization, Marriott had faced a suit by holders of preferred stock. Marriott said that the holders have agreed to dismiss their case and convert their preferred shares into common stock.

The suit by the group of bondholders, representing about a dozen institutional investors, is still pending, however. Under the reorganization plan, holders of about $1.5 billion in Marriott bonds would have the option to swap their notes for new notes of a unit of the new real-estate entity. The company will retain $2.1 billion of Marriott's $3 billion long-term debt and will own 139 hotels and other real-estate assets.

Larry Kill, attorney for the bondholders, said the suit would proceed despite the shareholder vote. "This was a very unfair transaction," he said.

As a separate company, Host Marriott would have had about $1.2 billion in sales in 1992, according to the company's estimates. Marriott International, Inc., the new hotel concern, will operate more than 760 hotels through Marriott's four hotel-management units and related management services. Marriott International would have had $7.8 billion in sales last year, the company estimates.

In 1992, Marriott had net income of $85 million, or 64 cents a share, on sales of $8.72 billion. It had about $3 billion in long-term debt as of Jan. 1.

Moody's Investors Service, Inc., downgraded its ratings on the senior unsecured debt of Marriott Corp., affecting about $2.3 billion in debt, to Ba-2 from single-B-2. Moody's said the bond-exchange plan will leave a Host Marriott unit highly leveraged "with modest debt protection." Moody's said it expects only gradual improvement in operating earnings, given the sluggish economy and glut of hotel rooms. Moody's said, however, that the Host Marriott unit will be well-positioned for increased earnings when the recovery hits full speed.

Source: Jyoti Thottam, "Marriott to Split, Making 2 Firms," *The Wall Street Journal*, July 26, 1993. Reprinted by permission of Dow Jones & Company, Inc., via Copyright Clearance Center, Inc. © 1993 Dow Jones & Company, Inc. All Rights Reserved Worldwide.

be issued subject to an indenture, and therefore might be referred to as either a bond or a note irrespective of the existence of an indenture. As in any profession, the jargon of investments is sometimes ambiguous.

11.7 Preferred Stock

preferred stock A security with a claim to dividend payments that is senior to common stock.

Preferred stock has some of the features of both bonds and common stock. Preferred stockholders have a claim to dividend payments that is senior to the claim of common stockholders—hence the term "preferred stock." However, their claim is subordinate to the claims of bondholders and other creditors. A typical preferred stock issue has the following basic characteristics:

1. Preferred stockholders do not normally participate with common stockholders in the election of a board of directors. However, a few preferred stock issues do grant voting rights to their holders.

2. Preferred stockholders are promised a stream of fixed dividend payments. Thus, preferred dividends resemble bond coupons.

3. Preferred stock normally has no specified maturity, but it is often callable by the issuer.

4. Management can suspend payment of preferred dividends without setting off a bankruptcy process, but only after suspending payment of all common stock dividends.

5. If preferred dividends have been suspended, all unpaid preferred dividends normally become a cumulative debt that must be paid in full before the corporation can resume any payment of common stock dividends. Preferred stock with this feature is termed *cumulative preferred.*

6. Some preferred stock issues have a conversion feature similar to convertible bonds. These are called *convertible preferred stock.*

Figure 11.6 is a *Wall Street Journal* announcement for an issue of convertible preferred stock by Omnipoint Corporation. Actually, it is an issue of depository shares, where each depository share represents a claim on one-twentieth of the underlying convertible preferred shares. The preferred shares may be converted at any time at a conversion price of $31.115 per depository share.

All else equal, preferred stock normally pays a lower interest rate to investors than do corporate bonds. This is because when most investors buy preferred stock, the dividends received are taxed at the same rate as bond interest payments. However, if a business corporation buys preferred stock, it can usually exclude at least 70 percent of the preferred dividends from income taxation. As a result, most preferred stock is owned by corporations that can take advantage of the preferential tax treatment of preferred dividends. However, companies that issue preferred stock must treat preferred dividends the same as common stock dividends for tax purposes, and therefore cannot deduct preferred dividends from their taxable income.

CHECK THIS

11.7a From the perspective of common stockholders and management, what are some of the advantages of issuing preferred stock instead of bonds or new shares of common stock?

11.8 Adjustable-Rate Bonds and Adjustable-Rate Preferred Stock

adjustable-rate bonds Securities that pay coupons that change according to a prespecified rule. Also called *floating-rate bonds* or simply *floaters.*

Many bond, note, and preferred stock issues allow the issuer to adjust the annual coupon according to a rule or formula based on current market interest rates. These securities are called **adjustable-rate bonds**; they are also sometimes called *floating-rate bonds* or *floaters.*

For example, a typical adjustment rule might specify that the coupon rate be reset annually to be equal to the current rate on 180-day maturity U.S. Treasury bills plus

Figure 11.6   Convertible Preferred Shares Issue

June 24, 1998

$325,000,000

Omnipoint
C O R P O R A T I O N

6,500,000 Shares

Depositary Shares Each Representing ¹/₂₀ of a Share of
7% Cumulative Convertible Preferred Stock
(Liquidation Preference equivalent to $50 per Depositary Share)

Each of the 6,500,000 Depositary Shares offered hereby (the "Offering") represents ownership of ¹/₂₀ of a share of 7% Cumulative Convertible Preferred Stock (the "Preferred Stock") of Omnipoint Corporation, a Delaware corporation (the "Company"), deposited with the Depositary and entitles the holder to all proportional rights and preferences of the Preferred Stock (including dividend, voting, conversion, redemption and liquidation rights and preferences). The proportionate Liquidation Preference of each Depositary Share is $50. The Depositary Shares are being offered hereby by the Initial Purchasers to qualified institutional buyers in reliance on Rule 144A under the Securities Act of 1933, as amended (the "Securities Act"). The Preferred Stock will be convertible at the option of the holder thereof into shares of Common Stock, par value $.01 per share, of the Company ("Common Stock"), at any time unless previously redeemed at a Conversion Price of $31.115 per Depositary Share subject to adjustment under certain circumstances.

The undersigned privately placed these securities with qualified institutional buyers pursuant to Rule 144A and outside the United States under the Securities Act of 1933.

Donaldson, Lufkin & Jenrette
Securities Corporation

BancAmerica Robertson Stephens

Bear, Stearns & Co. Inc.

Salomon Smith Barney

Allen & Company
Incorporated

Lehman Brothers

Raymond James & Associates, Inc.

Credit Suisse First Boston

Cowen & Company

2 percent. Alternatively, a more flexible rule might specify that the coupon rate on a bond issue cannot be set below 105 percent of the yield to maturity of newly issued five-year Treasury notes. Thus, if five-year Treasury notes have recently been sold to yield 6 percent, the minimum allowable coupon rate is $1.05 \times 6\% = 6.3\%$.

Adjustable rate bonds and notes are often putable at par value. For this reason, an issuer may set a coupon rate above an allowable minimum to discourage bondholders from selling their bonds back to the corporation.

CHECK THIS

11.8a How does an adjustable coupon rate feature affect the interest rate risk of a bond?

11.8b How might bondholders respond if the coupon rate on an adjustable-rate putable bond was set below market interest rates?

11.9 Corporate Bond Credit Ratings

credit rating An assessment of the credit quality of a bond issue based on the issuer's financial condition.

When a corporation sells a new bond issue to investors, it usually subscribes to several bond rating agencies for a credit evaluation of the bond issue. Each contracted rating agency then provides a **credit rating**—an assessment of the credit quality of the bond issue based on the issuer's financial condition. Rating agencies will normally provide a credit rating only if it is requested by an issuer and will charge a fee for this service. As part of the contractual arrangement between the bond issuer and the rating agency, the issuer agrees to allow a continuing review of its credit rating even if the rating deteriorates. Without a credit rating a new bond issue would be very difficult to sell to the public, which is why almost all bond issues originally sold to the general public have a credit rating assigned at the time of issuance. Also, most public bond issues have ratings assigned by several rating agencies.

Established rating agencies in the United States include Duff and Phelps, Inc. (D&P); Fitch Investors Service (Fitch); McCarthy, Crisanti and Maffei (MCM); Moody's Investors Service (Moody's); and Standard & Poor's Corporation (S&P). Of these, the two best known rating agencies are Moody's and Standard & Poor's. These companies publish regularly updated credit ratings for thousands of domestic and international bond issues.

It is important to realize that corporate bond ratings are assigned to particular bond issues, and not to the issuer of those bonds. For example, a senior bond issue is likely to have a higher credit rating than a subordinated issue even if both are issued by the same corporation. Similarly, a corporation with two bond issues outstanding may have a higher credit rating assigned to one issue because that issue has stronger covenant protection specified in the bond's indenture contract.

Seniority and covenant protection are not the only things affecting bond ratings. Bond rating agencies consider a number of factors before assigning a credit rating, including an appraisal of the financial strength of the issuer, the caliber of the issuer's management, and the issuer's position in an industry as well as the industry's position in the economy. In general, a bond rating is intended to be a comparative indicator of overall credit quality for a particular bond issue. The rating in itself is not a recommendation to buy or sell a bond.

Table 11.2 summarizes corporate bond rating symbols and definitions used by Moody's (first column), Duff and Phelps (second column), and Standard & Poor's

Table 11.2		**Corporate Bond Credit Rating Symbols**	
Rating Agency			
Moody's	Duff and Phelps	Standard & Poor's	Credit Rating Description
Investment-Grade Bond Ratings			
Aaa	1	AAA	Highest credit rating, maximum safety
Aa1	2	AA+	
Aa2	3	AA	High credit quality, investment-grade bonds
Aa3	4	AA−	
A1	5	A+	
A2	6	A	Upper-medium quality, investment-grade bonds
A3	7	A−	
Baa1	8	BBB+	
Baa2	9	BBB	Lower-medium quality, investment-grade bonds
Baa3	10	BBB−	
Speculative-Grade Bond Ratings			
Ba1	11	BB+	Low credit quality, speculative-grade bonds
Ba2	12	BB	
Ba3	13	BB−	
B1	14	B+	Very low credit quality, speculative-grade bonds
B2	15	B	
B3	16	B−	
Extremely Speculative-Grade Bond Ratings			
Caa	17	CCC+	Extremely low credit standing, high-risk bonds
		CCC	
		CCC−	
Ca		CC	Extremely speculative
C		C	
		D	Bonds in default

(third column). As shown, bond credit ratings fall into three broad categories: investment grade, speculative grade, and extremely speculative grade.

Why Bond Ratings Are Important

Bond credit ratings assigned by independent rating agencies are quite important to bond market participants. Only a few institutional investors have the resources and expertise necessary to properly evaluate a bond's credit quality on their own. Bond ratings provide investors with reliable, professional evaluations of bond issues at a reasonable cost. This information is indispensable for assessing the economic value of a bond.

prudent investment guidelines
Restrictions on investment portfolios stipulating that securities purchased must meet a certain level of safety.

Furthermore, many financial institutions have **prudent investment guidelines** stipulating that only securities with a certain level of investment safety may be included in their portfolios. For example, bond investments for many pension funds are limited to investment-grade bonds rated at least Baa by Moody's or at least BBB by Standard & Poor's. Bond ratings provide a convenient measure to monitor implementation of these guidelines.

Individual investors investing in bonds also find published bond ratings useful. Individual investors generally do not have the ability to diversify as extensively as do large institutions. With limited diversification opportunities, an individual should invest only in bonds with higher credit ratings.

11.10 Junk Bonds

high-yield bonds
Bonds with a speculative credit rating that is offset by a yield premium offered to compensate for higher credit risk. Also called *junk bonds*.

Bonds with a speculative or low grade rating—that is, those rated Ba or lower by Moody's or BB or lower by Standard & Poor's—are commonly called **high-yield bonds**, or, more colorfully, *junk bonds*. The designation "junk" is somewhat misleading and often unduly pejorative, since junk bonds *have* economic value. Junk bonds simply represent debt with a higher than average credit risk. To put the term in perspective, one should realize that most consumer debt and small business debt represents higher than average credit risk. Yet it is generally considered desirable from an economic and social perspective that credit be available to consumers and small businesses.

Junk bonds that were originally issued with an investment-grade credit rating that subsequently fell to speculative grade because of unforeseen economic events are called *fallen angels.* Another type, *original-issue junk,* is defined as bonds originally issued with a speculative-grade rating.

Junk bonds are attractive investments for many institutional investors with well-diversified portfolios. The logic of junk bond investing revolves around the possibility that the *yield premium* for junk bonds might be high enough to justify accepting the higher default rates of junk bonds. As an example of this logic, consider the following back-of-the-envelope calculations.

Suppose that the average yield on junk bonds is 10 percent when U.S. Treasury bonds yield 7 percent. In this case, the yield premium of junk bonds over default-free Treasury bonds is 3 percent. Further suppose that an investor expects about 4 percent of all outstanding junk bonds to default each year, and experience suggests that when junk bonds default bondholders on average receive 50 cents for each dollar of bond face value. Based on these rough assumptions, diversified junk bond investors expect to lose 2 percent ($.04 \times .50$) of their portfolio value each year through defaults. But with a junk bond yield premium of 3 percent, the junk bond portfolio is expected to outperform U.S. Treasury bonds by 1 percent per year. It is true that a junk bond portfolio is much more expensive to manage than a Treasury bond portfolio. However, for a $1 billion bond portfolio, a junk bond yield premium of 1 percent represents $10 million of additional interest income per year.

Of course, actual default rates could turn out to be much different than expected. History suggests that the major determinant of aggregate bond default rates is the state of economic activity. During an expansionary economic period, bond default rates are usually low. But in a recession, default rates can rise dramatically. For this reason, the investment performance of a junk bond portfolio largely depends on the health of the economy.

Prices and yields of selected junk bonds are published regularly in *The Wall Street Journal* in its "High-Yield Bonds" report. A sample report is displayed in Figure 11.7. Information reported for individual issues includes the name of the issuer, the type of bond and the current Standard & Poor's credit rating, the coupon rate and maturity of the bond, a dealer bid price and the change in the bid price from the previous day, and the bond's yield. The reported yield is either a *yield to maturity* or a *yield to call,* whichever is lower. Yield to call is calculated assuming that the bond issue will be called at the earliest possible call date, while the yield to maturity is calculated assuming that the bonds will not be called before maturity.

CHECK THIS

11.10a Can junk bond default risk be completely diversified away by large institutional bond investors?

11.10b From an investor's perspective, is there any importance in distinguishing between fallen angels and original-issue junk?

11.11 Bond Market Trading

Consistent with the need to hold bonds for predictable cash flows, most corporate bond investors buy and hold bonds until they mature. However, many investors need to liquidate some bonds before they mature and others wish to purchase outstanding bonds originally issued by a particular corporation several years earlier. For these and many other reasons, the existence of an active secondary market for corporate bonds is important for most bond investors. Fortunately, an active secondary market with a substantial volume of bond trading does exist to satisfy most of the liquidity needs of investors.

Figure 11.7

Junk Bond Trading

Source: Reprinted with permission from *The Wall Street Journal*, June 31, 1998, via Copyright Clearance Center, Inc. © 1998 Dow Jones & Company, Inc. All Rights Reserved Worldwide.

HIGH-YIELD BONDS

Tuesday, June 30, 1998

	Total Daily Return	Index Value	Average Price Change	Vol.
Flash Index	+ 0.15%	256.92	+ 0.06	M
Cash Pay	+ 0.15	269.10	+ 0.05	M
Deferred Int	+ 0.16	272.18	+ 0.12	M
Distressed	+ 0.16	44.96	unch	M
Bankrupt	+ 0.10	183.12	unch	M

Volume Key: H = Heavy, M = Moderate, L = Light
The Flash Index comprises more than 650 issues.
July 1, 1990 = 100

Key Gainers

	Type/Coup.	Mat.	3:00 P.M. Bid Price	Price Change	Principal Return	Yld.-y
Grand Casino	c/ 10.125	12/03	110	+ 7	+ 6.74	6.08
Metronet	e/ 0.000	6/08	61 1/2	+ 1	+ 1.65	10.02
fox family	a/ 9.250	11/07	100 1/2	+ 1 1/2	+ 1.49	9.150
Nextel Comm	e/ 0.000	9/07	67 3/4	+ 3/4	+ 1.12	9.86
Wiser Oil	b/ 9.500	5/07	93	+ 1/2	+ 0.53	10.74

Key Losers

None

Name	Type/Rating	Coup.	Mat.	3:00 P.M. Bid Price	Net Chg.	Yld.-y
AK Steel	a/BB-	9.125	12/06	104 5/8	+ 1/2	8.18
Advantica	a/B	11.250	1/08	105 1/2	unch	10.18

Name	Type/Rating	Coup.	Mat.	3 P.M. Bid	Net Chg.	Yld.-y
Brunos	b/NR	10.500	8/05	16 1/2	unch	68.61
Exide	a/NR	10.000	4/05	103	unch	9.04
Grand Casino	c/BB	10.125	12/03	110	+7	6.08
Grand Union	d/NR	12.000	9/04	58	unch	26.02
Gulf Canada	b/BB-	9.625	7/05	107 1/4	unch	7.83
Intl cable	e/B-	0.000	2/06	81 1/2	unch	9.53
K mart	a/BB	8.125	12/06	104	unch	7.47
Lenfest Comm	a/BB+	8.375	11/05	105 1/4	unch	7.43
NL Indust.	c/B	11.750	10/03	110 1/2	unch	7.27
Nextel Comm	e/CCC+	0.000	9/03	98 1/2 + 1/2		11.39
Paging Netwk	b/B	10.000	10/08	103 3/4	unch	9.19
Revlon	c/B-	0.000	3/01	77 3/4 + 3/8		9.54
Riverwood	a/B-	10.250	4/06	102 1/2	unch	9.67
Ryland Group	b/B+	10.500	7/02	104	unch	7.34
Sprint	a/B+	11.000	8/06	115 1/4	unch	7.06
Stone	a/B	9.875	2/01	102 3/8	unch	8.22
Teligent	a/CCC	11.500	12/07	101 1/2	unch	11.19
Tenet Hlth.	b/BB-	8.625	1/07	103	unch	8.02
Trump AC	c/B	11.250	5/06	96 3/4	unch	11.89
Viacom	f/BB-	8.000	7/06	103	unch	7.13
WCI Steel	c/B+	10.000	12/04	102 3/4 + 1/2		9.41

Volume indicators are based solely on the traders' subjective judgment given the relative level of inquiry and trading activity on any given day.

Bid Prices are indicative only and may not represent actual bids by a dealer.

Price quotes follow accrued interest conventions.

a-Senior. b-Senior Sub. c-Secured. d-Senior, Split Cpn. e-Senior, Zero To Full. f-Subordinated. y-yield is the lower of yield to maturity and yield to call. z-omitted for reset or bankrupt bonds, negative yields, or yields above 35%.

Source: Salomon Smith Barney

Almost as many different bond issues are listed on the New York Stock Exchange (NYSE) as there are different common stock issues. These NYSE-traded bond issues represent the most actively traded bonds of large corporations. However, there are many more thousands of different corporate debt issues outstanding. Most of these less actively traded debt issues trade in the over-the-counter (OTC) market. In fact, it is estimated that less than 1 percent of all corporate bond trading actually takes place on the New York Stock Exchange. While some bond trading activity occurs on the American Stock Exchange and other regional exchanges, corporate bond trading is characteristically an OTC activity. Nevertheless, bond trading on the New York Stock Exchange is watched by bond investors and traders throughout the world.

Every business day, *The Wall Street Journal* publishes an overview of corporate bond trading in its "New York Exchange Bonds" report. Figure 11.8 presents a partial sample daily report. As shown, part of this report is a summary of the prior day's bond trading activity, including data on trading volume, number of issues traded, and summary statistics describing general bond price movements. The remainder of the daily bond report lists information regarding trading of individual bond issues, including bond identification, current yield, trading volume, closing price, and the change in price from the previous day.

In Figure 11.8, bond identification is listed in the first column. Identification includes an abbreviated name of the issuer, the bond's coupon rate, and maturity. For example, several AT&T (ticker symbol ATT) bond issues are listed. The longest maturity AT&T bond pays an $8\frac{5}{8}$ percent coupon and matures in 2031. A bond dealer might refer to these bonds as "ATT $8\frac{5}{8}$s of 31."

When referring to the "New York Exchange Bonds" report, notice that corporate bond prices are conventionally stated as a percentage of par value. Thus, a quoted price of 97 indicates that a bond with a face value of $1,000 has a price of $970. Also notice that for corporate bonds, price fractions are true fractions. Thus, a price of $101\frac{5}{8}$ means that $10,000 of face value has a price of $10,000 \times 101\frac{5}{8}\% = \$10,162.50$.

As we saw in Chapter 10, current yield is defined as a bond's annual coupon payments divided by its current market price. Notice that current yields are not reported for those bonds where a current yield value is uninformative. This includes convertible bonds, indicated by *cv* in the current yield column, and floating-rate bonds and zero coupon bonds, indicated by *f* and *zr*, respectively, in the bond identification column.

CHECK THIS

11.11a All else equal, is an actively traded bond more or less risky as an investment than a thinly traded bond? (Hint: Is liquidity a good or a bad thing for a bond?)

11.11b Why might a current yield for a convertible bond be uninformative for the purpose of making a comparison between two or more bonds?

Figure 11.8

NYSE Bond Trading

Source: Reprinted with permission from *The Wall Street Journal,* December 30, 1998, via Copyright Clearance Center, Inc., © 1998 Dow Jones & Company, Inc. All Rights Reserved Worldwide.

NEW YORK EXCHANGE BONDS

Quotations as of 4 p.m. Eastern Time
Tuesday, December 29, 1998

Volume $14,538,000

SALES SINCE JANUARY 1
(000 omitted)

1998	1997	1996
$3,806,217	$5,053,564	$5,532,417

	Domestic		All Issues	
	Tue	Mon	Tue	Mon.
Issues Traded	199	205	205	214
Advances	81	86	85	92
Declines	79	84	81	86
Unchanged	39	35	39	36
New highs	2	3	2	3
New lows	7	4	7	5

Dow Jones Bond Averages

	−1997−		−1998−				−−−1998−−−			−−1997−−	
	High	Low	High	Low			Close	Chg.	%Yld	Close	Chg.
	105.13	101.09	107.17	104.42	20 Bonds		106.47	−0.12	6.63	105.13	unch
	102.89	97.64	104.71	101.88	10 Utilities		104.21	+0.08	6.74	102.79	−0.05
	107.49	104.54	109.81	106.48	10 Industrials		108.72	−0.32	6.51	107.47	+0.05

CORPORATION BONDS
Volume, $14,313,000

Bonds	Cur Yld.	Vol.	Close	Net Chg.
ATT 5⁷⁄₈01	5.1	50	100¹⁄₈	+ ¹⁄₂
ATT 7¹⁄₈02	6.8	18	105	+ ¹⁄₄
ATT 6³⁄₄04	6.4	10	106	...
ATT 8.2s05	7.9	35	103⁷⁄₈	...
ATT 8¹⁄₈22	7.6	22	106⁵⁄₈	− ⁵⁄₈
ATT 8¹⁄₂24	7.5	78	107³⁄₄	− ¹⁄₈
ATT 8⁵⁄₈31	7.8	18	110¹⁄₈	− ³⁄₄
AutDt zr12	...	25	101¹⁄₂	− ¹⁄₂
BankAm 8¹⁄₂99	8.5	10	100¹⁄₈	− ¹¹⁄₃₂
BellPa 7¹⁄₈12	7.0	25	101⁷⁄₈	− ¹⁄₈
BellsoT 6¹⁄₂00	6.4	30	101¹⁄₂	+ ¹⁄₄
BellsoT 6¹⁄₄03	6.0	22	103⁷⁄₈	...
BellsoT 6³⁄₈04	6.1	25	104¹⁄₈	− ¹⁄₄
BellsoT 5⁷⁄₈09	5.7	15	103⁷⁄₈	+ ⁵⁄₈
BellsoT 7s25	6.2	10	112³⁄₄	+ 1¹⁄₂
BellsoT 6³⁄₄33	6.6	53	102⁷⁄₈	+ ¹⁄₈
BellsoT 7⁵⁄₈35	6.8	20	111⁵⁄₈	+ ⁷⁄₈
BethSt 8.45s05	8.4	30	100	− ³⁄₈
Bordn 8³⁄₈16	8.2	56	101³⁄₄	+ 1¹⁄₄
BosCelts 6s38	10.0	16	59³⁄₄	+ ¹⁄₂
BoydGm 9¹⁄₄03	8.9	45	104	+ ¹⁄₄
BrnGp 9¹⁄₂06	9.0	55	105³⁄₄	+ ¹⁄₄
CaterpInc 9³⁄₄19	9.1	8	107	+ 1
ChaseM 8s04	7.9	30	101³⁄₄	− ¹⁄₄
ChaseM 7⁷⁄₈04	7.7	10	102	+ 1
ChaseM 6¹⁄₈08	6.0	20	103⁵⁄₈	− 1³⁄₈
ChaseM 6¹⁄₂09	6.2	10	105¹⁄₈	+ ⁵⁄₈
ChespkE 9⁵⁄₈05	13.3	40	72¹⁄₂	− 2¹⁄₂
ChespkE 9¹⁄₈01	13.1	92	69¹⁄₂	...
ChryF 13¹⁄₄99	12.6	100	105¹⁄₈	− ¹⁄₈
ChryF 12³⁄₄99	12.2	5	104³⁄₈	+ ¹⁄₄
Clardge 11³⁄₄02f	...	3	67	+ ¹⁄₄
ClrkOil 9¹⁄₂04	9.4	122	101	...
Coeur 6³⁄₈04	cv	106	56	+ 2¹⁄₂
CwE 8¹⁄₈07Jcld	...	5	101³⁄₄	− ¹⁄₃₂
CompUSA 9¹⁄₂00	9.3	18	101⁵⁄₈	− ³⁄₈
CompMgt 8s03	cv	96	21	− 1
CompMgt 8s03	cv	10	21¹⁄₈	− ³⁄₈
ConPort 10s06	14.3	20	70	+ 5
Convrse 7s04	cv	280	34	...
GMA 7¹⁄₈99	7.1	30	100⁵⁄₃₂	...
GMA 9⁵⁄₈00	9.2	19	104¹⁄₂	+ ³⁄₈
GMA 7s00	6.9	121	101³⁄₈	...
GMA 5¹⁄₂01	5.6	20	99	− ¹⁄₂
GMA 5⁵⁄₈01	5.7	5	99³⁄₈	− ¹⁄₈
GMA 6⁷⁄₈01	6.7	1	102¹⁄₈	− 1³⁄₈
GMA 7s02	6.7	30	104	+ ³⁄₈
GMA 6⁵⁄₈02	6.5	10	102¹⁄₂	− ¹⁄₂
GMA dc6s11	6.1	26	98	...

Bonds	Cur Yld.	Vol.	Close	Net Chg.
GMA zr12	...	13	391	− 4
GMA zr15	...	25	325¹⁄₂	− 3¹⁄₂
GenesisH 9³⁄₄05	9.9	39	98	+ ⁷⁄₈
GrnTrFn 10¹⁄₄02	9.6	5	107¹⁄₄	+ ¹⁄₈
HRPT 7¹⁄₂03	cv	62	96	− ¹⁄₂
HlthcrR 6.55s02	cv	96	91¹⁄₂	− ¹⁄₄
Hlthso 9¹⁄₂01	9.2	5	103³⁄₈	− ¹⁄₂
Hexcel 7s03	cv	20	83	+ 1
Hills 12¹⁄₂03f	...	44	68	+ 1³⁄₄
Hilton 5s06	cv	109	92	+ ⁵⁄₈
Hollngr 8⁵⁄₈05	7.9	15	109¹⁄₄	− ³⁄₄
Leucadia 7³⁄₄13	7.7	66	100¹⁄₈	− ¹⁄₈
Loews 3¹⁄₈07	cv	208	78⁵⁄₈	− 1³⁄₈
LglsLt 8.2s23	8.2	44	109³⁄₄	+ ¹⁄₂
LouGs 7¹⁄₂02	7.4	5	101³⁄₈	− ¹⁄₂
MBNA 8.28s26	8.3	90	99¹⁄₂	...
MDC Hld 8³⁄₈08	8.5	95	98³⁄₄	+ ³⁄₈
Mascotch 03	cv	108	80	...
McDnl 7³⁄₄02	7.3	25	101¹⁄₆	− 1¹⁄₂
McDnl 6³⁄₄03	6.6	5	103	+ 1⁷⁄₈
Medtrst 7¹⁄₂01	cv	40	93¹⁄₂	+ 1
MPac 5s45f	...	29	64¹⁄₄	...
Mobil 8³⁄₈01	7.9	5	106¹⁄₈	...
Motrla zr13	...	20	75	+ ⁵⁄₈
Nabis 8.3s99	8.3	11	100⁵⁄₁₆	− ¹⁄₃₂
NatData 5s03	cv	20	107	...
NETelTel 8⁵⁄₈01	8.1	25	106	...
NETelTel 4¹⁄₂02	4.6	5	97	− ¹⁄₄
NETelTel 6¹⁄₄03	6.1	65	103	+ ¹⁄₂
NETelTel 4⁵⁄₈05	4.8	10	97¹⁄₈	+ ¹⁄₈
NETelTel 7³⁄₈07	7.2	121	102¹⁄₂	− ¹⁄₄
NETelTel 6³⁄₈08	6.3	2	100¹⁄₂	− ¹⁄₄
NJBTI 7¹⁄₄11	7.1	20	101³⁄₄	...
NYTel 7¹⁄₄24	6.8	1	106³⁄₈	− ¹⁄₈
NYTel 7³⁄₈11	7.2	10	102⁵⁄₈	− ¹⁄₄
NYTel 7s25	6.7	8	104¹⁄₂	− ¹⁄₈
Noram 6s12	cv	7	96¹⁄₂	...
Novacr 5¹⁄₂2000	cv	112	75	+ 2¹⁄₄
OcciP 11¹⁄₈19	10.4	10	106⁷⁄₈	− ⁵⁄₈
OffDep zr07	...	2	100¹⁄₂	+ 1¹⁄₄
OffDep zr08	...	3	79	− 2
OreStl 11s03	10.6	185	103³⁄₄	+ ⁵⁄₈
Oryx 7¹⁄₄14	cv	65	99¹⁄₈	− ¹⁄₄
PacBell 6¹⁄₄05	6.0	37	103⁷⁄₈	+ ³⁄₈
PhilPt 9.18s21	8.4	5	109³⁄₈	...
PotEl 5s02	cv	15	96¹⁄₂	...
PotEl 7s18	cv	6	100⁵⁄₈	...
Pride 6¹⁄₄06	cv	46	81	− 1
PSEG 6s00	6.0	5	100¹⁄₂	− ¹⁄₂
PSEG 6¹⁄₄04	6.3	5	102⁷⁄₈	− 1⁷⁄₈
PSvEG 7s24	6.8	18	103	− ¹⁄₄
PSEG 8s37	7.2	5	111	...
Quanx 6.88s07	cv	11	95⁷⁄₈	+ 2⁷⁄₈
RJR Nb 8s01	7.9	30	101¹⁄₂	− 1
RJR Nb 8⁵⁄₈02	8.3	5	103⁵⁄₈	− ³⁄₈
RJR Nb 7⁵⁄₈03	7.6	130	100	+ ¹⁄₄
RJR Nb 8³⁄₄05	8.5	27	103³⁄₈	+ ¹⁄₂
RJR Nb 8³⁄₄07	8.5	210	103¹⁄₄	− ¹⁄₂
RJR Nb 9¹⁄₄13	8.7	802	106³⁄₈	+ ³⁄₄
RJR Nb 8.3s99	8.3	7	100⁵⁄₁₆	...
RJR Nb 8³⁄₄04	8.5	189	102³⁄₈	− 1¹⁄₄
Rallys 9⁷⁄₈00	12.4	20	79⁷⁄₈	+ 2⁵⁄₈
RalsP 9¹⁄₄09	7.8	5	119	− 4⁷⁄₈
RelGrp 9s00	8.6	30	104³⁄₈	+ ¹⁄₂
RelGrp 9³⁄₄03	9.4	15	103⁵⁄₈	+ ⁵⁄₈
Revl 9¹⁄₂99	9.4	74	100⁵⁄₈	...
Safwy 10s01	9.1	13	109³⁄₄	+ ¹⁄₈
Safwy 9⁷⁄₈07	8.1	10	121⁷⁄₈	+ 1⁷⁄₈
Sears 9¹⁄₂99	9.4	125	101⁹⁄₃₂	− 7⁄₃₂
SvcMer 8³⁄₈01f	...	350	42¹⁄₂	+ 2
SvcMer 9s04f	...	2643	19	+ 1¹⁄₈
Simula 8s04	cv	50	82	+ ¹⁄₂

Bonds	Cur Yld.	Vol.	Close	Net Chg.
SwBell 6¹⁄₈00	6.1	28	101	...
SwBell 7s15	6.5	40	108¹⁄₂	+ ⁷⁄₈
SwBell 7¹⁄₄25	6.8	58	106	+ 1¹⁄₂
StdCmcl 07	cv	12	76³⁄₄	+ ³⁄₄
StoneC 9⁷⁄₈01	9.8	43	100⁷⁄₈	...
StoneC 11¹⁄₂02A	11.2	69	100¹⁄₂	...
StoneC 10³⁄₄02O	10.4	12	103³⁄₈	+ ¹⁄₈
StoneCn 6³⁄₄07	cv	45	79⁵⁄₈	+ 2⁵⁄₈
SwiftE 6¹⁄₄06	cv	16	74¹⁄₈	− 1³⁄₈
TVA 6¹⁄₈03	6.0	50	101³⁄₈	...
TVA 8.05s24	8.0	31	101	...
TVA 8⁵⁄₈29	8.0	110	107⁷⁄₈	− ¹⁄₈
TVA 8¹⁄₄34	8.1	34	101³⁄₄	+ ¹⁄₄
TVA 7¹⁄₄43	6.8	17	106¹⁄₄	+ ¹⁄₄
TVA 7.85s44	7.3	26	107⁵⁄₈	+ ¹⁄₈
Tenet 8s03	7.7	2	103³⁄₈	− 2⁵⁄₈
Tenet 05	cv	40	83	− 2
Tenet 8s05	7.8	5	102	− 1¹⁄₂
Tenet 8⁵⁄₈07	8.2	37	105⁷⁄₈	− 1⁷⁄₈
TmeWar 7.98s04	7.4	3	108¹⁄₂	− ³⁄₈
TmeWar 8.11s06	7.2	7	112¹⁄₂	+ ³⁄₄
TmeWar 8.18s07	7.2	3	114	+ 1
TmeWar 9¹⁄₈13	7.4	41	123⁵⁄₈	− ¹⁄₈
TmeWar 9.15s23	7.1	22	128³⁄₄	+ 1¹⁄₈
TollCp 9¹⁄₂03	9.3	15	102³⁄₈	− ¹⁄₈
URS 6¹⁄₂12	cv	11	79	+ 6³⁄₄
UtdAir 10.67s04	9.0	5	118	− 2
US Filt 4¹⁄₂01	cv	100	94¹⁄₂	...
Viac 7s03Acld	...	25	99¹³⁄₁₆	− ¹⁄₃₂
Webb 9³⁄₄03	9.7	1	100⁵⁄₈	− 1³⁄₈
Webb 9s06	8.9	130	101³⁄₈	...
WebbDel 9³⁄₄09	9.6	73	98¹⁄₈	+ ¹⁄₄
Weirton 10³⁄₄99	10.9	63	100	+ ¹⁄₁₆
Weirton 11³⁄₈04	12.2	55	93¹⁄₈	+ 1¹⁄₂
Weirton 10³⁄₄05	12.6	24	85¹⁄₂	− ¹⁄₂
WhiPit 9³⁄₈03	8.6	14	108⁵⁄₈	− ³⁄₈

AMEX BONDS

Volume $705,000

SALES SINCE JANUARY 1

1998	1997	1996
$251,363,000	$358,270,000	$484,678,000

	Tue.	Mon.	Thu.	Wed.
Issues Traded	16	16	6	17
Advances	8	3	3	3
Declines	7	6	1	8
Unchanged	1	7	3	6
New highs	1	0	0	0
New lows	1	1	0	1

Bonds	Cur Yld.	Vol.	Close	Net Chg.
AltLiv 5¹⁄₄02	cv	35	114¹⁄₂	+ 8
ArchCm 10⁷⁄₈08f	...	12	58	− 4
AssisLiv cv02	7.7	225	78	+ 1¹⁄₂
Centrtrst 7¹⁄₂01	cv	41	93¹⁄₂	− ¹⁄₂
ChckFul 8s06	cv	9	100¹⁄₂	+ 1
FruitL 7s11	7.4	16	94	− 1
Greyhnd 8¹⁄₂03	cv	33	101¹⁄₂	+ 1
HaltMar 4¹⁄₂04	cv	111	57	− 2¹⁄₂
MagHunt 10s07	11.9	10	83⁷⁄₈	− ⁵⁄₈

NASDAQ

Convertible Debentures

Tuesday, December 29, 1998

Issue	Vol.	Close	Net Chg.
Agnico 3¹⁄₂04	18	60	− ¹⁄₄
Baker 7s02	92	67¹⁄₂	− ¹⁄₂
CalMicr 5¹⁄₄03	200	60	− 1
DrgEmp 7³⁄₄14	13	81	− 1
DuraPh 3¹⁄₂02	800	70¹⁄₂	...
Exectne 7¹⁄₂11	10	68	+ 5
Hechng 5¹⁄₂12	75	34¹⁄₂	− 1¹⁄₂
Hexcel 7s11	200	73³⁄₄	− 1¹⁄₄
Metamor 2.94s04	16	80	+ 13¹⁄₄
PhyCor 4¹⁄₂03	200	62	+ 4
Synetic 5s07	60	82³⁄₄	− 1¹⁄₄
SysSftwr 7s02	7	72¹⁄₂	+ 2
Telxon 7¹⁄₂12	100	78¹⁄₄	− ¹⁄₂
VLSI 8¹⁄₄05	200	93¹⁄₂	− ¹⁄₂

EXPLANATORY NOTES

(For New York and American Bonds) Yield is Current yield. cv-Convertible bond. cf-Certificates. cld-Called. dc-Deep discount. ec-European currency units. f-Dealt in flat. il-Italian lire. kd-Danish kroner. m-Matured bonds, negotiability impaired by maturity. na-No accrual. r-Registered. rp-Reduced principal. st, sd-Stamped. t-Floating rate. wd-When distributed. ww-With warrants. x-Ex interest. xw-Without warrants. zr-Zero coupon.

vi-In bankruptcy or receivership or being reorganized under the Bankruptcy Act, or securities assumed by such companies.

11.12 Summary and Conclusions

This chapter covers the important topic of corporate bonds, a major source of capital used by corporations. In this chapter we saw that:

1. A corporate bond represents a corporation's promise to pay bondholders a fixed sum of money at maturity, along with periodic payments of interest. The sum paid at maturity is the bond's principal, and the periodic interest payments are coupons. Most bonds pay fixed coupons, but some pay floating coupon rates adjusted regularly according to prevailing market interest rates.

2. Corporate bonds are usually callable, which means that the issuer has the right to buy back outstanding bonds before maturity. When a bond issue is called, bondholders surrender their bonds in exchange for a prespecified call price.

3. The largest category of corporate bond investors is life insurance companies, which own about a third of all outstanding corporate bonds. Remaining ownership shares are roughly equally distributed among individual investors, pension funds, banks, and foreign investors.

4. Debentures are the most common type of corporate bond. Debenture bonds represent the unsecured debt of a corporation. Mortgage bonds represent debt issued with a lien on specific property pledged as security for the bonds. Collateral trust bonds are characterized by a pledge of financial assets as security for a bond issue. Equipment trust certificates are issued according to a lease form of financing, where investors purchase equipment trust certificates and the proceeds from this sale are used to purchase equipment that is leased to a corporation.

5. A bond indenture is a formal agreement between the corporation and bondholders that spells out the legal rights and obligations of both parties with respect to a bond issue. An indenture typically specifies the seniority of a bond issue, along with any call provisions, put provisions, bond-to-stock conversion provisions, and sinking fund provisions.

6. When a corporation sells a new bond issue to the public, it usually has a credit rating assigned by several independent bond rating agencies. Without a credit rating, a new bond issue would be difficult to sell, which is why almost all bond issues sold to the public have credit ratings assigned.

7. Bonds with a speculative or lower grade rating, commonly called high-yield bonds, or junk bonds, represent corporate debt with higher than average credit risk. Credit ratings for junk bonds are frequently revised to reflect changing financial conditions.

8. The existence of an active secondary market for corporate bonds is important to most bond investors. More than 2,300 different bond issues are listed on the NYSE. These represent the most actively traded issues of large corporations. Many more thousands of different corporate debt issues trade in the OTC market. Indeed, the greatest total volume of bond trading occurs in the OTC market.

GET REAL

This chapter explored corporate bonds, an important type of investment for institutions such as life insurance companies and for individuals. It also covered convertible bonds and preferred stock. How should you put this information to work?

Now that you understand the most important features of corporate bonds, you need to buy a variety of them to experience the real-world gains and losses that come with managing a bond portfolio. So, with a simulated brokerage account (such as Stock-Trak), try putting equal (or approximately equal) dollar amounts in four or five different corporate issues. Be sure to include a range of credit ratings, including some junk bonds. To better understand the bonds you purchase, you should hit the library and look them up in a bond guide such as those published by Moody's and S&P. There you will find a brief description of the most important features.

As you monitor the prices of your bonds, notice how interest rates influence their values. You will also find, however, that for the lower quality issues, the stock price of the issuing company is an important influence. Why is this so?

You should also buy a couple of convertible bonds and several different preferred stocks. Once again, be sure to include a range of credit ratings.

With the convertible issues, the price will definitely be influenced by the underlying stock value, but the impact depends on whether the conversion feature is in the money or not, among other things. Once again, at the library, you can get the important features of the issue, including the conversion ratio. Find out whether your issues are in the money or not.

Key Terms

plain vanilla bonds 307
unsecured debt 307
debentures 307
mortgage bond 308
collateral trust bond 308
equipment trust certificate 308
indenture summary 310
prospectus 310
senior debentures 311
subordinated debentures 311
negative pledge clause 311
bond refunding 311
put bonds 313
convertible bonds 313
in-the-money bond 316

intrinsic bond value 317
exchangeable bonds 317
term bonds 317
serial bonds 317
sinking fund 319
protective covenants 321
event risk 322
private placement 322
preferred stock 323
adjustable-rate bonds 324
credit ratings 326
prudent investment guidelines 328
high-yield bonds 328

Chapter Review Problems and Self-Test

1. **Callable Bonds** A particular bond matures in 30 years. It is callable in 10 years at 110. The call price is cut by 1 percent of par each year until the call price reaches par. If the bond is called in 12 years, how much will you receive? Assume a $1,000 face value.

2. **Convertible Bonds** A convertible bond features a conversion ratio of 50. What is the conversion price? If the stock sells for $30 per share, what is the conversion value?

3. **Convertible Bonds** A convertible bond has an 8 percent coupon, paid semiannually, and will mature in 15 years. If the bond were not convertible, it would be priced to yield 9 percent. The conversion ratio on the bond is 40, and the stock is currently selling for $24 per share. What is the minimum value of this bond?

Answers to Self-Test Problems

1. The call price will be $110\% - 2 \times 1\% = 108\%$ of face value, or $1,080.

2. The conversion price is face value divided by the conversion ratio, $1,000/50 = $20. The conversion value is what the bond is worth on a converted basis, $50 \times $30 = $1,500.

3. The minimum value is the larger of the conversion value and the intrinsic bond value. The conversion value is $40 \times $24 = $960. To calculate the intrinsic bond value, note that we have a face value of $1,000 (by assumption), a semiannual coupon of $40, an annual yield of 9 percent (4.5 percent per half-year), and 15 years to maturity (30 half-years). Using the standard bond pricing formula from our previous chapter, the bond's price (be sure to verify this) if it were not convertible is $918.56. This convertible bond thus will sell for more than $960.

Test Your Investment Quotient

1. **Trust Certificates**   An airline elects to finance the purchase of some new airplanes using equipment trust certificates. Under the legal arrangement associated with such certificates, the airplanes are pledged as collateral, but which other factor applies? (*1990 CFA exam*)

    a. The airline still has legal title to the planes.
    b. Legal title to the planes resides with the manufacturer.
    c. The airline does not get legal title to the planes until the manufacturer is paid.
    d. Legal title to the planes resides with a third party, who then leases the planes to the airline.

2. **Callable Bonds**   What does the call feature of a bond mean? (*1988 CFA exam*)

    a. An investor can call for payment on demand.
    b. An investor can call only if the firm defaults on an interest payment.
    c. An issuer can call the bond issue prior to the maturity date.
    d. An issuer can call the issue during the first three years.

3. **Callable Bonds**   Who benefits from a call provision on a corporate bond? (*1989 CFA exam*)

    a. The issuer
    b. The bondholders
    c. The trustee
    d. Government regulators

4. **Callable Bonds**   Which of the following describes a bond with a call feature? (*1990 CFA exam*)

    a. It is attractive, because the immediate receipt of principal plus premium produces a high return.
    b. It is more likely to be called when interest rates are high, because the interest savings will be greater.
    c. It would usually have a higher yield than a similar noncallable bond.
    d. It generally has a higher credit rating than a similar noncallable bond.

5. **Convexity**   What does positive convexity on a bond imply? (*1991 CFA exam*)

    a. The direction of change in yield is directly related to the change in price.
    b. Prices increase at a faster rate as yields drop than they decrease as yields rise.
    c. Price changes are the same for both increases and decreases in yields.
    d. Prices increase and decrease at a faster rate than the change in yield.

6. **Indentures**   Which of the following is not a responsibility of a corporate trustee with regard to a bond's trust indenture? (*1992 CFA exam*)

    a. Checking compliance.
    b. Authenticating the bonds issued.
    c. Negotiating the terms.
    d. Declaring defaults.

7. **Refundings** The refunding provision of an indenture allows bonds to be retired unless: (*1989 CFA exam*)

   a. They are replaced with a new issue having a lower interest cost.
   b. The remaining time to maturity is less than five years.
   c. The stated time period in the indenture has not passed.
   d. The stated time period in the indenture has passed.

8. **Debentures** Holders of unsecured debentures with a negative pledge clause can claim which of the following assurances? (*1990 CFA exam*)

   a. No additional secured debt will be issued in the future.
   b. If any secured debt is issued in the future, the unsecured debentures must be redeemed at par.
   c. The debentures will be secured, but to a lesser degree than any secured debt issued in the future.
   d. The debentures will be secured at least equally with any secured debt issued in the future.

9. **Preferred Stock** Nonconvertible preferred stock has which of the following in comparison to common stock? (*1990 CFA exam*)

   a. Preferential claim on a company's earnings.
   b. A predetermined dividend rate.
   c. Preferential voting rights.
   d. All of the above.

10. **Preferred Stock** A preferred stock that is entitled to dividends in arrears is known as: (*1988 CFA exam*)

   a. Convertible
   b. Cumulative
   c. Extendible
   d. Participating

11. **Preferred Stock** Why does a firm's preferred stock often sell at yields below its bonds? (*1994 CFA exam*)

   a. Preferred stock generally carries a higher agency rating.
   b. Owners of preferred stock have a prior claim on the firm's earnings.
   c. Owners of preferred stock have a prior claim on the firm's assets in a liquidation.
   d. Corporations owning stock may exclude from income taxes most of the dividend income they receive.

12. **Convertible Bonds** Which one of the following statements about convertible bonds is true? (*1991 CFA exam*)

   a. The longer the call protection on a convertible, the less the security is worth.
   b. The more volatile the underlying stock, the greater the value of the conversion feature.
   c. The smaller the spread between the dividend yield on the stock and the yield to maturity on the bond, the more the convertible is worth.
   d. The collateral that is used to secure a convertible bond is one reason convertibles are more attractive than the underlying common stocks.

13. **Convertible Bonds** Which one of the following statements about convertible bonds is false? (*1993 CFA exam*)

   a. The yield on the convertible will typically be higher than the yield on the underlying common stock.
   b. The convertible bond will likely participate in a major upward movement in the price of the underlying common stock.
   c. Convertible bonds are typically secured by specific assets of the issuing company.
   d. A convertible bond can be valued as a straight bond with an attached option.

14. Convertible Bonds   Consider these possible advantages of convertible bonds for investors: (*1991 CFA exam*)

   i. The conversion feature enables the convertible to participate in major upward moves in the price of the underlying common stock.

   ii. The bonds are typically secured by specific assets of the issuing company.

   iii. Investors may redeem their bonds at the stated conversion price any time during the life of the issue.

   iv. The yield on the convertible will almost always be higher than the yield on the underlying common stock.

Which are true?

   a. i and ii only.
   b. ii and iii only.
   c. i and iii only.
   d. i and iv only.

15. Convertible Bonds   A convertible bond sells at $1,000 par with a conversion ratio of 40 and an accompanying stock price of $20 per share. The conversion price and conversion value are, respectively, (*1994 CFA exam*)

   a. $20 and $1,000
   b. $20 and $800
   c. $25 and $1,000
   d. $25 and $800

Questions and Problems

Core Questions

1. Bond Types   What are the four main types of corporate bonds?

2. Bond Features   What is a bond refunding? Is it the same thing as a call?

3. Callable Bonds   With regard to the call feature, what are call protection and the call premium? What typically happens to the call premium through time?

4. Put Bonds   What is a put bond? Is the put feature desirable from the investor's perspective? The issuer's?

5. Bond Yields   What is the impact on a bond's coupon rate from:

   a. A call feature?
   b. A put feature?

6. Convertible Bonds   A convertible bond has a $1,000 face value and a conversion ratio of 40. What is the conversion price?

7. Convertible Bonds   A convertible bond has a $1,000 face value and a conversion ratio of 80. If the stock sells for $10 per share, what is the conversion value?

8. Exchangeable Bonds   What is the difference between an exchangeable bond and a convertible bond?

9. Event Risk   What is event risk? In addition to protective covenants, what bond feature do you think best reduces or eliminates such risk?

10. Floaters   From the bondholder's perspective, what are the potential advantages and disadvantages of floating coupons?

Intermediate Questions

11. Put Bonds   What is the difference between put bonds and extendible bonds?

12. Callable Bonds   All else the same, callable bonds have less interest rate sensitivity than noncallable bonds. Why? Is this a good thing?

13. Convertible Bonds   A convertible bond has a 6 percent coupon, paid semiannually, and will mature in eight years. If the bond were not convertible, it would be priced to yield 9 percent. The conversion ratio on the bond is 20, and the stock is currently selling for $30 per share. What is the minimum value of this bond?

14. **Convertible Bonds** You own a convertible bond with a conversion ratio of 40. The stock is currently selling for $30 per share. The issuer of the bond has announced a call; the call price is 105. What are your options here? What should you do?

15. **Sinking Fund** Does the decision to include a sinking fund increase or decrease the coupon rate on a newly issued bond? Does your answer depend on the issuer?

16. **Inverse Floaters** An "inverse floater" is a bond with a coupon that is adjusted down when interest rates rise and up when rates fall. What is the impact of the floating coupon on the bond's price volatility?

STOCK-TRAK·
Portfolio Simulations

Trading Corporate Bonds with Stock-Trak

Stock-Trak supports trading in a select number of corporate bond issues. These bonds trade in sufficient volume for Stock-Trak to obtain timely price quotes. The list of available bonds changes from time to time, so you should consult the Stock-Trak website (www.mhhe.com/cj) for the most recent list. Ticker symbols for these bonds are not necessary, because Stock-Trak lists the bonds by issuer name, coupon, and maturity. These five bonds are shown as they were listed by Stock-Trak:

AT&T $8\frac{1}{8}$ 22

Ann Taylr $8\frac{3}{4}$ 10

Borden $8\frac{3}{8}$ 16

Chase M $6\frac{1}{8}$ 06

Converse 7s 04

Following standard practice, corporate bonds available for Stock-Trak trading have a face value denomination of $1,000 per bond.

Stock-Trak Exercises

1. Buy two different corporate bonds with maturities of at least 10 years. One bond should have a low coupon rate (but not a zero coupon) and the other should have a high coupon rate. Compare the two bonds by keeping a record of their weekly price changes.

2. Stock-Trak corporate bonds typically include several zero coupon issues. Two such bonds issued by Motorola and Office Depot were listed by Stock-Trak as

Motrla zr 13

Off Dep zr 08

Buy two zero coupon bonds and compare their performance by keeping a record of their weekly price changes.

12 Government Bonds

U.S. Treasury bonds are among the safest investments available because they are secured by the considerable taxing powers of the federal government. Many bonds issued by federal government agencies, and by state and local municipal governments, are also nearly free of default risk. Consequently, government bonds are generally excellent vehicles for conservative investment strategies seeking predictable investment results. ■ The largest and most important debt market is that for debt issued by the U.S. government. This market is truly global in character since a large share of federal debt is sold to foreign investors, and it thereby sets the tone for debt markets around the world. In contrast, the market for debt issued by states and municipalities is almost exclusively a domestic market since almost all U.S. municipal securities are owned by U.S. investors. These two broad categories make up the government bond market. In this chapter, we examine securities issued by federal, state, and local governments, which combined represent more than $7 trillion of oustanding securities.

12.1 Government Bond Basics

The U.S. federal government is the largest single borrower in the world. In 1999 the gross public debt of the U.S. government was more than $5 trillion. Part of this debt is financed internally, but the bulk is financed by the sale of a wide array of debt securities to the general public. Responsibility for managing outstanding government debt belongs to the U.S. Treasury, which acts as the financial agent of the federal government.

The U.S. Treasury finances government debt by issuing marketable securities and nonmarketable securities. Most of the gross public debt is financed by the sale of marketable securities at regularly scheduled Treasury auctions. Marketable securities include Treasury bills, Treasury notes, and Treasury bonds, often simply called T-bills, T-notes, and T-bonds, respectively. Outstanding marketable securities trade among investors in a large, active financial market called the Treasury market. Nonmarketable securities include U.S. Savings Bonds, Government Account Series, and State and Local Government Series. Many individuals are familiar with U.S. Savings Bonds since they are sold only to individual investors. Government Account Series are issued to federal government agencies and trust funds, in particular, the Social Security Administration trust fund. State and Local Government Series are purchased by municipal governments.

Treasury security ownership is registered with the U.S. Treasury. When an investor sells a U.S. Treasury security to another investor, registered ownership is officially transferred by notifying the U.S. Treasury of the transaction. However, only marketable securities allow registered ownership to be transferred. Nonmarketable securities do not allow a change of registered ownership and therefore cannot trade among investors. For example, a U.S. Savings Bond is a nonmarketable security. If an investor wishes to sell a U.S. Savings Bond, it must be redeemed by the U.S. Treasury. This is normally a simple procedure, since most banks handle the purchase and sale of U.S. Savings Bonds for their customers.

Another large market for government debt is the market for municipal government debt. There are more than 80,000 state and local governments in the United States, almost all of which have some form of outstanding debt. In a typical year, well over 10,000 new municipal debt issues are brought to market. Total municipal debt outstanding in the United States is about $2 trillion. Of this total, individual investors hold about half, either through direct purchase or indirectly through mutual funds. The remainder is split about equally between holdings of property and casualty insurance companies and commercial banks.

12.2 U.S. Treasury Bills, Notes, Bonds, and STRIPS

Treasury bills are short-term obligations that mature in one year or less. They are originally issued with maturities of 13, 26, or 52 weeks. A T-bill entitles its owner to receive a single payment at the bill's maturity, called the bill's **face value** or *redemption value.* The smallest denomination T-bill has a face value of $1,000. T-bills are sold on a **discount basis**, where a price is set at a discount from face value. For example, if a $10,000 bill is sold for $9,500, then it is sold at a discount of $500, or 5 percent. The discount represents the **imputed interest** on the bill.

face value The value of a bill, note, or bond at its maturity when a payment of principal is made. Also called *redemption value.*

discount basis
Method of selling a Treasury bill at a discount from face value.

imputed interest The interest paid on a Treasury bill determined by the size of its discount from face value.

STRIPS Treasury program allowing investors to buy individual coupon and principal payments from a whole Treasury note or bond. Acronym for *Separate Trading of Registered Interest and Principal of Securities.*

zero coupon bonds A note or bond paying a single cash flow at maturity. Also called *zeroes.*

Treasury notes are medium-term obligations with original maturities of 10 years or less, but more than 1 year. They are normally issued with original maturities of 2, 5, or 10 years, and they have face value denominations as small as $1,000. Besides a payment of face value at maturity, T-notes also pay semiannual coupons.

Treasury bonds are long-term obligations with much longer original-issue maturities. Since 1985, the Treasury has only issued T-bonds with a maturity of 30 years in its regular bond offerings. Like T-notes, T-bonds pay their face value at maturity, pay semiannual coupons, and have face value denominations as small as $1,000.

The coupon rate for T-notes and T-bonds is set according to interest rates prevailing at the time of issuance. For example, if the prevailing interest rate for a Treasury note of a certain maturity is 5 percent, then the coupon rate—that is, the annual coupon as a percentage of par value—for a new issue with that maturity is set at or near 5 percent. Thus, a $10,000 par value T-note paying a 5 percent coupon would pay two $250 coupons each year. Coupon payments normally begin six months after issuance and continue to be paid every six months until the last coupon is paid along with the face value at maturity. Once set, the coupon rate remains constant throughout the life of a U.S. Treasury note or bond.

Treasury STRIPS are derived from Treasury notes originally issued with maturities of 10 years and from Treasury bonds issued with 30-year maturities. Since 1985, the U.S. Treasury has sponsored the **STRIPS** program, an acronym for *Separate Trading of Registered Interest and Principal of Securities.* This program allows brokers to divide Treasury bonds and notes into *coupon strips* and *principal strips,* thereby allowing investors to buy and sell the strips of their choice. Principal strips represent face-value payments and coupon strips represent coupon payments. For example, a 30-year maturity T-bond can be separated into 61 strips, representing 60 semiannual coupon payments and a single face value payment. Under the Treasury STRIPS program, each of these strips can be separately registered to different owners.

The terms "STRIPS" and "strips" can sometimes cause confusion. The acronym STRIPS is used when speaking specifically about the Treasury STRIPS program. However, the term *strips* now popularly refers to any separate part of a note or bond issue broken down into its component parts. In this generic form, the term strips is acceptable.

Since each strip created under the STRIPS program represents a single future payment, STRIPS securities effectively become **zero coupon bonds** and are commonly called *zeroes.* The unique characteristics of Treasury zeroes make them an interesting investment choice. The potential benefits of STRIPS in an investor's portfolio are discussed in *The Wall Street Journal* article reprinted in the nearby Investment Updates box.

The yield to maturity of a zero coupon bond is the interest rate that an investor will receive if the bond is held until it matures. Table 12.1 lists bond prices for zero coupon bonds with a face value of $10,000, maturities of 5, 10, 20, and 30 years, and yields from 3 percent to 15 percent. As shown, a $10,000 face-value zero coupon bond with a term to maturity of 20 years and an 8 percent yield has a price of $2,082.89.

Figure 12.1 graphs prices of zero coupon bonds with a face value of $10,000. The vertical axis measures bond prices and the horizontal axis measures bond maturities. Bond prices for yields of 4, 8, and 12 percent are illustrated.

Table 12.1	Zero Coupon Bond Prices, $10,000 Face Value			
			Bond Maturity	
Yield to Maturity	**5 Years**	**10 Years**	**20 Years**	**30 Years**
3.0%	$8,616.67	$7,424.70	$5,512.62	$4,092.96
3.5	8,407.29	7,068.25	4,996.01	3,531.30
4.0	8,203.48	6,729.71	4,528.90	3,047.82
4.5	8,005.10	6,408.16	4,106.46	2,631.49
5.0	7,811.98	6,102.71	3,724.31	2,272.84
5.5	7,623.98	5,812.51	3,378.52	1,963.77
6.0	7,440.94	5,536.76	3,065.57	1,697.33
6.5	7,262.72	5,274.71	2,782.26	1,467.56
7.0	7,089.19	5,025.66	2,525.72	1,269.34
7.5	6,920.20	4,788.92	2,293.38	1,098.28
8.0	6,755.64	4,563.87	2,082.89	950.60
8.5	6,595.37	4,349.89	1,892.16	823.07
9.0	6,439.28	4,146.43	1,719.29	712.89
9.5	6,287.23	3,952.93	1,562.57	617.67
10.0	6,139.13	3,768.89	1,420.46	535.36
10.5	5,994.86	3,593.83	1,291.56	464.17
11.0	5,854.31	3,427.29	1,174.63	402.58
11.5	5,717.37	3,268.83	1,068.53	349.28
12.0	5,583.95	3,118.05	972.22	303.14
12.5	5,453.94	2,974.55	884.79	263.19
13.0	5,327.26	2,837.97	805.41	228.57
13.5	5,203.81	2,707.96	733.31	198.58
14.0	5,083.49	2,584.19	667.80	172.57
14.5	4,966.23	2,466.35	608.29	150.02
15.0	4,851.94	2,354.13	554.19	130.46

Figure 12.1	Zero Coupon Bond Prices ($10,000 Face Value)

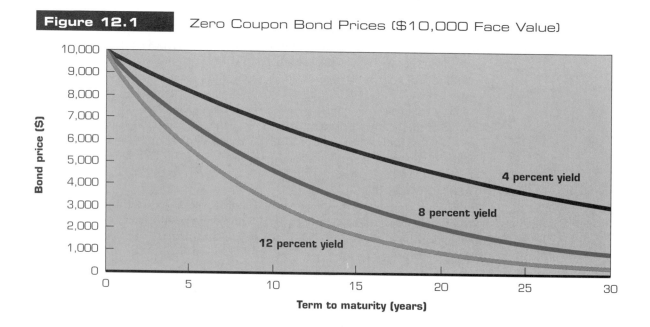

Zero-Coupon Bonds Offer Safety Net

With stock prices at dizzying levels, many individual investors are understandably nervous about keeping their balance if the long bull market suddenly stumbles.

But the traditional safety-net strategy of shifting some money into certificates of deposit and conventional bonds, or simply putting new money into such fixed-income investments, can seem fairly ho-hum.

For people looking for added security but with a touch of pizazz, some advisers are recommending long-term zero-coupon Treasury bonds, or "strips," as they are known.

Strips, which are created by investment firms that split Treasury bonds from their coupon payments, are sold at deep discounts to their face value. They don't make periodic interest payments. Instead, their value builds over the years, guaranteeing a predetermined compound rate of return to investors who hang on until maturity.

Along the way, prices of zero-coupon bonds can gyrate violently, rising sharply when interest rates fall and plunging when rates rise.

But for investors who can afford to wait out the price dips, the prospect of handsome profits if rates drift lower makes zeros a safety net with the bounce of a trampoline. "Your downside is protected, but your upside is unknown," says James E. Wilton, a Columbia, S.C., financial planner.

The best time to invest in strips is just after the bond market gets pummeled, when prices are low and yields are high. But even at today's prices, Treasury strips could deliver higher returns than stocks during the next few years, with considerably less risk, argues James Floyd, senior research analyst at Leuthold Group in Minneapolis.

The Ups and Downs Annual return on a new 20-year zero-coupon Treasury bond purchased with a yield of 7% and sold after one, three or five years when interest rates have fallen or risen.

Time Held	Gain at 6.5% Yield	Gain/Loss at 8% Yield
One year	21%	−7%
Three years	11	3
Five years	9	5

Source: The Leuthold Group.

Suppose you want at least $100,000 when you retire 20 years from now. You can buy 100 20-year Treasury strips, each with a face value of $1,000. Your cost: about $25,000, including a broker's markup of some $675. Your yield would be about 7%.

If rates drop this year, with new strips yielding 6.5%, you could sell yours, pocketing a 21% gain.

Of course, if interest rates rocket higher, with new strips yielding 8%, you would lose 7% if you sold. But even that would hurt less than a 10% to 35% plunge in the stock market, which Mr. Floyd figures is as much as stock prices could fall.

And if you held the strips until they matured—or until rates fell again—you would be guaranteed to gain. Stocks offer no such assurance.

CHECK THIS

12.2a What are some possible reasons why individual investors might prefer to buy Treasury STRIPS rather than common stocks?

12.2b What are some possible reasons why individual investors might prefer to buy individual Treasury STRIPS rather than whole T-notes or T-bonds?

12.2c For zero coupon bonds with the same face value and yield to maturity, is the price of a zero with a 15-year maturity larger or smaller than the average price of two zeroes with maturities of 10 years and 20 years? Why?

Treasury Bond and Note Prices

Figure 12.2 displays a partial *Wall Street Journal* listing of prices and other relevant information for Treasury securities. Notice that Treasury notes and bonds are listed together, but there are separate sections for Treasury bills and Treasury STRIPS. The sections for Treasury bills and STRIPS were discussed in detail in Chapter 9. We discuss the section for Treasury notes and bonds next.

Treasury bond and note price quotes are stated on a percentage of par basis where, for example, a price of 102 equals par value plus 2 percent. Fractions of a percent are stated in thirty-seconds. Thus a price stated as 102:28 is actually equal to 102 + 28/32, or 102.875. To illustrate, the first column in the section for notes and bonds in Figure 12.2 states the annual coupon rate. The next two columns report maturity in month–year format. Dealer bid and asked price quotes come next, followed by changes in ask quotes from the previous day. The last column gives the yield to maturity implied by an asked price quote. The letter *n* next to various maturity dates indicates a T-note. The absence of the letter *n* indicates a T-bond.

The quoted maturities for certain T-bonds have two years listed. For example, look at the bond issue with a maturity listed as Nov 09-14. This means that the bond matures in November 2014, but it is callable at par value any time after November 2009. When a T-bond is called, bondholders surrender their bonds to receive a cash payment equal to the bond's par value. Because the Nov 09-14 bond pays an 11.75 percent coupon but has a much lower yield to maturity, this bond has a price well above par value. It is likely that this bond will be called at its earliest possible call date in November 2009. Therefore, the reported asked yield is actually a yield to call. A **yield to call (YTC)** is the interest rate for a bond assuming the bond will be called at its earliest possible call date and the bondholder will hold the bond until it is called. When a callable T-bond has a price above par, the reported yield is a yield to call.

yield to call (YTC)
The interest rate on a bond that assumes the bond will be called at its earliest possible call date.

Since 1985, the Treasury has issued only noncallable bonds. Thus, the cluster of callable bonds in Figure 12.2 were all issued before 1985, and all listed bonds with a maturity of 2015 or later are noncallable bonds issued in 1985 or later.

Since Treasury bonds and notes pay semiannual coupons, bond yields are stated on a semiannual basis. The relationship between the price of a note or bond and its yield to maturity was discussed in Chapter 10. For convenience, the bond price formula from that chapter is restated here:

$$\text{Bond price} = \frac{\text{Annual coupon}}{YTM} \times \left[1 - \frac{1}{(1 + YTM/2)^{2M}}\right] + \frac{\text{Face value}}{(1 + YTM/2)^{2M}}$$

Figure 12.3 illustrates the relationship between the price of a bond and its yield to maturity for 2-year, 7-year, and 30-year terms to maturity. Notice that each bond has a price of 100 when its yield is 8 percent. This indicates that each bond has an 8 percent coupon rate, because when a bond's coupon rate is equal to its yield to maturity, its price is equal to its par value.

bid-ask spread The difference between a dealer's ask price and bid price.

The difference between a dealer's asked and bid prices is called the **bid-ask spread**. The bid-ask spread measures the dealer's gross profit from a single round-trip transaction of buying a security at the bid price and then selling it at the asked price.

Figure 12.2

U.S. Treasury Securities

Source: Reprinted with permission from *The Wall Street Journal,* via Copyright Clearance Center, January 14, 1999. © 1999 Dow Jones & Company, Inc. All Rights Reserved Worldwide.

TREASURY BONDS, NOTES & BILLS

Wednesday, January 13, 1999

Representative and Indicative Over-the-Counter quotations based on $1 million or more.

Treasury bond, note and bill quotes are as of mid-afternoon. Colons in bond and note bid-and-asked quotes represent 32nds; 101:01 means 101 1/32. Net changes in 32nds. Treasury bill quotes in hundredths, quoted in terms of a rate discount. Days to maturity calculated from settlement date. All yields are to maturity and based on the asked quote. Most recently auctioned treasury bonds and notes, and current 13-week and 26-week bills are boldfaced. For bonds callable prior to maturity, yields are computed to the earliest call date for issues quoted above par and to the maturity date for issues quoted below par. n-Treasury note. i-Inflation-indexed. wi-When issued. iw-Inflation-indexed when issued; daily change is expressed in basis points.

Source: Dow Jones/Cantor Fitzgerald.

U.S. Treasury strips as of 3 p.m. Eastern time, also based on transactions of $1 million or more. Colons in bid-and-asked quotes represent 32nds; 99:01 means 99 1/32. Net changes in 32nds. Yields calculated on the asked quotation. ci-stripped coupon interest. bp-Treasury bond, stripped principal. np-Treasury note, stripped principal. For bonds callable prior to maturity, yields are computed to the earliest call date for issues quoted above par and to the maturity date for issues below par.

Source: Bear, Stearns & Co. via Street Software Technology Inc.

GOVT. BONDS & NOTES

Rate	Maturity Mo./Yr.	Bid	Asked	Chg.	Ask Yld.
5 5/8	Feb 06n	104:29	104:31	+16	4.79
9 3/8	Feb 06	126:27	127:01	+19	4.83
6 7/8	May 06n	112:13	112:17	+18	4.82
7	Jul 06n	113:06	113:10	+16	4.86
6 1/2	Oct 06n	110:11	110:13	+17	4.87
3 3/8	Jan 07i	96:23	96:24	+2	3.85
6 1/4	Feb 07n	109:03	109:05	+18	4.87
7 5/8	Feb 02-07	107:28	107:30	+8	4.83
6 5/8	May 07n	111:26	111:30	+19	4.86
6 1/8	Aug 07n	108:20	108:22	+18	4.87
7 7/8	Nov 02-07	110:18	110:22	+9	4.79
3 5/8	Jan 08i	98:13	98:14	+5	3.83
5 1/2	Feb 08n	105:05	105:07	+19	4.78
5 5/8	May 08n	105:29	105:30	+21	4.83
8 3/8	Aug 03-08	114:07	114:11	+12	4.85
4 3/4	**Nov 08n**	**100:05**	**100:06**	**+22**	**4.73**
8 3/4	Nov 03-08	116:04	116:08	+13	4.93
3 7/8	Jan 09i	100:20	100:21	+1	3.80
9 1/8	May 04-09	119:08	119:12	+11	4.95
10 3/8	Nov 04-09	127:04	127:10	+15	4.93
11 3/4	Feb 05-10	135:07	135:13	+16	4.95
10	May 05-10	126:31	127:05	+16	4.95
12 3/4	Nov 05-10	144:18	144:24	+20	4.95
13 7/8	May 06-11	153:31	154:05	+20	4.97
14	Nov 06-11	157:20	157:26	+23	4.99
10 3/8	Nov 07-12	137:09	137:15	+21	5.06
12	Aug 08-13	151:27	152:01	+28	5.08
13 1/4	May 09-14	164:19	164:25	+29	5.10
12 1/2	Aug 09-14	159:19	159:25	+28	5.12
11 3/4	Nov 09-14	154:15	154:21	+27	5.11
11 1/4	Feb 15	163:10	163:16	+35	5.33
10 5/8	Aug 15	156:31	157:05	+33	5.38
9 7/8	Nov 15	148:26	149:00	+33	5.40
9 1/4	Feb 16	142:05	142:11	+32	5.42
7 1/4	May 16	120:05	120:09	+29	5.43
7 1/2	Nov 16	123:05	123:11	+30	5.44
8 3/4	May 17	137:31	138:05	+34	5.44
8 7/8	Aug 17	139:22	139:28	+34	5.44
9 1/8	May 18	143:14	143:20	+35	5.45
9	Nov 18	142:16	142:22	+37	5.45
8 7/8	Feb 19	141:04	141:10	+34	5.46
8 1/8	Aug 19	132:11	132:17	+33	5.47
8 1/2	Feb 20	137:12	137:18	+34	5.48
8 3/4	May 20	140:24	140:30	+36	5.47
8 3/4	Aug 20	140:30	141:04	+35	5.48
7 7/8	Feb 21	130:08	130:14	+34	5.48
8 1/8	May 21	133:19	133:25	+34	5.48
8 1/8	Aug 21	133:26	134:00	+35	5.48
8	Nov 21	132:14	132:20	+34	5.48
7 1/4	Aug 22	123:05	123:11	+33	5.48
7 5/8	Nov 22	128:09	128:15	+35	5.47
7 1/8	Feb 23	121:27	122:01	+32	5.47
6 1/4	Aug 23	110:17	110:19	+32	5.46
7 1/2	Nov 24	128:05	128:11	+34	5.44
7 5/8	Feb 25	130:05	130:11	+37	5.44
6 7/8	Aug 25	119:30	120:02	+35	5.44
6	Feb 26	107:30	108:00	+32	5.43
6 3/4	Aug 26	118:17	118:21	+35	5.44
6 1/2	Nov 26	115:03	115:07	+35	5.43
6 5/8	Feb 27	117:00	117:04	+36	5.43
6 3/8	Aug 27	113:23	113:27	+35	5.42
6 1/8	Nov 27	110:22	110:24	+34	5.39
3 5/8	Apr 28i	98:10	98:11	-2	3.72
5 1/2	Aug 28	103:17	103:18	+35	5.26
5 1/4	**Nov 28**	**101:17**	**101:18**	**+36**	**5.15**

U.S. TREASURY STRIPS

Mat.	Type	Bid	Asked	Chg.	Ask Yld.
Feb 99	ci	99:19	99:19	....	4.79
Feb 05	ci	74:19	74:23	+10	4.85
Feb 05	np	74:25	74:29	+10	4.81
Aug 05	ci	72:25	72:29	+10	4.86
Aug 05	bp	72:18	72:22	+10	4.90
Aug 05	np	73:09	73:14	+10	4.75
Nov 05	ci	72:00	72:05	+10	4.84
Nov 05	np	72:15	72:20	+10	4.74
Feb 06	ci	70:26	70:31	+13	4.90
Feb 06	bp	71:04	71:09	+13	4.84
Feb 06	np	71:12	71:17	+13	4.79
May 06	ci	69:31	70:04	+13	4.90
Aug 06	ci	69:08	69:13	+13	4.88
Nov 06	ci	68:18	68:23	+14	4.85
Feb 07	ci	67:06	67:11	+13	4.95
May 07	ci	66:13	66:18	+13	4.95
Aug 07	ci	65:20	65:26	+13	4.94
Nov 07	ci	65:02	65:07	+14	4.90
Feb 08	ci	63:17	63:22	+13	5.03
May 08	ci	62:22	62:27	+13	5.04
Aug 08	ci	61:29	62:02	+13	5.04
Nov 08	ci	60:26	60:31	+12	5.10
Feb 09	ci	59:22	59:27	+11	5.16
May 09	ci	58:25	58:31	+10	5.18
Aug 09	ci	57:28	58:02	+11	5.20
Nov 09	ci	57:00	57:06	+10	5.23
Nov 09	bp	56:14	56:19	+10	5.32
Feb 10	ci	56:02	56:08	+10	5.26
May 10	ci	55:07	55:13	+10	5.28
Aug 10	ci	54:11	54:17	+10	5.30
Nov 10	ci	53:17	53:23	+10	5.32
Feb 11	ci	52:21	52:27	+12	5.35
May 11	ci	51:27	52:01	+12	5.37
Aug 11	ci	51:01	51:07	+12	5.39
Nov 11	ci	50:07	50:13	+11	5.41
Feb 12	ci	49:13	49:19	+11	5.43
May 12	ci	48:20	48:27	+12	5.45
Aug 12	ci	47:27	48:01	+11	5.47
Nov 12	ci	47:03	47:09	+11	5.49
Feb 13	ci	46:09	46:15	+11	5.51
May 13	ci	45:18	45:24	+11	5.53
Aug 13	ci	44:27	45:01	+11	5.55
Nov 13	ci	44:05	44:11	+12	5.56
Feb 14	ci	43:14	43:20	+12	5.57
May 14	ci	42:24	42:30	+12	5.59
Aug 14	ci	42:02	42:08	+12	5.61
Nov 14	ci	41:13	41:19	+12	5.62
Feb 15	ci	40:24	40:30	+12	5.63
Feb 15	bp	41:03	41:09	+1	5.58
May 15	ci	40:03	40:09	+11	5.64
Aug 15	ci	39:14	39:20	+10	5.66
Aug 15	bp	39:14	39:20	+2	5.66
Nov 15	ci	38:26	39:00	+9	5.68
Nov 15	bp	38:19	38:26	+3	5.70
Feb 16	ci	38:05	38:11	+7	5.69
Feb 16	bp	38:05	38:11	+6	5.69
May 16	ci	37:19	37:25	+8	5.70
May 16	bp	37:27	38:01	+11	5.66
Aug 16	ci	37:01	37:07	+9	5.70
Nov 16	ci	36:16	36:22	+9	5.70
Nov 16	bp	36:25	36:31	+11	5.66
Feb 17	ci	35:30	36:04	+9	5.71
May 17	ci	35:14	35:20	+9	5.71
May 17	bp	35:18	35:24	+9	5.69
Aug 17	ci	34:30	35:04	+9	5.71
Aug 17	bp	35:02	35:08	+9	5.69
Nov 17	ci	34:14	34:20	+9	5.71
Feb 18	ci	33:31	34:05	+10	5.71
May 18	ci	33:16	33:22	+10	5.71
May 18	bp	33:17	33:23	+9	5.70
Aug 18	ci	33:03	33:09	+10	5.70
Nov 18	ci	32:17	32:23	+10	5.71
Nov 18	bp	32:19	32:25	+10	5.70
Feb 19	ci	32:00	32:06	+10	5.72
Feb 19	bp	32:04	32:10	+10	5.70
May 19	ci	31:19	31:25	+10	5.72
Aug 19	ci	31:04	31:10	+9	5.72
Aug 19	bp	31:08	31:14	+10	5.70
May 20	ci	29:28	30:02	+10	5.72
May 20	bp	29:30	30:04	+10	5.71
Aug 20	ci	29:14	29:20	+10	5.72
Aug 20	bp	29:16	29:22	+9	5.70
Nov 20	ci	29:01	29:07	+10	5.72
Feb 21	ci	28:20	28:26	+10	5.72
Feb 21	bp	28:26	29:00	+10	5.68
May 21	ci	28:08	28:14	+10	5.71
May 21	bp	28:11	28:17	+10	5.70
Aug 21	ci	27:28	28:02	+10	5.70
Aug 21	bp	28:00	28:06	+10	5.68
Nov 21	ci	27:18	27:24	+10	5.70
Nov 21	bp	27:22	27:28	+10	5.68
Feb 22	ci	27:07	27:13	+10	5.69
May 22	ci	26:28	27:02	+10	5.68
Aug 22	ci	26:17	26:23	+10	5.68
Aug 22	bp	26:27	27:01	+10	5.63
Nov 22	ci	26:06	26:12	+10	5.67
Nov 22	bp	26:14	26:20	+10	5.63
Feb 23	ci	26:01	26:07	+10	5.64
Feb 23	bp	26:09	26:15	+10	5.59
May 23	ci	25:24	25:29	+10	5.63
Aug 23	ci	25:15	25:21	+10	5.61
Aug 23	bp	25:27	26:01	+11	5.55
Nov 23	ci	25:05	25:11	+10	5.61
Feb 24	ci	25:08	25:14	+19	5.53
May 24	ci	24:21	24:27	+10	5.57
Aug 24	ci	24:11	24:17	+10	5.57
Nov 24	ci	24:04	24:10	+10	5.55
Nov 24	bp	24:11	24:17	+10	5.52
Feb 25	ci	23:30	24:04	+10	5.53
Feb 25	bp	24:03	24:09	+10	5.50
May 25	ci	23:20	23:26	+10	5.53
Aug 25	ci	23:10	23:16	+10	5.52
Aug 25	bp	23:15	23:21	+10	5.50
Nov 25	ci	23:03	23:08	+10	5.51
Feb 26	ci	22:21	22:26	+10	5.53
Feb 26	bp	23:01	23:07	+10	5.47
May 26	ci	22:12	22:18	+10	5.53
Aug 26	ci	22:03	22:09	+10	5.52
Aug 26	bp	22:10	22:16	+10	5.48
Nov 26	ci	21:27	22:01	+10	5.51
Nov 26	bp	22:01	22:06	+10	5.48
Feb 27	ci	21:18	21:24	+10	5.51
Feb 27	bp	21:27	22:01	+10	5.46
May 27	ci	21:07	21:13	+10	5.51
Aug 27	ci	21:08	21:14	+10	5.46
Aug 27	bp	21:19	21:24	+10	5.41
Nov 27	ci	21:19	21:24	+10	5.36
Nov 27	bp	21:23	21:29	+10	5.34

TREASURY BILLS

Maturity	Days to Mat.	Bid	Asked	Chg.	Ask Yld.
Jan 21 '99	7	4.94	4.86	+0.04	4.93
Jan 28 '99	14	4.52	4.44	−0.01	4.51
Feb 04 '99	21	4.66	4.58	−0.08	4.66
Feb 11 '99	28	4.53	4.45	+0.01	4.53
Feb 18 '99	35	4.49	4.45	−0.01	4.53
Feb 25 '99	42	4.48	4.44	....	4.53
Mar 04 '99	49	4.49	4.45	....	4.54
Mar 11 '99	56	4.43	4.39	−0.03	4.48
Mar 18 '99	63	4.39	4.37	−0.04	4.46
Mar 25 '99	70	4.38	4.36	−0.05	4.46
Apr 01 '99	77	4.37	4.35	−0.04	4.45
Apr 08 '99	84	4.34	4.32	−0.03	4.42
Apr 15 '99	**91**	**4.35**	**4.34**	**−0.03**	**4.45**
Apr 22 '99	98	4.34	4.32	−0.05	4.43
Apr 29 '99	105	4.33	4.31	−0.05	4.43
May 06 '99	112	4.33	4.31	−0.04	4.43
May 13 '99	119	4.27	4.25	−0.03	4.37
May 20 '99	126	4.31	4.29	−0.06	4.42
May 27 '99	133	4.32	4.30	−0.06	4.43
Jun 03 '99	140	4.29	4.27	−0.07	4.40
Jun 10 '99	147	4.29	4.27	−0.07	4.41
Jun 17 '99	154	4.28	4.26	−0.07	4.40
Jun 24 '99	161	4.26	4.24	−0.09	4.38
Jul 01 '99	168	4.26	4.24	−0.09	4.39
Jul 08 '99	175	4.26	4.24	−0.09	4.39
Jul 15 '99	**182**	**4.25**	**4.24**	**−0.09**	**4.39**
Jul 22 '99	189	4.26	4.24	−0.08	4.39
Aug 19 '99	217	4.25	4.23	−0.09	4.39
Sep 16 '99	245	4.26	4.24	−0.09	4.40
Oct 14 '99	273	4.27	4.25	−0.10	4.42
Nov 12 '99	302	4.29	4.27	−0.09	4.45
Dec 09 '99	329	4.29	4.27	−0.10	4.46
Jan 06 '00	357	4.25	4.24	−0.10	4.44

INFLATION-INDEXED TREASURY SECURITIES

Rate	Mat.	Bid/Asked	Chg.	*Yld.	Accr. Prin.
3.625	07/02	99-18/19	+03	3.740	1024
3.375	01/07	96-23/24	+02	3.841	1035
3.625	01/08	98-13/14	+05	3.823	1015
3.875	01/09	100-20/21	+01	3.792	1000

Figure 12.3   Bond Prices ($10,000 Face Value)

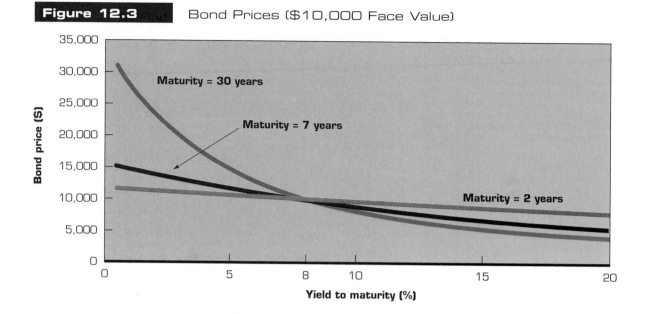

12.2d What would Figure 12.3 look like if the three bonds all had coupon rates of 6 percent or had coupon rates of 10 percent?

12.2e In Figure 12.2, which Treasury issues have the narrowest spreads? Why do you think this is so?

12.2f Examine the spreads between bid and asked prices for Treasury notes and bonds listed in a recent *Wall Street Journal.*

Inflation-Indexed Treasury Securities

In recent years, the U.S. Treasury has issued securities that guarantee a fixed rate of return in excess of realized inflation rates. These inflation-indexed Treasury securities pay a fixed coupon rate on their current principal and adjust their principal semiannually according to the most recent inflation rate.

For example, suppose an inflation-indexed note is issued with a coupon rate of 3.5 percent and an initial principal of $1,000. Six months later, the note will pay a coupon of $1,000 \times 3.5\%/2 = \$17.50$. Assuming 2 percent inflation over the six months since issuance, the note's principal is then increased to $1,000 \times 102\% = \$1,020$. Six months later, the note pays $1,020 \times 3.5\%/2 = \$17.85$ and its principal is again adjusted to compensate for recent inflation.

Price and yield information for inflation-indexed Treasury securities is reported in *The Wall Street Journal* in the same section with other Treasury securities, as shown in Figure 12.2. Locating the listing for inflation-indexed Treasury securities in Figure 12.2, we see that the first and second columns report the fixed coupon rate and maturity, respectively. The third and fourth columns report current bid/ask prices and the price change from the previous trading day. Prices for inflation-indexed securities are reported as a percentage of current accrued principal. The fifth and sixth columns list an inflation-adjusted yield to maturity and current accrued principal reflecting all cumulative inflation adjustments.

12.3 U.S. Treasury Auctions

The Federal Reserve Bank conducts regularly scheduled auctions for Treasury bills, notes, and bonds. Specifically, 13- and 26-week bills are auctioned on a weekly basis and 52-week bills are auctioned every four weeks. Two-year notes are auctioned monthly; longer maturity notes are auctioned each quarter. Bonds are sold three times per year. A statement regarding the face value quantity of bills, notes, or bonds to be offered is announced before each auction. Table 12.2 summarizes the auction schedule and purchase conditions for U.S. Treasury securities. However, from time to time the Treasury may change this schedule slightly.

At each Treasury auction, the Federal Reserve accepts sealed bids of two types: competitive bids and noncompetitive bids. Competitive bids for T-bills specify a bid price and a bid quantity. The bid price is what the bidder is willing to pay and the bid quantity is the face value amount that the bidder will purchase if the bid is accepted. Noncompetitive bids specify only a bid quantity since the price charged to noncompetitive bidders will be determined by the results of the competitive auction process. Individual investors can submit noncompetitive bids, but only Treasury securities dealers can submit competitive bids.

At the close of bidding, all sealed bids are forwarded to the U.S. Treasury for processing. As a first step, all noncompetitive bids are accepted automatically and are subtracted from the total issue amount. Then a **stop-out bid** is determined; this is the price at which all competitive bids are sufficient to finance the remaining issue amount. Competitive bids at or above the stop-out bid are accepted and bids below the stop-out bid are rejected.

stop-out bid The lowest competitive bid in a U.S. Treasury auction that is accepted.

Since 1998, all U.S. Treasury auctions have been single-price auctions in which all accepted competitive bids pay the stop-out bid. The stop-out bid is also the price paid by noncompetitive bidders. For example, suppose an auction for T-bills with $20 billion of face value receives $28 billion of competitive bids and $4 billion of noncompetitive bids. Noncompetitive bids are automatically accepted, leaving $16 billion for competitive bidders. Now suppose the stop-out bid for this $16 billion amount is $9,700 for a $10,000 face-value T-bill. Accepted competitive bidders and all noncompetitive bidders pay this price of $9,700.

Table 12.2	General Auction Pattern for U.S. Treasury Securities		
Security	Purchase Minimum	Purchase in Multiples of	General Auction Schedule
13-week bill	$1,000	$1,000	Weekly
26-week bill	1,000	1,000	Weekly
52-week bill	1,000	1,000	Every 4 weeks
2-year note	1,000	1,000	Monthly
5-year note	1,000	1,000	February, May, August, November
10-year note	1,000	1,000	February, May, August, November
30-year bond	1,000	1,000	February, August, November

The process is similar for T-bond and T-note issues, except that bids are made on a yield basis, where competitive bids state yields instead of prices. A coupon rate for the entire issue is then set according to the average competitive-bid yield.

CHECK THIS

12.3a The Federal Reserve announces an offering of Treasury bills with a face value amount of $25 billion. The response is $5 billion of noncompetitive bids, along with the following competitive bids:

Bidder	Price Bid	Quantity Bid
A	$9,500	$5 billion
B	9,550	5 billion
C	9,600	5 billion
D	9,650	5 billion
E	9,700	5 billion

In a single-price auction, which bids are accepted and what prices are paid by each bidder? How much money is raised by the entire offering?

12.4 U.S. Savings Bonds

The U.S. Treasury offers an interesting investment opportunity for individual investors in the form of savings bonds. Two types of savings bonds are currently available, Series EE and Series I. Other types exist, but they are either no longer available or can be obtained only by converting one type for another. For more information, you should consult the official U.S. Savings Bonds website (www.savingsbonds.gov), or the Bureau of Public Debt website (www.publicdebt.treas.gov).

Series EE Savings Bonds

Series EE bonds are available in face value denominations ranging from $50 to $10,000, but the original price of a Series EE bond is always set at exactly half its face value. Thus, Series EE bonds are sold to resemble zero coupon securities. However, individuals purchasing Series EE bonds receive semiannual interest accruals. Each May 1 and November 1, the Treasury sets the interest rate on EE bonds at 90 percent of the yield on newly issued five-year maturity T-notes. For example, suppose the yield on newly issued five-year maturity T-notes is 5.56 percent. In this case, the Treasury will set an interest rate of $.90 \times 5.56\% = 5.0\%$ on savings bonds for the next six months. This interest is paid as an accrual to the redemption value of the bond, where the current redemption value is the original price of the bond plus all prior accrued interest.

Series I Savings Bonds

Series I bonds are also available in face value denominations ranging from $50 to $10,000, but they are originally sold at face value. Each May 1 and November 1, the Treasury sets the interest rate on Series I bonds at a fixed rate plus the recent inflation rate. In this way, Series I bonds are indexed to inflation. For example, suppose the fixed rate is 3 percent, and the recent inflation rate is 2 percent. In this case, the Treasury will set an interest rate of $3\% + 2\% = 5\%$ for the next six months. This interest is paid as an accrual to the redemption value of the bond.

Savings bonds offer several tax advantages to individual investors. First, as with all U.S. Treasury securities, savings bonds are not subject to state or local taxes. Also, federal income tax payment on U.S. Savings Bond interest is deferred until the bonds are redeemed. With all factors considered, their overall attractiveness has led individual investors to hold almost $200 billion of U.S. Savings Bonds.

CHECK THIS

12.4a Compare the methods by which interest is paid for Series I savings bonds and inflation-indexed Treasury securities.

12.5 Federal Government Agency Securities

Most U.S. government agencies consolidate their borrowing through the Federal Financing Bank, which obtains funds directly from the U.S. Treasury. However, several federal agencies are authorized to issue securities directly to the public. For example, the Resolution Trust Funding Corporation, the World Bank, and the Tennessee Valley Authority issue notes and bonds directly to investors. Bonds issued by U.S. government agencies share an almost equal credit quality with U.S. Treasury issues. Although most agency debt does not carry an explicit guarantee of the U.S. government, a federal agency on the verge of default would probably receive government support to ensure timely payment of interest and principal on outstanding debt. This perception is supported by historical experience and the political reality that Congress would likely feel compelled to rescue an agency that it created if it became financially distressed.

What makes government agency notes and bonds attractive to many investors is that they offer higher yields than comparable U.S. Treasury securities. However, the market for agency debt is less active than the market for U.S. Treasury debt, and therefore the spread between dealers' bid and asked prices is greater for agency issues than for Treasury issues. For example, Figure 12.4 presents dealer price quotes for agency issues as reported in *The Wall Street Journal*. The listing format is the same as for Treasury notes and bonds described previously, except that callable bonds are indicated by an asterisk with only the maturity date shown.

If you compare bid and asked dealer price quotes for agency bonds listed in Figure 12.4 with similar Treasury bonds listed in Figure 12.2, you will find that agency bonds have a higher bid-ask spread than Treasury bonds. The reason for the higher bid-ask spread is that agency bond trading volume is much lower than Treasury bond trading volume. To compensate for the lower volume, dealers charge higher spreads. Thus, trading agency bonds is more costly than trading Treasury bonds. Consequently, agency bonds are usually purchased by institutional investors planning to hold the bonds until they mature. Another reason for the higher yields on agency bonds compared to Treasury bonds is that interest income from agency bonds is subject to state and local taxation, whereas Treasury interest payments are subject only to federal taxation.

To illustrate, we consider a specific bond issue from the Tennessee Valley Authority (TVA). The TVA is a federally-owned utility company operating in, you guessed it, the Tennessee River valley. In 1992, the TVA sold a $1 billion issue of 50-year maturity bonds in a public offering. This was the first time in several decades that a U.S. government-affiliated issuer sold bonds with a 50-year term to maturity. Pension funds and insurance companies purchased most of the bonds to match the 8.25 percent coupons with future contractual payments to retirees and insurance beneficiaries.

GOVERNMENT AGENCY ISSUES

Wednesday, January 13, 1999

Over-the-Counter mid-afternoon quotations based on large transactions, usually $1 million or more. Colons in bid-and-asked quotes represent 32nds; 101:01 means 101 1/32.

All yields are calculated to maturity, and based on the asked quote. * -- Callable issue, maturity date shown. For issues callable prior to maturity, yields are computed to the earliest call date for issues quoted above par, or 100, and to the maturity date for issues below par.

Source: Bear, Stearns & Co. via Street Software Technology Inc.

Federal Home Loan Bank

Rate	Mat.	Bid	Asked	Yld.
6.44	4-99	100:14	100:17	4.25
8.60	6-99	101:20	101:23	4.67
6.11	6-99	100:16	100:19	4.74
8.45	7-99	101:28	101:31	4.63
6.26	8-99	100:24	100:27	4.75
8.60	8-99	102:06	102:09	4.74
5.87	10-99	100:20	100:23	4.91
8.38	10-99	102:18	102:21	4.85
5.00	10-99*	100:00	100:03	4.87
5.80	11-99	100:17	100:20	4.99
8.60	1-00	103:19	103:22	4.87
5.53	2-00	100:16	100:19	4.95
5.78	5-00*	100:08	100:11	4.76
4.49	11-00	99:02	99:05	4.99
5.62	1-01	101:16	101:19	4.78
5.20	9-01	100:00	100:04	5.14
4.86	10-01	99:13	99:17	5.04
4.63	10-01	98:29	99:01	5.01
4.66	10-01	98:30	99:02	5.03
4.64	10-02	98:06	98:10	5.14
4.68	10-02	100:10	100:14	4.55
6.18	10-02	103:25	103:29	5.03
5.66	1-03	102:16	102:22	4.91
5.37	1-03	100:28	101:02	5.08
6.25	1-03*	99:26	100:00	6.25
5.42	1-03	101:28	102:02	4.85
6.07	1-03*	100:00	100:06	0.82
6.05	2-03*	100:01	100:07	2.83
6.03	5-03*	101:30	102:04	5.05
5.76	6-03	103:06	103:12	4.90
5.57	9-03	101:26	102:00	5.09
5.63	9-03	101:20	101:26	5.18
5.13	9-03	100:02	100:08	5.07
4.78	10-03	98:10	98:16	5.14
5.06	10-03*	99:27	100:01	5.05
6.02	10-03*	99:08	99:14	6.16
9.50	2-04	120:25	120:31	4.82
6.00	5-04*	99:08	99:14	6.13
7.00	7-07*	101:22	101:28	5.69
7.00	8-07*	101:30	102:04	5.57
5.80	9-08	102:28	103:04	5.38

Inter-Amer. Devel. Bank

Rate	Mat.	Bid	Asked	Yld.
7.13	9-99	101:16	101:19	4.74
8.50	5-01	106:28	107:00	5.22
6.13	3-06	106:13	106:19	5.01
6.63	3-07	109:31	110:05	5.09
12.25	12-08	151:00	151:08	5.48
8.88	6-09	126:20	126:28	5.45
8.40	9-09	123:28	124:04	5.39
8.50	3-11	125:21	125:29	5.54
7.13	3-23*	103:21	103:29	6.69
7.00	6-25	114:14	114:22	5.90
6.80	10-25	112:00	112:08	5.89

World Bank Bonds

Rate	Mat.	Bid	Asked	Yld.
8.38	10-99	102:18	102:21	4.53
8.13	3-01	107:04	107:08	4.51
6.38	5-01	103:20	103:24	4.67
6.75	1-02	104:20	104:24	5.02
12.38	10-02	123:08	123:14	5.38
5.25	9-03	101:31	102:05	4.73
6.38	7-05	107:18	107:24	4.97
6.63	8-06	109:30	110:06	4.99
8.25	9-16	126:08	126:16	5.82
8.63	10-16	130:11	130:19	5.84
9.25	7-17	138:07	138:15	5.83
7.63	1-23	124:31	125:07	5.69
8.88	3-26	139:20	139:28	5.91

Financing Corporation

Rate	Mat.	Bid	Asked	Yld.
10.70	10-17	151:27	152:03	6.02
9.80	11-17	145:31	146:07	5.75
9.40	2-18	137:31	138:07	6.01
9.80	4-18	147:12	147:20	5.69
10.00	5-18	149:07	149:15	5.73
10.35	8-18	153:04	153:12	5.76
9.65	11-18	146:07	146:15	5.70
9.90	12-18	148:21	148:29	5.74
9.60	12-18	145:07	145:15	5.74
9.65	3-19	146:06	146:14	5.73
9.70	4-19	146:18	146:26	5.75
9.00	6-19	137:18	137:26	5.81
8.60	9-19	133:10	133:18	5.79

Tennessee Valley Authority

Rate	Mat.	Bid	Asked	Yld.
8.38	10-99	101:27	101:30	5.53
6.00	11-00	101:13	101:16	5.11
6.50	8-01	103:09	103:13	5.08
6.38	6-05	105:18	105:24	5.31
3.38	1-07	95:28	96:02	3.96
8.05	7-24*	101:12	101:20	6.19
6.75	11-25	110:30	111:06	5.91
8.63	11-29*	103:18	103:26	8.28
8.25	9-34*	102:24	103:00	4.84
8.25	4-42*	113:26	114:02	6.90
7.25	7-43*	104:11	104:19	6.92
6.88	12-43*	105:19	105:27	6.27

Farm Credit Fin. Asst. Corp.

Rate	Mat.	Bid	Asked	Yld.
9.38	7-03	116:21	116:27	5.15
8.80	6-05	120:21	120:27	4.96
9.20	9-05*	107:22	107:28	4.34

Resolution Funding Corp.

Rate	Mat.	Bid	Asked	Yld.
8.13	10-19	131:27	132:03	5.51
8.88	7-20	142:07	142:15	5.49
9.38	10-20	143:03	143:11	5.83
8.63	1-21	139:12	139:20	5.50
8.63	1-30	136:31	137:07	5.97
8.88	4-30	148:04	148:12	5.58

GNMA Mtge. Issues Jan99

Rate	Mat.	Bid	Asked	Yld.
5.50	30Yr	96:16	96:18	6.00
6.00	30Yr	99:01	99:03	6.19
6.50	30Yr	100:31	101:01	6.37
7.00	30Yr	102:10	102:12	6.52
7.50	30Yr	103:04	103:06	6.52
8.00	30Yr	103:31	104:01	6.29
8.50	30Yr	106:03	106:05	5.72
9.00	30Yr	106:23	106:25	6.08
9.50	30Yr	107:06	107:08	6.91

Student Loan Marketing

Rate	Mat.	Bid	Asked	Yld.
5.52	6-99	100:08	100:11	4.63
5.66	2-00*	100:01	100:04	5.21
5.56	3-00*	100:02	100:05	4.41
7.50	3-00	102:21	102:24	4.99
6.05	9-00	101:27	101:30	4.82
7.00	12-02	106:24	106:30	5.01
7.30	8-12	118:26	119:02	5.31
0.00	10-22	24:14	24:22	5.99

Federal Farm Credit Bank

Rate	Mat.	Bid	Asked	Yld.
5.60	5-99	100:09	100:12	4.29
5.55	7-99	100:08	100:11	4.81
8.65	10-99	102:18	102:21	4.75
6.28	6-01	103:03	103:07	4.86
6.10	9-01	102:28	103:00	4.89
5.70	6-03	102:20	102:26	4.99
6.75	6-07	111:02	111:08	5.09

The TVA offering included $500 million of stripped coupon bonds and $500 million of bonds without a strips feature. The issue matures in 2042 but is callable after 20 years at a call price of 106. The call price is the amount bondholders will receive when the bond is called. "Nonstrippable" bonds were sold with a yield to maturity of 8.515 percent, or .58 percent more than the yield on then current 30-year maturity Treasury bonds. The principal strips were sold to yield 8.94 percent, and yields on coupon strips varied according to their payment dates.

The generous call price of 106 implies that, if the bonds are called at the earliest possible call date in 2012, their yield will be more than the originally stated yield to maturity. To evaluate a potential early call, bond investors often refer to a bond's yield to call. As discussed in Chapter 10, a bond's yield to call is the interest rate for a bond assuming that the bond is called at the earliest possible call date. The TVA bonds originally sold at an average price of about 96:30, or $96.9375, with a yield to call of 8.69 percent, or .175 percent more than the yield to maturity of 8.515 percent.

CHECK THIS

12.5a In Figure 12.4, find the price quotes for the Tennessee Valley Authority bond issue discussed immediately above maturing in 2042.

12.5b From a recent issue of *The Wall Street Journal*, find the price quotes for the Tennessee Valley Authority bond issue discussed immediately above. What is the spread between their bid and asked prices?

12.5c Examine spreads between bid and asked prices for government agency notes and bonds listed in a recent *Wall Street Journal*. What is the typical bid-ask spread?

12.6 Municipal Bonds

Municipal notes and bonds are intermediate- to long-term interest-bearing obligations of state and local governments or agencies of those governments. The defining characteristic of municipal notes and bonds, often called "munis," is that coupon interest is usually exempt from federal income tax. Consequently, the market for municipal debt is commonly called the *tax-exempt market*. Most of the 50 states also have an income tax, but their tax treatment of municipal debt interest varies. Only a few states exempt coupon interest on out-of-state municipal bonds from in-state income tax, but most states do allow in-state municipal debt interest an exemption from in-state income tax. In any case, state income tax rates are normally much lower than federal income tax rates, and state taxes can be used as an itemized deduction from federal taxable income. Consequently, state taxes are usually a secondary consideration for municipal bond investors.

The federal income tax exemption makes municipal bonds attractive to investors in the highest income tax brackets. This includes many individual investors, commercial banks, and property and casualty insurance companies—precisely those investors who actually hold almost all municipal debt. However, yields on municipal debt are less than on corporate debt with similar features and credit quality. This eliminates much, but not all, of the advantage of the tax exemption. Therefore, tax-exempt investors, including pension funds and retirement accounts of individuals, nonprofit institutions, and some life insurance companies, normally do not invest in municipal bonds. Instead, they prefer to invest in higher-yielding corporate bonds.

Municipal bonds are typically less complicated investments than corporate bonds. However, while municipal debt often carries a high credit rating, **default risk** does exist. Thus, investing in municipal debt requires more care than investing in U.S. Treasury securities.

default risk The risk that a bond issuer will cease making scheduled payments of coupons or principal or both.

To illustrate some standard features of a municipal bond issue, Table 12.3 summarizes the issue terms for a hypothetical bond issue by the city of Bedford Falls. We see that the bonds were issued in December 1999 and mature 30 years later in December 2029. Each bond has a face value denomination of $5,000 and pays an annual coupon equal to 6 percent of face value. The annual coupon is split between two semiannual payments each June and December. Based on the original offer price of 100, or 100 percent of par value, the bonds have a yield to maturity of 6 percent. Bedford Falls bonds are call-protected for 10 years, until January 2009. Thereafter, the bonds are callable any time at par value.

general obligation bonds (GOs) Bonds issued by a municipality that are secured by the full faith and credit of the issuer.

The Bedford Falls bonds are **general obligation bonds (GOs)**, which means that the bonds are secured by the full faith and credit of the city of Bedford Falls. "Full faith and credit" means the power of the municipality to collect taxes. The trustee for the bond issue is the Potters Bank of Bedford Falls. A trustee is appointed to represent the financial interests of bondholders and administer the sinking fund for the bond issue. A sinking fund requires a bond issuer to redeem for cash a fraction of an outstanding bond issue on a periodic basis. The sinking fund in this example requires that beginning 10 years after issuance, the city must redeem at par value $2.5 million of the bond issue each year. At each annual redemption, a fraction of the bond issue is called and the affected bondholders receive the par value call price.

Table 12.3	City of Bedford Falls General Obligation Bonds	
Issue amount	$50 million	Bond issue represents a total face value amount of $50 million
Issue date	12/15/99	Bonds will be offered to the public on December 15, 1999
Maturity date	12/31/29	All remaining principal must be paid at maturity on December 31, 2029
Par value	$5,000	Each bond has a face value of $5,000
Coupon rate	6%	Annual coupons of $300 per bond
Coupon dates	12/31, 6/30	Semiannual coupons of $150
Offering price	100	Offer price is 100% of par value
Yield to maturity	6%	Based on stated offer price
Call provision	Callable after 12/31/09	Bonds are call-protected for 10 years
Call price	100	Bonds are callable at par value
Trustee	Potters Bank of Bedford Falls	The trustee is appointed to represent the bondholders and administer the sinking fund
Sinking fund	$2.5 million annual par redemptions after 12/31/09	City must redeem at par value $2.5 million of the bond issue each year beginning in 2010

Municipal Bond Features

Municipal bonds are typically callable, pay semiannual coupons, and have a par value denomination of $5,000. Municipal bond prices are stated as a percentage of par value. Thus, a price of 102 indicates that a bond with a par value of $5,000 has a price of $5,100. By convention, however, municipal bond dealers commonly use yield quotes rather than price quotes in their trading procedures. For example, a dealer might quote a bid-yield of 6.25 percent for a 5 percent coupon bond with seven years to maturity, indicating a willingness to buy at a price determined by that yield. The actual dollar bid price in this example is $4,649.99, as shown in the following bond price calculation:

$$\frac{\$250}{.0625} \times \left[1 - \frac{1}{(1.03125)^{14}}\right] + \frac{\$5,000}{(1.03125)^{14}} = \$4,649.99$$

Because there are many thousands of different municipal bond issues outstanding, only a few large issues trade with sufficient frequency to justify having their prices reported in the financial press. A *Wall Street Journal* listing of some actively traded municipal bonds is seen in Figure 12.5. The listing reports the name of the issuer, the coupon rate and maturity of the issue, the most recent bid price quote and the change from an earlier price quote, and a yield to maturity based on a dealer's bid yield.

call provision Feature of a municipal bond issue that specifies when the bonds may be called by the issuer and the call price that must be paid.

A **call provision** is a standard feature of most municipal bond issues. A call provision allows an issuer to retire outstanding bonds before they mature, usually to refund with new bonds after a fall in market interest rates. When the bond is called, each bondholder receives the bond's call price in exchange for the bond. However, two bond features often limit an issuer's call privilege. First, callable municipal bonds usually offer a period of call protection following their original issue date. Since a bond issue is not callable during this period, the earliest possible call date is the end of the call protection period. Second, a call price is often specified with a call premium. A call premium is the difference between a bond's call price and its par value. A common arrangement is to specify a call premium equal to one year's coupons for a call occurring at the earliest possible call date. This is then followed by a schedule of call premium reductions, until about 5 to 10 years before maturity, when the call premium is eliminated entirely. Thereafter, the bond issue is callable any time at par value.

Figure 12.5

Municipal Securities

Source: Reprinted with permission from *The Wall Street Journal,* via Copyright Clearance Center, Inc. © 1999 Dow Jones & Company, Inc. All Rights Reserved Worldwide.

Tax-Exempt Bonds
Representative prices for several active tax-exempt revenue and refunding bonds, based on institutional trades. Changes rounded to the nearest one-eighth. Yield is to maturity. n-New. Source: The Bond Buyer.

ISSUE	COUPON	MAT	PRICE	CHG	BID YLD	ISSUE	COUPON	MAT	PRICE	CHG	BID YLD
Alabama Pub Sch Auth r	4.250	11-01-18	90 1/8	...	5.03	Mo. Hlth & Ed Fac	5.000	05-15-38	94 7/8	...	5.31
Austin TX Sub Lien 98A	4.250	05-15-28	87	...	5.10	NC Med Care Comm	5.000	06-01-28	97	— 1/8	5.20
Brazis Riv Auth Tx-n	5.050	11-01-18	99 3/8	— 1/4	5.10	NC Med Care Comm Hsp	4.750	12-01-28	92 3/8	— 1/8	5.25
CA Ed Facs Auth Ser 98	4.500	10-01-27	92 1/4	— 1/4	5.01	NYC Genl Oblig Bds	5.000	08-15-22	97	...	5.22
Cook Co Ill Ser 98A	5.000	11-15-22	98	— 1/8	5.15	NYC Genl Oblig Bds	5.000	08-15-28	96 3/8	— 1/8	5.22
Dallas Tx Wtrwrks-n	5.000	10-01-29	97 5/8	— 1/8	5.15	NYC Munl Wtr Fin Auth	5.000	06-15-27	97 5/8	— 1/8	5.16
Denver Colo Arpt-n	5.000	11-15-25	96 3/8	— 1/4	5.25	NYC Munl Wtr & Swr Ath	4.750	06-15-31	95 3/8	— 1/8	5.10
Denver Colo Arpt-n	5.000	11-15-25	97 5/8	— 3/8	5.16	PA of NY & NJ cnsldted	4.250	10-01-26	88 3/8	— 1/4	5.02
Fla St Bd Ed Cap	4.750	06-01-23	95 1/4	...	5.09	Portland Ore Sewer	4.500	06-01-18	93 1/2	...	5.02
Huston Tx Airport Sys	5.000	07-01-28	97 1/2	— 1/8	5.17	PR Elec Pwr Auth	4.750	07-01-21	97	...	4.97
Huston Tx Airport Sys	5.000	07-01-25	96 1/4	— 1/8	5.26	PR Hwy & Trans Auth	5.000	07-01-38	96 7/8	— 1/8	5.19
King Co Wash Ltd	5.000	01-01-30	96 3/4	— 1/8	5.21	Pub Hwy Auth Colo.	5.000	09-01-26	97 7/8	— 1/8	5.14
LI Pwr Auth NY	5.125	12-01-22	99 5/8	...	5.15	Sacramento Cty Fin Auth	4.750	05-01-23	96	— 1/8	5.03
Long Island Pwr Elec	4.750	04-01-18	96 1/2	— 1/8	5.03	So Miami Hlth Hosp Auth	5.000	11-15-28	97 3/4	— 1/8	5.14
Mass Tpk Auth Ser A	5.000	01-01-37	96 1/2	— 1/8	5.21	Tampa Bay Wtr Fla	4.750	10-01-27	94 7/8	— 1/8	5.09
Matagorda Co Tx-n	5.125	11-01-28	99 1/2	— 1/8	5.16	Triboro BTA NY	4.750	01-01-24	95 3/8	— 1/8	5.08
Metro Washn Arpts Auth	5.000	10-01-28	97 3/8	...	5.18	Wash Hlth Care Auth	5.000	11-15-28	96 3/8	— 1/8	5.24
Miami-Dade Co Sch Bd-n	5.000	08-01-25	97 3/4	— 1/8	5.15	Wash Hlth Care Fac-n	5.000	10-01-28	96 3/8	...	5.24
Miami-Dade Fla Avia	5.000	10-01-28	97 1/8	— 1/8	5.18	Washn Convntn Center	4.750	10-01-28	92 3/4	...	5.22
Mo. Hhh & Ed Fac	5.000	05-15-28	96 1/2	...	5.24	Wayne Chrtr Co MI Airp	5.000	12-01-28	96 1/8	— 1/8	5.26

serial bonds Bonds issued with maturity dates scheduled at intervals, so that a fraction of the bond issue matures in each year of a multiple-year period.

Municipal bonds are commonly issued with a serial maturity structure, hence the term **serial bonds**. In a serial bond issue, a fraction of the total issue amount is scheduled to mature in each year over a multiple-year period. As an example, a serial bond issue may contain bonds that mature in each year over a 5-year period, with the first group maturing 11 years after the original issue date, and the last group maturing 15 years after issuance. The purpose of a serial maturity structure is to spread out the principal repayment, thereby avoiding a lump-sum repayment at a single maturity date.

term bonds Bonds from an issue with a single maturity date.

When an entire bond issue matures on a single date, the bonds are called **term bonds**. Term bonds normally have a sinking fund provision. A sinking fund is a trustee-managed account to which the issuer makes regular payments. Account reserves are dedicated to redeeming a fraction of the bond issue on each of a series of scheduled redemption dates. Each redemption usually proceeds by lottery, where randomly selected bonds are called and the affected bondholders receive the sinking fund call price. Alternatively, scheduled redemptions can be implemented by purchasing bonds from investors at current market prices. This latter option is usually selected by the issuer when the bonds are selling at a discount from par value. The motive for a sinking fund provision is similar to that for a serial maturity structure; it provides a means for the issuer to avoid a lump-sum principal repayment at a single maturity date.

put bonds Bonds that can be sold back to the issuer.

Some municipal bonds are putable, and these are called **put bonds**. The holder of a put bond, also called a *tender offer bond,* has the option of selling the bond back to the issuer, normally at par value. Some put bonds can be tendered any time, whereas others can be tendered only on regularly scheduled dates. Weekly, monthly, quarterly, semiannual, and annual put date schedules are all used. Notice that with a put bond, maturity is effectively the choice of the bondholder. This feature protects bondholders from rising interest rates and the associated fall in bond prices. However, a putable bond will have a higher price than a comparable nonputable bond. The price differential simply reflects the value of the put option to sell back the bonds.

variable-rate notes Securities that pay an interest rate that changes according to market conditions. Also called *floaters.*

While most municipal bonds maintain a constant coupon rate (hence the term fixed-rate bonds), interest rate risk has induced many municipalities to issue **variable-rate notes**, often called *floaters.* For these debt issues, the coupon rate is adjusted periodically according to an index-based rule. For example, at each adjustment the coupon rate may be set at 60 percent of the prevailing rate on 91-day maturity U.S. Treasury bills. A variable-rate note may also be putable, in which case it is called a *variable-rate demand obligation,* often abbreviated to VRDO. A stipulation attached to most VRDOs allows the issuer to convert an entire variable-rate issue to a fixed-rate issue following a specified conversion procedure. Essentially, the issuer notifies each VRDO holder of the intent to convert the outstanding VRDO issue to a fixed-rate issue on a specific future date. In response, VRDO holders have the option of tendering their VRDOs for cash, or they can accept conversion of their VRDOs into fixed-rate bonds. In the late 1980s, following a decade of volatile interest rates, VRDOs made up about 10 percent of the total value of outstanding municipal bonds.

For the first time in 1993, several municipalities issued bonds with strippable coupons and principal, called *muni-strips.* Like the U.S. Treasury STRIPS program, muni-strips allow separate trading of registered interest and principal. *The Wall Street Journal* story of an issue of muni-strips offered by the government of Puerto Rico appears in the nearby Investment Updates box. Puerto Rico is a protectorate of the United States and bonds issued by the government of Puerto Rico are not subject to taxation of coupon interest. Another part of the Puerto Rico bond offering is composed of inverse floaters. Inverse floaters are like the variable- or floating-rate bonds discussed above. However, inverse floaters pay a variable

Puerto Rico Sells Municipal Bonds, Including "Designer" Securities

Puerto Rico sold a new kind of municipal bond yesterday that investors can buy or trade in bits and pieces.

As part of a well-received $961 million offering of general obligation municipal refunding bonds, Puerto Rico sold about $126 million of so-called bond payment obligations, or BPOs. The offering was the largest of a $2 billion slate of new municipal bonds sold yesterday.

Bond payment obligations can be broken down into separate pre-packaged parts at the will of the investor and distributed into different portfolios or even sold to other investors. Each of the parts comes with its own registration number to make trading easier. The BPO bond is the ultimate "designer security," said Gary Gray, a senior vice president at Lehman Brothers, the offering's lead underwriter.

But such flexibility comes at a price. Investors receive yields as much as 0.10 percentage points lower than similarly rated plain-vanilla bonds if they choose not to break the BPOs into separate parts, many of which would be riskier than regular bonds.

The BPOs were sold in maturities of 15, 16 and 17 years with yields ranging from 5.50% to 5.60%. Certain parts of the BPOs, when separated, would have significantly higher or lower yields depending on the direction of short-term interest rates, among other factors. The plain-vanilla fixed-rate bonds sold by Puerto Rico maturing in 14 years, by comparison, yielded 5.55%, 0.05 percentage points more than the 15-year BPO bonds.

Furthermore, some of the bonds could pay much less, or much more, than regular bonds depending on the direction of interest rates.

Indeed, the offering had been postponed in April due to rising interest rates as an inflation scare rushed through the bond market. But with interest rates moving lower again, Lehman and Puerto Rico decided that yesterday was time to come to market.

A handful of large mutual fund companies snapped up the BPOs and many of the plain-vanilla bonds, according to Lehman officials. Part of the reason for such strong demand is that interest payments from Puerto Rico's securities are exempt from federal, state and local taxes. Indeed, demand was so strong that the offering was increased from an anticipated $700 million. The bonds are rated Baa-1 by Moody's Investors Service, Inc., and single-A by Standard & Poor's Corp.

It wasn't the first time Lehman has sold BPOs, but it is the largest offering of its type ever. Earlier this year, Lehman sold about $60 million of BPOs for the Puerto Rico Telephone Agency and the Pennsylvania Housing Finance Agency.

All of these offerings are part of a program by Lehman to sell more exotic municipal bonds to sophisticated investors. The program, appropriately called "strips and pieces," is described in a brochure which speaks of "bull floaters" and "bear floaters," among other creatures.

According to Lehman officials, the BPOs were designed for investors looking to boost yields and plug holes in their portfolios left by bonds that were called away as interest rates dropped. They were also designed for investors hoping to hedge against other volatile bonds. Some of the pieces give the investor the right to claim a certain coupon or principal payment at some date in the future. Others are the popular inverse-floaters, called bull floaters in the brochure, which pay more than plain-vanilla bonds when short-term interest rates fall and less when they rise. On the other hand, the bear floaters pay more than plain-vanilla bonds when short-term rates rise and less when they fall. After five years, both bull and bear floaters convert to fixed-rate securities. The bear floaters would then have a fixed rate of 5.5% while the bull floaters would yield 3.5% or 1.5%, depending on which BPO package they are separated from.

The bonds sold yesterday could be purchased in denominations of $5,000, if bought in whole parts, as more than half of them were, according to Mr. Gray. Despite the low denominations, Lehman isn't actively marketing the BPOs to individual investors, Mr. Gray said. But some of the bits and pieces, like inverse floaters, for example, wouldn't be such a bad idea for individuals interested in holding them until maturity, he added.

Source: Thomas T. Vogel Jr., "Puerto Rico Sells Municipal Bonds Including 'Designer' Securities," *The Wall Street Journal*, June 24, 1993. Reprinted by permission of Dow Jones & Company, Inc., via Copyright Clearance Center, Inc. © 1993 Dow Jones & Company, Inc. All Rights Reserved Worldwide.

coupon rate that moves inversely with market interest rates. That is, higher interest is paid when market interest rates fall and lower interest is paid when market interest rates rise.

Inverse floaters are created by splitting the interest payments of a bond issue with fixed coupons. For example, suppose a municipality issues $10 million face value bonds paying fixed 6 percent coupons. The bonds are placed in a trust, and the fixed annual $600,000 coupons are used to pay interest on floaters and inverse floaters that are issued as claims on the trust. Initially, the interest payments may be split equally between the floaters and inverse floaters. Later, if market interest rates increase, interest payments on the floaters will rise and interest payments on the inverse floaters will fall. If market interest rates decrease, floater interest will fall and inverse floater interest will rise. Total interest payments to floaters and inverse floaters will remain constant.

Types of Municipal Bonds

There are two basic types of municipal bonds: revenue bonds and general obligation bonds, often referred to as GOs. General obligation bonds are issued by all levels of municipal governments, including states, counties, cities, towns, school districts, and water districts. They are secured by the general taxing powers of the municipalities issuing the bonds. For state governments and large city governments, tax revenue is collected from a diverse base of income taxes on corporations and individuals, sales taxes, and property taxes. In contrast, tax revenues for smaller municipalities are largely derived from property taxes, although sales taxes have become increasingly important. Because of their large, diverse tax bases, general obligation bonds issued by states and large cities are often called *unlimited tax bonds* or *full faith and credit bonds*.

However, some general obligation bonds are called *limited tax bonds*. The distinction between limited and unlimited tax bonds arises when a constitutional limit or other statutory limit is placed on the power of a municipality to assess taxes. For example, an amendment to the California state constitution, popularly known as Proposition 13 when it was enacted, placed rigid limits on the ability of California municipalities to assess taxes on real estate.

revenue bonds
Municipal bonds secured by revenues collected from a specific project or projects.

Revenue bonds constitute the bulk of all outstanding municipal bonds. **Revenue bonds** are bonds secured by proceeds collected from the projects they finance. Thus, the credit quality of a revenue bond issue is largely determined by the ability of a project to generate revenue. A few examples of the many different kinds of projects financed by revenue bonds are listed below.

Airport and seaport bonds: Used to finance development of airport and seaport facilities. Secured by user fees and lease revenues.

College dormitory bonds: Used to finance construction and renovation of dormitory facilities. Secured by rental fees.

Industrial development bonds: Used to finance development of projects ranging from factories to shopping centers. Secured by rental and leasing fees.

Multifamily housing bonds: Used to finance construction of housing projects for senior citizens or low-income families. Secured by rental fees.

Highway and road gas tax bonds: Used to finance highway construction. May be secured by specific toll revenues or general gas tax revenues.

Student loan bonds: Used to purchase higher education guaranteed student loans. Secured by loan repayments and federal guarantees.

hybrid bonds
Municipal bonds secured by project revenues with some form of general obligation credit guarantees.

Many municipal bonds possess aspects of both general obligation and revenue bonds; these are called **hybrid bonds**. Typically, a hybrid is a revenue bond secured by project-specific cash flows, but with additional credit guarantees. A common form of hybrid is the *moral obligation bond.* This is a state-issued revenue bond with provisions for obtaining general revenues when project-specific resources are inadequate. Usually, extra funds can be obtained only with approval of a state legislature, which is said to be "morally obligated" to assist a financially distressed state-sponsored project. However, a moral obligation is not a guarantee, and the likelihood of state assistance varies. Municipal bond credit analysts consider each state's history of assistance as well as current state financial conditions when evaluating the credit-quality enhancement of the moral obligation. In general, experienced municipal bond investors agree that a state will first service its own general obligation debt before providing service assistance to moral obligation debt. This is evidenced by the typically higher yields on moral obligation debt compared to general obligation debt.

Since 1983, all newly issued municipal bonds have had to be registered—that is, with the identity of all bondholders registered with the issuer. With registered bonds, the issuer sends coupon interest and principal payments only to the registered owner of a bond. Additionally, it is now standard practice for registered bonds to be issued in book entry form; bondholders are not issued printed bond certificates but instead receive notification that their ownership is officially registered. The actual registration record is maintained by the issuer in computer files. This contrasts with the now defunct practice (in the U.S.) of issuing bearer bonds, where coupon interest and principal were paid to anyone presenting the bond certificates.

Municipal Bond Credit Ratings

Municipal bond credit rating agencies provide investors with an assessment of the credit quality of individual bond issues. As part of the issuance and credit rating process, the rating agency is paid a fee to assign a credit rating to a new bond issue, to periodically reevaluate the issue, and to make these ratings available to the public. The three largest municipal bond credit rating agencies are Moody's Investors Service, Standard & Poor's Corporation, and Fitch Investors Service. Among them, they rate thousands of new issues each year. Table 12.4 compares and briefly describes the credit rating codes assigned by these three agencies.

The highest credit rating that can be awarded is "triple-A," which indicates that interest and principal are exceptionally secure because of the financial strength of the issuer. Notice that "triple-A" and "double-A" ratings are denoted as AAA and AA, respectively, by Standard & Poor's and Fitch, but as Aaa and Aa, respectively, by Moody's. Also notice that "triple-B" and "double-B" ratings—that is, BBB and BB, respectively—by Standard & Poor's and Fitch correspond to "B-double-a" and "B-single-a" ratings—Baa and Ba, respectively—by Moody's. The same pattern holds for C ratings.

The highest four credit ratings, BBB or Baa and above, designate investment-grade bonds. As a matter of policy, many financial institutions will invest only in investment-grade bonds. Lower rankings indicate successively diminishing levels of credit quality. Ratings of BB or Ba and below designate speculative-grade bonds. Individual investors should probably avoid speculative-grade bonds. A rating of C or below indicates that actual or probable default makes the bond issue unsuitable for most investors.

It is not unusual for the ratings assigned to a particular bond issue to differ slightly across credit rating agencies. For example, a bond issue may be rated AA by Standard &

Table 12.4	Municipal Bond Credit Ratings			
Rating Agency				
Standard & Poor's	**Moody's**	**Fitch**		**Credit Rating Description**
Investment-Grade Bond Ratings				
AAA	Aaa	AAA		Highest credit quality
AA	Aa	AA		High credit quality
A	A	A		Good credit quality
BBB	Baa	BBB		Satisfactory credit quality
Speculative-Grade Bond Ratings				
BB	Ba	BB		Speculative credit quality
B	B	B		Highly speculative quality
CCC	Caa	CCC		Poor credit quality
CC	Ca	CC		Probable default
Extremely Speculative-Grade Bond Ratings				
C	C	C		Imminent default
D		DDD		In default
		DD, D		

Poor's, Aa by Moody's, but only A by Fitch. When this occurs, it usually reflects a difference in credit rating methods rather than a disagreement regarding basic facts. For example, Moody's may focus on the budgetary status of the issuer when assigning a credit rating, while Standard & Poor's may emphasize the economic environment of the issuer. Remember that Standard & Poor's, Moody's, and Fitch are competitors in the bond rating business, and, like competitors in any industry, they try to differentiate their products.

Municipal Bond Insurance

insured municipal bonds Bonds secured by an insurance policy that guarantees bond interest and principal payments should the issuer default.

In the last two decades, it has become increasingly common for municipalities to obtain bond insurance for new bond issues. **Insured municipal bonds**, besides being secured by the issuer's resources, are also backed by an insurance policy written by a commercial insurance company. The policy provides for prompt payment of coupon interest and principal to municipal bondholders in the event of a default by the issuer. The cost of the insurance policy is paid by the issuer at the time of issuance. The policy cannot be canceled while any bonds are outstanding. With bond insurance, the credit quality of the bond issue is determined by the financial strength of the insurance company, not the municipality alone. Credit rating agencies are certainly aware of this fact. Consequently, a bond issue with insurance can obtain a higher credit rating than would be possible without insurance, and therefore sell at a higher price.

Municipal bond insurance companies manage default risk in three ways. First, they insure bond issues only from municipalities that have a good credit rating on their own. Second, municipal bond insurers diversify default risk by writing insurance policies for municipalities spread across a wide geographic area. Third, and perhaps most important, to compete in the municipal bond insurance business, insurers must maintain substantial investment portfolios as a source of financial reserves. Without sizable reserves, a company's insurance policies are not credible and municipalities will avoid purchasing insurance from them.

12.7 Equivalent Taxable Yield

Consider an individual investor who must decide whether to invest in a corporate bond paying annual coupon interest of 8 percent or a municipal bond paying annual coupon interest of 5 percent. Both bonds are new issues with a triple-A credit rating, both bonds sell at par value, and the investor plans to hold the bonds until they mature. Since both bonds are purchased at par value, their coupon rates are equal to their originally stated yields to maturity. For the municipal bond this is a tax-exempt yield, and for the corporate bond this is a taxable yield.

Clearly, if the investment was for a tax-exempt retirement account, corporate debt is preferred since the coupon interest is higher and tax effects are not a consideration. But if the investment is not tax-exempt, the decision should be made on an aftertax basis. Essentially, the investor must decide which investment provides the highest return after accounting for income tax on corporate debt interest. This is done by comparing the tax-exempt yield of 5 percent on municipal bonds with an equivalent taxable yield. An equivalent taxable yield depends on the investor's marginal tax rate and is computed as follows:

$$\text{Equivalent taxable yield} = \frac{\text{Tax-exempt yield}}{1 - \text{Marginal tax rate}}$$

For example, suppose the investor is in a 35 percent marginal tax bracket. Then a tax-exempt yield of 5 percent is shown to correspond to an equivalent taxable yield of 7.69 percent as follows:

$$\text{Equivalent taxable yield} = \frac{5\%}{1 - .35} = 7.69\%$$

In this case, the investor would prefer the taxable yield of 8 percent for the corporate bond rather than the equivalent taxable yield of 7.69 percent for the municipal bond.

Alternatively, the investor could compare the aftertax yield on the corporate bond with the tax-exempt yield on the municipal bond. An aftertax yield is computed as follows.

$$\text{Aftertax yield} = \text{Taxable yield} \times (1 - \text{Marginal tax rate})$$

To change the example, suppose that the investor is in a 40 percent marginal tax bracket. This results in an aftertax yield of 4.8 percent, as shown below.

$$\text{Aftertax yield} = 8\% \times (1 - .40) = 4.8\%$$

In this case, the tax-exempt yield of 5 percent on the municipal bond is preferred to the aftertax yield of 4.8 percent on the corporate bond.

Another approach is to compute the critical marginal tax rate that would leave an investor indifferent between a given tax-exempt yield on a municipal bond and a given taxable yield on a corporate bond. A critical marginal tax rate is found as follows:

$$\text{Critical marginal tax rate} = 1 - \frac{\text{Tax-exempt yield}}{\text{Taxable yield}}$$

For the example considered here, the critical marginal tax rate is 37.5 percent, determined as follows:

$$\text{Critical marginal tax rate} = 1 - \frac{5\%}{8\%} = 37.5\%$$

Investors with a marginal tax rate higher than the critical marginal rate would prefer the municipal bond, whereas investors in a lower tax bracket would prefer the corporate bond.

CHECK THIS

12.7a An investor with a marginal tax rate of 30 percent is interested in a tax-exempt bond with a yield of 6 percent. What is the equivalent taxable yield of this bond?

12.7b A taxable bond has a yield of 10 percent and a tax-exempt bond has a yield of 7 percent. What is the critical marginal tax rate for these two bonds?

Taxable Municipal Bonds

private activity bonds Taxable municipal bonds used to finance facilities used by private businesses.

The Tax Reform Act of 1986 imposed notable restrictions on the types of municipal bonds that qualify for federal tax exemption of interest payments. In particular, the 1986 act expanded the definition of **private activity bonds**. Private activity bonds include any municipal security where 10 percent or more of the issue finances facilities used by private entities and is secured by payments from private entities.

Interest on private activity bonds is tax-exempt only if the bond issue falls into a so-called qualified category. Qualified private activity bonds that still enjoy a tax-exempt interest privilege include public airport bonds, multifamily housing bonds, nonvehicular mass commuting bonds, and various other project bonds. The major types of private activity bonds that do not qualify for tax-exempt interest are those used to finance sports stadiums, convention facilities, parking facilities, and industrial parks. However, these taxable private activity bonds may still enjoy exemption from state and local income tax. In any case, as a result of the 1986 act and the continuing need to finance private activity projects, new issues of taxable municipal revenue bonds frequently are sold with yields similar to corporate bond yields.

12.9 Summary and Conclusions

This chapter covers the topic of government bonds, including U.S. Treasury bonds, notes, and bills, and state, city, county, and local municipal bonds. In this chapter, we saw that:

1. The U.S. federal government is the largest single borrower in the world, with over $5 trillion of debt. Responsibility for managing this debt belongs to the U.S. Treasury, which issues Treasury bills, notes, and bonds at regular auctions to finance government debt.

2. Treasury bills are short-term obligations that are sold on a discount basis. Treasury notes are medium-term obligations that pay fixed semiannual

coupons as well as payment of face value at maturity. Treasury bonds are long-term obligations that pay their face value at maturity and pay fixed semi-annual coupons.

3. The U.S. Treasury sponsors the STRIPS program, where Treasury bonds and notes are broken down into principal strips, which represent face value payments, and coupon strips, which represent individual coupon payments. Since each strip created under the STRIPS program represents a single future payment, strips effectively become zero coupon bonds.

4. Several federal agencies are authorized to issue securities directly to the public. Bonds issued by U.S. government agencies have a credit quality almost identical to U.S. Treasury issues, but agency notes and bonds are attractive to many investors because they offer higher yields than comparable U.S. Treasury securities. However, the market for agency debt is less active than the market for U.S. Treasury debt and investors are potentially subject to state income taxes on agency debt interest, while U.S. Treasury debt interest is not subject to state taxes.

5. Another large market for government debt is the market for municipal government debt. Total municipal debt outstanding currently exceeds $2 trillion, divided among almost all of the more than 80,000 state and local governments in the United States. Individual investors hold about half this debt, while the remainder is roughly split equally between holdings of property and casualty insurance companies and commercial banks.

6. Municipal notes and bonds are intermediate- to long-term interest-bearing obligations of state and local governments or agencies of those governments. Municipal debt is commonly called the tax-exempt market because the coupon interest is usually exempt from federal income tax, which makes municipal bonds attractive to investors in the highest income tax brackets. However, yields on municipal debt are less than yields on corporate debt with similar features and credit quality, thus eliminating much of the advantage of the tax exemption.

7. Most municipal bonds pay a constant coupon rate, but some municipal notes pay variable coupon rates that change according to prevailing market interest rates. Also, a call provision is a standard feature of most municipal bond issues. A call provision allows an issuer to retire outstanding bonds before they mature. When the bond is called, each bondholder receives the bond's call price in exchange for returning the bond to the issuer.

8. There are two basic types of municipal bonds: revenue bonds and general obligation bonds. Revenue bonds, which constitute the bulk of all outstanding municipal bonds, are secured by proceeds collected from the projects they finance. General obligation bonds, which are issued by all levels of municipal governments, are secured by the general taxing powers of the municipalities issuing the bonds.

9. As part of the process for issuing municipal bonds to the public, a rating agency is paid a fee to assign a credit rating to a new bond issue. In the last two decades, it has become increasingly common for municipalities to obtain bond insurance for new bond issues through an insurance policy written by a commercial

insurance company. With bond insurance, the credit quality of the bond issue is determined by the financial strength of the insurance company, not the municipality alone.

GET REAL

This chapter covered government bonds, a large and important market. How should you put your knowledge of bonds to work?

Begin by purchasing (in a simulated brokerage account) the various types of government securities that are out there. Observe their relative prices over time.

You should also learn more about buying Treasury securities. A great place to go is the Bureau of Public Debt's website, www.publicdebt.treas.gov. There you can examine and download the forms needed to bid in the regular auctions; you can obtain the current auction schedule; and you can inspect the results of previous auctions. You can also read about the *TreasuryDirect* program, which is probably the most convenient and least expensive way of purchasing Treasury issues.

Beyond this, you will find that there are special Treasury securities that we did not discuss in the chapter such as SLGS ("slugs"). Take a few minutes to read up on these less commonly encountered securities. You will also find detailed information about savings bonds.

If you try to purchase municipal bonds in a simulated brokerage account, you may find that you are not able to. The reason is that the market for municipals is so thin for any given issue that getting the needed price information isn't possible. The important practical implication is that the same municipal bond may be quoted at different prices by different dealers, so it pays to shop around. Also, if you ever wanted to sell a municipal issue, you would find that the lack of liquidity of the vast majority of issues leads to very large bid-ask spreads. Municipal bonds are thus best suited for buy and hold investors.

Key Terms

face value 340
discount basis 341
imputed interest 341
STRIPS 341
zero coupon bonds 341
yield to call (YTC) 344
bid-ask spread 344
stop-out bid 347
default risk 352

general obligation bonds (GOs) 352
call provision 353
serial bonds 354
term bonds 354
put bonds 354
variable-rate notes 354
revenue bonds 356
hybrid bonds 357
insured municipal bond 358
private activity bond 360

Chapter Review Problems and Self-Test

1. **Treasury Yields** A callable Treasury bond's price is 140:25. It has a coupon rate of 10 percent, makes semiannual payments, and matures in 21 years. What yield would be reported in the financial press?

2. Equivalent Yields A particular investor faces a 40 percent tax rate. If a AA-rated municipal bond yields 4 percent, what must a similar taxable issue yield for the investor to be impartial to them?

Answers to Self-Test Problems

1. First, note that this is a callable issue selling above par, so the yield to call will be reported. All callable Treasury bonds are callable at face value five years before they mature. Thus, to calculate the yield to call, all we have to do is pretend the bond has 16 years to maturity instead of 21. We therefore have a bond with a price of 140.78125 (after converting from thirty-seconds), a coupon of 10 percent paid semiannually, and a maturity of 16 years (or 32 periods). Verify using the standard bond formula from Chapter 10 that the semiannual yield to call is 3 percent, so the reported yield would be 6 percent.

2. The equivalent taxable yield is the municipal yield "grossed up" by one minus the tax rate:

$$\frac{4\%}{1 - .40} = 6.67\%$$

Test Your Investment Quotient

1. **Zero Coupon Bonds** What is the yield to maturity (YTM) on a zero coupon bond?
   a. The interest rate realized if the bond is held to maturity.
   b. The interest rate realized when the bond is sold.
   c. The coupon yield for an equivalent coupon bond.
   d. A fixed rate when the bond is issued.

2. **Treasury Notes** The coupon rate for a Treasury note is set
   a. The same for all Treasury note issues.
   b. By a formula based on the size of the Treasury note issue.
   c. According to prevailing interest rates at time of issuance.
   d. According to the supply and demand for money.

3. **Treasury Bonds** What is the dollar value of a U.S. Treasury bond quoted at 92:24? (*1990 CFA exam*)
   a. $922.75
   b. $922.40
   c. $927.50
   d. Indeterminable

4. **Treasury Bills** Treasury bills are sold on a discount basis, meaning that the difference between their issued price and their redemption value is
   a. The same for all T-bill issues.
   b. The imputed interest on the T-bill.
   c. Never less than the issued price.
   d. The bond equivalent yield for the T-bill.

5. **Treasury Auctions** Which of the following statements about single-price Treasury auctions is false?
   a. Competitive bidders pay the stop-out bid.
   b. Noncompetitive bidders pay the stop-out bid plus a small premium.
   c. Noncompetitive bidders pay the stop-out bid.
   d. All of the above are true.

6. Savings Bonds   The interest rate on Series I Savings Bonds is reset every six months as

  a. 90 percent of the rate on newly issued five-year T-notes.
  b. 90 percent of the rate on newly issued five-year T-notes plus the recent inflation rate.
  c. A fixed rate plus the recent inflation rate.
  d. An adjustable rate plus the recent inflation rate.

7. Agency Bonds   Which statement applies to a bond issued by an agency of the U.S. government? (*1992 CFA exam*)

  a. It is exempt from the federal income tax on interest.
  b. It becomes a direct obligation of the U.S. Treasury in case of default.
  c. It is secured by assets held by the agency.
  d. None of the above.

8. Agency Bonds   Which is true for bonds issued by all agencies of the U.S. government? (*1989 CFA exam*)

  a. They become direct obligations of the U.S. Treasury.
  b. They are secured bonds backed by government holdings.
  c. They are exempt from federal income tax.
  d. None of the above.

9. Municipal Bonds   Which of the following constitutes the bulk of all outstanding municipal bonds?

  a. Revenue bonds
  b. General obligation bonds
  c. Moral obligation bonds
  d. Private activity bonds

10. Revenue Bonds   A revenue bond is distinguished from a general obligation bond in that revenue bonds have which of the following characteristics? (*1990 CFA exam*)

  a. They are issued by counties, special districts, cities, towns, and state-controlled authorities, whereas general obligation bonds are issued only by the states themselves.
  b. They are typically secured by limited taxing power, whereas general obligation bonds are secured by unlimited taxing power.
  c. They are issued to finance specific projects and are secured by the revenues of the project being financed.
  d. They have first claim to any revenue increase of the tax authority issuing.

11. Insured Municipal Bonds   Which of the following is not a method used by municipal bond insurers to manage default risk?

  a. Only insure bonds from municipalities with a good credit rating.
  b. Diversify default risk by writing insurance policies for municipalities spread across a wide geographic area.
  c. Maintain substantial investment portfolios as a source of financial reserves.
  d. All of the above are used to manage default risk.

12. Insured Municipal Bonds   Which one of the following generally is not true of an insured municipal bond? (*1991 CFA exam*)

  a. The price on an insured bond is higher than that on an otherwise identical uninsured bond.
  b. The insurance can be canceled in the event the issuer fails to maintain predetermined quality standards.
  c. The insurance premium is a one-time payment made at the time of issuance.
  d. The insurance company is obligated to make all defaulted principal and/or interest payments in a prompt and timely fashion.

13. **Taxable Equivalent Yield**   A municipal bond carries a coupon of 6 3/4 percent and is trading at par. To a taxpayer in the 34 percent tax bracket, what would the taxable equivalent yield of this bond be? (*1992 CFA exam*)

   a. 4.5 percent
   b. 10.2 percent
   c. 13.4 percent
   d. 19.9 percent

14. **Taxable Equivalent Yield**   A 20-year municipal bond is currently priced at par to yield 5.53 percent. For a taxpayer in the 33 percent tax bracket, what equivalent taxable yield would this bond offer? (*1991 CFA exam*)

   a. 8.25 percent
   b. 10.75 percent
   c. 11.40 percent
   d. None of the above

15. **Taxable Equivalent Yield**   The coupon rate on a tax-exempt bond is 5.6 percent, and the coupon rate on a taxable bond is 8 percent. Both bonds sell at par. At what tax bracket (marginal tax rate) would an investor show no preference between the two bonds? (*1994 CFA exam*)

   a. 30.0 percent
   b. 39.6 percent
   c. 41.7 percent
   d. 42.9 percent

Questions and Problems

Core Questions

1. **Bills versus Bonds**   What are the key differences between T-bills and T-bonds?
2. **Notes versus Bonds**   What are the key differences between T-notes and T-bonds?
3. **Zeroes**   What two Treasury securities are zeroes?
4. **Spreads**   What are typical spreads for T-notes and T-bonds? Why do you think they differ from issue to issue?
5. **Agencies versus Treasuries**   From an investor's standpoint, what are the key differences between Treasury and agency issues?
6. **Municipals versus Treasuries**   From an investor's standpoint, what are the main differences between Treasury and municipal issues?
7. **Serial Bonds**   What are serial bonds? What purpose does this structure serve?
8. **VRNs**   In the context of the muni market, what are variable-rate notes? What is likely true about their risks compared to those of ordinary issues?
9. **Revenues versus General Obligation Munis**   What is the difference between a revenue bond and a general obligation bond?
10. **Private Activity Munis**   What is a private activity muni? What type of investor would be interested?

Intermediate Questions

11. **Treasury Prices**   A Treasury issue is quoted at 127:23 bid and 127:25 ask. What is the least you could pay to acquire a bond?
12. **Treasury Prices**   A noncallable Treasury bond has a quoted yield of 6.4 percent. It has a 6 percent coupon and 12 years to maturity. What is its price?

13. **Treasury Yields**   In Figure 12.2, locate the Treasury bond with the longest maturity (this is the so-called bellwether bond). Verify that, given the ask price, the reported yield is correct.

14. **Callable Treasury Bonds**   Examine the yields on the callable issues in Figure 12.2 that mature in 2014. Why do think the yields are so much smaller than those reported for the non-callable issues maturing in 2015?

15. **Tax Equivalent Yields**   A taxable corporate issue yields 7 percent. For an investor in a 28 percent tax bracket, what is the equivalent aftertax yield?

16. **Tax Rates**   A taxable issue yields 8 percent, and a similar municipal issue yields 6 percent. What is the critical marginal tax rate?

17. **Treasury versus Municipal Bonds**   Treasury and municipal yields are often compared to calculate critical tax rates. What concerns might you have about such a comparison? What do you think is true about the calculated tax rate?

18. **Callable Treasury Bonds**   For a callable Treasury bond selling above par, is it necessarily true that the yield to call will be less than the yield to maturity? Why or why not?

19. **Callable Agency Issues**   For a callable agency bond selling above par, is it necessarily true that the yield to call will be less than the yield to maturity? Why or why not?

20. **Callable Treasury Bonds**   Locate the callable bond with a final maturity of Nov 2014 in Figure 12.2. Verify that the reported yield is correct given the ask price of 154:21.

STOCK-TRAK·
Portfolio Simulations

Trading Government Bonds with Stock-Trak

U.S. Treasury bonds are available for trading through your Stock-Trak account. The list of available bonds changes from time to time, and you should consult the Stock-Trak website (www.mhhe.com/cj) for the most recent list. Ticker symbols for Treasury bonds are not necessary to submit buy and sell orders. However, special ticker symbols are used by Stock-Trak to identify Treasury bonds in your account statements. The following is a sample of some U.S. Treasury bonds and their Stock-Trak ticker symbols:

Ticker	Description	Explanation
B-T067	Jul 06 7	7 percent coupon, July 2006 maturity
B-T266	Feb 26 6	6 percent coupon, February 2026 maturity

Since all Treasury bonds are free of default risk, the only factors that affect their prices are related to the structure of interest rates in the economy. If you expect interest rates to increase, then you can benefit from the resulting fall in bond prices by short selling bonds. On the other hand, if you expect interest rates to decrease, you should buy bonds and wait for the resulting increase in bond prices.

Stock-Trak Exercises

1. Buy the longest- and shortest-maturity Treasury issues in equal dollar amounts. Observe which yields the greatest return over your investment period.

2. Invest equal amounts in similar-maturity Treasury bonds and corporate bonds. What is their yield spread? Observe which provides the highest return over your investment period.

3. If buying and selling Treasury bonds seems too conservative, you can get more bang for your buck by trading futures contracts on Treasury bonds. The futures contract on the 30-year T-bond has the ticker symbol US and requires only a $2,000 margin deposit for a contract on a $100,000 bond. If this high-powered form of T-bond trading interests you, then refer to the Stock-Trak section in Chapter 16 for details.

13 Mortgage-Backed Securities

The development of mortgage-backed securities represents an important innovation in the way that capital is raised to finance purchases in housing markets. The basic concept is simple. Collect a portfolio of mortgages into a mortgage pool. Then issue securities with pro rata claims on mortgage pool cash flows. These mortgage-backed securities have the attraction to investors that they represent a claim on a diversified portfolio of mortgages, and therefore are considerably less risky than individual mortgage contracts. ■ Owning your own home is a big part of the American dream. But few Americans can actually afford to buy a home outright. What makes home ownership possible for so many is a well-developed system of home mortgage financing. With mortgage financing, a home buyer makes only a down payment and borrows the remaining cost of a home with a mortgage loan. The mortgage loan is obtained from a mortgage originator, usually a local bank or other mortgage broker. Describing this financial transaction, we can say that a home buyer *issues* a mortgage and an originator *writes* a mortgage. The mortgage loan distinguishes itself from other loan contracts by a pledge of real estate as collateral for the loan.

This system has undergone many changes in recent decades. In this chapter, we carefully examine the basic investment characteristics of mortgage-backed securities.

13.1 A Brief History of Mortgage-Backed Securities

mortgage pass-throughs Bonds representing a claim on the cash flows of an underlying mortgage pool passed through to bondholders.

Traditionally, savings banks and savings and loans (S&Ls) wrote most home mortgages and then held the mortgages in their portfolios of interest-earning assets. This changed radically during the 1970s and 1980s when market interest rates ascended to their highest levels in American history. Entering this financially turbulent period, savings banks and S&Ls held large portfolios of mortgages written at low pre-1970s interest rates. These portfolios were financed from customers' savings deposits. When market interest rates climbed to near 20 percent levels in the early 1980s, customers flocked to withdraw funds from their savings deposits to invest in money market funds that paid higher interest rates. As a result, savings institutions were often forced to sell mortgages at depressed prices to satisfy the onslaught of deposit withdrawals. For this, and other reasons, the ultimate result was the collapse of many savings institutions.

Today, home buyers still commonly turn to local banks for mortgage financing, but few mortgages are actually held by the banks that originate them. After writing a mortgage, an originator usually sells the mortgage to a mortgage repackager who accumulates them into mortgage pools. To finance the creation of a mortgage pool, the mortgage repackager issues mortgage-backed bonds, where each bond claims a pro rata share of all cash flows derived from mortgages in the pool. A pro rata share allocation pays cash flows in proportion to a bond's face value. Essentially, each mortgage pool is set up as a trust fund and a servicing agent for the pool collects all mortgage payments. The servicing agent then passes these cash flows through to bondholders. For this reason, mortgage-backed bonds are often called **mortgage pass-throughs**, or simply *pass-throughs*. However, all securities representing claims on mortgage pools are generically called **mortgage-backed securities (MBSs)**. The primary collateral for all mortgage-backed securities is the underlying pool of mortgages.

mortgage-backed securities (MBSs) Securities whose investment returns are based on a pool of mortgages.

mortgage securitization The creation of mortgage-backed securities from a pool of mortgages.

The transformation from mortgages to mortgage-backed securities is called **mortgage securitization**. More than $3 trillion of mortgages have been securitized in mortgage pools. This represents tremendous growth in the mortgage securitization business, since in the early 1980s less than $1 billion of home mortgages were securitized in pools. Yet despite the multi–trillion dollar size of the mortgage-backed securities market, the risks involved with these investments are often misunderstood even by experienced investors.

13.2 Fixed-Rate Mortgages

fixed-rate mortgage Loan that specifies constant monthly payments at a fixed interest rate over the life of the mortgage.

Understanding mortgage-backed securities begins with an understanding of the mortgages from which they are created. Most home mortgages are 15-year or 30-year maturity **fixed-rate mortgages** requiring constant monthly payments. As an example of a fixed-rate mortgage, consider a 30-year mortgage representing a loan of $100,000 financed at an annual interest rate of 8 percent. This translates into a monthly interest rate of 8 percent / 12 months = .67%, and it requires a series of 360 monthly payments. The size of the monthly payment is determined by the requirement that the present value of all monthly payments based on the financing rate specified in the mortgage contract be equal to the original loan amount of $100,000. Mathematically, the constant monthly payment for a $100,000 mortgage is calculated using the following formula:

$$\text{Monthly payment} = \frac{\$100,000 \times r/12}{1 - \dfrac{1}{(1 + r/12)^{T \times 12}}} \qquad [13.1]$$

where

r = Annual mortgage financing rate

$r/12$ = Monthly mortgage financing rate

T = Mortgage term in years

$T \times 12$ = Mortgage term in months

In the example of a 30-year mortgage financed at 8 percent, the monthly payments are $733.76. This amount is calculated as follows.

$$\text{Monthly payment} = \frac{\$100,000 \times .08/12}{1 - \dfrac{1}{(1 + .08/12)^{360}}}$$
$$= \$733.76$$

Another example is a 15-year mortgage financed at 8 percent requiring 180 monthly payments of $955.65 calculated as follows:

$$\text{Monthly payment} = \frac{\$100,000 \times .08/12}{1 - \dfrac{1}{(1 + .08/12)^{180}}}$$
$$= \$955.65$$

Monthly mortgage payments are sensitive to the interest rate stipulated in the mortgage contract. Table 13.1 provides a schedule of monthly payments required for 5-year, 10-year, 15-year, 20-year, and 30-year mortgages based on annual interest rates ranging from 5 percent to 15 percent in increments of .5 percent. Notice that monthly payments required for a $100,000 thirty-year mortgage financed at 5 percent are only $536.82, while monthly payments for the same mortgage financed at 15 percent are $1,264.44.

CHECK THIS

13.2a The most popular fixed-rate mortgages among home buyers are those with 15-year and 30-year maturities. What might be some of the comparative advantages and disadvantages of these two mortgage maturities?

13.2b Suppose you were to finance a home purchase using a fixed-rate mortgage. Would you prefer a 15-year or 30-year maturity mortgage? Why?

Table 13.1	$100,000 Mortgage Loan Monthly Payments				
	Mortgage Maturity				
Interest Rate	**30-Year**	**20-Year**	**15-Year**	**10-Year**	**5-Year**
5.0%	$ 536.82	$ 659.96	$ 790.79	$1,060.66	$1,887.12
5.5	567.79	687.89	817.08	1,085.26	$1,910.12
6.0	599.55	716.43	843.86	1,110.21	1,933.28
6.5	632.07	745.57	871.11	1,135.48	1,956.61
7.0	665.30	775.30	898.83	1,161.08	1,980.12
7.5	699.21	805.59	927.01	1,187.02	2,003.79
8.0	733.76	836.44	955.65	1,213.28	2,027.64
8.5	768.91	867.82	984.74	1,239.86	2,051.65
9.0	804.62	899.73	1,014.27	1,266.76	2,075.84
9.5	840.85	932.13	1,044.22	1,293.98	2,100.19
10.0	877.57	965.02	1,074.61	1,321.51	2,124.70
10.5	914.74	998.38	1,105.40	1,349.35	2,149.39
11.0	952.32	1,032.19	1,136.60	1,377.50	2,174.24
11.5	990.29	1,066.43	1,168.19	1,405.95	2,199.26
12.0	1,028.61	1,101.09	1,200.17	1,434.71	2,224.44
12.5	1,067.26	1,136.14	1,232.52	1,463.76	2,249.79
13.0	1,106.20	1,171.58	1,265.24	1,493.11	2,275.31
13.5	1,145.41	1,207.37	1,298.32	1,522.74	2,300.98
14.0	1,184.87	1,243.52	1,331.74	1,552.66	2,326.83
14.5	1,224.56	1,280.00	1,365.50	1,582.87	2,352.83
15.0	1,264.44	1,316.79	1,399.59	1,613.35	2,378.99

Fixed-Rate Mortgage Amortization

mortgage principal
The amount of a mortgage loan outstanding, which is the amount required to pay off the mortgage.

Each monthly mortgage payment has two separate components. The first component represents payment of interest on outstanding **mortgage principal**. Outstanding mortgage principal is also called a mortgage's *remaining balance* or *remaining principal*. It is the amount required to pay off a mortgage before it matures. The second component represents a pay-down, or *amortization,* of mortgage principal. The relative amounts of each component change throughout the life of a mortgage. For example, a 30-year $100,000 mortgage financed at 8 percent requires 360 monthly payments of $733.76. The first monthly payment consists of a $666.67 payment of interest and a $67.09 pay-down of principal. The first month's interest payment, representing one month's interest on a mortgage balance of $100,000, is calculated as

$$\$100,000 \times .08/12 = \$666.67$$

After this payment of interest, the remainder of the first monthly payment, that is, $733.76 − $666.67 = $67.09, is used to amortize outstanding mortgage principal. Thus, after the first monthly payment, outstanding principal is reduced to $100,000 − $67.09 = $99,932.91.

The second monthly payment includes a $666.22 payment of interest calculated as

$$\$99,932.91 \times .08/12 = \$666.22$$

The remainder of the second monthly payment, that is, $733.76 − $666.22 = $67.54, is used to reduce mortgage principal to $99,932.91 − $67.54 = $99,865.37.

mortgage amortization The process of paying down mortgage principal over the life of the mortgage.

This process continues throughout the life of the mortgage. The interest payment component gradually declines and the payment of principal component gradually increases. Finally, the last monthly payment is divided into a $4.86 payment of interest and a final $728.90 pay-down of mortgage principal. The process of paying down mortgage principal over the life of a mortgage is called **mortgage amortization**.

Mortgage amortization is described by an amortization schedule. An amortization schedule states the remaining principal owed on a mortgage at any point in time and also states the scheduled principal payment and interest payment in any month. Amortization schedules for 15-year and 30-year $100,000 mortgages financed at a fixed rate of 8 percent are listed in Table 13.2. The payment month is given in the left-hand

Table 13.2	**$100,000, 8%, Mortgage Loan Amortization Schedules for 15-Year and 30-Year Mortgages**						
	30-Year Mortgage, $733.76 Monthly Payment				**15-Year Mortgage, $955.65 Monthly Payment**		
Payment Month	**Remaining Principal**	**Principal Reduction**	**Interest Payment**	**Payment Month**	**Remaining Principal**	**Principal Reduction**	**Interest Payment**
1	$99,932.28	$67.10	$666.66	1	$99,710.80	$288.98	$666.67
12	99,164.02	72.19	661.57	12	96,401.94	310.90	644.75
24	98,259.32	78.18	655.58	24	92,505.48	336.70	618.95
36	97,279.54	84.67	649.09	36	88,285.62	364.65	591.00
48	96,218.44	91.69	642.07	48	83,715.51	394.91	560.74
60	95,069.26	99.30	634.46	60	78,766.09	427.69	527.96
72	93,824.71	107.54	626.22	72	73,405.86	463.19	492.46
84	92,476.86	116.47	617.29	84	67,600.74	501.63	454.02
96	91,017.13	126.14	607.62	96	61,313.80	543.27	412.38
108	89,436.25	136.61	597.15	108	54,505.04	588.36	367.29
120	87,724.16	147.95	585.81	120	47,131.16	637.19	318.46
132	85,869.96	160.23	573.53	132	39,145.25	690.08	265.57
144	83,861.87	173.52	560.24	144	30,496.52	747.36	208.29
156	81,687.10	187.93	545.83	156	21,129.94	809.39	146.26
168	79,331.84	203.52	530.24	168	10,985.94	876.57	79.08
180	76,781.08	220.42	513.34	180	0.00	949.32	6.33
192	74,018.62	238.71	495.05				
204	71,026.87	258.52	475.24				
216	67,786.80	279.98	453.78				
228	64,277.82	303.22	430.54				
240	60,477.59	328.39	405.37				
252	56,361.94	355.64	378.12				
264	51,904.69	385.16	348.60				
276	47,077.50	417.13	316.63				
288	41,849.65	451.75	282.01				
300	36,187.89	489.25	244.51				
312	30,056.21	529.85	203.91				
324	23,415.61	573.83	159.93				
336	16,223.83	621.46	112.30				
348	8,435.14	673.04	60.72				
360	0.00	728.90	4.86				

column. Then, for each maturity, the first column reports remaining mortgage principal immediately after a monthly payment is made. Columns 2 and 3 for each maturity list the principal payment and the interest payment scheduled for each monthly payment. Notice that immediately after the 180th monthly payment for a 30-year $100,000 mortgage, $76,781.08 of mortgage principal is still outstanding. Notice also that as late as the 252nd monthly payment, the interest payment component of $378.12 still exceeds the principal payment component of $355.64.

The amortization process for a 30-year $100,000 mortgage financed at 8 percent interest is illustrated graphically in Figure 13.1. Figure 13.1A graphs the amortization of mortgage principal over the life of the mortgage. Figure 13.1B graphs the rising principal payment component and the falling interest payment component of the mortgage.

Figure 13.1

Mortgage Principal and Payments for a $100,000 Mortgage with an 8 Percent Interest Rate

A. Outstanding mortgage principal

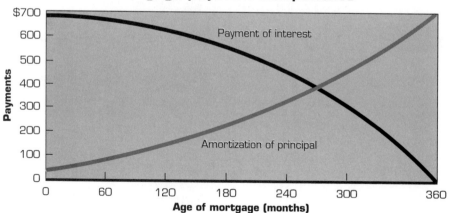

B. Mortgage payment components

Fixed-Rate Mortgage Prepayment and Refinancing

mortgage prepayment Paying off all or part of outstanding mortgage principal ahead of its amortization schedule.

A mortgage borrower has the right to pay off an outstanding mortgage at any time. This right is similar to the call feature on corporate bonds, whereby the issuer can buy back outstanding bonds at a prespecified call price. Paying off a mortgage ahead of its amortization schedule is called **mortgage prepayment**.

Prepayment can be motivated by a variety of factors. A homeowner may pay off a mortgage in order to sell the property when a family moves because of, say, new employment or retirement. After the death of a spouse, a surviving family member may pay off a mortgage with an insurance benefit. These are examples of mortgage prepayment for personal reasons. However, mortgage prepayments often occur for a purely financial reason: an existing mortgage loan may be refinanced at a lower interest rate when a lower rate becomes available.

Consider a 30-year $100,000 fixed-rate 8 percent mortgage with a monthly payment of $733.76. Suppose that 10 years into the mortgage, market interest rates have fallen and the financing rate on new 20-year mortgages is 6.5 percent. After 10 years (120 months), the remaining balance for the original $100,000 mortgage is $87,724.16. The monthly payment on a new 20-year $90,000 fixed-rate 6.5 percent mortgage is $671.01, which is $62.75 less than the $733.76 monthly payment on the old 8 percent mortgage with 20 years of payments remaining. Thus, a homeowner could profit by prepaying the original 8 percent mortgage and refinancing with a new 20-year 6.5 percent mortgage. Monthly payments would be lower by $62.75, and the $2,275.84 difference between the new $90,000 mortgage balance and the old $87,724.16 mortgage balance would defray any refinancing costs.

As this example suggests, during periods of falling interest rates, mortgage refinancings are an important reason for mortgage prepayments. The nearby Investment Updates box presents a *Wall Street Journal* article discussing the merits of mortgage refinancing.

The possibility of prepayment and refinancing is an advantage to mortgage borrowers but a disadvantage to mortgage investors. For example, consider investors who supply funds to write mortgages at a financing rate of 8 percent. Suppose that mortgage interest rates later fall to 6.5 percent, and, consequently, homeowners rush to prepay their 8 percent mortgages so as to refinance at 6.5 percent. Mortgage investors recover their outstanding investment principal from the prepayments, but the rate of return that they can realize on a new investment is reduced because mortgages can now be written only at the new 6.5 percent financing rate. The possibility that falling interest rates will set off a wave of mortgage refinancings is an ever-present risk that mortgage investors must face.

Government National Mortgage Association

Government National Mortgage Association (GNMA) Government agency charged with promoting liquidity in the home mortgage market.

In 1968, Congress established the **Government National Mortgage Association (GNMA)**, colloquially called "Ginnie Mae," as a government agency within the Department of Housing and Urban Development (HUD). GNMA was charged with the mission of promoting liquidity in the secondary market for home mortgages. Liquidity is the ability of investors to buy and sell securities quickly at competitive market prices. Essentially, mortgages repackaged into mortgage pools are a more liquid investment product than the original unpooled mortgages. GNMA has successfully sponsored the re-packaging of several trillion dollars of mortgages into hundreds of thousands of mortgage-backed securities pools.

It May Make Sense to Pay Down a Mortgage

Maybe this is the year to put it on the house.

Spooked by the stock market? Disenchanted with lowly bond yields? Consider taking some of your investment dollars and using them to pay down your mortgage.

Admittedly, making extra mortgage payments won't earn you dazzling returns. If your mortgage rate is 8%, that's your effective pretax rate of return on every additional dollar you add to your mortgage check.

Doesn't seem like much? Sure, it can't compare with the 11%-a-year total return for stocks since year-end 1925, and it pales beside the 31% annual stock-market gain of the past three calendar years, as calculated by Chicago's Ibbotson Associates.

But making extra mortgage payments can be a smart move for conservative investors who would otherwise buy bonds, money-market funds, and certificates of deposit.

The case for making extra mortgage payments has been bolstered by the recent drop in interest rates, which has squeezed yields on bonds and other conservative investments. In fact, interest rates have fallen so much that many folks are seizing the chance to refinance their mortgages and lock in lower rates.

For those homeowners who find it's not worth refinancing, extra-mortgage payments offer an alternative way of eliminating costly mortgage debt. By adding just a few dollars to each monthly check, you can save thousands of dollars in interest over the life of your mortgage.

Suppose you just borrowed $200,000 using a 30-year, $7\frac{1}{2}$% fixed-rate mortgage that requires a $1,400 monthly payment. By adding only $25 to each check, for a total of $8,425 over the life of the loan, you would save $22,500 in interest and pay off your mortgage almost two years early.

Adding a few dollars to the monthly check can also make sense if you have an adjustable-rate mortgage. But with an ARM, your extra $25 won't shorten the length of the loan. Instead, the additional dollars will lead to lower required monthly payments.

Still, before you tack an extra $25, $50 or $100 onto the next mortgage check, make sure you have already made the most of other options that promise a higher return. For instance, instead of paying down your mortgage, you are much better off getting rid of credit-card debt. Your cards may be costing you 18% a year and, unlike mortgage debt, the interest isn't tax-deductible.

Similarly, before you make any extra mortgage payments, you should invest the maximum possible in your employer's retirement-savings plan and fully fund a regular or Roth individual retirement account.

Once you have paid off high-cost debt and made full use of tax-sheltered retirement accounts, you may have additional money that you want to save. At that point, you might use the extra money to pay down your mortgage or, alternatively, you could use the cash to buy investments in a regular taxable account.

fully modified mortgage pool
Mortgage pool that guarantees timely payment of interest and principal.

prepayment risk
Uncertainty faced by mortgage investors regarding early payment of mortgage principal and interest.

GNMA mortgage pools are based on mortgages issued under programs administered by the Federal Housing Administration (FHA), the Veteran's Administration (VA), and the Farmer's Home Administration (FmHA). Mortgages in GNMA pools are said to be **fully modified** because GNMA guarantees bondholders full and timely payment of both principal and interest even in the event of default of the underlying mortgages. The GNMA guarantee augments guarantees already provided by the FHA, VA, and FmHA. Since GNMA, FHA, VA, and FmHA are all agencies of the federal government, GNMA mortgage pass-throughs are free of default risk. But while investors in GNMA pass-throughs do not face default risk, they still face **prepayment risk**.

GNMA operates in cooperation with private underwriters certified by GNMA to create mortgage pools. The underwriters originate or otherwise acquire the mortgages to form a pool. After verifying that the mortgages comply with GNMA requirements, GNMA authorizes the underwriter to issue mortgage-backed securities with a GNMA guarantee.

As a simplified example of how a GNMA pool operates, consider a hypothetical GNMA fully modified mortgage pool containing only a single mortgage. After obtaining approval from GNMA, the pool has a GNMA guarantee and is called a *GNMA bond.* The underwriter then sells the bond and the buyer is entitled to receive all mortgage payments, less servicing and guarantee fees. If a mortgage payment occurs ahead of schedule, the early payment is passed through to the GNMA bondholder. If a payment is late, GNMA makes a timely payment to the bondholder. If any mortgage principal is prepaid, the early payment is passed through to the bondholder. If a default occurs, GNMA settles with the bondholder by making full payment of remaining mortgage principal. In effect, to a GNMA bondholder mortgage default is the same thing as a prepayment.

When originally issued, the minimum denomination of a GNMA mortgage-backed bond is $25,000, with subsequent increments of $5,000. The minimum size for a GNMA mortgage pool is $1 million, although it could be much larger. Thus, for example, a GNMA mortgage pool might conceivably represent only 40 bonds with an initial bond principal of $25,000 par value per bond. However, initial bond principal only specifies a bond's share of mortgage pool principal. Over time, mortgage-backed bond principal declines because of scheduled mortgage amortization and mortgage prepayments.

GNMA Clones

Federal Home Loan Mortgage Corporation (FHLMC) and Federal National Mortgage Association (FNMA)
Government sponsored enterprises charged with promoting liquidity in the home mortgage market.

While GNMA is perhaps the best-known guarantor of mortgage-backed securities, two government-sponsored enterprises (GSEs) are also significant mortgage repackaging sponsors. These are the **Federal Home Loan Mortgage Corporation (FHLMC)**, colloquially called "Freddie Mac," and the **Federal National Mortgage Association (FNMA)**, called "Fannie Mae." FHLMC was chartered by Congress in 1970 to increase mortgage credit availability for residential housing. It was originally owned by the Federal Home Loan Banks operated under direction of the U.S. Treasury. But in 1989, FHLMC was allowed to become a private corporation with an issue of common stock. Freddie Mac stock trades on the New York Stock Exchange under the ticker symbol FRE.

The Federal National Mortgage Association was originally created in 1938 as a government-owned corporation of the United States. Thirty years later FNMA was split into two government corporations: GNMA and FNMA. Soon after, in 1970, FNMA was allowed to become a private corporation and has since grown to become one of the major financial corporations in the United States. Fannie Mae stock trades on the New York Stock Exchange under the ticker symbol FNM.

Like GNMA, both FHLMC and FNMA operate with qualified underwriters who accumulate mortgages into pools financed by an issue of bonds that entitle bondholders to cash flows generated by mortgages in the pools, less the standard servicing and guarantee fees. However, the guarantees on FHLMC and FNMA pass-throughs are not exactly the same as for GNMA pass-throughs. Essentially, FHLMC and FNMA are only government-sponsored enterprises, whereas GNMA is a government agency. Congress may be less willing to rescue a financially strapped GSE.

Before June 1990, FHLMC guaranteed timely payment of interest but only *eventual* payment of principal on its mortgage-backed bonds. However, beginning in June 1990, FHLMC began its Gold program whereby it guaranteed timely payment of both interest and principal. Therefore, FHLMC Gold mortgage-backed bonds are fully modified pass-through securities. FNMA guarantees timely payment of both interest and principal on its mortgage-backed bonds, and therefore these are also fully modified pass-through securities. But since FHLMC and FNMA are only GSEs, their fully modified pass-throughs do not carry the same default protection as GNMA fully modified pass-throughs.

 13.4 **Public Securities Association Mortgage Prepayment Model**

prepayment rate
The probability that a mortgage will be prepaid during a given year.

Mortgage prepayments are typically described by stating a **prepayment rate**, which is the probability that a mortgage will be prepaid in a given year. The greater the prepayment rate for a mortgage pool, the faster the mortgage pool principal is paid off, and the more rapid is the decline of bond principal for bonds supported by the underlying mortgage pool. Historical experience shows that prepayment rates can vary substantially from year to year depending on mortgage type and various economic and demographic factors.

Conventional industry practice states prepayment rates using a prepayment model specified by the Public Securities Association (PSA). According to this model, prepayment rates are stated as a percentage of a PSA benchmark. The PSA benchmark specifies an annual prepayment rate of .2 percent in month 1 of a mortgage, .4 percent in month 2, then .6 percent in month three, and so on. The annual prepayment rate continues to rise by .2 percent per month until reaching an annual prepayment rate of 6 percent in month 30 of a mortgage. Thereafter, the benchmark prepayment rate remains constant at 6 percent per year. This PSA benchmark represents a mortgage prepayment schedule called 100 PSA, which means 100 percent of the PSA benchmark. Deviations from the 100 PSA benchmark are stated as a percentage of the benchmark. For example, 200 PSA means 200 percent of the 100 PSA benchmark, and it doubles all prepayment rates relative to the benchmark. Similarly, 50 PSA means 50 percent of the 100 PSA benchmark, halving all prepayment rates relative to the benchmark. Prepayment rate schedules illustrating 50 PSA, 100 PSA, and 200 PSA are graphically presented in Figure 13.2.

seasoned mortgages
Mortgages over 30 months old.

Based on historical experience, the PSA prepayment model makes an important distinction between **seasoned mortgages** and **unseasoned mortgages**. In the PSA model, unseasoned mortgages are those less than 30 months old with rising prepayments rates. Seasoned mortgages are those over 30 months old with constant prepayment rates.

unseasoned mortgages
Mortgages less than 30 months old.

conditional prepayment rate (CPR) The prepayment rate for a mortgage pool conditional on the age of the mortgages in the pool.

Prepayment rates in the PSA model are stated as **conditional prepayment rates (CPRs)**, since they are conditional on the age of mortgages in a pool. For example, the CPR for a seasoned 100 PSA mortgage is 6 percent, which represents a 6 percent probability of mortgage prepayment in a given year. By convention, the probability of prepayment in a given month is stated as a *single monthly mortality (SMM)*. SMM is calculated using a CPR as follows:

$$SMM = 1 - (1 - CPR)^{1/12} \qquad [13.2]$$

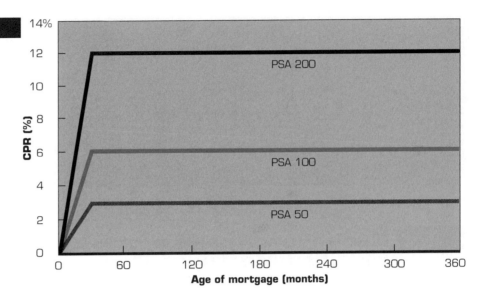

Figure 13.2

PSA
Prepayment
Model Showing
Conditional
Prepayment
Rates (CPR)

For example, the SMM corresponding to a seasoned 100 PSA mortgage with a 6 percent CPR is .5143 percent, which is calculated as

$$SMM = 1 - (1 - .06)^{1/12}$$
$$= .5143\%$$

As another example, the SMM corresponding to an unseasoned 100 PSA mortgage in month 20 of the mortgage with a 4 percent CPR is .3396 percent, which is calculated as

$$SMM = 1 - (1 - .04)^{1/12} = .3396\%$$

average life Average
time for a mortgage
in a pool to be paid
off.

Some mortgages in a pool are prepaid earlier than average, some are prepaid later than average, and some are not prepaid at all. The **average life** of a mortgage in a pool is the average time for a single mortgage in a pool to be paid off, either by prepayment or by making scheduled payments until maturity. Because prepayment shortens the life of a mortgage, the average life of a mortgage is usually much less than a mortgage's stated maturity. We can calculate a mortgage's projected average life by assuming a particular prepayment schedule. For example, the average life of a mortgage in a pool of 30-year mortgages assuming several PSA prepayment schedules is stated immediately below.

Prepayment Schedule	Average Mortgage Life (years)
50 PSA	20.40
100 PSA	14.68
200 PSA	8.87
400 PSA	4.88

Notice that an average life ranges from slightly less than 5 years for 400 PSA prepayments to slightly more than 20 years for 50 PSA prepayments.[1]

Bear in mind that these are expected averages given a particular prepayment schedule. Since prepayments are somewhat unpredictable, the average life of mortgages in any specific pool are likely to deviate somewhat from an expected average.

---

[1] Formulas used to calculate average mortgage life are complicated and depend on the assumed prepayment model. For this reason, average life formulas are omitted here.

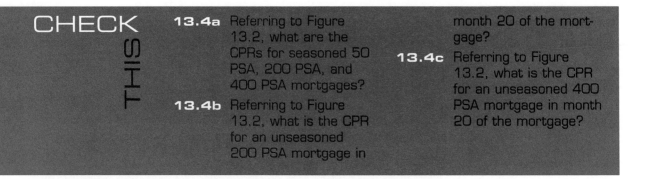

CHECK
THIS

13.4a Referring to Figure 13.2, what are the CPRs for seasoned 50 PSA, 200 PSA, and 400 PSA mortgages?

13.4b Referring to Figure 13.2, what is the CPR for an unseasoned 200 PSA mortgage in month 20 of the mortgage?

13.4c Referring to Figure 13.2, what is the CPR for an unseasoned 400 PSA mortgage in month 20 of the mortgage?

Cash Flow Analysis of GNMA Fully Modified Mortgage Pools

Each month, GNMA mortgage-backed bond investors receive pro rata shares of cash flows derived from fully modified mortgage pools. Each monthly cash flow has three distinct components:

1. Payment of interest on outstanding mortgage principal.
2. Scheduled amortization of mortgage principal.
3. Mortgage principal prepayments.

As a sample GNMA mortgage pool, consider a $10 million pool of 30-year 8 percent mortgages financed by the sale of 100 bonds at a par value price of $100,000 per bond. For simplicity, we ignore servicing and guarantee fees. The decline in bond principal for these GNMA bonds is graphed in Figure 13.3A for the cases of prepayment rates following 50 PSA, 100 PSA, 200 PSA, and 400 PSA schedules. In Figure 13.3A, notice that 50 PSA prepayments yield a nearly straight-line amortization of bond principal. Also notice that for the extreme case of 400 PSA prepayments, over 90 percent of bond principal is amortized within 10 years of mortgage pool origination.

Monthly cash flows for these GNMA bonds are graphed in Figure 13.3B for the cases of 50 PSA, 100 PSA, 200 PSA, and 400 PSA prepayment schedules. In Figure 13.3B, notice the sharp spike in monthly cash flows associated with 400 PSA prepayments at about month 30. Lesser PSA prepayment rates blunt the spike and level the cash flows.

As shown in Figures 13.3A and B, prepayments significantly affect the cash flow characteristics of GNMA bonds. However, these illustrations assume that prepayment schedules remain unchanged over the life of a mortgage pool. This can be unrealistic, since prepayment rates often change from those originally forecast. For example, sharply falling interest rates could easily cause a jump in prepayment rates from 100 PSA to 400 PSA. Since large interest rate movements are unpredictable, future prepayment rates can also be unpredictable. Consequently, GNMA mortgage-backed bond investors face substantial cash flow uncertainty. This makes GNMA bonds an unsuitable investment for many investors, especially relatively unsophisticated investors unaware of the risks involved. Nevertheless, GNMA bonds offer higher yields than U.S. Treasury bonds, which makes them attractive to professional fixed-income portfolio managers.

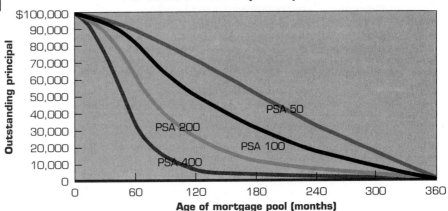

A. GNMA bond principal

Figure 13.3

Principal and
Cash Flows for
$100,000 Par
Value 30-Year
8 Percent
GNMA Bonds

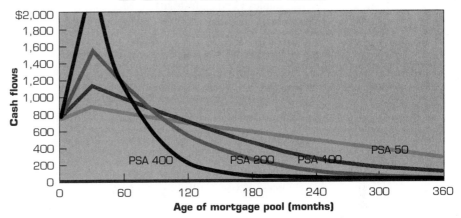

B. GNMA bond cash flows

CHECK THIS

13.5a GNMA bond investors face significant cash flow uncertainty. Why might cash flow uncertainty be a problem for many portfolio managers?

13.5b Why might cash flow uncertainty be less of a problem for investors with a very long term investment horizon?

Macaulay Durations for GNMA Mortgage-Backed Bonds

For mortgage pool investors, prepayment risk is important because it complicates the effects of interest rate risk. With falling interest rates, prepayments speed up and the average life of mortgages in a pool shortens. Similarly, with rising interest rates, pre-

Macaulay duration
A measure of interest rate risk for fixed-income securities.

payments slow down and average mortgage life lengthens. Recall from a previous chapter that interest rate risk for a bond is often measured by **Macaulay duration**. However, Macaulay duration assumes a fixed schedule of cash flow payments. But the schedule of cash flow payments for mortgage-backed bonds is not fixed because it is affected by mortgage prepayments, which in turn are affected by interest rates. For this reason, Macaulay duration is a deficient measure of interest rate risk for mortgage-backed bonds. The following examples illustrate the deficiency of Macaulay duration when it is unrealistically assumed that interest rates do not affect mortgage prepayment rates.[2]

1. *Macaulay duration for a GNMA bond with zero prepayments.* Suppose a GNMA bond is based on a pool of 30-year, 8 percent fixed-rate mortgages. Assuming an 8 percent interest rate, their price is equal to their initial par value of $100,000. The Macaulay duration for these bonds is 9.56 years.

2. *Macaulay duration for a GNMA bond with a constant 100 PSA prepayment schedule.* Suppose a GNMA bond based on a pool of 30-year 8 percent fixed-rate mortgages follows a constant 100 PSA prepayment schedule. Accounting for this prepayment schedule when calculating Macaulay duration, we obtain a Macaulay duration of 6.77 years.

Examples 1 and 2 illustrate how Macaulay duration can be affected by mortgage prepayments. Essentially, faster prepayments cause earlier cash flows and shorten Macaulay durations.

However, Macaulay durations are still misleading because they assume that prepayment schedules are unaffected by changes in interest rates. When falling interest rates speed up prepayments, or rising interest rates slow down prepayments, Macaulay durations yield inaccurate price-change predictions for mortgage-backed securities. The following examples illustrate the inaccuracy.

3. *Macaulay duration for a GNMA bond with changing PSA prepayment schedules.* Suppose a GNMA bond based on a pool of 30-year 8 percent fixed-rate mortgages has a par value price of $100,000, and that, with no change in interest rates, the pool follows a 100 PSA prepayment schedule. Further suppose that when the market interest rate for these bonds rises to 9 percent, prepayments fall to a 50 PSA schedule. In this case, the price of the bond falls to $92,644, representing a 7.36 percent price drop, which is more than .5 percent larger than the drop predicted by the bond's Macaulay duration of 6.77.

4. *Macaulay duration for a GNMA bond with changing PSA prepayment schedules.* Suppose a GNMA bond based on a pool of 30-year 8 percent fixed rate mortgages has a par value price of $100,000, and that with no change in interest rates the pool follows a 100 PSA prepayment schedule. Further suppose that when the market interest rate for these bonds falls to 7 percent, prepayments rise to a 200 PSA schedule. In this case, the bond price rises to $105,486, which is over 1.2 percent less than the price increase predicted by the bond's Macaulay duration of 6.77.

Examples 3 and 4 illustrate that simple Macaulay durations overpredict price increases and underpredict price decreases for changes in mortgage-backed bond prices caused by changing interest rates. These errors are caused by the fact that Macaulay duration does not account for prepayment rates changing in response to interest rate

---

[2] The Macaulay duration formula for a mortgage is not presented here since, as our discussion suggests, its usage is not recommended.

changes. The severity of these errors depends on how strongly interest rates affect prepayment rates. Historical experience indicates that interest rates significantly affect prepayment rates, and that Macaulay duration is a very conservative measure of interest rate risk for mortgage-backed securities.

To correct the deficiencies of Macaulay duration, a method often used in practice to assess interest rate risk for mortgage-backed securities is to first develop projections regarding mortgage prepayments. Projecting prepayments for mortgages requires analyzing both economic and demographic variables. In particular, it is necessary to estimate how prepayment rates will respond to changes in interest rates. Only then is it possible to calculate predicted prices for mortgage-backed securities based on hypothetical interest rate and prepayment scenarios. The task is easier to describe than accomplish, however, since historical experience indicates that the relationship between interest rates and prepayment rates can be unstable over time. For this reason, mortgage-backed securities analysis will always be part art and part science.

| CHECK THIS | 13.5c Why is it important for portfolio managers to know by how much a change in interest rates will affect mortgage prepayments? | 13.5d Why is it important for portfolio managers to know by how much a change in interest rates will affect mortgage-backed bond prices? |

13.6 Collateralized Mortgage Obligations

collateralized mortgage obligations (CMOs)
Securities created by splitting mortgage pool cash flows according to specific allocation rules.

When a mortgage pool is created, cash flows from the pool are often carved up and distributed according to various allocation rules. Mortgage-backed securities representing specific rules for allocating mortgage cash flows are called **collateralized mortgage obligations (CMOs)**. Indeed, a CMO is defined by the rule that created it. Like all mortgage pass-throughs, primary collateral for CMOs are the mortgages in the underlying pool. This is true no matter how the rules for cash flow distribution are actually specified.

The three best-known types of CMO structures using specific rules to carve up mortgage pool cash flows are (1) interest-only strips (IOs) and principal-only strips (POs), (2) sequential CMOs, and (3) protected amortization class securities (PACs). Each of these CMO structures is discussed immediately below. Before beginning, however, we retell an old Wall Street joke that pertains to CMOs: Question: "How many investment bankers does it take to *sell* a lightbulb?" Answer: "401; one to hit it with a hammer, and 400 to sell off the pieces."

The moral of the story is that mortgage-backed securities can be repackaged in many ways, and the resulting products are often quite complex. Even the basic types we consider here are significantly more complicated than the basic fixed income instruments we considered in earlier chapters. Consequently, we do not go into great detail regarding the underlying calculations for CMOs. Instead, we examine only the basic properties of the most commonly encountered CMOs.

Interest-Only and Principal-Only Mortgage Strips

**interest-only strips
(IOs)** Securities that
pay only the interest
cash flows to
investors.

**principal-only strips
(POs)** Securities that
pay only the principal
cash flows to
investors.

Perhaps the simplest rule for carving up mortgage pool cash flows is to separate payments of principal from payments of interest. Mortgage-backed securities paying only the interest component of mortgage pool cash flows are called **interest-only strips**, or simply **IOs.** Mortgage-backed securities paying only the principal component of mortgage pool cash flows are called **principal-only strips**, or simply **POs.** Mortgage strips are more complicated than straight mortgage pass-throughs. In particular, IO strips and PO strips behave quite differently in response to changes in prepayment rates and interest rates.

Let us begin an examination of mortgage strips by considering a $100,000 par value GNMA bond that has been stripped into a separate IO bond and a PO bond. The whole GNMA bond receives a pro rata share of all cash flows from a pool of 30-year 8 percent mortgages. From the whole bond cash flow, the IO bond receives the interest component and the PO bond receives the principal component. The sum of IO and PO cash flows reproduces the whole bond cash flow.

Assuming various PSA prepayment schedules, cash flows to IO strips are illustrated in Figure 13.4A and cash flows to PO strips are illustrated in Figure 13.4B. Holding the interest rate constant at 8 percent, IO and PO strip values for various PSA prepayment schedules are listed immediately below:

Prepayment Schedule	IO Strip Value	PO Strip Value
50 PSA	$63,102.80	$36,897.20
100 PSA	53,726.50	46,273.50
200 PSA	41,366.24	58,633.76
400 PSA	28,764.16	71,235.84

Notice that total bond value is $100,000 for all prepayment schedules because the interest rate is unchanged from its original 8 percent value. Nevertheless, even with no change in interest rates, faster prepayments imply *lower* IO strip values and *higher* PO strip values, and vice versa.

There is a simple reason why PO strip value rises with faster prepayments rates. Essentially, the only cash flow uncertainty facing PO strip holders is the timing of PO cash flows, not the total amount of cash flows. No matter what prepayment schedule applies, total cash flows paid to PO strip holders over the life of the pool will be equal to the initial principal of $100,000. Therefore, PO strip value increases as principal is paid earlier to PO strip holders because of the time value of money.

In contrast, IO strip holders face considerable uncertainty regarding the total amount of IO cash flows that they will receive. Faster prepayments reduce principal more rapidly, thereby reducing interest payments since interest is paid only on outstanding principal. The best that IO strip holders could hope for is that no mortgages are prepaid, which would maximize total interest payments. Prepayments reduce total interest payments. Indeed, in the extreme case, where all mortgages in a pool are prepaid, IO cash flows stop completely.

The effects of changing interest rates compounded by changing prepayment rates are illustrated by considering IO and PO strips from a $100,000 par value GNMA bond based on a pool of 30-year 8 percent mortgages. First, suppose that an interest rate of 8 percent yields a 100 PSA prepayment schedule. Also suppose that a lower interest rate of 7 percent yields 200 PSA prepayments, and a higher interest rate of 9 percent yields 50 PSA prepayments. The resulting whole bond values and separate IO and PO strip values for these combinations of interest rates and prepayment rates are listed immediately below:

Figure 13.4

Cash Flows for
$100,000 Par
Value 30-Year
8 Percent
Bonds

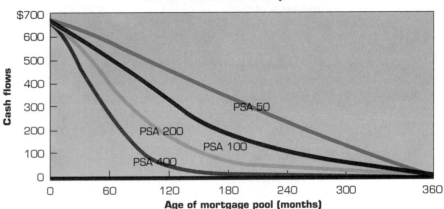

A. GNMA IO strip

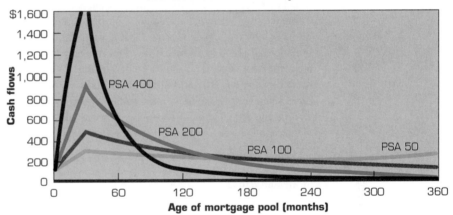

B. GNMA PO strip

Interest Rate	Prepayments	IO Strip Value	PO Strip Value	Whole Bond Value
9%	50 PSA	$59,124.79	$35,519.47	$94,644.26
8	100 PSA	53,726.50	46,273.50	100,000.00
7	200 PSA	43,319.62	62,166.78	105,486.40

When the interest rate increases from 8 percent to 9 percent, total bond value falls by $5,355.74. This results from the PO strip price *falling* by $10,754.03 and the IO strip price *increasing* by $5,398.29. When the interest rate decreases from 8 percent to 7 percent, total bond value rises by $5,486.40. This results from the PO strip price *increasing* by $15,893.28 and the IO strip price *falling* by $10,406.88. Thus, PO strip values change in the same direction as whole bond value, but the PO price change is larger. Notice that the IO strip price changes in the opposite direction of the whole bond and PO strip price change.

13.6a Suppose a $100,000 mortgage financed at 8 percent (.75 percent monthly) is paid off in the first month after issuance. In this case, what are the cash flows to an IO strip and a PO strip from this mortgage?

Sequential Collateralized Mortgage Obligations

sequential CMOs
Securities created by splitting a mortgage pool into a number of slices, called tranches.

One problem with investing in mortgage-backed bonds is the limited range of maturities available. An early method developed to deal with this problem is the creation of **sequential CMOs**. Sequential CMOs carve a mortgage pool into a number of tranches. *Tranche,* the French word for slice, is a commonly-used financial term to describe the division of a whole into various parts. Sequential CMOs are defined by rules that distribute mortgage pool cash flows to sequential tranches. While almost any number of tranches are possible, a basic sequential CMO structure might have four tranches: A-tranche, B-tranche, C-tranche, and Z-tranche. Each tranche is entitled to a share of mortgage pool principal and interest on that share of principal.

As a hypothetical sequential CMO structure, suppose a 30-year 8 percent GNMA bond initially represents $100,000 of mortgage principal. Cash flows to this whole bond are then carved up according to a sequential CMO structure with A-, B-, C-, and Z-tranches. The A-, B-, and C-tranches initially represent $30,000 of mortgage principal each. The Z-tranche initially represents $10,000 of principal. The sum of all four tranches reproduces the original whole bond principal of $100,000. The cash flows from the whole bond are passed through to each tranche according to the following rules:

Rule 1: Mortgage principal payments. All payments of mortgage principal, including scheduled amortization and prepayments, are first paid to the A-tranche. When all A-tranche principal is paid off, subsequent payments of mortgage principal are then paid to the B-tranche. After all B-tranche principal is paid off, all principal payments are then paid to the C-tranche. Finally, when all C-tranche principal is paid off, all principal payments go to the Z-tranche.

Rule 2: Interest payments. All tranches receive interest payments in proportion to the amount of outstanding principal in each tranche. Interest on A-, B-, and C-tranche principal is passed through immediately to A-, B-, and C-tranches. Interest on Z-tranche principal is paid to the A-tranche as cash in exchange for the transfer of an equal amount of principal from the A-tranche to the Z-tranche. After A-tranche principal is fully paid, interest on Z-tranche principal is paid to the B-tranche in exchange for an equal amount of principal from the B-tranche to the Z-tranche. This process continues sequentially through each tranche.

For example, the first month's cash flows from a single whole bond are allocated as follows. Scheduled mortgage payments yield a whole bond cash flow of $733.76, which is divided between $67.10 principal amortization and $666.66 payment of interest. All scheduled principal amortization is paid to the A-tranche and A-tranche principal is reduced by a like amount. Since outstanding principal was *initially* equal to $30,000 for the A-, B-, and C-tranche bonds, each of these tranches receives an interest payment of $30,000 × .08 / 12 = $200. In addition, the Z-tranche interest payment of $10,000 × .08 / 12 = $66.67 is paid to the A-tranche in cash in exchange for transferring $66.67 of principal to the Z-tranche. In summary, A-tranche principal is reduced by $67.10 + $66.67 = $133.77 plus any prepayments, and Z-tranche principal is increased by $66.67.

Remaining principal amounts for A-, B-, C-, and Z-tranches assuming 100 PSA prepayments are graphed in Figure 13.5A. Corresponding cash flows for A-, B-, C-, and Z-tranche assuming 100 PSA prepayments are graphed in Figure 13.5B.

Figure 13.5

Sequential CMO
Principal and
Cash Flows for
a $100,000
Par Value
GNMA Bond

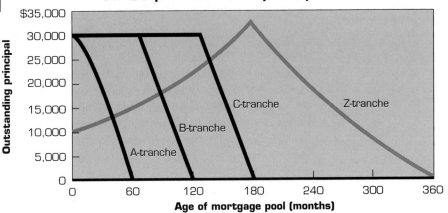

A. Sequential CMO principal

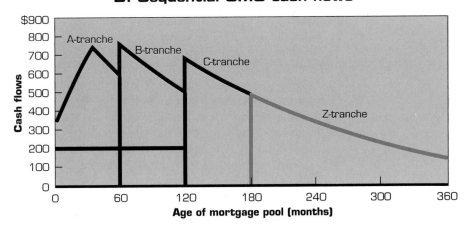

B. Sequential CMO cash flows

CHECK THIS

13.6b Figures 13.5A and 13.5B assume a 100 PSA prepayment schedule. How would these figures change for a 200 PSA prepayment schedule or a 50 PSA prepayment schedule?

13.6c While A-, B-, and C-tranche principal is being paid down, Z-tranche interest is used to acquire principal for the Z-tranche. What is the growth rate of Z-tranche principal during this period?

Protected Amortization Class Bonds

protected amortization class bond (PAC)
Mortgage-backed security that takes priority for scheduled payments of principal.

Another popular security used to alleviate the problem of cash flow uncertainty when investing in mortgage-backed bonds is a **protected amortization class (PAC) bond**, or simply **PAC.** Like all CMOs, PAC bonds are defined by specific rules that carve up cash flows from a mortgage pool. Essentially, a PAC bond carves out a slice of a mortgage pool's cash flows according to a rule that gives PAC bondholders first priority entitlement to promised PAC cash flows. Consequently, PAC cash flows are predictable so long as mortgage pool prepayments remain within a predetermined band. PAC bonds are attractive to investors who require a high degree of cash flow certainty from their investments.

PAC support bond
Mortgage-backed security that has subordinate priority for scheduled payments of principal. Also called *PAC companion bond.*

After PAC bondholders receive their promised cash flows, residual cash flows from the mortgage pool are paid to non-PAC bonds, often referred to as **PAC support bonds** or *PAC companion bonds*. In effect, almost all cash flow uncertainty is concentrated in the non-PAC bonds. The non-PAC bond supports the PAC bond and serves the same purpose as a Z-tranche bond in a sequential CMO structure. For this reason, a non-PAC bond is sometimes called a PAC Z-tranche.

PAC collar Range defined by upper and lower prepayment schedules of a PAC bond.

Creation of a PAC bond entails three steps. First, we must specify two PSA prepayment schedules that form the upper and lower prepayment bounds of a PAC bond. These bounds define a **PAC collar**. For example, suppose we create a single PAC bond from a new $100,000 par value GNMA bond based on a pool of 30-year fixed rate mortgages. The PAC collar specifies a 100 PSA prepayment schedule as a lower bound and a 300 PSA prepayment schedule as an upper bound. Cash flows to the PAC bond are said to enjoy protected amortization so long as mortgage pool prepayments remain within this 100–300 PSA collar.

Our second step in creating a PAC bond is to calculate principal-only (PO) cash flows from our 30-year $100,000 par value GNMA bond assuming 100 PSA and 300 PSA prepayment schedules. These PO cash flows, which include both scheduled amortization and prepayments, are plotted in Figure 13.6A. In Figure 13.6A, notice that principal-only cash flows for 100 PSA and 300 PSA prepayment schedules intersect in month 103. Before the 103rd month, 300 PSA PO cash flows are greater. After that month, 100 PSA PO cash flows are greater. PAC bond cash flows are specified by the 100 PSA schedule before month 103 and the 300 PSA schedule after month 103. Because the PAC bond is specified by 100 PSA and 300 PSA prepayment schedules, it is called a PAC 100/300 bond.

Our third step is to specify the cash flows to be paid to PAC bondholders on a priority basis. PAC bondholders receive payments of principal according to the PAC collar's lower PSA prepayment schedule. For the PAC 100/300 bond in this example, principal payments are made according to the 100 PSA prepayment schedule until month 103, when the schedule switches to the 300 PSA prepayment schedule. The sum of all scheduled principal to be paid to PAC 100/300 bondholders represents total initial PAC bond principal. In addition to payment of principal, a PAC bondholder also receives payment of interest on outstanding PAC principal. For example, if the mortgage pool financing rate is 9 percent, the PAC bondholder receives an interest payment of .75 percent per month of outstanding PAC principal.

Total monthly cash flows paid to the PAC bond including payments of principal and interest are graphed in Figure 13.6B. As shown, total cash flow reaches a maximum in month 30, thereafter gradually declining. So long as mortgage pool prepayments remain within the 100/300 PSA prepayment collar, PAC bondholders will receive these cash flows exactly as originally specified.

Figure 13.6

GNMA PAC 100/300 Cash Flows for $100,000 Par Value 30-Year 8 Percent Bond

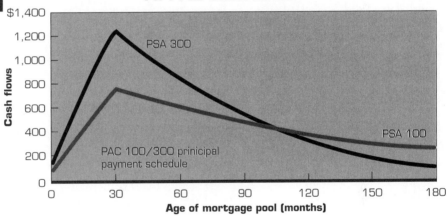

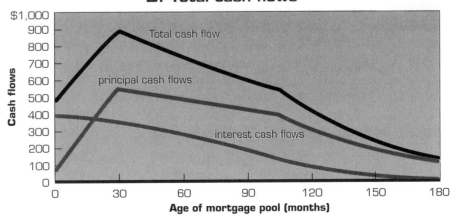

PAC collars are usually sufficiently wide so that actual prepayments move outside the collar only infrequently. In the event that prepayments move outside a collar far enough to interfere with promised PAC cash flows, PAC bonds normally specify the following two contingency rules:

PAC contingency rule 1. When actual prepayments fall below a PAC collar's lower bound, there could be insufficient cash flow to satisfy a PAC bond's promised cash flow schedule. In this case, the PAC bond receives all available cash flow, and any shortfall is carried forward and paid on a first-priority basis from future cash flows. Non-PAC bonds receive no cash flows until all cumulative shortfalls to PAC bonds are paid off.

PAC contingency rule 2. When actual prepayments rise above a PAC collar's upper bound, it is possible that all outstanding principal for the non-PAC support bonds is paid off before the PAC bond. When all non-PAC principal is paid off, the PAC cash flow schedule is abandoned and all mortgage pool cash flows are paid to PAC bondholders.

CHECK THIS

13.6d A PAC 100/300 bond based on a pool of fully modified 30-year fixed-rate mortgages switches payment schedules after 103 months. Would switching occur earlier or later for a PAC 50/300 bond? For a PAC 100/500 bond?

13.6e Figures 13.8A and 13.8B assume a PAC 100/300 bond based on a pool of fully modi-

fied 30-year fixed-rate mortgages. What would these figures look like for a PAC 50/300 and a PAC 100/500 bond?

13.6f How might a large change in market interest rates cause mortgage pool prepayments to move outside a PAC collar far enough and long enough to interfere with an originally stated PAC bond cash flow schedule?

13.7 Yields for Mortgage-Backed Securities and Collateralized Mortgage Obligations

Yields for mortgage-backed securities (MBSs) and collateralized mortgage obligations (CMOs) for representative GNMA, FHLMC, and FNMA mortgage pools are published daily in *The Wall Street Journal*. Figure 13.7 is a sample *Wall Street Journal* listing. In the panel labeled Mortgage-Backed Securities, the first column lists the type of mortgage pool. For example, the first mortgage pool type is 30-year FMAC (i.e., Freddie Mac) Gold paying 6 percent interest on outstanding principal. The second mortgage pool type is 30-year FMAC Gold paying 6.5 percent interest on outstanding principal. Column 2 reports the price (in percentage points and 32nds of a point) for the MBS. The third column is the change in the price from the previous day. The fourth column shows the estimated average life of the mortgages in the underlying pool. The fifth column gives the spread (in basis points) between the yield to maturity on the MBS and the yield on a U.S. Treasury

Figure 13.7

MBS Yields

The Wall Street Journal,
May 11, 1999. Reprinted by
permission of Dow Jones &
Company, Inc., via Copyright
Clearance Center, Inc.
© 1999 Dow Jones &
Company. All Rights
Reserved Worldwide.

MORTGAGE-BACKED SECURITITES

Indicative, not guaranteed; from Bear Stearns Cos./Street Pricing Service

		PRICE (Jan) (Pts-32ds)	PRICE CHANGE (32ds)	AVG LIFE (years)	SPRD TO AVG LIFE (Bps)	SPREAD CHANGE	PSA (Prepay Speed)	YIELD TO MAT.*
30-YEAR								
FMAC GOLD	6.0%	96-12	+ 02	9.4	112	unch	140	6.63%
FMAC GOLD	6.5%	98-30	+ 03	8	128	unch	175	6.74
FMAC GOLD	7.0%	101-02	+ 02	6.5	140	+ 1	225	6.81
FNMA	6.0%	96-10	+ 03	9.4	111	unch	140	6.62
FNMA	6.5%	98-27	+ 02	7.9	127	+ 1	175	6.72
FNMA	7.0%	100-30	+ 01	6.4	139	+ 2	225	6.79
GNMA	6.0%	96-07	+ 03	10.6	108	unch	110	6.61
GNMA	6.5%	98-25	+ 02	9.4	124	unch	135	6.75
GNMA	7.0%	101-02	+ 01	7.8	139	+ 1	175	6.84
15-YEAR								
FMAC GOLD	6.0%	98-24	+ 03	5.8	92	unch	155	6.30%
FNMA	6.0%	98-21	+ 03	5.7	91	unch	155	6.29
GNMA	6.0%	98-31	+ 03	5.9	87	unch	140	6.25

*Extrapolated from benchmarks based on projections from Bear Stearns prepayment model, assuming interest rates remain unchanged.

COLLATERALIZED MORTGAGE OBLIGATIONS

Spread of CMO yields above U.S. Treasury securities of comparable maturity, in basis points (100 basis points = 1 percentage point of interest)

MAT	SPREAD	CHG FROM PREV DAY
SEQUENTIALS		
2-year	94	unch
5-year	122	unch
7-year	138	unch
10-year	144	unch
20-year	115	unch
PACS		
2-year	73	unch
5-year	96	unch
7-year	109	unch
10-year	118	unch
20-year	110	unch

cash flow yield Yield
to maturity for a
mortgage-backed
security conditional on
an assumed
prepayment pattern.

note or bond with a maturity similar to the average life on the MBS. Column 6 shows the change in this spread from the previous day.

Column 7 shows the assumed PSA prepayment rate, and the final column shows the yield to maturity on the MBS calculated using the assumed prepayment rate, also known as the **cash flow yield**. Essentially, cash flow yield is the interest rate that equates the present value of all future cash flows on the mortgage pool to the current price of the pool, assuming a particular prepayment rate.

13.8 Summary and Conclusions

This chapter discusses the large and growing market for mortgage-backed securities. Many aspects of this market were covered, including the following items.

1. Most Americans finance their homes with mortgages. The buyer makes a down payment and borrows the remaining cost with a mortgage loan. Mortgages are often repackaged into mortgage-backed securities through a process called mortgage securitization. Currently, about half of all mortgages in the United States have been securitized, yet the risks involved in these investments are often misunderstood.

2. Most home mortgages are 15- or 30-year fixed-rate mortgages requiring constant monthly payments. The present value of all monthly payments is equal to the original amount of the mortgage loan. Each monthly payment has two components: payment of interest on outstanding mortgage principal and a scheduled pay-down of mortgage principal. The relative amounts of each component change throughout the life of a mortgage. The interest payment component gradually declines, and the pay-down of principal component gradually increases.

3. A mortgage borrower has the right to pay off a mortgage early, which is called mortgage prepayment. Borrowers frequently decide to prepay to refinance an existing mortgage at a lower interest rate. Prepayment and refinancing, advantages to mortgage borrowers, are disadvantages to mortgage investors. Thus, mortgage investors face prepayment risk.

4. In 1968, Congress established the Government National Mortgage Association (GNMA) as a government agency charged with promoting liquidity in the secondary market for home mortgages. GNMA is the largest single guarantor of mortgage-backed securities. Two government-sponsored enterprises (GSEs) are also significant mortgage repackaging sponsors: the Federal Home Loan Mortgage Corporation (FHLMC) and the Federal National Mortgage Association (FNMA).

5. Each month, GNMA, FHLMC, and FNMA mortgage-backed bond investors receive cash flows derived from fully modified mortgage pools. Each monthly cash flow has three distinct components: payment of interest on outstanding mortgage principal, scheduled amortization of mortgage principal, and mortgage principal prepayments.

6. Mortgage prepayments are stated as a prepayment rate. The greater the prepayment rate, the faster is mortgage pool principal paid off. Prepayment rates can vary substantially from year to year, depending on mortgage type and various economic and demographic factors. Conventional industry practice states prepayment rates using a prepayment model specified by the Public Securities Association (PSA). This model states prepayment rates as a percentage of a PSA benchmark, which represents an annual prepayment rate of 6 percent for seasoned mortgages, and is called 100 PSA. Deviations from the 100 PSA benchmark are stated as a percentage of the benchmark.

7. Prepayment risk complicates the effects of interest rate risk. Interest rate risk for a bond is related to its effective maturity as measured by Macaulay duration. However, Macaulay duration assumes a fixed schedule of cash flow payments. But the schedule of cash flow payments for mortgage-backed bonds is not fixed because it is affected by mortgage prepayments, which in turn are affected by interest rates. For this reason, Macaulay duration is a deficient measure of interest rate risk for mortgage-backed bonds.

8. Cash flows from mortgage pools are often carved up and distributed according to various rules. Mortgage-backed securities representing specific rules for allocating mortgage cash flows are called collateralized mortgage obligations (CMOs). The three best known types of CMO structures using specific rules to carve up mortgage pool cash flows are interest-only (IO) and principal-only (PO) strips, sequential CMOs, and protected amortization class securities (PACs).

9. Cash flow yields for mortgage-backed securities (MBSs) and collateralized mortgage obligations (CMOs) for GNMA, FHLMC, and FNMA mortgage pools are published daily in *The Wall Street Journal*. Cash flow yield for a mortgage-backed security corresponds to yield to maturity for an ordinary bond. Essentially, cash flow yield is the interest rate that discounts all future expected cash flows from a mortgage pool to be equal to the price of the mortgage pool.

GET REAL

This chapter covered one of the more complex investments available, mortgage-backed securities (MBSs). Ironically, these investments are fairly complicated, but unlike most exotic instruments, the basic types of MBS are very suitable for ordinary individual investors. In fact, GNMAs and similar investments are frequently recommended, and rightly so, for even very conservative investors.

However, as a practical matter, directly buying into mortgage pools is not practical for most individual investors. It is also probably unwise, because not all pools are equally risky in terms of prepayments, and analysis of individual pools is best left to experts. Instead, most investors in MBSs end up in mutual funds specializing in these instruments, and most of the major mutual fund families have such funds. A good place to learn more is a prospectus from such a fund.

An important real-world aspect in mortgage investing of any kind is that some of the cash flow received is typically principal and some is interest. In contrast, with a coupon bond, for example, no principal is returned until the bond matures or is called. When a mortgage matures, however, no principal is returned other than the amount contained in the final payment.

The reason this is important is that many investors have a policy of living on, or otherwise spending, the income (i.e., dividends and interest) from their portfolios. Such investors need to understand that with an amortizing investment, only a portion of a cash payment received is actually income. Unfortunately, unsophisticated investors sometimes focus only on the total amount received without recognizing this fact and, unfortunately, wake up to discover that all (or a substantial part) of the principal is spent and thus not available to generate future investment income.

Key Terms

Chapter Review Problems and Self-Test

1. **Mortgage Payments** What are the monthly payments on a 30-year $150,000 mortgage if the mortgage rate is 6 percent? What portion of the first payment is interest? Principal?

2. **Mortgage Balances**   Consider a 15-year $210,000 mortgage with a 7 percent interest rate. After 10 years, the borrower (the mortgage issuer) pays it off. How much will the lender receive?

Answers to Self-Test Problems

1. This is a standard time value of money calculation in which we need to find an annuity-type payment. The present value is $150,000. The interest rate is .06/12 = .005, or .5 percent, per month. There is a total of 360 payments. Using the formula from the text (generalized slightly), we have

$$\text{Monthly payment} = \frac{\text{Mortgage balance} \times r/12}{1 - \dfrac{1}{(1 + r/12)^{T \times 12}}}$$

Plugging in $r = .06$ and $T = 30$, we get a payment of $899.33. The interest portion for a month is equal to the mortgage balance at the beginning of the month ($150,000 in this case) multiplied by the interest rate per month (.5 percent), or $150,000 \times .005 = $750. The remaining portion of the payment, $899.33 - $750 = $149.33, goes to reduce the principal balance.

2. We first need to know the monthly payment. Here, the original balance is $210,000, the rate is 7 percent, and the original life is 15 years. Plugging in the numbers using the formula just above, check that we get a monthly payment of $1,887.54.
   From here, there are two ways to go. One is relatively easy, the other is relatively tedious. The tedious way would be to construct an amortization table for the mortgage and then locate the balance in the table. However, we need only a single balance, so there is a much faster way. After 10 years, we can treat this mortgage as though it were a 5-year mortgage with payments of $1,887.54 and an interest rate of 7 percent. We can then solve for the mortgage balance using the same formula:

$$\text{Monthly payment} = \frac{\text{Mortgage balance} \times .07/12}{1 - \dfrac{1}{(1 + .07/12)^{5 \times 12}}} = \$1,887.54$$

Solving for the mortgage balance gets us $95,324.50.

Test Your Investments Quotient

1. **Fixed-Rate Mortgages**   Which of the following statements about fixed rate mortgages is false?

   a. 15-year mortgages have higher monthly payments than 30-year mortgages.
   b. Scheduled monthly payments are constant over the life of the mortgage.
   c. Actual monthly payments may vary over the life of the mortgage.
   d. Absent defaults, actual monthly payments are never more than scheduled monthly payments.

2. **GNMA Bonds**   Mortgages in GNMA pools are said to be fully modified because GNMA guarantees bondholders which of the following?

   a. A minimum rate of return on their investment.
   b. A modified schedule of cash flows over the life of the pool.
   c. Full and timely payment of both principal and interest in the event of default.
   d. Eventual payment of both principal and interest in the event of default.

3. **GNMA Bonds**   Which of the following is not a source of risk for GNMA mortgage pool investors?

   a. Prepayment risk
   b. Default risk
   c. Interest rate risk
   d. Reinvestment risk

4. GNMA Bonds Which one of the following sets of features most accurately describes a GNMA mortgage pass-through security? (*1988 CFA exam*)

	Average Life	Payment Frequency	Credit Risk
a.	Predictable	Monthly	High
b.	Predictable	Semiannual	Low
c.	Unpredictable	Monthly	Low
d.	Unpredictable	Semiannual	Low

5. GNMA Bonds In contrast to original-issue U.S. Treasury securities, original-issue GNMA pass-through securities: (*1988 CFA exam*)

a. Provide quarterly payments to the investor.
b. Have a limited availability of maturities.
c. Are often issued in zero coupon form.
d. Have interest payments.

6. GNMA Bonds Which of the following should a bond portfolio manager who is looking for mortgage-backed securities that would perform best during a period of rising interest rates purchase: (*1989 CFA exam*)

a. A 12 percent GNMA with an average life of 5.6 years.
b. An 8 percent GNMA with an average life of 6.0 years.
c. A 10 percent GNMA with an average life of 8.5 years.
d. A 6 percent GNMA with an average life of 9.0 years.

7. GNMA Bonds Why will the effective yield on a GNMA bond be higher than that of a U.S. Treasury bond with the same quoted yield to maturity? Because: (*1991 CFA exam*)

a. GNMA yields are figured on a 360-day basis.
b. GNMAs carry higher coupons.
c. GNMAs have longer compounding periods.
d. GNMA interest is paid monthly.

8. Mortgage-Backed Bonds If a mortgage-backed bond is issued as a fully modified pass-through security, it means that: (*1991 CFA exam*)

a. Bondholders will receive full and timely payment of principal and interest even if underlying mortgage payments are not made.
b. The bond has been structured to include both conforming and nonconforming loans.
c. The interest rates on the underlying mortgages have been altered so that they equal the weighted-average coupon on the bond.
d. The security carries a balloon payment to ensure that the bond is fully amortized in a set time frame (12 to 15 years).

9. Prepayments Projecting prepayments for mortgage pass-through securities: (*1990 CFA exam*)

a. Requires only a projection of changes in the level of interest rates.
b. Requires analyzing both economic and demographic variables.
c. Is not necessary to determine a cash flow yield.
d. Is not necessary to determine duration.

10. Prepayments A bond analyst at Omnipotent Bank (OB) notices that the prepayment experience on his holdings of high-coupon GNMA issues has been moving sharply higher. What does this indicate? (*1989 CFA exam*)

a. Interest rates are falling.
b. The loans comprising OB's pools have been experiencing lower default rates.
c. The pools held by OB are older issues.
d. All of the above.

11. **Mortgage-Backed Bonds** Which of the following statements about mortgage pass-through securities is (are) correct? (*1991 CFA exam*)

   i. Pass-throughs offer better call protection than most corporates and Treasuries.
   ii. Interest and principal payments are made on a monthly basis.
   iii. It is common practice to use the weighted-average maturity on a pass-through in place of its duration.
   iv. Pass-throughs are relatively immune from reinvestment risk.

   a. i and iii only
   b. ii and iii only
   c. ii only
   d. iv only

12. **Mortgage-Backed Bonds** Which of the following are advantages of mortgage-backed securities (MBSs)? (*1991 CFA exam*)

   i. MBS yields are above those of similarly rated corporate and U.S. Treasury bonds.
   ii. MBSs have high-quality ratings, usually AAA, with some backed by the full faith and credit of the U.S. government.
   iii. MBSs have no call provision, thus protecting the investor from having to make a reinvestment decision before maturity.

   a. i and ii only
   b. ii and iii only
   c. i and iii only
   d. i, ii, and iii

13. **Mortgage-Backed Bonds** Which of the following are characteristics that would make mortgage-backed securities (MBSs) inappropriate for less sophisticated, conservative investors? (*1989 CFA exam*)

   i. The maturity of MBSs is quite variable and difficult to determine.
   ii. Due to their convexity, the realized total return on MBSs is often more dependent on interest rate levels than other bonds of similar maturity.
   iii. Due to a possible unfamiliarity with prepayment concepts, investors may not be able to evaluate the true yield on MBS issues.
   iv. Many MBS issues are not quoted widely and are difficult to monitor.

   a. i, ii and iii only
   b. i, iii and iv only
   c. ii and iv only
   d. All of the above

14. **Collateralized Mortgage Obligations** For a given mortgage pool, which of the following CMOs based on that pool is the riskiest investment?

   a. 100/300 PAC bond.
   b. A-tranche sequential CMO.
   c. Interest-only (IO) strip.
   d. Principal-only (PO) strip.

15. **Collateralized Mortgage Obligations** For a given mortgage pool, which of the following CMOs based on that pool is most likely to increase in price when market interest rates increase?

   a. 100/300 PAC bond.
   b. A-tranche sequential CMO.
   c. Interest-only (IO) strip.
   d. Principal-only (PO) strip.

Questions and Problems

Core
Questions

1. **Mortgage Securitization** How does mortgage securitization benefit borrowers?

2. **Mortgage Securitization** How does mortgage securitization benefit mortgage originators?

3. **Mortgage Payments** What is the monthly payment on a 30-year fixed rate mortgage if the original balance is $180,000 and the rate is 8 percent?

4. **Mortgage Payments** All else the same, will the payments be higher on a 15-year mortgage or a 30-year mortgage? Why?

5. **Ginnie, Freddie, and Fannie** From an investor's point of view, what is the difference between mortgage pools backed by GNMA, FHLMC, and FNMA?

6. **Mortgage Balances** If a mortgage has monthly payments of $1,000, a life of 30 years, and a rate of 6 percent per year, what is the mortgage amount?

7. **Mortgage Pools** What does it mean for a mortgage pool to be fully modified?

8. **Mortgage Interest** A 30-year $140,000 mortgage has a rate of 8 percent. What are the interest and principal portions in the first payment? In the second?

9. **Prepayments** What are some of the reasons that mortgages are paid off early? Under what circumstances are mortgage prepayments likely to rise sharply? Explain.

10. **Mortgage Balances** Consider a 30-year $200,000 mortgage with a 6.5 percent interest rate. After 10 years, the borrower (the mortgage issuer) pays it off. How much will the lender receive?

Intermediate
Questions

11. **Prepayments** Explain why the right to prepay a mortgage is similar to the call feature contained in most corporate bonds.

12. **Prepayments** Consider a 15-year $120,000 mortgage with a rate of 9 percent. Eight years into the mortgage, rates have fallen to 6 percent. What would be the monthly saving to a homeowner from refinancing the outstanding mortgage balance at the lower rate?

13. **Prepayments** Evaluate the following argument: "Prepayment is not a risk to mortgage investors because prepayment actually means that the investor is paid both in full and ahead of schedule." Is it always true or false?

14. **Prepayments** Consider a 30-year $140,000 mortgage with a rate of 6.375 percent. Five years into the mortgage, rates have fallen to 6 percent. Suppose the transaction cost of obtaining a new mortgage is $1,000. Should the homeowner refinance at the lower rate?

15. **CPRs** What are the conditional prepayment rates for seasoned 50 PSA, 200 PSA, and 400 PSA mortgages? How do you interpret these numbers?

16. **SMMs** What is the single-month mortality for seasoned 50 PSA, 200 PSA, and 400 PSA mortgages? How do you interpret these numbers?

17. **CMOs** What is a collateralized mortgage obligation? Why do they exist? What are three popular types?

18. **IO and PO Strips** What are IO and PO strips? Assuming interest rates never change, which is riskier?

19. **IO and PO Strips** Which has greater interest rate risk, an IO or a PO strip?

20. **Sequential CMOs** Consider a single whole bond sequential CMO. It has two tranches, an A-tranche and a Z-tranche. Explain how the payments are allocated to the two tranches. Which tranche is riskier?

21. **PACs** Explain in general terms how a protected amortization class CMO works.

22. **Duration and MBSs** Why is Macaulay duration an inadequate measure of interest rate risk for an MBS?

Options and Futures

14 Stock Options

Options have fascinated investors for centuries. The option concept is simple. Instead of buying stock shares today, you buy an option to buy the stock at a later date at a price specified in the option contract. You are not obligated to exercise the option, however, unless doing so benefits you. Moreover, the most you can lose is the original price of the option, which is normally only a fraction of the stock price. Sounds good, doesn't it? ■

Options on common stocks have traded in financial markets for about as long as have common stocks. However, it was not until 1973, when the Chicago Board Options Exchange was established, that options trading became a large and important part of the financial landscape. Since then, the success of options trading has been phenomenal.

Much of the success of options trading is attributable to the tremendous flexibility that options offer investors in designing investment strategies. For example, options can be used to reduce risk through hedging strategies or to increase risk through speculative strategies. As a result, when properly understood and applied, options are appealing both to conservative investors and to aggressive speculators.

In this chapter, we discuss options generally, but our primary focus is on options on individual common stocks. However, later in the chapter we also discuss options on stock market indexes, which are options on portfolios of common stocks. We begin by reviewing some of the ideas we touched on in Chapter 3, where we very briefly discussed options.

14.1 Options on Common Stocks

Option Basics

derivative security
Security whose value is derived from the value of another security. Options are a type of derivative security.

As we have discussed, options on common stock are a type of **derivative security** because the value of a stock option is "derived" from the value of the underlying common stock. For example, the value of an option to buy or sell IBM stock is derived from the value of IBM stock. However, the relationship between the value of a particular stock option and the value of the underlying stock depends on the specific type of option.

Recall that there are two basic option types: **call options** and **put options**. Call options are options to buy, and put options are options to sell. Thus, a call option on IBM stock is an option to buy IBM shares, and a put option on IBM stock is an option to sell IBM shares. More specifically, a call option on common stock grants the holder the right, but not the obligation, to buy the underlying stock at a given **strike price** before the option expiration date. Similarly, a put option on common stock grants the holder the right, but not the obligation, to sell the underlying stock at a given strike price before the option expiration date. The strike price, also called the *exercise price,* is the price at which stock shares are bought or sold to fulfill the obligations of the option contract.

call option On common stock, grants the holder the right, but not the obligation, to buy the underlying stock at a given **strike price.**

put option On common stock, grants the holder the right, but not the obligation, to sell the underlying stock at a given **strike price.**

Options are contracts, and, in practice, option contracts are standardized to facilitate convenience in trading and price reporting. Standardized stock options have a contract size of 100 shares of common stock per option contract. This means that a single call option contract involves an option to buy 100 shares of stock. Likewise, a single put option contract involves an option to sell 100 shares of stock.

Because options are contracts, an understanding of stock options requires that we know the specific contract terms. In general, options on common stock must stipulate at least the following six contract terms:

strike price Price specified in an option contract that the holder pays to buy shares (in the case of call options) or receives to sell shares (in the case of put options) if the option is exercised. Also called the *striking* or *exercise price.*

1. The identity of the underlying stock.
2. The strike price, also called the striking or exercise price.
3. The option expiration date, also called the option maturity.
4. The option contract size.
5. The option exercise style.
6. The delivery or settlement procedure.

First, a stock option contract requires that the specific stock issue be clearly identified. While this may seem to be stating the obvious, in financial transactions it is important that the "obvious" is in fact clearly and unambiguously understood by all concerned parties.

Second, the strike price, also called the exercise price, must be stipulated. The strike price is quite important, since the strike price is the price that an option holder will pay (in the case of a call option) or receive (in the case of a put option) if the option is exercised.

Third, the size of the contract must be specified. As stated earlier, the standard contract size for stock options is 100 stock shares per option.

The fourth contract term that must be stated is the option expiration date. An option cannot be exercised after its expiration date. If an option is unexercised and its expiration date has passed, the option becomes worthless.

Fifth, the option's exercise style determines when the option can be exercised. There are two basic exercise styles: American and European. **American options** can be exercised any time before option expiration, but **European options** can be exercised only on the day before option expiration. Options on individual stocks are normally American style, and stock index options are usually European style.

American option An option that can be exercised any time before expiration.

European option An option that can be exercised only on the day before option expiration.

Finally, in the event that a stock option is exercised, the settlement process must be stipulated. For stock options, standard settlement requires delivery of the underlying stock shares several business days after a notice of exercise is made by the option holder.

Stock options are traded in financial markets in a manner similar to the way that common stocks are traded. For example, there are organized options exchanges, and there are over-the-counter (OTC) options markets. The largest volume of stock options trading in the United States takes place at the Chicago Board Options •Exchange (CBOE). However, stock options are also actively traded at the Philadelphia Stock Exchange (PHLX), the New York Stock Exchange (NYSE), the American Stock Exchange (AMEX), and the Pacific Stock Exchange (PSE). Like a stock exchange, or, for that matter, any securities exchange, an options exchange is a marketplace where customer buy orders and sell orders are matched up with each other.

Option Price Quotes

Current prices for many stock options traded at the major options exchanges are reported each day in *The Wall Street Journal*. However, *The Wall Street Journal* reports prices for only the most heavily traded stock options. Figure 14.1 reproduces a section of the "Listed Options Quotations" page in *The Wall Street Journal*

In Figure 14.1, the table entitled "Most Active Contracts" reports data on selected option contracts with the highest trading volumes in the previous day's options trading. Reference information immediately above this table is useful for interpreting data in the options listings. In the table itself, the first three columns report the name of the option's underlying stock, the expiration month, and the strike price for the option. A "p" following the strike price indicates a put option; otherwise, it is a call option. The next two columns report volume, measured as the number of contracts traded on the previous day, and the exchange where that particular option contract is traded.

The column labeled "Last" reports the contract price for the last trade of the previous day, and the column labeled "Net Chg" reports the price change from the last price recorded a day earlier. The final column reports open interest, the total number of contracts outstanding. Notice that all option contracts listed in this table are sorted by trading volume.

The rest of the "Listed Options Quotations" page reports options trading data grouped by the underlying stock. For each underlying stock with options listed in Figure 14.1, the first column under a stock name is simply a repeated statement of the stock's current price. The second column states strike prices of the various options available for each stock. Notice that the range of available strike prices for stock options typically brackets a current stock price.

The third column states the expiration months of each available option contract. By convention, standardized stock options expire on the Saturday following the third Friday of their expiration month. Because of this convention, the exact date that an option expires can be known exactly by referring to a calendar to identify the third Friday of its expiration month.

Figure 14.1

Listed Options Quotations

Source: Reprinted by permission of *The Wall Street Journal,* January 15, 1999, via Copyright Clearance Center, Inc. © 1999 Dow Jones & Company, Inc. All Rights Reserved Worldwide.

Thursday, January 14, 1999

Composite volume and close for actively traded equity and LEAPS, or long-term options, with results for the corresponding put or call contract. Volume figures are unofficial. Open interest is total outstanding for all exchanges and reflects previous trading day. Close when possible is shown for the underlying stock on primary market. **CB**-Chicago Board Options Exchange. **AM**-American Stock Exchange. **PB**-Philadelphia Stock Exchange. **PC**-Pacific Stock Exchange. **NY**-New York Stock Exchange. **XC**-Composite. **p**-Put.

MOST ACTIVE CONTRACTS

Option/Strike			Vol	Exch	Last	Net Chg	a-Close	Open Int
DellCptr	Jan	80	15,323	AM	7/16	− 7/8	77 5/8	20,420
BostChkn	Jan	5	p 13,982	XC	4 3/8	− 1/8		54,490
MicrTc	Jan	70	8,147	XC	1 1/4	− 1 1/4	69 3/8	7,528
WasteMInc	Jan	25	8,107	XC	12 1/4	− 1/4		9,179
EKodak	Jul	70	p 8,026	CB	5 5/8	+ 1/4	70 5/16	1,022
CienaCp	Jan	20	7,814	XC	3/8	...	18 11/16	23,754
Schering	Jan	25	7,684	PC	26	+ 1/4	51 1/16	18,656
Intel	Jan	140	7,342	AM	1/4	− 1 7/8	133 3/4	11,378
Intel	Jan	135	7,303	AM	1 1/4	− 3 3/4	133 3/4	10,359
USA Wste	Jan 00	40	7,300	XC	16	+ 5 3/4	50 15/16	5,451
AT&T	Jan 00	80	p 5,581	CB	8 5/8	+ 5/8	82 1/16	2,858
AmOnline	Jan	150	5,534	XC	15/16	− 1 11/16	144 1/2	25,518
Compaq	Jan	45	5,380	XC	7/16	− 1 9/16	44 9/16	24,212
Iomega	May	7 1/2	p 4,951	XC	1 1/8	...	9	57,704
Intel	Jan	130	p 4,930	AM	1/2	+ 1/4	133 3/4	7,640
MCI Wrld	Jun	45	4,930	XC	26 3/4	− 3 3/4	71	664
Amazon	Feb	100	4,910	XC	46 5/8	− 4 3/8	138	22,224
BankAm	Feb	65	p 4,739	XC	5 1/2	+ 1 7/8	62 7/16	12,466
TelBrasH	Jan	40	p 4,548	XC	1/8	− 1/16	54 1/8	14,856
AppleC	Feb	45	4,536	XC	2 9/16	− 2 13/16	41 3/8	2,992

Option/Strike			Vol	Exch	Last	Net Chg	a-Close	Open Int
Citigroup	Mar	50	p 4,447	XC	4	+ 1/2	50 1/2	7,664
TycoLb	Jan	75	p 4,412	PB	3 1/8	− 1 1/2	72 1/8	4,412
EKodak	Jul	75	4,358	CB	4 3/4	− 3 7/8	70 5/16	153
Citigroup	Jan	50	p 4,177	XC	5/8	+ 1/8	50 1/2	14,168
Intel	Jan	135	p 4,123	AM	2 7/16	+ 1 5/16	133 3/4	5,436
AT&T	Jan 00	70	p 4,105	CB	5	+ 3/4	82 1/16	3,339
AscendC	Jan	80	3,997	XC	2 1/8	+ 1/2	82 1/8	26,240
M C I	Jan	25	3,997	XC	63	− 4 7/8		8,438
Cisco	Jan	100	3,951	XC	1/2	− 1/4	96 3/8	19,924
LockhdM	Feb	40	p 3,888	XC	3 3/8	+ 1 1/8	38 3/4	2,382
Amazon	Apr	110	3,840	XC	46 1/2	− 1 1/2	138	27,100
LockhdM	Jan	40	p 3,710	XC	1 3/8	+ 1/2	38 3/4	21,968
BankAm	Feb	65	3,680	XC	3 1/8	− 1 1/8	62 7/16	16,000
Micsft	Jan	150	3,659	PC	1/8	− 3/8	141 3/4	12,163
AmOnline	Jan	155	3,657	XC	3/8	− 7/8	144 1/2	19,041
DellCptr	Feb	80	3,594	AM	5 1/8	− 5/8	77 5/8	17,935
RJRNab	Mar	27 1/2	p 3,560	XC	2	+ 3/8	27 13/16	2,661
TelBrasH	Apr	100	3,545	XC	9/16	− 3/16	54 1/8	16,329
Motorola	Jan	70	3,506	AM	1/8	− 2 1/4	66 1/4	8,845
AmOnline	Jan	150	p 3,496	XC	6 1/8	− 7/8	144 1/2	24,048

WSJ.com Complete equity option listings and data are available in The Wall Street Journal Interactive Edition at **http://wsj.com** on the Internet's World Wide Web.

Option/Strike		Exp.	Call Vol.	Call Last	Put Vol.	Put Last
AES Cp	35	Feb	35	4 1/8	715	2 1/16
36 7/8	40	Feb	550	1 15/16	128	4 1/2
A M R	65	Jan	442	1/8	150	2 3/4
ASM Litho	45	Apr	...	...	560	8 5/8
AT&T	60	Jan	691	22	...	...
82 1/16	70	Jan	1379	12 1/2	...	...
82 1/16	75	Jan	1655	7	...	...
82 1/16	75	Feb	2519	9 1/4	448	1 1/2
82 1/16	75	Apr	370	11	30	3 1/8
82 1/16	80	Jan	1671	2 1/4	602	5/16
82 1/16	80	Feb	600	5 7/8	202	3 3/8
82 1/16	80	Apr	466	8	81	4 7/8
82 1/16	85	Feb	1351	3 1/4	15	5 1/2
82 1/16	90	Feb	610	1 1/2	20	9 1/4
82 1/16	90	Apr	464	3 1/2	...	...
AdvFibCm	10	Jan	435	3 3/4	...	...
13 1/2	12 1/2	Jan	1295	1 3/16	105	1/4
13 1/2	12 1/2	Feb	884	2 5/8	191	1 9/16
13 1/2	15	Feb	2409	1 5/8	16	2 3/4
A M D	20	Jan	568	2 1/2	487	1/8
22 3/8	20	Feb	280	4	2759	1 1/4
22 3/8	20	Apr	191	5	649	2 1/4
22 3/8	22 1/2	Jan	800	5/8	1368	1
22 3/8	22 1/2	Feb	707	2 7/8	614	2 1/2
22 3/8	22 1/2	Apr	434	3 1/2	145	3
22 3/8	25	Jan	1641	1/8	1627	2 3/4
22 3/8	25	Feb	2529	1 3/4	1119	4
22 3/8	25	Apr	611	2 7/8	1319	4 3/4
144 1/2	165	Feb	442	8 1/4	4	28 5/8
144 1/2	170	Jan	494	1/16	25	26
144 1/2	170	Feb	459	7	35	32
144 1/2	175	Feb	540	6 1/2	69	35 3/4
144 1/2	185	Feb	1091	4 5/8	20	45
AmBankrs	50	Feb	410	2 5/8	...	...
AmExpr	95	Jan	358	3/16	795	3 7/8
95 15/16	100	Feb	90	3 1/2	909	7 3/8
Am Hom	50	Jan	861	5 1/2	10	1/16
54 3/4	50	Feb	610	6	...	...
54 3/4	55	Jan	1023	1/2	32	1/2
AmIntG	80	Feb	1200	20 1/8	...	...
98 11/16	90	May	85	15 3/4	350	5
AmIntGr o	80	Jan	800	19 1/2	...	...
AppleC	17 1/2	Jan	959	1/16	40	3 1/8
41 3/8	30	Jan	341	11 1/4	...	...
41 3/8	35	Jan	398	6 1/2	20	1/16
41 3/8	40	Jan	3308	1 11/16	537	3/8
41 3/8	40	Feb	1247	4 1/2	660	2 7/8
41 3/8	40	Apr	501	6 3/4	167	4 3/8
41 3/8	42 1/2	Feb	587	3 1/2	161	4 1/8
41 3/8	42 1/2	Jan	1101	1/2	458	1 3/8
41 3/8	42 1/2	Feb	587	3 1/2	161	4 1/8
41 3/8	42 1/2	Apr	232	5 5/8	724	5 7/8
41 3/8	45	Jan	3205	3/16	290	3 1/4
41 3/8	45	Feb	4536	2 9/16	358	5 3/8
41 3/8	45	Apr	466	4 3/8	20	6 5/8
41 3/8	47 1/2	Jan	959	1/16	40	3 1/8
41 3/8	47 1/2	Feb	739	1 13/16	39	7 1/4
41 3/8	50	Feb	830	1 1/4	30	7 1/2
ApplMg	5	Jan	620	2 5/8	...	...
7 3/4	5	Apr	600	3 1/8	46	1/2
7 3/4	10	Apr	890	13/16	112	3 3/8
AplMat	40	Jan	380	13 5/8	100	1/16
53 1/4	55	Jan	438	7/16	375	2 3/8
AscendC	70	Jan	444	12 3/8	20	1/8
82 1/8	70	Feb	385	14 1/4	685	1 7/8
82 1/8	70	Mar	45	16	346	3 3/8
82 1/8	75	Jan	748	7	10	1/16
82 1/8	75	Feb	532	10 7/8	368	3 1/2
AgriBio	17 1/2	Feb	432	1	3	3 5/8
14 7/8	17 1/2	Apr	1016	1 1/2	95	5
14 7/8	20	Apr	545	1	...	...
Airtch	70	Feb	2855	12 1/8	600	1 7/8
78 13/16	75	Feb	101	7 1/2	448	3 1/8
78 13/16	80	Jan	539	3/4	125	1 7/8
78 13/16	80	Feb	1415	4 5/8	140	5 1/2
AmaxGl	25	Jan	...	...	600	4 1/8
...	25	Apr	...	...	600	5 1/2
Amazon	83 3/8	Jan	49	57 3/4	880	1/16
138	93 3/8	Feb	...	...	1051	6 1/4
138	100	Feb	4910	46 5/8	228	7 1/2
138	110	Jan	147	32 1/2	374	3/8
138	110	Feb	43	46	353	10
138	110	Apr	3840	46 1/2	48	15 5/8
138	113 3/8	Jan	33	26 3/4	466	1/4
138	120	Jan	52	25	1313	3/4
138	130	Jan	161	12	1023	2
138	130	Feb	195	28 1/2	357	16 7/8
BkrsTr	85	Feb	10	2 7/16	598	2 3/4
BarNbl	40	Jan	362	1/2	99	1 1/4
39 3/8	40	Feb	464	3 3/8	33	4
BarickG	20	Jan	741	3/16	327	5/16
bynd.com	40	Jun	414	9 1/2	...	...
BioPharm	30	Feb	...	...	500	3 5/8
Biogen	80	Jan	405	10 5/8	40	3/16
90 1/4	90	Jan	1658	1 3/4	38	1 1/2
90 1/4	90	Feb	754	6	19	6
Biovail	30	Jul	955	13	10	2 7/8
Block	45	Jan	806	1/8	760	1 7/16
43 7/8	45	Feb	750	1 9/16	760	2 1/4
Boeing	35	Jan	594	1/8	403	1 5/8
33 7/16	35	Feb	691	1 1/8	137	2 3/8
33 7/16	40	Jan	3	1/16	491	6 1/2
33 7/16	40	Feb	354	3/8	10	6 5/8
BostBeer	12 1/2	Mar	584	7/8	...	...
BostChkn	5	Jan	...	...	13982	4 3/8
BostSc	20	Jan	556	3 7/8	364	1/8
24	25	Jan	635	1/4	314	15/16
Broadcom	140	Jan	573	1 3/4	25	5 3/4
CBS Cp	32 1/2	Jan	535	2 1/8	...	...
34 3/8	35	Jan	712	3/8	625	15/16
34 3/8	37 1/2	Feb	179	1 1/8	500	3 1/2
CMGI	67 1/2	Mar	401	40 3/4	...	...
105	70	Jan	385	35	...	...
Cendant	15	Jan	1140	4 1/2	10	1/16
19 1/2	17 1/2	Jan	708	2 1/16	10	1/8
19 1/2	17 1/2	Feb	1197	2 3/4	839	5/8
19 1/2	20	Jan	2317	1/8	399	5/8
19 1/2	20	Feb	1101	1 7/16	659	1 5/8
19 1/2	25	Feb	373	1/4	...	...
Centocor	40	Jan	1011	1/4	186	7/8
39 9/16	40	Feb	37	3 1/8	435	3 1/8
39 9/16	45	Jan	11	1/16	388	5 1/4
Cephln	10	Jan	685	3/8	...	...
10 1/16	10	May	750	3 1/8	8	1 7/8
Chase n	60	Feb	20	11 1/8	497	1 11/16
68 1/8	65	Jan	294	3 1/2	844	5/16
68 1/8	65	Feb	1709	6 7/8	714	3
68 1/8	70	Jan	2685	9/16	339	1 13/16
68 1/8	70	Feb	694	4 1/4	553	5 5/8
68 1/8	75	Feb	875	2	144	8 3/8
ChinaTlc	35	Jun	1700	4 7/8	...	...
Chiron	25	Jan	608	1/16	54	1 5/8
Chryslr o	60	Jan	679	3 3/4	...	...
CienaCp	15	Jan	2101	3 5/8	366	1/16
18 11/16	15	Feb	388	4 3/4	149	15/16
18 11/16	17 1/2	Jan	3014	1 1/2	221	1/8
18 11/16	17 1/2	Feb	1083	3 5/8	143	1 3/4
AmOnline	12 1/2	Jan	2663	136	...	...
144 1/2	100	Jan	1870	46 1/8	...	...
144 1/2	120	Feb	44	30 5/8	1444	6 1/4
144 1/2	120	Apr	15	38 5/8	512	12 1/2
144 1/2	125	Feb	63	27 1/2	664	7
144 1/2	130	Feb	97	24 1/2	371	8 7/8
144 1/2	135	Jan	158	10 1/4	698	1/2
144 1/2	140	Jan	1366	5 1/2	2281	1 1/8
144 1/2	140	Feb	376	18 1/2	282	12 7/8
144 1/2	145	Jan	1704	2 9/16	1596	2 9/16
144 1/2	145	Feb	1309	16 1/4	497	15 1/2
144 1/2	150	Jan	5534	15/16	3496	6 1/8
144 1/2	150	Feb	1989	13 1/2	2097	18 3/8
144 1/2	155	Jan	3657	3/8	1498	10 7/8
144 1/2	155	Feb	638	12	106	22 1/8
144 1/2	160	Jan	2727	1/8	426	16
144 1/2	160	Feb	1314	10 1/8	192	24 5/8
144 1/2	165	Jan	585	1/16	14	20 1/8
96 3/8	105	Feb	1653	4 3/4	168	11 7/8
96 3/8	110	Feb	1062	3 3/8	79	15 1/4
96 3/8	110	Apr	915	6 3/4	...	...
96 3/8	110	Jul	402	11	...	...
96 3/8	115	Feb	677	2 1/4	...	...
Citigroup	45	Jan	217	5 3/4	523	1/16
50 1/2	45	Feb	194	7 1/4	697	1 1/2
50 1/2	47 1/2	Feb	54	5 1/2	624	2 1/16
50 1/2	47 1/2	Mar	69	6 3/4	480	2 3/4
50 1/2	50	Jan	3003	5/8	4177	5/8
50 1/2	50	Feb	675	4	1270	3 1/4
50 1/2	50	Mar	291	4 7/8	4447	4
50 1/2	55	Jan	1098	1/16	659	4 1/4
50 1/2	55	Feb	1865	1 7/8	803	6
50 1/2	55	Mar	510	2 7/8	118	6 1/2
50 1/2	60	Feb	1062	13/16	9	10 1/8
50 1/2	60	Mar	447	1 5/8	21	10 1/8
ClearCh	50	Apr	635	12 3/8	...	...
Clorox	110	Jan	324	3/8	1493	1 3/4
108 9/16	115	Jan	690	1/16	25	6 3/8
Coke	55	Feb	3	9 1/2	1795	3/4
63 11/16	60	Jan	344	3 1/4	246	3/16
63 11/16	60	Feb	221	5 3/4	896	1 1/2
63 11/16	65	Jan	481	3/16	1354	1 1/4
63 11/16	65	Feb	278	2 1/2	1609	3 1/4
63 11/16	70	Feb	357	3/4	220	6 3/4
CmpUSA	12 1/2	Feb	59	1 3/16	755	1 1/4
12 3/8	20	Feb	...	...	500	7 5/8
Compaq	5	Jan	769	1/16	13	2 5/8
44 9/16	30	Jan	1021	14 5/8	...	...
44 9/16	35	Jan	1371	9 3/4	...	...
44 9/16	35	Apr	362	11 1/2	197	1 1/4
44 9/16	37 1/2	Jan	418	7 1/8	...	...
44 9/16	37 1/2	Feb	60	8 3/8	397	1
44 9/16	40	Jan	2640	4 3/4	20	1/16
44 9/16	40	Feb	618	6 3/8	279	1 7/16
44 9/16	42 1/2	Jan	739	2 1/4	384	3/16
44 9/16	45	Jan	5380	7/16	1552	7/8
44 9/16	45	Feb	1653	3 1/2	410	3 3/8
44 9/16	45	Apr	760	5 1/8	76	4 5/8
44 9/16	47 1/2	Feb	368	2 1/2	5	4 5/8
44 9/16	50	Feb	1557	1 11/16	69	6
44 9/16	50	Apr	634	3 1/8	...	...
44 9/16	50	Jul	542	4 7/8	68	8 3/4
44 9/16	55	Feb	437	13/16	...	...
CompAssoc	40	Jan	401	4 5/8	355	1/16
44 5/8	45	Jan	550	7/16	384	7/8
44 5/8	55	Feb	625	1/2	...	...
Cmpuwr	70	Feb	391	5	13	7 1/4
66 13/16	75	Feb	1265	3 1/4	22	10 3/8
Cnseco	35	May	370	3 1/8	154	5

These first three contract terms—the identity of the underlying stock, the striking price, and the expiration month—will not change during the life of the option. However, since the price of a stock option depends on the price of the underlying stock, the price of an option changes as the stock price changes.

Option prices are reported in columns 5 and 7 in the stock options listing displayed in Figure 14.1. Column 5 gives call option prices, and column 7 gives put option prices. Option prices are stated on a per-share basis, but the actual price of an option contract is 100 times the per-share price. This is because each option contract represents an option on 100 shares of stock. Fractional contracts for, say, 50 shares, are not normally available.

In Figure 14.1, trading volume for each contract is reported in columns 4 and 6. Column 4 states the number of call option contracts traded for each available strike-maturity combination, while column 6 states the number of put option contracts traded for each strike-maturity combination.

CHECK THIS

14.1a What is a call option? What is a put option?

14.1b What are the six basic contract terms that an options contract must specify?

14.2 Why Options?

As a stock market investor, a basic question you might ask is: "Why buy stock options instead of shares of stock directly?" Good question! To answer it properly, we need to compare the possible outcomes from two investment strategies. The first investment strategy entails simply buying stock. The second strategy involves buying a call option that allows the holder to buy stock any time before option expiration.

For example, suppose you buy 100 shares of IBM stock at a price of $90 per share, representing an investment of $9,000. Afterwards, three things could happen: the stock price could go up, go down, or remain the same. If the stock price goes up, you make money; if it goes down, you lose money. Of course, if the stock price remains the same, you break even.

Now, consider the alternative strategy of buying a call option with a strike price of $90 expiring in three months at a per-share price of $5. This corresponds to a contract price of $500 since the standard option contract size is 100 shares. The first thing to notice about this strategy is that you have invested only $500, and therefore the most that you can lose is only $500.

To compare the two investment strategies just described, let's examine three possible cases for IBM's stock price at the close of trading on the third Friday of the option's expiration month. In case 1, the stock price goes up to $100. In case 2, the stock price goes down to $80. In case 3, the stock price remains the same at $90.

Case 1: If the stock price goes up to $100, and you originally bought 100 shares at $90 dollars per share, then your profit is $100 \times (\$100 - \$90) = \$1,000$. As a percentage of your original investment amount of $9,000, this represents a return on investment of $1,000 / $9,000 = 11.11\%$.

Alternatively, if you originally bought the call option, you can exercise the option and buy 100 shares at the strike price of $90 and sell the stock at the $100 market price. After accounting for the original cost of the option contract, your profit is $100 \times (\$100 - \$90) - \$500 = \$500$. As a percentage of your original investment of $500, this represents a return on investment of $500 / $500 = 100\%.

Case 2: If the stock price goes down to $80, and you originally bought 100 shares at $90 dollars per share, then your loss is $100 \times (\$80 - \$90) = -\$1,000$. As a percentage of your original investment, this represents a return of $-\$1,000 / \$9,000 = -11.11\%$.

If instead you originally bought the call option, it would not pay to exercise the option and it would expire worthless. You would then realize a total loss of your $500 investment and your return is -100 percent.

Case 3: If the stock price remains the same at $90, and you bought 100 shares, you break even and your return is zero percent.

However, if you bought the call option, it would not pay to exercise the option and it would expire worthless. Once again, you would lose your entire $500 investment.

As these three cases illustrate, the outcomes of the two investment strategies differ significantly, depending on subsequent stock price changes. Whether one strategy is preferred over another is a matter for each individual investor to decide. What is important is the fact that options offer an alternative means of formulating investment strategies.

Example 14.1 Stock Returns

Suppose you bought 100 shares of stock at $50 per share. If the stock price goes up to $60 per share, what is the percentage return on your investment? If, instead, the stock price falls to $40 per share, what is the percentage return on your investment?

If the stock goes to $60 per share, you make $10/$50 = 20%. If it falls to $40, you lose $10/$50 = 20%.

Example 14.2 Call Option Returns

In Example 14.1 just above, suppose that you bought one call option contract for $200. The strike price is $50. If the stock price is $60 just before the option expires, should you exercise the option? If you exercise the option, what is the percentage return on your investment? If you don't exercise the option, what is the percentage return on your investment?

If the stock price is $60, you should definitely exercise. If you do, you will make $10 per share, or $1,000, from exercising. Once we deduct the $200 original cost of the option, your net profit is $800. Your percentage return is $800/$200 = 400%. If you don't exercise, you lose your entire $200 investment, so your loss is 100 percent.

Example 14.3 More Call Option Returns

In Example 14.2, if the stock price is $40 just before the option expires, should you exercise the option? If you exercise the option, what is the percentage return on your investment? If you don't exercise the option, what is the percentage return on your investment?

If the stock price is $40, you shouldn't exercise since, by exercising, you will be paying $50 per share. If you did exercise, you would lose $10 per share, or $1,000, plus the $200 cost of the option, or $1,200 total. This would amount to a $1,200/$200 = 600% loss! If you don't exercise, you lose the $200 you invested, for a loss of 100 percent.

Of course, we can also calculate percentage gains and losses from a put option purchase. Here we make money if the stock price declines. So, suppose you buy a put option with a strike price of $20 for $.50. If you exercise your put when the stock price is $18, what is your percentage gain?

You make $2 per share since you are selling at $20 when the stock is worth $18. Your put contract cost $50, so your net profit is $200 − $50 = $150. As a percentage of your original $50 investment, you made $150 / $50 = 300%.

CHECK THIS

14.2a If you buy 100 shares of stock at $10 and sell out at $12, what is your percentage return?

14.2b If you buy one call contract with a strike of $10 for $100 and exercise it when the stock is selling for $12, what is your percentage return?

14.3 Option Payoffs and Profits

Options are appealing because they offer investors a wide variety of investment strategies. In fact, there is essentially no limit to the number of different investment strategies available using options. However, fortunately for us, only a small number of basic strategies are available and more complicated strategies are built from these. We discuss the payoffs from basic strategies in this section and the following section.

Option Writing

option writing Taking the seller's side of an option contract.

call writer One who has the obligation to sell stock at the option's strike price if the option is exercised.

put writer One who has the obligation to buy stock at the option's strike price if the option is exercised.

Thus far, we have discussed options from the standpoint of the buyer only. However, options are contracts, and every contract must link at least two parties. The two parties to an option contract are the buyer and the seller. The seller of an option is called the "writer," and the act of selling an option is referred to as **option writing**.

By buying an option you buy the right, but not the obligation, to exercise the option before the option's expiration date. By selling or writing an option you take the seller's side of the option contract. Option writing involves receiving the option price and, in exchange, assuming the obligation to satisfy the buyer's exercise rights if the option is exercised.

For example, a **call writer** is obligated to sell stock at the option's strike price if the buyer decides to exercise the call option. Similarly, a **put writer** is obligated to buy stock at the option's strike price if the buyer decides to exercise the put option.

Option Payoffs

It is useful to think about option investment strategies in terms of their initial cash flows and terminal cash flows. The initial cash flow of an option is the price of the option, also called the option *premium*. To the option buyer, the option price (or premium) is a cash outflow.

To the option writer, the option price (or premium) is a cash inflow. The terminal cash flow of an option is the option's payoff that could be realized from the exercise privilege. To the option buyer, a payoff entails a cash inflow. To the writer, a payoff entails a cash outflow.

For example, suppose the current price of IBM stock is $80 per share. You buy a call option on IBM with a strike price of $80. The premium is $4 per share. Thus, the initial cash flow is −$400 for you and +$400 for the option writer. What are the terminal cash flows for you and the option writer if IBM has a price of $90 when the option expires? What are the terminal cash flows if IBM has a price of $70 when the option expires?

If IBM is at $90, then you experience a cash inflow of $10 per share, whereas the writer experiences an outflow of $10 per share. If IBM is at $70, you both have a zero cash flow when the option expires because it is worthless. Notice that in both cases the buyer and the seller have the same cash flows, just with opposite signs. This shows that options are a "zero-sum game," meaning that any gains to the buyer must come at the expense of the seller and vice versa.

Payoff Diagrams

When investors buy options, the price that they are willing to pay depends on their assessment of the likely payoffs (cash inflows) from the exercise privilege. Likewise, when investors write options, an acceptable selling price depends on their assessment of the likely payoffs (cash outflows) resulting from the buyers' exercise privilege. Given this, a general understanding of option payoffs is critical for understanding how option prices are determined.

A payoff diagram is a very useful graphical device for understanding option payoffs. The payoffs from buying a call option and the payoffs from writing a call option are seen in the payoff diagram in Figure 14.2. The vertical axis of Figure 14.2 measures option payoffs, and the horizontal axis measures the possible stock prices on the option expiration date. These examples assume that the call option has a strike price of $50 and that the option will be exercised only on its expiration date.

In Figure 14.2, notice that the call option payoffs are zero for all stock prices below the $50 strike price. This is because the call option holder will not exercise the option to buy stock at the $50 strike price when the stock is available in the stock market at a lower price. In this case, the option expires worthless.

Figure 14.2

Call Option
Payoffs

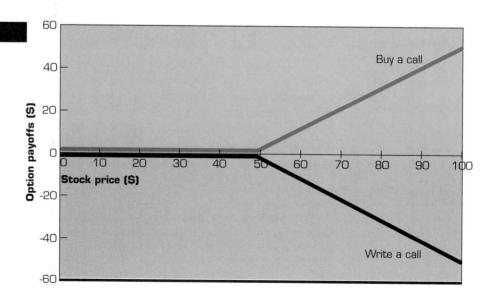

In contrast, if the stock price is higher than the $50 strike price, the call option payoff is equal to the difference between the market price of the stock and the strike price of the option. For example, if the stock price is $60, the call option payoff is equal to $10, which is the difference between the $60 stock price and the $50 strike price. This payoff is a cash inflow to the buyer, because the option buyer can buy the stock at the $50 strike price and sell the stock at the $60 market price. However, this payoff is a cash outflow to the writer, because the option writer must sell the stock at the $50 strike price when the stock's market price is $60.

Putting it all together, the distinctive "hockey-stick" shape of the call option payoffs shows that the payoff is zero if the stock price is below the strike price. Above the strike price, however, the buyer of the option gains $1 for every $1 increase in the stock price. Of course, as shown, the option writer loses $1 for every $1 increase in the stock price above the strike price.

Figure 14.3 is an example of a payoff diagram illustrating the payoffs from buying a put option and from writing a put option. As with our call option payoffs, the vertical axis measures option payoffs, and the horizontal axis measures the possible stock prices on the option expiration date. Once again, these examples assume that the put has a strike price of $50, and that the option will be exercised only on its expiration date.

In Figure 14.3, the put option payoffs are zero for all stock prices above the $50 strike price. This is because a put option holder will not exercise the option to sell stock at the $50 strike price when the stock can be sold in the stock market at a higher price. In this case, the option expires worthless.

In contrast, if the stock price is lower than the $50 strike price, the put option payoff is equal to the difference between the market price of the stock and the strike price of the option. For example, if the stock price is $40, the put option payoff is equal to $10, which is the difference between the $40 stock price and the $50 strike price. This payoff is a cash inflow to the buyer, because the option buyer can buy the stock at the $40 market price and sell the stock at the $50 strike price. However, this payoff is a cash outflow to the writer, because the option writer must buy the stock at the $50 strike price when the stock's market price is $40.

Our payoff diagrams illustrate an important difference between the maximum possible gains and losses for puts and calls. Notice that if you buy a call option, there is no upper limit to your potential profit because there is no upper limit to the stock price. However, with

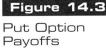

Figure 14.3

Put Option
Payoffs

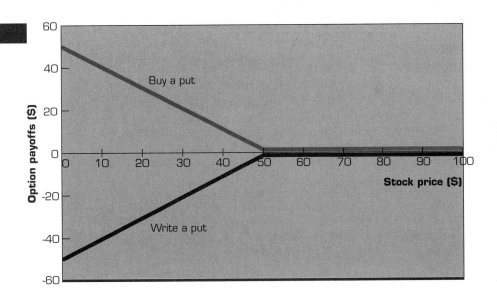

a put option, the most you can make is the strike price. In other words, the best thing that can happen to you if you buy a put is for the stock price to go to zero. Of course, whether you buy a put or a call, your potential loss is limited to the option premium you pay.

Similarly, as shown in Figure 14.2, if you write a call, there is no limit to your possible loss, but your potential gain is limited to the option premium you receive. As shown in Figure 14.3, if you write a put, both your gain and loss are limited, although the potential loss could be substantial.

Options Profits

Between them, Figures 14.2 and 14.3 tell us essentially everything we need to know about the payoffs from the four basic strategies involving options, buying and writing puts and calls. However, these figures give the payoffs at expiration only and so do not consider the original cash inflow or outflow. Option profit diagrams are an extension of payoff diagrams that do take into account the initial cash flow.

As we have seen, the profit from an option strategy is the difference between the option's terminal cash flow (the option payoff) and the option's initial cash flow (the option price, or premium). An option profit diagram simply adjusts option payoffs for the original price of the option. This means that the option premium is subtracted from the payoffs from buying an option and added to payoffs from writing options.

To illustrate, Figures 14.4 and 14.5 are profit diagrams corresponding to the four basic investment strategies for options. In each diagram, the vertical axis measures option profits, and the horizontal axis measures possible stock prices. Each profit diagram assumes that the option's strike price is $50 and that the put and call option prices are both $10. Notice that in each case the characteristic hockey-stick shape is maintained; the "stick" is just shifted up or down.

CHECK THIS

14.3a What is option writing?

14.3b What are the payoffs from writing call options?

14.3c What are the payoffs from writing put options?

14.4 Option Strategies

Thus far, we have considered the payoffs and profits from buying and writing individual calls and puts. In this section, we consider what happens when we start to combine puts, calls, and shares of stock. There are numerous combinations that we could examine, but we will stick to just a few of the most basic and most important strategies.

The Protective Put Strategy

Suppose you own a share of TelMex (Telephonos de México) stock, currently worth $50. Suppose you additionally purchase a put option with a strike price of $50 for $2. What is the net effect of this purchase?

To answer, we can compare what happens if TelMex stock stays at or above $50 to what happens if it drops below $50. If TelMex stays at or above $50, your put will expire worthless since you would choose not to exercise it. You would be out the $2.

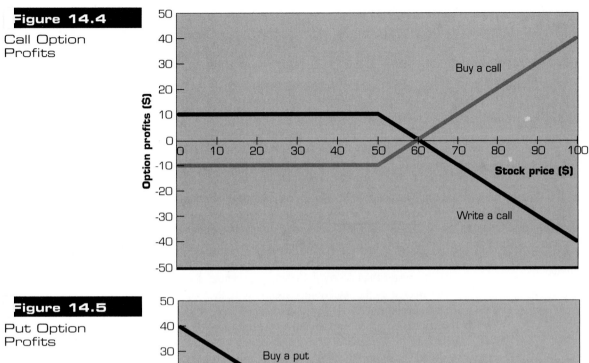

Figure 14.4

Call Option
Profits

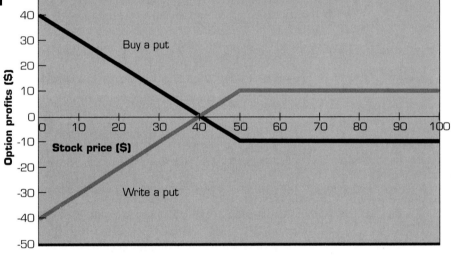

Figure 14.5

Put Option
Profits

However, if TelMex falls below $50, you would exercise your put, and the put writer would pay you $50 for your stock. No matter how far below $50 the price falls, you have guaranteed that you will receive $50 for your stock.

Thus, by purchasing a put option, you have protected yourself against a price decline. In the jargon of Wall Street, you have paid $2 to eliminate the "downside risk." For this reason, a strategy of buying a put option on a stock you own is called a **protective put** strategy.

Notice that this use of a put option *reduces* the overall risk faced by an investor, so it is a conservative strategy. This is a good example of how options, or any derivative asset, can be used to decrease risk rather than increase it. Stated differently, options can be used to hedge as well as speculate, so they do not inherently increase risk.

Buying a put option on an asset you own is just like buying term insurance. When you buy car insurance, for example, you are effectively buying a put option on your car. If, because of an accident or theft, your car's value declines, you "exercise" your option, and the insurance company essentially pays for the decline in value.

protective put
Strategy of buying a put option on a stock already owned. This protects against a decline in value.

The Covered Call Strategy

Another conservative option strategy is to write call options on stock you already own. For example, again suppose you own some TelMex stock currently selling at $50. Now, instead of buying a put, consider selling a call option for, say, $2, with an exercise price of $55. What is the effect of this transaction?

To answer, we can compare what happens if TelMex stays below $55 (the exercise price on the option you sold) to what happens if it rises above $55. If TelMex stays below $55, the option will expire worthless, and you pocket the $2 premium you received. If the stock rises above $55, the option will be exercised against you, and you will deliver the stock in exchange for $55.

Thus, when you sell a call option on stock you already own, you keep the option premium no matter what. The worst thing that can happen to you is that you will have to sell your stock at the exercise price. Since you already own the stock, you are said to be "covered," and this strategy is known as a **covered call** strategy.

covered call Strategy of selling a call option on stock already owned.

With our covered call strategy, the stock is currently selling for $50. Since the strike price on the option is $55, the net effect of the strategy is to give up the possibility of a profit greater than $5 on the stock in exchange for the certain option premium of $2. This decreases the uncertainty surrounding the return on the investment and therefore decreases its risk.

In the jargon of Wall Street, a covered call exchanges "upside" potential for current income. In contrast, a strategy of selling call options on stock you do not own is a "naked" call strategy and, as we saw earlier, has unlimited potential losses. Thus, selling call options is either quite risky or else acts to reduce risk, depending on whether you are covered or naked. This is important to understand.

Straddles

Suppose a share of stock is currently selling at $50. You think the price is going to make a major move, but you are uncertain about the direction. What could you do? One answer is buy a call *and* buy a put, both with a $50 exercise price. That way, if the stock goes up sharply, your call will pay off; if it goes down sharply, your put will pay off. This is an example of a long **straddle**.

straddle Buying or selling a call and a put with the same exercise price. Buying is a *long straddle;* selling is a *short straddle.*

This is called a "straddle" because you have, in effect, straddled the current $50 stock price. It is a long straddle because you bought both options. If you thought the stock price was *not* going to move in either direction, you might sell a put and a call, thereby generating some income. As long as the stock price stays at $50, both options would expire worthless. This is an example of a short straddle.

There are many other strategies, with colorful names such as strips, strangles, collars, and spreads, but we need to move on. In our next section, we discuss some upper and lower bounds on option values.

Example 14.4 Option Strategies

You own a share of stock worth $80. Suppose you sell a call option with a strike price of $80 and also buy a put with a strike of $80. What is the net effect of these transactions on the risk of owning the stock?

Notice that what you have done is combine a protective put and a covered call strategy. To see the effect of doing this, suppose that at option expiration, the stock is selling for more than $80. In this case, the put is worthless. The call will be exercised against you, and you will receive $80 for your stock. If the stock is selling for less than $80, then the call is worthless. You would exercise your put and sell the stock for $80. In other words, the net effect is that you have guaranteed that you will exchange the stock for $80 no matter what happens, so you have created a riskless asset!

CHECK THIS

14.4a What is a protective put strategy? A covered call strategy?

14.4b What is a short straddle? When might it be appropriate?

14.5 Option Prices, Intrinsic Values, and Arbitrage

There are strict limits to the range of values that an option price can attain in competitive options markets. We will have much to say about the determinants of an option's value in the next chapter. Here we touch on the subject by discussing some basic boundaries for the price of an option.

The Upper Bound for a Call Option Price

What is the most a call option could sell for? To answer, suppose we have a call option on a share of stock. The current stock price is $60. Without more information, we can't say a lot about the price of the call option, but we do know one thing: The price of the option must be less than $60!

If you think about it, the right to buy a share of stock cannot be worth more than the share itself. To illustrate, suppose the call option was actually selling for $65 when the stock was selling at $60. What would you do?

What you would do is get very rich, very fast. You would sell call options at $65 and buy stock at $60. You pocket the $5 difference. The worst thing that can happen to you is the options are exercised and you receive the exercise price. In this case, you make an unlimited amount of money at no risk.

This is an example of a true *arbitrage* opportunity. An arbitrage is an opportunity that (1) requires no net investment on your part, (2) has no possibility of loss, and (3) has at least the potential for a gain. The case of a call option selling for more than its underlying asset is a particularly juicy arbitrage because it puts money in your pocket today, and later either leaves you with stock you acquired at no cost or else leaves you with the exercise price on the option. Very nice, indeed! But too good to be true.

The Upper Bound for a Put Option

We've seen that a call option cannot sell for more than the underlying stock. How about a put option? To answer, suppose again that the stock price is $60. If a put sells for $65, is there an arbitrage opportunity?

It may look a little odd, but, without more information, we can't tell if there is an arbitrage or not. To see this, suppose the exercise price on the put option is $1,000. The right to sell a share of stock for $1,000 when its current worth is only $60 is obviously valuable, and it is obviously worth more than $65.

As this example suggests, the upper bound on a put option's price depends on the strike price. To illustrate, suppose we have a put option with an exercise price of $50 and a price of $60. What would you do?

This situation is an arbitrage opportunity. You would simply sell puts at $60 and put the money in the bank. The worst thing that could happen to you is that you would have to buy the stock for $50 a share, leaving you with stock and $10 per share in cash (the difference between the $60 you received and the $50 you paid for the stock). So you would either end up with stock that cost you nothing to acquire plus some cash or, if the option expires worthless, you would keep the entire $60. We therefore conclude that a put option must sell for less than its strike price.

The Lower Bounds on Option Prices

Having established the most a call or put could sell for, we now want to know what is the least they could sell for. We observe that an option cannot have a negative value, since, by definition, an option can simply be discarded.

intrinsic value The payoff that an option holder receives assuming the underlying stock price remains unchanged from its current value.

To further address this question, it is useful to define what is known as the **intrinsic value** of an option. The intrinsic value of an option is the payoff that an option holder receives if the underlying stock price does not change from its current value. Equivalently, it is what the option would be worth if it were expiring immediately.

For example, suppose a certain call option contract specifies a strike price of $50, and the underlying stock price for the option is currently $45. Suppose the option was about to expire. With the stock price at $45 and the strike at $50, this option would have no value. Thus, this call option's intrinsic value is zero.

Alternatively, suppose the underlying stock price is currently $55. If the option was about to expire, it would be exercised, yielding a payoff of $5. This $5, which is simply the difference between the $55 stock price and the $50 strike price, is the call option's intrinsic value.

As another example of intrinsic value, suppose a put option has a strike price of $50, and the current stock price is $55. If the put were about to expire, it would be worthless. In this case, the put option's intrinsic value is zero.

Alternatively, suppose the underlying stock price was $45. The put option would be exercised, yielding a payoff of $5, which is the difference between the $50 strike price and the $45 stock price. In this case, the put option's intrinsic value is $5.

Based on our examples, the intrinsic value of a call option and a put option can be written as follows, where S is a current stock price and K is the option's strike price. The term *"max"* is a shorthand notation for maximum.

$$\text{Call option intrinsic value} = max\,[0, S - K]$$
$$\text{Put option intrinsic value} = max\,[0, K - S]$$

This notation simply means that the intrinsic value of a call option is equal to $S - K$ or zero, whichever is bigger. Similarly, the intrinsic value of a put option is equal to $K - S$ or zero, whichever is bigger.

An option with a positive intrinsic value is said to be "in the money," and an option with a zero intrinsic value is said to be "out of the money" or "out the money." If the stock price and the strike price are essentially equal, the option is said to be "at the money." Thus, a call option is in the money when the stock price is greater than the strike price, and a put option is in the money when the stock price is less than the strike price.

Having defined an option's intrinsic value, we now ask: Is it possible for an option to sell for less than its intrinsic value? The answer is no. To see this, suppose a current stock price is S = $60, and a call option with a strike price of K = $50 has a price of C = $5. Clearly, this call option is in the money, and the $5 call price is less than the option's intrinsic value of $S - K$ = $10.

If you are actually presented with these stock and option prices, you have an arbitrage opportunity to obtain a riskless arbitrage profit by following a simple three-step strategy. First, buy the call option at its price of C = $5. Second, immediately exercise the call option and buy the stock from the call writer at the strike price of K = $50. At this point, you have acquired the stock for $55, which is the sum of the call price plus the strike price.

As a third and final step, simply sell the stock at the current market price of S = $60. Since you acquired the stock for $55 and sold the stock for $60, you have earned an arbitrage profit of $5. Clearly, if such an opportunity continued to exist, you would repeat these three steps over and over until you became bored with making easy money (as if that could ever happen!). But realistically, such easy arbitrage opportunities do not exist, and it therefore follows that a call option price is never less than its intrinsic value.

A similar arbitrage argument applies to put options. For example, suppose a current stock price is S = $40, and a put option with a strike price of K = $50 has a price of P = $5. This $5 put price is less than the option's intrinsic value of $K - S$ = $10. To exploit this opportunity, you first buy the put option at its price of P = $5, and then buy the stock at its current price of S = $40. At this point, you have acquired the stock for $45, which is the sum of the put price plus the stock price. Now you immediately exercise the put option, thereby selling the stock to the option writer at the strike price of S = $50. Since you acquired the stock for $45 and sold the stock for $50, you have earned an arbitrage profit of $5. Again, you would not realistically expect such an easy arbitrage opportunity to actually exist, and therefore we conclude that a put option's price is never less than its intrinsic value.

Our conclusion that call option and put option prices are never less than their intrinsic values can be stated as follows, where the mathematical symbol "≥" means "greater than or equal to":

$$\text{Call option price} \geq max\ [0, S - K]$$
$$\text{Put option price} \geq max\ [0, K - S]$$

In plain English, these equations simply state that an option's price is never less than the intrinsic value of the option.

There is an important caveat concerning our lower bounds on option values. If you pick up *The Wall Street Journal,* it is relatively easy to find cases in which it appears an option is selling for less than its intrinsic value, at least by a small amount. However, if you tried to actually exploit the apparent arbitrage, you would find that the prices in the *Journal* are not the ones you could actually trade at! There are a variety of reasons for this, but, at a minimum, keep in mind that the prices you see for the stock and the option are probably not synchronous, so the two prices may never have existed at the same point in time.

CHECK THIS

14.5a What is the most a call option could be worth? The least?

14.5b What is the most a put option could be worth? The least?

14.5c What is an out-of-the-money put option?

14.6 Stock Index Options

Following the tremendous success of stock options trading on the Chicago Board Options Exchange, the exchange looked for other new financial products to offer to investors and portfolio managers. In 1982, the CBOE created stock index options, which, at the time, represented a new type of option contract.

Index Options: Features and Settlement

stock index option
An option on a stock market index. The most popular stock index options are options on the S&P 100 index, S&P 500 index, and Dow Jones Industrials index.

A **stock index option** is an option on a stock market index. The first stock index options were contracts on the Standard & Poor's index of 100 large companies representative of American industry. This index is often simply called the "S&P 100." S&P 100 index options trade under the ticker symbol OEX, and S&P 100 index options are referred to as "OEX options." The second stock index options introduced by the CBOE were contracts on the Standard & Poor's index of 500 companies, the "S&P 500." S&P 500 index options trade under the ticker symbol SPX and are referred to as "SPX options." In 1997, the CBOE introduced options on the Dow Jones Industrial Average (DJIA), which trade under the ticker symbol DJX.

Besides the different underlying indexes, the major difference between SPX, DJX, and OEX contracts are that OEX options are American style, whereas SPX and DJX options are European style. As we noted earlier, American-style options can be exercised any time before expiration, whereas European-style options can be exercised only on the last day before option expiration.

Before stock index options could be introduced, one very important detail that had to be worked out was what to do when an option is exercised. It was obvious to exchange officials that actual delivery of all stocks comprising a stock index was impractical. Instead, a cash settlement procedure was adopted for stock index options. With cash settlement, when a stock index option is exercised, the option writer pays a cash amount to the option buyer based on the difference between the exercise date index level and the option's strike price. For example, suppose you had purchased an SPX call option with a strike price of $920, and the S&P 500 index was $940 on the day before option expiration. The difference between the index level and the strike price is $940 − $920 = $20. Since the contract size for SPX options is 100 times the S&P 500 index, the option writer must pay 100 × $20 = $2,000, which you receive as the option holder.

In the example above, the contract size for SPX options was stated to be 100 times the S&P 500 index. In fact, the contract size for almost all standardized stock index options is 100 times the underlying index. Thus, the actual price of a stock index option is 100 times the price stated on an index level basis. There are only a few exceptions to this rule. For example, the CBOE offers so-called Reduced Value index options with a contract size that is one-tenth the size of standard index options. Reduced Value index options are appealing to some individual investors, but they represent only a minuscule share of all index options trading.

Index Option Price Quotes

There now exists a wide variety of stock market indexes for which options are available. Each business day, *The Wall Street Journal* provides a summary of the previous day's activity in stock index options. Figure 14.6, "Index Options Trading", excerpts this column.

Figure 14.6

Index Options Trading

Source: Reprinted by permission of *The Wall Street Journal,* July 3, 1998. Via Copyright Clearance Center, Inc. © 1998 Dow Jones & Company, Inc. All Rights Reserved Worldwide.

Thursday, July 2, 1998

Volume, last, net change and open interest for all contracts. Volume figures are unofficial. Open interest reflects previous trading day. p-Put c-Call

CHICAGO

RANGES FOR UNDERLYING INDEXES

Thursday, July 2, 1998

	High	Low	Close	Net Chg.	From Dec. 31	% Chg.
DJ Indus (DJX)	90.48	90.03	90.25	− 0.24	+ 11.17	+ 14.1
DJ Trans (DTX)	351.42	349.53	350.65	− 0.81	+ 25.00	+ 7.7
DJ Util (DUX)	294.32	292.79	293.84	− 0.30	+ 20.77	+ 7.6
S&P 100 (OEX)	560.60	557.82	559.38	− 1.22	+ 99.44	+ 21.6
S&P 500 -A.M.(SPX)	1148.56	1142.99	1146.42	− 2.14	+ 175.99	+ 18.1
CB-Tech (TXX)	282.55	275.84	277.35	− 5.20	+ 61.56	+ 28.5
CB-Mexico (MEX)	103.01	101.99	102.57	− 0.33	− 24.41	− 19.2
CB-Lps Mex (VEX)	10.30	10.20	10.26	− 0.03	− 2.44	− 19.2
MS Multintl (NFT)	636.03	632.61	633.94	− 2.09	+ 102.39	+ 19.3
GSTI Comp (GTC)	183.71	179.85	180.23	− 3.48	+ 36.77	+ 25.6
Nasdaq 100 (NDX)	1356.14	1331.84	1332.53	− 23.61	+ 341.73	+ 34.5
NYSE (NYA)	586.08	584.08	585.80	+ 0.20	+ 74.61	+ 14.6
Russell 2000 (RUT)	459.85	457.91	458.31	− 1.51	+ 21.29	+ 4.9
Lps S&P 100 (OEX)	112.12	111.56	111.88	− 0.24	+ 19.89	+ 21.6
Lps S&P 500 (SPX)	114.86	114.30	114.64	− 0.21	+ 17.60	+ 18.1
S&P Midcap (MID)	366.32	365.07	365.42	− 0.24	+ 32.05	+ 9.6
Major Mkt (XMI)	960.41	954.45	956.39	− 4.02	+ 119.54	+ 14.3
HK Fltg (HKO)	172.76	172.71	172.71	+ 6.42	− 41.85	− 19.5
IW Internet (IIX)	396.38	385.60	390.24	− 4.76	+ 129.99	+ 50.0
AM-Mexico (MXY)	113.86	112.31	113.66	+ 0.79	− 27.87	− 19.7
Institu'l -A.M.(XII)	645.27	642.46	644.41	− 0.50	− 405.75	− 38.6
Japan (JPN)			170.39	+ 1.16	+ 12.75	+ 8.1
MS Cyclical (CYC)	521.91	517.08	519.66	− 2.25	+ 44.65	+ 9.4
MS Consumr (CMR)	525.13	522.57	524.89	+ 0.94	+ 79.25	+ 17.8
MS Hi Tech (MSH)	608.08	591.64	596.38	− 11.70	+ 148.86	+ 33.3
Pharma (DRG)	676.84	672.43	676.62	+ 2.97	+ 142.88	+ 26.8
Biotech (BTK)	145.33	142.24	142.44	− 2.34	− 19.98	− 12.3
Comp Tech (XCI)	569.38	558.18	558.45	− 10.93	+ 119.46	+ 27.2
Gold/Silver (XAU)	70.15	68.35	68.80	− 1.93	− 5.39	− 7.3
OTC (XOC)	980.51	964.32	965.14	− 15.37	+ 227.19	+ 30.8
Utility (UTY)	327.09	325.12	326.11	− 0.98	+ 16.08	+ 5.2
Value Line (VLE)	958.08	955.16	956.62	− 1.46	+ 79.78	+ 9.1
Bank (BKX)	881.61	872.21	880.89	+ 5.36	+ 125.54	+ 16.6
Semicond (SOX)	252.75	245.24	245.61	− 7.14	− 18.02	− 6.8
Top 100 (TPX)	1104.79	1100.38	1103.40	− 0.92	+ 193.78	+ 21.3
Oil Service (OSX)	92.53	89.47	92.04	+ 2.43	− 22.33	− 19.5
PSE Tech (PSE)	350.20	343.88	345.21	− 5.04	+ 54.65	+ 18.8

(Tables of strike, volume, last, net change, and open interest for CB MEXICO INDEX (MEX), CB TECHNOLOGY (TXX), DJ INDUS AVG (DJX), NASDAQ-100 (NDX), S&P 100 INDEX (OEX), S&P 500 INDEX-AM (SPX) option contracts follow.)

The most prominent component of this column is the box entitled "Ranges for Underlying Indexes," which contains information on the more than 35 major stock market indexes for which index options are now available. In the first column of this box, the name of each index and (in parentheses), its ticker symbol are listed. Columns 2, 3, 4, and 5 report the corresponding high, low, close, and net change values, respectively, for each stock market index from the previous day's trading. For each stock index, the columns labeled "From Dec. 31" and "% Chg." report the dollar value change and percentage value change, respectively, since the beginning of the current year.

Outside the ranges box, index options trading data are reported separately for each options exchange and index. Figure 14.6 contains information for options on several indexes. The first set of index options data is for the Chicago Board Mexico Index (MEX). MEX index option contracts were first introduced in 1994.

The first column of MEX data reports contract expiration months, and the second column reports strike prices. The letters next to each strike price denote whether the option is a call or a put. The third column reports trading volume measured as the number of contracts traded during the previous day's trading. The fourth column, labeled "Last," reports the contract price for the last trade of the previous day, and the fifth column, labeled "Net Chg.," reports the price change from the last price on the previous day. Finally, the sixth column, labeled "Open Int.," lists the total number of contracts outstanding.

At the bottom of the MEX listing, total call volume and open interest are reported, followed by put volume and open interest. Trading volume is measured by the number of contracts traded on a given day. Open interest is measured by the total number of contracts outstanding on a given day.

The vast majority of all trading in stock index options is conducted on the Chicago Board Options Exchange. In fact, most index options activity is concentrated in the S&P 100 and S&P 500 contracts traded on the CBOE. OEX trading volume is often almost twice as large as SPX trading volume, but SPX open interest is usually twice as large as OEX open interest. Figure 14.6 provides OEX and SPX information. Notice the large number of strike prices available for these contracts.

Example 14.5 Index Options

Suppose you bought 10 July 990 SPX call contracts at a quoted price of $5. How much did you pay in total? At option expiration, suppose the S&P 500 is at 1000. What would you receive?

The price per SPX contract is 100 times the quoted price. Since you bought 10 contracts, you paid a total of $5 × 100 × 10 = $5,000. If, at expiration, the S&P 500 is at 1000, you would receive $100 × (1000 − 990) = $1,000 per contract, or $10,000 in all. This $10,000 would be paid to you in cash, since index options feature cash settlement.

CHECK THIS

14.6a In addition to the underlying asset, what is the major difference between any ordinary stock option and a stock index option?

14.6b In addition to the underlying index, what is the major difference between the OEX and SPX option contracts?

14.7 The Options Clearing Corporation

Suppose that you ordered a new car through a local dealer and paid a $2,000 deposit. Further suppose that two weeks later you receive a letter informing you that your dealer had entered bankruptcy. No doubt, you would be quite upset at the prospect of losing your $2,000 deposit.

Now consider a similar situation where you pay $2,000 for several call options through a broker. On the day before expiration you tell your broker to exercise the options, since they would produce, say, a $5,000 payoff. Then, a few days later, your broker tells you that the call writer entered bankruptcy proceedings and that your $2,000 call premium and $5,000 payoff were lost. No doubt, this would also be quite upsetting. However, if your options were traded through a registered options exchange, the integrity of your options investment would be guaranteed by the **Options Clearing Corporation (OCC).**

Options Clearing Corporation (OCC)
Private agency that guarantees that the terms of an option contract will be fulfilled if the option is exercised; issues and clears all option contracts trading on U.S. exchanges.

The Options Clearing Corporation is the clearing agency for all options exchanges in the United States. Both the exchanges and the clearing agency are subject to regulation by the Securities and Exchange Commission (SEC). Most options investors are unaware of the OCC because only member firms of an options exchange deal directly with it. However, in fact, all option contracts traded on U.S. options exchanges are originally issued, guaranteed, and cleared by the OCC. Brokerage firms merely act as intermediaries between investors and the OCC.

To better understand the function of the OCC, let us examine a hypothetical order to buy options. In this example, assume that you instruct your broker to buy, say, 10 August 100 put options on IBM. For simplicity, let us also assume that your broker works for a member firm of the CBOE and therefore can relay your order directly to the CBOE.

When the order arrives at the CBOE, it is directed to one of several dealers for IBM options. The CBOE dealer accepts the order by taking the position of a writer for the 10 put contracts. The order is then transferred to the OCC. Once the OCC verifies that there are matching orders from a buyer and a writer, for a small fee it takes over the dealer's position as the writer for your 10 August 100 puts.

By assuming the writer's obligation, the clearing corporation guarantees that the terms of your put contracts will be fulfilled if you later decide to exercise the options. From the CBOE dealer's perspective, the clearing corporation becomes the buyer of the 10 August 100 puts. As such, the CBOE dealer becomes obligated to the clearing corporation as the writer of 10 August 100 put options.

In this way, all dealer default risk is transferred to the clearing corporation. Ultimately, the OCC ensures the performance of all options traded on all registered options exchanges in the United States. Without the OCC, these options exchanges could not function nearly as efficiently as they do in practice.

14.8 Summary and Conclusions

In 1973, organized stock options trading began when the Chicago Board Options Exchange (CBOE) was established. Since then, options trading has grown enormously. In this chapter, we examined a number of concepts and issues surrounding stock options. We saw that:

1. Options on common stock are derivative securities because the value of a stock option is derived from the value of the underlying common stock. There are two basic types of options: call options and put options. Call options are options to buy, and put options are options to sell.

2. Options are contracts. Standardized stock options represent a contract size of 100 shares of common stock per option contract. We saw how standardized option prices are quoted in the financial press.

3. Various strategies exist with options, ranging from buying and selling individual puts and calls to combination strategies involving calls, puts, and the underlying stock. There are many common strategies, including protective puts and covered calls.

4. Option prices have boundaries enforced by arbitrage. A call option cannot sell for more than the underlying asset, and a put option cannot sell for more than the strike price on the option.

5. An option's intrinsic value is a lower bound for an option's price. The intrinsic value of an option is the payoff that an option holder receives if the underlying stock price does not change from its current value.

6. A stock index option is an option on a stock market index such as the S&P 500. All stock index options use a cash settlement procedure when they are exercised. With a cash settlement procedure, when a stock index option is exercised, the option writer pays a cash amount to the option buyer.

7. The Options Clearing Corporation (OCC) is the clearing agency for all options exchanges in the United States. It guarantees that the terms of an option contract are fulfilled if the option is exercised.

GET REAL

This chapter added to your understanding of put and call options. In addition to covering the rights, obligations, and potential gains and losses involved, the chapter covered some basic option/stock strategies and stock index options. How should you put this information to work?

Now that you understand the most important features of stock and stock index options, you need to buy and sell a variety of them to experience the relatively large percentage real-world gains and losses that options can provide. So, with a simulated brokerage account (such as *Stock-Trak*), you should first execute each of the basic option transactions (buy a call, sell a call, buy a put, sell a put) for a variety of underlying stocks. To experience a wide range of possible outcomes, it is best to do each of these with out-the-money, at-the-money, and in-the-money options, so a total of a dozen transactions will be needed at a minimum. Pay careful attention to your commissions; they can be quite large as a percentage, particularly for small option purchases.

Once your option positions are established, follow the stock and option prices for a period of several weeks and then close. Calculate the percentage gains and losses on both the stock and the options.

The second types of trades to become familiar with are the covered call and protective put strategies, so execute these. You might also try a protective call on a short position (this trade is discussed in the end-of-chapter problems). A long and short straddle will round out your understanding of basic option trades.

A very common use of stock index put options is to insure an entire portfolio against adverse market movements. Execute such a transaction for your portfolio and evaluate its effectiveness. How large a purchase should you make? The answer is that it depends on how much insurance you want, but it is important not to create too large a position because then you are essentially speculating on a market drop instead of just protecting against one.

Key Terms

derivative security 402
call option 402
put option 402
strike price 402
American option 403
European option 403
option writing 407
call writer 407

put writer 407
protective put 411
covered call 412
straddle 412
intrinsic value 414
stock index option 416
Options Clearing Corporation (OCC) 419

Chapter Review Problems and Self-Test

1. **Call Option Payoffs**   Suppose you purchase 15 call contracts on Scholes Co. stock. The strike price is $220, and the premium is $10. If the stock is selling for $240 per share at expiration, what are your call options worth? What is your net profit? What if the stock were selling for $230? $220?

2. **Stock versus Options**   Stock in Black Manufacturing is currently priced at $90 per share. A call option with a $90 strike and 60 days to maturity is quoted at $5. Compare the percentage gains and losses from a $9,000 investment in the stock versus the option in 90 days for stock prices of $60, $90, and $120.

Answers to Self-Test Problems

1. The stock is selling for $240. You own 15 contracts, each of which gives you the right to buy 100 shares at $220. Your options are thus worth $20 per share on 1,500 shares, or $30,000. The option premium was $10, so you paid $1,000 per contract, or $15,000 total. Your net profit is $15,000. If the stock is selling for $230, your options are worth $15,000, so your net profit is exactly zero. If the stock is selling for $220, your options are worthless and you lose the entire $15,000 you paid.

2. The stock costs $90 per share, so if you invest $9,000, you'll get 100 shares. The option premium is $5, so an option contract costs $500. If you invest $9,000, you'll get $9,000/$500 = 18 contracts. If the stock is selling for $120 in 90 days, your profit on the stock is $30 per share, or $3,000 total. The percentage gain is $3,000/$9,000 = 33.33%.

   Similarly, in this case, your options are worth $30 per share, or $3,000 per contract. However, you have 18 contracts, so your options are worth $54,000 in all. Since you paid $9,000 for the 18 contracts, your profit is $45,000. Your percentage gain is a whopping $45,000/$9,000 = 500%.

   If the stock is selling for $90, your profit is $0 on the stock, so your percentage return is 0 percent. Your options are worthless (why?); the percentage loss is −100 percent. If the stock is selling for $60, verify that your percentage loss on the stock is −33.33 percent and your loss on the option is again −100 percent.

Test Your Investment Quotient

1. **Option Contracts**   Which of the following is not specified by a stock option contract?

   a. Price of the underlying stock.
   b. Contract size.
   c. Exercise style.
   d. Contract settlement procedure.

2. **Option Contracts** A July 50 call option contract for YXZ stock is identified by which ticker symbol?

   a. YXZ-JG
   b. YXZ-JS
   c. YXZ-GJ
   d. YXZ-SJ

3. **Option Contracts** An April 40 put option contract for YXZ stock is identified by which ticker symbol?

   a. YXZ-HD
   b. YXZ-HP
   c. YXZ-DH
   d. YXZ-PH

4. **Option Strategies** Which of the following stock option strategies has the potential for the largest loss?

   a. Writing a covered call.
   b. Writing a covered put.
   c. Writing a naked call.
   d. Writing a naked put.

5. **Option Strategies** Which statement describes an at-the-money protective put position (comprised of owning the stock and the put)? (*1992 CFA Exam*)

   a. It protects against loss at any stock price below the strike price of the put.
   b. It has limited profit potential when the stock price rises.
   c. It returns any increase in the stock's value, dollar for dollar, less the cost of the put.
   d. It provides a pattern of returns similar to a stop-loss order at the current stock price.

6. **Option Strategies** Which of the following yields a defensive/protective strategy?

   a. Writing a naked put.
   b. Buying a put on stock you currently own.
   c. Writing a call against stock you currently hold short.
   d. Buying a call on a stock you own.

7. **Option Strategies** Investor A uses options for defensive and income reasons. Investor B uses options as an aggressive investment strategy. What is an appropriate use of options for investors A and B respectively? (*1990 CFA Exam*)

   a. Writing covered calls / buying puts on stock not owned.
   b. Buying out-of-the-money calls / buying puts on stock owned.
   c. Writing naked calls / buying in-the-money calls.
   d. Selling puts on stock owned / buying puts on stock not owned.

8. **Option Strategies** How is a long straddle position constructed?

   a. Write a call and write a put.
   b. Buy a call and buy a put.
   c. Write a call and buy a put.
   d. Buy a call and write a put.

9. **Option Strategies** Which one of the following option combinations best describes a straddle? Buy both a call and a put on the same stock with (*1994 CFA Exam*)

   a. Different exercise prices and the same expiration date.
   b. The same exercise price and different expiration dates.
   c. The same exercise price and the same expiration date.
   d. Different exercise prices and different expiration. dates.

10. **Option Strategies** Which is the riskiest options transaction if the underlying stock price is expected to increase substantially?

   a. Writing a naked call.
   b. Writing a naked put.
   c. Buying a call.
   d. Buying a put.

11. **Option Gains and Losses** You create a "strap" by buying two calls and one put on ABC stock, all with a strike price of $45. The calls cost $5 each, and the put costs $4. If you close your position when ABC stock is priced at $55, what is your per-share gain or loss? (*1993 CFA Exam*)

   a. $4 loss
   b. $6 gain
   c. $10 gain
   d. $20 gain

12. **Option Gains and Losses** A put on XYZ stock with a strike price of $40 is priced at $2.00 per share, while a call with a strike price of $40 is priced at $3.50. What is the maximum per-share loss to the writer of the uncovered put and the maximum per-share gain to the writer of the uncovered call? (*1993 CFA Exam*)

	Maximum Loss to Put Writer	Maximum Gain to Call Writer
a.	$38.00	$3.50
b.	$38.00	$36.50
c.	$40.00	$3.50
d.	$40.00	$40.00

13. **Option Pricing** If a stock is selling for $25, the exercise price of a put option on that stock is $20, and the time to expiration of the option is 90 days, what are the minimum and maximum prices for the put today? (*1991 CFA Exam*)

   a. $0 and $5
   b. $0 and $20
   c. $5 and $20
   d. $5 and $25

14. **Option Strategies** Which of the following strategies is most suitable for an investor wishing to eliminate "downside" risk from a stock?

   a. long straddle
   b. short straddle
   c. covered call
   d. protective put

15. **Index Options** What is the ticker symbol for the S&P 100 index?

   a. SPC
   b. SPM
   c. SPX
   d. OEX

16. **Index Options** What is the ticker symbol for the S&P 500 index?

   a. SPC
   b. SPM
   c. SPX
   d. OEX

Questions and Problems

Core
Questions

1. **Basic Properties of Options**   What is a call option? A put option? Under what circumstances might you want to buy each? Which one has greater potential profit? Why?

2. **Calls versus Puts**   Complete the following sentence for each of these investors:

   a. A buyer of call options.
   b. A buyer of put options.
   c. A seller (writer) of call options.
   d. A seller (writer) of put options.

   The (buyer/seller) of a (put/call) option (pays/receives) money for the (right/obligation) to (buy/sell) a specified asset at a fixed price for a fixed length of time.

3. **Call Option Payoffs**   Suppose you purchase five call contracts on Macron Technology stock. The strike price is $50, and the premium is $2. If, at expiration, the stock is selling for $60 per share, what are your put options worth? What is your net profit?

4. **Put Option Payoffs**   Suppose you purchase eight put contracts on Testaburger Co. The strike price is $30, and the premium is $3. If, at expiration, the stock is selling for $20 per share, what are your call options worth? What is your net profit?

5. **Stock versus Options**   Stock in Cheezy-Poofs Manufacturing is currently priced at $100 per share. A call option with a $100 strike and 90 days to maturity is quoted at $5. Compare the percentage gains and losses from a $10,000 investment in the stock versus the option in 90 days for stock prices of $80, $100, and $120.

Use the following options quotations to answer questions 6 through 9:

Option & NY Close	Strike Price	Expiration	Calls		Puts	
			Vol.	Last	Vol.	Last
Hendreeks						
86	80	Feb	72	7	50	3/4
86	80	Mar	41	8 1/8	29	1 9/16
86	80	May	16	9 7/8	10	2 7/8
86	80	Aug	8	12	2	4 1/4

6. **Calculating Option Payoffs**   Suppose you buy 60 February 80 call option contracts. How much will you pay, ignoring commissions?

7. **Calculating Option Payoffs**   In Problem 6, suppose that Hendreeks stock is selling for $95 per share on the expiration date. How much is your options investment worth? What if the terminal stock price is $86?

8. **Calculating Option Payoffs**   Suppose you buy 25 August 80 put option contracts. What is your maximum gain? On the expiration date, Hendreeks is selling for $55 per share. How much is your options investment worth? What is your net gain?

9. **Calculating Option Payoffs**   In Problem 8, suppose you write 25 of the August 80 put contracts. What is your net gain or loss if Hendreeks is selling for $55 at expiration? For $100? What is the break-even price, that is, the terminal stock price that results in a zero profit?

10. **Option Breakeven**   In general, if you buy a call option, what stock price is needed for you to break even on the transaction ignoring taxes and commissions? If you buy a put option?

Intermediate
Questions

11. **Protective Puts**   Buying a put option on a stock is sometimes called "stock price insurance." Why?

12. **Defining Intrinsic Value**   What is the intrinsic value of a call option? How do we interpret this value?

13. **Defining Intrinsic Value**   What is the intrinsic value of a put option? How do we interpret this value?

14. **Call Option Writing** Suppose you write 20 call option contracts with a $40 strike. The premium is $2. Evaluate your potential gains and losses at option expiration for stock prices of $30, $40, and $50.

15. **Put Option Writing** Suppose you write 10 put option contracts with a $20 strike. The premium is $1. Evaluate your potential gains and losses at option expiration for stock prices of $10, $20, and $30.

16. **Index Options** Suppose you buy one SPX option contract with a strike of $1,300. At maturity, the S&P 500 index is at 1350. What is your net gain or loss if the premium you paid was $20?

17. **Arbitrage and Options** You notice that shares of stock in the Patel Corporation are going for $50 per share. Call options with an exercise price of $35 per share are selling for $10. What's wrong here? Describe how you could take advantage of this mispricing if the option expires today.

Use the following options quotations to answer questions 18 through 21:

Option & NY Close	Strike Price	Expiration	Calls		Puts	
			Vol.	Last	Vol.	Last
Milson						
59	55	Mar	98	$3\frac{1}{2}$	66	$1\frac{1}{16}$
59	55	Apr	54	$6\frac{1}{4}$	40	$1\frac{15}{16}$
59	55	Jul	25	$8\frac{5}{8}$	17	$3\frac{5}{8}$
59	55	Oct	10	$10\frac{1}{4}$	5	$3\frac{1}{4}$

18. **Interpreting Options Quotes** How many options contracts on Milson stock were traded with an expiration date of July? How many underlying shares of stock do these options contracts represent?

19. **Interpreting Options Quotes** Are the call options in the money? What is the intrinsic value of a Milson Corp. call option?

20. **Interpreting Options Quotes** Are the put options in the money? What is the intrinsic value of a Milson Corp. put option?

21. **Interpreting Options Quotes** Two of the options are clearly mispriced. Which ones? At a minimum, what should the mispriced options sell for? Explain how you could profit from the mispricing in each case.

22. **Option Strategies** Recall the options strategies of a protective put and covered call discussed in the text. Suppose you have sold short some shares of stock. Discuss analogous option strategies and how you would implement them. (Hint: They're called protective calls and covered puts.)

STOCK-TRAK·
Portfolio Simulations

Trading Stock Options with Stock-Trak

Once you know how to trade common stocks and understand the basics of stock options, you should try your hand at trading stock options. You can buy, sell, and write stock options with your Stock-Trak account. There are some limitations, however, since options are not available for all stocks, and Stock-Trak restricts stock options trading to short-term options with maturities of less than one year. But these restrictions are quite minor.

There are four basic types of stock option trades:

1. Buy an option to open or increase a long position.
2. Sell an option to close or reduce a long position.
3. Write an option to open or increase a short position.
4. Buy an option to cover or reduce a short position.

We will here discuss by example the first two types of option trades: "buying" an option to take a long position, and "selling" an option to close all or part of a long position. Until you have acquired extensive experience with these trade types, you should avoid options writing.

To trade a particular stock option, you must first know the stock ticker symbol for the underlying stock. Then you must also know the ticker extension representing the strike price and maturity month of the specific contract you wish to trade. The process of obtaining this information is described next.

Suppose you want to buy five call option contracts for Coca-Cola (KO) and four put option contracts for Disney (DIS). Further suppose that both options have a $50 strike price and a March expiration month. Your orders might be abbreviated to look like this:

Buy 5 KO-CJ

Buy 4 DIS-OJ

Notice that in addition to the stock ticker symbols, these option tickers have a two-letter extension denoting the option type—call or put—and the strike price and expiration month. The first letter represents the option type and expiration month. The second letter represents the strike price.

Converting option type, expiration month, and strike price to the correct two-letter ticker extension is easily done using Table ST.1. When the strike price is greater than 100, simply subtract 100 and use the result to specify a strike code; for example a strike of 135 has the strike code G, the same as for a strike of 35.

Notice in Table ST.1 that the 12 letters A–L denote the 12 expiration months January through December for call options. Similarly, the 12 letters M–X denote the 12 expiration months for put options. The 20 letters A–T represent the strike prices 5 through 100 in five-dollar increments. The six letters U–Z are reserved for the six strikes 7.5, 12.5, 17.5, 22.5, 27.5, and 32.5, respectively.

Table ST.1	Stock Option Ticker Symbol Codes						
Expiration Month	**Calls**	**Puts**	**Strike**		**Strike**		
January	A	M	5	A	70	N	
February	B	N	10	B	75	O	
March	C	O	15	C	80	P	
April	D	P	20	D	85	Q	
May	E	Q	25	E	90	R	
June	F	R	30	F	95	S	
July	G	S	35	G	100	T	
August	H	T	40	H	7.5	U	
September	I	U	45	I	12.5	V	
October	J	V	50	J	17.5	W	
November	K	W	55	K	22.5	X	
December	L	X	60	L	27.5	Y	
			65	M	32.5	Z	

Options exchanges use special option tickers for NASDAQ stocks, which have four or more letters in their ticker symbols. Stock-Trak insulates its customers from this inconvenience and accepts the full NASDAQ stock ticker for option orders. This is also standard practice among brokerage firms accepting customer orders. Table ST.2 provides several examples of Stock-Trak option tickers and their corresponding options exchange versions.

If you are interested in seeing more options exchange tickers, a complete list can be found at the CBOE website (www.cboe.com).

Table ST.2	**Exchange and Stock-Trak Tickers for July 40 Call (GH) Options**		
	NASDAQ Company (Ticker)	**Exchange Ticker**	**Stock-Trak Ticker**
	Microsoft (MSFT)	MSQ-GH	MSFT-GH
	Novell (NOVL)	NKQ-GH	NOVL-GH
	Sun Microsystems (SUNW)	SUQ-GH	SUNW-GH

Stock-Trak Exercises

1. What are the option types, expiration months, and strike prices for the following Micron Technology (MU) options: MU-FF, MU-RF, MU-HK, MU-TL?

2. What are the two-letter ticker extensions for the following options: January 80 calls, July 25 puts, April 12.5 calls, October 27.5 puts?

Trading Dow Jones Index Options with Stock-Trak

In addition to trading stock options with your Stock-Trak account, you can also trade options on many stock market indexes. To trade stock index options, you must first decide which particular stock index you want to use for options trading and find the ticker symbol for that index. You must also know the ticker extension for the strike price and maturity month. Also be aware that the ticker extensions for stock index options may not be the same as for stock options.

The best known stock index in the world is the Dow Jones Industrial Average (DJIA). The standard ticker symbol for this index is DJX, and DJX options trade on the Chicago Board Options Exchange (CBOE). Strike prices for DJX options are stated in unit increments representing 1/100 of the underlying index level. For example, strike prices of 100, 101, and so on, correspond to index levels of 10,000, 10,100, and so on, which are 100 times the stated strike price. However, the contract value for a single DJX option contract corresponds to the full value of the index, which we hope will be over 10,000 when you read this.

For example, suppose you bought three September 101 DJX call options. If at expiration the DJIA was at, say, 10,250, your payoff would be 3 contracts × (10,250 − 10,100) = $450. As another example, suppose you bought four July 119 DJX put options and at expiration the DJIA was 11,825. Then your payoff would be 4 contracts × (11,900 − 11,825) = $300.

DJX option tickers also have two-letter extensions denoting the option type (call or put), strike price, and expiration month. Just like stock options, the first letter represents the option type and expiration month, and the second letter represents the strike price. The letter codes for the option type and expiration month are the same as for stock options. However, DJX options have special strike price codes. These DJX strike codes are listed in Table ST.3.

For example, orders to buy three DJX September 133 calls and four DJX July 131 puts might be abbreviated as

Buy 3 DJX-IC contracts

Buy 4 DJX-SA contracts

Notice that just like stock options, September calls and July puts are denoted by the letters I and S, respectively. However, letter codes for the 133 and 131 strike prices are C and A, respectively, as indicated in the table.

In addition to options on the DJIA, you can also trade options on the Dow Jones Transportation Average (DJTA) and the Dow Jones Utilities Average (DJUA). The ticker symbols for these indexes are DJT and DJU, respectively, and their strike price codes are identical to those used for DJX options.

For more information on these options, consult the CBOE website (www.cboe.com).

Stock-Trak Exercises

1. What are the two-letter ticker extensions for the following Dow Jones index options: January 106 calls, July 111 puts, April 136 calls, October 116 puts?

2. Given an index level of 11,000, what are the option types, expiration months, and strike prices for the following options on the Dow Jones Industrial Average: DJX-EO, DJX-QY, DJX-JL, DJX-HW? (Hint: When a strike code might refer to several strikes, assume the strike nearest the current index level.)

Trading Standard and Poor's Index Options with Stock-Trak

The two most popular stock indexes for options trading are Standard & Poor's indexes, specifically the S&P 100 and S&P 500 indexes. Standard ticker symbols for these indexes are OEX for the S&P 100 and SPX for the S&P 500. OEX and SPX option tickers use the same

Table ST.3	Dow Jones Averages Strike Price Codes				
Code			Strike price		
A	27	53	79	105	131
B	28	54	80	106	132
C	29	55	81	107	133
D	30	56	82	108	134
E	31	57	83	109	135
F	32	58	84	110	136
G	33	59	85	111	137
H	34	60	86	112	138
I	35	61	87	113	139
J	36	62	88	114	140
K	37	63	89	115	141
L	38	64	90	116	142
M	39	65	91	117	143
N	40	66	92	118	144
O	41	67	93	119	145
P	42	68	94	120	146
Q	43	69	95	121	147
R	44	70	96	122	148
S	45	71	97	123	149
T	46	72	98	124	150
U	47	73	99	125	151
V	48	74	100	126	152
W	49	75	101	127	153
X	50	76	102	128	154
Y	51	77	103	129	155
Z	52	78	104	130	156

two-letter extensions as stock options to specify the option type (call or put), strike price, and expiration month. Thus like stock options, the first letter represents the option type and expiration month, and the second letter represents the strike price.

At the time this was written, SPX and OEX levels were around 1,300 and 650, respectively, and options for both indexes had available strike prices spanning more than 100 points. This created a problem when specifying option tickers that distinguished between, say, the 1,360 and 1,460 strikes. To handle this problem, the SPX ticker was split between the designations SPX and SPB. The SPX ticker was used for strikes in the 1300s and the SPB ticker was used for strikes in the 1400s. Likewise, the OEX ticker was split between OEX and OEW designations. OEX was used for strikes in the 600s, and OEW was used for strikes in the 700s.

For example, SPX-SJ referred to July 1350 puts and SPB-GJ referred to July 1450 calls. Likewise, OEX-PL referred to April 660 puts and OEW-DL referred to April 760 calls. The designations in effect when you want to trade SPX and OEX options will depend on the current SPX and OEX index levels. You should consult the CBOE website (www.cboe.com) for the necessary information.

Stock-Trak Exercises

1. What are the two-letter ticker extensions for the following SPX index options: January 1390 calls, July 1375 puts, April 1410 calls, October 1420 puts?

2. Given an index level of 1350, what are the option types, expiration months, and strike prices for the following options on the S&P 500 index: SPX-EO, SPB-QF, SPX-JL, SPB-VB?

15 Option Valuation

Just what is an option worth? Actually, this is one of the more difficult questions in finance. Option valuation is an esoteric area of finance since it often involves complex mathematics. Fortunately, just like most options professionals, you can learn quite a bit about option valuation with only modest mathematical tools. But no matter how far you might wish to delve into this topic, you must begin with the Black-Scholes-Merton option pricing model. This model is the core from which all other option pricing models trace their ancestry. ■ The previous chapter introduced the basics of stock options. From an economic standpoint, perhaps the most important subject was the expiration date payoffs of stock options. Bear in mind that when investors buy options today, they are buying risky future payoffs. Likewise, when investors write options today, they become obligated to make risky future payments. In a competitive financial marketplace, option prices observed each day are collectively agreed on by buyers and writers assessing the likelihood of all possible future payoffs and payments and setting option prices accordingly.

In this chapter, we discuss stock option prices. This discussion begins with a statement of the fundamental relationship between call and put option prices and stock prices known as put-call parity. We then turn to a discussion of the Black-Scholes-Merton option pricing model. The Black-Scholes-Merton option pricing model is widely regarded by finance professionals as the premier model of stock option valuation.

15.1 Put-Call Parity

put-call parity
Theorem asserting a certain parity relationship between call and put prices for European-style options with the same strike price and expiration date.

Put-call parity is perhaps the most fundamental parity relationship among option prices. **Put-call parity** states that the difference between a call option price and a put option price for European-style options with the same strike price and expiration date is equal to the difference between the underlying stock price and the discounted strike price. The put-call parity relationship is algebraically represented as

$$C - P = S - Ke^{-rT} \qquad \qquad 15.1$$

where the variables are defined as follows:

C = Call option price P = Put option price

S = Current stock price K = Option strike price

r = Risk-free interest rate T = Time remaining until option expiration

The logic behind put-call parity is based on the fundamental principle of finance stating that two securities with the same riskless payoff on the same future date must have the same price. To illustrate how this principle is applied to demonstrate put-call parity, suppose we form a portfolio of risky securities by following these three steps:

1. Buy 100 shares of Microsoft stock (MSFT).
2. Write one Microsoft call option contract.
3. Buy one Microsoft put option contract.

Both Microsoft options have the same strike price and expiration date. We assume that these options are European style, and therefore cannot be exercised before the last day prior to their expiration date.

Table 15.1 states the payoffs to each of these three securities based on the expiration date stock price, denoted by S_T. For example, if the expiration date stock price is greater than the strike price, that is, $S_T > K$, then the put option expires worthless and the call option requires a payment from writer to buyer of $(S_T - K)$. Alternatively, if the stock price is less than the strike price, that is, $S_T < K$, the call option expires worthless and the put option yields a payment from writer to buyer of $(K - S_T)$.

In Table 15.1, notice that no matter whether the expiration date stock price is greater or less than the strike price, the payoff to the portfolio is always equal to the strike price. This means that the portfolio has a risk-free payoff at option expiration equal to the

Table 15.1	**Put-Call Parity**		
		Expiration Date Payoffs	
Expiration Date Stock Price		$S_T > K$	$S_T < K$
Buy stock		S_T	S_T
Write one call option		$-(S_T - K)$	0
Buy one put option		0	$(K - S_T)$
Total portfolio expiration date payoff		K	K

strike price. Since the portfolio is risk-free, the cost of acquiring this portfolio today should be no different from the cost of acquiring any other risk-free investment with the same payoff on the same date. One such riskless investment is a U.S. Treasury bill.

The cost of a U.S. Treasury bill paying K dollars at option expiration is the discounted strike price Ke^{-rT}, where r is the risk-free interest rate and T is the time remaining until option expiration, which together form the discount factor e^{-rT}. By the fundamental principle of finance stating that two riskless investments with the same payoff on the same date must have the same price, it follows that this cost is also equal to the cost of acquiring the stock and options portfolio. Since this portfolio is formed by (1) buying the stock, (2) writing a call option, and (3) buying a put option, its cost is the sum of the stock price, plus the put price, less the call price. Setting this portfolio cost equal to the discounted strike price yields this equation:

$$S + P - C = Ke^{-rT}$$

By a simple rearrangement of terms we obtain the originally stated put-call parity equation, thereby validating our put-call parity argument:

$$C - P = S - Ke^{-rT}$$

The put-call parity argument stated above assumes that the underlying stock paid no dividends before option expiration. If the stock does pay a dividend before option expiration, then the put-call parity equation is adjusted as follows, where the variable D represents the present value of the dividend payment:

$$C - P = S - Ke^{-rT} - D \qquad\qquad 15.2$$

The logic behind this adjustment is the fact that a dividend payment reduces the value of the stock, since company assets are reduced by the amount of the dividend payment. When the dividend payment occurs before option expiration, investors adjust the effective stock price determining option payoffs to be made after the dividend payment. This adjustment reduces the value of the call option and increases the value of the put option.

CHECK THIS

15.1a The argument supporting put-call parity is based on the fundamental principle of finance that two securities with the same riskless payoff on the same future date must have the same price. Restate the demonstration of put-call parity based on this fundamental principle. (Hint: Start by recalling and explaining the contents of Table 15.1.)

15.1b Exchange-traded options on individual stock issues are American style, and therefore put-call parity does not hold exactly for these options. In the "Listed Options Quotations" page of *The Wall Street Journal*, compare the differences between selected call and put option prices with the differences between stock prices and discounted strike prices. How closely does put-call parity appear to hold for these American-style options?

Two U.S. Economists Win the Nobel Prize for Work on Options

Two economists with close ties to Wall Street, Robert C. Merton and Myron S. Scholes, won the Nobel Memorial Prize in Economic Science for pathbreaking work that helped spawn the $148 billion stock-options industry.

The Nobel economics prize is given to innovators whose work breaks new ground and sires whole bodies of economic research. But this year, the prize committee chose laureates not only with distinguished academic records, but also with especially pragmatic bents, to split the $1 million award. Prof. Merton, 53 years old, teaches at Harvard Business School, while Prof. Scholes, 56, has emeritus status from the Stanford Graduate School of Business.

In the early 1970s, Prof. Scholes, with the late mathematician Fischer Black, invented an insightful method of pricing options and warrants at a time when most investors and traders still relied on educated guesses to determine the value of various stock-market products. Prof. Merton later demonstrated the broad applicability of the Black-Scholes options-pricing formula, paving the way for the incredible growth of markets in options and other derivatives.

The Black-Scholes Formula

In their paper, Black and Scholes obtained exact formulas for pricing options.

$$C = SN(d) - Ke^{-rt}N(d - \sigma\sqrt{T})$$

According to the formula, the value of the call option C is given by the difference between the expected share value (the first term on the right-hand-side of the equation) and the expected cost (the second term) if the option is exercised at maturity.

"Thousands of traders and investors now use this formula every day to value stock options in markets throughout the world," the Royal Swedish Academy of Sciences said yesterday.

The Black-Scholes option-pricing model "is really the classic example of an academic innovation that has been adopted widely in practice," said Gregg Jarrell, professor of economics at the University of Rochester's William E. Simon Business School and former chief economist at the Securities and Exchange Commission. "It is one of the most elegant and precise models that any of us has ever seen."

Options allow investors to trade the future rights to buy or sell assets—such as stocks—at a set price. An investor who holds 100 shares of International Business Machines Corp. stock today,

---

15.2 The Black-Scholes-Merton Option Pricing Model

Option pricing theory made a great leap forward in the early 1970s with the development of the Black-Scholes option pricing model by Fischer Black and Myron Scholes. Recognizing the important theoretical contributions by Robert Merton, many finance professionals knowledgeable in the history of option pricing theory refer to an extended version of the model as the Black-Scholes-Merton option pricing model. In 1997, Myron Scholes and Robert Merton were awarded the Nobel Prize in Economics for their pioneering work in option pricing theory. Unfortunately, Fischer Black had died two years earlier and so did not share the Nobel Prize, which cannot be awarded posthumously. The nearby Investment Updates box presents *The Wall Street Journal* story of the Nobel Prize award.

The Black-Scholes-Merton option pricing model states the value of a stock option as a function of these six input factors:

1. The current price of the underlying stock.
2. The dividend yield of the underlying stock.

for example, might buy an option giving them the right to sell 100 IBM shares at a fixed price in three months' time. The investor is therefore partially protected against a fall in the stock price during the life of the option.

Until the Black-Scholes model gained acceptance, the great minds of economics and finance were unable to develop a method of putting an accurate price on those options. The problem was how to evaluate the risk associated with options, when the underlying stock price changes from moment to moment. The risk of an option depends on the price of the stock underlying the option.

That breakthrough allowed the economists to create a pricing formula that included the stock price, the agreed sale or "strike" price of the option, the stock's volatility, the risk-free interest rate offered with a secure bond, and the time until the option's expiration. They published their work in 1973, the same year the Chicago Board Options Exchange turned the scattered world of options trading into a more formal market.

Prof. Merton himself forged a formal theoretical framework for the Black-Scholes formula, and extended the analysis to other derivative products—financial instruments in which the value of the security depends on the value of another indicator, such as mortgage, interest or exchange rates. More broadly, his work allowed economists and financial professionals to view a wide variety of commonly traded financial instruments— such as corporate bonds—as derivatives and to price them using the ideas first expounded by Dr. Black and Prof. Scholes. "For the most part, the thing was conceived entirely in theory," said Prof. Merton.

The practical implications soon became apparent, however, as market participants flocked to the Black-Scholes-Merton approach to determine how much options are worth. "It's just a terrific yardstick for investors to help make that judgment," said Bill Kehoe, vice president and manager of the options marketing group at Merrill Lynch & Co., and an options trader since 1961.

Options markets have grown astronomically in the quarter century since the formula reached trading floors around the country. The value of U.S. exchange-traded options in 1995 was $118 billion. Last year, it surged to $148 billion, and in the first nine months of 1997, the figure hit $155 billion. More than 100,000 options series are now available. "Even now, we calculate the value of options world-wide using the Black-Scholes formula," said Yair Orgler, chairman of the Tel Aviv Stock Exchange.

Source: Michael M. Phillips, "Two U.S. Economists Win Nobel Prize," *The Wall Street Journal*, October 15, 1997. Reprinted by permission of Dow Jones & Company, Inc., via Copyright Clearance Center, Inc. © 1997 Dow Jones & Company, Inc. All Rights Reserved Worldwide

3. The strike price specified in the option contract.

4. The risk-free interest rate over the life of the option contract.

5. The time remaining until the option contract expires.

6. The price volatility of the underlying stock.

The six inputs are algebraically defined as follows:

S = Current stock price

y = Stock dividend yield

K = Option strike price

r = Risk-free interest rate

T = Time remaining until option expiration

σ = Sigma, representing stock price volatility

In terms of these six inputs, the Black-Scholes-Merton formula for the price of a call option on a single share of common stock is

$$C = Se^{-yT}N(d_1) - Ke^{-rT}N(d_2) \qquad 15.3$$

The Black-Scholes-Merton formula for the price of a put option on a share of common stock is

$$P = Ke^{-rT}N(-d_2) - Se^{-yT}N(-d_1)$$ 15.4

In these call and put option formulas, the numbers d_1 and d_2 are calculated as

$$d_1 = \frac{\ln(S/K) + (r - y + \sigma^2/2)T}{\sigma\sqrt{T}} \quad \text{and} \quad d_2 = d_1 - \sigma\sqrt{T}$$

In the formulas above, call and put option prices are algebraically represented by C and P, respectively. In addition to the six input factors S, K, r, y, T, and σ, the following three mathematical functions are used in the call and put option pricing formulas:

1. e^x, or $exp(x)$, denoting the natural exponent of the value of x.

2. $ln(x)$, denoting the natural logarithm of the value of x.

3. $N(x)$, denoting the standard normal probability of the value of x.

Clearly, the Black-Scholes-Merton call and put option pricing formulas are based on relatively sophisticated mathematics. While we recommend that the serious student of finance make an effort to understand these formulas, we realize that this is not an easy task. The goal, however, is to understand the economic principles determining option prices. Mathematics is simply a tool for strengthening this understanding. In writing this chapter, we have tried to keep this goal in mind.

Many finance textbooks state that calculating option prices using the formulas given here is easily accomplished with a hand calculator and a table of normal probability values. We emphatically disagree. While hand calculation is possible, the procedure is tedious and subject to error. Instead, we suggest that you use the Black-Scholes-Merton Options Calculator computer program included with this textbook (or a similar program obtained elsewhere). Using this program, you can easily and conveniently calculate option prices and other option-related values for the Black-Scholes-Merton option pricing model. We encourage you to use this options calculator and to freely share it with your friends.

CHECK THIS

15.2   Consider the following inputs to the Black-Scholes-Merton option pricing model.

$S = \$50$ $y = 0\%$
$K = \$50$ $r = 5\%$
$T = 60$ days $\sigma = 25\%$

These input values yield a call option price of $2.22 and a put option price of $1.81.

Verify the above option prices using the options calculator. (Note: The options calculator computes numerical values with a precision of about three decimal points, but in this textbook prices are normally rounded to the nearest penny.)

15.3 Varying the Option Price Input Values

An important goal of this chapter is to provide an understanding of how option prices change as a result of varying each of the six input values. Table 15.2 summarizes the sign effects of the six inputs on call and put option prices; the plus sign

Table 15.2	**Six Inputs Affecting Option Prices**			
		Sign of Input Effect		
Input		**Call**	**Put**	**Common Name**
Underlying stock price (S)		+	−	Delta
Strike price of the option contract (K)		−	+	
Time remaining until option expiration (T)		+	+	Theta
Volatility of the underlying stock price (σ)		+	+	Vega
Risk-free interest rate (r)		+	−	Rho
Dividend yield of the underlying stock (y)		−	+	

indicates a positive effect and the minus sign indicates a negative effect. Where the magnitude of the input impact has a commonly used name, this is stated in the rightmost column.

The two most important inputs determining stock option prices are the stock price and the strike price. However, the other input factors are also important determinants of option value. We next discuss each input factor separately.

Varying the Underlying Stock Price

Certainly, the price of the underlying stock is one of the most important determinants of the price of a stock option. As the stock price increases, the call option price increases and the put option price decreases. This is not surprising, since a call option grants the right to buy stock shares and a put option grants the right to sell stock shares at a fixed strike price. Consequently, a higher stock price at option expiration increases the payoff of a call option. Likewise, a lower stock price at option expiration increases the payoff of a put option.

For a given set of input values, the relationship between call and put option prices and an underlying stock price is illustrated in Figure 15.1. In Figure 15.1, stock prices are measured on the horizontal axis and option prices are measured on the vertical axis. Notice that the graph lines describing relationships between call and put option prices and the underlying stock price have a convex (bowed) shape. Convexity is a fundamental characteristic of the relationship between option prices and stock prices.

Figure 15.1

Put and Call Option Prices

Input values:
K = $100
T = ¼ year
r = 5%
σ = 25%
y = 0%

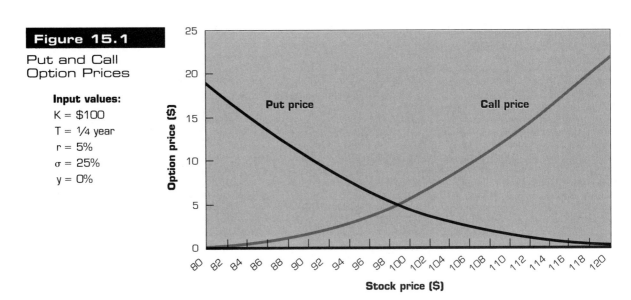

Varying the Option's Strike Price

As the strike price increases, the call price decreases and the put price increases. This is reasonable, since a higher strike price means that we must pay a higher price when we exercise a call option to buy the underlying stock, thereby reducing the call option's value. Similarly, a higher strike price means that we will receive a higher price when we exercise a put option to sell the underlying stock, thereby increasing the put option's value. Of course this logic works in reverse also; as the strike price decreases, the call price increases and the put price decreases.

Varying the Time Remaining until Option Expiration

Time remaining until option expiration is an important determinant of option value. As time remaining until option expiration lengthens, both call and put option prices normally increase. This is expected, since a longer time remaining until option expiration allows more time for the stock price to move away from a strike price and increase the option's payoff, thereby making the option more valuable. The relationship between call and put option prices and time remaining until option expiration is illustrated in Figure 15.2, where time remaining until option expiration is measured on the horizontal axis and option prices are measured on the vertical axis.

Varying the Volatility of the Stock Price

Stock price volatility (sigma, σ) plays an important role in determining option value. As stock price volatility increases, both call and put option prices increase. This is as expected, since the more volatile the stock price, the greater is the likelihood that the stock price will move farther away from a strike price and increase the option's payoff, thereby making the option more valuable. The relationship between call and put option prices and stock price volatility is graphed in Figure 15.3, where volatility is measured on the horizontal axis and option prices are measured on the vertical axis.

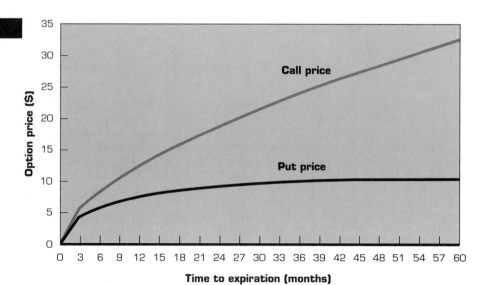

Figure 15.2

Option Prices and Time to Expiration

Input values:
S = $100
K = $100
r = 5%
σ = 25%
y = 0%

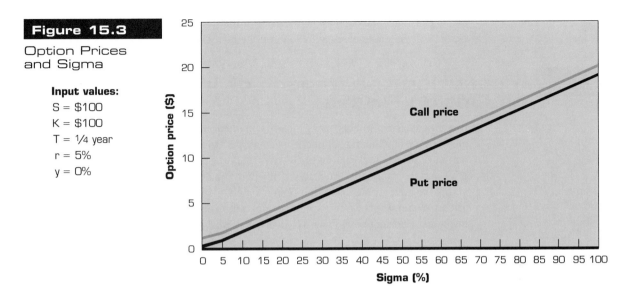

Figure 15.3

Option Prices and Sigma

Input values:
S = $100
K = $100
T = ¼ year
r = 5%
y = 0%

Varying the Interest Rate

Although seemingly not as important as the other inputs, the interest rate still noticeably affects option values. As the interest rate increases, the call price increases and the put price decreases. This is explained by the time value of money. A higher interest rate implies a greater discount, which lowers the present value of the strike price that we pay when we exercise a call option or receive when we exercise a put option. Figure 15.4 graphs the relationship between call and put option prices and interest rates, where the interest rate is measured on the horizontal axis and option prices are measured on the vertical axis.

Varying the Dividend Yield

A stock's dividend yield has an important effect on option values. As the dividend yield increases, the call price decreases and the put price increases. This follows from the fact that when a company pays a dividend, its assets are reduced by the amount of the div-

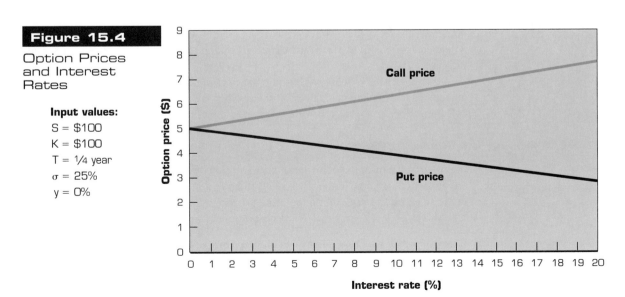

Figure 15.4

Option Prices and Interest Rates

Input values:
S = $100
K = $100
T = ¼ year
σ = 25%
y = 0%

idend, causing a like decrease in the price of the stock. Then, as the stock price decreases, the call price decreases and the put price increases.

15.4 Measuring the Impact of Input Changes on Option Prices

delta Measure of the dollar impact of a change in the underlying stock price on the value of a stock option. Delta is positive for a call option and negative for a put option.

Investment professionals using options in their investment strategies have standard methods to state the impact of changes in input values on option prices. The two inputs that most affect stock option prices over a short period, say, a few days, are the stock price and the stock price volatility. The approximate impact of a stock price change on an option price is stated by the option's **delta**. In the Black-Scholes-Merton option pricing model, expressions for call and put option deltas are stated as follows, where the mathematical functions e^x and $N(x)$ were previously defined:

$$Call\ option\ delta = e^{-yT}N(d_1) > 0$$
$$Put\ option\ delta = -e^{-yT}N(-d_1) < 0$$

As shown above, a call option delta is always positive and a put option delta is always negative. This corresponds to Table 15.2, where $+$ indicates a positive effect for a call option and $-$ indicates a negative effect for a put option resulting from an increase in the underlying stock price.

eta Measure of the percentage impact of a change in the underlying stock price on the value of a stock option. Eta is positive for a call option and negative for a put option.

The approximate percentage impact of a stock price change on an option price is stated by the option's **eta.** In the Black-Scholes-Merton option pricing model, expressions for call and put option etas are stated as follows, where the mathematical functions e^x and $N(x)$ were previously defined:

$$Call\ option\ eta = e^{-yT}N(d_1)S/C > 1$$
$$Put\ option\ eta = -e^{-yT}N(-d_1)S/P < -1$$

In the Black-Scholes-Merton option pricing model, a call option eta is greater than $+1$ and a put option eta is less than -1.

vega Measure of the impact of a change in stock price volatility on the value of a stock option. Vega is positive for both a call option and a put option.

The approximate impact of a volatility change on an option's price is measured by the option's **vega**.[1] In the Black-Scholes-Merton option pricing model, vega is the same for call and put options and is stated as follows, where the mathematical function $n(x)$ represents a standard normal density.

$$Vega = Se^{-yT}n(d_1)\sqrt{T} > 0$$

As shown above, vega is always positive. Again this corresponds with Table 15.2, where $+$ indicates a positive effect for both a call option and a put option from a volatility increase.

As with the Black-Scholes-Merton option pricing formula, these so-called "greeks" are tedious to calculate manually; fortunately they are easily calculated using an options calculator.

Interpreting Option Deltas

Interpreting the meaning of an option delta is relatively straightforward. Delta measures the impact of a change in the stock price on an option price, where a one-dollar change in the stock price causes an option price to change by approximately delta dollars. For

---

[1] Those of you who are scholars of the Greek language recognize that "vega" is not a Greek letter like the other option sensitivity measures. (It is a star in the constellation Lyra.) Alas, the term vega has entered the options professionals' vocabulary and is in widespread use.

example, using the input values stated immediately below, we obtain a call option price of \$2.22 and a put option price of \$1.81. We also get a call option delta of $+.55$ and a put option delta of $-.45$.

$S = \$50$	$y = 0\%$
$K = 50$	$r = 5\%$
$T = 60$ days	$\sigma = 25\%$

Now if we change the stock price from \$50 to \$51, we get a call option price of \$2.81 and a put option price of \$1.41. Thus, a $+\$1$ stock price change increased the call option price by \$.59 and decreased the put option price by \$.40. These price changes are close to, but not exactly equal to, the original call option delta value of $+.55$ and put option delta value of $-.45$.

Interpreting Option Etas

Eta measures the percentage impact of a change in the stock price on an option price, where a 1 percent change in the stock price causes an option price to change by approximately eta percent. For example, the input values stated above yield a call option price of \$2.22, a put option price of \$1.81, a call option eta of 12.42, and a put option eta of -12.33. If the stock price changes by 1 percent from \$50 to \$50.50, we get a call option price of \$2.51 and a put option price of \$1.60. Thus, a 1 percent stock price change increased the call option price by 13.06 percent and decreased the put option price by 11.60 percent. These percentage price changes are close to the original call option eta value of $+12.42$ and put option eta value of -12.33.

Interpreting Option Vegas

Interpreting the meaning of an option vega is also straightforward. Vega measures the impact of a change in stock price volatility on an option price, where a 1 percent change in sigma changes an option price by approximately the amount vega. For example, using the same input values stated earlier we obtain call and put option prices of \$2.22 and \$1.82, respectively. We also get an option vega of $+.08$. If we change the stock price volatility to $\sigma = 26\%$, we then get call and put option prices of \$2.30 and \$1.89. Thus, a $+1$ percent stock price volatility change increased both call and put option prices by \$.08, exactly as predicted by the original option vega value.

Interpreting an Option's Gamma, Theta, and Rho

gamma Measure of delta sensitivity to a stock price change.

theta Measure of the impact on an option price of time remaining until option expiration lengthening by one day.

rho Measure of option price sensitivity to a change in the interest rate.

In addition to delta, eta, and vega, options professionals commonly use three other measures of option price sensitivity to input changes: gamma, theta, and rho.

Gamma measures delta sensitivity to a stock price change, where a one-dollar stock price change causes delta to change by approximately the amount gamma. In the Black-Scholes-Merton option pricing model, gammas are the same for call and put options.

Theta measures option price sensitivity to a change in time remaining until option expiration, where a one-day change causes the option price to change by approximately the amount theta. Since a longer time until option expiration normally implies a higher option price, thetas are usually positive.

Rho measures option price sensitivity to a change in the interest rate, where a 1 percent interest rate change causes the option price to change by approximately the amount rho. Rho is positive for a call option and negative for a put option.

Implied Standard Deviations

implied standard deviation (ISD) An estimate of stock price volatility obtained from an option price.

implied volatility (IVOL) Another term for implied standard deviation.

The Black-Scholes-Merton stock option pricing model is based on six inputs: a stock price, a strike price, an interest rate, a dividend yield, the time remaining until option expiration, and the stock price volatility. Of these six factors, only the stock price volatility is not directly observable and must be estimated somehow. A popular method to estimate stock price volatility is to use an implied value from an option price. A stock price volatility estimated from an option price is called an **implied standard deviation** or **implied volatility**, often abbreviated as **ISD** or **IVOL**, respectively. Implied volatility and implied standard deviation are two terms for the same thing.

Calculating an implied volatility requires that all input factors have known values, except sigma, and that a call or put option value be known. For example, consider the following option price input values, absent a value for sigma:

$$S = \$50 \qquad y = 0\%$$
$$K = 50 \qquad r = 5\%$$
$$T = 60 \text{ days}$$

Suppose we also have a call price of $C = \$2.22$. Based on this call price, what is the implied volatility? In other words, in combination with the input values stated above, what sigma value yields a call price of $C = \$2.22$? The answer is a sigma value of .25, or 25 percent.

Now suppose we wish to know what volatility value is implied by a call price of $C = \$3$. To obtain this implied volatility value, we must find the value for sigma that yields this call price. If you use the options calculator program, you can find this value by varying sigma values until a call option price of $3 is obtained. This should occur with a sigma value of 34.68 percent. This is the implied standard deviation (ISD) corresponding to a call option price of $3.

You can easily obtain an estimate of stock price volatility for almost any stock with option prices reported in *The Wall Street Journal*. For example, suppose you wish to obtain an estimate of stock price volatility for Microsoft common stock. Since Microsoft stock trades on Nasdaq under the ticker MSFT, stock price and dividend yield information are obtained from the "Nasdaq National Market Issues" pages. Microsoft options information is obtained from the "Listed Options Quotations" page. Interest rate information is obtained from the "Treasury Bonds, Notes and Bills" column.

The following information was obtained for Microsoft common stock and Microsoft options from *The Wall Street Journal*:

Stock price = $89	Dividend yield = 0%
Strike price = $90	Interest rate = 5.54%
Time until contract expiration = 73 days	Call price = $8.25

To obtain an implied standard deviation from these values using the options calculator program, first set the stock price, dividend yield, strike, interest rate, and time values as specified above. Then vary sigma values until a call option price of $8.25 is obtained. This should occur with a sigma value of 52.1 percent. This implied standard deviation represents an estimate of stock price volatility for Microsoft stock obtained from a call option price.

15.6 Hedging a Stock Portfolio with Stock Index Options

Hedging is a common use of stock options among portfolio managers. In particular, many institutional money managers make some use of stock index options to hedge the equity portfolios they manage. In this section, we examine how an equity portfolio manager might hedge a diversified stock portfolio using stock index options.

To begin, suppose that you manage a $10 million diversified portfolio of large-company stocks and that you maintain a portfolio beta of 1 for this portfolio. With a beta of 1, changes in the value of your portfolio closely follow changes in the Standard & Poor's 500 index. Therefore, you decide to use options on the S&P 500 index as a hedging vehicle. S&P 500 index options trade on the Chicago Board Options Exchange (CBOE) under the ticker symbol SPX. SPX option prices are reported daily in the "Index Options Trading" column of *The Wall Street Journal.* Each SPX option has a contract value of 100 times the current level of the S&P 500 index.

SPX options are a convenient hedging vehicle for an equity portfolio manager because they are European style and because they settle in cash at expiration. For example, suppose you hold one SPX call option with a strike price of 910, and at option expiration, the S&P 500 index stands at 917. In this case, your cash payoff is 100 times the difference between the index level and the strike price, or $100 \times (917 - 910) = \$700$. Of course, if the expiration date index level falls below the strike price, your SPX call option expires worthless.

Hedging a stock portfolio with index options requires first calculating the number of option contracts needed to form an effective hedge. While you can use either put options or call options to construct an effective hedge, we here assume that you decide to use call options to hedge your $10 million equity portfolio. Using stock index call options to hedge an equity portfolio involves writing a certain number of option contracts. In general, the number of stock index option contracts needed to hedge an equity portfolio is stated by the equation

$$\text{Number of option contracts} = \frac{\text{Portfolio beta} \times \text{Portfolio value}}{\text{Option delta} \times \text{Option contract value}} \qquad 15.5$$

Money Managers Use Options to Hedge Portfolios

Traders and money managers began using options to hedge their portfolios yesterday after spending the past week ignoring defensive strategies to speculate on earnings and stock price movements.

The turning point came late in the morning when the Standard & Poor's 500 index slid below 1140. This wiped out many S&P 500 index futures positions and market professionals responded by buying S&P 500 index options to protect their portfolios from the market's volatility.

This hedging activity marked a change in the approach they have taken to the market. Many professionals recently stopped hedging their portfolios because the stock market has quickly corrected in the past. They spent money for hedges they ultimately didn't need.

"A lot of people were completely unhedged when the decline began," said Leon Gross, Salomon Smith Barney's options strategist. He noted that the S&P 500 index's rise to 1186 from 1086 took six weeks, while it dropped 50 points in only four days.

The fear in the options market spiked higher as the S&P index fell along with the Dow Jones Industrial Average.

The option market's fear gauge, the Chicago Board Options Exchange Volatility Index, rose 1.72, or 7.5%, to 24.66. "This is an indication that people are getting nervous and paying for puts," Mr. Gross said.

Options prices reflected this discomfort, which made hedging portfolios even more expensive than normal. For more aggressive traders, such as hedge funds, high options prices created opportunities to short sell puts and sectors.

The Nasdaq index of the 100 largest nonfinancial stocks was a popular way to short the technology sector. Other traders sold put options because they think the fear is overdone and they'll be able to buy the contracts back for less money.

In your particular case, you have a portfolio beta of 1 and a portfolio value of $10 million. You now need to calculate an option delta and option contract value.

The option contract value for an SPX option is simply 100 times the current level of the S&P 500 index. Checking the "Index Options Trading" column in *The Wall Street Journal* you see that the S&P 500 index has a value of 928.80, which means that each SPX option has a current contract value of $92,880.

To calculate an option delta, you must decide which particular contract to use. You decide to use options with an October expiration and a strike price of 920, that is, the October 920 SPX contract. From the "Index Options Trading" column, you find the price for these options is 35 3/8, or 35.375. Options expire on the Saturday following the third Friday of their expiration month. Counting days on your calendar yields a time remaining until option expiration of 70 days. The interest rate on Treasury bills maturing closest to option expiration is 5 percent. The dividend yield on the S&P 500 index is not normally reported in *The Wall Street Journal*. Fortunately, the S&P 500 trades in the form of depository shares on the American Stock Exchange (AMEX) under the ticker SPY. SPY shares represent a claim on a portfolio designed to match as closely as possible the S&P 500. By looking up information on SPY shares on the Internet, you find that the dividend yield is 1.5 percent.

With the information now collected, you enter the following values into an options calculator: $S = 928.80$, $K = 920$, $T = 70$, $r = 5\%$, and $y = 1.5\%$. You then adjust the sigma value until you get the call price of $C = 35.375$. This yields an implied standard deviation of 17 percent, which represents a current estimate of S&P 500 index volatility. Using this sigma value of 17 percent then yields a call option delta of .599. You now have sufficient information to calculate the number of option contracts needed to effectively hedge your equity portfolio. By using the equation above, we can calculate the number of October 920 SPX options that you should write to form an effective hedge as

$$\frac{1.0 \times \$10,000,000}{.599 \times \$92,880} \approx 180 \text{ contracts}$$

Furthermore, by writing 180 October 920 call options, you receive $180 \times 100 \times 35.375 = \$636,750$.

To assess the effectiveness of this hedge, suppose the S&P 500 index and your stock portfolio both immediately fall in value by 1 percent. This is a loss of $100,000 on your stock portfolio. After the S&P 500 index falls by 1 percent, its level is 919.51, which then yields a call option price of $C = 30.06$. Now, if you were to buy back the 180 contracts, you would pay $180 \times 100 \times 30.06 = \$541,080$. Since you originally received $636,750 for the options, this represents a gain of $636,750 - \$541,080 = \$95,670$, which cancels most of the $100,000 loss on your equity portfolio. In fact, your final net loss is only $4,330, which is a small fraction of the loss that would have been realized on an unhedged portfolio.

To maintain an effective hedge over time, you will need to rebalance your options hedge on, say, a weekly basis. Rebalancing simply requires calculating anew the number of option contracts needed to hedge your equity portfolio, and then buying or selling options in the amount necessary to maintain an effective hedge. The nearby Investment Updates box contains a brief *Wall Street Journal* report on hedging strategies using stock index options.

CHECK THIS

15.6a In the hedging example above, suppose instead that your equity portfolio had a beta of 1.5. What number of SPX call options would be required to form an effective hedge?

15.6b Alternatively, suppose that your equity portfolio had a beta of .5. What number of SPX call options would then be required to form an effective hedge?

15.7 Implied Volatility Skews

We earlier defined implied volatility (IVOL) and implied standard deviation (ISD) as the volatility value implied by an option price and stated that implied volatility represents an estimate of the price volatility (sigma, σ) of the underlying stock. We further noted that implied volatility is often used to estimate a stock's price volatility over the period remaining until option expiration. In this section, we examine the phenomenon of implied **volatility skews**—the relationship between implied volatilities and strike prices for options.

volatility skew

Description of the relationship between implied volatilities and strike prices for options. Also called *volatility smiles.*

To illustrate the phenomenon of implied volatility skews, Table 15.3 presents option information for IBM stock options observed in October 1998 for options expiring 43 days later in November 1998. This information includes strike prices, call option prices, put option prices, and call and put implied volatilities calculated separately for each option. Notice how the individual implied volatilities differ across different strike prices. Figure 15.5 provides a visual display of the relationship between implied volatilities and strike prices for these IBM options. The steep negative slopes for call and put implied volatilities might be called volatility skews.

Table 15.3	Volatility Skews for IBM Options				
Strikes	**Calls**	**Call ISD (%)**	**Puts**	**Put ISD (%)**	
115	$17\frac{1}{4}$	58.14	$4\frac{5}{8}$	58.62	
120	$13\frac{1}{8}$	51.77	$5\frac{3}{4}$	53.92	
125	$9\frac{3}{4}$	48.28	$7\frac{3}{8}$	50.41	
130	$6\frac{7}{8}$	45.27	$9\frac{3}{4}$	48.90	
135	$4\frac{5}{8}$	43.35	$11\frac{3}{4}$	42.48	
140	$2\frac{7}{8}$	40.80	$15\frac{3}{8}$	42.83	

Other information: $S = 127.3125$, $y = 0.07\%$, $T = 43$ days, $r = 3.6\%$.

Logically, there can be only one stock price volatility since price volatility is a property of the underlying stock, and each option's implied volatility should be an estimate of a single underlying stock price volatility. That this is not the case is well known to options professionals, who commonly use the terms volatility smile and volatility skew to describe the anomaly. Why do volatility skews exist? Many suggestions have been proposed regarding possible causes. However, there is widespread agreement that the major factor causing volatility skews is **stochastic volatility**. Stochastic volatility is the phenomenon of stock price volatility changing over time, where the price volatility changes are largely random.

The Black-Scholes-Merton option pricing model assumes that stock price volatility is constant over the life of the option. Therefore, when stock price volatility is stochastic, the Black-Scholes-Merton option pricing model yields option prices that may differ from observed market prices. Nevertheless, the simplicity of the Black-Scholes-Merton model makes it an excellent working model of option prices and many options professionals consider it an invaluable tool for analysis and decision making. Its simplicity is an advantage especially because option pricing models that account for stochastic volatility can be quite complex, and therefore difficult to work with. Furthermore, even

stochastic volatility
The phenomenon of stock price volatility changing randomly over time.

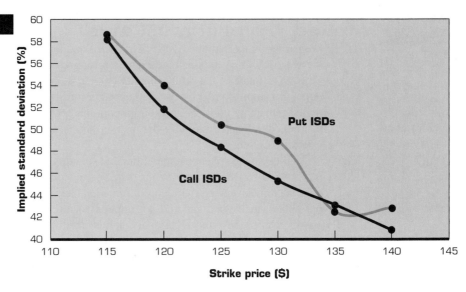

Figure 15.5

Volatility Skews for IBM Options

when volatility is stochastic, the Black-Scholes-Merton option pricing model yields accurate option prices for options with strike prices close to a current stock price. For this reason, when using implied volatility to estimate an underlying stock price volatility it is best to use at-the-money options—that is, options with a strike price close to the current stock price.

CHECK THIS

15.7 Using information from a recent *Wall Street Journal*, calculate IBM implied volatilities for options with at least one month until expiration.

15.8 Summary and Conclusions

In this chapter, we examined stock option prices. Many important aspects of option pricing were covered, including the following:

1. Put-call parity states that the difference between a call price and a put price for European style options with the same strike price and expiration date is equal to the difference between the stock price less a dividend adjustment and the discounted strike price. Put-call parity is based on the fundamental principle that two securities with the same riskless payoff on the same future date must have the same price today.

2. The Black-Scholes-Merton option pricing formula states that the value of a stock option is a function of the current stock price, the stock dividend yield, option strike price, risk-free interest rate, time remaining until option expiration, and the stock price volatility.

3. The two most important determinants of the price of a stock option are the price of the underlying stock and the strike price of the option. As the stock price increases, call prices increase and put prices decrease. Conversely, as the strike price increases, call prices decrease and put prices increase.

4. Time remaining until option expiration is an important determinant of option value. As time remaining until option expiration lengthens, both call and put option prices normally increase. Stock price volatility also plays an important role in determining option value. As stock price volatility increases, both call and put option prices increase.

5. Although less important, the interest rate can noticeably affect option values. As the interest rate increases, call prices increase and put prices decrease. A stock's dividend yield also affects option values. As the dividend yield increases, call prices decrease and put prices increase.

6. The two input factors that most affect stock option prices over a short period, say, a few days, are the stock price and the stock price volatility. The impact of a stock price change on an option price is measured by the option's delta. The impact of a volatility change on an option's price is measured by the option's vega.

7. A call option delta is always positive and a put option delta is always negative. Delta measures the impact of a stock price change on an option price, where a one-dollar change in the stock price causes an option price to change by approximately delta dollars.

8. Vega measures the impact of a change in stock price volatility (sigma, σ) on an option price, where a 1 percent change in volatility changes an option price by approximately the amount vega.

9. Of the six input factors to the Black-Scholes-Merton option pricing model, only the stock price volatility is not directly observable and must be estimated somehow. A stock price volatility estimated from an option price is called an implied volatility or an implied standard deviation, which are two terms for the same thing.

10. Options on the S&P 500 index are a convenient hedging vehicle for an equity portfolio because they are European style and because they settle for cash at option expiration. Hedging a stock portfolio with index options requires calculating the number of option contracts needed to form an effective hedge.

11. To maintain an effective hedge over time, you should rebalance the options hedge on a regular basis. Rebalancing requires recalculating the number of option contracts needed to hedge an equity portfolio, and then buying or selling options in the amount necessary to maintain an effective hedge.

12. Volatility skews, or volatility smiles, occur when individual implied volatilities differ across call and put options with different strike prices. Volatility skews commonly appear in implied volatilities for stock index options and also appear in implied volatilities for options on individual stocks. The most important factor causing volatility skews is stochastic volatility, the phenomenon of stock price volatility changing over time in a largely random fashion.

13. The Black-Scholes-Merton option pricing model assumes a constant stock price volatility and yields option prices that may differ from stochastic volatility option prices. Nevertheless, even when volatility is stochastic, the Black-Scholes-Merton option pricing model yields accurate option prices for options with strike prices close to a current stock price. Therefore, when using implied volatility to estimate an underlying stock price volatility, it is best to use at-the-money options.

GET REAL

This chapter began by introducing you to the put-call parity condition, one of the most famous pricing relationships in finance. Using it, we can establish the relative prices of puts, calls, the underlying stock, and a T-bill. In practice, if you were to use closing prices and rates published in, say, *The Wall Street Journal*, you would find numerous apparent violations. However, if you tried to execute the trades needed to profit from these violations, you would essentially always find that you can't get the printed prices. One reason for this is that the prices you see are not even contemporaneous because the markets close at different times. Thus, trying to make money pursuing put-call parity violations is probably not a good idea.

We next introduced the Nobel Prize–winning Black-Scholes-Merton option pricing formula. We saw that the formula and its associated concepts are fairly complex, but, despite that complexity, the formula is very widely used by traders and money managers.

To learn more about the real-world use of the concepts we discussed, you should purchase a variety of stock and index options and then compare the prices you pay to the theoretical prices from the the option pricing formula. You will need to come up with a volatility estimate. A good way to do this is to calculate some implied standard deviations from a few days earlier. You should also compute the various "greeks" and observe how well they describe what actually happens to some of your option prices. How well do they work?

Another important use for option pricing theory is to gain some insight into stock market volatility, both on an overall level and for individual stocks. Remember that in Chapter 1 we discussed the probabilities associated with returns equal to the average plus or minus a particular number of standard deviations for a small number of indexes. Implied standard deviations (ISDs) provide a means of broadening this analysis to anything with traded options. Try calculating a few ISDs for both stock index options and some high-flying, technology-related stocks. You might be surprised how volatile the market thinks individual stocks can be. The ISDs on high-tech stocks serve as a warning to investors about the risks of loading up on such investments compared to investing in a broadly diversified market index.

Key Terms

put-call parity 432
delta 440
eta 440
vega 440
gamma 441
theta 441

rho 441
implied standard deviation (ISD) 442
implied volatility (IVOL) 442
volatility skew 445
stochastic volatility 446

Chapter Review Problems and Self-Test

1. **Put-Call Parity** A call option sells for $4. It has a strike price of $40 and six months to maturity. If the underlying stock currently sells for $30 per share, what is the price of a put option with a $40 strike and six months to maturity? The risk-free interest rate is 5 percent.

2. **Black-Scholes**   What is the value of a call option if the underlying stock price is $200, the strike price is $180, the underlying stock volatility is 40 percent, and the risk-free rate is 4 percent? Assume the option has 60 days to expiration.

Answers to Self-Test Problems

1. Using the put-call parity formula, we have

$$C - P = S - Ke^{-rT}$$

Rearranging to solve for P, the put price, and plugging in the other numbers gets us

$$P = C - S + Ke^{-rT}$$
$$= \$4 - \$30 + \$40e^{-.05(.5)}$$
$$= \$13.01$$

2. We will simply use the options calculator supplied with this book to calculate the answer to this question. The inputs are

S =	Current stock price	= $200
K =	Option strike price	= $180
r =	Risk-free interest rate	= .04
σ =	Stock volatility	= .40
T =	Time to expiration	= 60 days

Notice that, absent other information, the dividend yield is zero. Plugging these values into the options calculator produces a value of $25.63.

Test Your Investment Quotient

1. **Put-Call Parity**   According to put-call parity, a risk-free portfolio is formed by buying 100 stock shares and:

   a. Writing one call contract and buying one put contract.
   b. Buying one call contract and writing one put contract.
   c. Buying one call contract and buying one put contract.
   d. Writing one call contract and writing one put contract.

2. **Black-Scholes-Merton Model**   In the Black-Scholes-Merton option pricing model, the value of an option contract is a function of six input factors. Which of the following is not one of these factors?

   a. The price of the underlying stock.
   b. The strike price of the option contract.
   c. The expected return on the underlying stock.
   d. The time remaining until option expiration.

3. **Black-Scholes Formula**   In the Black-Scholes option valuation formula, an increase in a stock's volatility: (*1992 CFA exam*)

   a. Increases the associated call option value.
   b. Decreases the associated put option value.
   c. Increases or decreases the option value, depending on the level of interest rates.
   d. Does not change either the put or call option value because put-call parity holds.

4. **Option Prices** Which of the following variables influence the value of options? (*1990 CFA exam*)

   i. Level of interest rates.
   ii. Time to expiration of the option.
   iii. Dividend yield of underlying stock.
   iv. Stock price volatility.

   a. i and iv only
   b. ii and iii only
   c. i, iii, and iv only
   d. i, ii, iii, and iv

5. **Option Prices** Which of the following factors does not influence the market price of options on a common stock? (*1989 CFA exam*)

   a. The expected return on the underlying stock.
   b. The volatility of the underlying stock.
   c. The relationship between the strike price of the options and the market price of the underlying stock.
   d. The option's expiration date.

6. **Option Prices** Which one of the following will increase the value of a call option? (*1993 CFA exam*)

   a. An increase in interest rates.
   b. A decrease in time to expiration of the call.
   c. A decrease in the volatility of the underlying stock.
   d. An increase in the dividend rate of the underlying stock.

7. **Option Prices** Which one of the following would tend to result in a high value of a call option? (*1988 CFA exam*)

   a. Interest rates are low.
   b. The variability of the underlying stock is high.
   c. There is little time remaining until the option expires.
   d. The exercise price is high relative to the stock price.

8. **Option Price Factors** Which of the following incorrectly states the signs of the impact of an increase in the indicated input factor on call and put option prices?

	Call	Put
a. Risk-free interest rate	+	−
b. Underlying stock price	+	−
c. Dividend yield of the underlying stock	−	+
d. Volatility of the underlying stock price	+	−

9. **Option Price Factors** Which of the following correctly states the signs of the impact of an increase in the indicated input factor on call and put option prices?

	Call	Put
a. Strike price of the option contract	+	−
b. Time remaining until option expiration	+	−
c. Underlying stock price	+	−
d. Volatility of the underlying stock price	+	−

10. **Option Price Sensitivities** Which of the following measures the impact of a change in the stock price on an option price?

   a. Vega
   b. Rho
   c. Delta
   d. Theta

11. **Option Price Sensitivities** Which of the following measures the impact of a change in time remaining until option expiration on an option price?

    a. Vega
    b. Rho
    c. Delta
    d. Theta

12. **Option Price Sensitivities** Which of the following measures the impact of a change in the underlying stock price volatility on an option price?

    a. Vega
    b. Rho
    c. Delta
    d. Theta

13. **Option Price Sensitivities** Which of the following measures the impact of a change in the interest rate on an option price?

    a. Vega
    b. Rho
    c. Delta
    d. Theta

14. **Hedging with Options** You wish to hedge a stock portfolio, where the portfolio beta is 1, the portfolio value is $10 million, the hedging index call option delta is .5, and the hedging index call option contract value is $100,000. Which of the following hedging transactions is required to hedge the portfolio?

    a. Write 200 call option contracts.
    b. Write 100 call option contracts.
    c. Buy 200 call option contracts.
    d. Buy 100 call option contracts.

15. **Hedging with Options** You wish to hedge a stock portfolio, where the portfolio beta is .5, the portfolio value is $10 million, the hedging index call option delta is .5, and the hedging index call option contract value is $100,000. Which of the following hedging transactions is required to hedge the portfolio?

    a. Write 200 call option contracts.
    b. Write 100 call option contracts.
    c. Buy 200 call option contracts.
    d. Buy 100 call option contracts.

Questions and Problems

Core Questions

1. **Option Prices** What are the six factors that determine an option's price?

2. **Options and Expiration Dates** What is the impact of lengthening the time to expiration on an option's value? Explain.

3. **Options and Stock Price Volatility** What is the impact of an increase in the volatility of the underlying stock on an option's value? Explain.

4. **Options and Dividend Yields** How do dividend yields affect option prices? Explain.

5. **Options and Interest Rates** How do interest rates affect option prices? Explain.

6. **Put-Call Parity** A call option is currently selling for $10. It has a strike price of $80 and three months to maturity. What is the price of a put option with an $80 strike price and three months to maturity? The current stock price is $85, and the risk-free interest rate is 6 percent.

7. **Put-Call Parity** A call option currently sells for $10. It has a strike price of $80 and three months to maturity. A put with the same strike and expiration date sells for $8. If the risk-free interest rate is 4 percent, what is the current stock price?

8. **Call Option Prices** What is the value of a call option if the underlying stock price is $100, the strike price is $70, the underlying stock volatility is 30 percent, and the risk-free rate is 5 percent? Assume the option has 30 days to expiration.

9. **Call Option Prices** What is the value of a call option if the underlying stock price is $20, the strike price is $22, the underlying stock volatility is 50 percent, and the risk-free rate is 4 percent? Assume the option has 60 days to expiration and the underlying stock has a dividend yield of 2 percent.

10. **Call Option Prices** What is the value of a put option if the underlying stock price is $60, the strike price is $65, the underlying stock volatility is 25 percent, and the risk-free rate is 5 percent? Assume the option has 180 days to expiration.

Intermediate Questions

11. **Put-Call Parity** A put and a call option have the same maturity and strike price. If both are at the money, which is worth more? Prove your answer and then provide an intuitive explanation.

12. **Put-Call Parity** A put and a call option have the same maturity and strike price. If they also have the same price, which one is in the money?

13. **Put-Call Parity** One thing the put-call parity equation tells us is that given any three of a stock, a call, a put, and a T-bill, the fourth can be synthesized or replicated using the other three. For example, how can we replicate a share of stock using a put, a call, and a T-bill?

14. **Delta** What does an option's delta tell us? Suppose a call option with a delta of .60 sells for $2.00. If the stock price rises by $1, what will happen to the call's value?

15. **Eta** What is the difference between an option's delta and its eta? Suppose a call option has an eta of 12. If the underlying stock rises from $100 to $102, what will be the impact on the option's price?

16. **Vega** What does an option's vega tell us? Suppose a put option with a vega of .60 sells for $12.00. If the underlying volatility rises from 50 to 51 percent, what will happen to the put's value?

17. **American Options** A well-known result in option pricing theory is that it will never pay to exercise a call option on a non–dividend-paying stock before expiration. Why do you suppose this is so? Would it ever pay to exercise a put option before maturity?

18. **ISDs** A call option has a price of $2.57. The underlying stock price, strike price, and dividend yield are $100, $120, and 3 percent, respectively. The option has 100 days to expiration, and the risk-free interest rate is 6 percent. What is the implied volatility?

19. **Hedging with Options** Suppose you have a stock market portfolio with a beta of 1.4 that is currently worth $150 million. You wish to hedge against a decline using index options. Describe how you might do so with puts and calls. Suppose you decide to use SPX calls. Calculate the number of contracts needed if the contract you pick has a delta of .50, and the S&P 500 index is at 1200.

20. **Calculating the Greeks** Using an options calculator, calculate the price and the following "greeks" for a call and a put option with one year to expiration: delta, gamma, rho, eta, vega, and theta. The stock price is $80, the strike price is $75, the volatility is 40 percent, the dividend yield is 3 percent, and the risk-free interest rate is 5 percent.

16 Futures Contracts

Trading in futures contracts adds a time dimension to commodity markets. A futures contract separates the date of the agreement—when the delivery price is specified—from the date when delivery and payment actually occur. By separating these dates, buyers and sellers achieve an important and flexible tool for risk management. So fundamental is this underlying principle that it has been practiced for several millennia and is likely to be around for several more. ■ A hallmark of ancient civilizations was the trading of commodities at an officially designated marketplace. Indeed, the Forum and the Agora defined Rome and Athens as centers of civilization as much as the Pantheon and the Parthenon. While commodities trading was normally conducted on the basis of barter or coin-and-carry, the use of what are known as forward contracts dates at least to ancient Babylonia, where they were regulated by Hammurabi's Code.

This chapter covers modern-day versions of these activities. The first sections discuss the basics of futures contracts and how their prices are quoted in the financial press. From there, we move into a general discussion of how futures contracts are used and the relationship between current cash prices and futures prices.

Futures Contracts Basics

forward contract
Agreement between a buyer and a seller, who both commit to a transaction at a future date at a price set by negotiation today.

futures contract
Contract between a seller and a buyer specifying a commodity or financial instrument to be delivered and paid for at contract maturity. Futures contracts are managed through an organized futures exchange.

futures price Price negotiated by buyer and seller at which the underlying commodity or financial instrument will be delivered and paid for to fulfill the obligations of a futures contract.

By definition, a **forward contract** is a formal agreement between a buyer and a seller who both commit to a commodity transaction at a future date at a price set by negotiation today. The genius of forward contracting is that it allows a producer to sell a product to a willing buyer before it is actually produced. By setting a price today, both buyer and seller remove price uncertainty as a source of risk. With less risk, buyers and sellers mutually benefit and commerce is stimulated. This principle has been understood and practiced for centuries.

Futures contracts represent a step beyond forward contracts. Futures contracts and forward contracts accomplish the same economic task, which is to specify a price today for future delivery. This specified price is called the **futures price**. However, while a forward contract can be struck between any two parties, futures contracts are managed through an organized futures exchange. Sponsorship through a futures exchange is a major distinction between a futures contract and a forward contract.

History of Futures Trading

History buffs will be interested to know that organized futures trading appears to have originated in Japan during the early Tokugawa era—that is, the seventeenth century. As you might guess, these early Japanese futures markets were devoted to trading contracts for rice. Tokugawa rule ended in 1867, but active rice futures markets continue on to this day.

The oldest organized futures exchange in the United States is the Chicago Board of Trade (CBOT). The CBOT was established in 1848 and grew with the westward expansion of American ranching and agriculture. Today, the CBOT is the largest, most active futures exchange in the world. Other early American futures exchanges still with us today include the MidAmerica Commodity Exchange (founded in 1868), New York Cotton Exchange (1870), New York Mercantile Exchange (1872), Chicago Mercantile Exchange (1874), New York Coffee Exchange (1882), and the Kansas City Board of Trade (1882).

For more than 100 years, American futures exchanges devoted their activities exclusively to commodity futures. However, a revolution began in the 1970s with the introduction of financial futures. Unlike commodity futures which call for delivery of a physical commodity, financial futures require delivery of a financial instrument. The first financial futures were foreign currency contracts introduced in 1972 at the International Monetary Market (IMM), a division of the Chicago Mercantile Exchange (CME).

Next came interest rate futures, introduced at the Chicago Board of Trade in 1975. An interest rate futures contract specifies delivery of a fixed-income security. For example, an interest rate futures contract may specify a U.S. Treasury bill, note, or bond as the underlying instrument. Finally, stock index futures were introduced in 1982 at the Kansas City Board of Trade (KBT), the Chicago Mercantile Exchange, and the New York Futures Exchange (NYFE). A stock index futures contract specifies a particular stock market index as its underlying instrument.

Financial futures have been so successful that they now constitute the bulk of all futures trading. This success is largely attributed to the fact that financial futures have become an indispensable tool for financial risk management by corporations and portfolio managers. As we will see, futures contracts can be used to reduce risk through hedging strategies or to increase risk through speculative strategies. In this chapter, we discuss futures contracts generally, but, since this text deals with financial markets, we will ultimately focus on financial futures.

Futures Contract Features

Futures contracts are a type of derivative security because the value of the contract is derived from the value of an underlying instrument. For example, the value of a futures contract to buy or sell gold is derived from the market price of gold. However, because a futures contract represents a zero-sum game between a buyer and a seller, the net value of a futures contract is always zero. That is, any gain realized by the buyer is exactly equal to a loss realized by the seller, and vice versa.

Futures are contracts, and, in practice, exchange-traded futures contracts are standardized to facilitate convenience in trading and price reporting. Standardized futures contracts have a set contract size specified according to the particular underlying instrument. For example, a standard gold futures contract specifies a contract size of 100 troy ounces. This means that a single gold futures contract obligates the seller to deliver 100 troy ounces of gold to the buyer at contract maturity. In turn, the contract also obligates the buyer to accept the gold delivery and pay the negotiated futures price for the delivered gold.

To properly understand a futures contract, we must know the specific terms of the contract. In general, futures contracts must stipulate at least the following five contract terms:

1. The identity of the underlying commodity or financial instrument.
2. The futures contract size.
3. The futures maturity date, also called the expiration date.
4. The delivery or settlement procedure.
5. The futures price.

First, a futures contract requires that the underlying commodity or financial instrument be clearly identified. This is stating the obvious, but it is important that the obvious is clearly understood in financial transactions.

Second, the size of the contract must be specified. As stated earlier, the standard contract size for gold futures is 100 troy ounces. For U.S. Treasury note and bond futures, the standard contract size is $100,000 in par value notes or bonds, respectively.

The third contract term that must be stated is the maturity date. Contract maturity is the date on which the seller is obligated to make delivery and the buyer is obligated to make payment.

Fourth, the delivery process must be specified. For commodity futures, delivery normally entails sending a warehouse receipt for the appropriate quantity of the underlying commodity. After delivery, the buyer pays warehouse storage costs until the commodity is sold or otherwise disposed.

Finally, the futures price must be mutually agreed on by the buyer and seller. The futures price is quite important, since it is the price that the buyer will pay and the seller will receive for delivery at contract maturity.

For financial futures, delivery is often accomplished by a transfer of registered ownership. For example, ownership of U.S. Treasury bill, note, and bond issues is registered at the Federal Reserve in computerized book-entry form. Futures delivery is accomplished by a notification to the Fed to effect a change of registered ownership.

Other financial futures feature cash settlement, which means that the buyer and seller simply settle up in cash with no actual delivery. We discuss cash settlement in more detail when we discuss stock index futures. The important thing to remember for now is that delivery procedures are selected for convenience and low cost. Specific delivery procedures are set by the futures exchange and may change slightly from time to time.

Futures Prices

The largest volume of futures trading in the United States takes place at the Chicago Board of Trade, which accounts for about half of all domestic futures trading. However, futures trading is also quite active at other futures exchanges. Current futures prices for contracts traded at the major futures exchanges are reported each day in *The Wall Street Journal*. Figure 16.1 reproduces a portion of the daily "Futures Prices" report of *The Wall Street Journal*.

This section of the *Journal* contains a box labeled "Exchange Abbreviations," which lists the major world futures exchanges and their exchange abbreviation codes. Elsewhere, the information is divided into sections according to categories of *The* underlying commodities or financial instruments. For example, the section, "Grains and Oilseeds," lists futures price information for wheat, oats, soybeans, and similar crops. The section "Metals and Petroleum" reports price information for copper, gold, and petroleum products. There are separate sections for financial futures, which include "Currency," "Interest Rate," and "Index" categories.

Each section states the contract name, futures exchange, and contract size, along with price information for various contract maturities. For example, under "Metals and Petroleum" we find the Copper contract traded at the Commodities Exchange (COMEX) Division of the New York Mercantile Exchange (CMX.Div.NYM). The standard contract size for copper is 25,000 pounds per contract. The futures price is quoted in cents per pound.

Example 16.1 Futures Quotes

In Figure 16.1, locate the gold contract. Where is it traded? What does one contract specify?

The gold contract, like the copper contract, trades on the COMEX. One contract calls for delivery of 100 troy ounces. The futures price is quoted in dollars per ounce.

The reporting format for each futures contract is similar. For example, the first column of a price listing gives the contract delivery/maturity month. For each maturity month, the next five columns report futures prices observed during the previous day at the opening of trading ("Open"), the highest intraday price ("High"), the lowest intraday price ("Low"), the price at close of trading ("Settle"), and the change in the settle price from the previous day ("Change").

The next two columns ("Lifetime," "High" and "Low") report the highest and lowest prices for each maturity observed over the previous year. Finally, the last column reports open interest for each contract maturity, which is the number of contracts outstanding at the end of that day's trading. The last row below these eight columns summarizes trading activity for all maturities by reporting aggregate trading volume and open interest for all contract maturities.

By now, we see that four of the contract terms for futures contracts are stated in the futures prices listing. These are:

1. The identity of the underlying commodity or financial instrument.

2. The futures contract size.

3. The futures maturity date.

4. The futures price.

Figure 16.1 Futures Prices

Monday, February 22, 1999

Open Interest Reflects Previous Trading Day.

GRAINS AND OILSEEDS

CORN (CBT) 5,000 bu.; cents per bu.

	Open	High	Low	Settle	Change	Lifetime High	Lifetime Low	Open Interest
Mar	215	215	212	214	− 1	305	209½	98,822
May	220½	221	217½	219¾	− 1	299	217	94,627
July	225¾	226¼	222½	224¾	− 1	312	222½	84,185
Sept	232¼	233	230	231¾	− ¾	280	229¾	19,717
Dec	240	241	237½	239¾	− ¾	291½	235	49,538
Mr00	248½	248½	245½	247½	− ¾	270	242½	6,418
July	256¼	256¼	254½	256	− ¼	278½	250½	1,924
Dec	254½	254½	251½	254	− 1½	279½	250	1,585

Est vol 87,000; vol Fr 57,765; open int 357,221, −5,946.

OATS (CBT) 5,000 bu.; cents per bu.

	Open	High	Low	Settle	Change	Lifetime High	Lifetime Low	Open Interest
Mar	101½	101¾	100½	101½	− ¼	166½	99¾	4,795
May	105¼	105½	104¼	105¼	− ¼	161	103¾	5,834
July	109	109	107½	108½	− ½	150	107½	3,274
Sept	111¾	111¾	110¾	111¼	− 1¼	140	110¾	1,050
Dec	117	117¼	116½	117	− ½	147	116½	2,088

Est vol 3,700; vol Fr 1,448; open int 17,056, −110.

SOYBEANS (CBT) 5,000 bu.; cents per bu.

	Open	High	Low	Settle	Change	Lifetime High	Lifetime Low	Open Interest
Mar	477¾	478¼	464½	474	− 4¼	694	464½	42,942
May	483	483	470	478¼	− 4½	671	470	40,596
July	489	489½	476	484½	− 5	728	476	39,086
Aug	489½	490	480	486	− 5¼	618¼	480	11,578
Sept	488	488½	483	488½	− 4½	616½	483	4,533
Nov	500½	501	489¾	496½	− 5	680	489¾	23,425
Ja00	506	506½	501	506¼	− 5¼	632	501	732
Mar	515½	516	509	515¼	− 6¾	594	509	200

Est vol 80,000; vol Fr 55,886; open int 163,969, −3,230.

SOYBEAN MEAL (CBT) 100 tons; $ per ton.

	Open	High	Low	Settle	Change	Lifetime High	Lifetime Low	Open Interest
Mar	129.90	129.90	126.60	128.90	− .90	195.00	126.60	28,229
May	129.20	129.20	126.50	128.70	− .80	192.50	126.50	35,410
July	130.00	131.90	129.00	130.90	− 1.40	188.00	129.00	32,602
Aug	133.20	133.20	130.60	132.00	− 1.40	178.90	130.60	10,428
Sept	134.50	134.50	132.30	134.00	− 1.20	183.50	132.30	8,522
Oct	135.00	135.00	134.00	134.80	− 1.50	180.50	134.00	3,548
Dec	138.30	138.30	136.70	138.00	− 1.60	181.50	136.70	8,909

Est vol 30,000; vol Fr 28,476; open int 127,982, −2,370.

SOYBEAN OIL (CBT) 60,000 lbs.; cents per lb.

	Open	High	Low	Settle	Change	Lifetime High	Lifetime Low	Open Interest
Mar	18.91	18.91	18.28	18.89	− .02	28.80	18.28	31,340
May	19.19	19.19	18.52	19.06	− .13	28.30	18.52	41,969
July	19.40	19.40	18.77	19.33	− .11	27.50	18.77	25,482
Aug	19.55	19.55	18.95	19.49	− .07	26.20	18.95	5,991
Sept	19.65	19.70	19.10	19.61	− .09	26.20	19.10	5,988
Oct	19.80	19.80	19.30	19.68	− .14	26.20	19.30	3,372
Dec	20.01	20.01	19.40	19.95	− .08	26.20	19.40	15,534

Est vol 40,000; vol Fr 33,825; open int 135,189, +3,164.

WHEAT (CBT) 5,000 bu.; cents per bu.

	Open	High	Low	Settle	Change	Lifetime High	Lifetime Low	Open Interest
Mar	255½	255¾	248½	251¾	− 3	384½	247	38,292
May	265	265¾	259¼	262¼	− 2½	355	258	35,931
July	275	275	269	271¾	− 3¼	389	268	45,474
Sept	283½	284	279½	282	− 3½	344	278¼	4,180
Dec	300	300	293	296¼	− 3¼	365	292	6,197

Est vol 34,000; vol Fr 35,475; open int 130,968, −955.

WHEAT (KC) 5,000 bu., cents per bu.

	Open	High	Low	Settle	Change	Lifetime High	Lifetime Low	Open Interest
Mar	284¼	285½	281½	284¼	− ¾	410½	281½	18,816
May	294	295¼	292	294	− 1	370	291¾	17,192
July	304½	305	301½	304½	− 1	370	301½	19,826
Sept	312	314	311	312¾	− 1¼	360	311	3,003
Dec	325	326	323	325	− ¾	368	323	2,699

Est vol 13,582; vol Fr 21,834; open int 61,907, −1,598.

WHEAT (MPLS) 5,000 bu.; cents per bu.

	Open	High	Low	Settle	Change	Lifetime High	Lifetime Low	Open Interest
Mar	332½	334	330	332	− 1½	398	319	7,259
May	339½	340	336¾	339	− 1½	401	326	11,698
July	344	345½	342½	344	− 1	385	337	5,014
Sept	347	349¼	346	347½	− ½	387	345	2,210

Est vol 7,278; vol Fr 8,043; open int 26,792, +1,556.

METALS AND PETROLEUM

COPPER-HIGH (Cmx.Div.NYM)-25,000 lbs.; cents per lb.

	Open	High	Low	Settle	Change	Lifetime High	Lifetime Low	Open Interest
Feb	61.50	61.50	61.20	61.25	− .45	94.60	61.20	323
Mar	61.50	62.30	61.15	61.35	− .55	98.20	61.15	31,830
Apr	62.00	62.05	61.70	61.85	− .50	96.00	61.70	2,630
May	62.90	62.90	62.00	62.20	− .60	98.50	62.00	14,632
June	62.70	63.00	62.50	62.60	− .60	91.00	62.50	1,514
July	63.30	63.30	62.90	63.00	− .55	95.75	62.90	7,454
Aug	63.40	63.45	63.40	63.40	− .55	90.50	63.40	1,408
Sept	64.10	64.20	63.90	63.80	− .50	94.60	63.90	4,209
Oct	64.35	64.35	64.35	64.15	− .50	90.00	64.35	1,033
Nov	64.80	64.80	64.70	64.45	− .50	86.90	64.70	931
Dec	65.30	65.30	64.95	64.80	− .50	86.00	64.95	5,812
Ja00	65.75	65.75	65.75	65.05	− .50	83.80	65.75	301
Feb	66.00	66.00	66.00	65.30	− .50	79.50	66.00	383
Mar	66.00	66.30	66.00	65.60	− .50	83.00	66.00	834
Apr	66.40	66.40	66.40	65.85	− .50	80.50	66.40	171
May	67.00	67.00	66.80	66.10	− .50	77.70	66.80	260
June		....	....	66.40	− .50	77.50	69.50	224
July	67.00	67.10	67.00	66.60	− .50	78.10	67.00	619
Sept		....	....	67.15	− .50	78.60	68.70	453
Oct		....	....	67.45	− .50	71.95	71.95	120
Dec		....	....	68.00	− .50	74.00	69.00	185

Est vol 27,000; vol Fr 11,179; open int 75,498, +1,656.

GOLD (Cmx.Div.NYM)-100 troy oz.; $ per troy oz.

	Open	High	Low	Settle	Change	Lifetime High	Lifetime Low	Open Interest
Feb	289.50	291.50	288.80	289.00	− .50	349.50	277.50	632
Mar		....	....	288.00	− 1.00	294.00	284.50	2
Apr	289.40	289.80	287.60	288.50	− 1.00	351.20	280.00	105,319
June	291.00	291.00	289.70	290.40	− 1.00	520.00	282.00	25,992
Aug	292.00	292.50	292.00	292.40	− 1.00	327.00	288.40	6,816
Oct		....	....	294.30	− 1.00	308.40	287.00	2,838
Dec	296.00	296.00	295.00	296.10	− 1.00	506.00	286.50	12,910
Fb00	297.50	297.50	297.50	297.30	− 1.00	512.00	294.00	7,406
Apr		....	....	299.10	− 1.00	311.00	298.00	1,120
June		....	....	300.90	− 1.00	473.50	290.50	10,330

HEATING OIL NO. 2 (NYM) 42,000 gal.; $ per gal.

	Open	High	Low	Settle	Change	Lifetime High	Lifetime Low	Open Interest
Mar	.3065	.3115	.3040	.3087	+ .0053	.5830	.2920	33,460
Apr	.3125	.3160	.3100	.3138	+ .0042	.5900	.2965	33,712
May	.3180	.3225	.3170	.3198	+ .0042	.5330	.3040	16,016
June	.3250	.3280	.3230	.3258	+ .0042	.5300	.3115	17,077
July	.3320	.3360	.3300	.3333	+ .0042	.5290	.3220	12,887
Aug	.3435	.3440	.3435	.3418	+ .0042	.5120	.3320	10,492
Sept	.3540	.3540	.3540	.3508	+ .0037	.5200	.3420	5,932
Oct	.3630	.3630	.3630	.3598	+ .0037	.5200	.3510	5,301
Nov	.3660	.3695	.3660	.3678	+ .0037	.5235	.3605	4,417
Dec	.3750	.3780	.3745	.3758	+ .0032	.5275	.3680	12,898
Ja00	.3800	.3835	.3800	.3813	+ .0032	.5170	.3700	11,983
Feb	.3830	.3830	.3825	.3813	+ .0032	.4960	.3750	2,531
Mar	.3820	.3825	.3820	.3808	+ .0032	.5060	.3760	723

Est vol 30,359; vol Fri 43,323; open int 170,451, +4,242.

GASOLINE-NY Unleaded (NYM)) 42,000 gal.; $ per gal.

	Open	High	Low	Settle	Change	Lifetime High	Lifetime Low	Open Interest
Mar	.3410	.3500	.3375	.3470	+ .0061	.5230	.3240	27,285
Apr	.3700	.3790	.3700	.3759	+ .0060	.5500	.3580	32,891
May	.3810	.3905	.3810	.3866	+ .0052	.5500	.3710	18,595
June	.3915	.3995	.3900	.3949	+ .0043	.5250	.3815	16,562
July	.3985	.4060	.3985	.4009	+ .0036	.5260	.3900	15,739
Aug	.4040	.4085	.4040	.4049	+ .0036	.5215	.3950	3,622
Sept	.4100	.4100	.4060	.4064	+ .0036	.5065	.3950	3,560
Oct	....	....	....	.3989	+ .0036	.4696	.3890	2,345

Est vol 30,624; vol Fri 39,654; open int 124,488, +2,511.

NATURAL GAS, (NYM) 10,000 MMBtu.; $ per MMBtu's

	Open	High	Low	Settle	Change	Lifetime High	Lifetime Low	Open Interest
Mar	1.750	1.760	1.690	1.704	− .041	2.600	1.690	44,724
Apr	1.765	1.770	1.690	1.702	− .063	2.440	1.690	45,979
May	1.800	1.805	1.730	1.740	− .060	2.380	1.730	18,405
June	1.830	1.830	1.770	1.778	− .052	2.384	1.770	17,069
July	1.855	1.865	1.810	1.818	− .044	2.390	1.810	15,887
Aug	1.890	1.895	1.845	1.856	− .037	2.390	1.845	12,504
Sept	1.920	1.920	1.885	1.894	− .029	2.380	1.885	13,966
Oct	1.965	1.965	1.935	1.938	− .029	2.415	1.935	9,754
Nov	2.145	2.150	2.120	2.123	− .024	2.535	2.115	10,038
Dec	2.315	2.315	2.285	2.290	− .025	2.680	2.213	13,649
Ja00	2.385	2.385	2.350	2.360	− .025	2.680	2.295	14,857
Feb	2.310	2.310	2.285	2.290	− .020	2.565	2.240	6,844
Mar	2.235	2.235	2.210	2.220	− .014	2.475	2.119	5,344
Apr	2.150	2.152	2.130	2.138	− .014	2.360	2.015	4,652
May	2.115	2.120	2.110	2.113	− .014	2.339	1.960	4,691
June	2.130	2.130	2.120	2.123	− .016	2.320	2.001	7,326
July	2.138	2.138	2.120	2.132	− .016	2.325	2.005	2,613
Aug	2.137	2.140	2.135	2.136	− .016	2.320	2.005	2,214
Sept	2.140	2.141	2.140	2.138	− .016	2.370	2.100	2,166
Oct	2.168	2.168	2.158	2.157	− .016	2.346	2.100	2,159
Nov	2.285	2.285	2.283	2.282	− .013	2.469	2.240	1,962
Dec	....	....	....	2.419	− .016	2.620	2.380	2,737
Ja01	....	....	....	2.470	− .015	2.675	2.400	3,733
Feb	....	....	....	2.385	− .013	2.522	2.305	2,402
Mar	....	....	....	2.295	− .010	2.420	2.210	1,897
Apr	....	....	....	2.202	− .010	2.315	2.120	1,934
May	2.193	2.193	2.193	2.183	− .010	2.305	2.119	1,495
June	2.196	2.200	2.196	2.190	− .010	2.301	2.095	834
July	2.202	2.206	2.201	2.196	− .010	2.310	2.095	1,456
Aug	2.211	2.211	2.211	2.201	− .010	2.280	2.102	789
Sept	2.220	2.220	2.220	2.210	− .100	2.290	2.137	697
Oct	....	....	....	2.236	− .010	2.320	2.133	944

Est vol 96,797; vol Fri 43,415; open int 283,310, +2,366.

BRENT CRUDE (IPE) 1,000 net bbls.; $ per bbl.

	Open	High	Low	Settle	Change	Lifetime High	Lifetime Low	Open Interest
Apr	10.50	10.59	10.35	10.58	+ .18	16.15	9.90	76,675
May	10.62	10.76	10.55	10.75	+ .18	16.17	10.10	44,010
June	10.78	10.92	10.77	10.92	+ .17	17.30	10.30	36,149
Ju01		....	....	13.22	+ .03	16.53	13.58	3,445
Dec		....	....	13.57	+ .01	15.56	13.75	5,031

Est vol 35,000; vol Fr 33,393; open int 240,759, −936.

CURRENCY

JAPAN YEN (CME)-12.5 million yen; $ per yen (.00)

	Open	High	Low	Settle	Change	Lifetime High	Lifetime Low	Open Interest
Mar	.8193	.8350	.8185	.8296	+ .0014	.9319	.6997	83,112
June	.8295	.8450	.8295	.8397	+ .0015	.9430	.7086	5,984
Sept	.8540	.8545	.8490	.8502	+ .0016	.9500	.7680	1,550
Dec	.8595	.8658	.8595	.8607	+ .0017	.9600	.8590	405

Est vol 30,160; vol Fri 26,780; open int 91,051, +2,606.

DEUTSCHEMARK (CME)-125,000 marks; $ per mark

	Open	High	Low	Settle	Change	Lifetime High	Lifetime Low	Open Interest
Mar	.5642	.5666	.5615	.5648	− .0015	.6347	.5540	59,951
June	.5658	.5681	.5654	.5676	− .0015	.6285	.5620	1,703
Sept	....	....	....	.5706	− .0015	.6300	.5795	167

Est vol 11,267; vol Fri 16,378; open int 61,889, +741.

CANADIAN DOLLAR (CME)-100,000 dlrs.; $ per Can $

	Open	High	Low	Settle	Change	Lifetime High	Lifetime Low	Open Interest
Mar	.6716	.6725	.6672	.6684	− .0034	.7247	.6290	72,367
June	.6724	.6725	.6673	.6686	− .0034	.7170	.6300	4,833
Sept	.6707	.6707	.6685	.6690	− .0034	.7080	.6310	1,101
Dec	.6694	.6694	.6690	.6694	− .0034	.6751	.6320	1,204

Est vol 6,674; vol Fri 7,412; open int 79,666, −1,039.

BRITISH POUND (CME)-62,500 pds.; $ per pound

	Open	High	Low	Settle	Change	Lifetime High	Lifetime Low	Open Interest
Mar	1.6198	1.6264	1.6168	1.6256	+ .0048	1.7150	1.5950	58,997
June	1.6188	1.6254	1.6170	1.6248	+ .0048	1.7060	1.5880	1,963
Sept		....	....	1.6250	+ .0048	1.6980	1.6180	230

Est vol 5,754; vol Fri 13,663; open int 61,220, +4,481.

SWISS FRANC (CME)-125,000 francs; $ per franc

	Open	High	Low	Settle	Change	Lifetime High	Lifetime Low	Open Interest
Mar	.6902	.6928	.6870	.6919	− .0009	.7890	.6635	61,580
June	.6971	.6989	.6953	.6984	− .0009	.7930	.6700	698
Sept	....	....	....	.7049	− .0009	.7650	.7045	249

Est vol 11,156; vol Fri 24,138; open int 62,533, +5,480.

AUSTRALIAN DOLLAR (CME)-100,000 dlrs.; $ per A.$

	Open	High	Low	Settle	Change	Lifetime High	Lifetime Low	Open Interest
Mar	.6384	.6418	.6355	.6402	− .0003	.6545	.5785	28,614

Est vol 1,002; vol Fri 1,159; open int 28,675, +32.

MEXICAN PESO (CME)-500,000 new Mex. peso, $ per MP

	Open	High	Low	Settle	Change	Lifetime High	Lifetime Low	Open Interest
Mar	.09930	.09975	.09915	.09945	+ 00030	.10565	.07000	11,583
June	.09360	.09420	.09360	.09405	+ 00040	.10220	.06900	6,510
Sept	....	....	....	.08950	+ 00035	.09510	.06350	636
Dec	.08560	.08560	.08560	.08560	+ 00045	.84345	.06700	199

Est vol 1,021; vol Fri 2,386; open int 18,928, −312.

BRAZILIAN REAL (CME)-100,000 Braz. reals; $ per reals

	Open	High	Low	Settle	Change	Lifetime High	Lifetime Low	Open Interest
Mar	.05200	.05200	.05150	.05150	− 00010	.08090	.04800	4,986
Apr	.05100	.05100	.05090	.05070	− 00007	.79760	.48000	1,271
June	....	....	....	.04890	− 00006	.07560	.04750	1,757

Est vol 265; vol Fri 433; open int 8,066, +40.

INTEREST RATE

TREASURY BONDS (CBT)-$100,000; pts. 32nds of 100%

	Open	High	Low	Settle	Change	Lifetime High	Lifetime Low	Open Interest
Mar	123-13	123-26	122-29	123-23	+ 13	134-26	103-04	566,811
June	122-19	123-11	122-18	123-08	+ 12	134-02	110-07	266,550
Sept	....	....	....	122-26	+ 11	131-06	115-11	8,520
Dec	....	....	....	122-06	+ 11	128-28	118-07	3,299

Est vol 310,000; vol Fr 422,127; open int 845,180, −16,461.

TREASURY BONDS (MCE)-$50,000; pts. 32nds of 100%

	Open	High	Low	Settle	Change	Lifetime High	Lifetime Low	Open Interest
Mar	123-01	123-26	123-00	123-23	+ 14	134-28	122-23	13,023

Est vol 3,300; vol Fr 6,511; open int 13,152, +418.

TREASURY NOTES (CBT)-$100,000; pts. 32nds of 100%

	Open	High	Low	Settle	Change	Lifetime High	Lifetime Low	Open Interest
Mar	116-00	116-09	115-22	116-08	+ 9	123-22	112-04	453,315
June	116-09	116-15	115-30	115-29	+ 10	120-21	113-18	116,902

Est vol 145,000; vol Fr 220,856; open int 570,962, +1,388.

5 YR TREAS NOTES (CBT)-$100,000; pts. 32nds of 100%

	Open	High	Low	Settle	Change	Lifetime High	Lifetime Low	Open Interest
Mar	111-07	111-14	11-025	11-135	+ 5.5	116-15	111-03	234,745
June	11-315	12-095	11-315	112-09	+ 6.0	116-08	11-295	35,145

Est vol 66,000; vol Fr 70,977; open int 269,895, −5,180.

2 YR TREAS NOTES (CBT)-$200,000, pts. 32nds of 100%

	Open	High	Low	Settle	Change	Lifetime High	Lifetime Low	Open Interest
Mar	05-105	05-047	105-00	05-045	+ 2.7	106-30	04-302	29,751

Est vol 6,600; vol Fr 13,269; open int 40,124, +679.

30-DAY FEDERAL FUNDS (CBT)-$5 million; pts. of 100%

	Open	High	Low	Settle	Change	Lifetime High	Lifetime Low	Open Interest
Feb	95.250	95.255	95.250	95.250	− .010	95.710	94.310	6,059
Mar	95.23	95.23	95.22	95.22	− .01	95.78	94.38	4,993
Apr	95.23	95.23	95.23	95.23	....	95.76	94.43	2,115
May	95.22	95.22	95.20	95.20	....	95.82	94.61	1,526
June	95.19	95.19	95.18	95.18	− .02	95.60	0.12	1,200

Est vol 888; vol Fr 1,027; open int 16,428, −219.

MUNI BOND INDEX (CBT)-$1,000; times Bond Buyer MBI

	Open	High	Low	Settle	Change	Lifetime High	Lifetime Low	Open Interest
Mar	125-02	125-25	125-02	125-23	+ 16	129-27	122-25	23,816
June	124-16	125-03	124-16	125-03	+ 17	125-04	123-12	2,427

Est vol 1,000; vol Fr 1,326; open int 26,245, +183.

The index: Close 125-07; Yield 5.28.

TREASURY BILLS (CME)-$1 mil.; pts. of 100%

	Open	High	Low	Settle	Chg	Discount Settle	Discount Chg	Open Interest
Mar	95.61	95.61	95.57	95.58	− .03	4.42	+ .03	2,510
June	95.69	95.69	95.67	95.67	− .02	4.33	+ .02	710

Est vol 438; vol Fr 125; open int 3,220, +32.

LIBOR-1 MO. (CME)-$3,000,000; points of 100%

	Open	High	Low	Settle	Chg	Discount Settle	Discount Chg	Open Interest
Mar	95.03	95.04	95.03	95.03	....	4.97	....	5,702
Apr	95.05	95.05	95.05	95.05	+ .05	4.95	− .05	2,909
May	95.03	95.04	95.03	95.04	....	4.96	....	2,383
June	....	....	....	94.99	....	5.01	....	450
July	....	....	....	94.98	....	5.02	....	264

Est vol 1,161; vol Fr 948; open int 12,317, +143.

INDEX

DJ INDUSTRIAL AVERAGE (CBOT)-$10 times average

	Open	High	Low	Settle	Chg	High	Low	Open Interest
Mar	9363	9592	9340	9576	+ 213	9760	7220	16,535
June	9425	9670	9420	9655	+ 216	9810	7670	1,376
Sept		....	....	9737	+ 218	9891	7875	913
Dec		....	....	9820	+ 219	9974	7987	862
Dc00		....	....	10198	+ 223	10300	8100	50

Est vol 12,000; vol Fri 10,783; open int 19,736, −119.

Idx prl: High 9558.28; Low 9331.16; Close 9552.68 +212.73

S&P 500 INDEX (CME)-$250 times index

	Open	High	Low	Settle	Chg	High	Low	Open Interest
Mar	124300	127650	124050	127450	+ 31.00	129420	902.85	375,060
June	125500	128800	125300	128640	+ 31.20	130250	914.85	24,522
Sept	126900	130100	126500	129870	+ 31.70	131370	927.35	2,732
Dec	128300	131320	127720	131090	+ 31.70	132520	960.70	1,859
Mr00	130400	132520	128920	132350	+ 32.30	133850	970.00	259
June		....	....	133750	+ 32.30	135200	980.00	495
Dec	134200	136420	132820	136250	+ 32.30	137750	126650	682

Est vol 100,941; vol Fri 94,319; open int 405,609, −1,703.

Idx prl: High 1272.22; Low 1239.22; Close 1272.14 +32.92

MINI S&P 500 (CME)-$50 times index

	Open	High	Low	Settle	Chg	High	Low	Open Interest
Mar	124250	127675	124050	127450	+ 31.00	129425	939.50	20,401

Vol Fri 28,132; open int 20,502, −604.

S&P MIDCAP 400 (CME)-$500 times index

	Open	High	Low	Settle	Chg	High	Low	Open Interest
Mar	359.50	366.00	359.00	366.00	+ 6.65	398.90	274.30	15,643
June	363.00	369.40	363.00	369.45	+ 6.65	402.25	278.95	600

Est vol 446; vol Fri 999; open int 16,243, −13.

Idx prl: High 364.95; Low 357.21; Close 364.95 +6.37

EXCHANGE ABBREVIATIONS
(for commodity futures and futures options)

CBT-Chicago Board of Trade; CME-Chicago Mercantile Exchange; CSCE-Coffee, Sugar & Cocoa Exchange, New York; CMX-COMEX (Div. of New York Mercantile Exchange); CTN-New York Cotton Exchange; EUREX-European Exchange; FINEX-Financial Exchange (Div. of New York Cotton Exchange; IPE-International Petroleum Exchange; KC-Kansas City Board of Trade; LIFFE-London International Financial Futures Exchange; MATIF-Marche a Terme International de France; ME-Montreal Exchange; MCE-MidAmerica Commodity Exchange; MPLS-Minneapolis Grain Exchange; NYFE-New York Futures Exchange (Sub. of New York Cotton Exchange); NYM-New York Mercantile Exchange; SIMEX-Singapore International Monetary Exchange Ltd.; SFE-Sydney Futures Exchange; TFE-Toronto Futures Exchange; WPG-Winnipeg CommodityExchange. CBT, CME, NYMX/CMX, CTN, FINEX, NYFE reflect overnight trading.

Exact contract terms for the delivery process are available from the appropriate futures exchange on request.

Example 16.2 Futures Prices

In Figure 16.1, locate the soybean contract with the greatest open interest. Explain the information provided.

The soybean (or just "bean") contract with the greatest open interest is specified by the contract maturity with the greatest number of contracts outstanding, so the March contract is the one we seek. One contract calls for delivery of 5,000 bushels of beans (a bushel, of course, is four pecks). The closing price for delivery at that maturity is stated as a quote in cents per bushel. Since there are 5,000 bushels in a single contract, the total contract value is the quoted price per bushel times 5,000, or $23,700 for the March contract.

To get an idea of the magnitude of financial futures trading, take a look at the first entry under "Interest Rate" in Figure 16.1, the CBT Treasury bond contract. One contract calls for the delivery of $100,000 in par value bonds. The total open interest in this one contract is often close to half a million contracts. Thus, the total face value represented by these contracts is close to half a *trillion* dollars.

Who does all this trading? The orders originate from money managers around the world and are sent to the various exchanges' trading floors for execution. On the floor, the orders are executed by professional traders who are quite aggressive at getting the best prices. On the floor and off, futures traders can be recognized by their colorful jackets. As *The Wall Street Journal* article in the nearby Investment Updates box reports, these garish jackets add a touch of clamor to the trading pits. In the next section we will discuss how and why futures contracts are used for speculation and hedging.

CHECK THIS

16.1a What is a forward contract? A futures contract?

16.1b What is a futures price?

16.2 Why Futures?

Futures contracts can be used for speculation or for hedging. Certainly, hedging is the major economic purpose for the existence of futures markets. However, a viable futures market cannot exist without participation by both hedgers and speculators. Hedgers transfer price risk to speculators, and speculators absorb price risk. Hedging and speculating are complementary activities. We next discuss speculating with futures; then we discuss hedging with futures.

Garish Jackets Add to Clamor of Chicago Pits

For the inhabitants of Chicago's futures and options trading pits, dressing for success means throwing good taste to the wind.

Take James Oliff, a trader in the Chicago Mercantile Exchange's newly opened Mexican peso futures pit. Daily, he dons a multicolored jacket bedecked with cacti and sombreros, in keeping, he says, with the "theme" of the product he trades.

Twisting and turning to display his gaudy garb, the veteran currency options trader explains: "I wanted a jacket that would be easy to pick out in the crowd. Runners get orders to me more quickly, and clerks find me faster when I'm trying to do trades."

It's important to have what veterans of the mayhem describe as "pit presence" to make money in the crowded and noisy trading pits of the Merc and the Chicago Board of Trade. That elusive quality, they say, involves such stratagems as finding the best spot in the pit from which to communicate with clerks and other traders, maintaining good posture and using a loud, well-projected voice and forceful hand signals to attract attention.

Increasingly, in places such as the CBOT's bond pit, where hundreds of people cram into a space only slightly larger than a tennis court, garb is being used to grab attention. Hence the insatiable demand for magenta, lime-green, and silver-lamé jackets, featuring designs that run the gamut from the Mighty Morphin Power Rangers to bucolic farmhouses and sunflowers.

"I'd come in buck naked if I could," says Thomas Burke, a trader in the CBOT's overpopulated bond-futures pit. "As it is, the more obnoxious the jacket, the better. The louder it is, the more I can rest my voice and let my jacket draw the attention."

Chicago's exchanges quietly tolerate the proliferation of the garish trading jackets. Dress codes ban jeans and still require members to wear shirts with collars and don ties (although some of these may be little more than strings, having been worn daily for more than a decade). The rules also say that trading jackets must have sleeves that come below the elbow and contain pockets into which the traders stuff their trading cards and other documents. But during the past decade, traders say, exchange efforts to regulate the color and design of the jackets, or gently encourage their wearers to opt for something in quiet good taste, have been dropped as an exercise in futility.

Robert Pierce, who trades corn options at the CBOT, says the old brown jackets made him look like a UPS delivery man. "When someone gave me a UPS cap on the floor one day as a joke, I decided it was time for a change of style," he says. The switch, to a comparatively tasteful multicolored geometric pattern, has the added advantage of disguising pen and pencil marks, adds his wife, Cathy.

Dawn Guera, a former clerk at the CBOT, has spun the traders' need to stand out in the crowd into a four-year-old business designing and manufacturing custom trading jackets. Traders wander into her storefront operation next door to the CBOT to choose from dozens of fabrics with designs ranging from a subdued Harvard University crest on a crimson background to a slinky leopard skin pattern or turquoise frogs cavorting on a neon-pink background.

"Everyone has their own hobbies and interests and want the jackets to reflect that," she explains, pointing to fabrics with designs of dice and cards aimed at traders willing to acknowledge their addiction to gambling in the markets. "It's like a vanity license plate."

And, at $50 a pop, traders are willing, even eager, to order multiple jackets, Ms. Guera says, especially since many believe that washing or dry cleaning a "lucky" jacket will launder out the luck in it. Some, like the CBOT's Gilbert Leistner, take a seasonal approach to jackets: in summer and fall he wears a brightly colored turquoise and aquamarine jacket decorated with tropical fish, but switches to a Southwestern theme come Thanksgiving.

"It's my version of going south for the winter," he says, adding he's contemplating donning something in gold lamé for New Year's celebrations.

Ms. Guera, a former sportswear designer in New York, says traders have a long way to go before they'll pull themselves off the worst-dressed lists. To be sure, some of the early emphasis on flashiness is easing a bit, she says, and demands for fluorescent geometric patterns are giving way to a new trend favoring subtler paisley-type patterns with lapels, cuffs, and pockets in a contrasting, solid color.

"I think it would be great if we could really push the fashion envelope here and remove the collar and cuffs from the jackets, or even persuade the exchanges to let traders wear vests instead," she says. "I'm looking for a way of making this whole trading process more artistic and creative."

Speculating with Futures

Suppose you are thinking about speculating on commodity prices because you believe you can accurately forecast future prices most of the time. The most convenient way to speculate is with futures contracts. If you believe that the price of gold will go up, then you can speculate on this belief by buying gold futures. Alternatively, if you think gold will fall in price, you can speculate by selling gold futures. To be more precise, you think that the current futures price is either too high or too low relative to what gold prices will be in the future.

Buying futures is often referred to as "going long," or establishing a **long position**. Selling futures is often called "going short," or establishing a **short position**. A **speculator** accepts price risk in order to bet on the direction of prices by going long or short.

long position In futures jargon, refers to the contract buyer. A long position profits from a futures price increase.

To illustrate the basics of speculating, suppose you believe the price of gold will go up. In particular, the current futures price for delivery in three months is $400 per ounce. You think that gold will be selling for more than that three months from now, so you go long 100 three-month gold contracts. Each gold contract represents 100 troy ounces, so 100 contracts represents 10,000 ounces of gold with a total contract value of 10,000 × $400 = $4,000,000. In futures jargon, this is a $4 million long gold position.

short position In futures jargon, refers to the seller. A short position profits from a futures price decrease.

Now, suppose your belief turns out to be correct and at contract maturity the market price of gold is $420 per ounce. From your long futures position, you accept delivery of 10,000 troy ounces of gold at $400 per ounce and immediately sell the gold at the market price of $420 per ounce. Your profit is $20 per ounce, or 10,000 × $20 = $200,000, less applicable commissions.

speculator Trader who accepts price risk by going long or short to bet on the future direction of prices.

Of course, if your belief turned out wrong and gold fell in price, you would lose money since you must still buy the 10,000 troy ounces at $400 per ounce to fulfill your futures contract obligations. Thus, if gold fell to, say, $390 per ounce, you would lose $10 per ounce, or 10,000 × $10 = $100,000. As this example suggests, futures speculation is risky, but it is potentially rewarding if you can accurately forecast the direction of future commodity price movements.

As another example of commodity speculation, suppose an analysis of weather patterns has convinced you that the coming winter months will be warmer than usual, and that this will cause heating oil prices to fall as unsold inventories accumulate. You can speculate on this belief by selling heating oil futures.

Figure 16.1 reveals that the standard contract size for heating oil is 42,000 gallons. Suppose you go short 10 contracts at a futures price of 55 cents per gallon. This represents a short position with a total contract value of 10 × 42,000 × $.55 = $231,000.

If, at contract maturity, the price of heating oil is, say, 50 cents per gallon, you could buy 420,000 gallons for delivery to fulfill your futures commitment. Your profit would be 5 cents per gallon, or 10 × 42,000 × $.05 = $21,000, less applicable commissions. Of course, if heating oil prices rise by 5 cents per gallon, you would lose $21,000 instead. Again, speculation is risky but rewarding if you can accurately forecast the weather.

Example 16.3 What Would Juan Valdez Do?

After an analysis of political currents in Central and South America, you conclude that future coffee prices will be lower than currently indicated by futures prices. Would you go long or short? Analyze the impact of a swing in coffee prices of 10 cents per pound in either direction if you have a 10-contract position, where each contract calls for delivery of 37,500 pounds of coffee.

You would go short since you expect prices to decline. You're short 10 contracts, so you must deliver 10 × 37,500 = 375,000 pounds of coffee. If coffee prices fall to 10 cents below your originally contracted futures price, then you make 10 cents per pound, or $37,500. Of course, if you're wrong and prices are 10 cents higher, you lose $37,500.

Hedging with Futures

hedger Trader who seeks to transfer price risk by taking a futures position opposite to an existing position in the underlying commodity or financial instrument.

Many businesses face price risk when their activities require them to hold a working inventory. For example, suppose you own a regional gasoline distributorship and must keep a large operating inventory of gas on hand, say, 5 million gallons. In futures jargon, this gasoline inventory represents a long position in the underlying commodity.

If gas prices go up, your inventory goes up in value; but if gas prices fall, your inventory value goes down. Your risk is not trivial, since even a 5-cent fluctuation in the gallon price of gas will cause your inventory to change in value by $250,000. Because you are in the business of distributing gas, and not speculating on gas prices, you would like to remove this price risk from your business operations. Acting as a **hedger**, you seek to transfer price risk by taking a futures position opposite to an existing position in the underlying commodity or financial instrument. In this case, the value of your gasoline inventory can be protected by selling gasoline futures contracts.

Gasoline futures are traded on the New York Mercantile Exchange (NYM), and the standard contract size for gasoline futures is 42,000 gallons per contract. Since you wish to hedge 5 million gallons, you need to sell 5,000,000 / 42,000 = 119 gasoline contracts. With this hedge in place, any change in the value of your long inventory position is canceled by an approximately equal but opposite change in value of your short futures position. Because you are using this short position for hedging purposes, it is called a **short hedge**.

short hedge Sale of futures to offset potential losses from falling prices.

By hedging, you have greatly reduced or even eliminated the possibility of a loss from a decline in the price of gasoline. However, you have also eliminated the possibility of a gain from a price increase. This is an important point. If gas prices rise, you would have a substantial loss on your futures position, offsetting the gain on your inventory. Overall, you are long the underlying commodity because you own it; you offset the risk in your long position with a short position in futures.

Of course, your business activities may also include distributing other petroleum products like heating oil and natural gas. Futures contracts are available for these petroleum products also, and therefore they may be used for inventory hedging purposes.

Example 16.4 Short Hedging

Suppose you have an inventory of 1.2 million pounds of soybean oil. Describe how you would hedge this position.

Since you are long in the commodity, bean oil, you need to go short in (sell) futures. A single bean oil contract calls for delivery of 60,000 pounds of oil. To hedge your position, you need to sell 1.2 million / 60,000 = 20 futures contracts.

long hedge Purchase of futures to offset potential losses from rising prices.

The opposite of a short hedge is a **long hedge**. In this case, you do not own the underlying commodity, but you need to acquire it in the future. You can lock in the price you will pay in the future by buying, or going long in, futures contracts. In effect, you are short the underlying commodity because you must buy it in the future. You offset your short position with a long position in futures.

Example 16.5 More Hedging

You need to buy 600,000 pounds of orange juice in three months. How can you hedge the price risk associated with this future purchase? What price will you effectively lock in? One orange juice contract calls for delivery of 15,000 pounds of juice concentrate.

You are effectively short orange juice since you don't currently own it but plan to buy it. To offset the risk in this short position, you need to go long in futures. You should buy 600,000/15,000 = 40 contracts. The price you lock in is the original futures price.

Example 16.6 Even More Hedging

Suppose your company will receive payment of £10 million in six months, which will then be converted to U.S. dollars. What is the standard futures contract size for British pounds? Describe how you could use futures contracts to lock in an exchange rate from British pounds to U.S. dollars for your planned receipt of £10 million, including how many contracts are required.

Your company will be receiving £10 million, so you are effectively long pounds. To hedge, you need to short (sell) futures contracts. Put differently, you will want to exchange pounds for dollars. By selling a futures contract, you obligate yourself to deliver the underlying commodity, in this case currency, in exchange for payment in dollars. One British pound contract calls for delivery of £62,500. You will therefore sell £10 million / £62,500 = 160 contracts.

CHECK
THIS

16.2a What is a long position in futures? A short position? For a speculator, when is each appropriate?

16.2b What is a long hedge? A short hedge?

16.3 Futures Trading Accounts

A futures exchange, like a stock exchange, allows only exchange members to trade on the exchange. Exchange members may be firms or individuals trading for their own accounts, or they may be brokerage firms handling trades for customers. Some firms conduct both trading and brokerage operations on the exchange. In this section, we discuss the mechanics of a futures trading account as it pertains to a customer with a trading account at a brokerage firm.

The biggest customer trading accounts are those of corporations that use futures to manage their business risks and money managers who hedge or speculate with clients' funds. Many individual investors also have futures trading accounts of their own, although speculation by individual investors is not recommended without a full understanding of all risks involved. Whether a futures trading account is large or small, the mechanics of account trading are essentially the same.

futures margin
Deposit of funds in a futures trading account dedicated to covering potential losses from an outstanding futures position.

initial margin
Amount required when a futures contract is first bought or sold. Initial margin varies with the type and size of a contract, but it is the same for long and short futures positions.

marking-to-market In futures trading accounts, the process whereby gains and losses on outstanding futures positions are recognized on a daily basis.

maintenance margin
The minimum margin level required in a futures trading account at all times.

margin call
Notification to increase the margin level in a trading account.

reverse trade A trade that closes out a previously established futures position by taking the opposite position.

There are several essential things to know about futures trading accounts. The first thing to know about a futures trading account is that margin is required. In this way, futures accounts resemble the stock margin accounts we discussed in Chapter 2; however, the specifics are quite different. **Futures margin** is a deposit of funds in a futures trading account dedicated to covering potential losses from an outstanding futures position. An **initial margin** is required when a futures position is first established. The amount varies according to contract type and size, but margin requirements for futures contracts usually range between 2 percent to 5 percent of total contract value. Initial margin is the same for both long and short futures positions.

The second thing to know about a futures trading account is that contract values in outstanding futures positions are marked to market on a daily basis. **Marking-to-market** is a process whereby gains and losses on outstanding futures positions are recognized at the end of each day's trading.

For example, suppose one morning you call your broker and instruct her to go long five U.S. Treasury bond contracts for your account. A few minutes later, she calls back to confirm order execution at a futures price of 110. Since the Treasury bond contract size is $100,000 par value, contract value is $110\% \times \$100,000 = \$110,000$ per contract. Thus, the total position value for your order is $550,000, for which your broker requires $25,000 initial margin. In addition, your broker requires that at least $20,000 in **maintenance margin** be present at all times. The necessary margin funds are immediately wired from a bank account to your futures account.

Now, at the end of trading that day Treasury bond futures close at a price of 108. Overnight, all accounts are marked to market. Your Treasury bond futures position is marked to $108,000 per contract, or $540,000 total position value, representing a loss of $10,000. This loss is deducted from your initial margin to leave only $15,000 of margin funds in your account.

Since the maintenance margin level on your account is $20,000, your broker will issue a **margin call** on your account. Essentially, your broker will notify you that you must immediately restore your margin level to the initial margin level of $25,000, or else she will close out your Treasury bond futures position at whatever trading price is available at the exchange.

This example illustrates what happens when a futures trading account is marked to market and the resulting margin funds fall below the maintenance margin level. The alternative, and more pleasant experience occurs when a futures price moves in your favor, and the marking-to-market process adds funds to your account. In this case, marking-to-market gains can be withdrawn from your account so long as remaining margin funds are not less than the initial margin level.

The third thing to know about a futures trading account is that a futures position can be closed out at any time; you do not have to hold a contract until maturity. A futures position is closed out by simply instructing your broker to close out your position. To actually close out a position, your broker will enter a **reverse trade** for your account.

A reverse trade works like this: Suppose you are currently short five Treasury bond contracts, and you instruct your broker to close out the position. Your broker responds by going long five Treasury bond contracts for your account. In this case, going long five contracts is a reverse trade because it cancels exactly your previous five-contract short position. At the end of the day of your reverse trade, your account will be marked to market at the futures price realized by the reverse trade. From then on, your position is closed out and no more gains or losses will be realized.

This example illustrates that closing out a futures position is no more difficult than initially entering into a position. There are two basic reasons to close out a futures position before contract maturity. The first is to capture a current gain or loss, without realizing further price risk. The second is to avoid the delivery requirement that comes from holding a futures contract until it matures. In fact, over 98 percent of all futures contracts are closed out before contract maturity, which indicates that less than 2 percent of all futures contracts result in delivery of the underlying commodity or financial instrument.

Before closing this section, let's briefly list the three essential things to know about a futures trading account as discussed above:

1. Margin is required.
2. Futures accounts are marked to market daily.
3. A futures position can be closed out any time by a reverse trade.

Understanding the items in this list is important to anyone planning to use a futures trading account.

CHECK THIS

16.3a What are the three essential things you should know about a futures trading account?

16.3b What is meant by initial margin for a futures position? What is meant by maintenance margin for a futures position?

16.3c Explain the process of marking-to-market a

futures trading account. What is a margin call, and when is one issued?

16.3d How is a futures position closed out by a reverse trade? What proportion of all futures positions are closed out by reverse trades rather than by delivery at contract maturity?

16.4 Cash Prices versus Futures Prices

We now turn to the relationship between today's price of some commodity or financial instruments and its futures price. We begin by examining current cash prices.

Cash Prices

cash price Price of a commodity or financial instrument for current delivery. Also called the *spot price.*

cash market Market in which commodities or financial instruments are traded for essentially immediate delivery. Also called the *spot market.*

The **cash price** of a commodity or financial instrument is the price quoted for current delivery. The cash price is also called the *spot price,* as in "on the spot." In futures jargon, terms like "spot gold" or "cash wheat" are used to refer to commodities being sold for current delivery in what is called the **cash market** or the *spot market.*

Figure 16.2 reproduces the "Cash Prices" column of *The Wall Street Journal,* published the same day as the "Futures Prices" column seen in Figure 16.1. The column is divided into sections according to commodity categories. For example, the first section, "Grains and Feeds," lists spot price information for wheat, corn, soybeans, and similar crops. Other commodity sections include "Foods," "Fats and Oils," "Metals," and "Precious Metals." Each section gives commodity names along with cash market prices for the last two days of trading and one year earlier.

Figure 16.2

Commodity Cash Prices

Source: Reprinted by permission of *The Wall Street Journal*, Febuary 23, 1999, via Copyright Clearance Center, Inc. © 1999 Dow Jones & Company, Inc. All Rights Reserved Worldwide

CASH PRICES

Monday, February 22, 1999
(Closing Market Quotations)

GRAINS AND FEEDS	Mon	Fri	Year Ago
Barley, top-quality Mpls., bu	u220-25	220-25	z
Bran, wheat middlings, KC ton	u54-7	51-55	71.50
Corn, No. 2 yel. Cent. Ill. bu	bpu2.04½	2.05	2.57½
Corn Gluten Feed, Midwest, ton	53.00	55-69	71.50
Cottonseed Meal, Clksdle, Miss. ton	100.00	97.50	127.50
Hominy Feed, Cent. Ill. ton	52.00	54.00	77.00
Meat-Bonemeal, 50% pro. Ill. ton.	140-45	145.00	170.00
Oats, No. 2 milling, Mpls., bu	u1.16½	1.16¾	1.69¾
Sorghum, (Milo) No. 2 Gulf cwt	u407-13	408-14	5.02½
Soybean Meal, Cent. Ill., rail, ton 44%	u122-4	123-5	173.50
Soybean Meal, Cent. Ill., rail, ton 48%	u129-32	131-3	183.00
Soybeans, No. 1 yel Cent.-Ill. bu	bpu4.64	4.78	6.57½
Wheat, Spring 14%-pro Mpls. bu	u354-72	3.72	4.14¾
Wheat, No. 2 sft red, St.Lou. bu	bpu2.26	2.29½	3.23
Wheat, hard KC, bu	2.85¾	2.86½	3.56½
Wheat, No. 1 sft wht, del Port Ore	u3.08	3.11	3.53
FOODS			
Beef, Carcass, Equiv.Index Value, choice 1-3,550-700lbs.	u94.04	94.17	89.93
Beef, Carcass, Equiv.Index Value, select 1-3,550-700lbs.	u91.12	90.81	87.31
Broilers, Dressed "A" lb.	ux.5745	.5581	.5488
Broilers, 12-Cty Comp Wtd Av	u.5789	.5816	.5772
Butter, AA, Chgo., lb.	u1.34	1.34	1.40
Cheddar Cheese, barrels, Chgo lb.	n129.50	129.50	143.00
Cheddar Cheese, blocks, Chgo lb.	n133.00	133.00	142.75
Cocoa, Ivory Coast, $metric ton	1,491	1,502	1,711
Coffee, Brazilian, NY lb.	n1.00½	1.01½	1.91½
Coffee, Colombian, NY lb.	n1.10½	1.11½	2.01½
Eggs, Lge white, Chgo doz.	u.58-63	.58-63	.61½
Flour, hard winter KC cwt	8.60	8.65	9.75
Hams, 17-20 lbs, Mid-US lb fob	u.48-51	.48	.58½
Hogs, Iowa-S.Minn. avg. cwt	u27.26	25.50	34.00
Hogs, S. Dakota avg. cwt	u28.26	27.63	33.00
Pork Bellies, 12-14 lbs Mid-US lb	u.47	z	.44⅝
Pork Loins, 13-19 lbs. Mid-US lb	u.85-90	.82-91	1.01
Steers, Tex.-Okla. ch avg cwt	uz	z	z
Steers, Feeder, Okl Cty, av cwt	u82.13	83.38	87.00
Sugar, cane, raw, world, lb. fob	7.08	7.02	10.59
FATS AND OILS			
Coconut Oil, crd, N. Orleans lb.	xxn.35	.35	.26½
Corn Oil, crd wet/dry mill, Chgo.	u24¾-5¼	24¾-5¼	.28
Grease, choice white, Chgo lb.	z	z	.12½
Lard, Chgo lb.	.14¼	.14¼	.16
Palm Oil, ref. bl. deod. N.Orl. lb.	n.28½	.28½	.32½
Soybean Oil, crd, Central Ill. lb.	u1869-79	1871-81	.2691
Tallow, bleachable, Chgo lb.	.11	.11	.16
Tallow, edible, Chgo lb.	.14	.14	.18
METALS			
Aluminum ingot lb. del. Midwest	p.58½-9½	.58½-9½	.70⅛
Copper high gr lb., Cmx sp price	.61	.62	.73
Copper Scrap, No 2 wire NY lb	h.50	.50	.60
Lead, lb.	p.43769	.43784	.44876
Mercury 76 lb. flask NY	q155-80	155-80	170
Steel Scrap 1 hvy mlt EC ton	79-80	79-80	140.5
Tin composite lb.	q3.5649	3.5773	3.6034
Zinc Special High grade lb	q.52332	.52332	.50250
PRECIOUS METALS			
Gold, troy oz			
Engelhard indust bullion	288.34	287.49	293.85
Engelhard fabric prods	302.76	301.86	308.54
Handy & Harman base price	287.20	286.35	292.70
Handy & Harman fabric price	301.56	300.67	307.34
London fixing AM 287.20 PM	287.20	286.35	292.70
Krugerrand, whol	a296.00	297.00	300.00
Maple Leaf, troy oz.	a297.00	298.00	304.00
American Eagle, troy oz.	a297.00	298.00	304.00
Platinum, (Free Mkt.)	374.50	377.00	377.00
Platinum, indust (Engelhard)	376.00	381.00	377.00
Platinum, fabric prd (Engelhard)	476.00	481.00	477.00
Palladium, indust (Engelhard)	355.00	360.00	238.00
Palladium, fabrc prd (Englhard)	370.00	375.00	253.00
Silver, troy ounce			
Engelhard indust bullion	5.540	5.580	6.500
Engelhard fabric prods	6.205	6.250	7.280
Handy & Harman base price	5.570	5.590	6.480
Handy & Harman fabric price	6.238	6.261	7.258
London Fixing (in pounds) Spot (U.S. equiv.$5.5750)	3.4414	3.4282	3.9565
Coins, whol $1,000 face val	a5,255	5,350	4,423

a-Asked. b-Bid. bp-Country elevator bids to producers. c-Corrected. h-Reuters. n-Nominal. na-Not available. p-Producer price via Platt's Metals Week. q-Platt's Metals Week. r-Rail bids. u-U.S. Dept. of Agriculture. x-Less than truckloads. z-Not quoted. xx-f.o.b. tankcars.

OIL PRICES

Monday, February 22, 1999

CRUDE GRADES	Mon	Fri	Yr. Ago
OFFSHORE-d			
European "spot" or free market prices			
Arab lt.	8.55	8.66	12.12
Arab hvy.	7.75	7.86	10.02
Iran, lt.	9.75	9.86	12.72
Forties	10.00	10.11	14.20
Brent	10.10	10.21	14.02
Bonny lt.	10.10	10.21	14.02
Urals-Medit.	9.35	9.46	13.02
DOMESTIC-f			
Spot market			
W. Tex. Int Cush (900-1125) (Mar)	11.98	11.78	15.18
W.Tx.sour, Midl (575-1000) ..	10.63	10.40	13.18
La. sw. St.Ja (800-1076)	11.20	10.98	14.88
Al. No. Slope Pacific Del	10.48	10.28	12.40

Open-market crude oil values in Northwest Europe around 17:50 GMT in dlrs per barrel, for main loading ports in country of origin for prompt loading, except as indicated.

REFINED PRODUCTS	Mon	Fri	Yr. Ago
Fuel Oil, No. 2 NY gal.	.3025	.2912	.4193
Diesel Fuel, 0.05 S. NY harbor low sulfur	.3185	.3072	.4398
Gasoline, unlded, premium NY gal. non-oxygenated ...	.3633	.3572	.4791
Gasoline, unlded, premium NY gal. oxygenated	.3683	.3622	.4894
Gasoline, unlded, reg. NY gal. non-oxygenated ...	.3108	.3072	.4424
Gasoline, unlded, reg. NY gal. oxygenated	.3208	.3147	.4644
Propane, non-tet, Mont Belvieu, Texas, gal.	.2263	.2238	.3005
Propane, wet-tet, Mont Belvieu, Texas, gal.	.2578	.2238	.2981
Butane, normal, Mont Belvieu, Texas, gal.	.2875	.2875	.3650
RAW PRODUCTS			
Natural Gas Henry Hub, $ per mmbtu .	1.775	1.785	2.185

a-Asked. b-Bid. c-Corrected. d-as of 11 a.m. est in Northwest Europe. f-As of 4 p.m. est. Refiners' posted buying prices are in parentheses. n.a.-Not available. z-Not quoted. n-Nominal. r-Revised. Source: Dow Jones Energy Service

Cash-Futures Arbitrage

Intuitively, you might think that there is a close relationship between the cash price of a commodity and its futures price. If you do, then your intuition is quite correct. In fact, your intuition is backed up by strong economic argument and more than a century of experience observing the simultaneous operation of cash and futures markets.

As a routine matter, cash and futures prices are closely watched by market professionals. To understand why, suppose you notice that spot gold is trading for $400 per ounce while the two-month futures price is $450 per ounce. Do you see a profit opportunity?

You should, because buying spot gold today at $400 per ounce while simultaneously selling gold futures at $450 per ounce locks in a $50 per ounce profit. True, gold has storage costs (you have to put it somewhere), and a spot gold purchase ties up capital that could be earning interest. However, these costs are small relative to the $50 per ounce gross profit, which works out to be $50 / $400 = 12.5% per two months, or about 100 percent per year (with compounding). Furthermore, this profit is risk-free! Alas, in reality, such easy profit opportunities are the stuff of dreams.

cash-futures arbitrage Strategy for earning risk-free profits from an unusually large difference between cash and futures prices.

Earning risk-free profits from an unusual difference between cash and futures prices is called **cash-futures arbitrage**. In a competitive market, cash-futures arbitrage has very slim profit margins. In fact, the profit margins are almost imperceptible when they exist at all.

Comparing cash prices for commodities in Figure 16.2 with their corresponding futures prices reported in Figure 16.1, you will find that cash prices and futures prices are seldom equal. In futures jargon, the difference between a cash price and a futures price is called **basis**.[1]

basis The difference between the cash price and the futures price for a commodity, i.e., basis = cash price − futures price.

For commodities with storage costs, the cash price is usually less than the futures price. This is referred to as a **carrying-charge market**. Sometimes, however, the cash price is greater than the futures price and this is referred to as an **inverted market**. We can summarize this discussion of carrying-charge markets, inverted markets, and basis as follows:

carrying-charge market The case where the futures price is greater than the cash price; i.e., the basis is negative.

Carrying-charge market: Basis = Cash price − Futures price < 0 **16.1**

Inverted market: Basis = Cash price − Futures price > 0

inverted market The case where the futures price is less than the cash price; i.e., the basis is positive.

A variety of factors can lead to an economically justifiable difference between a commodity's cash price and its futures price, including availability of storage facilities, transportation costs, and seasonal price fluctuations. However, the primary determinants of cash-futures bases are storage costs and interest costs. Storage cost is the cost of holding the commodity in a storage facility, and interest cost refers to interest income forgone because funds are being used to buy and hold the commodity.

If a futures price rises far enough above a cash price to more than cover storage costs and interest expense, commodity traders will undertake cash-futures arbitrage by buying in the cash market and selling in the futures market. This drives down the futures price and drives up the cash price until the basis is restored to an economically justifiable level.

Similarly, if a futures price falls far enough relative to a cash price, traders will undertake cash-futures arbitrage by short selling in the cash market and buying in the futures market. This drives down the cash price and drives up the futures price until an economically justifiable basis is restored. In both cases, arbitrage ensures that the basis is kept at an economically appropriate level.

---

[1] Confusingly, basis is sometimes presented as the futures price less the cash price. The official Commodity Trading Manual of the Chicago Board of Trade defines basis as the difference between the cash and the futures price, i.e., basis = cash price − futures price. We will be consistent with the CBOT definition.

Spot-Futures Parity

We can be a little bit more precise concerning the relationship between spot and futures prices for financial futures. To illustrate, suppose we had a futures contract on shares of common stock in a single company (actually there are no such contracts in the U.S.). This particular stock does not pay dividends.

For concreteness, suppose the contract calls for delivery of 1,000 shares of stock in one year. The current (i.e., cash or spot) price is $50 per share. Also, 12-month T-bills are yielding 6 percent. What should the futures price be? To answer, notice that you can buy 1,000 shares of stock for $50 per share, or $50,000 total. You can eliminate all of the risk associated with this purchase by selling one futures contract. The net effect of this transaction is that you have created a risk-free asset. Since the risk-free rate is 6 percent, your investment must have a future value of $50,000 \times 1.06 = $53,000$. In other words, the futures price should be $53 per share.

Suppose the futures price is, in fact, $52 per share. What would you do? To make a great deal of money, you would short 1,000 shares of stock at $50 per share and invest the $50,000 proceeds at 6 percent.[2] Simultaneously, you would buy one futures contract.

At the end of the year, you would have $53,000. You would use $52,000 to buy the stock to fulfill your obligation on the futures contract and then return the stock to close out the short position. You pocket $1,000. This is just another example of cash-futures arbitrage.

More generally, if we let F be the futures price, S be the spot price, and r be the risk-free rate, then our example illustrates that

$$F = S(1 + r) \qquad \textbf{16.2}$$

spot-futures parity
The relationship between spot prices and futures prices that holds in the absence of arbitrage opportunities.

In other words, the futures price is simply the future value of the spot price, calculated at the risk-free rate. This is the famous **spot-futures parity** condition. This condition must hold in the absence of cash-futures arbitrage opportunities.

More generally, if r is the risk-free rate per period, and the futures contract matures in T periods, then the spot-futures parity condition is

$$F = S(1 + r)^T \qquad \textbf{16.3}$$

Notice that T could be a fraction of one period. For example, if we have the risk-free rate per year, but the futures contract matures in six months, T would be 1/2.

Example 16.7 Parity Check

A non–dividend-paying stock has a current price of $12 per share. The risk-free rate is 4 percent per year. If a futures contract on the stock matures in three months, what should the futures price be?

From our spot-futures parity condition, we have

$$\begin{aligned} F &= S(1 + r)^T \\ &= \$12(1.04)^{1/4} \\ &= \$12.12 \end{aligned}$$

---

[2] For the sake of simplicity, we ignore the fact that individual investors don't earn interest on the proceeds from a short sale.

The futures price should be $12.12. Notice that T, the number of periods, is 1/4 because the contract matures in one quarter.

More on Spot-Futures Parity

In our spot-futures parity example just above, we assumed that the underlying financial instrument (the stock) had no cash flows (no dividends). If there are dividends (for a stock future) or coupon payments (for a bond future), then we need to modify our spot-futures parity condition.

For a stock, we let D stand for the dividend, and we assume that the dividend is paid in one period, at or near the end of the futures contract's life. In this case, the spot-futures parity condition becomes

$$F = S(1 + r) - D \qquad \text{16.4}$$

Notice that we have simply subtracted the amount of the dividend from the future value of the stock price. The reason is that if you buy the futures contract, you will not receive the dividend, but the dividend payment will reduce the stock price.

An alternative, and very useful, way of writing the dividend-adjusted spot-futures parity result in Equation 16.4 is to define d as the dividend yield on the stock. Recall that the dividend yield is just the upcoming dividend divided by the current price. In our current notation, this is just $d = D/S$. With this in mind, we can write the dividend-adjusted parity result as

$$F = S(1 + r) - D\,(S/S) \qquad \text{16.5}$$

$$= S(1 + r) - S\,(D/S)$$

$$= S(1 + r) - Sd$$

$$= S(1 + r - d)$$

Finally, as above, if there is something other than a single period involved, we would write

$$F = S(1 + r - d)^T \qquad \text{16.6}$$

where T is the number of periods (or fraction of a period).

For example, suppose there is a futures contract on a stock with a current price of $80. The futures contract matures in six months. The risk-free rate is 7 percent per year, and the stock has an annual dividend yield of 3 percent. What should the futures price be?

Plugging in to our dividend-adjusted parity equation, we have

$$F = S(1 + r - d)^T$$

$$= \$80(1 + .07 - .03)^{1/2}$$

$$= \$81.58$$

Notice that we set T equal to 1/2 since the contract matures in six months.

CHECK THIS

16.4a What is the spot price for a commodity?

16.4b With regard to futures contracts, what is the basis?

16.4c What is an inverted market?

16.4d What is the spot-futures parity condition?

16.5 Stock Index Futures

While there are no futures contracts on individual stocks, there are a number of contracts on stock market indexes. Because these contracts are particularly important, we devote this entire section to them. We first describe the contracts and then discuss some trading and hedging strategies involving their use.

Basics of Stock Index Futures

Locate the section labeled "Index" in Figure 16.1. Here we see various stock index futures contracts. The second contract listed, on the S&P 500 index, is the most important. With this contract, actual delivery would be very difficult or impossible because the seller of the contract would have to buy all 500 stocks in exactly the right proportions to deliver. Clearly, this is not practical, so this contract features cash settlement.

To understand how stock index futures work, suppose you bought one S&P 500 contract at a futures price of 1,300. The contract size is $250 times the level of the index. What this means is that, at maturity, the buyer of the contract will pay the seller $250 times the difference between the futures price of 1,300 and the level of the S&P 500 index at contract maturity.

For example, suppose that at maturity the S&P had actually fallen to 1,270. In this case, the buyer of the contract must pay $250 \times (1,300 - 1,270) = $7,500$ to the seller of the contract. In effect, the buyer of the contract has agreed to purchase 250 "units" of the index at a price of $1,300 per unit. If the index is below 1,300, the buyer will lose money. If the index is above that, then the seller will lose money.

Example 16.8 Index Futures

Suppose you are convinced that Midcap stocks are going to skyrocket in value. Consequently, you buy 20 S&P Midcap 400 contracts maturing in six months at a price of 395. Suppose that the S&P Midcap 400 index is at 410 when the contracts mature. How much will you make or lose?

The futures price is 395, and the contract size is $500 times the level of the index. If the index is actually at 410, you make $500 \times (410 - 395) = $7,500$ per contract. With 20 contracts, your total profit is $150,000.

Index Arbitrage

index arbitrage
Strategy of monitoring the futures price on a stock index and the level of the underlying index to exploit deviations from parity.

The spot-futures parity relation we developed above is the basis for a common trading strategy known as **index arbitrage**. Index arbitrage refers to monitoring the futures price on a stock index along with the level of the underlying index. The trader looks for violations of parity and trades as appropriate.

For example, suppose the S&P 500 futures price for delivery in one year is 1,340. The current level is 1,300. The dividend yield on the S&P is projected to be 3 percent per year, and the risk-free rate is 5 percent. Is there a trading opportunity here?

From our dividend-adjusted parity equation (16.6), the futures price should be

$$F = S(1 + r - d)^T$$
$$= 1,300(1 + .05 - .03)^1$$
$$= 1,326$$

Thus, based on our parity calculation, the futures price is too low. We want to buy low, sell high, so we sell the index and simultaneously buy the futures contract.

program trading
Computer-assisted monitoring of relative prices of financial assets; it sometimes includes computer submission of buy and sell orders to exploit perceived arbitrage opportunities.

Index arbitrage is often implemented as a **program trading** strategy. While this term covers a lot of ground, it generally refers to the monitoring of relative prices by computer to more quickly spot opportunities. In some cases it includes submitting the needed buy and sell orders using a computer to speed up the process.

Whether a computer is used in program trading is not really the issue; instead, a program trading strategy is any coordinated, systematic procedure for exploiting (or trying to exploit) violations of parity or other arbitrage opportunities. Such a procedure is a trading "program" in the sense that whenever certain conditions exist, certain trades are made. Thus, the process is sufficiently mechanical that it can be automated, at least in principle.

Technically, the NYSE defines program trading as the simultaneous purchase or sale of at least 15 different stocks with a total value of $1 million or more. Program trading accounts for about 15 percent of total trading volume on the NYSE, and about 20 percent of all program trading involves stock-index arbitrage.

There is another phenomenon often associated with index arbitrage and, more generally, futures and options trading. S&P 500 futures contracts have four expiration months per year, and they expire on the third Friday of those months. On these same four Fridays, options on the S&P index and various individual stock options also expire. These Fridays have been dubbed the "triple witching hour" because all three types of contracts expire, sometimes leading to unusual price behavior.

In particular, on triple witching hour Fridays, all positions must be liquidated, or "unwound." To the extent that large-scale index arbitrage and other program trading has taken place, enormous buying or selling sometimes occurs late in the day on such Fridays, as positions are closed out. Large price swings and, more generally, increased volatility often are seen. To curtail this problem to a certain extent, the exchanges have adopted rules regarding the size of a position that can be carried to expiration, and other rules have been adopted as well.

Hedging Stock Market Risk with Futures

We earlier discussed hedging using futures contracts in the context of a business protecting the value of its inventory. We now discuss some hedging strategies available to portfolio managers based on financial futures. Essentially, an investment portfolio is an inventory of securities, and financial futures can be used to reduce the risk of holding a securities portfolio.

We consider the specific problem of an equity portfolio manager wishing to protect the value of a stock portfolio from the risk of an adverse movement of the overall stock market. Here, the portfolio manager wishes to establish a short hedge position to reduce risk and must determine the number of futures contracts required to properly hedge a portfolio.

In this hedging example, you are responsible for managing a broadly diversified stock portfolio with a current value of $100 million. Analysis of market conditions leads you to believe that the stock market is unusually susceptible to a price decline during the next few months. Of course, nothing is certain regarding stock market fluctuations, but still you are sufficiently concerned to believe that action is required.

cross-hedge Hedging a particular spot position with futures contracts on a related, but not identical commodity or financial instrument.

A fundamental problem exists for you, however, in that there is no futures contract that exactly matches your particular portfolio. As a result, you decide to protect your stock portfolio from a fall in value caused by a falling stock market using stock index futures. This is an example of a **cross-hedge**, where a futures contract on a related, but not identical, commodity or financial instrument is used to hedge a particular spot position.

Thus, to hedge your portfolio, you wish to establish a short hedge using stock index futures. To do this, you need to know how many index futures contracts are required to form an effective hedge. There are three basic inputs needed to calculate the number of stock index futures contracts required to hedge a stock portfolio:

1. The current value of your stock portfolio.

2. The beta of your stock portfolio.

3. The contract value of the index futures contract used for hedging.

Based on our discussion in Chapter 6, you are familiar with the concept of beta as a measure of market risk for a stock portfolio. Essentially, beta measures portfolio risk relative to the overall stock market. We will assume that you have maintained a beta of 1.25 for your $100 million stock portfolio.

You decide to establish a short hedge using futures contracts on the Standard & Poor's index of 500 stocks (S&P 500), since this is the index you used to calculate the beta for your portfolio. From *The Wall Street Journal,* you find that the S&P 500 futures price for three-month maturity contracts is currently, say, 1,300. Since the contract size for S&P 500 futures is 250 times the index, the current value of a single index futures contract is $250 × 1,300 = $325,000.

You now have all inputs required to calculate the number of contracts needed to hedge your stock portfolio. The number of stock index futures contracts needed to hedge a stock portfolio is determined as follows:

$$\text{Number of contracts} = \frac{\beta_P \times V_P}{V_F} \qquad \textbf{16.7}$$

where β_P = Beta of the stock portfolio

V_P = Value of the stock portfolio

V_F = Value of a single futures contract

For your particular hedging problem, β_P = 1.25, V_P = $100 million, and V_F = $325,000, thereby yielding this calculation:

$$\text{Number of contracts} = \frac{1.25 \times \$100,000,000}{\$325,000} \approx 385$$

Thus you can establish an effective short hedge by going short 385 S&P 500 index futures contracts. This short hedge will protect your stock portfolio against the risk of a general fall in stock prices during the life of the futures contracts.

Example 16.9 Hedging with Stock Index Futures

How many futures contracts are required to hedge a $250 million stock portfolio with a portfolio beta of .75 using S&P 500 futures with a futures price of 1,200?

Using the formula for the number of contracts, we have

$$\text{Number of contracts} = \frac{.75 \times \$250,000,000}{\$300,000} = 625$$

You therefore need to sell 625 contracts to hedge this $250 million portfolio.

Hedging Interest Rate Risk with Futures

Having discussed hedging a stock portfolio, we now turn to hedging a bond portfolio. As we will see, the bond portfolio hedging problem is similar to the stock portfolio hedging problem. Once again, we will be cross-hedging, but this time using futures contracts on U.S. Treasury notes. Here, our goal is to protect the bond portfolio against changing interest rates.

In this example, you are responsible for managing a bond portfolio with a current value of $100 million. Recently, rising interest rates have caused your portfolio to fall in value slightly, and you are concerned that interest rates may continue to trend upward for the next several months. You decide to establish a short hedge based on 10-year Treasury note futures.

The formula for the number of U.S. Treasury note futures contracts needed to hedge a bond portfolio is

$$\text{Number of contracts} = \frac{D_P \times V_P}{D_F \times V_F} \qquad \textbf{16.8}$$

where D_P = Duration of the bond portfolio

V_P = Value of the bond portfolio

D_F = Duration of the futures contract

V_F = Value of a single futures contract

We already know the value of the bond portfolio, which is $100 million. Also, suppose that the duration of the portfolio is given as eight years. Next, we must calculate the duration of the futures contract and the value of the futures contract.

As a useful rule of thumb, the duration of an interest rate futures contract is equal to the duration of the underlying instrument plus the time remaining until contract maturity:

$$D_F = D_U + M_F \qquad \textbf{16.9}$$

where D_F = Duration of the futures contract

D_U = Duration of the underlying instrument

M_F = Time remaining until contract maturity

For smplicity, let us suppose that the duration of the underlying U.S. Treasury note is 6 1/2 years and the futures contract has a maturity of 1/2 year, yielding a futures contract duration of 7 years.

The value of a single futures contract is the current futures price times the futures contract size. The standard contract size for U.S. Treasury note futures contracts is $100,000 par value. Now suppose that the futures price is 98, or 98 percent of par value. This yields a futures contract value of $100,000 \times .98 = $98,000.

You now have all inputs required to calculate the number of futures contracts needed to hedge your bond portfolio. The number of U.S. Treasury note futures contracts needed to hedge the bond portfolio is calculated as follows:

$$\text{Number of contracts} = \frac{8 \times \$100,000,000}{7 \times \$98,000} = 1,166$$

Thus, you can establish an effective short hedge by going short 1,166 futures contracts for 10-year U.S. Treasury notes. This short hedge will protect your bond portfolio against the risk of a general rise in interest rates during the life of the futures contracts.

Example 16.10 Hedging with U.S. Treasury Note Futures

How many futures contracts are required to hedge a $250 million bond portfolio with a portfolio duration of 5 years using 10-year U.S. Treasury note futures with a duration of 7.5 years and a futures price of 105?

Using the formula for the number of contracts, we have

$$\text{Number of contracts} = \frac{5 \times \$250,000,000}{7.5 \times \$105,000} = 1{,}587$$

You therefore need to sell 1,587 contracts to hedge this $250 million portfolio.

Futures Contract Delivery Options

cheapest-to-deliver option Seller's option to deliver the cheapest instrument when a futures contract allows several instruments for delivery. For example, U.S. Treasury note futures allow delivery of any Treasury note with a maturity between 6 1/2 and 10 years.

Many futures contracts have a delivery option, whereby the seller can choose among several different "grades" of the underlying commodity or instrument when fulfilling delivery requirements of a futures contract. Naturally, we expect the seller to deliver the cheapest among available options. In futures jargon, this is called the **cheapest-to-deliver option**. The cheapest-to-deliver option is an example of a broader feature of many futures contracts, known as a "quality" option. Of course, futures buyers know about the delivery option, and therefore the futures prices reflects the value of the cheapest-to-deliver instrument.

As a specific example of a cheapest-to-deliver option, the 10-year Treasury note contract allows delivery of *any* Treasury note with a maturity between 6 1/2 and 10 years. This complicates the bond portfolio hedging problem. For the portfolio manager trying to hedge a bond portfolio with U.S. Treasury note futures, the cheapest-to-deliver feature means that a note can be hedged only based on an assumption about which note will actually be delivered. Furthermore, through time the cheapest-to-deliver note may vary, and, consequently, the hedge will have to be monitored regularly to make sure that it correctly reflects the note issue that is most likely to be delivered. Fortunately, because this is a common problem, many commercial advisory services provide this information to portfolio managers and other investors.

CHECK THIS

16.5a What is a cross-hedge?

16.5b What are the three basic inputs required to calculate the number of stock index futures contracts needed to hedge an equity portfolio?

16.5c What are the basic inputs required to calculate the number of U.S. Treasury note futures contracts needed to hedge a bond portfolio?

16.5d What is the cheapest-to-deliver option?

16.6 Summary and Conclusions

This chapter surveyed the basics of futures contracts. In it, we saw that:

1. A forward contract is an agreement between a buyer and a seller for a future commodity transaction at a price set today. Futures contracts are a step beyond forward contracts. Futures contracts and forward contracts accomplish the same

task, but a forward contract can be struck between any two parties, while standardized futures contracts are managed through organized futures exchanges.

2. Commodity futures call for delivery of a physical commodity. Financial futures require delivery of a financial instrument or, in some cases, cash. Futures contracts are a type of derivative security, because the value of the contract is derived from the value of an underlying instrument.

3. Hedging is the major economic reason for the existence of futures markets. However, a viable futures market requires participation by both hedgers and speculators. Hedgers transfer price risk to speculators, and speculators absorb price risk. Hedging and speculating are thus complementary activities.

4. Futures trading accounts have three essential features: margin is required, futures accounts are marked to market daily, and a futures position can be closed out any time by a reverse trade.

5. The cash price of a commodity or financial instrument is the price quoted for current delivery. The cash price is also called the spot price.

6. The difference between a cash price and a futures price is called basis. For commodities with storage costs, the cash price is usually less than the futures price. This is referred to as a carrying-charge market. Sometimes the cash price is greater than the futures price, and this case is referred to as an inverted market.

7. There is a simple relationship between cash and futures prices known as spot-futures parity. Violations of parity give rise to arbitrage opportunities, including index arbitrage, which involves stock index futures.

8. Cross-hedging refers to using futures contracts on a related commodity or instrument to hedge a particular spot position. Stock index futures, for example, can be used to hedge an equities portfolio against general declines in stock prices, and U.S. Treasury note futures can be used to hedge a bond portfolio.

GET

This chapter covered the essentials of what many consider to be a complex subject, futures contracts. As we hope you realize, futures contracts per se are not complicated at all; in fact, they are, for the most part, quite simple. This doesn't mean that they're for everybody, of course. Because of the tremendous leverage possible, very large gains and losses can (and do) occur with great speed.

To experience some of the gains and losses from outright speculation, you should buy and sell a variety of contracts in a simulated brokerage account such as Stock-Trak. Be sure to go both long and short and pick a few of each major type of contract.

As we discussed, in addition to speculation, futures contracts are enormously useful as a hedging tool. Try using the S&P contract to hedge your stock portfolio for a week or two. To determine the number of contracts, you will either need to calculate your stock portfolio's beta or just assume your portfolio has a beta of 1. Either way, you will sell contracts. Next, observe how well the hedge works. As a practical matter (as long as the number of contracts is in the right ballpark), you will likely find that the hedge is quite effective.

Similarly, try using T-bond contracts to hedge your bond portfolio. Here you need to know two durations, but you can just assume the needed durations are equal to about 10 for the T-bond contract and, assuming you own long-term bonds, maybe 9 for your bond portfolio. Once again, as a practical matter, you will probably find that the hedge is quite effective in reducing both your losses and your gains.

Key Terms

Chapter Review Problems and Self-Test

1. **Futures Gains and Losses** Suppose you purchase 10 orange juice contracts today at the settle price of $1 per pound. How much do these 10 contracts cost you? If the settle price is lower tomorrow by 2 cents per pound, how much do you make or lose?

2. **Spot-Futures Parity** Suppose a futures contract exists on Microsoft stock, which is currently selling at $200 per share. The contract matures in two months; the risk-free rate is 5 percent annually. The current dividend yield on the stock is 0 percent. What does the parity relationship imply the futures price should be?

Answers to Self-Test Problems

1. If you go long (purchase) 10 contracts, you pay nothing today (you will be required to post margin, but a futures contract is an agreement to exchange cash for goods later, not today). If the settle price drops by 2 cents per pound, you lose 15,000 pounds (the contract size) $\times$ $.02 = $300 per contract. With 10 contracts, you lose $3,000.

2. The spot-futures parity condition is

$$F = S(1 + r - d)^T$$

where S is the spot price, r is the risk-free rate, d is the dividend yield, F is the futures price, and T is the time to expiration measured in years.

   Plugging in the numbers we have, with zero for the dividend yield and 1/6 for the number of years (2 months out of 12), gets us

$$F = \$200(1 + .05)^{1/6} = \$201.63$$

Test Your Investment Quotient

1. **Futures Exchanges** Which of the following is the oldest and currently the most active futures exchange in the United States?

   a. Kansas City Board of Trade (KBOT).

   b. Chicago Mercantile Exchange (CME).

   c. New York Mercantile Exchange (NYMX).

   d. Chicago Board of Trade (CBOT).

2. **Futures Exchanges** The first financial futures contracts, introduced in 1972, were

   a. Currency futures at the CME.
   b. Interest rate futures at the CBOT.
   c. Stock index futures at the KBOT.
   d. Wheat futures at the CBOT.

3. **Futures versus Forward Contracts** Which of the following statements is true regarding the distinction between futures contracts and forward contracts?

   a. Futures contracts are exchange-traded, whereas forward contracts are OTC-traded.
   b. All else equal, forward prices are higher than futures prices.
   c. Forward contracts are created from baskets of futures contracts.
   d. Futures contracts are cash-settled at maturity, whereas forward contracts result in delivery.

4. **Futures versus Forward Contracts** In which of the following ways do futures contracts differ from forward contracts? (*1993 CFA exam*)

   i. Futures contracts are standardized.
   ii. For futures, performance of each party is guaranteed by a clearinghouse.
   iii. Futures contracts require a daily settling of any gains or losses.

   a. i and ii only
   b. i and iii only
   c. ii and iii only
   d. i, ii, and iii

5. **Futures Margin** Initial margin for a futures contract is usually

   a. Regulated by the Federal Reserve.
   b. Less than 2 percent of contract value.
   c. In the range between 2 percent to 5 percent of contract value.
   d. In the range between 5 percent to 15 percent of contract value.

6. **Futures Margin** Which of the following statements is false about futures account margin?

   a. Initial margin is higher than maintenance margin.
   b. A margin call results when account margin falls below maintenance margin.
   c. Marking-to-market of account margin occurs daily.
   d. A margin call results when account margin falls below initial margin.

7. **Futures Contracts** Which of the following contract terms changes daily during the life of a futures contract?

   a. Futures price.
   b. Futures contract size.
   c. Futures maturity date.
   d. Underlying commodity.

8. **Futures Trading Accounts** Which of the following is the least essential thing to know about a futures trading account?

   a. Margin is required.
   b. Futures accounts are marked-to-market daily.
   c. A futures position can be closed by a reverse trade.
   d. A commission is charged for each trade.

9. **Futures Delivery** On the maturity date, stock index futures contracts require delivery of (*1993 CFA exam*)

   a. Common stock.
   b. Common stock plus accrued dividends.
   c. Treasury bills.
   d. Cash.

10. **Futures Delivery** On the maturity date, Treasury note futures contracts require delivery of
    a. Treasury notes plus accrued coupons over the life of the futures contract.
    b. Treasury notes.
    c. Treasury bills.
    d. Cash.

11. **Spot-Futures Parity** A Treasury bond futures contract has a quoted price of 100. The underlying bond has a coupon rate of 7 percent and the current market interest rate is 7 percent. Spot-futures parity then implies a cash bond price of
    a. 93
    b. 100
    c. 107
    d. 114

12. **Spot-Futures Parity** A stock index futures contract maturing in one year has a currently traded price of $1,000. The cash index has a dividend yield of 2 percent and the interest rate is 5 percent. Spot-futures parity then implies a cash index level of
    a. $933.33
    b. $970.87
    c. $1,071
    d. $1,029

13. **Futures Hedging** You manage a $100 million stock portfolio with a beta of .8. Given a contract size of $100,000 for a stock index futures contract, how many contracts are needed to hedge your portfolio?
    a. 8
    b. 80
    c. 800
    d. 8,000

14. **Futures Hedging** You manage a $100 million bond portfolio with a duration of 9 years. You wish to hedge this portfolio against interest rate risk using T-bond futures with a contract size of $100,000 and a duration of 12 years. How many contracts are required?
    a. 750
    b. 1,000
    c. 133
    d. 1,333

15. **Futures Hedging** Which of the following is not an input needed to calculate the number of stock index futures contracts required to hedge a stock portfolio?
    a. The value of the stock portfolio.
    b. The beta of the stock portfolio.
    c. The contract value of the index futures contract.
    d. The initial margin required for each futures contract.

Questions and Problems

Core Questions

1. **Understanding Futures Quotations** Using Figure 16.1, answer the following questions:
   a. How many exchanges trade wheat futures contracts?
   b. If you have a position in 10 gold futures, what quantity of gold underlies your position?
   c. If you are short 20 oat futures contracts and you opt to make delivery, what quantity of oats must you supply?
   d. Which maturity of the unleaded gasoline contract has the largest open interest? Which one has the smallest open interest?

2. **Understanding Futures Quotations**   Using Figure 16.1, answer the following questions:

   a. What was the settle price for September 1999 corn futures on this date? What is the total dollar value of this contract at the close of trading for the day?

   b. What was the settle price for March 1999 Treasury bond futures on this date? If you held 10 contracts, what is the total dollar value of your futures position?

   c. Suppose you held an open position of 25 S&P Midcap 400 index futures on this day. What is the change in the total dollar value of your position for this day's trading? If you held a long position, would this represent a profit or a loss to you?

   d. Suppose you are short 10 July 1999 soybean oil futures contracts. Would you have made a profit or a loss on this day?

3. **Futures Profits and Losses**   You are long 20 March 1999 oats futures contracts. Calculate your dollar profit or loss from this trading day.

4. **Futures Profits and Losses**   You are short 15 December 1999 corn futures contracts. Calculate your dollar profit or loss from this trading day.

5. **Futures Profits and Losses**   You are short 30 June 1999 five-year Treasury note futures contracts. Calculate your profit or loss from this trading day.

6. **Hedging with Futures**   Kellogg's, the breakfast cereal manufacturer, uses large quantities of corn in its manufacturing operation. Suppose the near-term weather forecast for the corn-producing states is droughtlike conditions, so that corn prices are expected to rise. To hedge its costs, Kellogg's has decided to use the Chicago Board of Trade's corn futures contract. Should the company be a short hedger or a long hedger?

7. **Hedging with Futures**   Suppose one of Fidelity's mutual funds closely mimics the S&P 500 index. The fund has done very well during the year, and, in November, the fund manager wants to lock in the gains he has made using stock index futures. Should he take a long or short position in S&P 500 index futures?

8. **Hedging with Futures**   A mutual fund that predominantly holds long-term Treasury bonds plans on liquidating the portfolio in three months. However, the fund manager is concerned that interest rates may rise from current levels and wants to hedge the price risk of the portfolio. Should she buy or sell Treasury bond futures contracts?

9. **Hedging with Futures**   An American electronics firm imports its completed circuit boards from Japan. The company signed a contract today to pay for the boards in Japanese yen upon delivery in four months; the price per board in yen was fixed in the contract. Should the importer buy or sell Japanese yen futures contracts?

10. **Hedging with Futures**   Jed Clampett just dug another oil well, and, as usual, it's a gusher. Jed estimates that in 2 months, he'll have two million barrels of crude oil to bring to market. However, Jed would like to lock in the value of this oil at today's prices, since the oil market has been skyrocketing recently. Should Jed buy or sell crude oil futures contracts?

**Intermediate
Questions**

11. **Open Interest**   Referring to Figure 16.1, what is the total open interest on the Deutsche mark contract? Does it represent long positions or short positions or both? Based on the settle price on the March contract, what is the dollar value of the open interest?

12. **Margin Call**   Suppose the initial margin on heating oil futures is $1,000, the maintenance margin is $750 per contract, and you establish a long position of five contracts today (see Figure 16.1 for contract specifications). Tomorrow, the contract settles down .01 from .36 to .35. Are you subject to a margin call? What is the maximum price decline on the contract that you can sustain without getting a margin call?

13. **Future Markets**   Is it true that a futures contract is a zero-sum game, meaning that the only way for a buyer to win is for a seller to lose, and vice versa?

14. **Marking-to-Market** You are short 20 gasoline futures contracts, established at an initial settle price of .545 (see Figure 16.1 for contract specifications). Your initial margin to establish the position is $1,200 per contract and the maintenance margin is $800 per contract. Over the subsequent four trading days, the settle price is .555, .560, .540, and .520, respectively. Compute the balance in your margin account at the end of each of the four trading days, and compute your total profit or loss at the end of the trading period.

15. **Spot-Futures Parity** Suppose a futures contract exists on IBM stock, which is currently selling at $90 per share. The contract matures in three months, the risk-free rate is 6 percent annually, and the current dividend yield on the stock is 4 percent. What does the parity relationship imply the futures price should be?

16. **Index Arbitrage** Suppose the CAC-40 index (a widely followed index of French stock prices) is currently at 1,800, the expected dividend yield on the index is 3 percent per year, and the risk-free rate in France is 6 percent annually. If the futures that expire in six months are currently trading at 1,850, what program trading strategy would you recommend?

17. **Cross-Hedging** You have been assigned to implement a three-month hedge for a stock mutual fund portfolio that primarily invests in medium-sized companies. The mutual fund has a beta of 1.15 measured relative to the S&P Midcap 400, and the net asset value of the fund is $200 million. Should you be long or short in the futures contracts? Using the quotations in Figure 16.1 for the March contract, determine the appropriate number of futures to use in designing your cross-hedge strategy.

18. **Program Trading** Program traders closely monitor relative futures and cash market prices, but program trades are not actually made on a fully mechanical basis. What are some of the complications that might make program trading using, for example, the S&P 500 contract more difficult than the spot-futures parity formula indicates?

19. **Spot-Futures Parity** Suppose the 90-day S&P 500 futures price is 1,200 while the cash price is 1,194. What is the implied difference between the risk-free interest rate and the dividend yield on the S&P 500?

20. **Hedging Interest Rate Risk** Suppose you want to hedge a $600 million bond portfolio with a duration of 6 years using 10-year Treasury note futures with a duration of 9 years, a futures price of 102, and 90 days to expiration. How many contracts do you buy or sell?

STOCK-TRAK
Portfolio Simulations

Trading Commodity Futures with Stock-Trak

Commodity futures trading is popular among many individual investors. Stock-Trak allows its customers to trade a large number of different commodity futures: corn, wheat, gold, silver, oil, and many others. If you are interested in trying your hand at commodities trading with Stock-Trak, simply select the commodities you wish to trade from *The Wall Street Journal* "Futures" column, and then note the contract size for those commodities before deciding how many contracts you wish to trade. Table ST.1 lists contract sizes and ticker symbols for some popular commodities futures contracts.

Table ST. 1	**Commodity Futures Contract Size and Tickers**			
Instrument	**Ticker**		**Instrument**	**Ticker**
Corn (5,000 bushels)	C		Copper (25,000 lb)	HG
Soybeans (5,000 bushels)	S		Gold (100 oz)	GC
Wheat (5,000 bushels)	W		Platinum (50 oz)	PL
Coffee (37,500 lb)	KC		Crude oil (1,000 bbl)	CL
Sugar (112,000 lb)	SB		Heating oil (42,000 gal)	HO
Orange juice (15,000 lb)	JO		Unleaded gas (42,000 gal)	HU

Suppose you wish to take a long position in 100,000 pounds of copper in the hope that copper prices will go up, and at the same time assume a short position in 300,000 pounds of coffee in the belief that coffee prices are about to fall. You would then buy four copper contracts and sell eight coffee contracts. But before submitting these orders, you must decide on a contract maturity month. For Stock-Trak trading, it is convenient to pick a month at or after the end of the semester, say, December or June.

Commodity futures tickers have two-character extensions denoting the contract expiration date. The first character is a letter representing the expiration month, and the second character is a number representing the expiration year. Futures ticker extensions for contracts expiring in 1999 are specified in Table ST.2.

There are four basic types of futures trades:

1. Buy to open or increase a long position.

2. Sell to open or increase a short position.

3. Sell to close or decrease a long position.

4. Buy to close or decrease a long position.

Examples of the first two types of trades are orders to go long 4 June 1999 copper contracts and go short 8 December 2000 coffee contracts. Using standard futures ticker symbols, these orders are stated as:

> Buy 4 C-M9 contracts
>
> Sell 8 KC-Z0 contracts

Examples of the next two trade types are orders that close out these positions:

> Sell 4 C-M9 contracts
>
> Buy 8 KC-Z0 contracts

Stock-Trak Exercise

1. What are the complete tickers for the following commodity futures contracts: September 2000 orange juice, March 1999 unleaded gas, June 2001 gold?

Table ST.2	**Futures Ticker Extension Codes (1999 Expirations)**			
Expiration Month	**Code**		**Expiration Month**	**Code**
January	F9		July	N9
February	G9		August	Q9
March	H9		September	U9
April	J9		October	V9
May	K9		November	X9
June	M9		December	Z9

Trading Stock Index Futures with Stock-Trak

Once you have mastered the basics of trading commodity futures, you may wish to begin trading stock index futures. Your Stock-Trak account allows you to trade futures on a number of different stock market indexes. To trade stock index futures, you first choose the stock index you want to use and find the ticker symbol for that index. You must also know the ticker extension for the maturity month of the futures contract.

The most popular stock market indexes are the Dow Jones Industrial Average (DJIA) and the Standard & Poor's 500 (S&P 500). Futures contracts for the DJIA trade under the futures ticker symbol DJ. Futures contracts for the S&P 500 trade under the futures ticker symbol SP.

At the time this was written, the contract value for a single DJ futures contract was 10 times the underlying index level, and the contract value for the SP futures contract was 250 times the underlying index level. However, these contract values may change and you should consult the Stock-Trak website for the latest contract specifications. If you wish to know more detail about contract specifications, you should consult the Chicago Board of Trade website (www.cbot.com).

For example, suppose you go short a single DJ futures contract when the futures price is 10,150, and then at contract maturity the underlying index has a value of 10,025. Your dollar gain is then $10 \times (10,150 - 10,025) = \$1,250$. Alternatively, suppose you go long a single SP futures contract when the futures price is 1,310, and then at contract maturity the S&P 500 index is at 1,302. Your dollar loss is then $250 \times (1,310 - 1,302) = \$2,000$.

Futures tickers for stock indexes have a two-character extension denoting the contract expiration date. Just like commodity futures, the first character is a letter representing the expiration month, and the second character is an integer representing the expiration year. Futures ticker extensions for contracts expiring in 2000 are listed in Table ST.3.

For example, orders to go long 2 DJ June 1999 futures contract and go short 4 SP December 2000 futures contracts are abbreviated as

Buy 2 DJ-M9 contracts

Sell 4 SP-Z0 contracts

Stock-Trak Exercise

1. What are the complete tickers for the following stock index futures contracts: DJIA March 1999, S&P 500 September 2000?

Trading Interest Rate Futures with Stock-Trak

You can trade on interest rate changes using interest rate futures with your Stock-Trak account. The most widely used interest rate futures contracts are based on Eurodollar rates and rates on U.S. Treasury bills, notes, and bonds. To trade interest rate futures with Stock-Trak, you first select the desired instrument and the number of futures contracts. Table ST.4 lists futures contract sizes and ticker symbols for several interest rate contracts.

Table ST.3	Futures Ticker Extension Codes (2000 Expirations)			
Expiration Month	**Code**		**Expiration Month**	**Code**
January	FO		July	NO
February	GO		August	QO
March	HO		September	UO
April	JO		October	VO
May	KO		November	XO
June	MO		December	ZO

Table ST.4	Interest Rate Futures Contract Size and Tickers			
	Instrument	Ticker	Instrument	Ticker
	5-year T-note ($100,000)	FV	13-week T-bills ($1 million)	TB
	10-year T-note ($100,000)	TY	Eurodollar ($1 million)	ED
	30-year T-bond ($100,000)	US	LIBOR ($3 million)	EM

For example, orders to go long 3 Treasury bill June 1999 futures contracts and go short 2 Eurodollar December 2000 futures contracts are abbreviated as

Buy 3 TB-M9 contracts

Sell 2 ED-Z0 contracts

Going long implies buying the underlying instrument and going short implies selling the underlying instrument. The futures price specifies the price paid upon delivery at contract expiration. Detailed contract specifications for interest rate futures are available at the Chicago Board of Trade website (www.cbot.com) and the Chicago Mercantile Exchange website (www.cme.com).

Stock-Trak Exercises

1. What are the complete tickers for the following interest rate futures contracts: 5-year Treasury note September 2000, LIBOR March 1999, 30-year Treasury bond June 2001?

2. Through the website for this text book (www.mhhe.com/cj), go to the Stock-Trak website and review the latest information about trading futures contracts through Stock-Trak.

17

Diversification and Asset Allocation

Intuitively, we all know that diversification is important for managing investment risk. But how exactly does diversification work, and how can we be sure we have an efficiently diversified portfolio? Insightful answers can be gleaned from the modern theory of diversification and asset allocation. ■ In this chapter, we examine the role of diversification and asset allocation in investing. Most of us have a strong sense that diversification is important. After all, "Don't put all your eggs in one basket" is a bit of folk wisdom that seems to have stood the test of time quite well. Even so, the importance of diversification has not always been well understood. For example, noted author and market analyst Mark Twain recommended: "Put all your eggs in the one basket and—WATCH THAT BASKET!" This chapter shows why this was probably not Twain's best piece of advice.[1]

---

[1] This quote has been attributed to both Mark Twain (*The Tragedy of Pudd'nhead Wilson*, 1894) and Andrew Carnegie (*How to Succeed in Life*, 1903).

As we will see, diversification has a profound effect on portfolio risk and return. The role and impact of diversification were first formally explained in the early 1950s by financial pioneer Harry Markowitz, who shared the 1986 Nobel Prize in Economics for his insights. The primary goal of this chapter is to explain and explore the implications of Markowitz's remarkable discovery.

17.1   Expected Returns and Variances

In Chapter 1, we discussed how to calculate average returns and variances using historical data. We now begin to discuss how to analyze returns and variances when the information we have concerns future possible returns and their probabilities.

Expected Returns

We start with a straightforward case. Consider a period of time such as a year. We have two stocks, say Netcap and Jmart. Netcap is expected to have a return of 25 percent in the coming year; Jmart is expected to have a return of 20 percent during the same period.

In a situation such as this, if all investors agreed on these expected return values, why would anyone want to hold Jmart? After all, why invest in one stock when the expectation is that another will do better? Clearly, the answer must depend on the different risks of the two investments. The return on Netcap, although it is *expected* to be 25 percent, could turn out to be significantly higher or lower. Similarly, Jmart's *realized* return could be significantly higher or lower than expected.

For example, suppose the economy booms. In this case, we think Netcap will have a 70 percent return. But if the economy tanks and enters a recession, we think the return will be −20 percent. In this case, we say that there are *two states of the economy,* which means that there are two possible outcomes. This scenario is oversimplified of course, but it allows us to illustrate some key ideas without a lot of computational complexity.

Suppose we think boom and recession are equally likely to happen, that is, a 50–50 chance of each outcome. Table 17.1 illustrates the basic information we have described and some additional information about Jmart. Notice that Jmart earns 30 percent if there is a recession and 10 percent if there is a boom.

Obviously, if you buy one of these stocks, say, Jmart, what you earn in any particular year depends on what the economy does during that year. Suppose these probabilities stay the same through time. If you hold Jmart for a number of years, you'll earn 30 percent about half the time and 10 percent the other half. In this case, we say your **expected return** on Jmart, $E(R_J)$, is 20 percent:

expected return
Average return on a risky asset expected in the future.

$$E(R_J) = .50 \times 30\% + .50 \times 10\% = 20\%$$

In other words, you should expect to earn 20 percent from this stock, on average.

Table 17.1	States of the Economy and Stock Returns			
			Security Returns if State Occurs	
State of Economy	**Probability of State of Economy**		**Netcap**	**Jmart**
Recession	.50		−20%	30%
Boom	.50		70	10
	1.00			

Table 17.2	**Calculating Expected Returns**					
			Netcap		Jmart	
(1)	(2)	(3) Return if	(4)	(5) Return if	(6)
State of Economy	Probability of State of Economy	State Occurs	Product (2) × (3)	State Occurs	Product (2) × (5)
Recession	.50	−20%	−.10	30%	.15
Boom	.50	70	.35	10	.05
	1.00		$E(R_N) = 25\%$		$E(R_J) = 20\%$

For Netcap, the probabilities are the same, but the possible returns are different. Here we lose 20 percent half the time, and we gain 70 percent the other half. The expected return on Netcap, $E(R_N)$ is thus 25 percent:

$$E(R_N) = .50 \times -20\% + .50 \times 70\% = 25\%$$

Table 17.2 illustrates these calculations.

In Chapter 1, we defined a risk premium as the difference between the returns on a risky investment and a risk-free investment, and we calculated the historical risk premiums on some different investments. Using our projected returns, we can calculate the *projected* or *expected risk premium* as the difference between the expected return on a risky investment and the certain return on a risk-free investment.

For example, suppose risk-free investments are currently offering 8 percent. We will say that the risk-free rate, which we label R_f, is 8 percent. Given this, what is the projected risk premium on Jmart? On Netcap? Since the expected return on Jmart, $E(R_J)$, is 20 percent, the projected risk premium is

$$\text{Risk premium} = \text{Expected return} - \text{Risk-free rate} \qquad \textbf{17.1}$$
$$= E(R_J) - R_f$$
$$= 20\% - 8\%$$
$$= 12\%$$

Similarly, the risk premium on Netcap is $25\% - 8\% = 17\%$.

In general, the expected return on a security or other asset is simply equal to the sum of the possible returns multiplied by their probabilities. So, if we have 100 possible returns, we would multiply each one by its probability and then add up the results. The sum would be the expected return. The risk premium would then be the difference between this expected return and the risk-free rate.

Example 17.1 Unequal Probabilities.

Look again at Tables 17.1 and 17.2. Suppose you thought a boom would occur 20 percent of the time instead of 50 percent. What are the expected returns on Netcap and Jmart in this case? If the risk-free rate is 10 percent, what are the risk premiums?

The first thing to notice is that a recession must occur 80 percent of the time (1 − .20 = .80) since there are only two possibilities. With this in mind, Jmart has a 30 percent return in 80 percent of the years and a 10 percent return in 20 percent of the years. To calculate the expected return, we just multiply the possibilities by the probabilities and add up the results:

$$E(R_J) = .80 \times 30\% + .20 \times 10\% = 26\%$$

Table 17.3 summarizes the calculations for both stocks. Notice that the expected return on Netcap is −2 percent.

Table 17.3	**Calculating Expected Returns**					
			Netcap		Jmart	
(1)	**(2)**	**(3)**	**(4)**	**(5)**	**(6)**
State of Economy	**Probability of State of Economy**	**Return if State Occurs**	**Product (2) × (3)**	**Return if State Occurs**	**Product (2) × (5)**
Recession	.80	−20%	−.16	30%	.24
Boom	.20	70	.14	10	.02
	1.00		$E(R_N) = -2\%$		$E(R_J) = 26\%$

The risk premium for Jmart is 26% − 10% = 16% in this case. The risk premium for Netcap is negative: −2% − 10% = −12%. This is a little unusual, but, as we will see, it's not impossible.

Calculating the Variance

To calculate the variances of the returns on our two stocks, we first determine the squared deviations from the expected return. We then multiply each possible squared deviation by its probability. Next we add these up, and the result is the variance.

To illustrate, one of our stocks above, Jmart, has an expected return of 20 percent. In a given year, the return will actually be either 30 percent or 10 percent. The possible deviations are thus 30% − 20% = 10% or 10% − 20% = −10%. In this case, the variance is

$$\text{Variance} = \sigma^2 = .50 \times (10\%)^2 + .50 \times (-10\%)^2 = .01$$

The standard deviation is the square root of this:

$$\text{Standard deviation} = \sigma = \sqrt{.01} = .10 = 10\%$$

Table 17.4 summarizes these calculations and the expected return for both stocks. Notice that Netcap has a much larger variance. Netcap has the higher return, but Jmart has less risk. You could get a 70 percent return on your investment in Netcap, but you could also lose 20 percent. Notice that an investment in Jmart will always pay at least 10 percent.

Which of these stocks should you buy? We can't really say; it depends on your personal preferences regarding risk and return. We can be reasonably sure, however, that some investors would prefer one and some would prefer the other.

You've probably noticed that the way we calculated expected returns and variances here is somewhat different from the way we did it in Chapter 1 (and, probably, different from the way you learned it in "sadistics"). The reason is that we were examining historical returns in Chapter 1, so we estimated the average return and the variance based on some actual events. Here, we have projected *future* returns and their associated probabilities, so this is the information with which we must work.

Table 17.4	**Expected Returns and Variances**		
		Netcap	**Jmart**
Expected return, $E(R)$		25%	20%
Variance, σ^2		.2025	.0100
Standard deviation, σ		45%	10%

Example 17.2 More Unequal Probabilities

Going back to Table 17.3 in Example 17.1, what are the variances on our two stocks once we have unequal probabilities? What are the standard deviations?

We can summarize the needed calculations as follows:

(1) State of Economy	(2) Probability of State of Economy	(3) Return Deviation from Expected Return	(4) Squared Return Deviation	(5) Product (2) × (4)
Netcap				
Recession	.80	$-.20 - (-.02) = -.18$	.0324	.02592
Boom	.20	$.70 - (-.02) = .72$	.5184	.10368
				$\sigma_N^2 = .12960$
Jmart				
Recession	.80	$.30 - .26 = .04$	.0016	.00128
Boom	.20	$.10 - .26 = -.16$	.0256	.00512
				$\sigma_J^2 = .00640$

Based on these calculations, the standard deviation for Netcap is $\sigma_N = \sqrt{.1296} = 36\%$. The standard deviation for Jmart is much smaller, $\sigma_J = \sqrt{.0064}$, or 8 percent.

CHECK THIS

17.1a How do we calculate the expected return on a security?

17.1b In words, how do we calculate the variance of an expected return?

17.2 Portfolios

portfolio Group of assets such as stocks and bonds held by an investor.

Thus far in this chapter, we have concentrated on individual assets considered separately. However, most investors actually hold a **portfolio** of assets. All we mean by this is that investors tend to own more than just a single stock, bond, or other asset. Given that this is so, portfolio return and portfolio risk are of obvious relevance. Accordingly, we now discuss portfolio expected returns and variances.

Portfolio Weights

portfolio weight Percentage of a portfolio's total value invested in a particular asset.

There are many equivalent ways of describing a portfolio. The most convenient approach is to list the percentages of the total portfolio's value that are invested in each portfolio asset. We call these percentages the **portfolio weights**.

For example, if we have $50 in one asset and $150 in another, then our total portfolio is worth $200. The percentage of our portfolio in the first asset is $50/$200 = .25. The percentage of our portfolio in the second asset is $150/$200 = .75. Notice that the weights sum up to 1.00 since all of our money is invested somewhere.[2]

---

[2] Some of it could be in cash, of course, but we would then just consider cash to be another of the portfolio assets.

Portfolio Expected Returns

Let's go back to Netcap and Jmart. You put half your money in each. The portfolio weights are obviously .50 and .50. What is the pattern of returns on this portfolio? The expected return?

To answer these questions, suppose the economy actually enters a recession. In this case, half your money (the half in Netcap) loses 20 percent. The other half (the half in Jmart) gains 30 percent. Your portfolio return, R_P, in a recession will thus be

$$R_P = .50 \times -20\% + .50 \times 30\% = 5\%$$

Table 17.5 summarizes the remaining calculations. Notice that when a boom occurs, your portfolio would return 40 percent:

$$R_P = .50 \times 70\% + .50 \times 10\% = 40\%$$

As indicated in Table 17.5, the expected return on your portfolio, $E(R_P)$, is 22.5 percent.

We can save ourselves some work by calculating the expected return more directly. Given these portfolio weights, we could have reasoned that we expect half our money to earn 25 percent (the half in Netcap) and half of our money to earn 20 percent (the half in Jmart). Our portfolio expected return is thus

$$E(R_P) = .50 \times E(R_N) + .50 \times E(R_J)$$

$$= .50 \times 25\% + .50 \times 20\%$$

$$= 22.5\%$$

This is the same portfolio return that we calculated in Table 17.5.

This method of calculating the expected return on a portfolio works no matter how many assets there are in the portfolio. Suppose we had n assets in our portfolio, where n is any number at all. If we let x_i stand for the percentage of our money in Asset i, then the expected return is

$$E(R_P) = x_1 \times E(R_1) + x_2 \times E(R_2) + \cdots + x_n \times E(R_n) \qquad \textbf{17.2}$$

This says that the expected return on a portfolio is a straightforward combination of the expected returns on the assets in that portfolio. This seems somewhat obvious, but, as we will examine next, the obvious approach is not always the right one.

Table 17.5	**Expected Portfolio Return**			
	(1)	**(2)**	**(3)**	**(4)**
	State of Economy	**Probability of State of Economy**	**Portfolio Return if State Occurs**	**Product (2) × (3)**
	Recession	.50	$.50 \times -20\% + .50 \times 30\% = 5\%$	.025
	Boom	.50	$.50 \times 70\% + .50 \times 10\% = 40\%$	.200
				$E(R_P) = 22.5\%$

Example 17.3 More Unequal Probabilities

Suppose we had the following projections on three stocks:

State of Economy	Probability of State of Economy	Returns		
		Stock A	Stock B	Stock C
Boom	.50	10%	15%	20%
Bust	.50	8	4	0

We want to calculate portfolio expected returns in two cases. First, what would be the expected return on a portfolio with equal amounts invested in each of the three stocks? Second, what would be the expected return if half of the portfolio were in A, with the remainder equally divided between B and C?

From our earlier discussion, the expected returns on the individual stocks are

$$E(R_A) = 9.0\% \qquad E(R_B) = 9.5\% \qquad E(R_C) = 10.0\%$$

(Check these for practice.) If a portfolio has equal investments in each asset, the portfolio weights are all the same. Such a portfolio is said to be *equally weighted*. Since there are three stocks in this case, the weights are all equal to 1/3. The portfolio expected return is thus

$$E(R_P) = 1/3 \times 9.0\% + 1/3 \times 9.5\% + 1/3 \times 10.0\% = 9.5\%$$

In the second case, check that the portfolio expected return is 9.375%.

Portfolio Variance

From the preceding discussion, the expected return on a portfolio that contains equal investments in Netcap and Jmart is 22.5 percent. What is the standard deviation of return on this portfolio? Simple intuition might suggest that half of our money has a standard deviation of 45 percent, and the other half has a standard deviation of 10 percent. So the portfolio's standard deviation might be calculated as follows:

$$\sigma_P = .50 \times 45\% + .50 \times 10\% = 27.5\%$$

Unfortunately, this approach is *completely incorrect!*

Let's see what the standard deviation really is. Table 17.6 summarizes the relevant calculations. As we see, the portfolio's variance is about .031, and its standard deviation is less than we thought—it's only 17.5 percent. What is illustrated here is that the variance on a portfolio is *not* generally a simple combination of the variances of the assets in the portfolio.

We can illustrate this point a little more dramatically by considering a slightly different set of portfolio weights. Suppose we put 2/11 (about 18 percent) in Netcap and the other 9/11 (about 82 percent) in Jmart. If a recession occurs, this portfolio will have a return of

$$R_P = 2/11 \times -20\% + 9/11 \times 30\% = 20.91\%$$

If a boom occurs, this portfolio will have a return of

$$R_P = 2/11 \times 70\% + 9/11 \times 10\% = 20.91\%$$

Notice that the return is the same no matter what happens. No further calculation is needed: This portfolio has a *zero* variance and no risk!

Table 17.6		**Calculating Portfolio Variance**		
(1)	**(2)**	**(3)**	**(4)**	**(5)**
State of Economy	**Probability of State of Economy**	**Portfolio Returns if State Occurs**	**Squared Deviation from Expected Return**	**Product (2) × (4)**
Recession	.50	5%	$(.05 - .225)^2 = .030625$	.0153125
Boom	.50	40	$(.40 - .225)^2 = .030625$	.0153125
				$\sigma_P^2 = .030625$
				$\sigma_P = \sqrt{.030625} = 17.5\%$

This is a nice bit of financial alchemy. We take two quite risky assets and by mixing them just right, we create a riskless portfolio. It seems very clear that combining assets into portfolios can substantially alter the risks faced by an investor. This is a crucial observation, and we will begin to explore its implications in the next section.[3]

Example 17.4 Portfolio Variance and Standard Deviations

In Example 17.3, what are the standard deviations of the two portfolios?

To answer, we first have to calculate the portfolio returns in the two states. We will work with the second portfolio, which has 50 percent in Stock A and 25 percent in each of stocks B and C. The relevant calculations are summarized as follows:

State of Economy	Probability of State of Economy	Returns			
		Stock A	**Stock B**	**Stock C**	**Portfolio**
Boom	.50	10%	15%	20%	13.75%
Bust	.50	8	4	0	5.00

The portfolio return when the economy booms is calculated as

$$R_P = .50 \times 10\% + .25 \times 15\% + .25 \times 20\% = 13.75\%$$

The return when the economy goes bust is calculated the same way. Check that it's 5 percent and also check that the expected return on the portfolio is 9.375%. The variance is thus

$$\sigma_P^2 = .50 \times (.1375 - .09375)^2 + .50 \times (.05 - .09375)^2 = .0019141$$

The standard deviation is thus about 4.375 percent. For our equally weighted portfolio, redo these calculations and check that the standard deviation is about 5.5 percent.

CHECK THIS

17.2a What is a portfolio weight?

17.2b How do we calculate the variance of an expected return?

---

[3] Earlier, we had a risk-free rate of 8 percent. Now we have, in effect, a 20.91 percent risk-free rate. If this situation actually existed, there would be a very profitable arbitrage opportunity! In reality, we expect that all riskless investments would have the same return.

17.3 Diversification and Portfolio Risk

Our discussion to this point has focused on some hypothetical securities. We've seen that portfolio risks can, in principle, be quite different from the risks of the assets that make up the portfolio. We now look more closely at the risk of an individual asset versus the risk of a portfolio of many different assets. As we did in Chapter 1, we will examine some stock market history to get an idea of what happens with actual investments in U.S. capital markets.

The Effect of Diversification: Another Lesson from Market History

In Chapter 1, we saw that the standard deviation of the annual return on a portfolio of large common stocks was about 20 percent per year. Does this mean that the standard deviation of the annual return on a typical stock in that group is about 20 percent? As you might suspect by now, the answer is no. This is an extremely important observation.

To examine the relationship between portfolio size and portfolio risk, Table 17.7 illustrates typical average annual standard deviations for equally weighted portfolios that contain different numbers of randomly selected NYSE securities.

In column 2 of Table 17.7, we see that the standard deviation for a "portfolio" of one security is just under 50 percent per year at 49.24 percent. What this means is that if you randomly select a single NYSE stock and put all your money into it, your standard

Table 17.7	Portfolio Standard Deviations		
(1) **Number of Stocks in Portfolio**	**(2)** **Average Standard Deviation of Annual Portfolio Returns**	**(3)** **Ratio of Portfolio Standard Deviation to Standard Deviation of a Single Stock**
1	49.24%	1.00
2	37.36	.76
4	29.69	.60
6	26.64	.54
8	24.98	.51
10	23.93	.49
20	21.68	.44
30	20.87	.42
40	20.46	.42
50	20.20	.41
100	19.69	.40
200	19.42	.39
300	19.34	.39
400	19.29	.39
500	19.27	.39
1,000	19.21	.39

Source: These figures are from Table 1 in Meir Statman, "How Many Stocks Make a Diversified Portfolio?" *Journal of Financial and Quantitative Analysis* 22 (September 1987), pp. 353–64. They were derived from E.J. Elton and M.J. Gruber, "Risk Reduction and Portfolio Size: An Analytic Solution," *Journal of Business* 50 (October 1977), pp. 415–37.

deviation of return would typically have been about 50 percent per year. Obviously, such a strategy has significant risk! If you were to randomly select two NYSE securities and put half your money in each, your average annual standard deviation would have been about 37 percent.

The important thing to notice in Table 17.7 is that the standard deviation declines as the number of securities is increased. By the time we have 100 randomly chosen stocks (and 1 percent invested in each), the portfolio's volatility has declined by 60 percent, from 50 percent per year to 20 percent per year. With 500 securities, the standard deviation is 19.27 percent per year, similar to the 20 percent per year we saw in Chapter 1 for large common stocks. The small difference exists because the portfolio securities, portfolio weights, and the time periods covered are not identical.

The Principle of Diversification

Figure 17.1 illustrates the point we've been discussing. What we have plotted is the standard deviation of the return versus the number of stocks in the portfolio. Notice in Figure 17.1 that the benefit in terms of risk reduction from adding securities drops off as we add more and more. By the time we have 10 securities, most of the diversification effect is already realized, and by the time we get to 30 or so, there is very little remaining benefit. In other words, the benefit of further diversification increases at a decreasing rate, so the "law of diminishing returns" applies here as it does in so many other places.

Figure 17.1 illustrates two key points. First, some of the riskiness associated with individual assets can be eliminated by forming portfolios. The process of spreading an investment across assets (and thereby forming a portfolio) is called *diversification*. The **principle of diversification** tells us that spreading an investment across many assets will eliminate some of the risk. Not surprisingly, risks that can be eliminated by diversification are called "diversifiable" risks.

principle of diversification
Spreading an investment across a number of assets will eliminate some, but not all, of the risk.

The second point is equally important. There is a minimum level of risk that cannot be eliminated by simply diversifying. This minimum level is labeled "nondiversifiable risk" in Figure 17.1. Taken together, these two points are another important lesson from

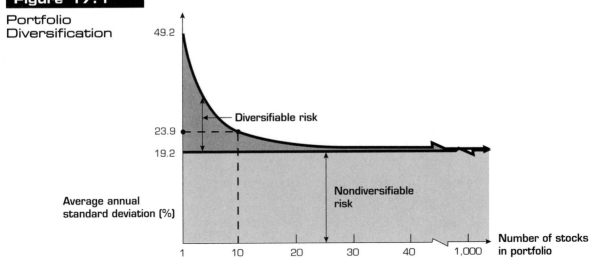

Figure 17.1

Portfolio
Diversification

financial market history: Diversification reduces risk, but only up to a point. Put another way, some risk is diversifiable and some is not.

CHECK THIS

17.3a What happens to the standard deviation of return for a portfolio if we increase the number of securities in the portfolio?

17.3b What is the principle of diversification?

Correlation and Diversification

We've seen that diversification is important. What we haven't discussed is how to get the most out of diversification. For example, in our previous section, we investigated what happens if we simply spread our money evenly across randomly chosen stocks. We saw that significant risk reduction resulted from this strategy, but you might wonder whether even larger gains could be achieved by a more sophisticated approach. As we begin to examine that question here, the answer is yes.

Why Diversification Works

correlation The tendency of the returns on two assets to move together.

Why diversification reduces portfolio risk as measured by the portfolio standard deviation is important and worth exploring in some detail. The key concept is **correlation**, which is the extent to which the returns on two assets move together. If the returns on two assets tend to move up and down together, we say they are *positively* correlated. If they tend to move in opposite directions, we say they are *negatively* correlated. If there is no particular relationship between the two assets, we say they are *uncorrelated*.

The *correlation coefficient,* which we use to measure correlation, ranges from -1 to $+1$, and we will denote the correlation between the returns on two assets, say A and B, as $\text{Corr}(R_A, R_B)$. The Greek letter ρ (rho) is often used to designate correlation as well. A correlation of $+1$ indicates that the two assets have a *perfect* positive correlation. For example, suppose that whatever return Asset A realizes, either up or down, Asset B does the same thing by exactly twice as much. In this case, they are perfectly correlated because the movement on one is completely predictable from the movement on the other. Notice, however, that perfect correlation does not necessarily mean they move by the same amount.

A zero correlation means that the two assets are uncorrelated. If we know that one asset is up, then we have no idea what the other one is likely to do; there simply is no relation between them. Perfect negative correlation [$\text{Corr}(R_A, R_B) = -1$] indicates that they always move in opposite directions. Figure 17.2 illustrates the three benchmark cases of perfect positive, perfect negative, and zero correlation.

Diversification works because security returns are generally not perfectly correlated. We will be more precise about the impact of correlation on portfolio risk in just a moment. For now, it is useful to simply think about combining two assets into a portfolio. If the two assets are highly correlated (the correlation is near $+1$), then they have a strong tendency to move up and down together. As a result, they offer limited diversification benefit. For example, two stocks from the same industry, say, General Motors and Ford, will tend to be relatively highly correlated since the companies are in essentially the same business, and a portfolio of two such stocks is not likely to be very diversified.

Figure 17.2 Correlations

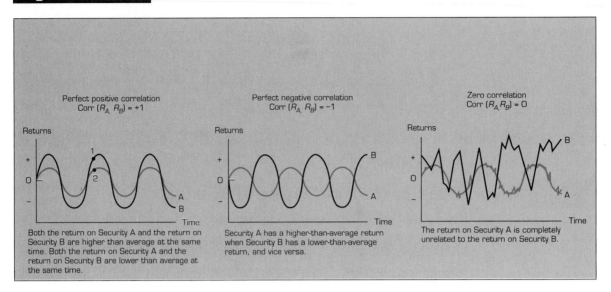

Perfect positive correlation
Corr $(R_A, R_B) = +1$

Both the return on Security A and the return on Security B are higher than average at the same time. Both the return on Security A and the return on Security B are lower than average at the same time.

Perfect negative correlation
Corr $(R_A, R_B) = -1$

Security A has a higher-than-average return when Security B has a lower-than-average return, and vice versa.

Zero correlation
Corr $(R_A, R_B) = 0$

The return on Security A is completely unrelated to the return on Security B.

In contrast, if the two assets are negatively correlated, then they tend to move in opposite directions; whenever one zigs, the other tends to zag. In such a case, there will be substantial diversification benefit because variation in the return on one asset tends to be offset by variation in the opposite direction from the other. In fact, if two assets have a perfect negative correlation [Corr(R_A, R_B) $= -1$], then it is possible to combine them such that all risk is eliminated. Looking back at our example involving Jmart and Netcap in which we were able to eliminate all of the risk, what we now see is that they must be perfectly negatively correlated.

To further illustrate the impact of diversification on portfolio risk, suppose we observed the actual annual returns on two stocks, A and B, for the years 1995–1999. We summarize these returns in Table 17.8. In addition to actual returns on stocks A and B, we also calculated the returns on an equally weighted portfolio of A and B in Table 17.8. We label this portfolio as AB. In 1996, for example, Stock A returned 10 percent and Stock B returned 15 percent. Since Portfolio AB is half invested in each, its return for the year was

$$1/2 \times 10\% + 1/2 \times 15\% = 12.5\%$$

The returns for the other years are calculated similarly.

Table 17.8 **Annual Returns on Stocks A and B**

Year	Stock A	Stock B	Portfolio AB
1995	10%	15%	12.5%
1996	30%	−10%	10%
1997	−10%	25%	7.5%
1998	5%	20%	12.5%
1999	10%	15%	12.5%
Average returns	9%	13%	11%
Standard deviations	14.3%	13.5%	2.2%

At the bottom of Table 17.8, we calculated the average returns and standard deviations on the two stocks and the equally weighted portfolio. These averages and standard deviations are calculated just as they were in Chapter 1 (check a couple just to refresh your memory). The impact of diversification is apparent. The two stocks have standard deviations in the 13 percent to 14 percent per year range, but the portfolio's volatility is only 2.2 percent. In fact, if we compare the portfolio to Stock B, it has a higher return (11 percent vs. 9 percent) and much less risk.

Figure 17.3 illustrates in more detail what is occurring with our example. Here we have three bar graphs showing the year-by-year returns on Stocks A and B and Portfolio AB. Examining the graphs, we see that in 1996, for example, Stock A earned 30 percent while Stock B lost 10 percent. The following year, Stock B earned 25 percent while A lost 10 percent. These ups and downs tend to cancel out in our portfolio, however, with the result that there is much less variation in return from year to year. In other words, the correlation between the returns on stocks A and B is relatively low.

Calculating the correlation between stocks A and B·is not difficult, but it would require us to digress a bit. Instead, we will explain the needed calculation in the next chapter, where we build on the principles developed here.

Calculating Portfolio Risk

We've seen that correlation is an important determinant of portfolio risk. To further pursue this issue, we need to know how to calculate portfolio variances directly. For a portfolio of two assets, A and B, the variance of the return on the portfolio, σ^2_P, is given by Equation 17.3:

$$\sigma_P^2 = x_A^2\sigma_A^2 + x_B^2\sigma_B^2 + 2x_Ax_B\sigma_A\sigma_B\text{Corr}(R_A,R_B) \qquad 17.3$$

In this equation, x_A and x_B are the percentages invested in assets A and B. Notice that $x_A + x_B = 1$. (Why?)

Figure 17.3   Impact of Diversification

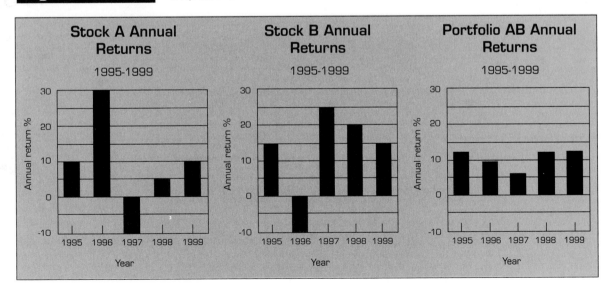

Equation 17.3 looks a little involved, but its use is straightforward. For example, suppose Stock A has a standard deviation of 40 percent per year and Stock B has a standard deviation of 60 percent per year. The correlation between them is .15. If you put half your money in each, what is your portfolio standard deviation?

To answer, we just plug the numbers into Equation 17.3. Note that x_A and x_B are each equal to .50, while σ_A and σ_B are .40 and .60, respectively. Taking $\text{Corr}(R_A, R_B) = .15$, we have

$$\sigma_P^2 = .50^2 \times .40^2 + .50^2 \times .60^2 + 2 \times .50 \times .50 \times .40 \times .60 \times .15$$

$$= .25 \times .16 + .25 \times .36 + .018$$

$$= .148$$

Thus, the portfolio variance is .148. As always, variances are not easy to interpret since they are based on squared returns, so we calculate the standard deviation by taking the square root:

$$\sigma_P = \sqrt{.148} = .3847 = 38.47\%$$

Once again, we see the impact of diversification. This portfolio has a standard deviation of 38.47 percent, which is less than either of the standard deviations on the two assets that are in the portfolio.

Example 17.5 Portfolio Variance and Standard Deviation

In the example we just examined, Stock A has a standard deviation of 40 percent per year and Stock B has a standard deviation of 60 percent per year. Suppose now that the correlation between them is .35. Also suppose you put one-fourth of your money in stock A. What is your portfolio standard deviation?

If you put 1/4 (or .25) in Stock A, you must have 3/4 (or .75) in Stock B, so $x_A = .25$ and $x_B = .75$. Making use of our portfolio variance equation (17.3), we have

$$\sigma_P^2 = .25^2 \times .40^2 + .75^2 \times .60^2 + 2 \times .25 \times .75 \times .40 \times .60 \times .35$$

$$= .0625 \times .16 + .5625 \times .36 + .0315$$

$$= .244$$

Thus the portfolio variance is .244. Taking the square root, we get

$$\sigma_P = \sqrt{.244} = .49396 \approx 49\%$$

This portfolio has a standard deviation of 49 percent, which is between the individual standard deviations. This shows that a portfolio's standard deviation isn't necessarily less than the individual standard deviations.

To illustrate why correlation is an important, practical, real-world consideration, suppose that as a very conservative, risk-averse investor, you decide to invest all of your money in a bond mutual fund. Based on your analysis, you think this fund has an expected return of 6 percent with a standard deviation of 10 percent per year. A stock fund is available, however, with an expected return of 12 percent, but the standard deviation of 15 percent is too high for your taste. Also, the correlation between the returns on the two funds is about .10.

Is the decision to invest 100 percent in the bond fund a wise one, even for a very risk-averse investor? The answer is no; in fact, it is a bad decision for any investor. To see why, Table 17.9 shows expected returns and standard deviations available from different combinations of the two mutual funds. In constructing the table, we begin with 100 percent in the stock fund and work our way down to 100 percent in the bond fund by reducing the percentage in the stock fund in increments of .05. These calculations are all done just like our examples just above; you should check some (or all) of them for practice.

Beginning on the first row in Table 17.9, we have 100 percent in the stock fund, so our expected return is 12 percent, and our standard deviation is 15 percent. As we begin to move out of the stock fund and into the bond fund, we are not surprised to see both the expected return and the standard deviation decline. However, what might be surprising to you is the fact that the standard deviation falls only so far and then begins to rise again. In other words, beyond a point, adding more of the lower risk bond fund actually *increases* your risk!

The best way to see what is going on is to plot the various combinations of expected returns and standard deviations calculated in Table 17.9 as we do in Figure 17.4. We simply placed the standard deviations from Table 17.9 on the horizontal axis and the corresponding expected returns on the vertical axis.

Examining the plot in Figure 17.4 on page 504, we see that the various combinations of risk and return available all fall on a smooth curve (in fact, for the geometrically inclined, it's a hyperbola). This curve is called an **investment opportunity set** because it shows the possible combinations of risk and return available from portfolios of these two assets. One important thing to notice is that, as we have shown, there is a portfolio that has the smallest standard deviation (or variance—same thing) of all. It is labeled "minimum variance portfolio" in Figure 17.4. What are (approximately) its expected return and standard deviation?

investment opportunity set
Collection of possible risk–return combinations available from portfolios of individual assets.

Table 17.9	Risk and Return with Stocks and Bonds		
Portfolio Weights			
Stocks	**Bonds**	**Expected Return**	**Standard Deviation**
1.00	.00	12.00%	15.00%
.95	.05	11.70	14.31
.90	.10	11.40	13.64
.85	.15	11.10	12.99
.80	.20	10.80	12.36
.75	.25	10.50	11.77
.70	.30	10.20	11.20
.65	.35	9.90	10.68
.60	.40	9.60	10.28
.55	.45	9.30	9.78
.50	.50	9.00	9.42
.45	.55	8.70	9.12
.40	.60	8.40	8.90
.35	.65	8.10	8.75
.30	.70	7.80	8.69
.25	.75	7.50	8.71
.20	.80	7.20	8.82
.15	.85	6.90	9.01
.10	.90	6.60	9.27
.05	.95	6.30	9.60
.00	1.00	6.00	10.00

Egg Basket Analysis

Diversify. Don't put all your eggs in one basket. We have all heard the wisdom, but few of us heed it in picking mutual funds. People who own the Fidelity Contrafund, say, may branch out to Fidelity Growth & Income with their next fund purchase, thinking they're diversifying. They aren't.

In the statistical scheme of things, these are two peas in a pod. They may both prove to be good funds, but the likelihood is that in a month when one goes up, the other will, too, and when one goes down, so will the other.

So, too, with almost any pair of big-company stock funds—Fidelity Magellan and Vanguard Index 500, Fidelity Destiny I and Vanguard Windsor. They tend to track pretty closely. You don't accomplish a lot by dividing your eggs between those two baskets. You might as well put all your money in the one blue-chip fund you like the most.

So, too, any two long-term domestic bond funds are likely to match each other's ups and downs pretty well, even if they have seemingly different objectives—one junk bonds and the other Ginnie Mae, one a Treasury bond fund and the other a corporate fund.

Surprisingly, most bond funds have in recent years become similar to most stock funds in the general timing of their up and down movements. Look at what has happened on Wall Street recently. Last year interest rates went down, sending bond funds up and stock funds with them. In early April the process reversed. They crashed in unison.

If you want true diversity, therefore, make sure you spread your money among funds that do not move in lockstep with each other. The Benham Treasury Note Fund and the Lexington Strategic Silver Fund are one such pair. When inflation perks up, so, most of the time, do silver prices and interest rates. That makes the T-note fund do badly and the Silver fund do well. The reverse is also true.

Heartland Value Fund and MFS World Governments-A bond fund are another intriguing pair. When one zigs, the other zags. These two funds are not mirror opposites, to be sure, but they really do travel on different wavelengths.

Here's yet another pair of funds that tend to veer off in different directions: GAM International Fund and Vanguard GNMA Fund.

How did we find these diversifications? With a computer. We fed it monthly returns since 1986 for 560 funds and asked it to calculate, for each pair, what statisticians call the correlation coefficient. That's a measure of how closely two data series track each other.

If you want to apply correlation analysis to your fund portfolio, try Fund Analyzer, recently out from Value Line. You feed the program two or more fund names. It tells you the risk and return of each fund over the past ten years, as well as the risk and return of a blend (see graphs).

The Value Line software assumes that you, like any warm-blooded investor, want two things from your portfolio: high return and low risk. Alas, you usually have to trade one of these objectives off against the other. A stock fund will have high risk (high volatility) and a high expected return. A short-term bond fund will be low on both scores. A 50/50 blend will be in the middle on both measures.

You don't need a fancy computer program to tell you how large a position you need in the short bond fund to blend with your stock fund. It's a matter of taste for risk. The short fund, being less vulnerable to interest rate changes, is the less volatile. So throw enough of it into your mix to enable you to sleep well at night. You can do that in your head or on the back of an old charge slip.

But that won't give you true diversity. For that you need funds that have a low degree of correlation with

Now we see clearly why a 100 percent bonds strategy is a poor one. With a 10 percent standard deviation, the bond fund offers an expected return of 6 percent. However, Table 17.9 shows us that a combination of about 60 percent stocks and 40 percent bonds has almost the same standard deviation, but a return of about 9.6 percent. Comparing 9.6 percent to 6 percent, we see that this portfolio has a return that is fully 60 percent greater ($6\% \times 1.6 = 9.6\%$) with the same risk. Our conclusion? Asset allocation matters.

Given the apparent importance of asset allocation, it is not too surprising to learn that this analysis is becoming widespread in investment practice. The nearby Investment Updates box presents an article from *Forbes* discussing its use for mutual fund investors. Notice how closely the discussion tracks our development.

each other. Then diversification really pays. The return of a 50/50 blend lies right on the midpoint of the two funds' returns, but their combined risk level is a bit *lower* than an average of the two funds' risk levels.

Look at the Heartland Value/ MFES World pair in the lower-right graph. The returns for the funds over the past ten years have averaged 14.3% and 11.8%, respectively. A blend would have earned you 13%, right in the middle. But the risk of the blend is below the average of the two funds' risk measures.

This, graphically, is what you gain by not putting all your eggs in one basket.

Source: Forbes, May 6, 1996.

Balancing Funds. Start with upper left and go clockwise. Fidelity Contrafund + Fidelity Growth & Income: Two eggs, one basket. Less return, less risk. Gain from diversification? Zilch. Fidelity Magellan + Fidelity Ginnie Mae: Just a small gain from diversification. Heartland Value + MFS World Governments-A: Give up some return, but see the risk dramatically decline. Lexington Strategic Silver + Benham Treasury Note: Dramatic diversification. When one wiggles, the other waggles.

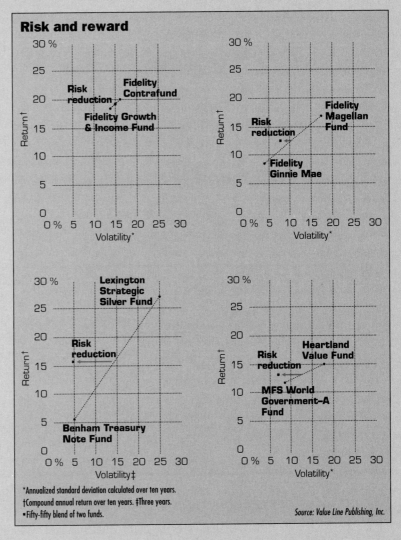

Risk and reward

*Annualized standard deviation calculated over ten years.
†Compound annual return over ten years. ‡Three years.
▪Fifty-fifty blend of two funds.

Source: Value Line Publishing, Inc.

efficient portfolio A portfolio that offers the highest return for its level of risk.

Going back to Figure 17.4, notice that any portfolio that plots below the minimum variance portfolio is a poor choice because, no matter which one you pick, there is another portfolio with the same risk and a much better return. In the jargon of finance, we say that these undesirable portfolios are *dominated* and/or *inefficient*. Either way, we mean that given their level of risk, the expected return is inadequate compared to some other portfolio of equivalent risk. A portfolio that offers the highest return for its level of risk is said to be an **efficient portfolio**. In Figure 17.4, the minimum variance portfolio and all portfolios that plot above it are therefore efficient.

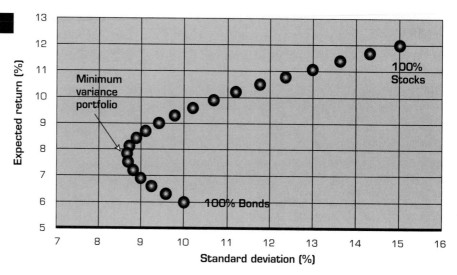

Figure 17.4

Risk and Return with Stocks and Bonds

Example 17.6 More Portfolio Variance and Standard Deviation

Looking at Table 17.9, suppose you put 57.627 percent in the stock fund. What is your expected return? Your standard deviation? How does this compare with the bond fund?

If you put 57.627 percent in stocks, you must have 42.373 percent in bonds, so $\chi_A = .57627$ and $\chi_B = .42373$. Making use of our portfolio variance equation (17.3), we have

$$\sigma_P^2 = .57627^2 \times .15^2 + .42373^2 \times .10^2 + 2 \times .57627 \times .42373 \times .15 \times .10 \times .10$$
$$= .332 \times .0225 + .180 \times .01 + .0007325$$
$$= .01$$

Thus, the portfolio variance is .01, so the standard deviation is .1, or 10 percent. Check that the expected return is 9.46 percent. Compared to the bond fund, the standard deviation is now identical, but the expected return is almost 350 basis points higher.

More on Correlation and the Risk-Return Trade-Off

Given the expected returns and standard deviations on the two assets, the shape of the investment opportunity set in Figure 17.4 depends on the correlation. The lower the correlation, the more bowed to the left the investment opportunity set will be. To illustrate, Figure 17.5 shows the investment opportunity for correlations of $-1, 0$, and $+1$ for two stocks, A and B. Notice that Stock A has an expected return of 12 percent and a standard deviation of 15 percent, while Stock B has an expected return of 6 percent and a standard deviation of 10 percent. These are the same expected returns and standard deviations we used to build Figure 17.4, and the calculations are all done the same way; just the correlations are different. Notice also that we use the symbol ρ to stand for the correlation coefficient.

In Figure 17.5, when the correlation is $+1$, the investment opportunity set is a straight line connecting the two stocks, so, as expected, there is little or no diversification benefit. As the correlation declines to zero, the bend to the left becomes pronounced. For correlations between $+1$ and zero, there would simply be a less pronounced bend.

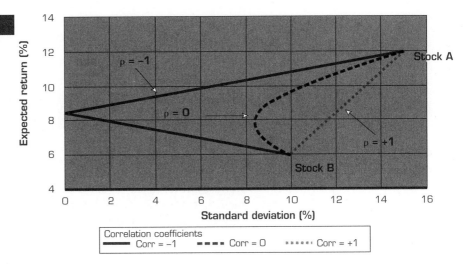

Figure 17.5

Risk and Return
with Two
Assets

Finally, as the correlation becomes negative, the bend becomes quite pronounced, and the investment opportunity set actually becomes two straight-line segments when the correlation hits −1. Notice that the minimum variance portfolio has a *zero* variance in this case.

It is sometimes desirable to be able to calculate the percentage investments needed to create the minimum variance portfolio. We will just state the result here, but a problem at the end of the chapter asks you to show that the weight on Asset A in the minimum variance portfolio, x_A^*, is

$$x_A^* = \frac{\sigma_B^2 - \sigma_A \sigma_B \, \text{Corr}(R_A, R_B)}{\sigma_A^2 + \sigma_B^2 - 2\sigma_A\sigma_B \, \text{Corr}(R_A, R_B)}$$ **17.4**

In Equation 17.4, we will take Asset A to be the one with the larger standard deviation. If the standard deviations happened to be the same, then Asset A could be either.

Example 17.7 **Finding the Minimum Variance Portfolio**

Looking back at Table 17.9, what combination of the stock fund and the bond fund has the lowest possible standard deviation? What is the minimum possible standard deviation?

Recalling that the standard deviations for the stock fund and bond fund were .15 and .10, respectively, and noting that the correlation was .1, we have

$$x_A^* = \frac{.10^2 - .15 \times .10 \times .10}{.15^2 + .10^2 - 2 \times .15 \times .10 \times .10}$$

$$= .288136$$

$$\approx 28.8\%$$

Thus, the minimum variance portfolio has 28.8 percent in stocks and the balance, 71.2 percent, in bonds. Plugging these into our formula for portfolio variance, we have

$$\sigma_P^2 = .288^2 \times .15^2 + .712^2 \times .10^2 + 2 \times .288 \times .712 \times .15 \times .10 \times .10$$

$$= .007551$$

The standard deviation is the square root of .007551, about 8.7 percent. Notice that this is where the minimum occurs in Figure 17.5.

17.5 The Markowitz Efficient Frontier

In the previous section, we looked closely at the risk-return possibilities available when we consider combining two risky assets. Now we are left with an obvious question: What happens when we consider combining three or more risky assets? As we will see, at least on a conceptual level, the answer turns out to be a straightforward extension of our previous analysis.

Risk and Return with Multiple Assets

When we consider multiple assets, the formula for computing portfolio standard deviation becomes cumbersome; indeed, a great deal of calculation is required once we have much beyond two assets. As a result, although the required calculations are not difficult, they can be very tedious and are best relegated to a computer. We therefore will not delve into how to calculate portfolio standard deviations when there are many assets.

Figure 17.6 shows the result of calculating the expected returns and portfolio standard deviations when there are three assets. To illustrate the importance of asset allocation, we calculated expected returns and standard deviations from portfolios composed of three key investment types: U.S. stocks, foreign (non-U.S.) stocks, and U.S. bonds. These asset classes are not highly correlated in general; we assume a zero correlation in all cases. The expected returns and standard deviations are as follows:

	Expected Returns	**Standard Deviations**
Foreign stocks	18%	35%
U.S. stocks	12	22
U.S. bonds	8	14

Figure 17.6

Markowitz Efficient Portfolio

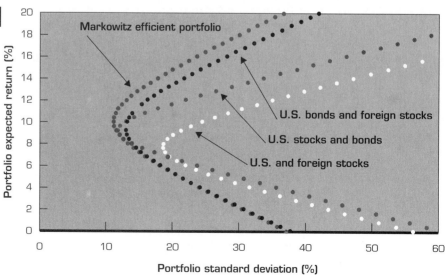

In Figure 17.6, each point plotted is a possible risk-return combination. Comparing the result with our two-asset case in Figure 17.4, we see that now not only do some assets plot below the minimum variance portfolio on a smooth curve, but we have portfolios plotting inside as well. Only combinations that plot on the upper left-hand boundary are efficient; all the rest are inefficient. This upper left-hand boundary is called the **Markowitz efficient frontier**, and it represents the set of portfolios with the maximum return for a given standard deviation.

Markowitz efficient frontier The set of portfolios with the maximum return for a given standard deviation.

Once again, Figure 17.6 makes it clear that asset allocation matters. For example, a portfolio of 100 percent U.S. stocks is highly inefficient. For the same standard deviation, there is a portfolio with an expected return almost 400 basis points, or 4 percent, higher. Or, for the same expected return, there is a portfolio with about half as much risk!

The analysis in this section can be extended to any number of assets or asset classes. In principle, it is possible to compute efficient frontiers using thousands of assets. As a practical matter, however, this analysis is most widely used with a relatively small number of asset classes. For example, most investment banks maintain so-called model portfolios. These are simply recommended asset allocation strategies typically involving three to six asset categories.

A primary reason that the Markowitz analysis is not usually extended to large collections of individual assets has to do with data requirements. The inputs into the analysis are (1) expected returns on all assets; (2) standard deviations on all assets; and (3) correlations between every pair of assets. Moreover, these inputs have to be measured with some precision, or we just end up with a garbage-in, garbage-out (GIGO) system.

Suppose we just look at 2,000 NYSE stocks. We need 2,000 expected returns and standard deviations. This is already a problem since returns on individual stocks cannot be predicted with precision at all. To make matters worse, however, we need to know the correlation between every *pair* of stocks. With 2,000 stocks, there are $2,000 \times 1,999 / 2 = 1,999,000$, or almost 2 million unique pairs![4] Also, as with expected returns, correlations between individual stocks are very difficult to predict accurately. We will return to this issue in our next chapter, where we show that there may be an extremely elegant way around the problem.

CHECK THIS

17.5a What is the Markowitz efficient frontier?

17.5b Why is Markowitz portfolio analysis most commonly used to make asset allocation decisions?

17.6 Summary and Conclusions

In this chapter, we covered the basics of diversification and portfolio risk and return. From this material we saw that:

1. A portfolio's expected return is a simple weighted combination of the expected returns on the assets in the portfolio, but the standard deviation on a portfolio is not.

---

[4] With 2,000 stocks, there are $2,000^2 = 4,000,000$ possible pairs. Of these, 2,000 involve pairing a stock with itself. Further, we recognize that the correlation between A and B is the same as the correlation between B and A, so we only need to actually calculate half of the remaining 3,998,000 correlations.

2. Diversification is a very important consideration. The principle of diversification tells us that spreading an investment across many assets can reduce some, but not all, of the risk. Based on U.S. stock market history, for example, about 60 percent of the risk associated with owning individual stocks can be eliminated by naive diversification.

3. Diversification works because asset returns are not perfectly correlated. All else the same, the lower the correlation, the greater is the gain from diversification.

4. When we consider the possible combinations of risk and return available from portfolios of assets, we find that some are inefficient (or dominated), meaning that they offer too little return for their risk.

5. Finally, for any group of assets, there is a set that is efficient. That set is known as the Markowitz efficient frontier.

The most important thing to carry away from this chapter is an understanding of diversification and why it works. Once you understand this, then the importance of asset allocation follows immediately. Our story is not complete, however, because we have not considered one important asset class: riskless assets. This will be the first task in our next chapter.

GET REAL

This chapter explained diversification, a very important consideration for real-world investors and money managers. The chapter also explored the famous Markowitz efficient portfolio concept, which shows how (and why) asset allocation affects portfolio risk and return.

Building a diversified portfolio is not a trivial task. Of course, as we discussed many chapters ago, mutual funds provide one way for investors to build diversified portfolios, but there are some significant caveats concerning mutual funds as a diversification tool. First of all, investors sometimes assume a fund is diversified simply because it holds a relatively large number of stocks. However, with the exception of some index funds, most mutual funds will reflect a particular style of investing, either explicity, as stated in the fund's objective, or implicitly, as favored by the fund manager. For example, in the mid-to late-1990s, stocks as a whole did very well, but mutual funds that concentrated on smaller stocks generally did not do well at all.

It is tempting to buy a number of mutual funds to ensure broad diversification, but even this may not work. Within a given fund family, the same manager may actually be responsible for multiple funds. In addition, managers within a large fund family frequently have similar views about the market and individual companies.

Thinking just about stocks for the moment, what does an investor need to consider to build a well-diversified portfolio? At a minimum, such a portfolio probably needs to be diversified across industries, with no undue concentrations in particular sectors of the economy; it needs to be diversified by company size (small, midcap, and large), and it needs to be diversified across "growth" (i.e., high-P/E) and "value" (low-P/E) stocks. Perhaps the most controversial diversification issue concerns international diversification. The correlation between international stock exchanges is surprisingly low, suggesting large benefits from diversifying globally.

Perhaps the most disconcerting fact about diversification is that it leads to the following paradox: A well-diversified portfolio will always be invested in something that does not do well! Put differently, such a portfolio will almost always have both winners and losers. In many ways, that's the whole idea. Even so, it requires a lot of financial discipline to stay diversified when some portion of your portfolio seems to be doing poorly. The payoff is that, over the long run, a well-diversified portfolio should provide much steadier returns and be much less prone to abrupt changes in value.

Key Terms

expected return 488
portfolio 491
portfolio weight 491
principle of diversification 496

correlation 497
investment opportunity set 501
efficient portfolio 503
Markowitz efficient frontier 507

Chapter Review Problems and Self-Test

Use the following table of states of the economy and stock returns to answer the review problems:

State of Economy	Probability of State of Economy	Security Returns if State Occurs	
		Roten	Bradley
Bust	.40	−10%	30%
Boom	.60	40	10
	1.00		

1. **Expected Returns** Calculate the expected returns for Roten and Bradley.
2. **Standard Deviations** Calculate the standard deviations for Roten and Bradley.
3. **Portfolio Expected Returns** Calculate the expected return on a portfolio of 50 percent Roten and 50 percent Bradley.
4. **Portfolio Volatility** Calculate the volatility of a portfolio of 50 percent Roten and 50 percent Bradley.

Answers to Self-Test Problems

1. We calculate the expected return as follows:

		Roten		Bradley	
(1)	**(2)**	**(3)**	**(4)**	**(5)**	**(6)**
State of Economy	Probability of State of Economy	Return if State Occurs	Product (2) × (3)	Return if State Occurs	Product (2) × (5)
Bust	.40	−10%	−.04	30%	.12
Boom	.60	40%	.24	10%	.06
			$E(R) = 20\%$		$E(R) = 18\%$

2. We calculate the standard deviation as follows:

(1)	**(2)**	**(3)**	**(4)**	**(5)**
State of Economy	Probability of State of Economy	Return Deviation from Expected Return	Squared Return Deviation	Product (2) × (4)
Roten				
Bust	.40	−.30	.09	.036
Boom	.60	.20	.04	.024
				$\sigma^2 = .06$
Bradley				
Bust	.40	.12	.0144	.00576
Boom	.60	−.08	.0064	.00384
				$\sigma^2 = .0096$

Taking square roots, the standard deviations are 24.495 percent and 9.798 percent.

3. We calculate the expected return on a portfolio of 50 percent Roten and 50 percent Bradley as follows:

(1) State of Economy	(2) Probability of State of Economy	(3) Portfolio Return if State Occurs	(4) Product (2) × (3)
Bust	.40	10%	.04
Boom	.60	25	.15

$$E(R_p) = 19\%$$

4. We calculate the volatility of a portfolio of 50 percent Roten and 50 percent Bradley as follows:

(1) State of Economy	(2) Probability of State of Economy	(3) Portfolio Returns if State Occurs	(4) Squared Deviation from Expected Return	(5) Product (2) × (4)
Bust	.40	.10	.0081	.00324
Boom	.60	.25	.0036	.00216

$$\sigma_P^2 = .0054$$
$$\sigma_P = 7.3485\%$$

Test Your Investment Quotient

1. **Diversification**   Netcap has an expected return of 25 percent and Jmart has an expected return of 20 percent. What is the likely investment decision for a risk-averse investor?

   a. Invest all funds in Netcap.
   b. Invest all funds in Jmart.
   c. Do not invest any funds in Netcap and Jmart.
   d. Invest funds partly in Netcap and partly in Jmart.

2. **Return Standard Deviation**   Netcap experiences returns of 5 percent or 45 percent, each with an equal probability. What is the return standard deviation for Netcap?

   a. 30 percent
   b. 25 percent
   c. 20 percent
   d. 10 percent

3. **Return Standard Deviation**   Jmart experiences returns of 0 percent, 25 percent, or 50 percent, each with a one-third probability. What is the approximate return standard deviation for Jmart?

   a. 30 percent
   b. 25 percent
   c. 20 percent
   d. 10 percent

CFA

4. **Expected Return** An analyst estimates that a stock has the following return probabilities and returns depending on the state of the economy:

State of Economy	Probability	Return
Good	.1	15%
Normal	.6	13
Poor	.3	7

What is the expected return of the stock? (*1994 CFA Exam*)

a. 7.8 percent
b. 11.4 percent
c. 11.7 percent
d. 13.0 percent

5. **Risk Premium** Netcap has an expected return of 25 percent, Jmart has an expected return of 20 percent, and the risk-free rate is 5 percent. You invest half your funds in Netcap and the other half in Jmart. What is the risk premium for your portfolio?

a. 20 percent
b. 17.5 percent
c. 15 percent
d. 12.5 percent

6. **Return Standard Deviation** Both Netcap and Jmart have the same return standard deviation of 20 percent, and Netcap and Jmart returns have zero correlation. You invest half your funds in Netcap and the other half in Jmart. What is the return standard deviation for your portfolio?

a. 20 percent
b. 14.14 percent
c. 10 percent
d. 0 percent

7. **Return Standard Deviation** Both Netcap and Jmart have the same return standard deviation of 20 percent, and Netcap and Jmart returns have a correlation of +1. You invest half your funds in Netcap and the other half in Jmart. What is the return standard deviation for your portfolio?

a. 20 percent
b. 14.14 percent
c. 10 percent
d. 0 percent

8. **Return Standard Deviation** Both Netcap and Jmart have the same return standard deviation of 20 percent, and Netcap and Jmart returns have a correlation of −1. You invest half your funds in Netcap and the other half in Jmart. What is the return standard deviation for your portfolio?

a. 20 percent
b. 14.14 percent
c. 10 percent
d. 0 percent

9. **Minimum Variance Portfolio** Both Netcap and Jmart have the same return standard deviation of 20 percent, and Netcap and Jmart returns have zero correlation. What is the minimum attainable return variance for a portfolio of Netcap and Jmart?

a. 20 percent
b. 14.14 percent
c. 10 percent
d. 0 percent

10. **Minimum Variance Portfolio**   Both Netcap and Jmart have the same return standard deviation of 20 percent, and Netcap and Jmart returns have a correlation of -1. What is the minimum attainable return variance for a portfolio of Netcap and Jmart?

    a. 20 percent
    b. 14.14 percent
    c. 10 percent
    d. 0 percent

11. **Minimum Variance Portfolio**   Stocks A, B, and C each have the same expected return and standard deviation. The following shows the correlations between returns on these stocks:

	Stock A	Stock B	Stock C
Stock A	+1.0		
Stock B	+0.9	+1.0	
Stock C	+0.1	−0.4	+1.0

    Given these correlations, which of the following portfolios constructed from these stocks would have the lowest risk? (*1994 CFA Exam*)

    a. One equally invested in stocks A and B.
    b. One equally invested in stocks A and C.
    c. One equally invested in stocks B and C.
    d. One totally invested in stock C.

12. **Markowitz Efficient Frontier**   Which of the following portfolios cannot lie on the efficient frontier as described by Markowitz? (*1994 CFA Exam*)

	Portfolio	Expected Return	Standard Deviation
a.	W	9%	21%
b.	X	5	7
c.	Y	15	36
d.	Z	12	15

Questions and Problems

Core Questions

1. **Expected Returns**   Use the following information on states of the economy and stock returns to calculate the expected return for Dingaling Telephone:

State of Economy	Probability of State of Economy	Security Return if State Occurs
Recession	.20	−10%
Normal	.50	20
Boom	.30	30
	1.00	

2. **Standard Deviations**   Using the information in the previous question, calculate the standard deviation of return.

3. **Expected Returns and Deviations** Repeat Questions 1 and 2 assuming that all three states are equally likely.

Use the following information on states of the economy and stock returns to answer Questions 4–7:

State of Economy	Probability of State of Economy	Security Returns if State Occurs	
		Roll	**Ross**
Bust	.30	−10%	40%
Boom	.70	50	10
	1.00		

4. **Expected Returns** Calculate the expected returns for Roll and Ross by filling in the following:

		Roll		Ross	
(1)	**(2)**	**(3)**	**(4)**	**(5)**	**(6)**
State of Economy	Probability of State of Economy	Return if State Occurs	Product (2) × (3)	Return if State Occurs	Product (2) × (5)
Bust					
Boom					

5. **Standard Deviations** Calculate the standard deviations for Roll and Ross by filling in the following:

(1)	**(2)**	**(3)**	**(4)**	**(5)**
State of Economy	Probability of State of Economy	Return Deviation from Expected Return	Squared Return Deviation	Product (2) × (4)
Roll				
Bust				
Boom				
Ross				
Bust				
Boom				

6. **Portfolio Expected Returns** Calculate the expected return on a portfolio of 40 percent Roll and 60 percent Ross by filling in the following:

(1)	**(2)**	**(3)**	**(4)**
State of Economy	Probability of State of Economy	Portfolio Return if State Occurs	Product (2) × (3)
Bust			
Boom			

7. **Portfolio Volatility** Calculate the volatility of a portfolio of 70 percent Roll and 30 percent Ross by filling in the following:

(1)	(2)	(3)	(4)	(5)
	Probability of	**Portfolio**	**Squared Deviation**	
State of	**State of**	**Returns if**	**from Expected**	**Product**
Economy	**Economy**	**State Occurs**	**Return**	**(2) × (4)**
Bust			$\sigma_P^2 =$	
Boom			$\sigma_P =$	

8. **Diversification and Market History** Based on market history, what is the average annual standard deviation of return for a single, randomly chosen stock? What is the average annual standard deviation for an equally weighted portfolio of many stocks?

9. **Interpreting Correlations** If the returns on two stocks are highly correlated, what does this mean? If they have no correlation? If they are negatively correlated?

10. **Efficient Portfolios** What is an efficient portfolio?

11. **Portfolio Returns and Volatilities** Fill in the missing information in the following table. Assume that Portfolio AB is 40 percent invested in Stock A.

	Annual Returns		
Year	**Stock A**	**Stock B**	**Portfolio AB**
1995	15%	55%	
1996	35%	−40%	
1997	−15%	45%	
1998	20%	00%	
1999	00%	10%	
Average returns			
Standard deviations			

Intermediate Questions

12. **Portfolio Returns and Volatilities** Given the following information, calculate the expected return and standard deviation for a portfolio that has 40 percent invested in Stock A, 30 percent in Stock B, and the balance in Stock C.

	Probability of	**Returns**		
State of	**State of**			
Economy	**Economy**	**Stock A**	**Stock B**	**Stock C**
Boom	.40	15%	18%	20%
Bust	.60	5	0	−5

13. **Portfolio Variance** Use the following information to calculate the expected return and standard deviation of a portfolio that is 40 percent invested in Kuipers and 60 percent invested in SuCo:

	Kuipers	**SuCo**
Expected return, $E(R)$	30%	26%
Standard deviation, σ	65	45
Correlation		.30

14. **More Portfolio Variance**   In the previous question, what is the standard deviation if the correlation is $+1$? 0? -1? As the correlation declines from $+1$ to -1 here, what do you see happening to portfolio volatility? Why?

15. **Minimum Variance Portfolio**   In problem 13, what are the expected return and standard deviation on the minimum variance portfolio?

16. **Asset Allocation**   Fill in the missing information assuming a correlation of $-.10$.

Portfolio Weights		Expected Return	Standard Deviation
Stocks	**Bonds**		
1.00		14%	20%
.80			
.60			
.40			
.20			
.00		5%	8%

17. **Expected Returns**   True or false: If the two stocks have the same expected return of 12 percent, then any portfolio of the two stocks will also have an expected return of 12 percent.

18. **Portfolio Volatility**   True or false: If the two stocks have the same standard deviation of 45 percent, then any portfolio of the two stocks will also have a standard deviation of 45 percent.

19. **Portfolio Variance**   Suppose two assets have perfect positive correlation. Show that the standard deviation on a portfolio of the two assets is simply

$$\sigma_p = x_A \times \sigma_A + x_B \times \sigma_B$$

(Hint: Look at the expression for the variance of a two-asset portfolio. If the correlation is $+1$, the expression is a perfect square.)

20. **Portfolio Variance**   Suppose two assets have perfect negative correlation. Show that the standard deviation on a portfolio of the two assets is simply

$$\sigma_p = \pm (x_A \times \sigma_A - x_B \times \sigma_B)$$

(Hint: See previous problem.)

21. **Portfolio Variance**   Using the result in problem 20, show that whenever two assets have perfect negative correlation it is possible to find a portfolio with a zero standard deviation. What are the portfolio weights? (Hint: Let x be the percentage in the first asset and $(1 - x)$ be the percentage in the second. Set the standard deviation to zero and solve for x.)

22. **Portfolio Variance**   Suppose two assets have zero correlation and the same standard deviation. What is true about the minimum variance portfolio?

23. **Portfolio Variance**   Derive our expression in the chapter for the portfolio weight in the minimum variance portfolio. (Danger! Calculus required!) (Hint: Let x be the percentage in the first asset and $(1 - x)$ the percentage in the second. Take the derivative with respect to x and set it to zero. Solve for x.)

18 Return, Risk, and the Security Market Line

An important insight of modern financial theory is that some investment risks yield an expected reward, while other risks do not. Essentially, risks that can be eliminated by diversification do not yield an expected reward, and risks that cannot be eliminated by diversification do yield an expected reward. Thus, financial markets are somewhat fussy regarding what risks are rewarded and what risks are not. ■ Chapter 1 presented some important lessons from capital market history. The most noteworthy, perhaps, is that there is a reward, on average, for bearing risk. We called this reward a *risk premium*. The second lesson is that this risk premium is positively correlated with an investment's risk.

In this chapter, we return to an examination of the reward for bearing risk. Specifically, we have two tasks to accomplish. First, we have to define risk more precisely and then discuss how to measure it. Once we have a better understanding of just what we mean by "risk," we will go on to quantify the relation between risk and return in financial markets.

When we examine the risks associated with individual assets, we find there are two types of risk: systematic and unsystematic. This distinction is crucial because, as we will see, systematic risk affects almost all assets in the economy, at least to some degree, whereas unsystematic risk affects at most only a small number of assets. This observation allows us to say a great deal about the risks and returns on individual assets. In particular, it is the basis for a famous relationship between risk and return called the *security market line,* or SML. To develop the SML, we introduce the equally famous beta coefficient, one of the centerpieces of modern finance. Beta and the SML are key concepts because they supply us with at least part of the answer to the question of how to go about determining the expected return on a risky investment.

18.1   Announcements, Surprises, and Expected Returns

In our previous chapter, we discussed how to construct portfolios and evaluate their returns. We now begin to describe more carefully the risks and returns associated with individual securities. Thus far, we have measured volatility by looking at the difference between the actual return on an asset or portfolio, R, and the expected return, $E(R)$. We now look at why those deviations exist.

Expected and Unexpected Returns

To begin, consider the return on the stock of a hypothetical company called Flyers. What will determine this stock's return in, say, the coming year?

The return on any stock traded in a financial market is composed of two parts. First, the normal, or expected, return from the stock is the part of the return that investors predict or expect. This return depends on the information investors have about the stock, and it is based on the market's understanding today of the important factors that will influence the stock in the coming year.

The second part of the return on the stock is the uncertain, or risky, part. This is the portion that comes from unexpected information revealed during the year. A list of all possible sources of such information would be endless, but here are a few basic examples:

News about Flyers's product research.

Government figures released on gross domestic product.

The results from the latest arms control talks.

The news that Flyers's sales figures are higher than expected.

A sudden, unexpected drop in interest rates.

Based on this discussion, one way to express the return on Flyers stock in the coming year would be

$$\text{Total return} - \text{Expected return} = \text{Unexpected return} \qquad \textbf{18.1}$$

or $$R - E(R) = U$$

where R stands for the actual total return in the year, $E(R)$ stands for the expected part of the return, and U stands for the unexpected part of the return. What this says is that the actual return, R, differs from the expected return, $E(R)$, because of surprises that occur during the year. In any given year, the unexpected return will be positive or negative, but, through time, the average value of U will be zero. This simply means that, on average, the actual return equals the expected return.

Announcements and News

We need to be careful when we talk about the effect of news items on stock returns. For example, suppose Flyers's business is such that the company prospers when gross domestic product (GDP) grows at a relatively high rate and suffers when GDP is relatively stagnant. In this case, in deciding what return to expect this year from owning stock in Flyers, investors either implicitly or explicitly must think about what GDP is likely to be for the coming year.

When the government actually announces GDP figures for the year, what will happen to the value of Flyers stock? Obviously, the answer depends on what figure is released. More to the point, however, the impact depends on how much of that figure actually represents new information

At the beginning of the year, market participants will have some idea or forecast of what the yearly GDP figure will be. To the extent that shareholders have predicted GDP, that prediction will already be factored into the expected part of the return on the stock, $E(R)$. On the other hand, if the announced GDP is a surprise, then the effect will be part of U, the unanticipated portion of the return.

As an example, suppose shareholders in the market had forecast that the GDP increase this year would be .5 percent. If the actual announcement this year is exactly .5 percent, the same as the forecast, then the shareholders don't really learn anything, and the announcement isn't news. There will be no impact on the stock price as a result. This is like receiving redundant confirmation about something that you suspected all along; it reveals nothing new.

To give a more concrete example, on June 24, 1996, Nabisco announced it was taking a massive $300 million charge against earnings for the second quarter in a sweeping restructuring plan. The company also announced plans to cut its workforce sharply by 7.8 percent, eliminate some package sizes and small brands, and relocate some of its operations. This all seems like bad news, but the stock price didn't even budge. Why? Because it was already fully expected that Nabisco would take such actions and the stock price already reflected the bad news.

A common way of saying that an announcement isn't news is to say that the market has already discounted the announcement. The use of the word "discount" here is different from the use of the term in computing present values, but the spirit is the same. When we discount a dollar to be received in the future, we say it is worth less to us today because of the time value of money. When an announcement or a news item is discounted into a stock price, we say that its impact is already a part of the stock price because the market already knew about it.

Going back to Flyers, suppose the government announces that the actual GDP increase during the year has been 1.5 percent. Now shareholders have learned something, namely, that the increase is 1 percentage point higher than they had forecast. This difference between the actual result and the forecast, 1 percentage point in this example, is sometimes called the *innovation* or the *surprise*.

This distinction explains why what seems to be bad news can actually be good news. For example, Gymboree, a retailer of children's apparel, had a 3 percent decline in same-store sales for the month of July 1996, yet its stock price shot up 13 percent on the news. In the retail business, same-store sales, which are sales by existing stores in operation at least a year, are a crucial barometer, so why was this decline good news? The reason was that analysts had been expecting significantly sharper declines, so the situation was not as bad as previously thought.

A key fact to keep in mind about news and price changes is that news about the future is what matters. For example, on May 8, 1996, America Online (AOL) announced third-quarter earnings that exceeded Wall Street's expectations. That seems like good news, but America Online's stock price promptly dropped 10 percent. The reason was that America Online also announced a new discount subscriber plan, which analysts took as an indication that future revenues would be growing more slowly. Similarly, shortly thereafter, Microsoft reported a 50 percent jump in profits, exceeding projections. That seems like *really* good news, but Microsoft's stock price proceeded to decline sharply. Why? Because Microsoft warned that its phenomenal growth could not be sustained indefinitely, so its 50 percent increase in current earnings was not such a good predictor of future earnings growth.

To summarize, an announcement can be broken into two parts, the anticipated, or expected, part plus the surprise, or innovation:

$$\text{Announcement} = \text{Expected part} + \text{Surprise} \qquad \textbf{18.2}$$

The expected part of any announcement is the part of the information that the market uses to form the expectation, $E(R)$, of the return on the stock. The surprise is the news that influences the unanticipated return on the stock, U.

Our discussion of market efficiency in Chapter 8 bears on this discussion. We are assuming that relevant information known today is already reflected in the expected return. This is identical to saying that the current price reflects relevant publicly available information. We are thus implicitly assuming that markets are at least reasonably efficient in the semistrong-form sense. Henceforth, when we speak of news, we will mean the surprise part of an announcement and not the portion that the market had expected and therefore already discounted.

Example 18.1 In the News

Suppose Intel were to announce that earnings for the quarter just ending were up by 40 percent relative to a year ago. Do you expect that the stock price would rise or fall on the announcement?

The answer is you can't really tell. Suppose the market was expecting a 60 percent increase. In this case, the 40 percent increase would be a negative surprise, and we would expect the stock price to fall. On the other hand, if the market was expecting only a 20 percent increase, there would be a positive surprise, and we would expect the stock to rise on the news.

CHECK THIS

18.1a What are the two basic parts of a return on common stock?

18.1b Under what conditions will an announcement have no effect on common stock prices?

18.2 Risk: Systematic and Unsystematic

It is important to distinguish between expected and unexpected returns because the unanticipated part of the return, that portion resulting from surprises, is the significant risk of any investment. After all, if we always receive exactly what we expect, then the investment is perfectly predictable and, by definition, risk-free. In other words, the risk of owning an asset comes from surprises—unanticipated events.

There are important differences, though, among various sources of risk. Look back at our previous list of news stories. Some of these stories are directed specifically at Flyers, and some are more general. Which of the news items are of specific importance to Flyers?

Announcements about interest rates or GDP are clearly important for nearly all companies, whereas the news about Flyers's president, its research, or its sales is of specific interest to Flyers investors only. We distinguish between these two types of events, because, as we will see, they have very different implications.

Systematic and Unsystematic Risk

systematic risk Risk that influences a large number of assets. Also called *market risk.*

The first type of surprise, the one that affects most assets, we label **systematic risk**. A systematic risk is one that influences a large number of assets, each to a greater or lesser extent. Because systematic risks have marketwide effects, they are sometimes called *market risks*.

The second type of surprise we call **unsystematic risk**. An unsystematic risk is one that affects a single asset, or possibly a small group of assets. Because these risks are unique to individual companies or assets, they are sometimes called *unique* or *asset-specific risks.* We use these terms interchangeably.

unsystematic risk Risk that influences a single company or a small group of companies. Also called *unique* or *asset-specific risk.*

As we have seen, uncertainties about general economic conditions, such as GDP, interest rates, or inflation, are examples of systematic risks. These conditions affect nearly all companies to some degree. An unanticipated increase, or surprise, in inflation, for example, affects wages and the costs of supplies that companies buy; it affects the value of the assets that companies own; and it affects the prices at which companies sell their products. Forces such as these, to which all companies are susceptible, are the essence of systematic risk.

In contrast, the announcement of an oil strike by a particular company will primarily affect that company and, perhaps, a few others (such as primary competitors and suppliers). It is unlikely to have much of an effect on the world oil market, however, or on the affairs of companies not in the oil business, so this is an unsystematic event.

Systematic and Unsystematic Components of Return

The distinction between a systematic risk and an unsystematic risk is never really as exact as we would like it to be. Even the most narrow and peculiar bit of news about a company ripples through the economy. This is true because every enterprise, no matter how tiny, is a part of the economy. It's like the tale of a kingdom that was lost because one horse lost a shoe. This is mostly hairsplitting, however. Some risks are clearly much more general than others.

The distinction between the two types of risk allows us to break down the surprise portion, U, of the return on the Flyers stock into two parts. Earlier, we had the actual return broken down into its expected and surprise components: $R - E(R) = U$. We now recognize that the total surprise component for Flyers, U, has a systematic and an unsystematic component, so

$$R - E(R) = \text{Systematic portion} + \text{Unsystematic portion} \qquad \textbf{18.3}$$

Because it is traditional, we will use the Greek letter epsilon, ϵ, to stand for the unsystematic portion. Because systematic risks are often called "market" risks, we use the letter m to stand for the systematic part of the surprise. With these symbols, we can rewrite the formula for the total return:

$$R - E(R) = U = m + \epsilon \qquad\qquad \textbf{18.4}$$

The important thing about the way we have broken down the total surprise, U, is that the unsystematic portion, ϵ, is more or less unique to Flyers. For this reason, it is unrelated to the unsystematic portion of return on most other assets. To see why this is important, we need to return to the subject of portfolio risk.

Example 18.2 Systematic versus Unsystematic Events

Suppose Intel were to unexpectedly announce that its latest computer chip contains a significant flaw in its floating point unit that left it unable to handle numbers bigger than a couple of gigatrillion (meaning that, among other things, the chip cannot calculate Intel's quarterly profits). Is this a systematic or unsystematic event?

Obviously, this event is for the most part unsystematic. However, it would also benefit Intel's competitors to some degree and, at least potentially, harm some users of Intel products such as personal computer makers. Thus, as with most unsystematic events, there is some spillover, but the effect is mostly confined to a relatively small number of companies.

CHECK THIS

18.2a What are the two basic types of risk?

18.2b What is the distinction between the two types of risk?

18.3 Diversification, Systematic Risk, and Unsystematic Risk

In the previous chapter, we introduced the principle of diversification. What we saw was that some of the risk associated with individual assets can be diversified away and some cannot. We are left with an obvious question: Why is this so? It turns out that the answer hinges on the distinction between systematic and unsystematic risk.

Diversification and Unsystematic Risk

By definition, an unsystematic risk is one that is particular to a single asset or, at most, a small group of assets. For example, if the asset under consideration is stock in a single company, such things as successful new products and innovative cost savings will tend to increase the value of the stock. Unanticipated lawsuits, industrial accidents, strikes, and similar events will tend to decrease future cash flows and thereby reduce share values.

Here is the important observation: If we hold only a single stock, then the value of our investment will fluctuate because of company-specific events. If we hold a large portfolio, on the other hand, some of the stocks in the portfolio will go up in value because of positive company-specific events and some will go down in value because of negative events. The net effect on the overall value of the portfolio will be relatively small, however, because these effects will tend to cancel each other out.

Now we see why some of the variability associated with individual assets is eliminated by diversification. When we combine assets into portfolios, the unique, or unsystematic, events—both positive and negative—tend to "wash out" once we have more than just a few assets. This is an important point that bears repeating:

Unsystematic risk is essentially eliminated by diversification, so a portfolio with many assets has almost no unsystematic risk.

In fact, the terms *diversifiable risk* and *unsystematic risk* are often used interchangeably.

Diversification and Systematic Risk

We've seen that unsystematic risk can be eliminated by diversification. What about systematic risk? Can it also be eliminated by diversification? The answer is no because, by definition, a systematic risk affects almost all assets. As a result, no matter how many assets we put into a portfolio, systematic risk doesn't go away. Thus, for obvious reasons, the terms *systematic risk* and *nondiversifiable risk* are used interchangeably.

Because we have introduced so many different terms, it is useful to summarize our discussion before moving on. What we have seen is that the total risk of an investment can be written as

$$\text{Total risk} = \text{Systematic risk} + \text{Unsystematic risk} \qquad \textbf{18.5}$$

Systematic risk is also called *nondiversifiable risk* or *market risk*. Unsystematic risk is also called *diversifiable risk, unique risk,* or *asset-specific risk.* Most important, for a well-diversified portfolio, unsystematic risk is negligible. For such a portfolio, essentially all risk is systematic.

CHECK THIS

18.3a Why is some risk diversifiable? Why is some risk not diversifiable?

18.3b Why can't systematic risk be diversified away?

18.4 Systematic Risk and Beta

We now begin to address another question: What determines the size of the risk premium on a risky asset? Put another way, why do some assets have a larger risk premium than other assets? The answer, as we discuss next, is also based on the distinction between systematic and unsystematic risk.

The Systematic Risk Principle

systematic risk principle The reward for bearing risk depends only on the systematic risk of an investment.

Thus far, we've seen that the total risk associated with an asset can be decomposed into two components: systematic and unsystematic risk. We have also seen that unsystematic risk can be essentially eliminated by diversification. The systematic risk present in an asset, on the other hand, cannot be eliminated by diversification.

Based on our study of capital market history in Chapter 1, we know that there is a reward, on average, for bearing risk. However, we now need to be more precise about what we mean by risk. The **systematic risk principle** states that the reward for bearing risk depends only on the systematic risk of an investment.

The underlying rationale for this principle is straightforward: Because unsystematic risk can be eliminated at virtually no cost (by diversifying), there is no reward for bearing it. In other words, the market does not reward risks that are borne unnecessarily.

The systematic risk principle has a remarkable and very important implication:

The expected return on an asset depends only on its systematic risk.

There is an obvious corollary to this principle: No matter how much total risk an asset has, only the systematic portion is relevant in determining the expected return (and the risk premium) on that asset.

Measuring Systematic Risk

beta coefficient (β)
Measure of the relative systematic risk of an asset. Assets with betas larger (smaller) than 1 have more (less) systematic risk than average.

Because systematic risk is the crucial determinant of an asset's expected return, we need some way of measuring the level of systematic risk for different investments. The specific measure we will use is called the **beta coefficient**, designated by the Greek letter β. A beta coefficient, or just beta for short, tells us how much systematic risk a particular asset has relative to an average asset. By definition, an average asset has a beta of 1.0 relative to itself. An asset with a beta of .50, therefore, has half as much systematic risk as an average asset. Likewise, an asset with a beta of 2.0 has twice as much systematic risk.

Table 18.1 presents the estimated beta coefficients for the stocks of some well-known companies. (This particular source rounds numbers to the nearest .05.) The range of betas in Table 18.1 is typical for stocks of large U.S. corporations. Betas outside this range occur, but they are less common.

The important thing to remember is that the expected return, and thus the risk premium, on an asset depends only on its systematic risk. Because assets with larger betas have greater systematic risks, they will have greater expected returns. Thus, from Table 18.1, an investor who buys stock in Exxon, with a beta of .65, should expect to earn less, on average, than an investor who buys stock in General Motors, with a beta of about 1.15.

One cautionary note is in order: Not all betas are created equal. For example, in Table 18.1, the source used, *Value Line,* reports a beta for Harley-Davidson of 1.65. At the same time, however, another widely used source, *S&P Stock Reports,* puts Harley-Davidson's beta at 1.13, substantially smaller. The difference derives from the different procedures used to come up with beta coefficients. We will have more to say on this subject when we explain how betas are calculated in a later section.

Example 18.3 Total Risk versus Beta

Consider the following information on two securities. Which has greater total risk? Which has greater systematic risk? Greater unsystematic risk? Which asset will have a higher risk premium?

	Standard Deviation	Beta
Security A	40%	.50
Security B	20	1.50

From our discussion in this section, Security A has greater total risk, but it has substantially less systematic risk. Because total risk is the sum of systematic and unsystematic risk. Security A must have greater unsystematic risk. Finally, from the systematic risk principle, Security B will have a higher risk premium and a greater expected return, despite the fact that it has less total risk.

Table 18.1	Beta Coefficients	
Source: *Value Line* Investment survey.	**Company**	**Beta β**
	Exxon	.65
	AT&T	.90
	IBM	.95
	Wal-Mart	1.10
	General Motors	1.15
	Microsoft	1.30
	Harley-Davidson	1.65
	America Online	2.40

Portfolio Betas

Earlier, we saw that the riskiness of a portfolio has no simple relation to the risks of the assets in the portfolio. By contrast, a portfolio beta can be calculated just like a portfolio expected return. For example, looking again at Table 18.1, suppose you put half of your money in AT&T and half in General Motors. What would the beta of this combination be? Because AT&T has a beta of .90 and General Motors has a beta of 1.15, the portfolio's beta, β_p, would be

$$\beta_P = .50 \times \beta_{AT\&T} + .50 \times \beta_{GM}$$
$$= .50 \times .90 + .50 \times 1.15$$
$$= 1.025$$

In general, if we had a large number of assets in a portfolio, we would multiply each asset's beta by its portfolio weight and then add the results to get the portfolio's beta.

Example 18.4 Portfolio Betas

Suppose we have the following information:

Security	Amount Invested	Expected Return	Beta
Stock A	$1,000	8%	.80
Stock B	2,000	12	.95
Stock C	3,000	15	1.10
Stock D	4,000	18	1.40

What is the expected return on this portfolio? What is the beta of this portfolio? Does this portfolio have more or less systematic risk than an average asset?

To answer, we first have to calculate the portfolio weights. Notice that the total amount invested is $10,000. Of this, $1,000/$10,000 = 10% is invested in Stock A. Similarly, 20 percent is invested in Stock B, 30 percent is invested in Stock C, and 40 percent is invested in Stock D. The expected return, $E(R_P)$, is thus

$$E(R_P) = .10 \times E(R_A) + .20 \times E(R_B) + .30 \times E(R_C) + .40 \times E(R_D)$$
$$= .10 \times 8\% + .20 \times 12\% + .30 \times 15\% + .40 \times 18\%$$
$$= 14.9\%$$

Similarly, the portfolio beta, β_P, is

$$\beta_P = .10 \times \beta_A + .20 \times \beta_B + .30 \times \beta_C + .40 \times \beta_D$$
$$= .10 \times .80 + .20 \times .95 + .30 \times 1.10 + .40 \times 1.40$$
$$= 1.16$$

This portfolio thus has an expected return of 14.9 percent and a beta of 1.16. Because the beta is larger than 1, this portfolio has greater systematic risk than an average asset.

CHECK THIS

18.4a What is the systematic risk principle?

18.4b What does a beta coefficient measure?

18.4c How do you calculate a portfolio beta?

18.4d True or false: The expected return on a risky asset depends on that asset's total risk. Explain.

18.5 The Security Market Line

We're now in a position to see how risk is rewarded in the marketplace. To begin, suppose that Asset A has an expected return of $E(R_A) = 20\%$ and a beta of $\beta_A = 1.6$. Further suppose that the risk-free rate is $R_f = 8\%$. Notice that a risk-free asset, by definition, has no systematic risk (or unsystematic risk), so a risk-free asset has a beta of zero.

Beta and the Risk Premium

Consider a portfolio made up of Asset A and a risk-free asset. We can calculate some different possible portfolio expected returns and betas by varying the percentages invested in these two assets. For example, if 25 percent of the portfolio is invested in Asset A, then the expected return is

$$E(R_P) = .25 \times E(R_A) + (1 - .25) \times R_f$$
$$= .25 \times 20\% + .75 \times 8\%$$
$$= 11\%$$

Similarly, the beta on the portfolio, β_P, would be

$$\beta_P = .25 \times \beta_A + (1 - .25) \times 0$$
$$= .25 \times 1.6$$
$$= .40$$

Notice that, because the weights have to add up to 1, the percentage invested in the risk-free asset is equal to 1 minus the percentage invested in Asset A.

One thing that you might wonder about is whether it is possible for the percentage invested in Asset A to exceed 100 percent. The answer is yes. This can happen if the investor borrows at the risk-free rate and invests the proceeds in stocks. For example, suppose an investor has $100 and borrows an additional $50 at 8 percent, the risk-free rate. The total investment in Asset A would be $150, or 150 percent of the investor's wealth. The expected return in this case would be

$$E(R_P) = 1.50 \times E(R_A) + (1 - 1.50) \times R_f$$
$$= 1.50 \times 20\% - .50 \times 8\%$$
$$= 26\%$$

The beta on the portfolio would be

$$\beta_P = 1.50 \times \beta_A + (1 - 1.50) \times 0$$
$$= 1.50 \times 1.6$$
$$= 2.4$$

We can calculate some other possibilities, as follows:

Percentage of Portfolio in Asset A	Portfolio Expected Return	Portfolio Beta
0%	8%	.0
25	11	.4
50	14	.8
75	17	1.2
100	20	1.6
125	23	2.0
150	26	2.4

In Figure 18.1A, these portfolio expected returns are plotted against portfolio betas. Notice that all the combinations fall on a straight line.

The Reward-to-Risk Ratio

What is the slope of the straight line in Figure 18.1A? As always, the slope of a straight line is equal to the rise over the run. In this case, as we move out of the risk-free asset into Asset A, the beta increases from zero to 1.6 (a run of 1.6). At the same time, the expected return goes from 8 percent to 20 percent, a rise of 12 percent. The slope of the line is thus 12% / 1.6 = 7.5%.

Notice that the slope of our line is just the risk premium on Asset A, $E(R_A) - R_f$ divided by Asset A's beta, β_A:

$$\text{Slope} = \frac{E(R_A) - R_f}{\beta_A}$$
$$= \frac{20\% - 8\%}{1.6}$$
$$= 7.50\%$$

What this tells us is that Asset A offers a *reward-to-risk* ratio of 7.5 percent.[1] In other words, Asset A has a risk premium of 7.50 percent per "unit" of systematic risk.

The Basic Argument

Now suppose we consider a second asset, Asset B. This asset has a beta of 1.2 and an expected return of 16 percent. Which investment is better, Asset A or Asset B? You might think that we really cannot say—some investors might prefer A; some investors might prefer B. Actually, however, we can say: A is better because, as we will demonstrate, B offers inadequate compensation for its level of systematic risk, at least relative to A.

To begin, we calculate different combinations of expected returns and betas for portfolios of Asset B and a risk-free asset, just as we did for Asset A. For example, if we

---

[1] This ratio is sometimes called the *Treynor index*, after one of its originators.

put 25 percent in Asset B and the remaining 75 percent in the risk-free asset, the portfolio's expected return will be

$$E(R_P) = .25 \times E(R_B) + (1 - .25) \times R_f$$
$$= .25 \times 16\% + .75 \times 8\%$$
$$= 10\%$$

Similarly, the beta on the portfolio, β_P, would be

$$\beta_P = .25 \times \beta_B + (1 - .25) \times 0$$
$$= .25 \times 1.2$$
$$= .30$$

Some other possibilities are as follows:

Percentage of Portfolio in Asset B	Portfolio Expected Return	Portfolio Beta
0%	8%	.0
25	10	.3
50	12	.6
75	14	.9
100	16	1.2
125	18	1.5
150	20	1.8

When we plot these combinations of portfolio expected returns and portfolio betas in Figure 18.1B, we get a straight line just as we did for Asset A.

The key thing to notice is that when we compare the results for Assets A and B, as in Figure 18.1C, the line describing the combinations of expected returns and betas for Asset A is higher than the one for Asset B. What this tells us is that for any given level of systematic risk (as measured by beta), some combination of Asset A and the risk-free asset always offers a larger return. This is why we were able to state that Asset A is a better investment than Asset B.

Another way of seeing that Asset A offers a superior return for its level of risk is to note that the slope of our line for Asset B is

$$\text{Slope} = \frac{E(R_B) - R_f}{\beta_B}$$
$$= \frac{16\% - 8\%}{1.2}$$
$$= 6.67\%$$

Thus, Asset B has a reward-to-risk ratio of 6.67 percent, which is less than the 7.5 percent offered by Asset A.

The Fundamental Result

The situation we have described for Assets A and B could not persist in a well-organized, active market because investors would be attracted to Asset A and away from Asset B. As a result, Asset A's price would rise and Asset B's price would fall. Because prices expected returns move in opposite directions, A's expected return would decline and B's would rise.

This buying and selling would continue until the two assets plotted on exactly the same line, which means they would offer the same reward for bearing risk. In other words, in an active, competitive market, we must have the situation that

$$\frac{E(R_A) - R_f}{\beta_A} = \frac{E(R_B) - R_f}{\beta_B}$$ **18.6**

This is the fundamental relation between risk and return.

Figure 18.1

Betas and
Portfolio
Returns

A. Portfolio expected returns and betas for Asset A

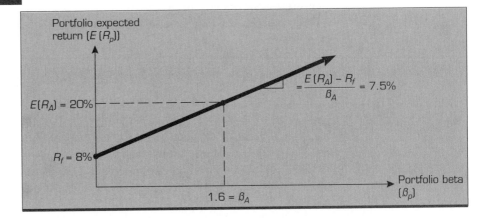

B. Portfolio expected returns and betas for Asset B

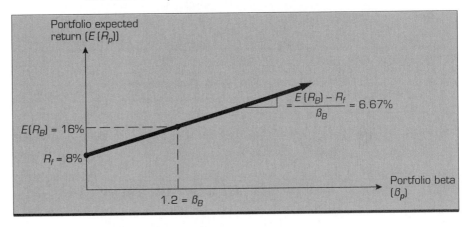

C. Portfolio expected returns and betas for both assets

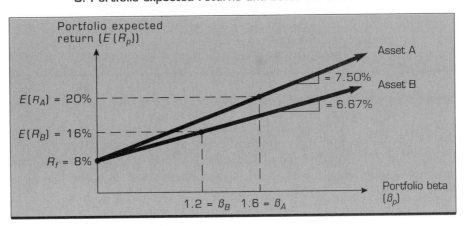

Our basic argument can be extended to more than just two assets. In fact, no matter how many assets we had, we would always reach the same conclusion:

The reward-to-risk ratio must be the same for all assets in a competitive financial market.

This result is really not too surprising. What it says is that, for example, if one asset has twice as much systematic risk as another asset, its risk premium will simply be twice as large.

Because all assets in the market must have the same reward-to-risk ratio, they all must plot on the same line. This argument is illustrated in Figure 18.2, where the subscript i on the return R_i and beta β_i indexes Assets A, B, C, and D. As shown, Assets A and B plot directly on the line and thus have the same reward-to-risk ratio. If an asset plotted above the line, such as C in Figure 18.2, its price would rise and its expected return would fall until it plotted exactly on the line. Similarly, if an asset plotted below the line, such as D in Figure 18.2, its expected return would rise until it too plotted directly on the line.

The arguments we have presented apply to active, competitive, well-functioning markets. Active financial markets, such as the NYSE, best meet these criteria. Other markets, such as real asset markets, may or may not. For this reason, these concepts are most useful in examining active financial markets.

Example 18.5 Buy Low, Sell High

A security is said to be *overvalued* relative to another security if its price is too high given its expected return and risk. Suppose you observe the following situation:

Security	Beta	Expected Return
Melan Co.	1.3	14%
Choly Co.	.8	10

The risk-free rate is currently 6 percent. Is one of the two securities overvalued relative to the other?

To answer, we compute the reward-to-risk ratio for both. For Melan, this ratio is (14% − 6%)/1.3 = 6.15%. For Choly, this ratio is 5 percent. What we conclude is that Choly offers an insufficient expected return for its level of risk, at least relative to Melan. Because its expected return is too low, its price is too high. In other words, Choly is overvalued relative to Melan, and we would expect to see its price fall relative to Melan. Notice that we could also say Melan is *undervalued* relative to Choly.

The Security Market Line

The line that results when we plot expected returns and beta coefficients is obviously of some importance, so it's time we gave it a name. This line, which we use to describe the relationship between systematic risk and expected return in financial markets, is usually called the **security market line (SML)**, and it is one of the most important concepts in modern finance.

security market line (SML) Graphical representation of the linear relationship between systematic risk and expected return in financial markets.

Market Portfolios   We will find it very useful to know the equation of the SML. Although there are many different ways we could write it, we will discuss the most frequently seen version. Suppose we consider a portfolio made up of all of the assets in the market. Such a portfolio is called a *market portfolio,* and we will express the expected return on this market portfolio as $E(R_M)$.

Figure 18.2

Expected
Returns and
Systematic Risk

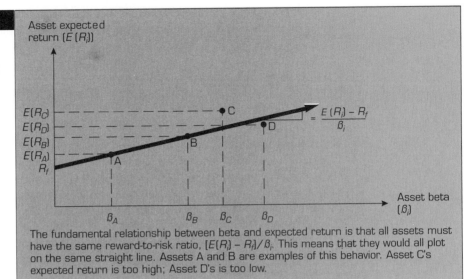

The fundamental relationship between beta and expected return is that all assets must
have the same reward-to-risk ratio, $[E(R_i) - R_f]/\beta_i$. This means that they would all plot
on the same straight line. Assets A and B are examples of this behavior. Asset C's
expected return is too high; Asset D's is too low.

Because all the assets in the market must plot on the SML, so must a market portfolio made up of those assets. To determine where it plots on the SML, we need to know
the beta of the market portfolio, β_M. Because this portfolio is representative of all of the
assets in the market, it must have average systematic risk. In other words, it has a beta
of 1. We could therefore express the slope of the SML as

$$\text{SML slope} = \frac{E(R_M) - R_f}{\beta_M} = \frac{E(R_M) - R_f}{1} = E(R_M) - R_f$$

**market risk
premium** The risk
premium on a market
portfolio; i.e., a
portfolio made of all
assets in the market.

The term $E(R_M) - R_f$ is often called the **market risk premium** because it is the risk
premium on a market portfolio.

The Capital Asset Pricing Model   To finish up, if we let $E(R_i)$ and β_i stand for
the expected return and beta, respectively, on any asset in the market, then we know that
asset must plot on the SML. As a result, we know that its reward-to-risk ratio is the
same as that of the overall market:

$$\frac{E(R_i) - R_f}{\beta_i} = E(R_M) - R_f$$

If we rearrange this, then we can write the equation for the SML as

$$E(R_i) = R_f + [E(R_M) - R_f] \times \beta_i \qquad \textbf{18.7}$$

**capital asset pricing
model (CAPM)** A
theory of risk and
return for securities
on a competitive
capital market.

This result is the famous **capital asset pricing model (CAPM)**.[2]

What the CAPM shows is that the expected return for an asset depends on three
things:

---

[2] Our discussion of the CAPM is actually closely related to the more recent development, arbitrage pricing
theory (APT). The theory underlying the CAPM is more complex than we have indicated here, and it has
implications beyond the scope of this discussion. As we present it here, the CAPM has essentially identical
implications to those of the APT, so we don't distinguish between them.

1. *The pure time value of money.* As measured by the risk-free rate, R_f, this is the reward for merely waiting for your money, without taking any risk.

2. *The reward for bearing systematic risk.* As measured by the market risk premium, $E(R_M) - R_f$, this component is the reward the market offers for bearing an average amount of systematic risk.

3. *The amount of systematic risk.* As measured by β_i, this is the amount of systematic risk present in a particular asset relative to that in an average asset.

By the way, the CAPM works for portfolios of assets just as it does for individual assets. In an earlier section, we saw how to calculate a portfolio's beta in the CAPM equation.

Figure 18.3 summarizes our discussion of the SML and the CAPM. As before, we plot expected return against beta. Now we recognize that, based on the CAPM, the slope of the SML is equal to the market risk premium, $E(R_M) - R_f$.

This concludes our presentation of concepts related to the risk-return trade-off. Table 18.2 summarizes the various concepts in the order in which we discussed them.

Example 18.6   Risk and Return

Suppose the risk-free rate is 4 percent, the market risk premium is 8.6 percent, and a particular stock has a beta of 1.3. Based on the CAPM, what is the expected return on this stock? What would the expected return be if the beta were to double?

With a beta of 1.3, the risk premium for the stock is 1.3 × 8.6%, or 11.18 percent. The risk-free rate is 4 percent, so the expected return is 15.18 percent. If the beta were to double to 2.6, the risk premium would double to 22.36 percent, so the expected return would be 26.36 percent.

Figure 18.3

Security
Market Line
(SML)

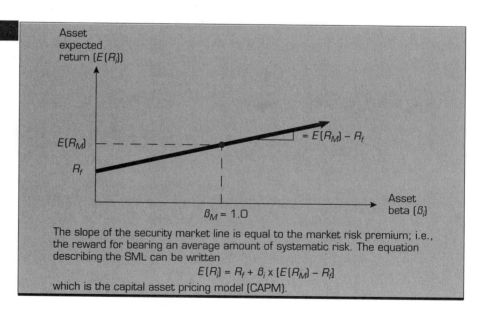

The slope of the security market line is equal to the market risk premium; i.e., the reward for bearing an average amount of systematic risk. The equation describing the SML can be written

$$E(R_i) = R_f + \beta_i \times [E(R_M) - R_f]$$

which is the capital asset pricing model (CAPM).

Table 18.2	**Risk and Return Summary**

1. **Total risk.** The *total risk* of an investment is measured by the variance or, more commonly, the standard deviation of its return.

2. **Total return.** The *total return* on an investment has two components: the expected return and the unexpected return. The unexpected return comes about because of unanticipated events. The risk from investing stems from the possibility of an unanticipated event.

3. **Systematic and unsystematic risks.** *Systematic risks* (also called *market risks*) are unanticipated events that affect almost all assets to some degree because the effects are economy-wide. *Unsystematic risks* are unanticipated events that affect single assets or small groups of assets. Unsystematic risks are also called *unique* or *asset-specific risks*.

4. **The effect of diversification.** Some, but not all, of the risk associated with a risky investment can be eliminated by diversification. The reason is that unsystematic risks, which are unique to individual assets, tend to wash out in a large portfolio, but systematic risks, which affect all of the assets in a portfolio to some extent, do not.

5. **The systematic risk principle and beta.** Because unsystematic risk can be freely eliminated by diversification, the *systematic risk principle* states that the reward for bearing risk depends only on the level of systematic risk. The level of systematic risk in a particular asset, relative to the average, is given by the *beta* of that asset.

6. **The reward-to-risk ratio and the security market line.** The *reward-to-risk ratio* for Asset i is the ratio of its risk premium, $E(R_i) - R_f$, to its beta, β_i:

$$\frac{E(R_i) - R_f}{\beta_i}$$

In a well-functioning market, this ratio is the same for every asset. As a result, when asset expected returns are plotted against asset betas, all assets plot on the same straight line, called the *security market line* (SML).

7. **The capital asset pricing model.** From the SML, the expected return on Asset i can be written

$$E(R_i) = R_f + [E(R_M) - R_f] \times \beta_i$$

This is the *capital asset pricing model* (CAPM). The expected return on a risky asset thus has three components. The first is the pure time value of money (R_f), the second is the market risk premium [$E(R_M) - R_f$], and the third is the beta for that asset (β_i).

CHECK THIS

18.5a What is the fundamental relationship between risk and return in active markets?

18.5b What is the security market line? Why must all assets plot directly on it in a well-functioning market?

18.5c What is the capital asset pricing model (CAPM)? What does it tell us about the required return on a risky investment?

18.6 More on Beta

In our last several sections, we discussed the basic economic principles of risk and return. We found that the expected return on a security depends on its systematic risk, which is measured using the security's beta coefficient, β. In this final section, we examine beta in more detail. We first illustrate more closely what it is that beta measures. We then show how betas can be estimated for individual securities, and we discuss why it is that different sources report different betas for the same security.

A Closer Look at Beta

Going back to the beginning of the chapter, we discussed how the actual return on a security, R, could be written as follows:

$$R - E(R) = m + \epsilon \qquad \qquad 18.8$$

Recall that in Equation 18.8, m stands for the systematic or marketwide portion of the unexpected return. Based on our discussion of the CAPM, we can now be a little more precise about this component.

Specifically, the systematic portion of an unexpected return depends on two things. First, it depends on the size of the systematic effect. We will measure this as $R_M - E(R_M)$, which is simply the difference between the actual return on the overall market and the expected return. Second, as we have discussed, some securities have greater systematic risk than others, and we measure this risk using beta. Putting it together, we have

$$m = \beta \times [R_M - E(R_M)] \qquad \qquad 18.9$$

In other words, the marketwide or systematic portion of the return on a security depends on both the size of the marketwide surprise, $R_M - E(R_M)$, and the sensitivity of the security to such surprises, β.

Now, if we combine equations 18.8 and 18.9, we have

$$R - E(R) = m + \epsilon$$
$$= \beta \times [R_M - E(R_M)] + \epsilon \qquad \qquad 18.10$$

Equation 18.10 gives us some additional insight into beta by telling us why some securities have higher betas than others. A high-beta security is simply one that is relatively sensitive to overall market movements, whereas a low-beta security is one that is relatively insensitive. In other words, the systematic risk of a security is just a reflection of its sensitivity to overall market movements.

A hypothetical example is useful for illustrating the main point of Equation 18.10. Suppose a particular security has a beta of 1.2, the risk-free rate is 5 percent, and the expected return on the market is 12 percent. From the CAPM, we know that the expected return on the security is

$$E(R) = R_f + [E(R_M) - R_f] \times \beta$$
$$= .05 + (.12 - .05) \times 1.2$$
$$= .134$$

Thus, the expected return on this security is 13.4 percent. However, we know that in any year the actual return on this security will be more or less than 13.4 percent because of unanticipated systematic and unsystematic events.

Columns 1 and 2 of Table 18.3 list the actual returns on our security, R, for a five-year period along with the actual returns for the market as a whole, R_M, for the same period. Given these actual returns and the expected returns on the security (13.4 percent) and the market as a whole (12 percent), we can calculate the unexpected returns on the security, $R - E(R)$, along with the unexpected return on the market as a whole, $R_M - E(R_M)$. The results are shown in columns 3 and 4 of Table 18.3

Next we decompose the unexpected returns on the security—that is, we break them down into their systematic and unsystematic components in columns 5 and 6. From Equation 18.9, we calculate the systematic portion of the unexpected return by taking the security's beta, 1.2, and multiplying it by the market's unexpected return:

$$\text{Systematic portion} = m = \beta \times [R_M - E(R_M)]$$

Finally, we calculate the unsystematic portion by subtracting the systematic portion from the total unexpected return:

$$\text{Unsystematic portion} = \epsilon = R - E(R) - \beta \times [R_M - E(R_M)]$$

Notice that the unsystematic portion is essentially whatever is left over after we account for the systematic portion. For this reason, it is sometimes called the "residual" portion of the unexpected return.

Figure 18.4 illustrates the main points of this discussion by plotting the unexpected returns on the security in Table 18.3 against the unexpected return on the market as a whole. These are the individual points in the graph, each labeled with its year. We also plot the systematic portions of the unexpected returns in Table 18.3 and connect them with a straight line. Notice that the slope of the straight line is equal to 1.2, the beta of the security. As indicated, the distance from the straight line to an individual point is the unsystematic portion of the return, ϵ, for a particular year.

Where Do Betas Come From?

As our discussion to this point shows, beta is a useful concept. It allows us to estimate the expected return on a security, it tells how sensitive a security's return is to unexpected market events, and it lets us separate out the systematic and unsystematic portions of a security's return. In our example just above, we were given that the beta was 1.2, so the required calculations were all pretty straightforward. Suppose, however, that we didn't have the beta ahead of time. In this case, we would have to estimate it.

A security's beta is a measure of how sensitive the security's return is to overall market movements. That sensitivity depends on two things: (1) how closely correlated the security's return is with the overall market's return, and (2) how volatile the security is relative to the market. Specifically, going back to our previous chapter, let $\text{Corr}(R_i, R_M)$

Table 18.3			Decomposition of Total Returns into Systematic and Unsystematic Portions			
	Actual Returns		**Unexpected Returns**		**Systematic Portion**	**Unsystematic Portion (ϵ)**
Year	R	R_M	$R - E(R)$	$R_M - E(R_M)$	$[R_M - E(R_M)] \times \beta$	$R - [R_M - E(R_M)] \times \beta$
1995	20%	15%	6.6%	3%	3.6%	3%
1996	−24.6	−3	−38	−15	−18	−20
1997	23	10	9.6	−2	−2.4	12
1998	36.8	24	23.4	12	14.4	9
1999	3.4	7	−10	−5	−6	−4

Figure 18.4

Unexpected
Returns and
Beta

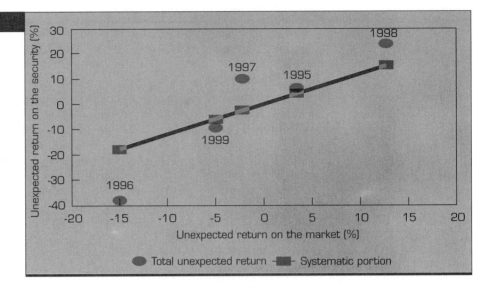

stand for the correlation between the return on a particular security i and the overall market. As before, let σ_i and σ_M be the standard deviations on the security and the market, respectively. Given these numbers, the beta for the security, β_i, is simply

$$\beta_i = \text{Corr}(R_i, R_M) \times \sigma_i / \sigma_M \qquad \textbf{18.11}$$

In other words, the beta is equal to the correlation multiplied by the ratio of the standard deviations.

From previous chapters, we know how to calculate the standard deviations in Equation 18.11. However, we have not yet discussed how to calculate correlations. This is our final task for this chapter. The simplest way to proceed is to construct a worksheet like Table 18.4.

The first six columns of Table 18.4 are familiar from Chapter 1. The first two contain five years of returns on a particular security and the overall market. We add these up and divide by 5 to get the average returns of 10 percent and 12 percent for the security and the market, respectively, as shown in the table. In the third and fourth columns we calculate the return deviations by taking each individual return and subtracting out the average return. In columns 5 and 6 we square these return deviations. To calculate the variances, we total these squared deviations and divide by $5 - 1 = 4$. We calculate the standard deviations by taking the square roots of the variances, and we find that the standard deviations for the security and the market are 18.87 percent and 15.03 percent, respectively.

Now we come to the part that's new. In the last column of Table 18.4, we have calculated the *product* of the return deviations by simply multiplying columns 3 and 4. When

covariance A measure of the tendency of two things to move or vary together.

we total these products and divide by $5 - 1 = 4$, the result is called the **covariance**.

Covariance, as the name suggests, is a measure of the tendency of two things to vary together. If the covariance is positive, then the tendency is to move in the same direction, and vice versa for a negative covariance. A zero covariance means there is no particular relation. For our security in Table 18.4, the covariance is $+204$, so the security tends to move in the same direction as the market.

A problem with covariances is that, like variances, the actual numbers are hard to interpret (the sign, of course, is not). For example, our covariance is 204, but, just from this number, we can't really say if the security has a strong tendency to move with the

Table 18.4	Calculating Beta							
	Returns		**Return Deviations**		**Squared Deviations**			
Year	**Security**	**Market**	**Security**	**Market**	**Security**	**Market**	**Product of Deviations**	
1995	10%	8%	0%	−4%	0	16	0	
1996	−8	−12	−18	−24	324	576	432	
1997	−4	16	−14	4	196	16	−56	
1998	40	26	30	14	900	196	420	
1999	12	22	2	10	4	100	20	
Totals	50	60	0	0	1,424	904	816	

	Average Returns	**Variances**	**Standard Deviations**
Security	50/5 = 10%	1,424/4 = 356	$\sqrt{356}$ = 18.87%
Market	60/5 = 12%	904/4 = 226	$\sqrt{226}$ = 15.03%

Covariance = $Cov(R_i, R_M)$ = 816/4 = 204
Correlation = $Corr(R_i, R_M)$ = 204/(18.87 × 15.03) = .72
Beta = β = .72 × (18.87/15.03) = .9031 ≈ .9

market or only a weak one. To fix this problem, we divide the covariance by the product of the two standard deviations. The result is the correlation coefficient, introduced in the previous chapter.

From Table 18.4, the correlation between our security and the overall market is .72. Recalling that correlations range from −1 to +1, this .72 tells us that the security has a fairly strong tendency to move with the overall market, but that tendency is not perfect.

Now, we have reached our goal of calculating the beta coefficient. As shown in the last row of Table 18.4, from Equation 18.11, we have

$$\beta_i = Corr(R_i, R_M) \times \sigma_i / \sigma_M$$

$$= .72 \times (18.87 / 15.03)$$

$$= .90$$

We find that this security has a beta of .9, so it has slightly less than average systematic risk.

Why Do Betas Differ?

Finally, we consider why different sources report different betas. The important thing to remember is that betas are estimated from actual data. Different sources estimate differently, possibly using different data. We discuss some of the key differences next.

First, there are two issues concerning data. Betas can be calculated using daily, weekly, month, quarterly, or annual returns. In principle, it does not matter which is chosen, but with real data, different estimates will result. Second, betas can be estimated over relatively short periods such as a few weeks or over long periods of 5 to 10 years or even more.

The trade-off here is not hard to understand. Betas obtained from high-frequency returns, such as daily returns, are less reliable than those obtained from less frequent returns, such as monthly returns. This argues for using monthly or longer returns. On the other hand, any time we estimate something, we would like to have a large number of recent observations. This argues for using weekly or daily returns. There is no ideal balance; the most common choices are three to five years of monthly data or a single year of weekly data. The betas we get from a year of weekly data are more current in the sense that they reflect only the previous year, but they tend to be less stable than those obtained from longer periods.

Another issue has to do with choice of a market index. All along, we have discussed the return on the "overall market," but we have not been very precise about how to measure this. By far the most common choice is to use the S&P 500 stock market index to measure the overall market, but this is not the only alternative. Different sources use different indexes to capture the overall market, and different indexes will lead to different beta estimates.

You might wonder whether some index is the "correct" one. The answer is yes, but a problem comes up. In principle, in the CAPM, when we speak of the overall market, what we really mean is the market for *every* risky asset of every type. In other words, what we would need is an index that included all the stocks, bonds, real estate, precious metals, and everything else in the entire world (not just the United States). Obviously, no such index exists, so instead we must choose some smaller index to proxy for this much larger one.

Last, a few sources (including *Value Line,* the source for Table 18.1) calculate betas the way we described in Table 18.4, but then they go on to adjust them for statistical reasons. The nature of the adjustment goes beyond our discussion, but such adjustments are another reason why betas differ across sources.

18.7 Summary and Conclusions

This chapter has covered the essentials of risk and return. Along the way, we have introduced a number of definitions and concepts. The most important of these is the security market line, or SML. The SML is important because it tells us the reward offered in financial markets for bearing risk.

Because we have covered quite a bit of ground, it's useful to summarize the basic economic logic underlying the SML as follows:

1. Based on capital market history, there is a reward for bearing risk. This reward is the risk premium on an asset.

2. The total risk associated with an asset has two parts: systematic risk and unsystematic risk. Unsystematic risk can be freely eliminated by diversification (this is the principle of diversification), so only systematic risk is rewarded. As a result, the risk premium on an asset is determined by its systematic risk. This is the systematic risk principle.

3. An asset's systematic risk, relative to the average, can be measured by its beta coefficient, β_i. The risk premium on an asset is then given by its beta coefficient multiplied by the market risk premium, $[E(R_M) - R_f] \times \beta_i$.

4. The expected return on an asset, $E(R_i)$, is equal to the risk-free rate, R_f, plus the risk premium:

$$E(R_i) = R_f + [E(R_M) - R_f] \times \beta_i$$

This is the equation of the SML, and it is often called the capital asset pricing model (CAPM).

Finally, to close out the chapter we showed how betas are calculated, and we discussed some of the main reasons different sources report different beta coefficients.

GET REAL

This chapter introduced you to the famous capital asset pricing model, or CAPM for short. For investors, the CAPM has a stunning implication: What you earn, through time, on your portfolio depends only on the level of systematic risk you bear. The corollary is equally striking: As a diversified investor, you don't need to be concerned with the total risk or volatility of any individual asset in your portfolio—it is simply irrelevant.

An immediate implication of the CAPM is that you, as an investor, need to be aware of the level of systematic risk you are carrying. Look up the betas of the stocks you hold in your simulated brokerage account and compute your portfolio's systematic risk. Is it bigger or smaller than 1.0? More important, is the portfolio's beta consistent with your desired level of portfolio risk?

Betas are particularly useful for understanding mutual fund risk and return. Since most mutual funds are at least somewhat diversified (the exceptions being sector funds and other specialized funds), they have relatively little unsystematic risk and their betas can be measured with some precision. Look at the funds you own and learn their betas (www.morningstar.com is a good source). Are the risk levels what you intended? As you study mutual fund risk, you will find some other measures exist, most of which are closely related to the measures discussed in this chapter. Take a few minutes to understand these as well.

Of course, we should note that the CAPM is a theory, and, as with any theory, whether it is correct or not is a question for the data. So does the CAPM work or not? Put more directly, does expected return depend on beta, and beta alone, or do other factors come into play? There is no more hotly debated question in all of finance, and the research that exists to date is inconclusive. (Some researchers would dispute this!) At a minimum, it appears that beta is a useful measure of market-related volatility, but whether it is a useful measure of expected return (much less a comprehensive one) awaits more research. Lots more research.

Key Terms

systematic risk 521	security market line (SML) 530
unsystematic risk 521	market risk premium 531
systematic risk principle 523	capital asset pricing model (CAPM) 531
beta coefficient (β) 524	covariance 536

Chapter Review Problems and Self-Test

1. **Risk and Return**   Suppose you observe the following situation:

Security	Beta	Expected Return
Sanders	1.8	22.00%
Janicek	1.6	20.44

If the risk-free rate is 7 percent, are these two stocks correctly priced relative to each other? What must the risk-free rate be if they are correctly priced?

2. CAPM Suppose the risk-free rate is 8 percent. The expected return on the market is 16 percent. If a particular stock has a beta of .7, what is its expected return based on the CAPM? If another stock has an expected return of 24 percent, what must its beta be?

Answers to Self-Test Problems

1. If we compute the reward-to-risk ratios, we get $(22\% - 7\%)/1.8. = 8.33\%$ for Sanders versus 8.4% for Janicek. Relative to Sanders, Janicek's expected return is too high, so its price is too low.

If they are correctly priced, then they must offer the same reward-to-risk ratio. The risk-free rate would have to be such that

$$\frac{22\% - R_f}{1.8} = \frac{20.44\% - R_f}{1.6}$$

With a little algebra, we find that the risk-free rate must be 8 percent:

$$22\% - R_f = (20.44\% - R_f)(1.8/1.6)$$
$$22\% - 20.44\% \times 1.125 = R_f - R_f \times 1.125$$
$$R_f = 8\%$$

2. Because the expected return on the market is 16 percent, the market risk premium is $16\% - 8\% = 8\%$ (the risk-free rate is 8 percent). The first stock has a beta of .7, so its expected return is $8\% + .7 \times 8\% = 13.6\%$.

For the second stock, notice that the risk premium is $24\% - 8\% = 16\%$. Because this is twice as large as the market risk premium, the beta must be exactly equal to 2. We can verify this using the CAPM:

$$E(R_i) = R_f + [E(R_M) - R_f] \times \beta_i$$
$$24\% = 8\% + (16\% - 8\%) \times \beta_i$$
$$\beta_i = 16\%/8\% = 2.0$$

Test Your Investment Quotient

1. Portfolio Return According to the CAPM, what is the rate of return of a portfolio with a beta of 1? *(1994 CFA Exam)*

a. Between R_M and R_f.
b. The risk-free rate, R_f.
c. Beta $\times (R_M - R_f)$.
d. The return on the market, R_M.

2. Stock Return The return on a stock is said to have which two of the following basic parts?

a. An expected return and an unexpected return.
b. A measurable return and an unmeasurable return.
c. A predicted return and a forecast return.
d. A total return and a partial return.

3. News Components A news announcement about a stock is said to have which two of the following parts?

a. An expected part and a surprise.
b. Public information and private information.
c. Financial information and product information.
d. A good part and a bad part.

4. **News Effects** A company announces that its earnings have increased 50 percent over the previous year, which matches analysts' expectations. What is the likely effect on the stock price?

   a. The stock price will increase.
   b. The stock price will decrease.
   c. The stock price will rise and then fall after an overreaction.
   d. The stock price will not be affected.

5. **News Effects** A company announces that its earnings have decreased 25 percent from the previous year, but analysts only expected a small increase. What is the likely effect on the stock price?

   a. The stock price will increase.
   b. The stock price will decrease.
   c. The stock price will rise and then fall after an overreaction.
   d. The stock price will not be affected.

6. **News Effects** A company announces that its earnings have increased 25 percent from the previous year, but analysts actually expected a 50 percent increase. What is the likely effect on the stock price?

   a. The stock price will increase.
   b. The stock price will decrease.
   c. The stock price will rise and then fall after an overreaction.
   d. The stock price will not be affected.

7. **News Effects** A company announces that its earnings have decreased 50 percent from the previous year, but analysts only expected a 25 percent decrease. What is the likely effect on the stock price?

   a. The stock price will increase.
   b. The stock price will decrease.
   c. The stock price will rise and then fall after an overreaction.
   d. The stock price will not be affected.

8. **Security Risk** The systematic risk of a security is also called its

   a. Perceived risk.
   b. Unique or asset-specific risk.
   c. Market risk.
   d. Fundamental risk.

9. **Security Risk** The unsystematic risk of a security is also called its

   a. Perceived risk.
   b. Unique or asset-specific risk.
   c. Market risk.
   d. Fundamental risk.

10. **Security Risk** Which type of risk is essentially eliminated by diversification?

    a. Perceived risk.
    b. Market risk.
    c. Systematic risk.
    d. Unsystematic risk.

11. **Security Risk** The systematic risk principle states that

    a. Systematic risk doesn't matter to investors.
    b. Systematic risk can be essentially eliminated by diversification.
    c. The reward for bearing risk is independent of the systematic risk of an investment.
    d. The reward for bearing risk depends only on the systematic risk of an investment.

12. **Security Risk** The systematic risk principle has an important implication, which is that

    a. Systematic risk is preferred to unsystematic risk.
    b. Systematic risk is the only risk that can be reduced by diversification.
    c. The expected return on an asset is independent of its systematic risk.
    d. The expected return on an asset depends only on its systematic risk.

13. **Security Risk**   The systematic risk of a stock is measured by its

   a. Beta coefficient.
   b. Correlation coefficient.
   c. Return standard deviation.
   d. Return variance.

14. **CAPM**   A financial market's security market line (SML) describes

   a. The relationship between systematic risk and expected returns.
   b. The relationship between unsystematic risk and expected returns.
   c. The relationship between systematic risk and unexpected returns.
   d. The relationship between unsystematic risk and unexpected returns.

15. **CAPM**   In the capital asset pricing model (CAPM), a security's expected return is

   a. The return on the market portfolio.
   b. The risk-free rate plus the return on the market portfolio.
   c. The return on the market portfolio plus a market risk premium.
   d. The risk-free rate plus a market risk premium.

Questions and Problems

**Core
Questions**

1. **Diversifiable Risk**   In broad terms, why is some risk diversifiable? Why are some risks nondiversifiable? Does it follow that an investor can control the level of unsystematic risk in a portfolio, but not the level of systematic risk?

2. **Announcements and Prices**   Suppose the government announces that, based on a just-completed survey, the growth rate in the economy is likely to be 2 percent in the coming year, compared to 5 percent for the year just completed. Will security prices increase, decrease, or stay the same following this announcement? Does it make any difference whether the 2 percent figure was anticipated by the market? Explain.

3. **Announcements and Risk**   Classify the following events as mostly systematic or mostly unsystematic. Is the distinction clear in every case?

   a. Short-term interest rates increase unexpectedly.
   b. The interest rate a company pays on its short-term debt borrowing is increased by its bank.
   c. Oil prices unexpectedly decline.
   d. An oil tanker ruptures, creating a large oil spill.
   e. A manufacturer loses a multimillion-dollar product liability suit.
   f. A Supreme Court decision substantially broadens producer liability for injuries suffered by product users.

4. **Announcements and Risk**   Indicate whether the following events might cause stocks in general to change price, and whether they might cause Big Widget Corp.'s stock to change price.

   a. The government announces that inflation unexpectedly jumped by 2 percent last month.
   b. Big Widget's quarterly earnings report, just issued, generally fell in line with analysts' expectations.
   c. The government reports that economic growth last year was at 3 percent, which generally agreed with most economists' forecasts.
   d. The directors of Big Widget die in a plane crash.
   e. Congress approves changes to the tax code that will increase the top marginal corporate tax rate. The legislation had been debated for the previous six months.

5. **Diversification and Risk**   True or false: The most important characteristic in determining the expected return of a well-diversified portfolio is the variances of the individual assets in the portfolio. Explain.

6. **Portfolio Betas**   You own a stock portfolio invested 30 percent in Stock Q, 20 percent in Stock R, 10 percent in Stock S, and 40 percent in Stock T. The betas for these four stocks are 1.2, .6, 1.5, and .8, respectively. What is the portfolio beta?

7. **Stock Betas** You own a portfolio equally invested in a risk-free asset and two stocks. If one of the stocks has a beta of 1.6 and the total portfolio is exactly as risky as the market, what must the beta be for the other stock in your portfolio?

8. **Expected Returns** A stock has a beta of 1.2, the expected return on the market is 17 percent, and the risk-free rate is 8 percent. What must the expected return on this stock be?

9. **Stock Betas** A stock has an expected return of 13 percent, the risk-free rate is 7 percent, and the market risk premium is 8 percent. What must the beta of this stock be?

10. **Market Returns** A stock has an expected return of 17 percent, its beta is .9, and the risk-free rate is 7.5 percent. What must the expected return on the market be?

11. **Risk-Free Rates** A stock has an expected return of 22 percent and a beta of 1.6, and the expected return on the market is 16 percent. What must the risk-free rate be?

12. **Portfolio Weights** A stock has a beta of .9 and an expected return of 13 percent. A risk-free asset currently earns 7 percent.
    a. What is the expected return on a portfolio that is equally invested in the two assets?
    b. If a portfolio of the two assets has a beta of .6, what are the portfolio weights?
    c. If a portfolio of the two assets has an expected return of 11 percent, what is its beta?
    d. If a portfolio of the two assets has a beta of 1.80, what are the portfolio weights? How do you interpret the weights for the two assets in this case? Explain.

Intermediate Questions

13. **Portfolio Risk and Return** Asset W has an expected return of 25 percent and a beta of 1.6. If the risk-free rate is 7 percent, complete the following table for portfolios of Asset W and a risk-free asset. Illustrate the relationship between portfolio expected return and portfolio beta by plotting the expected returns against the betas. What is the slope of the line that results?

Percentage of Portfolio in Asset W	Portfolio Expected Return	Portfolio Beta
0%		
25		
50		
75		
100		
125		
150		

14. **Relative Valuation** Stock Y has a beta of 1.59 and an expected return of 25 percent. Stock Z has a beta of .44 and an expected return of 12 percent. If the risk-free rate is 6 percent and the market risk premium is 11.3 percent, are these stocks correctly priced?

15. **Relative Valuation** In the previous problem, what would the risk-free rate have to be for the two stocks to be correctly priced?

16. **CAPM** Using the CAPM, show that the ratio of the risk premiums on two assets is equal to the ratio of their betas.

17. **Relative Valuation** Suppose you observe the following situation:

Security	Beta	Expected Return
Oxy Co.	1.35	23%
More-On Co.	.90	17

Assume these securities are correctly priced. Based on the CAPM, what is the expected return on the market? What is the risk-free rate?

18. **Announcements** As indicated by examples in this chapter, earnings announcements by companies are closely followed by, and frequently result in, share price revisions. Two issues should come to mind. First, earnings announcements concern past periods. If the market values stocks based on expectations of the future, why are numbers summarizing past performance relevant? Second, these announcements concern accounting earnings. Such earnings may have little to do with cash flow, so, again, why are they relevant?

19. **Beta**   Is it possible that a risky asset could have a beta of zero? Explain. Based on the CAPM, what is the expected return on such an asset? Is it possible that a risky asset could have a negative beta? What does the CAPM predict about the expected return on such an asset? Can you give an explanation for your answer?

20. **Relative Valuation**   Suppose you identify a situation in which one security is overvalued relative to another. How would you go about exploiting this opportunity? Does it matter if the two securities are both overvalued relative to some third security? Are your profits certain in this case?

21. **Calculating Beta**   Show that another way to calculate beta is to take the covariance between the security and the market and divide by the variance of the market's return.

22. **Calculating Beta**   Fill in the following table, supplying all the missing information. Use this information to calculate the security's beta.

Year	Returns Security	Returns Market	Return Deviations Security	Return Deviations Market	Squared Deviations Security	Squared Deviations Market	Product of Deviations
1995	12%	6%					
1996	−9	−12					
1997	−6	0					
1998	30	−4					
1999	18	30					
Totals	45	20					

19 International Finance and Investments

Investing overseas adds an international flavor to your portfolio. You can invest in an Argentine telephone company, an Italian auto company, or a Japanese electronics company as easily as you can invest in a U.S. book publishing company. Your overseas investments can increase your portfolio's diversification, but they also add a new risk element—you have to watch out for adverse exchange rate movements. ■ The rapid growth of global financial markets has made a knowledge of international finance and investments more important than ever before. Foreign currency markets are by far the most active markets in the world, with more than $1 trillion of currency transactions occurring daily among commercial banks. In comparison, daily trading on the New York Stock Exchange is only a relatively small fraction of that amount.

Despite the increasing integration of international financial markets, almost all countries maintain their own legal system and central bank, and they pursue their own fiscal and monetary policies. Moreover, global economic and political structures are evolving rapidly in directions that are often unpredictable. The immediate implication for investors is that investments in other countries have unique risk and return characteristics that must be dealt with. Coping with the international investment environment is a challenging task for money managers everywhere. Nevertheless, despite the difficulties involved, many international investment managers have succeeded brilliantly.

The purpose of this chapter is to familiarize you with some of the most important aspects of international finance and investments. Although reading this chapter does not guarantee that you will become a brilliant international investor, it is at least a first step. Perhaps the most important thing to realize before you begin your journey is that all that you already know about investments generally applies to international investments. International investors around the world all face similar problems and often adopt similar solutions that differ only in the details. The more you learn about international finance and investments, the more you will come to realize this. *Bon voyage!*

19.1 Currency Exchange Rates

The first salient fact distinguishing international investments from investments generally is that almost all countries maintain their own financial system and issue their own currency. The Mexican peso, Canadian dollar, Japanese yen, and British pound are all well-known currencies. However, the Swedish krona, Portuguese escudo, Irish punt, and Korean won are lesser known currencies even among world travelers.

A country may not have a currency of its own but instead use the currency of a neighbor. As examples of this practice, Liechtenstein uses the Swiss franc, Monaco uses the French franc, and San Marino uses the Italian lira. However, such examples are rare and typically occur only for very small countries.

Sometimes a group of countries agrees to use a common currency. The euro is a spectacular example. In January 1999, the 11 countries that compose the European Economic and Monetary Union (EMU) officially adopted the euro as a common currency. At first, the euro will be used as a currency for securities transactions, but over a period of several years it will replace the individual currencies of these 11 countries completely.

exchange rate The price of a country's currency stated in units of another country's currency, e.g., the exchange rate of U.S. dollars for British pounds.

An **exchange rate** is the price of a country's currency stated in units of another country's currency. Notice, however, that between any two currencies we can state two exchange rates. The exchange rate of U.S. dollars for British pounds might be stated as 1.55 dollars per pound. Alternatively, the exchange rate of British pounds for U.S. dollars may be stated as .645 pound per dollar, since .645 = 1/1.55. Both exchange rates actually say the same thing, which is the value of U.S. dollars and British pounds relative to each other. The fact that an exchange rate between any two currencies can be stated in two ways is something you may already know from personal travel experiences.

Most major currencies are freely traded in world currency markets, where their exchange rates are determined by the economic forces of supply and demand. These exchange rates are published daily in the financial press. Figure 19.1 presents a sample "Currency Trading" column from *The Wall Street Journal.* This column reports exchange rates between the major world currencies for transactions among New York City commercial banks. Notice that these exchange rates are reported in two ways: first as the U.S. dollar price of a foreign currency, and second as a foreign currency price of the U.S. dollar. For example, the U.S. dollar price of the euro is reported as 1.088, while the euro price of the U.S. dollar is reported as .9184. Of course, both quoted rates present the same information, which is the relative value of U.S. dollars and euros.

Figure 19.1

Exchange Rates

Source: *The Wall Street Journal,* March 4, 1999. Reprinted with permission from *The Wall Street Journal,* via Copyright Clearance Center, Inc. © 1999 Dow Jones & Company, Inc. All Rights Reserved Worldwide.

CURRENCY TRADING

Wednesday, March 3, 1999

EXCHANGE RATES

The New York foreign exchange mid-range rates below apply to trading among banks in amounts of $1 million and more, as quoted at 4 p.m. Eastern time by Telerate and other sources. Retail transactions provide fewer units of foreign currency per dollar. Rates for the 11 Euro currency countries are derived from the latest dollar-euro rate using the exchange ratios set 1/1/99.

Country	U.S. $ equiv. Wed	Tue	Currency per U.S. $ Wed	Tue
Argentina (Peso)	1.0002	1.0002	.9998	.9998
Australia (Dollar)	.6217	.6227	1.6086	1.6060
Austria (Schilling)	.07913	.07947	12.638	12.584
Bahrain (Dinar)	2.6525	2.6386	.3770	.3790
Belgium (Franc)	.02699	.02711	37.050	36.891
Brazil (Real)	.4673	.4630	2.1400	2.1600
Britain (Pound)	1.6138	1.6160	.6197	.6188
1-month forward	1.6129	1.6152	.6200	.6191
3-months forward	1.6121	1.6146	.6203	.6193
6-months forward	1.6122	1.6151	.6203	.6192
Canada (Dollar)	.6551	.6570	1.5265	1.5220
1-month forward	.6550	.6570	1.5267	1.5222
3-months forward	.6550	.6569	1.5268	1.5223
6-months forward	.6550	.6567	1.5268	1.5226
Chile (Peso)	.002002	.001989	499.45	502.65
China (Renminbi)	.1208	.1208	8.2789	8.2789
Colombia (Peso)	.0006419	.0006409	1557.94	1560.40
Czech. Rep. (Koruna) ...				
Commercial rate	.02897	.02906	34.518	34.414
Denmark (Krone)	.1464	.1471	6.8285	6.7995
Ecuador (Sucre)				
Floating rate	.0001002	.0001002	9984.50	9984.50
Finland (Markka)	.1831	.1839	5.4608	5.4373
France (Franc)	.1660	.1667	6.0246	5.9987
1-month forward	.1663	.1670	6.0148	5.9889
3-months forward	.1668	.1675	5.9961	5.9702
6-months forward	.1677	.1684	5.9641	5.9382
Germany (Mark)	.5567	.5591	1.7963	1.7886
1-month forward	.5576	.5600	1.7934	1.7856
3-months forward	.5593	.5618	1.7878	1.7801
6-months forward	.5623	.5648	1.7783	1.7705
Greece (Drachma)	.003385	.003396	295.38	294.51
Hong Kong (Dollar)	.1290	.1291	7.7495	7.7477
Hungary (Forint)	.004288	.004330	233.22	230.96
India (Rupee)	.02352	.02352	42.515	42.515
Indonesia (Rupiah)	.0001002	.0001127	8885.00	8870.00
Ireland (Punt)	1.3826	1.3885	.7233	.7202
Israel (Shekel)	.2468	.2470	4.0522	4.0488
Italy (Lira)	.0005623	.0005647	1778.35	1770.71

Country	U.S. $ equiv. Wed	Tue	Currency per U.S. $ Wed	Tue
Japan (Yen)	.008207	.008317	121.84	120.23
1-month forward	.008241	.008352	121.34	119.73
3-months forward	.008311	.008419	120.33	118.78
6-months forward	.008417	.008532	118.81	117.21
Jordan (Dinar)	1.4055	1.4045	.7115	.7120
Kuwait (Dinar)	3.2819	3.2819	.3047	.3047
Lebanon (Pound)	.0006616	.0006616	1511.50	1511.50
Malaysia (Ringgit-b)	.2632	.2632	3.8000	3.8000
Malta (Lira)	2.5387	2.5419	.3939	.3934
Mexico (Peso)				
Floating rate	.1005	.1005	9.9475	9.9490
Netherland (Guilder)	.4941	.4962	2.0240	2.0153
New Zealand (Dollar)	.5278	.5291	1.8947	1.8900
Norway (Krone)	.1260	.1264	7.9343	7.9108
Pakistan (Rupee)	.01957	.01952	51.110	51.235
Peru (new Sol)	.2946	.2948	3.3940	3.3925
Philippines (Peso)	.02558	.02561	39.100	39.050
Poland (Zloty)	.2516	.2521	3.9745	3.9670
Portugal (Escudo)	.005431	.005454	184.13	183.34
Russia (Ruble) (a)	.04361	.04369	22.930	22.890
Saudi Arabia (Riyal)	.2666	.2666	3.7510	3.7506
Singapore (Dollar)	.5754	.5771	1.7380	1.7328
Slovak Rep. (Koruna)	.02498	.02499	40.037	40.010
South Africa (Rand)	.1603	.1602	6.2400	6.2430
South Korea (Won)	.0008135	.0008168	1229.30	1224.35
Spain (Peseta)	.006544	.006572	152.82	152.16
Sweden (Krona)	.1211	.1213	8.2595	8.2440
Switzerland (Franc)	.6849	.6866	1.4601	1.4565
1-month forward	.6871	.6888	1.4555	1.4517
3-months forward	.6913	.6929	1.4466	1.4431
6-months forward	.6978	.6996	1.4331	1.4293
Taiwan (Dollar)	.03021	.03023	33.100	33.075
Thailand (Baht)	.02654	.02664	37.685	37.535
Turkey (Lira)	.00000280	.00000281	357340.00	356480.00
United Arab (Dirham)	.2723	.2700	3.6730	3.7040
Uruguay (New Peso)				
Financial	.09046	.09095	11.055	10.995
Venezuela (Bolivar)	.001736	.001736	576.00	576.00
SDR	1.3599	1.3592	.7353	.7357
Euro	1.0888	1.0935	.9184	.9145

Special Drawing Rights (SDR) are based on exchange rates for the U.S., German, British, French, and Japanese currencies. Source: International Monetary Fund.

a-Russian Central Bank rate. Trading band lowered on 8/17/98. b-Government rate.

The Wall Street Journal daily foreign exchange data from 1996 forward may be purchased through the Readers' Reference Service (413) 592-3600.

Key Currency Cross Rates Late New York Trading March 3, 1999

	Dollar	Euro	Pound	SFranc	Guilder	Peso	Yen	Lira	D-Mark	FFranc	CdnDlr
Canada	1.5265	1.6621	2.4635	1.0455	.75420	.15346	.01253	.00086	.84980	.25338	....
France	6.0246	6.5596	9.7225	4.1262	2.9766	.60564	.04945	.00339	3.3539	....	3.9467
Germany	1.7963	1.9558	2.8989	1.2303	.88750	.18058	.01474	.00101	....	.29816	1.1767
Italy	1778.4	1936.3	2869.9	1218.0	878.63	178.77	14.596	....	990.01	295.18	1165.0
Japan	121.84	132.66	196.63	83.446	60.198	12.248	....	.06851	67.828	20.224	79.817
Mexico	9.9475	10.831	16.053	6.8129	4.9148	....	.08164	.00559	5.5378	1.6511	6.5165
Netherlands	2.0240	2.2037	3.2663	1.3862	....	.20347	.01661	.00114	1.1268	.33596	1.3259
Switzerland	1.4601	1.5898	2.3563	....	.72139	.14678	.01198	.00082	.81284	.24236	.95650
U.K.	.61966	.67468	....	.42439	.30615	.06229	.00509	.00035	.34496	.10285	.40593
Euro	.91844	....	1.4822	.62903	.45378	.09233	.00754	.00052	.51130	.15245	.60167
U.S.	....	1.0888	1.6138	.68488	.49407	.10053	.00821	.00056	.55670	.16599	.65509

Source: Telerate

A more detailed listing of currency exchange rates is published weekly in *The Wall Street Journal.* Figure 19.2 is a sample "World Value of the Dollar" column. Almost all exchange rates listed here are stated as a foreign currency price of the U.S. dollar. However, those currencies marked with an asterisk are stated as a U.S. dollar price of the foreign currency. For example, the United Kingdom has its pound sterling currency marked with an asterisk, indicating an exchange rate stated as a U.S. dollar price of the British pound.

Figure 19.2

More Exchange
Rates

Source: *The Wall Street
Journal,* February 22, 1999.
Reprinted with permission
from *The Wall Street Journal,*
via Copyright Clearance
Center, Inc. © 1999 Dow
Jones & Company, Inc. All
Rights Reserved Worldwide.

World Value of the Dollar

The table below, compiled by Bank of America, gives the rates of exchange for the U.S. dollar against various currencies as of Friday, February 19, 1999. Unless otherwise noted, all rates listed are middle rates of interbank bid and asked quotes, and are expressed in foreign currency units per one U.S. dollar. The rates are indicative and aren't based on, nor intended to be used as a basis for, particular transactions.

BankAmerica International doesn't trade in all the listed foreign currencies.

Country (Currency)	Value 2/19	Value 2/12	Country (Currency)	Value 2/19	Value 2/12
Afghanistan (Afghani -c)	4750.00	4750.00	Lebanon (Pound)	1508.00	1508.00
Albania (Lek)	139.55	139.70	Lesotho (Maloti)	6.2225	6.095
Algeria (Dinar)	63.5833	63.4022	Liberia (Dollar)	1.00	1.00
Andorra (Peseta -7)	148.7316	148.0303	Libya (Dinar -21)	0.45	0.45
Andorra (Franc -8)	5.8636	5.0269	Liechtenstein (Franc)	1.4294	1.4235
Angola (Readjust Kwanza)	257128.00	257128.00	Lithuania (Litas)	4.0015	4.0018
Antigua (E Caribbean $)	2.70	2.70	Luxembourg (Lux.Franc -11)	36.0596	35.8896
Argentina (Peso)	0.9999	0.9999	Macao (Pataca)	8.0042	8.0055
Aruba (Florin)	1.79	1.79	Madagascar DR (Franc)	5220.00	5220.00
Australia (Australia Dollar)	1.568	1.5576	Malawi (Kwacha)	43.81	43.625
Austria (Schilling -14)	12.3003	12.2423	Malaysia (Ringgit)	3.795	3.80
Azerbaijan (Manat)	3950.00	3950.00	Maldive (Rufiyaa)	11.77	11.77
Bahamas (Dollar)	1.00	1.00	Mali Rep (C.F.A. Franc)	586.3565	502.6868
Bahrain (Dinar)	0.38	0.38	Malta (Lira *)	2.6355	2.6355
Bangladesh (Taka)	48.50	48.50	Martinique (Franc -8)	5.8636	5.0269
Barbados (Dollar)	2.00	2.00	Mauritania (Ouguiya)	204.44	204.44
Belgium (Franc -9)	36.0596	35.8896	Mauritius (Rupee)	24.875	24.925
Belize (Dollar)	2.00	2.00	Mexico (New Peso)	9.92	10.005
Benin (C.F.A. Franc)	586.3565	502.6868	Monaco (Franc -8)	5.8636	5.0269
Bermuda (Dollar)	1.00	1.00	Mongolia (Tugrik -o-29)	817.61	817.61
Bhutan (Ngultrum)	42.4205	42.4475	Montserrat (E Caribbean $)	2.70	2.70
Bolivia (Boliviano -o)	5.69	5.68	Morocco (Dirham)	9.562	9.5065
Bolivia (Boliviano -f)	5.70	5.69	Mozambique (Metical)	11495.00	11495.00
Botswana (Pula)	4.6449	4.5872	Namibia (Rand -c)	6.2225	6.095
Bouvet Island (Norwegian Krone)	7.7905	7.6765	Nauru Islands (Australia Dollar)	1.568	1.5576
Brazil (Real)	1.91	1.91	Nepal (Rupee)	67.675	67.675
Brunei (Dollar)	1.7067	1.6932	Netherlands (Guilder -10)	1.9699	1.9606
Bulgaria (Lev)	1741.85	1734.30	Netherlands Ant'les (Guilder)	1.79	1.79
Burkina Faso (C.F.A. Franc)	586.3565	502.6868	New Zealand (N.Z.Dollar)	1.8442	1.8283
Burma (Kyat)	6.2926	6.1047	Nicaragua (Gold Cordoba)	11.3443	11.3407
Burundi (Franc)	503.33	499.95	Niger Rep (C.F.A. Franc)	586.3565	502.6868
Cambodia (Riel)	3770.00	3775.00	Nigeria (Naira -o)	21.886	21.886
Cameroon (C.F.A. Franc)	586.3565	502.6868	Nigeria (Naira -m)	87.50	87.20
Canada (Dollar)	1.4881	1.4927	Norway (Norwegian Krone)	7.7905	7.6765
Cape Verde Isl (Escudo -20)	94.71	94.71	Oman, Sultanate of (Rial)	0.385	0.385
Cayman Islands (Dollar)	0.8333	0.8333	Pakistan (Rupee -27)	51.16	51.05
Centrl African Rp (C.F.A. Franc)	586.3565	502.6868	Panama (Balboa)	1.00	1.00
Chad (C.F.A. Franc)	586.3565	502.6868	Papua N.G. (Kina)	2.2222	2.2099
Chile (Peso -m)	496.54	493.26	Paraguay (Guarani -d)	2910.00	2910.00
Chile (Peso -o)	477.20	475.15	Peru (New Sol -d)	3.3895	3.3963
China (Renminbi Yuan)	8.2787	8.2776	Philippines (Peso)	38.87	38.65
Colombia (Peso -o-2)	1561.50	1564.20	Pitcairn Island (N.Z.Dollar)	1.8442	1.8283
Commnwlth Ind Sts (Rouble -m-17)	23.09	23.20	Poland (Zloty -o)	3.811	3.757
Comoros (Franc)	439.7674	377.0151	Portugal (Escudo -6)	179.2098	178.3648
Congo, People Rp (C.F.A. Franc)	586.3565	502.6868	Puerto Rico (U.S. $)	1.00	1.00
Costa Rica (Colon)	275.35	274.78	Qatar (Rival)	3.6405	3.65
Croatia (Kuna)	6.7353	6.6728	Repub of Macedonia (Denar)	53.9586	53.5759
Cuba (Peso -1)	23.00	23.00	Republic of Yemen (Rial -a-25)	141.34	136.66
Cyprus (Pound *)	1.9275	1.9359	Reunion, Ile de la (Franc -8)	5.8636	5.0269
Czech (Koruna)	33.706	33.513	Romania (Leu)	12319.00	12207.00
Denmark (Danish Krone)	6.646	6.6155	Rwanda (Franc)	320.34	320.63
Equatorial Guinea (C.F.A. Franc)	586.3565	502.6868	San Marino (Lira -13)	1730.8215	1722.6601
Estonia (Kroon)	13.9871	13.9224	Sao Tome & Principe (Dobra)	2390.00	2390.00
Ethiopia (Birr -o)	6.9875	6.9875	Saudi Arabia (Riyal)	3.7533	3.7507
Faeroe Islands (Danish Krone)	6.646	6.6155	Senegal (C.F.A. Franc)	586.3565	502.6868
Falkland Islands (Pound *)	1.6345	1.6259	Seychelles (Rupee)	5.359	5.42
Fiji (Dollar -31)	1.9688	1.9379	Sierra Leone (Leone)	1450.00	1571.00
Finland (Markka -16)	5.3149	5.2898	Singapore (Dollar)	1.7067	1.6932
France (Franc -8)	5.8636	5.0269	Slovak (Koruna -15)	39.199	38.226
French Guiana (Franc -8)	5.8636	5.0269	Slovenia (Tolar)	169.898	169.3312
French Pacific Isl (C.F.P. Franc)	106.6102	91.3975	Solomon Islands (Solomon Dollar)	4.8402	4.9455
Gabon (C.F.A. Franc)	586.3565	502.6868	Somali Rep (Shilling -d)	2620.00	2620.00
Gambia (Dalasi)	10.975	10.975	South Africa (Rand -c)	6.2225	6.095
Germany (Mark -12)	1.7483	1.7401	Spain (Peseta -7)	148.7316	148.0303
Ghana (Cedi)	2387.50	2387.50	Sri Lanka (Rupee)	69.29	69.095
Gibraltar (Pound *)	1.6345	1.6259	Sudan Rep (Pound -c)	1960.00	1960.00
Greece (Drachma)	286.855	286.475	Sudan Rep (Dinar)	196.00	196.00
Greenland (Danish Krone)	6.646	6.6155	Surinam (Guilder)	401.00	401.00
Grenada (E Caribbean $)	2.70	2.70	Swaziland (Lilangeni)	6.2225	6.095
Guadeloupe (Franc -8)	5.8636	5.0269	Sweden (Krona)	7.963	7.945
Guam (U.S. $)	1.00	1.00	Switzerland (Franc)	1.4294	1.4235
Guatemala (Quetzal)	6.8348	6.9241	Syria (Pound)	46.25	46.25
Guinea Bissau (C.F.A. Franc -23)	586.3565	502.6868	Taiwan (Dollar -o)	32.54	32.275
Guinea Rep (Franc)	1300.00	1300.00	Tanzania (Shilling)	691.35	688.25
Guyana (Dollar)	162.80	157.00	Thailand (Baht)	37.425	36.95
Haiti (Gourde)	16.8341	16.7883	Togo, Rep (C.F.A. Franc)	586.3565	502.6868
Honduras Rep (Lempira -d)	14.01	13.985	Tonga Islands (Pa'anga)	1.5883	1.5671
Hong Kong (Dollar)	7.7485	7.7498	Trinidad & Tobago (Dollar)	6.2525	6.2525
Hungary (Forint)	224.81	221.76	Tunisia (Dinar)	1.1369	1.13
Iceland (Krona)	71.32	70.74	Turkey (Lira)	347710.50	343810.00
India (Rupee -m)	42.4205	42.4475	Turks & Caicos (U.S. $)	1.00	1.00
Indonesia (Rupiah)	8850.00	8725.00	Tuvalu (Australia Dollar)	1.568	1.5576
Iran (Rial -o)	3000.00	3000.00	Uganda (Shilling)	1233.50	1233.50
Iraq (Dinar -o-26)	0.3109	0.3109	Ukraine (Hryvnia -18)	3.875	4.015
Ireland (Punt * -5)	1.4205	1.4272	United Arab Emir (Dirham)	3.673	3.6731
Israel (New Shekel)	4.0647	4.0617	United Kingdom (Pound Sterling *)	1.6345	1.6259
Italy (Lira -13)	1730.8215	1722.6601	Uruguay (Peso Uruguayo -m)	10.965	10.92
Ivory Coast (C.F.A. Franc)	586.3565	502.6868	Vanuatu (Vatu)	128.54	127.41
Jamaica (Dollar -o)	36.65	36.65	Vatican City (Lira -13)	1730.8215	1722.6601
Japan (Yen)	119.805	114.855	Venezuela (Bolivar -d-3)	577.00	577.255
Jordan (Dinar)	0.709	0.709	Vietnam (Dong -o-28)	13882.00	13881.50
Kenya (Shilling)	62.95	61.87	Virgin Is, Br (U.S. $)	1.00	1.00
Kiribati (Australia Dollar)	1.568	1.5576	Virgin Is, US (U.S. $)	1.00	1.00
Korea, North (Won)	2.20	2.20	Yugoslavia (New Dinar -19)	10.4179	10.3666
Korea, South (Won -30)	1204.50	1175.55	Zaire Rep (New Zaire)	245000.00	245000.00
Kuwait (Dinar)	0.3039	0.3029	Zambia (Kwacha)	2150.00	2487.50
Laos, People DR (Kip)	4203.50	4203.50	Zimbabwe (Dollar)	38.50	38.70
Latvia (Lat)	0.5788	0.5755			

In the United States, we often prefer to state an exchange rate as the U.S. dollar price of a unit of foreign currency. For example, we might state the exchange rate for Canadian dollars as 65 cents, because one Canadian dollar costs about U.S. $.65. However, we often reverse this practice and state an exchange rate as the foreign currency price of a U.S. dollar. For example, we might state the dollar exchange rate with Japanese yen as 121 yen, because 1 U.S. dollar can be bought for 121 yen. The fact that we often flip directions when stating various exchange rates is a common source of confusion for novices of international finance.

Further confusion can arise from the fact that exchange rates are often stated as cross rates. A **cross rate** is an exchange rate between two foreign currencies. For example, from the viewpoint of a U.S. resident, the exchange rate between German marks and British pounds is a cross rate. Similarly, from the viewpoint of a German resident, the exchange rate between U.S. dollars and British pounds is a cross rate. In this book, we assume the reader is a resident of the United States and that a cross rate is an exchange rate between any two currencies other than the U.S. dollar.

Cross rates among the major world currencies are reported daily in *The Wall Street Journal*'s "Key Currency Cross Rates" box, as shown at the bottom of Figure 19.1. The leftmost column of this box lists country names, while the top row lists the names of their currencies. The first column of exchange rates lists foreign currency prices of the U.S. dollar. For example, the exchange rate in the upper left corner is the Canadian dollar price of the U.S. dollar. The bottom row of exchange rates lists U.S. dollar prices of foreign currencies. For example, the exchange rate in the lower right corner is the U.S. dollar price of Canadian dollars. Except for the first column and the bottom row, all other exchange rates are cross rates between foreign currencies.

cross rate Exchange rate between two foreign currencies; e.g., for a U.S. resident, the exchange rate between German marks and British pounds.

CHECK THIS

19.1a Find the "Currency Trading" section in a recent *Wall Street Journal*. What are the U.S. dollar prices of the British pound, euro, French franc, German mark, and Japanese yen?

19.1b In a recent *Wall Street Journal*, find the "Key Currency Cross Rates" box. What are the British pound prices of the Canadian dollar, euro, and Japanese yen? What are the Japanese yen prices of the British pound, Canadian dollar, and the euro?

19.2 Exchange Rate Changes

exchange rate appreciation Increase in the value of one currency relative to another currency. *Exchange rate depreciation* occurs when one currency decreases in value relative to another currency.

In discussions of international financial markets, we often hear the term **exchange rate appreciation**—and its apparent opposite, *exchange rate depreciation*. Be forewarned, these terms are potentially confusing because an appreciation of, say, the British pound against the U.S. dollar is simultaneously a depreciation of the U.S. dollar against the British pound, and vice versa. Furthermore, the exchange rate between U.S. dollars and British pounds can be stated as either a dollar price of pounds or a pound price of dollars. To avoid confusing appreciation and depreciation, observe the rule that when the dollar price of pounds goes down this is exchange rate appreciation, and when the dollar price of pounds goes up this is exchange rate depreciation. Even better, state a decrease in the dollar price of pounds as a dollar appreciation and an increase in the dollar price of pounds as a dollar depreciation.

Now suppose the exchange rate of U.S. dollars for euros is originally U.S.$1.10 per euro, which then changes to U.S.$1.05 per euro. This is an example of exchange rate appreciation because we are stating the exchange rate as the U.S. dollar price of euros, and euros became cheaper when bought with U.S. dollars. Of course, it's clearer to say that the U.S. dollar appreciated against the euro or, equivalently, that the euro depreciated against the U.S. dollar. As another example, suppose the exchange rate of Japanese yen for U.S. dollars, originally ¥121 per $1, changes to ¥116 per $1. This is best stated as a dollar depreciation, but it is equivalently stated as a yen appreciation since the yen became more expensive when bought with U.S. dollars.

Experienced international investors know that the uncertainty of exchange rates appreciating or depreciating is an important source of risk. For example, suppose you invest in British gilts with a current value of £1 million. Gilts are bonds issued by the government of England and are denominated in British pounds. Assuming an original exchange rate of $1.50 per pound, gilts with a value of £1 million have a dollar value of $1.5 million. Now suppose that six months later these gilts have the same value in pounds, that is, £1 million, but the dollar depreciated to $1.60 per pound. In this case, £1 million in gilts can be sold and converted into $1.6 million, thereby yielding a $100,000 profit on the dollar depreciation. Alternatively, suppose that the dollar appreciated against the pound to $1.40 per pound. In this case, £1 million in gilts can be converted back to only $1.4 million, thereby yielding a $100,000 loss on the dollar appreciation. In international investments, the uncertainty associated with exchange rate movements can produce considerable investment risk.

Since exchange rate changes are largely unpredictable, holding assets denominated in a foreign currency involves **exchange rate risk**, or *currency risk*. From the standpoint of a U.S. investor, appreciation of the dollar against a foreign currency causes a decrease in value of an investment denominated in the foreign currency. Similarly, depreciation of the dollar against a foreign currency causes an increase in value of an investment denominated in the foreign currency.

To gain further insight into how exchange rate changes can affect investment returns, suppose that one year ago, when a single dollar cost 1.5 Deutsche marks (abbreviated DM), you purchased German bunds for DM15 million. As you might guess, *bund* is German for bond. This means the German bunds originally cost $10 million, that is, DM15 million/1.5. Now one year later, the value of the bunds is DM18 million and a dollar costs DM1.8. In this case, the mark value of the bunds increased by 20 percent, but the mark depreciated by 20 percent also. As a result, your total investment return is zero because the bunds can be converted back into only $10 million, that is, DM18 million/1.8. If instead the mark appreciated 20 percent to DM1.2 per dollar, your total investment return would be 50 percent since the bunds could be converted into $15 million, that is, DM18 million/1.2. As these examples suggest, exchange rate changes can have a dramatic effect on investments denominated in foreign currencies. Experienced international investors are well aware of this fact. You should be too!

exchange rate risk
The risk that an investment denominated in a foreign currency will change in value because of unpredicted changes in exchange rates. Also called *currency risk*.

CHECK THIS

19.2a The cross rate of francs for pounds changes from 9.5 to 10.2. Which currency appreciated and which currency depreciated?

19.2b The cross rate of yen for francs changes from 19 to 16. Which currency appreciated and which currency depreciated?

19.2c Suppose you buy German bunds and subsequently the dollar appreciates 10 percent against the mark. Did the dollar appreciation increase or decrease the dollar value of your investment?

19.2d Suppose you buy French OATs (*Obligations Assimilables du Trésor,* Treasury obligations) and subsequently the dollar depreciates 10 percent against the franc. Did the dollar depreciation increase or decrease the dollar value of your investment?

19.2e Suppose you purchased Japanese securities for ¥100 million one year ago when a dollar cost ¥100. What is your total investment return (based on U.S. dollars) if the value of the securities is now ¥110 million and a dollar now costs ¥110? What is your return if a dollar now costs ¥90 instead?

19.3 Triangular Arbitrage

triangular arbitrage
A round-trip sequence of three currency transactions at exchange rates that yield an arbitrage profit; e.g., dollars buy pounds, pounds buy francs, francs buy dollars.

Exchange rates among freely traded currencies follow a fundamental relationship referred to as **triangular arbitrage**. Actually, a more accurate description would be "no triangular arbitrage," since it is the general absence of triangular arbitrage opportunities that characterizes exchange rates determined in competitive currency markets.

As an example of what is meant by a triangular arbitrage, suppose that you observe the following three exchange rates among dollars, pounds, and francs:

$$\$1.5/\pounds1 \qquad \pounds.13/Fr1 \qquad Fr5/\$1$$

Next, suppose that you perform the following sequence of transactions beginning with a cash amount of $1,000:

1. With $1,000, buy £666.67 at $1.5 per pound.
2. With £666.67, buy Fr5,128.21 at £.13 per franc.
3. With Fr1,025.64, buy $1,025.64 at Fr5 per dollar.

Voila! You began with $1,000 but through the three transactions you end up with $1,025.46! This is an arbitrage profit of $25.46. If $25.46 seems like a small amount, consider performing the same sequence of transactions instead beginning with $1,000,000. In this case, your arbitrage profit is $25,460—not bad for a few minutes work! This is an example of triangular arbitrage.

Unfortunately, triangular arbitrage opportunities are rare in competitive currency markets. Certainly, if triangular arbitrage were possible on a regular basis, then everyone would be doing it. But, in fact, currency dealers trade only at currency prices that do not allow triangular arbitrage, since they are the ones who would lose money to the triangular arbitragers. Indeed, to avoid such mistakes the computers used by currency dealers are programmed to prevent entering an exchange rate that allows triangular arbitrage.

At this point, knowing that triangular arbitrage is implausible, you might wonder why you should care to learn about it. This is a legitimate question. The answer is that the absence of triangular arbitrage imposes a strong restriction on exchange rate structures. If at some future date you must deal with multiple exchange rates, you will need to understand these structures.

If triangular arbitrage opportunities existed, they would be easy to identify. You can determine whether a sequence of three exchange rates allows triangular arbitrage by simply calculating the product of the three rates that represent transactions making a round trip back to the starting currency. If the product is not equal to 1, then triangular arbitrage is possible. But if the product is equal to 1, triangular arbitrage is not possible.

For example, the no-triangular-arbitrage condition for the three exchange rates mentioned earlier is formally stated as follows:

$$S(\$/\pounds) \times S(\pounds/Fr) \times S(Fr/\$) = 1$$

where S is the current exchange rate, and the three exchange rates are

$S(\$/\pounds)$ = Dollar price of the pound

$S(\pounds/Fr)$ = Pound price of the franc

$S(Fr/\$)$ = Franc price of the dollar

Using the numerical values above, the product of the three exchange rates is calculated as

$$1.5 \times .13 \times 5 = .975$$

This product is not equal to 1, and therefore an arbitrage opportunity exists for these three exchange rates. But if the franc price of dollars was 5.13, then the product of the three exchange rates would be

$$1.5 \times .13 \times 5.13 = 1.000$$

Since this product is equal to 1, no arbitrage opportunity exists for these three exchange rates.

CHECK THIS

19.3a From a recent *Wall Street Journal*, find the dollar price of pounds, the pound price of francs, and the franc price of dollars. Check to see if the product of these three exchange rates is equal to 1.

19.3b From a recent *Wall Street Journal*, obtain the dollar price of marks, the mark price of yen, and the yen price of dollars. Check to see if the product of these three exchange rates is equal to 1.

19.4 Forward Currency Contracts

Exchange rate risk is a real concern for investors holding securities denominated in more than one currency. Suppose that you are a portfolio manager and have purchased commercial paper issued by a British company that will pay £10 million in six months. At the current exchange rate of $1.50 per pound, this payment can be converted into $15 million. However, you are concerned that the pound might depreciate against the dollar over the next six months. If, for example, the exchange rate depreciates to, say, $1.40 per pound, the £10 million payment could be converted into only $14 million. This represents a $1 million exchange rate loss. Of course, it is possible that the exchange rate could appreciate, in which case you would realize an exchange rate gain.

Seeing the possibilities, you are inclined to not speculate on an exchange rate change and therefore decide to hedge the transaction with a **forward currency contract**. Forward currency contracts are widely used by international investors to hedge exchange rate risk. A forward currency contract is an agreement to transact an exchange of currencies on a future date at a prespecified **forward exchange rate**. International commercial banks are major dealers in forward currency contracts. Thus, if you decide to hedge exchange rate risk with a forward currency contract, most likely you will enter into a forward contract with a commercial bank offering this service.

For your particular hedging problem, you wish to set an exchange rate today at which you can convert the £10 million payment into U.S. dollars six months from now. Suppose your bank agrees to a forward contract to buy £10 million from you in six months at a forward exchange rate of $1.55 per pound. This forward contract sets a dollar value for your pound payment of $15.5 million.

As another example, suppose you buy a block of shares in a French company for Fr50 million. You believe the franc value of your investment will rise in the next six months, but you are concerned that the franc will depreciate, thereby reducing or even eliminating your investment gains. To avoid currency risk you enter into a forward contract to sell Fr50 million in six months at a forward rate of Fr5.2 per dollar. This contract guarantees that you can sell Fr50 million for about $9.6 million, thereby removing most of the currency risk from your investment.

forward currency contract An agreement to transact a currency exchange on a future date at a prespecified exchange rate.

forward exchange rate A prespecified exchange rate for a future currency exchange.

CHECK THIS

19.4a You buy Japanese notes paying ¥700 million at maturity in one year. Explain how you would hedge the currency risk of this payment assuming a forward rate of ¥100 per dollar.

19.5 Interest Rate Parity

interest rate parity A relationship between interest rates in two countries and spot and forward exchange rates between the two countries' currencies.

spot exchange rate An exchange rate for an immediate currency exchange.

Interest rate parity specifies a fundamental relationship between the interest rates in two countries and the forward and **spot exchange rates** of the two countries' currencies. The interest rate parity condition is based on the fundamental principle that two risk-free investments held over the same time period should have the same rate of return. To illustrate the interest rate parity condition, suppose that you can choose between a risk-free investment denominated in U.S. dollars and a risk-free investment denominated in British pounds where currency risk is eliminated by the use of a forward currency contract. Since both investment strategies are risk-free, in competitive capital markets both investments should offer the same risk-free return.

The structure of interest rate parity between dollars and pounds is stated formally by the equation

$$[1 + r(\$)]^T = [1 + r(£)]^T \times \frac{F_T(\$/£)}{S(\$/£)}$$

where

$r(\$)$ = Risk-free interest rate for U.S. dollars
$r(£)$ = Risk-free interest rate for British pounds
$S(\$/£)$ = Spot exchange rate stated as a dollar price of the British pound
$F_T(\$/£)$ = Forward exchange rate for delivery T years from now

This equation may look intimidating, but it is in fact simple. The left side of the equation states the future value of a one-dollar investment earning the U.S. interest rate for T years. The right side of the equation states the future value of a one-dollar investment earning the interest rate for British pounds, where the investment is first converted into pounds at the spot exchange rate and later converted back to dollars at the forward exchange rate.

As a numerical example, suppose the dollar interest rate is $r(\$) = 5\%$ for a one-year investment, that is, $T = 1$. This means that a $1,000 investment will be worth $1,000 × 1.05 = $1,050 one year from now. Also suppose that the pound interest rate is $r(£) = 7\%$ and the spot exchange rate of dollars for pounds is $S(\$/£) = 1.5$. This means that $1,000 can be converted into $1,000/1.5 = £666.667 today and after earning interest will be worth £666.667 × 1.07 = £713.333 one year from now. Currency risk is eliminated with a forward contract to convert £713.333 back into dollars one year from now. The unique one-year forward rate that eliminates currency risk and satisfies interest rate parity is calculated as follows:

$$F_1(\$/£) = \frac{[1 + r(\$)] \times S(\$/£)}{1 + r(£)}$$

$$= \frac{1.05 \times 1.5}{1.07}$$

$$= 1.472$$

In this case, a one-year forward rate of $F_1(\$/£) = 1.472$ will convert £713.333 back into $1,050, since 1.472 × £713.333 = $1,050. Any other forward rate produces a different rate of return for the two risk-free investment strategies.

As another example, suppose the dollar interest rate is $r(\$) = 4\%$ per year for a six-month investment, that is, $T = 1/2$. Thus, $1,000 compounds to $1,000 × $1.04^{1/2} = $1,019.80 six months from now. Also suppose the pound interest rate is $r(£) = 7\%$ per year and the spot exchange rate is $S(\$/£) = 1.5$, meaning that converting $1,000 into $1,000/1.5 = £666.667 today and earning interest for six months yields £666.667 × $1.07^{1/2} = £689.606. The appropriate six-month forward rate is calculated as

$$F_{1/2}(\$/£) = \left[\frac{1 + r(\$)}{1 + r(£)}\right]^{1/2} \times S(\$/£)$$

$$= \left(\frac{1.04}{1.07}\right)^{1/2} \times 1.5$$

$$= 1.479$$

Only this six-month forward rate of $F_{1/2}(\$/£) = 1.479$ will convert £689.606 back into $1,019.80. Any other forward rate produces a different rate of return for the two risk-free investment strategies.

Of course, if two different risk-free investment strategies offer different returns, the choice is simple—select the strategy with the highest return. However, interest rates and exchange rates set by international banks are extremely competitive and do not allow for significant differences in risk-free returns. Thus, at least for commercial bank transactions, interest rate parity holds almost exactly.

19.5a Suppose the spot rate of dollars for marks is $S(\$/DM) = 1.6$ and one-year interest rates are $r(\$) = 7\%$ and $r(DM) = 3\%$. What one-year forward rate satisfies the interest rate parity condition?

19.5b Suppose the spot rate of yen for dollars is $S(¥/\$) = 100$ and one-year interest rates are $r(\$) = 7\%$ and $r(¥) = 5\%$. What one-year for-ward rate satisfies the interest rate parity con-dition? Hint: When the exchange rate is stated as the foreign currency price of the dollar, say, the yen/dollar rate, the interest rate parity equation is stated as

$$[1 + r(\$)]^T =$$
$$[1 + r(¥)]^T \times \frac{S(¥/\$)}{F_T(¥/\$)}$$

since $S(¥/\$) = 1/S(\$/¥)$ and $F(¥/\$) = 1/F(\$/¥)$.

19.6 Purchasing Power Parity

The absence of triangular exchange rate arbitrage and the interest rate parity relation-ship described earlier both have immediate importance for international investors since they describe relationships that almost always hold exactly. An exchange rate rela-tionship that does not always hold exactly, but which is important nonetheless, is **purchasing power parity**. Purchasing power parity asserts that countries with above-average rates of inflation will typically experience a depreciation of their currency. Likewise, countries with below-average inflation rates will generally experience cur-rency appreciation. For example, if the United States experiences 3 percent inflation and Canada experiences 7 percent inflation, then purchasing power parity asserts that we should expect to see the Canadian dollar depreciate against the U.S. dollar by about 4 percent, which is the difference between the Canadian and U.S. inflation rates. Similarly, if over the same period Mexico experiences 20 percent inflation, then we should expect to see the Mexican peso depreciate against the U.S. dollar by 17 percent and against the Canadian dollar by 13 percent.

purchasing power parity Theoretical relationship linking rates of inflation in different countries and exchange rate changes (e.g., above average inflation leads to currency depreciation, and vice versa).

The link between inflation rates and exchange rates asserted by purchasing power parity has been known to international economists for several centuries. However, it is a simple fact that purchasing power parity does not always hold exactly in the real world. Two countries with almost the same inflation rates may, and often do, experience significant changes in exchange rates between their two currencies. This is contrary to the predictions of purchasing power parity. Indeed, during periods of departure from purchasing power parity we frequently hear advice like "now would be a good time to take an overseas vacation because the dollar is strong," or conversely that "now would be a good time to forgo an overseas vacation because the dollar is weak." This does not mean, however, that purchasing power parity is a concept without practical usefulness. Quite the contrary; it is well known that purchasing power parity holds fairly well in the long run, say, three to five years. In the short run, say, one year or less, purchasing power parity is less reliable as a predictor of exchange rate changes.

For international investors selecting long-term international investments, deviations from purchasing power parity may provide timely opportunities to buy or sell securities denominated in foreign currencies. For example, a dollar that is strong against the

Japanese yen may suggest that the time is right to buy Japanese stocks and bonds. Suppose that over the last six months the yen depreciated against the dollar by 20 percent while Japanese inflation was about the same as United States inflation. This might be a good time to vacation in Japan or to buy Japanese stocks and bonds, since the dollar prices are about 20 percent cheaper than they would be had the yen not depreciated against the dollar. Conversely, suppose that the yen appreciated against the dollar by 20 percent. This might be a bad time to vacation in Japan but could be a good time to sell Japanese stocks and bonds since the dollar prices are about 20 percent higher than they would be had the yen not depreciated. Of course, the savvy international investor would not depend entirely on deviations from purchasing power parity to make investment decisions. But such considerations can be important, especially for long-term investment decisions.

CHECK THIS

19.6a Suppose the Conch Republic Bank offers 50 percent annual interest on five-year certificates of deposit denominated in conch shells. What does this suggest about future inflation in the Conch Republic and future changes in exchange rates for conch shells?

19.7 International Diversification

The most important reason to invest internationally is to diversify your portfolio. International investments provide excellent opportunities to broaden the base of securities available for inclusion in a portfolio. By diversifying a portfolio across a broader base of securities, the overall risk of the portfolio can be reduced without affecting the expected returns of the portfolio.

Experienced international investors agree that allocating some portion of a portfolio to a selection of international investments is a smart move. There is disagreement, however, as to how large that allocation should be. Professional money managers commonly suggest allocations ranging from about 10 percent to 60 percent of a portfolio to international investments. This wide range clearly reflects how subjective opinion on this important issue is. In fact, the international allocation decision will always be a subjective matter, depending to some degree on investor sentiment concerning world safety. For example, the history of world capital markets over the last 50 years might suggest a 60 percent allocation to international investments. But an investor looking back at the last 100 years might feel quite uncomfortable with even a 10 percent allocation. Recall that in the first 50 years of the twentieth century, the capital markets of Europe and Japan were devastated by war—in some cases twice! Will it happen again? We don't know. It might be prudent, however, for U.S. residents to keep at least half of their investment portfolio in U.S. investments.

After deciding on a specific portfolio allocation to international investments, the next step is to decide where to invest internationally. Each geographic region—Europe, Asia, Africa, South America, and so on—has its proponents, as do many individual countries. As a general rule, U.S. investors can find the greatest opportunities for risk-reducing diversification in those countries with stock market returns that are least correlated with U.S. stock market returns. A U.S. investor will find greater opportunities for risk-reducing international diversification by investing in, say, Chile or Malaysia, than in Canada or Mexico. This is because the economies of

Canada and Mexico are more closely linked to the United States economy than are the economies of Chile and Malaysia. Thus, Canadian and Mexican stock market returns are more highly correlated with U.S. stock market returns than are Malaysian and Chilean stock market returns.

Discussions of international diversification often make use of the statistical concept of correlation. In the context of these discussions, correlation measures the degree to which two stock markets tend to move together. Correlations are reported as a number between +1.0 and −1.0. A correlation of +1.0 indicates perfectly synchronized movements, while a correlation of −1.0 indicates perfectly synchronized movements in opposite directions. A correlation of zero indicates that the two markets move independently of each other. As rules of thumb, correlations below about .25 suggest good opportunities for risk-reducing diversification, whereas correlations above .50 indicate limited opportunities for risk-reducing diversification.

To illustrate why correlations matter, consider how portfolio risk declines as we diversify across world stock markets. For example, suppose we invest equal shares of our portfolio in each of a number of country stock market indexes, where all pairs of country indexes have the same correlation. Figure 19.3 shows how portfolio risk declines as the number of country indexes increases from 1 to 50 indexes for various hypothetical correlation values. In Figure 19.3, the horizontal axis measures the number of country indexes represented in the portfolio. The vertical axis is standardized such that the risk of investing in only a single index is equal to 1. The curved lines show how portfolio risk as a fraction of the risk of a single index portfolio declines as the number of indexes in the portfolio increases. Notice that each correlation determines a lower limit to risk-reducing diversification. This limit represents world systematic risk that cannot be removed from a portfolio by further diversification. Notice also that no matter which correlation we look at, most of the benefits of diversification are obtained with as few as 10 country indexes in the portfolio. Taken together, these two observations illustrate that good international diversification can be achieved by investing in a relatively small number of countries with low correlations. Conversely, good international diversification cannot be achieved by investing in a large number of highly correlated stock markets.

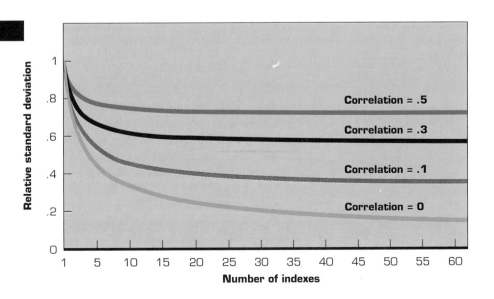

Figure 19.3

Gains from International Diversification

A Cushion Overseas Is But a Dream

You've heard the message: Investing in foreign stocks lowers your risk and increases your returns.

Well, there's a good chance your overseas portfolio isn't as diversified as you think. Some money managers, in fact, warn that if Wall Street tanks, most U.S. foreign-stock portfolios could tumble with it. That's because they are heavily invested in European markets that tend to rise and fall in tandem with U.S. share prices and are underinvested in Japan, which has a low correlation to U.S. stocks.

Roughly 69% of the $257.6 billion that Americans have invested in major stock markets outside of North America is in Europe and only 18% in Japan, according to a new report on the stock holdings of the 2,200 biggest U.S. institutional investors by Technimetrics Inc., a New York–based firm that tracks shareholder ownership. That compares with market-capitalization weightings of 50% for Europe and 41% for Japan, according to Morgan Stanley Capital International's Europe AustralAsia Far East index of 20 major stock markets, the main benchmark against which portfolio managers are measured.

What's more, a fifth of the money is invested in the British stock market and 16% in the Dutch market, both of which are especially highly correlated with the U.S. market. U.S. investors are also heavily overweight in the Swedish, Hong Kong, and Australian stock markets, which closely track the U.S.

The big question, say experts, is whether this mix will cushion the blow of a falling U.S. stock market. "You think you own foreign stocks, but if what you own is closely correlated to the U.S. economic and flow of funds cycle, it just won't do what you want it to do," says Nicholas Carn, chief investment officer of Draycott Partners in London. "And if the story in Japan is that of a domestic recovery, which is what we think it is, you lose out there."

The reason U.S. portfolios are so lopsided has less to do with well-thought-out decisions than American provincialism. U.S. investors "aren't particularly familiar with all the subtle differences in offshore markets," says William L. Wilby, a portfolio manager at Oppenheimer Funds Inc. in New York. "Therefore, their investment decision is driven primarily on the basis of comfort and cultural familiarity."

A look at some of Americans' favorite foreign investments offers additional clues. Spain's Telefonica de Espana SA, French oil company Total SA, Swiss drug giant Roche Holding AG, and Australian media company News Corp. represent "themes that are driving the U.S. economy," says Anne M. Tatlock, president of Fiduciary Trust Co. International in New York. At the same time, nearly half of all U.S. institutions own Royal Dutch Petroleum Co. shares, mostly because it is in Standard & Poor's 500-stock index, says John Vogt, a Technimetrics vice president in New York.

Led by names such as Royal Dutch, SmithKline Beecham PLC, British Petroleum Co., Telefon AB, L.M. Ericsson and Unilever Group, nine of the 10 biggest U.S. foreign investments—and 16 of the top 25—are European companies. Not one is Japanese.

"Each company on the list is a household name, a highly liquid stock, and most have a large presence in the U.S. in terms of their products," says Deborah Fuhr, a director of international accounts at Technimetrics in London. She adds that most of the companies have active investor-relations programs, are researched by big U.S. brokers, and either are listed on the New York Stock Exchange or trade in the form of American depositary receipts.

The last fact "drives a lot of the investment decisions, because many institutions lack overseas custodial arrangements and, therefore, can't own foreign stocks unless they trade in the U.S.," says Mr. Wilby.

Unfortunately, most correlations between international stock market indexes are greater than .50, suggesting limited international diversification opportunities. Table 19.1 presents some sample correlations between selected foreign stock market indexes and the U.S. Standard & Poor's 500 index over the period 1990 through 1995.

Table 19.1	Foreign Stock Market Correlations with S&P 500 Index					
Austria	.72	Hong Kong	.85	South Africa	.75
France	.76	Italy	−.36	England	.89
Germany	.70	Japan	.23		

Meanwhile, the low level of Japan investment reflects several years of poor corporate earnings and "tells you there isn't a high degree of confidence in a Japanese company being a global leader in any core industry," says Ms. Tatlock of Fiduciary Trust. Japanese companies are also "very reluctant to issue ADRs" because "they are highly sensitive to institutional investors' stances on issues of corporate governance," adds Mr. Vogt.

In some ways, the "overweight Europe, underweight Japan" portfolio has worked. Over the past five years, MSCI's Europe index posted a 12.1% average annual return in dollars, compared with just 5.7% for Japan. But noting that the stocks Americans own essentially represent a "U.S. bull-market portfolio" of pharmaceuticals, brand names, cellular telephones, and technology, one money manager argues that Americans might just as well have stayed home. Indeed, the S&P 500 returned 16.5% a year over the same period. That's 70% better than EAFE's 9.7% annual return and 36% higher than MSCI's Europe index.

The future might not be any brighter. Ms. Tatlock of Fiduciary Trust concedes that if an investor believes Continental Europe will follow the U.S. recovery, "there's good reason to be in" the big European companies owned by Americans. But she says that Japanese companies could outperform them, because they could generate faster earnings growth.

Others worry about the narrow concentration of Americans' overseas bets. Just three companies—Royal Dutch, Unilever, and Philips Electronics NV—account for 72% of all U.S. investment in Dutch stocks. Five—SmithKline, BP, Reuters Holdings PLC, Vodafone Group PLC, and Hanson PLC—make up 43% of their British portfolio. Oy Nokia accounts for 71% of all Finnish holdings, and Nestle SA, Roche, and Ciba-Geigy AG represent 52% of all Swiss holdings.

America's Favorites U.S. Institutions' Biggest Overseas Investments

Company	Amount (billions)
Royal Dutch Petroleum	$22.3
SmithKline Beecham	7.1
British Petroleum	5.9
Ericsson	5.0
Unilever	4.4
Nokia	4.2
Telefonas de Mexico	3.8
Reuters Holdings	3.3
Astra	3.2
Vodafone Group	3.2

Source: Technimetrics Inc.

All these big-company stocks are fairly valued, note money managers. Yet they point out that part of the logic behind investing abroad is to find inefficiently priced stocks. Instead of playing just the big names, investors should look for "new businesses and new industries in foreign countries that are at their emerging stages, some of which are older industries in the U.S.," says Oppenheimer's Mr. Wilby. A good example, he says, is private hospitals.

Nonetheless, change won't come quickly, especially regarding the underweighting of Japanese shares. "There's too much skepticism on Japan," says Chris A. Nowakowski, president of InterSec Research Corp. a Stamford Conn., investment advisory firm. "You've got to be a real hero to buy a market that has fallen by more than half in the past several years, and money managers are generally not heroes."

Source: Michael R. Sesit, "A Cushion Overseas Is But a Dream," *The Wall Street Journal*, June 13, 1996. Reprinted with permission from *The Wall Street Journal*, © 1996 Dow Jones & Company, Inc. All Rights Reserved Worldwide.

Notice that most of these correlations are greater than .70, indicating somewhat limited opportunities for risk-reducing diversification in these countries. However, the correlation with Japan is fairly small, suggesting good risk-reducing opportunities. The correlation for Italy is actually negative, suggesting even better diversification opportunities. While it is true that other factors should be considered, these correlations strongly suggest including Japan and Italy in a well-diversified international portfolio.

Unfortunately, most U.S. investors tend to ignore correlations when making international diversification decisions and actually tend to invest in countries with high correlations with U.S. stock markets. For example, about 20 percent of U.S. investments abroad are allocated to British stock markets, which are highly correlated with U.S.

International Investing Raises Questions

As Yogi Berra might say, the problem with international investing is that it's so darn foreign.

Currency swings? Hedging? International diversification? What's that?

Here are answers to five questions that I'm often asked:

- Foreign stocks account for some 60% of world stock-market value, so shouldn't you have 60% of your stock-market money overseas?

The main reason to invest abroad isn't to replicate the global market or to boost returns. Instead, "what we're trying to do by adding foreign stocks is to reduce volatility," explains Robert Ludwig, chief investment officer at money manager SEI Investments.

Foreign stocks don't move in sync with U.S. shares and, thus, they may provide offsetting gains when the U.S. market is falling. But to get the resulting risk reduction, you don't need anything like 60% of your money abroad.

- So, how much foreign exposure do you need to get decent diversification?

Based on the volatility of foreign markets and the correlation between markets, we think an optimal portfolio is 70% in the U.S., 20% in developed foreign markets and 10% in emerging markets," Mr. Ludwig says.

Why not put even more in foreign stocks? If your aim is to reduce a portfolio's risk level, "there are diminishing marginal benefits as the international equity exposure rises," explains Laurence Smith, a managing director with J.P. Morgan's investment management subsidiary.

He argues that once you have a third of your stock portfolio in foreign shares, there's no point in putting more money abroad unless you believe that overseas markets will outperform U.S. equities.

Even with a third of your stock-market money in foreign issues, you may find that the risk-reduction benefits aren't all that reliable. Unfortunately, when U.S. stocks get really pounded, it seems foreign shares also tend to tumble.

Experts have suggested that investors can better diversify their U.S. portfolios if, instead of emphasizing large foreign companies, they favor emerging markets, smaller foreign concerns, and stocks that are cheap based on value yardsticks, such as price-to-earnings or price-to-book value.

"I do agree that there's a return advantage and a diversification benefit from emerging markets," Mr. Ludwig says. "But when people say that value stocks outperform or small stocks outperform, I think they're extrapolating from a very small data series, and that's dangerous."

- Can U.S. companies with global operations give you international diversification?

"When you look at these multinationals, the factor that drives their performance is their home market," says Mark Riepe, a vice president with Ibbotson Associates, a Chicago research firm.

How come? U.S. multinationals tend to be owned by U.S. investors, who will be swayed by the ups and downs of the U.S. market. In addition, Mr. Riepe notes that while multinationals may derive substantial profits and revenue abroad, most of their costs—especially labor costs—will be incurred in the U.S.

stock markets. The nearby Investment Updates box presents an article from *The Wall Street Journal* that discusses the results of a survey of portfolio allocations to overseas investments made by U.S. institutional investors. The survey reports that these institutional investors overallocate to high-correlation countries and underallocate to low-correlation countries, thereby forgoing much of the benefit of international diversification.

While international diversification will continue to reduce investors' risk, other benefits are likely to diminish in the future. This is because international stock market indexes are becoming more highly correlated as international economies steadily become more integrated. The second nearby Investment Updates box presents an article published in *The Wall Street Journal* that discusses some of the problems associated with international investments and portfolio diversification.

Offsetting the reduced benefits of international diversification is the much increased ease of investing internationally. At one time international investments entailed substantial transaction costs because few foreign securities actually traded in U.S. financial markets. Today, several thousand foreign securities are traded in U.S. financial markets.

- Does international diversification come from the foreign stocks or the foreign currency?

"It comes from both in roughly equal pieces," Mr. Riepe says. "Those who choose to hedge their foreign currency raise the correlation with U.S. stocks, and so the diversification benefit won't be nearly as great."

Indeed, you may want to think twice before investing in a foreign-stock fund that frequently hedges its currency exposure in an effort to mute the impact of—and make money from—changes in foreign-exchange rates.

"The studies that we've done show that stock managers have hurt themselves more than they've helped themselves by actively managing currencies," Mr. Ludwig says.

- Should you divvy up your money among foreign countries depending on the size of each national stock market?

At issue is the nagging question of how much to put in Japan. If you replicated the market weightings of Morgan Stanley Capital International's Europe, Australasia, and Far East index, you would currently have around a third of your overseas money in Japan.

That's the sort of weighting you find in international index funds, which seek to track the performance of the EAFE or similar international indexes. Actively managed foreign-stock funds, by contrast, pay less attention to market weights and, on average, these days have just 14% in Japan.

So, who's right, the actively managed funds or the index funds? If you look at performance, it's a tough call.

In the 1980s, most funds lagged behind the Morgan Stanley index, which was bolstered by the dazzling performance of the Japanese market. But in the 1990s, the tables were turned. Actively managed funds have triumphed, as the index was dragged down by its large stake in the tumbling Tokyo market.

An honorable draw? Not quite. If your focus is risk reduction rather than performance, the index—and the funds that track it—are the clear winners. Japan performs quite unlike the U.S. market, so it provides good diversification for U.S. investors, says Tricia Rothschild, international editor at *Morningstar Mutual Funds*, a Chicago newsletter.

"But correlations aren't static," she adds. "There's always a problem with taking what happened over the past 20 years and projecting it out over the next 20 years."

CHECK THIS

19.7a How do correlations among world financial markets affect international diversification opportunities?

19.7b What is a typical correlation between United States and European financial markets?

19.8 American Depository Receipts

American Depository Receipts (ADRs)
Shares issued as a claim on foreign company stock shares held in a trust.

United States investors can invest in a large number of foreign companies through the purchase of **American Depository Receipts**, which are often simply called **ADRs.** ADRs represent foreign stock shares held in a local custodial account, where each ADR is equivalent to a certain number of shares of the underlying foreign company's stock. Several well-known banks serve as local custodians for ADR issues, including

Citibank, Bank of New York, and Morgan Guarantee Trust Company of New York. ADRs are a convenient way to invest in foreign companies, since ADR shares trade on U.S. stock exchanges or on Nasdaq. As a practical matter, the purchase of ADR shares is economically equivalent to owning the original underlying stock shares. We next discuss some significant details.

The two main types of ADRs are sponsored and unsponsored. Some older ADR issues are unsponsored, which simply means that the ADR issue was originally created without the explicit approval of the underlying foreign company. Since 1983, Securities and Exchange Commission rules require that all new ADR issues be sponsored by the foreign company.

There are three types of sponsored ADRs. Level I ADRs are not allowed to trade on a U.S. stock exchange because the underlying company does not provide detailed financial information to investors. Instead, they trade among brokers and dealers in the over-the-counter market. More than half of all ADRs circulating in the United States are Level I ADRs. Unless you are comfortable investing in a company unwilling to provide detailed financial information about itself, it may be best to avoid this type of ADR.

In contrast, foreign companies sponsoring Level II ADRs provide investors annual reports written in English, reporting financial information in the same format as U.S. companies. Consequently, Level II ADRs are allowed to trade on Nasdaq or on any of the organized stock exchanges in the United States. No new stock shares are issued to create a Level II ADR issue. Instead, a Level II ADR issue is created when a securities firm purchases a block of foreign company shares in an overseas market to hold in a trust and then issues ADRs representing claims on the foreign shares.

A Level III ADR issue is created when the foreign company issues new stock shares to be used as the basis for the new ADR issue. In this case, the company must satisfy requirements set by the SEC for an initial public offering. All Level II and Level III ADRs have prices stated in U.S. dollars and pay dividends in U.S. dollars.

Sometimes a popular foreign company will have more than one ADR issue trading in U.S. stock markets. For example, Telephonos de México, often simply called TelMex, has one ADR issue traded on the NYSE under the ticker symbol TMX and has another ADR issue traded on Nasdaq under the ticker symbol TFONY. Each TFONY ADR represents a single share of TelMex, whereas each TMX ADR represents 20 shares of TelMex. Thus, TMX ADR shares cost about 20 times as much as TFONY ADR shares. Of course, Telephonos de México stock shares also trade on the Mexican stock market, but these Mexican shares can only be owned by Mexican nationals.

CHECK THIS

19.8a What are sponsored ADRs? What are unsponsored ADRs?

19.8b What are Level I ADRs and where are they traded?

19.8c What is the difference between Level II ADRs and Level III ADRs?

19.9 World Equity Benchmark Shares

World Equity Benchmark Shares (WEBS) Depository trust shares, where the trust contains a basket of foreign company stock shares representative of a particular national stock market.

American investors interested in investing internationally without picking individual foreign company stocks can instead purchase **World Equity Benchmark Shares,** commonly called **WEBS.** WEBS represent depository shares held in a trust, where the trust is composed of a basket of stocks from a specific country. WEBS trade on the American Stock Exchange under their own ticker symbols. For example, Japan WEBS trade under the ticker symbol EWJ and are shares in a trust of Japanese stocks representative of the Japanese stock market. Investing in EWJ shares is similar to investing in a Japanese index mutual fund. Unlike mutual fund shares, however, WEBS can be sold short or traded on margin just like common stocks.

WEBS typically reflect about 60 percent of the capitalization of a country's stock market. They thus provide investment results that correspond to the aggregate performance of shares in the larger publicly traded companies in specific country markets. Countries for which WEBS are available for trading and their AMEX ticker symbols are listed in Table 19.2.

WEBS allow investors to construct an international stock portfolio without the need to purchase stocks of individual companies. For example, an aggressive international investor may wish to place, say, 15 percent of her portfolio in Japan, 5 percent in Germany, and 10 percent in Italy. By using WEBS, she can achieve exactly the proportions desired. Furthermore, changing these proportions at a later date is no more trouble than buying and selling individual common stocks.

CHECK THIS

19.9a What are WEBS and where are they traded?

19.9b How might WEBS be useful to an investor?

Table 19.2

WEBS on the AMEX

Country	Ticker Symbol	Country	Ticker Symbol
Australia	EWA	Malaysia	EWM
Austria	EWO	Mexico	EWW
Belgium	EWK	Netherlands	EWN
Canada	EWC	Singapore	EWS
France	EWQ	Spain	EWP
Germany	EWG	Sweden	EWD
Hong Kong	EWH	Switzerland	EWL
Italy	EWI	United Kingdom	EWU
Japan	EWJ		

Summary and Conclusions

Almost all countries issue their own national currency and maintain their own fiscal and monetary policies. So long as countries maintain separate monetary identities, international finance will continue to be an important body of knowledge for international investors and money managers. This chapter discusses the following topics within this body of knowledge:

1. Currency markets are the most active markets in the world, with over $1 trillion of currency transactions occurring daily. An exchange rate is the price of one country's currency in terms of another country's currency. An exchange rate can also be stated as a cross rate, which is an exchange rate between two foreign currencies.

2. Exchange rate appreciation and exchange rate depreciation occur simultaneously, so follow this rule: For the U.S. dollar price of euros, exchange rate appreciation means that euros are less expensive when bought with U.S. dollars. But for the euro price of U.S. dollars, exchange rate appreciation means that euros are more expensive when bought with U.S. dollars.

3. The uncertainty of exchange rates appreciating or depreciating is called exchange rate risk or currency risk. If you invest in British gilts denominated in British pounds and these gilts later have the same pound value but the dollar has depreciated against the pound, then you have realized a dollar profit on the depreciation. Alternatively, if the dollar appreciated against the pound, you would realize a dollar loss on the appreciation.

4. Forward currency contracts—agreements to exchange currencies on a future date at a prespecified forward exchange rate—are widely used to hedge exchange rate risks.

5. Exchange rates follow a fundamental relationship determined by an absence of triangular arbitrage. This relationship implies that the product of three exchange rates is equal to 1.

6. Interest rate parity specifies a fundamental relationship between interest rates in two countries and their currencies' spot and forward exchange rates. The structure of interest rate parity between dollars and pounds is stated by this equation:

$$[1 + r(\$)]^T = [1 + r(£)]^T \times \frac{F_T(\$/£)}{S(\$/£)}$$

Interest rate parity holds almost exactly for interest rates and exchange rates quoted by commercial banks.

7. Purchasing power parity asserts that countries with above-average inflation experience currency depreciation and countries with below-average inflation experience currency appreciation. Purchasing power parity is not a reliable exchange rate predictor in the short run, but it holds reasonably well in the long run.

8. The most important reason to invest internationally is enhanced portfolio diversification. Discussions of diversification use the statistical concept of correlation, where correlations below .25 suggest good diversification opportunities, while correlations above .50 indicate limited diversification opportunities.

9. U.S. investors can invest in many foreign companies through the purchase of ADRs, which represent depository shares held in trust. ADR shares typically trade on a stock exchange or on Nasdaq and are economically equivalent to owning the underlying foreign stock shares.

10. U.S. investors not wishing to pick individual foreign company stocks can purchase WEBS. WEBS represent depository shares held in a trust, where the trust is composed of a basket of stocks from a specific country. WEBS trade on the American Stock Exchange.

GET REAL

This chapter covered some international aspects of investing. In general, the case for international diversification is a strong one. However, in recent years, international diversification would have been a significant drag on the performance of a U.S. investor's stock portfolio. In broader terms, the extent to which an investor should diversify internationally is an open question. Theoretical considerations suggest enormous benefits, but are the benefits real or theoretical? Only time and study will tell.

One important thing to keep in mind about international investing is that exchange rate risk really does matter. Even if a particular market or stock does well measured in its home currency, the gain or loss experienced by a U.S. investor will depend on what happens to the exchange rate as well. An unfavorable exchange rate movement can turn a gain into a loss (or vice versa). Here is a question to ponder: If you own securities denominated in non-U.S. currencies, would you benefit from a strengthening or a weakening of the dollar? It may seem counterintuitive at first, but the answer is you would benefit from a weakening of the dollar. The reason: If the dollar weakens, each unit of foreign currency you receive from your investment will get you more dollars.

For now, it is important to gain some experience with international investing. There are three fairly straightforward ways to do this. First, purchasing ADRs is the most direct means of investing in non-U.S. companies, so choose a few (from different countries) for your portfolio. Second, use the web to investigate WEBS; try the American stock exchange at www.amex.com. These are country-specific baskets of stocks that are traded in the United States; they provide an easy and inexpensive way to invest in specific countries. Buy several of these. Finally, from many chapters ago, we know that some mutual funds specialize in international investing. Try investing in a few "emerging markets" funds or single-country funds specializing in less developed countries to experience some of the tremendous volatility that such markets sometimes display.

Key Terms

Chapter Review Problems and Self-Test

1. **Cross Rates**   Suppose the U.S. dollar/British pound exchange rate is $1.50 = £1, and the Japanese yen/U.S. dollar exchange rate is ¥120 = $1. What is the implied yen/pound exchange rate?

2. **Interest Rate Parity**   Suppose that the interest rate on one-year risk-free investments in the United States is 6 percent. The U.S. dollar/Swiss franc exchange rate is $1 = SFr 1.50. The one-year forward exchange rate is $1 = SFr 1.52. In the absence of arbitrage, what is the risk-free interest rate in Switzerland?

Answers to Self-Test Problems

1. One pound will buy you $1.50. One dollar will buy you ¥120, so £1 will buy $1.50 × 120 = ¥180. The cross rate is 180 yen per pound.

2. Interest rate parity requires that

$$[1 + r(\$)]^T = [1 + r(\text{SFr})]^T \times \frac{F_T(\$/\text{SFr})}{S(\$/\text{SFr})}$$

Noting that $T = 1$ and filling in the other numbers, we get

$$1.06 = [1 + r(\text{SFr})] \times \frac{1/1.52}{1/1.50}$$

The only thing that's a little tricky here is that we had to invert the exchange rates because they are quoted in dollars per franc in the formula while the question quotes them in francs per dollar. Solving for the Swiss interest rate, $r(\text{SFr})$, we get $1.06 \times (1.52/1.50) - 1 = 7.41\%$.

Test Your Investment Quotient

1. **Exchange Rates**   The U.S. dollar price of British pounds is $1.50, and the British pound price of French francs is £.5. Assuming an absence of triangular arbitrage, what is the franc price of dollars?

   a. Fr3.0
   b. Fr.333
   c. Fr1.333
   d. Fr.75

2. **Exchange Rates**   The U.S. dollar price of British pounds is $1.50, and the British pound price of Deutsche marks is £2. Assuming an absence of triangular arbitrage, what is the mark price of dollars?

   a. DM 3
   b. DM .333
   c. DM 1.333
   d. DM .75

3. **Exchange Rates**   You purchased British securities for £2,000 one year ago when the pound cost $1.50. What is your total return (based on U.S. dollars) if the value of the securities is now £2,400 and the pound is still worth $1.50?

   a. 16.7 percent
   b. 20.0 percent
   c. 28.6 percent
   d. 40.0 percent

4. **Exchange Rates** You purchased British securities for £2,000 one year ago when the pound cost $1.50. What is your total return (based on U.S. dollars) if the value of the securities is still £2,000 and the pound is now worth $1.75?

   a. 16.7 percent
   b. 20.0 percent
   c. 28.6 percent
   d. 40.0 percent

5. **Exchange Rates** You purchased British securities for £2,000 one year ago when the pound cost $1.50. What is your total return (based on U.S. dollars) if the value of the securities is now £2,400 and the pound is now worth $1.75?

   a. 16.7 percent
   b. 20.0 percent
   c. 28.6 percent
   d. 40.0 percent

6. **Interest Rate Parity** Risk-free interest rates for one-year deposits in the United States and England are 5 percent and 10 percent, respectively. The spot price of British pounds is $1.47. Which one-year forward price of pounds best satisfies interest rate parity?

   a. $1.40
   b. $1.45
   c. $1.50
   d. $1.54

7. **International Diversification** Why is investing internationally desirable? (*1988 CFA exam*)

   a. There is a direct relationship between the value of the U.S. dollar and U.S. stock market returns.
   b. Foreign currencies are more stable than the U.S. dollar.
   c. Investors benefit from the increased diversification.
   d. Foreign stocks pay higher dividends.

8. **International Diversification** A U.S. equity money manager wishing to acquire the greatest benefit from international diversification should do which of the following? (*1993 CFA exam*)

   i. Invest directly in foreign stocks.
   ii. Invest in U.S. multinational firms.
   iii. Short sell foreign stocks.

   a. i only
   b. ii only
   c. ii and iii
   d. i and ii

9. **International Diversification** Why is international diversification of equity portfolios desirable for U.S. investors? (*1989 CFA exam*)

   i. Foreign stocks offer U.S. investors substantial tax advantages.
   ii. Foreign stocks offer opportunities for U.S. investors to protect themselves against a decline in the value of the dollar relative to foreign currencies.
   iii. Increasing internationalization of the world economy leads to greater correlation in returns among U.S. and foreign common stocks.
   iv. Portfolio risk is reduced.

   a. i and iv only
   b. ii and iii only
   c. ii and iv only
   d. iii and iv only

10. **International Diversification**   The correlation coefficient between the returns on a broad index of U.S. stocks and the returns on stock indexes of other industrialized countries are mostly _____, and the correlation coefficient between the returns on various diversified portfolios of U.S. stocks are mostly _____. (*1992 CFA exam*)

a. less than .8; greater than .8
b. greater than .8; less than .8
c. less than 0; greater than 0
d. greater than 0; less than 0

11. **Currency Risk**   A U.S. investor in foreign government bonds is most likely to want to hedge against

a. Depreciation of the U.S. dollar.
b. Appreciation of the U.S. dollar.
c. Default risk.
d. Taxation.

12. **Currency Risk**   A U.S. investor in British gilts (government bonds) can hedge against depreciation of the pound by

a. Buying pounds in the forward market.
b. Selling pounds in the forward market.
c. Buying pounds in the spot market.
d. Depositing U.S. dollars in a London bank.

13. **Currency Risk**   An investor in common stocks of companies in a foreign country may wish to hedge against _____ of the investor's home currency and can do so by _____ the foreign currency in the forward market. (*1992 CFA exam*)

a. depreciation; selling
b. appreciation; purchasing
c. appreciation; selling
d. depreciation; purchasing

14. **American Depository Receipts**   Which of the following most accurately describes American Depository Receipts?

a. Depository shares of foreign company stocks traded in foreign markets.
b. Depository shares of American company stocks traded in U.S. markets.
c. Depository shares of foreign company stocks traded in U.S. markets.
d. Depository shares of American company stocks traded in foreign markets.

15. **American Depository Receipts**   Which type of unsponsored ADR does not trade on U.S. stock exchanges, but instead trades in the over-the-counter market?

a. Level I
b. Level II
c. Level III
d. Level IV

Questions and Problems

**Core
Questions**

1. **Exchange Rates**   Take a look back at Figure 19.2 to answer the following questions:

a. If you have $100, how many Italian lira can you get?
b. How much is one lira worth?
c. If you have Lit 5 million (Lit stands for Italian lira), how many dollars do you have?

2. **Exchange Rates**   Take a look back at Figure 19.2 to answer the following questions:

a. Which is worth more, a New Zealand dollar or a Singapore dollar?
b. Which is worth more, a Mexican peso or a Chilean peso?
c. Per unit, what is the most valuable currency listed? The least valuable?

3. **Cross Rates**   Use the information in Figure 19.2 to answer the following questions:
   a. Which would you rather have, $100 or £100? Why?
   b. Which would you rather have, Fr 100 or £100? Why?
   c. What is the cross rate for French francs in terms of British pounds? For pounds in terms of francs?

4. **Interest Rate Parity**   Suppose that the interest rate on one-year risk-free investments in the United States is 4 percent. The Japanese yen/U.S. dollar exchange rate is ¥1 = $.008. The one-year forward exchange rate is ¥1 = $.0078. In the absence of arbitrage, what is the risk-free interest rate in Japan?

5. **International Investing**   Suppose you buy shares in a mutual fund that tracks the overall stock market in South Korea. What impact does the exchange rate have on your return from this investment?

6. **Exchange Rate Changes**   What does it mean for one currency to strengthen or appreciate relative to another? If a currency does appreciate in value, what happens to the exchange rate?

7. **Exchange Rate Changes**   Suppose the yen/dollar exchange rate changes from ¥110 to ¥105. Has the yen appreciated or depreciated relative to the dollar? Why?

8. **International Investing**   It is often argued that international investing offers significant benefits to U.S. investors. Why?

9. **International Risks**   Investing internationally introduces another element of risk because of exchange rates. Explain.

10. **Interest Rate Parity**   Suppose that the interest rate on one-year risk-free investments in the United States is 5 percent. The German mark/U.S. dollar exchange rate is DM 1 = $.50. If the risk-free rate in Germany is 4 percent, what is the one-year forward exchange rate?

Intermediate Questions

11. **Exchange Rate Changes**   Over the week covered in Figure 19.2, did the Greek drachma appreciate or depreciate relative to the dollar? What about the British pound?

12. **Exchange Rate Changes**   In the previous question, did the drachma appreciate or depreciate relative to the pound?

13. **Triangular Arbitrage**   Suppose the dollar/French franc exchange rate is $1 = Fr 6 and the dollar/Swiss franc exchange rate is $1 = SFr 1.5. Further, the Swiss franc/French franc cross rate is quoted at Fr 5 = SFr 1. Is there an arbitrage here? How much can you make in a single round trip if you begin with $100? Explain step by step the necessary transactions.

14. **Interest Rate Parity**   Suppose that the annual interest rate on 90-day T-bills in the United States is 6 percent. The Japanese yen/U.S. dollar exchange rate is ¥1 = $.007. The 90-day forward exchange rate is ¥1 = $.00705. In the absence of arbitrage, what is the 90-day risk-free interest rate in Japan?

15. **International Investing**   Suppose you invest $10,000 in Korean stocks. At the time you make the investment, the U.S. dollar/South Korean won exchange rate is $.01. Over the next year, the value of your investment, measured in won, increases 60 percent. However, the exchange rate falls to W1 = $.008. What was the return on your investment in dollars?

16. **International Investing**   Suppose you invest $200,000 in Belgian stocks. At the time you make the investment, the Belgian franc/U.S. dollar exchange rate is BFr 40 = $1. Over the next year, the value of your investment, measured in francs, increases 10 percent, and the exchange rises to BFr 42 = $1. What was the return on your investment in dollars?

17. **Interest Rates**   Our discussion of interest rate parity clearly implies that different countries will generally have different risk-free rates, but how is it possible for two risk-free rates to exist at the same time?

18. **Purchasing Power Parity**   Suppose the U.S. dollar/Canadian dollar exchange rate is U.S.$.80/Can$1. If the rate of inflation in Canada is 6 percent compared to 4 percent in the United States, what do you predict will happen to the exchange rate. Why?

19. **International Diversification**   In the late 1990s, the U.S. stock market significantly outperformed most of the other major stock markets. Because of this, some market strategists argued that U.S. investors should invest exclusively in the United States. Evaluate this argument.

20. **International Diversification**   Is it possible to diversify a stock portfolio internationally without purchasing foreign-listed stocks or ADRs? (Hint: Yes, to a certain extent.) How?

STOCK-TRAK·
Portfolio Simulations

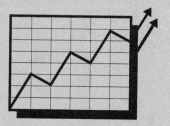

Trading Foreign Company Stocks with Stock-Trak

Hundreds of foreign company stocks are listed for trading in the United States. All of the foreign stocks listed on the NYSE, AMEX, or Nasdaq can be traded through your Stock-Trak account. You can view lists of these foreign company stocks by referring to the websites of the NYSE (www.nyse.com) and combined Nasdaq-AMEX (www.nasdaq-amex.com). The names and ticker symbols for some of the hundreds of foreign stocks listed on these websites are found in Table ST.1.

Table ST. 1	Foreign Stock Listings	
NYSE Foreign Company Stocks		**Nasdaq Foreign Company Stocks**
Telefonica de Argentina (TAR)		Banco de Galicia y Buenos Aires (BGALY)
National Australia Bank (NAB)		Atlas Pacific (APCFY)
British Steel (BST)		British Biotech (BBIOY)
Laboratorio Chile (LBC)		Compania Cervacerias Unidas (CCUUY)
Deutsche Telekom AG (DT)		Realax Software (RLAXY)
Hellenic Telecom (OTE)		Royal Olympic Cruise Lines (ROCLF)
Brilliance China Automotive (CBA)		Nam Tai Electronics (NTAIF)
Allied Irish Banks (AIB)		Hibernia Foods (HIBNY)
Blue-Square Israel (BSI)		Better Online Solutions (BOSCF)
Hitachi (HIT)		Japan Air Lines (JAPNY)
Royal Dutch Petroleum (RD)		Sapiens International (SPNSF)
New Zealand Telecom (NZT)		Tranz Rail Holdings (TNZR)

Stock-Trak Exercises

1. Explore the NYSE (www.nyse.com) and combined Nasdaq-AMEX (www.nasdaq-amex.com) websites and find their listings of foreign company stocks.

2. Notice that the Nasdaq ticker symbols for foreign company stocks normally have five letters, where the last letter is either a Y or an F. The Y indicates that they are ADR shares, while the F simply indicates that they are directly listed foreign company shares.

Trading Foreign Currency Futures with Stock-Trak

Currency futures are widely used to trade on exchange rate movements. The most popular currency futures contracts are those based on exchange rates between the U.S. dollar and several major world currencies. Stock-Trak allows you to trade currency futures for these exchange rates.

To trade currency futures with Stock-Trak, you need only select the desired exchange rate and the number of futures contracts. However, before trading currency futures, you should review the Stock-Trak exercises for commodity futures found in Chapter 16.

You will need to know the appropriate ticker symbols for the exchange rate you wish to trade. Table ST.2 lists the contract sizes and ticker symbols for exchange rate futures between the U.S. dollar and selected world currencies.

Table ST.2 — **Futures Contract Size and Tickers for Selected Currencies**

Currency	Ticker	Currency	Ticker
Australian dollar ($100,000)	AD	French franc (Fr250,000)	FF
British pound (£62,500)	BP	Japanese yen (¥12.5 million)	JY
Canadian dollar ($100,000)	CD	Swiss franc (SFr125,000)	SF
German mark (DM125,000)	DM	Mexican peso (Pe500,000)	MP

Currency futures tickers also have two-character extensions denoting the contract expiration date. These are the same codes used with commodity futures, where the first character is a letter representing the expiration month, and the second character is a number representing the expiration year. To refresh your memory, futures ticker extensions for contracts expiring in 1999 are specified in Table ST.3.

Table ST.3 — **Futures Ticker Extension Codes (1999 Expirations)**

Expiration Month	Code	Expiration Month	Code
January	F9	July	N9
February	G9	August	Q9
March	H9	September	U9
April	J9	October	V9
May	K9	November	X9
June	M9	December	Z9

For example, orders to go long 5 Australian dollar June 1999 futures contracts and go short 3 Deutsche mark December 2000 futures contracts are abbreviated as

Buy 5 AD-M9 contracts
Sell 3 DM-Z0 contracts

Going long implies buying the foreign currency and going short implies selling the foreign currency. The futures price specifies the price paid on delivery at contract expiration. Detailed contract specifications for currency futures are available at the Chicago Mercantile Exchange (CME) website (www.cme.com).

Stock-Trak Exercise

1. What are the complete tickers for the following currency futures contracts: British pound March 1999, Japanese yen September 2001, Mexican peso June 2000?

Answers to Test Your Investment Quotient Questions

Chapter 1

1-1   b
1-2   a
1-3   c
1-4   b (*Source:* 1994 Level I CFA Study Guide © 1994)
1-5   a
1-6   a
1-7   b
1-8   a
1-9   d
1-10   d
1-11   d
1-12   a
1-13   c (*Source:* 1994 Level I CFA Study Guide © 1994)
1-14   b
1-15   d

Chapter 2

2-1   c
2-2   c
2-3   c
2-4   c
2-5   b
2-6   b
2-7   b
2-8   a
2-9   c
2-10   b
2-11   a
2-12   c
2-13   c
2-14   c
2-15   d

Chapter 3

3-1   d
3-2   a
3-3   c
3-4   a
3-5   c
3-6   c
3-7   b
3-8   c
3-9   c
3-10   c

Chapter 4

4-1   d
4-2   d
4-3   d
4-4   d
4-5   a
4-6   b
4-7   a
4-8   c
4-9   b
4-10   d
4-11   c
4-12   a
4-13   a
4-14   b
4-15   d

Chapter 5

5-1   a
5-2   b
5-3   c
5-4   d
5-5   b (*Source:* 1991 Level I CFA Study Guide © 1991)
5-6   c
5-7   c (*Source:* 1991 Level I CFA Study Guide © 1991)
5-8   a (*Source:* 1991 Level I CFA Study Guide © 1991)
5-9   d
5-10   b
5-11   c
5-12   a (*Source:* 1991 Level I CFA Study Guide © 1991)
5-13   b (*Source:* 1990 Level I CFA Study Guide © 1990)
5-14   c (*Source:* 1990 Level I CFA Study Guide © 1990)

Chapter 6

6-1 c
6-2 a (*Source:* 1994 Level I CFA Study Guide © 1994)
6-3 a
6-4 b (*Source:* 1994 Level I CFA Study Guide © 1994)
6-5 b (*Source:* 1994 Level I CFA Study Guide © 1994)
6-6 c (*Source:* 1994 Level I CFA Study Guide © 1994)
6-7 d (*Source:* 1994 Level I CFA Study Guide © 1994)
6-8 d
6-9 c
6-10 c (*Source:* 1994 Level I CFA Study Guide © 1994)
6-11 a (*Source:* 1991 Level I CFA Study Guide © 1991)
6-12 c (*Source:* 1994 Level I CFA Study Guide © 1994)
6-13 a
6-14 d
6-15 d

Chapter 7

7-1 b
7-2 d
7-3 a
7-4 a
7-5 a
7-6 a
7-7 a
7-8 c
7-9 c
7-10 b (*Source:* 1994 Level I CFA Study Guide © 1994)
7-11 c (*Source:* 1994 Level I CFA Study Guide © 1994)
7-12 b (*Source:* 1994 Level I CFA Study Guide © 1994)
7-13 a (*Source:* 1994 Level I CFA Study Guide © 1994)
7-14 b (*Source:* 1994 Level I CFA Study Guide © 1994)
7-15 c

Chapter 8

8-1 d (*Source:* 1994 Level I CFA Study Guide © 1994)
8-2 c
8-3 d
8-4 b
8-5 a
8-6 b
8-7 d
8-8 a
8-9 d
8-10 c
8-11 d
8-12 c
8-13 a
8-14 a
8-15 a

Chapter 9

9-1 b
9-2 a
9-3 a
9-4 d (*Source:* 1988 Level I CFA Study Guide © 1988)
9-5 b
9-6 a
9-7 c (*Source:* 1991 Level I CFA Study Guide © 1991)
9-8 a
9-9 a
9-10 d (*Source:* 1993 Level I CFA Study Guide © 1993)
9-11 a (*Source:* 1988 Level I CFA Study Guide © 1988)
9-12 b (*Source:* 1989 Level I CFA Study Guide © 1989)
9-13 a (*Source:* 1992 Level I CFA Study Guide © 1992)
9-14 b
9-15 d (*Source:* 1994 Level I CFA Study Guide © 1994)

Chapter 10

10-1 b (*Source:* 1993 Level I CFA Study Guide © 1993)
10-2 c (*Source:* 1989 Level I CFA Study Guide © 1989)
10-3 d (*Source:* 1992 Level I CFA Study Guide © 1992)
10-4 b (*Source:* 1991 Level I CFA Study Guide © 1991)
10-5 a (*Source:* 1991 Level I CFA Study Guide © 1991)
10-6 b (*Source:* 1992 Level I CFA Study Guide © 1992)
10-7 a (*Source:* 1994 Level I CFA Study Guide © 1994)
10-8 c (*Source:* 1988 Level I CFA Study Guide © 1988)
10-9 c (*Source:* 1990 Level I CFA Study Guide © 1990)
10-10 c (*Source:* 1992 Level I CFA Study Guide © 1992)
10-11 a (*Source:* 1991 Level I CFA Study Guide © 1991)
10-12 a (*Source:* 1992 Level I CFA Study Guide © 1992)
10-13 b (*Source:* 1992 Level I CFA Study Guide © 1992)
10-14 a (*Source:* 1992 Level I CFA Study Guide © 1992)
10-15 d (*Source:* 1994 Level I CFA Study Guide © 1994)

Chapter 11

11-1 d (*Source:* 1990 Level I CFA Study Guide © 1990)
11-2 c (*Source:* 1988 Level I CFA Study Guide © 1988)
11-3 a (*Source:* 1989 Level I CFA Study Guide © 1989)
11-4 c (*Source:* 1990 Level I CFA Study Guide © 1990)
11-5 b (*Source:* 1991 Level I CFA Study Guide © 1991)
11-6 c (*Source:* 1992 Level I CFA Study Guide © 1992)
11-7 a (*Source:* 1989 Level I CFA Study Guide © 1989)
11-8 d (*Source:* 1990 Level I CFA Study Guide © 1990)
11-9 b (*Source:* 1990 Level I CFA Study Guide © 1990)
11-10 b (*Source:* 1988 Level I CFA Study Guide © 1988)
11-11 d (*Source:* 1994 Level I CFA Study Guide © 1994)
11-12 b (*Source:* 1991 Level I CFA Study Guide © 1991)
11-13 c (*Source:* 1993 Level I CFA Study Guide © 1993)
11-14 c (*Source:* 1991 Level I CFA Study Guide © 1991)
11-15 d (*Source:* 1994 Level I CFA Study Guide © 1994)

Chapter 12

12-1 a
12-2 c
12-3 c (*Source:* 1990 Level I CFA Study Guide © 1990)
12-4 b
12-5 b
12-6 c
12-7 d (*Source:* 1992 Level I CFA Study Guide © 1992)
12-8 d (*Source:* 1989 Level I CFA Study Guide © 1989)
12-9 a
12-10 c (*Source:* 1990 Level I CFA Study Guide © 1990)
12-11 d
12-12 b (*Source:* 1991 Level I CFA Study Guide © 1991)
12-13 b (*Source:* 1992 Level I CFA Study Guide © 1992)
12-14 a (*Source:* 1991 Level I CFA Study Guide © 1991)
12-15 a (*Source:* 1994 Level I CFA Study Guide © 1994)

Chapter 13

13-1 d
13-2 c
13-3 b
13-4 c
13-5 b (*Source:* 1988 Level I CFA Study Guide © 1988)
13-6 a (*Source:* 1989 Level I CFA Study Guide © 1989)
13-7 d (*Source:* 1991 Level I CFA Study Guide © 1991)
13-8 a (*Source:* 1991 Level I CFA Study Guide © 1991)
13-9 b (*Source:* 1990 Level I CFA Study Guide © 1990)
13-10 a (*Source:* 1989 Level I CFA Study Guide © 1989)
13-11 c (*Source:* 1991 Level I CFA Study Guide © 1991)
13-12 a
13-13 d
13-14 c
13-15 c

Chapter 14

14-1 a
14-2 c
14-3 d
14-4 c
14-5 c - (*Source:* 1992 Level I CFA Study Guide © 1992)
14-6 b
14-7 a - (*Source:* 1990 Level I CFA Study Guide © 1990)
14-8 b
14-9 c - (*Source:* 1994 Level I CFA Study Guide © 1994)
14-10 a
14-11 b - (*Source:* 1993 Level I CFA Study Guide © 1993)
14-12 a
14-13 b - (*Source:* 1991 Level I CFA Study Guide © 1991)
14-14 d
14-15 d
14-16 c

Chapter 15

15-1 a
15-2 c
15-3 a (*Source:* 1992 Level I CFA Study Guide © 1992)
15-4 d (*Source:* 1990 Level I CFA Study Guide © 1990)
15-5 a (*Source:* 1989 Level I CFA Study Guide © 1989)
15-6 a (*Source:* 1993 Level I CFA Study Guide © 1993)
15-7 b (*Source:* 1988 Level I CFA Study Guide © 1988)
15-8 d
15-9 a
15-10 c
15-11 d
15-12 a
15-13 b
15-14 a
15-15 b

Chapter 16

16-1 d
16-2 a
16-3 a
16-4 d (*Source:* 1993 Level I CFA Study Guide © 1993)
16-5 c
16-6 d
16-7 a
16-8 d
16-9 c (*Source:* 1993 Level I CFA Study Guide © 1993)
16-10 b
16-11 b
16-12 b
16-13 c
16-14 a
16-15 d

Chapter 17

17-1 d
17-2 c
17-3 c
17-4 b (*Source:* 1994 Level I CFA Study Guide © 1994)
17-5 b
17-6 b
17-7 a
17-8 d
17-9 b
17-10 d
17-11 c (*Source:* 1994 Level I CFA Study Guide © 1994)
17-12 a (*Source:* 1994 Level I CFA Study Guide © 1994)

Chapter 18

18-1 d (*Source:* 1994 Level I CFA Study Guide © 1994)
18-2 a
18-3 a
18-4 d
18-5 b
18-6 b
18-7 b
18-8 c
18-9 b
18-10 d
18-11 d
18-12 d
18-13 a
18-14 a
18-15 d

Chapter 19

19-1 c
19-2 b
19-3 b
19-4 a
19-5 d
19-6 d
19-7 c (*Source:* 1988 Level I CFA Study Guide © 1988)
19-8 a (*Source:* 1993 Level I CFA Study Guide © 1993)
19-9 c (*Source:* 1989 Level I CFA Study Guide © 1989)
19-10 a (*Source:* 1992 Level I CFA Study Guide © 1992)
19-11 b
19-12 b
19-13 c (*Source:* 1992 Level I CFA Study Guide © 1992)
19-14 c
19-15 a

Appendix B

Answers to Selected Questions and Problems

Chapter 1

1-1 Dollar return = −$1,720
1-2 Capital gains yield = −26.19%
Dividend yield = 5.71%
Total rate of return = −20.48%
1-3 Dollar return = $15,300
Capital gains yield = 42.86%
Dividend yield = 5.71%
Total rate of return = 48.57%
1-4 **a.** Average return = 5.41%, average risk premium = 1.31%
b. Average return = 4.10%, average risk premium = 0.0%
c. Average return = 12.83%, average risk premium = 8.73%
d. Average return = 17.21%, average risk premium = 13.11%
1-5 Jurassic average return = 11.4%; Stonehenge average return = 9.4%
1-6 **a.** Average return = 6.20%, variance = .00627, standard deviation = 7.92%
b. Average return = 9.40%, variance = .03413, standard deviation = 18.47%
1-8 Plus or minus one standard deviation, so about two years out of three
1-10 Prob(Return < −2.94) ≈ 1/6
95% level: 5.41 ± 2σ = 5.41 ± 2(8.35) = −11.29% to 22.11%
99% level: 5.41 ± 3σ = 5.41 ± 3(8.35) = −19.64% to 30.46%

Chapter 2

2-9 Maximum margin = 50%; $15,000/$75 per share = 200 shares
2-13 Interest on loan = $356.16
Dividends received = $450
Proceeds from stock sale = $33,000
Dollar return = $3,093.84
Rate of return = 33.3% per year
2-14 $24,000/$80 = 300 shares
Initial margin = 60%
Margin loan = $16,000
Price = $45.71
2-15 Interest on loan = $1,040
a. Proceeds from sale = $50,000
Dollar return = $8,960
Rate of return = 37.3%
Without margin, rate of return = 25%

b. Proceeds from sale = $40,000
Dollar return = −$1,040
Rate of return = −4.3%
Without margin, rate of return = 0%
c. Proceeds from sale = $30,000
Dollar return = −$11,040
Rate of return = −46.0%
Without margin, rate of return = −25%
2-18 Proceeds from short sale = $70,000
Cost of covering short = $50,000
Cost of covering dividends = $1,000
Dollar profit = $19,000
Rate of return = 27.1%
2-19 Proceeds from short sale = $125,000
Margin deposit = $75,000
Total liabilities plus account equity = $200,000
Price = $28.57

Chapter 3

3-5 Dividend yield = .046; P_0 = $78.26 ≈ 78¼
Stock closed down 3/8, so yesterday's closing price = 78⅝
7,295 round lots of stock were traded
3-6 P/E = 16; EPS = $4.89; NI = $24.45 million
3-11 Preferred A: dividend yield = 10.3%
Preferred B: dividend yield = 9.4%
Preferred A: maximum dividend yield = 11.4%
Preferred B: maximum dividend yield = 9.8%
3-13 The bond matures in the year 2011; next payment = $984.38
3-16 Initial value of position = $639,150
Final value of position = $671,625
Dollar profit = $32,475
3-19 Case 1: Payoff = $8 per share; dollar return = $6,937.5
Return on investment per 3 months = 137.04%
Annualized return on investment = 3,157%
Case 2: Payoff = $0; dollar return = −$5,062.50
Return on investment = −100%

Chapter 4

4-5 NAV = $33.33
4-6 Since the price quote is higher than NAV, this is a load fund.
Load = 7.5%
4-7 NAV = $54.60; market value of assets = $682.5 million

4-9 Initial shares = 25,000
Final shares = 26,725
Final NAV = $1 as this is a money market fund
4-14 Management fee = $10.2 million
Miscellaneous and administrative expenses = $4.8 million
4-15 Initial NAV = $17.625
Final NAV = $20.56
Sale proceeds per share = $19.94
Total return = 6.4%
You earned 6.4 percent even though the fund's investments grew by 18%!
4-16 Initial NAV = $18.75
Final NAV = $21.97
Total return = 17.15%
4-17 Municipal fund aftertax yield = 4.42%
Taxable fund aftertax yield = 4.28%
New Jersey municipal fund aftertax yield = 4.5%
4-18 Municipal fund aftertax yield = 4.8%
Taxable fund aftertax yield = 4.88%
New Jersey municipal fund aftertax yield = 4.5%
4-20 NAV at IPO = $9.10
Price = $8.19
Value of your investment = $40,950

Chapter 5

5-13 a. 1/1/98: Index value = 40
b. 1/1/99: Index value = 45
1998 return = 12.5%
1/1/00: Index value = 45
1999 return = 0%
c. Total two-year index return = 12.5%
5-15 a. 1/1/98: Index value = 1200
b. 1/1/99: Index value = 1350
1998 return = 12.5%
1/1/00: Index value = 1650
1999 return = 22.2%
c. Total two-year index return = 37.5%
5-17 1998: Douglas McDonnell return = 25%
Dynamics General return = 25%
International Rockwell return = −12.5%
1998: Index return = 12.5%
1/1/99: Index value = 112.5%
1998: Douglas McDonnell return = −20%
Dynamics General return = 60%
International Rockwell return = 0%
1999: Index return = 13.33%
1/1/00: Index value = 127.50
Total two-year index return = 27.5%

Chapter 6

6-5 $V(0) = \$39.75$
6-6 $V(0) = \$50$
Liquidating dividend = $53.28
6-8 $V(0) = \$25; D = \$3.47$
6-10 $V(0) = \$70; k = 9.71\%$
6-11 $V(0) = \$25; g = 9.524\%$
6-12 $V(0) = \$85; D(1) = \$2.55; D(3) = \$2.81$
6-13 Retention ratio = .60
Sustainable growth rate = 12%

6-15 $V(5) = \$112, V(0) = \$55.68$
6-17 $V(4) = \$13.50, V(0) = \$14.84$
6-18 $V(6) = \$111, V(3) = \$80.77, V(0) = \$52.68$
6-20 $k = 14.35\%$; Historical average dividend growth rate = 10.15%; $V(0) = \$31.47$

Chapter 7

7-16 Gross margin = 33.1%; Operating margin = 8.9%
7-17 ROA = 11.6%; ROE = 20%
7-20 BVPS × P/B = $28.03
EPS × P/E = $32.20
CFPS × P/CF = $29.03

Chapter 8

8-15 The market is not weak-form efficient.
8-16 Unlike gambling, the stock market is a positive-sum game; everybody can win. Also, speculators provide liquidity to markets and thus help promote efficiency.

Chapter 9

9-11 $d = .055; P = \$986,403$
9-12 $y = 5.653\%$
9-15 EAR = 5.318%

Chapter 10

10-9 Price = $894.16
10-10 Price = $1,225; $r = 3.805\%$; YTM = 7.61%; Current yield = 8.37%
10-11 Price = $860; $C = \$39.08$; Coupon rate = 7.82%
10-12 Price = $1,097.91
10-13 Price = $960; $r = 5.073\%$; YTM = 10.15%
10-16 X: $P_0 = \$1,183.92; P_1 = \$1,176.67; P_5 = \$1,142.12; P_{10} = \$1,083.17; P_{14} = \$1,019.00; P_{15} = \$1,000$
Y: $P_0 = \$755.67; P_1 = \$763.86; P_5 = \$804.88; P_{10} = \$881.31; P_{14} = \$971.91; P_{15} = \$1,000$
10-19 Current yield = 9.01%; $P_0 = \$1,109.88$
10-20 Maturity is indeterminate; a bond selling at par can have any maturity length.
10-21 a. $P_0 = \$1,100; r = 4.248\%$; YTM = 8.50%
b. $P_2 = \$1,251.22; P_0 = \$1,100; r = 7.614\%$; Yield = 15.23%
10-23 Price = $937.10; $r = 5.249\%$; YTM = 10.498%
Duration = 2.715 years; Modified duration = 2.58 years

Chapter 11

11-6 Conversion price = $25
11-7 Conversion value = $800

Chapter 12

12-11 Minimum face value = $1,000; Ask price = 127:25
12-15 Equivalent aftertax yield = 5.04%
12-16 Marginal tax rate = 25%

Chapter 13

13-3 Monthly payments = $1,320.78
13-6 Mortgage balance = $166,791.61

13-7 It means that timely payment of both principal and interest are guaranteed.

13-10 Payment = $1,264.136; Loan balance = $169,552.25

Chapter 14

14-2 **a.** The buyer of a call option pays money for the right to buy.
b. The buyer of a put option pays money for the right to sell.
c. The seller of a call option receives money for the obligation to sell.
d. The seller of a put option receives money for the obligation to buy.

14-6 60 contracts at $700 per contract = $42,000

14-7 Stock price = $95; Option value = $90,000
Stock price = $86; Option value = $36,000

14-8 Initial cost = $10,625; Maximum gain = $189,375
Terminal value = $62,500; Net gain = $51,875

14-9 Stock price = $55; Net loss = −$51,875
Stock price = $100; Net gain = $10,625
Break-even stock price = $75.75

14-12 The intrinsic value of a call option is max $(S - K, 0)$.

14-13 The value of a put option at expiration is max $(K - S, 0)$.

14-18 Forty-two contracts were traded (25 calls and 17 puts), representing options on 4,200 shares.

14-19 The calls are in the money, with intrinsic value = $4.

14-20 The puts are out of the money, with intrinsic value = $0.

Chapter 15

15-1 Six factors; stock price, strike price, time to expiration, risk-free interest rate, stock price volatility, and dividend yield

15-6 Put price = $3.81

15-7 Stock price = $81.20

15-8 Call option price = $30.29

15-9 Call option price = $.90

15-10 Put option price = $6.24

15-18 ISD = 40%

15-19 Need to sell = 3,500 contracts

Chapter 16

16-3 Long position loses $250

16-4 Short position gains $562.50

16-5 Short position loses = $5,625

Chapter 17

17-1 17%

17-2 $\sigma = 14.1774\%$

17-3 $\sigma = 17.3877\%$

17-5 Standard deviations are 27.4955 percent and 13.7477 percent.

17-10 An efficient portfolio is one that has the highest return for its level of risk.

17-12 $E(R_p) = 7.26\%$; $\sigma_p = 8.2793\%$

17-13 $E(R_p) = 27.6\%$; $\sigma_p = 42.73\%$

17-15 $E(R_p) = 27.02\%$; $\sigma_p = 41.6\%$

17-17 True

17-22 An equally weighted portfolio has minimum variance in this case.

Chapter 18

18-3 **a.** Systematic
b. Unsystematic
c. Both; probably mostly systematic
d. Unsystematic
e. Unsystematic
f. Systematic

18-5 False. Expected returns depend on systematic risk, not total risk.

18-6 $\beta_p = .95$

18-8 $E(r_i) = .188$

18-16 $[E(r_A) - r_f]/\beta_A = [E(r_B) - r_f]/\beta_B$
$\beta_A/\beta_B = [E(r_A) - r_f]/[E(r_B) - r_f]$

18-22

	Average returns	Standard Deviations
Security	9%	16.43%
Market	4	15.9

Covariance = 105; Correlation = .40, Beta = .41

Chapter 19

19-1 **a.** 173,082
b. $.00058
c. $2,888.80

19-2 **a.** New Zealand dollar is worth $.542; Singapore dollar is worth $.59.
b. Mexican peso is worth more.
c. Least valuable is Turkish lira at almost 348,000 per dollar; most valuable is Kuwaiti dinar at about .3 per dollar.

19-3 **a.** £100 is worth about $163.45.
b. French francs are worth about $17.
c. £1 is worth Fr 9.6.

19-4 Japanese interest rate, $r(¥) = 6.67\%$

19-7 It takes fewer yen to buy a dollar, so the yen has appreciated.

19-8 The primary benefit is diversification.

19-12 The cross rate moved from 472.75 drachma per pound to 478.20, so the drachma depreciated relative to the pound.

19-14 Japanese interest rate, $r(¥) = 3.02\%$

19-15 Your return was 28 percent measured in dollars.

19-16 Your return was 4.76 percent measured in dollars.

Name Index

Equation Index

Subject Index

DATE DUE

DEMCO 38-296

Please remember that this is a library book,
and that it belongs only temporarily to each
person who uses it. Be considerate. Do
not write in this, or any, library book.